1992-1993
HOCKEY
Scouting Report

1992-1993

HOCKEY

Scouting Report

Frank Brown
Sherry Ross

Douglas & McIntyre
Vancouver/Toronto

Douglas & McIntyre Ltd.
1615 Venables Street
Vancouver, British Columbia V5L 2H1

Cover photograph by Bruce Bennett
Cover design by Eric Ansley & Associates
Printed and bound in Canada

To Ren, and especially, Stimpy.

Acknowledgement

We would like to thank all of the people who helped us, by name, but we can't do that. The National Hockey League general managers, assistant general managers, coaches, assistant coaches, directors of player personnel, scouts and players who were our sources for the information in this book were promised anonymity for their honest assessments. Twenty years after Watergate, "Deep Throat" lives on.

We can thank the 22 (soon to be 24) team directors of media information, many of whom responded to our cries for help with player bios, playoff guides and post-season notes. Thanks also to the NHL Communications Department, whose excellent "Year in Review" was an invaluable source for those Traktor Chelyabinsk statistics.

We would also like to thank our families, friends and pets, for putting up with our negligence and cranky behavior while we locked ourselves away with a computer and piles of notebooks and tapes, and glasses of iced tea. We hope when you assess the authors, your scouting report will read:

Played bigger than their size. Were never intimidated. Finished all their checks.

Frank Brown

Contents

About the authors:

FRANK BROWN, 40, published his first story in 1970, about five years after being bitten by the hockey bug. For the past eleven years he has been senior hockey writer and columnist for the New York *Daily News*, which he joined after a seven-year career as national hockey editor at the Associated Press. Brown remains devoted to studying the game, and every Monday night is reserved for goaltending with the New York Hockey Media All-Stars, also known as the Zeroes of Hockey. Brown lives in New York City with his wife, Rhoda, and the world's smartest dog, Chuck.

SHERRY ROSS became the first female broadcaster in the history of the National Hockey League when she began working as the radio color analyst for the New Jersey Devils in December, 1991. She was one of the first women sportswriters to cover a major professional sports beat when she began covering the New York Rangers in 1978. Ross has worked for such newspapers as the Bergen *Record*, *Newsday* and *The National*, and her work has appeared in *Beckett Hockey Monthly* and *Goal* magazine. She is Secretary-Treasurer of the Professional Hockey Writers Association. Ross lives in New Jersey with her cat, Jolie, and Cody, the Wonder Horse.

BOSTON BRUINS

BRENT ASHTON

Yrs. of NHL service: 13
Born: Saskatoon, Sask.; May 18, 1960
Position: Left wing
Height: 6-1
Weight: 210
Uniform no.: 18
Shoots: Left

Career statistics:

GP	G	A	TP	PIM
940	274	332	606	583

1991-92 statistics:

GP	G	A	TP	+/-	PIM	PP	SH	GW	GT	S	PCT
68	18	22	40	−7	51	6	1	1	1	130	13.8

LAST SEASON

Acquired from Winnipeg for Petri Skriko, Oct. 29, 1991.

THE FINESSE GAME

Ashton does nothing well, but does everything adequately. He can play all three forward positions, which makes him valuable to a team, and his experience is another bonus since he is a pretty smart and economical player.

He does have good skating speed, which may be one of the major reasons why he has been able to stick around the NHL for so long without any dazzling ability. Ashton has good snap and wrist shots, both of which he disguises effectively. He catches goalies unaware. He also likes to use his backhand shot frequently. He is very effective in traffic, finding loose pucks and maintaining his footing.

Ashton's speed is another reason for his effectiveness. He has good balance and hand skills to keep tempo with his skating. However, he is not as deadly on breakaways as he should be since he tends to over-handle the puck.

THE PHYSICAL GAME

Ashton is an underrated player physically. He is a solid, sound checker who takes his man without making a big, noisy hit. His strength comes from his skating balance, which helps him in battles with stronger players. He won't be mistaken for a power forward, though, lacking the intensity that the position needs.

THE INTANGIBLES

Ashton has always had a tough time keeping a job with one team (the Bruins are his seventh organization). Still, he is the very definition of a journeyman player and should stick around the NHL for a few more seasons, chipping in his 40 or so points a year. His career will gain a few seasons thanks to expansion.

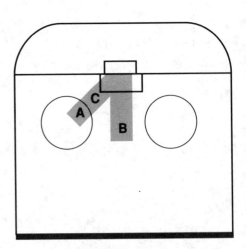

RAY BOURQUE

Yrs. of NHL service: 13
Born: Montreal, Que.; Dec. 28, 1960
Position: Right defense
Height: 5-11
Weight: 210
Uniform no.: 77
Shoots: Left

Career statistics:

GP	G	A	TP	PIM
950	272	743	1015	759

1991-92 statistics:

GP	G	A	TP	+/-	PIM	PP	SH	GW	GT	S	PCT
80	21	60	81	11	56	7	1	2	0	334	6.3

LAST SEASON

Named to NHL First All-Star Team. 1992 Norris Trophy finalist. One of two Bruins to play in all 80 games. Third among NHL defensemen in scoring. Third in NHL in shots. Led team in plus-minus and shots. Second on team in assists and points. Points three-season low. Became third defenseman in NHL history to score more than 1,000 career points.

THE FINESSE GAME

Bourque is one of the few NHL defenseman whose skills outshine those of most top forwards.

His scoring "slump" should be attributed more to the Bruins' holes up front (like the Bruins, Bourque missed the physical presence of Cam Neely in front of the net). It wasn't due to any deficiency on his part. He has a low, heavy slap from the point, an accurate snap shot from mid-range that he can keep along the ice or pick a top corner, and an excellent touch when he ventures in deep for a deflection. Bourque won the shooting accuracy competition at the All-Star Game with a remarkable display of precision. If he wanted to apply himself solely to the scoresheet, his numbers through the years would have been dazzling, but he is proudest of the work he does in his own zone.

Bourque's skating is simply gorgeous. Watch when he rushes the puck from his own end of the rink, going deep into his edges right and left to elude checkers. He does it at such velocity and with great agility . . . then makes a pass or takes a shot.

None of the these skills would mean much if Bourque weren't as smart as he is; he possesses great hockey sense. Speed, power, instincts, courage — it's all there in one package.

THE PHYSICAL GAME

Bourque's offensive skills are so dazzling that the best part of his game is overshadowed. He is big and strong enough to clear out the front of his net and create terror in the corners, and quick and agile enough to handle a speedy attacker in open ice. You can't beat him along the boards because he is so strong, and you can't beat him one-on-one in open ice because of his astute positioning and skating ability.

A workhorse who logs almost as much ice time as the officials, Bourque is a superbly conditioned athlete who devotes most of his off-season to preparing for the new season. Only once in his 13 seasons has he failed to play more than 60 games. The Bruins have to be concerned that the wear and tear will catch up to him, but so far he has shown no sign of faltering.

THE INTANGIBLES

Bourque's season was even more remarkable considering the plethora of injuries to key Bruins players. Playing most of the season with minor leaguers and kids, his leadership qualities became even more apparent. He remains one of the game's premier defensemen and crunch-time players. Even though Brian Leetch won the Norris Trophy last season, Bourque is still the best all-around defenseman.

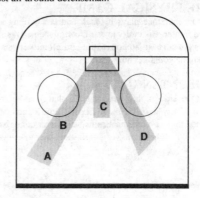

GLEN FEATHERSTONE

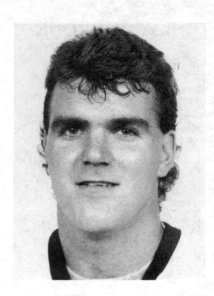

Yrs. of NHL service: 4
Born: Toronto, Ont.; July 8, 1968
Position: Left defense
Height: 6-4
Weight: 216
Uniform no.: 6
Shoots: Left

Career statistics:

GP	G	A	TP	PIM
152	6	29	35	391

1991-92 statistics:

GP	G	A	TP	+/-	PIM	PP	SH	GW	GT	S	PCT
8	1	0	1	−2	20	0	0	0	0	8	12.5

LAST SEASON

Signed as free agent July 25, 1991. Underwent back surgery for injury suffered early in season and played in career low games.

THE FINESSE GAME

Since Featherstone missed almost the entire season (and playoffs), we'll have to turn back to last season's Hockey Scouting Report to sum him up.

He has good size and strength, and is a powerful skater. Fast for a big man, he does lack agility and quickness.

Featherstone doesn't generate much offense, but should, since he has some significant hand skills. His problem is play selection. When there is no screen in front, he takes something off his shot and the goalie can handle it easily. When he has a screen, he sends in a screamer that usually hits someone in front and bounces away.

Defensively, Featherstone is a very sound, positional player. He reads plays well, and holds the blue line as well as anyone. He sometimes overplays the man, but is gaining maturity and making wiser decisions.

THE PHYSICAL GAME

Featherstone plays it tough and is a willing and good fighter. His injury may affect him mentally, since he might not be as anxious to put himself into a position where he could get hurt again.

THE INTANGIBLES

We said in last year's HSR that Featherstone would likely be on the move from St. Louis and he did indeed end up with the Bruins. If he can come back from his injury (no pun intended), he will find the small ice surface of Boston Garden to his liking. Featherstone showed some promise while with the Blues, but his development will depend on his recovery from his injury.

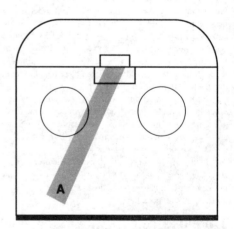

STEVE HEINZE

Yrs. of NHL service: 0
Born: Lawrence, Mass.; Jan. 30, 1970
Position: Right wing
Height: 5-11
Weight: 190
Uniform no.: 45
Shoots: Right

Career statistics:

GP	G	A	TP	PIM
14	3	4	7	6

1991-92 statistics:

GP	G	A	TP	+/-	PIM	PP	SH	GW	GT	S	PCT
14	3	4	7	−1	6	0	0	2	0	29	10.3

LAST SEASON

Made NHL debut with Bruins after 1992 Olympics.

THE FINESSE GAME

Heinze is a smooth skater with agility, balance and acceleration, and he has very good outside speed.

He doesn't have 57 varieties of shots, but he does possess a pretty good assortment. He can use a good, accurate wrist shot or a long slapshot. He lacks some offensive instincts but shows a willingness to go to the net. He is also a good playmaker, and passes equally well to either side. He leads a teammate nicely with his passes.

Heinze plays well at both ends of the rink. He anticipates the play well. In his own zone, he will tie up his man or use a poke check well. He plays an intelligent game.

THE PHYSICAL GAME

Heinze likes to hit, and likes to do it early in a game to get himself involved. He lacks the power of bigger forwards but uses his size well. Watching his first few shifts will indicate how involved Heinze will be in the game. He finishes every check and has overcome some injury problems and seems to be willing to pay the physical price to make the NHL.

THE INTANGIBLES

Heinze played well after joining the Bruins following the Olympics, but many players come into the NHL on Olympic adrenaline and are never able to sustain their play through an entire season. What Heinze has shown so far is promising. Strength may determine whether he has a good NHL career.

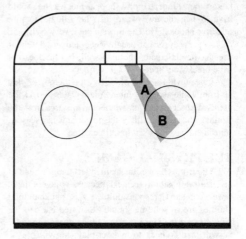

5

JOE JUNEAU

Yrs. of NHL service: 0
Born: Pont-Rouge, Que.; Jan. 5, 1968
Position: Center/left wing
Height: 6-0
Weight: 175
Uniform no.: 49
Shoots: Right

Career statistics:

GP	G	A	TP	PIM
14	5	14	19	4

1991-92 statistics:

GP	G	A	TP	+/-	PIM	PP	SH	GW	GT	S	PCT
14	5	14	19	6	4	2	0	0	0	38	13.2

LAST SEASON

Made NHL debut with Bruins after 1992 Olympics.

THE FINESSE GAME

A clever, creative playmaker, Juneau should be able to overcome the cozy confines of Boston Garden. He is willing to go into traffic to make plays and his skating quickness helps him in tight quarters. He sees the entire ice well and makes his play selections smartly.

Juneau handles the puck well and has good offensive instincts. Possibly because he felt obliged to give the puck up to Ray Bourque or Adam Oates whenever he saw them, Juneau didn't shoot as much as he should have. When the awe wears off, he will be a more effective shooter. He one-times a puck very well.

Not speedy, he can usually get a step on a defender because he anticipates the play well, but he does not have breakaway speed.

Juneau will see a lot of ice time on the power play up front while another center, Adam Oates, works the points. Expect great improvement in this area from the Bruins, who ranked 12th on the power play last season. Juneau can also be used to kill penalties.

THE PHYSICAL GAME

The Bruins broke Juneau in at left wing instead of his natural position (center) because wingers have fewer defensive responsibilities. His puckhandling abilities are so solid he should be shifted back to the pivot to start the season. Although he doesn't initiate, he will take a check to make a play; he will not be intimidated. He is a hard worker, but needs to improve his defense. He has the smarts, and it shouldn't take him long to gain the experience. Juneau is a blue chip prospect.

THE INTANGIBLES

When contracts talks between the Bruins and Juneau seemed to reach an impasse, the youngster threatened to play in Switzerland. Boston GM Harry Sinden responded by saying Juneau had better learn to yodel. Now the Bruins are singing Juneau's praises after coming to terms and after the strong performance by the Canadian Olympian in his brief NHL stint. A caveat: many players come into the league on an Olympic high but aren't able to recapture the post-Games magic during the regular season. Both Heinze and Juneau came out of the same Bruins draft (1988), which could go down as a great year for their scouts.

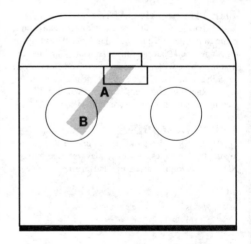

STEPHEN LEACH

Yrs. of NHL service: 7
Born: Cambridge, Mass.; Jan. 16, 1966
Position: Right wing
Height: 5-11
Weight: 180
Uniform no.: 27
Shoots: Right

Career statistics:

GP	G	A	TP	PIM
324	74	83	157	469

1991-92 statistics:

GP	G	A	TP	+/-	PIM	PP	SH	GW	GT	S	PCT
78	31	29	60	−8	147	12	0	4	0	243	12.8

LAST SEASON

Acquired from Washington for Randy Burridge, June 21, 1991. Second on team in power-play goals. Tied for second in game-winning goals. Games played, all scoring totals and PIM career highs. Missed two games with flu.

THE FINESSE GAME

Leach's shot is fast, heavy and accurate, and he loves to shoot. His philosophy is that if he throws the puck at the net, anything could happen, and good things happened for Leach after the 1991 trade that sent him to his hometown. He can catch goalies by surprise because he will shoot from the unlikeliest angle and then follow the puck in to the net looking for a rebound. He doesn't have a great scoring touch, but is always going towards the net.

Leach uses the boards well, where he can intimidate with his barrelling style. One of his favorite plays is to give himself a pass off the boards and just keep heading for the net.

He saw more ice time on the power play than in any other year in his career. He needs to work with a playmaker who will get him the puck, and skated well with Vladimir Ruzicka as his center. Leach is fundamentally sound, plays his position, and doesn't do anything out of the ordinary. He has a solid work ethic. He can also kill penalties.

THE PHYSICAL GAME

Leach's game is well-suited to his small home rink. He is an up-and-down winger and, while not big, he is powerfully built and uses his strength well. Leach gets a great deal of drive from his legs, and churns in the corners as he battles for the puck. He is very strong along the wall and in front of the net.

THE INTANGIBLES

Leach's role in Washington was as a part-time, fourth-line winger. The Bruins needed him more, and he became an important full-time, two-way forward. The increased ice time led to increased confidence. He was sent out on the first power-play unit and responded by producing. Some players wilt under pressure in their hometowns; Leach's career has been revived.

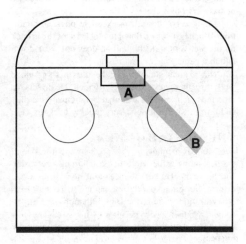

ANDY MOOG

Yrs. of NHL service: 11
Born: Penticton, B.C.; Feb. 18, 1960
Position: Goaltender
Height: 5-8
Weight: 170
Uniform no.: 35
Catches: Left

Career statistics:

GP	MINS	GA	SO	GAA	A	PIM
441	24769	1381	14	3.35	20	142

1991-92 statistics:

GP	MINS	GAA	W	L	T	SO	GA	S	SAPCT	PIM
62	3640	3.23	28	22	9	1	196	1727	.887	52

LAST SEASON

Fifth in NHL in wins. Games and minutes played career high. Wins matches career high (1986-87). GAA five-season high. Missed four games with knee injury. Missed one game with hip injury.

THE PHYSICAL GAME

Moog has always been smart enough to play a sound technical game so that his small size is neutralized. When he is on the top of his game, Moog is at the top of his crease, taking away as much of the net from the shooters as he can. He is more effective than some bigger goalies since he plays the angles so well.

He relied on his reflexes to get him into the NHL, and they are now complemented by his technical play. Moog's physical skills are somewhat limited now. He is weak on the glove side and five hole. Like most small goalies, he is tough to beat down low because he has very quick feet.

Moog keeps himself in excellent physical condition. When he does go down to block a shot, he is back on his feet very quickly, and he does not wear down late in a game.

Not a great stickhandler, he uses a short game well, directing pucks to his defensemen. He directs his rebounds well, and his teammates anticipate this play and turn the attack around very quickly back up ice.

THE MENTAL GAME

Moog is mentally a very tough competitor, one of the best in the game. He is dedicated to his profession and his team. He can bounce right back from a bad effort to turn in a sparkler the net night. He has great concentration through traffic, although he can be screened rather easily because of his size. The new crease rules helped Moog a lot, since in the past the opposition's game plans was to get in on Moog and try to take him off his game by bouncing him around. He is not easily rattled.

THE INTANGIBLES

Although he looks younger, Moog will be 33 during the season. The Bruins have asked a lot of him in the past, and his skills may start to erode quickly if he has to see a lot of action without much support again this season.

GORD MURPHY

Yrs. of NHL service: 4
Born: Willowdale, Ont.; Mar. 23, 1967
Position: Right defense
Height: 6-2
Weight: 195
Uniform no.: 28
Shoots: Right

Career statistics:

GP	G	A	TP	PIM
303	34	103	137	305

1991-92 statistics:

GP	G	A	TP	+/-	PIM	PP	SH	GW	GT	S	PCT
73	5	14	19	-2	84	0	0	0	1	132	3.8

LAST SEASON

Acquired from Philadelphia with Brian Dobbin and 1992 third-round draft choice for Garry Galley and Wes Walz, Jan. 2, 1992. Goals three-season low. Assists and points career lows.

THE FINESSE GAME

Murphy has a nice package of finesse skills, but never seems to put his entire game together to wrap a ribbon around them.

He is a strong, mobile and agile skater, forward and backward, and he adjusted well to the smaller ice surface at Boston Garden because he can make tight turns and accelerate in just a stride or two. He can move men out of his crease because of his good balance, and then take off to join a rush. Murphy plays well in both ends of the ice.

He is a very good stickhandler, and doesn't just get rid of the puck. Murphy will hold it and try to make a play, and he usually makes a good one. He has a good shot from the point with either a slap or a strong snap. He has a long reach and likes to use it to poke check or tie up an opponent.

THE PHYSICAL GAME

Murphy does not use his size as well as he might. He is not a good open-ice hitter, probably because he does not read plays well coming at him. When he is able to force an attacker to the wall, Murphy does make good takeouts, but doesn't always prevent the skater from getting back into the play. He could be much more forceful.

THE INTANGIBLES

Murphy has to become mentally tougher to become a more effective defenseman. Playing with Ray Bourque may help him, as Bourque has helped improve that part of Glen Wesley's game. Murphy has shown some offensive flair in the past, and with more confidence that aspect of his game should renew itself.

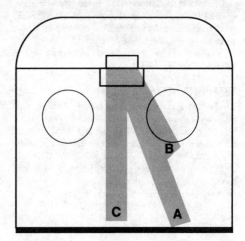

GLEN MURRAY

Yrs. of NHL service: 0
Born: Halifax, N.S.; Nov. 1, 1972
Position: Right wing
Height: 6-2
Weight: 200
Uniform no.: 44
Shoots: Right

Career statistics:

GP	G	A	TP	PIM
5	3	1	4	0

1991-92 statistics:

GP	G	A	TP	+/-	PIM	PP	SH	GW	GT	S	PCT
5	3	1	4	2	0	1	0	0	0	20	15.0

LAST SEASON

Made NHL debut with Bruins late in season.

THE FINESSE GAME

Murray's short game is outstanding. As a shooter, he has a quick release and a strong wrist shot. As a playmaker, he protects the puck with his body and moves it crisply. He has been a consistent player throughout his junior career and showed in his brief stint with the Bruins (late in the season and in the playoffs) that he should be ready for the big time.

His skating may be the only part of his game that is not NHL calibre. Still, he is not exactly a plodder and the lack of speed doesn't hurt in the offensive zone, since he likes to camp out near the goal. He has fairly good acceleration, but has trouble end-to-end, which hurts him getting back defensively.

Murray was the Bruins' first-round draft pick in 1991, and he could prove to be a gem.

THE PHYSICAL GAME

Murray loves to bang, and happily dives into the fray on the goalie's doorstep in search of goals. He is absolutely fearless around the net and in the corners. He is not a fighter, but he won't be intimidated. If he has to drop his gloves (which he probably will have to do to prove himself early in his career), Murray can handle himself. His work ethic is unquestioned and his intensity is consistently high every night.

THE INTANGIBLES

While the Bruins looked at Cam Neely on the sidelines and wondered what might have been, they could look at Glen Murray on the ice and wonder what might be. Murray has the potential to be the kind of power forward Neely was before his injury. He has the skills, but does he have Neely's heart?

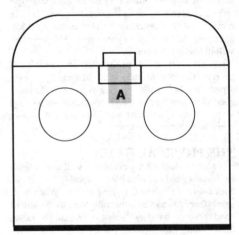

CAM NEELY

Yrs. of NHL service: 9
Born: Comox, B.C.; June 6, 1965
Position: Right wing
Height: 6-1
Weight: 210
Uniform no.: 8
Shoots: Right

Career statistics:

GP	G	A	TP	PIM
573	281	234	515	1059

1991-92 statistics:

GP	G	A	TP	+/-	PIM	PP	SH	GW	GT	S	PCT
9	9	3	12	9	16	1	0	2	0	30	30.0

LAST SEASON

Games played career low due to missing 71 games with surgery and complications from a calcification on his thigh.

THE FINESSE GAME

Neely was the reason the Ulf Samuelsson "Wanted" posters were hanging in Boston Garden during the 1992 Wales Conference final against Pittsburgh. It was Samuelsson whose controversial knee check took Neely out of the 1991 playoff, but the Bruins didn't "get" Samuelsson, and they haven't got Neely back, either.

Neely's playing time was limited to a handful of games last season, and his career is in doubt. When he is healthy, he is one of the NHL's top power forwards.

Since we didn't see much of Neely this season, we'll repeat some of what we told you in last year's HSR: Neely has superb scoring instincts and a great shot. He can score anywhere from the top of the circles in.

THE PHYSICAL GAME

Few NHL players have combined Neely's 50-goal scoring touch with his toughness. He has great size and strength, and uses it. He works the corners and the boards. He burrows his way into the front of the net. Only the very strongest of the league's defensemen can stop him when Neely gets up a head of steam, but since so much of his power is derived from his lower body, his leg injury is bound to impact his playing style.

He used to be one of the game's most vicious fighters; few have challenged that reputation in recent seasons, allowing Neely the freedom to terrorize goalies.

THE INTANGIBLES

Neely's injury has left his NHL future very much in doubt. At his physical peak, Neely is one of the premier power forwards in the league. His attitude and character will be able to help him through some of the rough going as he continues to rehabilitate, but Neely's health is a big, big question mark.

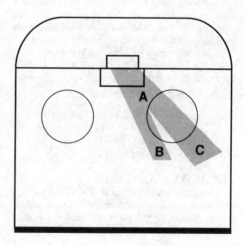

ADAM OATES

Yrs. of NHL service: 7
Born: Weston, Ont.; Aug. 27, 1962
Position: Center
Height: 5-11
Weight: 189
Uniform no.: 12
Shoots: Right

Career statistics:

GP	G	A	TP	PIM
467	122	393	515	146

1991-92 statistics:

GP	G	A	TP	+/-	PIM	PP	SH	GW	GT	S	PCT
80	20	79	99	−9	22	6	0	4	2	191	10.5

LAST SEASON

Acquired from St. Louis for Craig Janney and Stephane Quintal, Feb. 7, 1992. Fourth in NHL in assists. Led team in assists and points. One of two Bruins to play in all 80 games. Goals and points two-season lows.

THE FINESSE GAME

One of the game's best playmakers, Oates is a master at controlling the puck and the pace. He can slow a rush down to a tortoise pace, then suddenly spot an open teammate and thread a crisp pass through the defense. He creates a lot of space for himself with his creative moves. One of the great reasons for Brett Hull's success was his partnership with Oates in St. Louis.

Because Oates rarely shoots (he has a decent shot that he should utilize more), the defense can overplay him, knowing he is going to pass and tempt him by daring him to shoot. They cut down his passing lanes and Oates is neutralized. He is unselfish to a fault.

Oates has terrific hockey sense and was immediately asked to help out the Bruins' power play by working on the point. His value there is not as a shooter, but as a passer who can work the puck in low.

Oates is a good penalty killer because of his head, not his feet. He is not fast, but has adequate skating speed. At even strength, he is weak defensively. He knows better, but usually tries to make a risky play because he thinks offense so much.

THE PHYSICAL GAME

Oates likes playing in small rinks (his home rink and Buffalo's, also in the Adams Division, are smaller than regulation size) because he handles the puck more. He is very strong and while he doesn't play what would be characterized as a physical game, he plays the body well. Oates plays in traffic and is willing to take a hit to make a play. He is wiry and looks like he's a pushover, but he's not.

THE INTANGIBLES

Oates' impact in Boston cannot be fairly measured until he gets a sniper to feed. He was obtained with Cam Neely in mind, but Neely's status is very doubtful due to his injury. Oates was teamed with some of the Bruins' younger players, but so far none has made anyone forget Hull. The Bruins were willing to give up five years (Janney is 24) to acquire Oates.

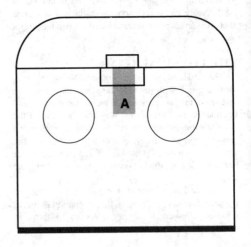

DAVE POULIN

Yrs. of NHL service: 9
Born: Timmins, Ont.; Dec. 17, 1958
Position: Center
Height: 5-11
Weight: 190
Uniform no.: 19
Shoots: Left

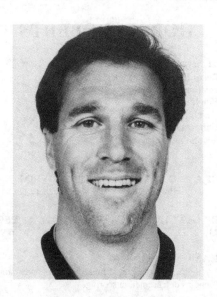

Career statistics:

GP	G	A	TP	PIM
548	179	268	447	358

1991-92 statistics:

GP	G	A	TP	+/-	PIM	PP	SH	GW	GT	S	PCT
18	4	4	8	−2	18	0	1	1	0	31	12.9

LAST SEASON

Groin injury limited playing time to career-low 18 games played.

THE FINESSE GAME

Poulin's skills, never his strong suit, are beginning to decline as age and injury take their toll. He must play physical to be effective. The few goals he gets come from digging around the front of the net. He works hard every shift.

A very good penalty killer, he plays on Boston's first unit when healthy. He is the team's best forechecker, aggressive and with great instincts and anticipation. He is frequently matched against bigger and stronger stars, but seldom fails to turn in a capable job.

Poulin is a very strong skater with speed and acceleration. He gets in quickly on a puck carrier when he is forechecking. He can carry the puck as well, but doesn't overhandle it. Poulin likes a fast, short game, and is effective in deep and in traffic. He has a strong wrist shot and also likes to go to his backhand.

THE PHYSICAL GAME

Poulin has always played bigger than his size, which is why he is so frequently sidelined; the guy doesn't know when to quit. He is a checker who will take the body. Still very good on face-offs, he will tie up the opposing forward and keep him from getting into the play if he cannot win the draw cleanly. He is an intense competitor and will use his stick without regret.

THE INTANGIBLES

The most important part of Poulin's game is his heart, which seems too big and indestructible to be housed in such a fragile shell. His experience and his work ethic will earn him a place in the lineup for as long as he is able to bend over and lace up his skates.

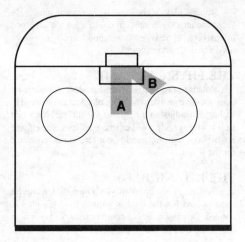

GORDIE ROBERTS

Yrs. of NHL service: 13
Born: Detroit, Mich.; Oct. 2, 1957
Position: Left defense
Height: 6-0
Weight: 190
Uniform no.: 28
Shoots: Left

Career statistics:

GP	G	A	TP	PIM
973	55	341	396	1437

1991-92 statistics:

GP	G	A	TP	+/-	PIM	PP	SH	GW	GT	S	PCT
73	2	22	24	19	87	1	0	1	0	29	6.9

LAST SEASON

Signed as free agent in June, 1992. Second among Penguins defensemen in scoring.

THE FINESSE GAME

Roberts has a love affair with the left wing glass. His main play is to bank a clearing attempt off the near glass — even if he has skated across to the right side to pick up a puck. He will backtrack behind his own net to be able to make the play up the left side.

With no speed carrying the puck, he will look to make the quick outlet pass, and his forwards have to be alert to coming back for the puck when he is on the ice.

Roberts plays a conservative defensive game. He keeps the attacker wide, and doesn't get too involved offensively, so he is seldom trapped. He won't leave his defensive partner outmanned.

THE PHYSICAL GAME

Roberts plays bigger than his size, although he does not have an overwhelming physical presence. He will have to adjust to the smaller ice surface, but since he is a willing body checker who positions himself and reads plays well, he should be a reliable defenseman for the Bruins.

THE INTANGIBLES

Roberts is a support player. Once in a while he steps up and has the kind of game where his play is noticed. Otherwise, he is a complementary player who can be used to partner a defenseman with more skill and speed. He gets little attention, but his work ethic makes him a valuable player. It also never hurts to have a winner in your lineup, and Roberts can show off his two Stanley Cup rings, both won with the Penguins.

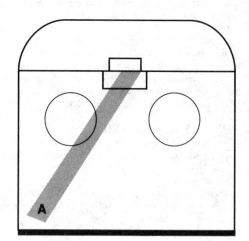

VLADIMIR RUZICKA

Yrs. of NHL service: 3
Born: Most, Czechoslovakia; June 6, 1963
Position: Center
Height: 6-3
Weight: 212
Uniform no.: 38
Shoots: Left

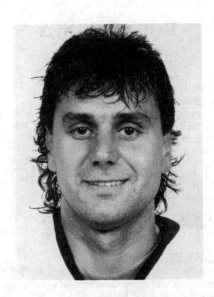

Career statistics:

GP	G	A	TP	PIM
131	58	50	108	77

1991-92 statistics:

GP	G	A	TP	+/-	PIM	PP	SH	GW	GT	S	PCT
77	39	36	75	-10	48	18	0	6	3	228	17.1

LAST SEASON
Games played and all scoring totals career highs. Led team in goals and power-play goals. Third on team in scoring. Missed one game with back injury. Missed two games with charley horse.

THE FINESSE GAME
Wingers have to be alert playing with Ruzicka. He can mesmerize with his puckhandling, doing a dipsy-doodle and then dishing off when his teammates least expect it. Ruzicka is especially good on the power play. He is so much better with the extra man than at even strength that he is close to being considered purely a power-play specialist, but the undermanned Bruins can ill afford that luxury.

He is an effortless skater, but picks his spots. Ruzicka does not go all-out unless he senses a good scoring chance.

Ruzicka has all the skills, size, strength and good hockey sense. So why has he been a marginal NHL player through much of his career? Because he lacks the inner drive to make himself more than an average player.

THE PHYSICAL GAME
Ruzicka does not get involved at all physically, although he has the build to be more effective with his body. He prefers open ice where he can elude checkers with his skating ability. He plays soft, and will avoid corners and traffic areas at all costs—even if it means passing up on a scoring opportunity. If there comes a choice between getting his and giving up the puck, Ruzicka will cough it up almost every time.

THE INTANGIBLES
Ruzicka gets easily frustrated on nights when things aren't going his way. Coach Rick Bowness benched Ruzicka at time during the playoffs, because "Rosie" was useless to his team unless he was scoring. Bowness is gone, but new coach Brian Sutter is at least as demanding defensively.

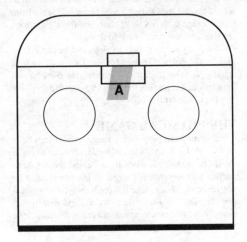

BOB SWEENEY

Yrs. of NHL service: 6
Born: Concord, Mass.; Jan. 25, 1964
Position: Center
Height: 6-3
Weight: 200
Uniform no.: 20
Shoots: Left

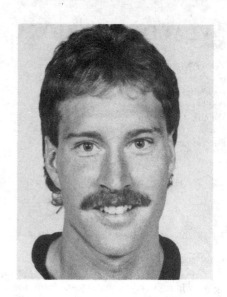

Career statistics:

GP	G	A	TP	PIM
382	81	112	193	504

1991-92 statistics:

GP	G	A	TP	+/-	PIM	PP	SH	GW	GT	S	PCT
63	6	14	20	−9	103	0	1	1	0	70	8.6

LAST SEASON

Missed one game with foot injury. Missed 11 games with knee injury. Games played and all scoring totals career lows for full season.

THE FINESSE GAME

Sweeney's hand skills are very good, but they are hampered by his lack of offensive flair. He carries the puck well and likes to hang on to it, but doesn't move it with any alertness. He is a better one-on-one player than a playmaker, but he doesn't have the skating ability to beat many defenders that way.

He is at his best in traffic, where he can use his hands, balance and tremendous reach. Sweeney has a fair shot from in tight, but most of his goals result from scrambles. He tries to beat goalies time and again from longer range with his wrist shot, but there's little on the shot and few goalies are fooled.

Sweeney reacts slowly to plays and he can't compensate for that weakness with his skating, since he's equally sluggish in that department. He does have a long stride, but it takes too long to get going.

He is fair on faceoffs.

THE PHYSICAL GAME

Sweeney can play a very tough game when he is motivated. He can't always move fast enough to make the hit he wants, but when he is behind the net or in traffic, Sweeney has his target at his mercy, and he can make the check, take the puck away, and make a play. He also has a little mean streak, and will fight if provoked. Most opponents are aware of this and leave Sweeney unchallenged.

THE INTANGIBLES

Sweeney had a poor season, complicated by injuries. He is a player who needs someone on his case all the time. New coach Brian Sutter may provide that whip, but more of his commitment to the game has to be self-generated.

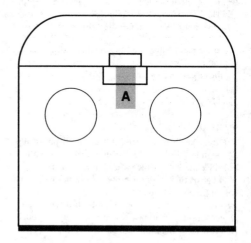

DON SWEENEY

Yrs. of NHL service: 4
Born: St. Stephen, N.B.; Aug. 17, 1966
Position: Defense
Height: 5-11
Weight: 170
Uniform no.: 32
Shoots: Left

Career statistics:

GP	G	A	TP	PIM
246	17	34	51	219

1991-92 statistics:

GP	G	A	TP	+/-	PIM	PP	SH	GW	GT	S	PCT
75	3	11	14	−9	74	0	0	1	0	92	3.3

LAST SEASON

Goals matched career low. Missed three games with knee injury.

THE FINESSE GAME

Sweeney is a good skater but a poor decision-maker. He is quick and can move the puck out of his zone smartly. He has to, to avoid getting pasted, especially in Boston's small rink. However, he sometimes rushes his outlet pass and ends up staring at a counterattack. When he is facing the play, Sweeney tends to become mesmerized by the puck. This might be because he is too small to play a very physical game, and hopes to outfox the puck carrier with a sweep check or an intercepted pass, but Sweeney doesn't always have the timing for that play.

He has better offensive instincts, but few skills to go with them. Sweeney will join the rush, but doesn't have the playmaking skill to generate much. His shot from the point is adequate. He will cheat in to the top of the circles but no deeper.

THE PHYSICAL GAME

Sweeney is one of the smallest defensemen in the NHL. He is overpowered when he has to go one-on-one with the league's bigger forwards, and has to rely on anticipation and stick-checking to stay away from those mismatches. He is scrappy, and his work ethic is outstanding; he can be a pesky critter to play against.

THE INTANGIBLES

Sweeney is a fill-in player who makes a good fifth or sixth defenseman because of his competitive nature, but his ice time will always be limited.

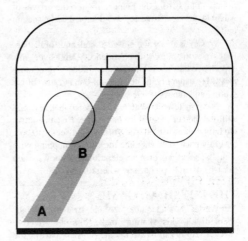

GLEN WESLEY

Yrs. of NHL service: 5
Born: Red Deer, Alta.; Oct. 2, 1968
Position: Defense
Height: 6-1
Weight: 195
Uniform no.: 26
Shoots: Left

Career statistics:

GP	G	A	TP	PIM
392	55	161	216	310

1991-92 statistics:

GP	G	A	TP	+/-	PIM	PP	SH	GW	GT	S	PCT
78	9	37	46	−9	54	4	0	1	0	211	4.3

LAST SEASON

Assists career high. Missed two games with knee injury.

THE FINESSE GAME

Wesley's offensive instincts match his skills, which are considerable. He has a good, quick shot from the point. His wrist shot is his best, and he plays the point well because his shot will get through in front to where it can be re-directed. He is also sharp enough to make plays from the point, although the arrival of Adam Oates means Wesley was demoted to the second unit.

Wesley is smart and poised at both ends of the ice. He carries the puck with confidence. Defensively, his experience has given him great confidence in reading plays. He cannot be beaten one-on-one because of his skating and smarts.

He is a terrific skater with speed, balance and agility, whether in open ice or in tight. He can control the tempo of a rush, starting off at what seems to be a leisurely pace, then catching the defense napping with a quick pass or his own acceleration. He knows when to rush, when to pinch, and when to back off.

THE PHYSICAL GAME

Wesley has adequate size and strength, which, coupled with his skating, make him an effective checker. He doesn't care for the physical part of the game. He makes himself do it because he knows it is the price to pay for playing his position in the NHL. Wesley still has trouble on the boards against bigger forwards. He needs more mental and physical toughness to lift him to the next level.

THE INTANGIBLES

There were great expectations after Wesley was drafted third overall in 1987, and the general impression is that he has never lived up to them. Okay, he's no Ray Bourque. But who is? All Wesley has done is improve steadily, season by season, to move from being an average defenseman to being just below the league's elite. He will never be an All-Star, he will never score 80 points a season, but he will be a solid, consistent performer.

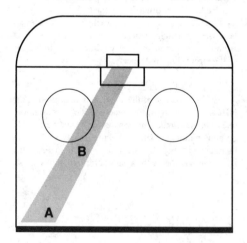

BUFFALO SABRES

DAVE ANDREYCHUK

Yrs. of NHL service: 10
Born: Hamilton, Ont.; Sept. 29, 1963
Position: Left wing
Height: 6-3
Weight: 220
Uniform no.: 25
Shoots: Right

Career statistics:

GP	G	A	TP	PIM
711	319	391	710	516

1991-92 statistics:

GP	G	A	TP	+/-	PIM	PP	SH	GW	GT	S	PCT
80	41	50	91	−9	71	28	0	2	2	337	12.2

LAST SEASON

Third in team scoring. Led NHL in power-play goals. Shots on goal total was second in NHL. Point total was career high. Scored at least 40 goals second time in three years. Plus-minus dropped 20. Had 29 points in first half, 62 points in second half.

THE FINESSE GAME

You have to know Dave Andreychuk has not played 10 seasons in the NHL because he's a pretty skater to watch. In fact, he is pretty much a horror show when you compare him to some of the dancers in today's NHL. He does not turn well and cannot change direction quickly. His best direction is straight-ahead. He doesn't have much acceleration; how do you accelerate to ponderous?

But what a pair of hands! What Andreychuk lacks in foot speed, he more than makes up for with hand speed and finishing skill. In close, he is pure magic. He loves the wraparounds, on which he can use his size and strength and muscle. He buries the second-chance plays—the rebounds, the scrambles. He's got the wrist shot and the snap. He is devastating from the slot and closer.

Andreychuk has enough hands to win any face-off, and almost guarantees possession on the important draws in the defensive zone late in the game. He also has enough hands to beat one checker; he doesn't have enough hand/foot skills, however, to beat a second. Still, where he works, you usually only need to beat one man, and you only need enough speed to get to the scrambles in front.

THE PHYSICAL GAME

Andreychuk is, simply, a moose. He is strong as one, about as big and slow, and just about as hard to move; Andreychuk's balance is so good, it's like he's four-legged. You have to tackle him to bring him down, but you still better tie up his arms or he'll try to shoot. Andreychuk uses his large frame to protect the puck and his long arms for extra reach.

THE INTANGIBLES

Andreychuk is the Sabres' go-to guy when they need a goal. According to the Sabres' statistics, he has 42 'clutch' goals over the past six seasons—a clutch goal defined as one scored in the third period with the Sabres down no more than two goals or up no more than one . . . plus, of course, overtime. He had nine such tallies in each of the past two seasons, leading the team. Every time he touches the puck, it's a potential scoring chance.

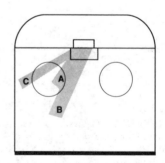

DONALD AUDETTE

Yrs. of NHL service: 1
Born: Laval, Que.; Sept. 23, 1969
Position: Right wing
Height: 5-8
Weight: 182
Uniform no.: 28
Shoots: Right

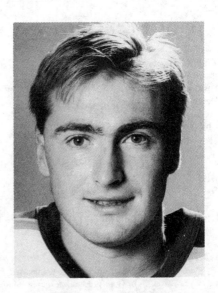

Career statistics:

GP	G	A	TP	PIM
71	35	20	55	79

1991-92 statistics:

GP	G	A	TP	+/-	PIM	PP	SH	GW	GT	S	PCT
63	31	17	48	−1	75	5	0	6	1	153	20.3

LAST SEASON

First in NHL. Led NHL rookies in game-winning goals. Was third among NHL freshmen in goals, sixth in power-play goals. Was fifth among rookies in shots but second in shooting percentage.

THE FINESSE GAME

This is a little guy with a lot of talent, someone who wants to score a goal every night and will find a way to do it. He barely saw any power-play time, yet still could have scored 40 goals, even in the 63 games he played.

Audette's biggest asset is his quickness. He takes quick, choppy strides, has quick feet, accelerates rapidly to top speed and makes everything seem sped-up —like a silent movie. The tempo picks up when he's out there.

Audette starts the transition game to offense very nicely. He gets the puck, identifies the best passing option and passes crisply. If he loses the puck, he works hard to get it back.

While he plays at a high pace, Audette remains in command of his skills. He has soft hands and good balance, controls well on the backhand when he curls in front from behind the net. He makes nice one-on-one moves at high speed.

Not far behind his quickness is Audette's great shot 'upstairs.' He can park a puck under the crossbar with the best in the league. He's up there with Steve Yzerman in that regard. Even the goalies know that's where Audette is going to aim, but they still have to stop it; few can, because the shot, of course, is quick, too.

THE PHYSICAL GAME

Audette will go to the physical areas of the ice and sometimes will go looking for trouble. He is borderline obnoxious in the goalmouth; Audette will hack and jab away, trying to free the puck while a goalie is trying to smother it. Sometimes he keeps chopping after the whistle, which is like begging to get pounded.

Audette will forecheck and give a hit, will scrap if sufficiently provoked. But his eye is out more for goals and opportunities to score them.

THE INTANGIBLES

Audette has been able to get by on tremendous offensive skills and his work ethic, but he's got to learn to be more physical. He has to build full-body strength and work on his stamina.

The sad thing is, major reconstructive knee is expected to keep him out until December at least. He's still worth a late pick, you poolsters.

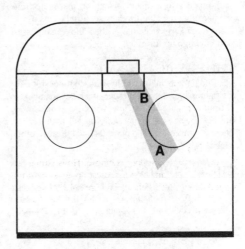

DOUG BODGER

Yrs. of NHL service: 8
Born: Chemainus, B.C.; June 18, 1966
Position: Left defense
Height: 6-2
Weight: 210
Uniform no.: 8
Shoots: Left

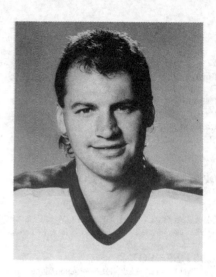

Career statistics:

GP	G	A	TP	PIM
562	70	266	336	570

1991-92 statistics:

GP	G	A	TP	+/-	PIM	PP	SH	GW	GT	S	PCT
73	11	35	46	1	108	4	0	1	0	180	6.1

LAST SEASON

Led team defensemen in scoring. Games played was five-season high. Goal production increased six. Plus-minus improved nine goals.

THE FINESSE GAME

Bodger skates well enough to be an asset in a small building. He can stop-and-start and move the puck in a tiny space, he is mobile and agile to either side, and he covers lots of ground laterally. He goes behind the net, collects the puck and sets the form of the breakout — both on the power play and at even strength. He is the quarterback, the steady focal point of his team's transition from defense to offense.

Under those responsibilities, Bodger is smooth and steady. He has a good view of the ice and picks the best passing option most of the time, hitting the target with a sharp first pass. If there is no pass, Bodger carries well enough to beat the first man and gain the red line, or weave to the attacking blue line and make a read.

He has a good shot from the point, and is especially good at one-timers, which he makes accurate and hard, but tippable. Bodger keeps the shots down, keeps them away from the goalie's gloves so possession might go up for grabs.

THE PHYSICAL GAME

Bodger gets involved physically but doesn't have the fight in him. He is not especially nasty to attackers in front of his net, although he will chop at ankles. He finishes checks, but is more of a pusher than a hitter. There are times when he plays the puck instead of the man.

THE INTANGIBLES

Bodger seemed a lot happier when Phil Housley was the offensive mainstay of the Buffalo defense corps, and could be a lot happier now that Petr Svoboda begins his first full season on the Sabres' blue line. Bodger is not a spotlight guy. He accepted its glare, but never sought it, even though there were nights he clearly was the best defenseman on the team. With Svoboda on board, Bodger can return to the shadows, where it is much more comfortable and relaxed, and could have one of his finest seasons. He is not too old to still be one of best.

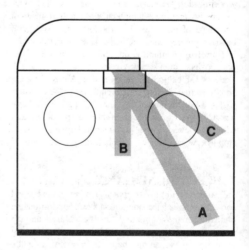

TOM DRAPER

Yrs. of NHL service: 1
Born: Outremont, Que.; Nov. 20, 1966
Position: Goaltender
Height: 5-11
Weight: 180
Uniform no.: 35
Catches: Left

Career statistics:

GP	MINS	GA	SO	GAA	A	PIM
34	1,522	113	1	4.45	2	2

1991-92 statistics:

GP	MINS	GAA	W	L	T	SO	GA	S	SAPCT	PIM
26	1,043	3.21	10	9	5	1	75	712	.895	2

LAST SEASON

Summoned permanently from Rochester (AHL), Jan. 28, 1992.

THE PHYSICAL GAME

There are times when Draper plays the shooter's body instead of the puck, which becomes a hardship because he often is a stand-there kind of goalie who tends to let the puck hit him. There is nothing wrong with that style, but if you aren't going to move much on the puck, you have to protect the shooting angle better than Draper often does.

Draper frequently is too deep in the crease, and it costs him—especially up high. Other times, he over-challenges and simply throws his body at the puck. There is a middle ground to be reached, a sense needed of when to come out and when to stay put, but takes playing time to figure out.

Draper's skating is fair to average. He doesn't get to all the hard-arounds but moves fairly well laterally. In his stance, Draper stays nicely over his edges, which keeps his feet mobile for low shots, and he keeps the five hole closed well. He anticipates pretty well, is alert, but sometimes buys fakes most other NHL goalies know enough to ignore.

Draper is fairly active in using his stick as a defensive tool. When players try to stuff the puck at his right post, Draper uses the big sweep attempt to whack the puck away. He will use the poke check on breakaways, and will recover well if there is a second shot to face. He moves the puck up ice only when he has lots of time; otherwise, he pretty much stays in the net.

THE MENTAL GAME

Draper makes some saves he shouldn't be expected to make, but also lets in shots he properly could be expected to stop. Soft goals against came at killer times, especially in the playoffs against Boston, and left questions about his ability to focus over full games at high pressure.

Again, though, inexperience could be the main issue, and the only cure could be playing time.

THE INTANGIBLES

At this stage of his development, Draper probably would be a tremendous backup goaltender, who could handle 30 or so games, win his share and ease gradually into a bigger workload as he earned the ice time.

DALE HAWERCHUK

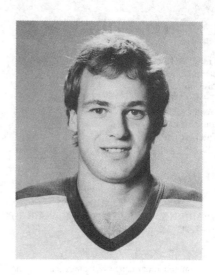

Yrs. of NHL service: 11
Born: Toronto, Ont.; April 4, 1963
Position: Center
Height: 5-11
Weight: 185
Uniform no.: 10
Shoots: Left

Career statistics:

GP	G	A	TP	PIM
870	433	683	1,116	527

1991-92 statistics:

GP	G	A	TP	+/-	PIM	PP	SH	GW	GT	S	PCT
77	23	75	98	-22	27	13	0	4	0	242	9.5

LAST SEASON

Assist total was fifth in NHL. Led team in scoring. Point total increased by 10. Shots increased by 48. Plus-minus declined 24 goals.

THE FINESSE GAME

Hawerchuk uses his wits and his experience to make himself a better player. As the pass is on the way to him from the corners, Hawerchuk will sneak a look at the slot, at the goalie, and know precisely what he's going to do when the puck arrives.

Similarly, he will use measured speed as he approaches the attacking blue line with the puck. All his wings have to do is drive up their lanes; they can be confident he'll find a way to get them the puck. If they're covered, Hawerchuk can crank the speed up a notch — it isn't a big notch, but it's enough to get the job done — and go one-on-one with a defenseman. Hawerchuk may not have overwhelming speed, but he remains elusive and can more than hold his own in a one-on-one matchup.

Hawerchuk has a very nice passing touch. He can be very accurate with a backhand pass, and can feather a forehand pass straight through a defender's legs. Hawerchuk also uses that view of the ice, plus his puck skills, while he helps run the power play from the point.

He decoys his shots well, never tips his hand as to where he's going to put it, and remains extremely calm on breakaways.

THE PHYSICAL GAME

You want to be first to the puck? Go ahead. Hawerchuk will let you get to the boards first, maybe even corral the puck. But he won't give you any place to go, and he'll be chopping between your skates for the puck until it's his.

THE INTANGIBLES

He missed all of three games last season, which means a total of 13 in 11 NHL campaigns. He's going to give you games, he's going to give you minutes, he's going to give you points, he's going to give you mature, intelligent play. And in his spare time, he's going to make your power play better.

In these diet-conscious times, he also will give you something called Defense Lite, which is a little less defense than normal.

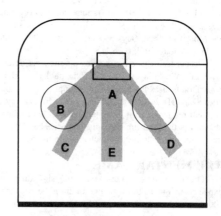

PAT LaFONTAINE

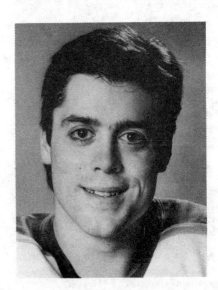

Yrs. of NHL service: 9
Born: St. Louis, Mo.; Feb. 22, 1963
Position: Center
Height: 5-10
Weight: 175
Uniform no.: 16
Shoots: Right

Career statistics:

GP	G	A	TP	PIM
587	333	326	659	407

1991-92 statistics:

GP	G	A	TP	+/-	PIM	PP	SH	GW	GT	S	PCT
57	46	47	93	10	98	23	0	5	1	203	22.7

LAST SEASON

Obtained from the Islanders, Oct. 25, 1991, with Randy Wood and Randy Hillier for Uwe Krupp, Pierre Turgeon, Dave McLlwain and Benoit Hogue. Goal total led team, point total was second. Plus-minus improved 16 goals.

THE FINESSE GAME

Straight-ahead speed is the name of the game for LaFontaine, who likes to get low as he drives to the net so his center of gravity drops and it becomes harder for defensemen to knock him off his feet. Of course, that preference cost him a broken jaw and any number of other facial difficulties after his unfortunate collision with Jamie Macoun's stick.

Nonetheless, LaFontaine returned with the same hustle and grit — the same combination of balance, acceleration and agility. He did not change his game; in fact, he may have stood up for himself more after returning from the long recovery process. He continued to break beautifully to open ice and he continued to bring the puck to the net, either up the middle or from either side.

Most of the time, it doesn't even matter if the goalies know what is coming. One of his favorite breakaway moves is one all goalies know but few can defend: LaFontaine comes straight in, throws a backhand fake, then strides to his right and slides a forehand around the goaltender's dive.

LaFontaine sprints for pucks when they're up for grabs. He comes back all the way to the front of his defensive net. He plays a responsible defensive game which is enhanced by good body positioning more than muscular gusto. And he is a smart penalty killer: instead of just rifling the puck down ice when he gains possession, LaFontaine will look to start a safe play that will slice more seconds off the clock.

On the power play, meanwhile, he gravitates toward the left-wing side, keeping his forehand open for slam-dunks.

THE PHYSICAL GAME

LaFontaine is extremely strong on his skates and on his stick. He can disrupt an opposition scoring chance by pinning the stick of a larger, seemingly stronger opponent. Naturally, he won't win all the size matchups, but LaFontaine unmistakably plays a larger game and he finishes a heckuva lot of checks.

THE INTANGIBLES

After a bitter parting with the Islanders, LaFontaine found a team he could grab by the scruff of the neck and carry with his determination and drive. He would not be stopped by the jaw fracture, and he would not let his teammates be stopped, either.

Also interesting is the fact that on the Islanders, LaFontaine was not exactly known for making his wings better players, or getting them to 'stretch the envelope.' But once he got to Buffalo, LaFontaine turned that trick — just ask Alexander Mogilny — and is a solid bet to keep doing so. At least as important, LaFontaine already has the intensity and focus the Sabres were waiting for Pierre Turgeon to develop.

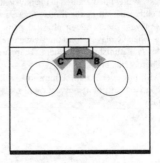

GRANT LEDYARD

Yrs. of NHL service: 8
Born: Winnipeg, Man.; Nov. 19, 1961
Position: Left defense
Height: 6-2
Weight: 200
Uniform no.: 3
Shoots: Left

Career statistics:

GP	G	A	TP	PIM
483	55	140	195	489

1991-92 statistics:

GP	G	A	TP	+/-	PIM	PP	SH	GW	GT	S	PCT
50	5	16	21	−4	45	0	0	0	0	87	5.7

LAST SEASON

Games played declined 10 games to four-season low. Plus-minus declined by 17 goals.

THE FINESSE GAME

Ledyard has good range and mobility, and uses those commodities to cut off the ice well on an intruder and angle him off to the corners. Balance and agility allow him to shift easily from forward skating to backward, to lateral to forward again.

Ledyard also uses his foot skills to advantage on offense. He can skate the puck up ice, can spin and shoot and make the occasional fancy play, but he is more likely to join a rush than to lead it. He has a nice change of speeds that keeps opposing defensemen guessing, and his straight-ahead power enables him to catch an attacker who has a head start in the race.

On defense, Ledyard makes use of his experience. He is more of a threat to step up on a play than to punish. He will use the fundamentally proper poke check, retaining his balance and keeping a first-step option open if the poke try does not succeed. There are times, though, when his vision of the ice is a bit limited and a back-door play against him succeeds.

THE PHYSICAL GAME

Ledyard is a finesse player with some strength and willingness. While fairly limited in the physical aspect, Ledyard is the one setting the limits. There are nights when he plays a mean, tough physical game. There are nights when he plays a solid physical game, finishing checks if not punishing with them. There are nights when he barely hits at all.

He will, however, sacrifice himself—will throw his body in front of point shots and will take a hit to make a play.

THE INTANGIBLES

Ledyard sometimes seems to be fighting himself, questioning himself. More mental toughness, more confidence in his abilities, would lead to more consistently productive play and keep him in the lineup on a more regular basis. Sometimes, he just squeezes the stick too tight.

CLINT MALARCHUK

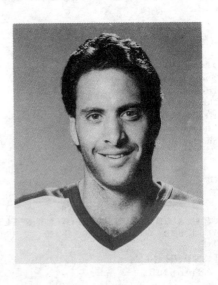

Yrs. of NHL service: 9
Born: Grand Prairie, Alta.; May 1, 1961
Position: Goaltender
Height: 6-0
Weight: 187
Uniform no.: 30
Catches: Left

Career statistics:

GP	MINS	GA	SO	GAA	A	PIM
338	19,030	1,100	12	3.47	14	134

1991-92 statistics:

GP	MINS	GAA	W	L	T	SO	GA	S	SAPCT	PIM
29	1,639	3.73	10	13	3	0	102	903	.887	6

LAST SEASON

Victory total was lowest since 1983-84. GAA was seven-season high.

THE PHYSICAL GAME

Quickness is one of the outstanding features of Malarchuk's game, and quickness of wit is included in the package. Malarchuk thinks the game extremely well, reads the situation, anticipates, and uses polished physical tools to get the job done.

Malarchuk positions himself well in the net, backs into the painted half-circle only on rare occasions. He challenges and moves side to side well. He plays a stand-up style but also is able to kick out quickly at the low shots. He does leave a fair number of rebounds, though, and doesn't control them all.

Malarchuk is a good skater who can reach the pucks drilled around the board and move them fairly effectively to teammates. He is always prepared to use the stick on defense against passes from the corner or behind the net.

In emergencies, he can stack the pads and slide across the crease. But Malarchuk mostly stays on his feet, uses his positioning well and lets the puck hit him.

THE MENTAL GAME

Malarchuk has won a lot of games with critical saves at the key times; he is a goalie who generally can be trusted to provide smart, workmanlike play. He is a battler, a real cowboy. When he gets knocked off his horse by a bad goal or a bad game, the only thing Malarchuk knows how to do is jump right back in the saddle.

THE INTANGIBLES

Malarchuk has faced a world of adversity over the last few seasons and has persevered through it all. He is a player to pull for. It's time a few things went right for him.

27

BRAD MAY

Yrs. of NHL service: 1
Born: Toronto, Ont.; Nov. 29, 1971
Position: Left wing
Height: 6-0
Weight: 209
Uniform no.: 27
Shoots: Left

Career statistics:

GP	G	A	TP	PIM
69	11	6	17	309

1991-92 statistics:

GP	G	A	TP	+/-	PIM	PP	SH	GW	GT	S	PCT
69	11	6	17	-12	309	1	0	3	0	82	13.4

LAST SEASON

First in NHL.

THE FINESSE GAME

While he is a very good passer, May's statistics last season and his scoring past make him appear at least as good a finisher as he is a playmaker. May gets most of his points through determined play around the goalmouth, and his penalty-minute total underscores his willingness to use his body to advantage.

May is effective with the slap shot or the wrist shot, although he spent more time creating loose pucks last season than shooting them. He also has good hockey sense — a nice combination of timing and anticipation.

He does not skate especially well. May has some mobility, but does not turn well or accelerate with great success. He scores his goals by going to the net; any defenseman who tries to stop him is going to have to pay a price.

THE PHYSICAL GAME

May brings to each game an eagerness to play up to and beyond his size. He is more than happy to take a hit if it will open a play, and there are times when the person who goes to check May ends up with the bad end of the deal.

He will drive the play right up the wall, go shoulder-to-shoulder with a defenseman and generally has the balance to remain standing after the inevitable collision.

THE INTANGIBLES

May did last season what rookies have to do. He earned his stripes, earned his sweater virtually every night and dared himself to do it again this season. He had 300-plus penalty minutes his final year in junior and even more last season, which means he has served 10 games' worth of punishment in two campaigns. While he still has dues to pay, the expectation is that May will help his team more this season by staying on the ice a bit more.

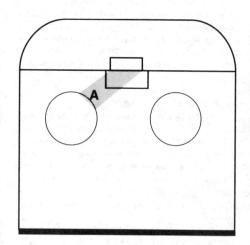

ALEXANDER MOGILNY

Yrs. of NHL service: 3
Born: Khabarovsk, Russia; Feb. 18, 1969
Position: Left wing
Height: 5-11
Weight: 195
Uniform no.: 89
Shoots: Left

Career statistics:

GP	G	A	TP	PIM
194	84	107	191	105

1991-92 statistics:

GP	G	A	TP	+/-	PIM	PP	SH	GW	GT	S	PCT
67	39	45	84	7	73	15	0	2	0	236	16.5

LAST SEASON

Was fourth on team in scoring. Goal total increased second consecutive season. Plus-minus declined seven. Produced 12 more power-play goals. Games played was career best.

THE FINESSE GAME

Mogilny has magic hands to go with dancing feet. He can get off a strong shot after a 360-degree spin. He can move the puck through a defenseman's skates in a confined area. He is the equal of anybody in the game as far as offensive, finesse skills are concerned, although he only deploys those skills when he's in the mood.

He is a skater of stunning acceleration, speed, quickness and agility, and he generally uses those assets to drive to the front of the net. Mogilny loves the give-and-go, and now he plays with Pat LaFontaine, who loves the same style. So they give-and-zoom all over the place, swirling and weaving so that LaFontaine can move to the left side and keep his forehand open while Mogilny slithers to the right to keep his forehand open. You know somebody's going to get a chance at a one-timer off a pass to the other.

One-on-one, Mogilny will cut inside and drive to the net; that route gets him there more quickly than having to drive outside a defenseman and then work all the way back in front for one of his super-strong wrist shots. Then there are the one-on-ones against goalies, who try to ignore the first three fakes so they can concentrate on Mogilny's fourth and fifth. It looks like he has the puck on a string—sometimes, too much so. Sometimes, he overhandles and a scoring chance gets wasted; sometimes he should only try to beat every member of the opposition only once per rush instead of twice.

THE PHYSICAL GAME

There are times when Mogilny seems to hear footsteps, but he generally does not give up the puck without a fight. He likes playing with it and has good strength to keep it, along with solid balance and strength on his skates.

He rubs out, eliminates, bumps, gets involved. He does not blast you into next week.

THE INTANGIBLES

It's still a matter of whether Mogilny shows up on a given night and wants to play, whether Mogilny wants to realize how much talent he has and how good he can be. It's a matter of North America still being a candy store and Mogilny being the kid in it; he's still having too much fun to be serious about anything right now, so he scratches the surface of his talent and puts up numbers most players can only envy. This should be a 100-point season for him. Superstardom awaits.

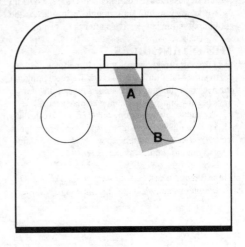

WAYNE PRESLEY

Yrs. of NHL service: 7
Born: Detroit, Mich.; Mar. 23, 1965
Position: Right wing
Height: 5-11
Weight: 180
Uniform no.: 18
Shoots: Right

Career statistics:

GP	G	A	TP	PIM
414	103	109	212	628

1991-92 statistics:

GP	G	A	TP	+/-	PIM	PP	SH	GW	GT	S	PCT
59	10	16	26	-27	133	3	0	1	0	135	7.4

LAST SEASON

Obtained from San Jose, March 9, 1992, for Dave Snuggerud. Plus-minus plunged 38 goals.

THE FINESSE GAME

Presley has good scoring skills. He handles himself well in front of the net, will get a puck 10 feet in front, make a decent fake and score. But he also will score on deflections, screens and gut-goals off turnovers, using the snap shot or the half-snap. He also fires the big slap shot with good results.

A strong skater, Presley may not look it, but he's fast. He uses that speed to advantage while driving down the wing, while on the forecheck and while killing penalties. His defensive concentration clearly could use improvement.

Presley is not big but he is gutty. And he can hit; if sufficiently ticked off, he will chase a guy down the ice and crank him in the back of the head.

THE PHYSICAL GAME

Presley is a tenacious forechecker. He shows up for work every night. He is tough, gritty, keeps the pot boiling in the jaw-festivals after the whistle.

THE INTANGIBLES

Okay, draftniks, here's your sleeper pick. It's our job to go out on a limb for you, and we're sticking out our necks on this guy for 20 goals, if not 25 — if he stays healthy and sees some power-play time.

A gamble, by definition, carries risks; Presley has not shown much consistency and sometimes lacks focus. You know he's going to work, you never know if he's going to think.

Nonetheless, Presley is a scorer. He loves to be in situations when it matters. He is underrated offensively and he's going to surprise this season; with Don Audette out until Christmas or so, Presley probably will get a big chance to show his scoring stuff.

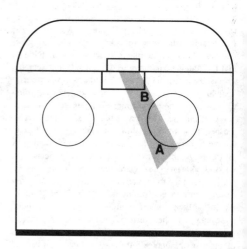

DAREN PUPPA

Yrs. of NHL service: 6
Born: Kirkland Lake, Ont.; March 23, 1963
Position: Goaltender
Height: 6-3
Weight: 205
Uniform no.: 31
Catches: Right

Career statistics:

GP	MINS	GA	SO	GAA	A	PIM
191	10,458	590	5	3.38	13	30

1991-92 statistics:

GP	MINS	GAA	W	L	T	SO	GA	S	SAPCT	PIM
33	1,757	3.89	11	14	4	0	114	932	.878	2

LAST SEASON

Totals for games played and victories were four-season low, GAA was four-season high.

THE PHYSICAL GAME

Puppa does an excellent job of making himself look impossibly huge in the net. He is a big boy, wears those big pads. You face him as you come down the wing and it is all you can do to find the net at all behind him.

Because that size advantage diminishes when he drops to the ice, Puppa tries to stay on his feet and play his angles. He has a good glove and uses it to his advantage. Whether shooters want to admit it or not, they get into certain habits and one favored tendency is to shoot stick-side, high; because most goalies catch with the left hand, shooters tend to shoot to the upper right. Except Puppa catches with his right hand, as does Grant Fuhr, and is quick enough to snare the shots.

He gets to a lot of the low ones, too, with those long legs and his tendency to butterfly. But in tight, Puppa sometimes gets caught in between; shots gets over his stick and between his legs as he drops in front of them. Other times, a faked shot will drop Puppa and leave him vulnerable.

Just as defensemen use their reach, though, Puppa exploits his long arms and uses his reach for poke checks against breakaways and cut-ins.

THE MENTAL GAME

Puppa's work ethic seemed to drop off last season and a load of talent went to waste. The talent was there, the drive didn't seem to be.

THE INTANGIBLES

Injuries have troubled him the past few seasons, and the punctuation mark in summing him up is turning from exclamation point to question mark. If he stays healthy, if he stays confident, if his development resumes, the Sabres will be in good shape. However, 'if' can be a very dangerous word for a team that wants to build on the promise of last season's second half.

MIKE RAMSEY

Yrs. of NHL service: 13
Born: Minneapolis, Minn.; Dec. 3, 1960
Position: Left defense
Height: 6-3
Weight: 195
Uniform no.: 5
Shoots: Left

Career statistics:

GP	G	A	TP	PIM
878	71	248	319	904

1991-92 statistics:

GP	G	A	TP	+/-	PIM	PP	SH	GW	GT	S	PCT
66	3	14	17	8	67	0	0	1	0	55	5.5

LAST SEASON

Games played was three-season low. Has scored fewer goals only once in his career.

THE FINESSE GAME

Ramsey has subjected his body to tremendous punishment over 13 seasons of blocking shots and banging bodies in the small corners and tiny neutral zones of the Adams Division rinks. His skating is skidding, but he spends more than half the season performing on ponds where range is not as critical.

Ramsey has tremendous defensive instincts. He will dive to the ice to destroy the passing lane when confronted with a two-on-one break. He will throw himself in front of any shot. There are times when he will block a shot with his shins and start a counterattack, harkening back to the days when HE was the offensive defenseman on his pair; but now, Ramsey generally stays back and lets the quicker guys do that job.

In the attacking zone, he will take the occasional chance to cheat into the slot to capitalize on confusion during a scramble. He won't take that risk, generally, if there is a chance the puck could turn over before he gets there.

THE PHYSICAL GAME

Ramsey still throws the big open-ice hits — still steps way up on the play in the neutral zone. He times the play well and catches opponents with their heads down. He plays a punishing game, sometimes seeming to punish himself as much as his opponent.

THE INTANGIBLES

Ramsey is heart, soul and character, an extremely likeable teammate; he has never stolen a paycheck. Used properly, he could play another two seasons.

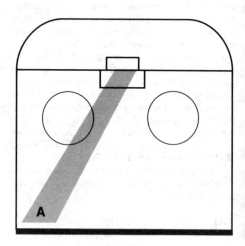

KEN SUTTON

Yrs. of NHL service: 1
Born: Edmonton, Alta.; May 11, 1969
Position: Left defense
Height: 6-0
Weight: 190
Uniform no.: 41
Shoots: Left

Career statistics:

GP	G	A	TP	PIM
79	5	24	29	84

1991-92 statistics:

GP	G	A	TP	+/-	PIM	PP	SH	GW	GT	S	PCT
64	2	18	20	5	71	0	0	0	0	81	2.5

LAST SEASON

First full season in NHL.

THE FINESSE GAME

Sutton is a defensive defenseman with occasional offensive flair, a surprisingly smooth player for someone so short of big-league experience. He is skilled, not overskilled, in all areas. He has some agility, and pivots pretty well, for instance, but his feet are rather heavy. Sometimes, he's so smooth, you don't notice him; other times, you can't miss the plays he makes.

Sutton is not going to carry the puck all the time, but when he does, he will make a nice rush. He has enough balance to make a tight, quick turn—even do a 360 — then made a quick breakout pass from the defensive zone. In the offensive zone, Sutton can drive to the net for a Paul Coffey-type goal.

Sutton has an average release but a hard, heavy shot; he really drives through the puck. But he also uses his hockey sense: he shoots in a manner that the puck can be deflected, and also looks in front before he lets loose. If he sees someone just outside the goal mouth, he will slide the puck down low instead of shooting.

THE PHYSICAL GAME

Sutton is efficient in front of his net, but is not strong or physical. He works hard, though, and stays within himself.

THE INTANGIBLES

Sutton is still improving. The biggest thing about his character is, he has a real steady, positive personality. He doesn't ride the mental elevator up and down. You know what to expect from him: steady efficiency.

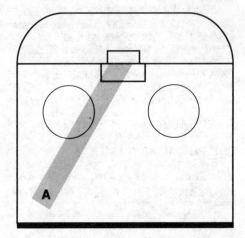

PETR SVOBODA

Yrs. of NHL service: 8
Born: Most, Czechoslovakia; Feb. 14, 1966
Position: Right defense
Height: 6-1
Weight: 170
Uniform no.: 7
Shoots: Left

Career statistics:

GP	G	A	TP	PIM
547	40	196	236	813

1991-92 statistics:

GP	G	A	TP	+/-	PIM	PP	SH	GW	GT	S	PCT
71	6	22	28	1	146	1	0	3	0	111	5.4

LAST SEASON

Obtained from Montreal, March 10, 1992, for Kevin Haller.

THE FINESSE GAME

Svoboda is not hugely strong on his skates, but he remains difficult to knock down because of quickness, exceptional balance and agility. He has excellent lateral movement and is an extremely capable backward skater. He can stop, pivot and start again very smoothly.

Svoboda also has straight-ahead pursuit power. From behind, he will catch an opponent who seems to be skating twice as fast and twice as hard.

His stick skills are strong. Svoboda carries the puck well and joins the rush well enough to create considerable offense. He has a hard, quick, low shot and is expert at getting one-timers on net during power plays. Svoboda also will use the wrist shot and can reach the net with it from the blue line. His view of the ice is improving, as are his reads of the play.

THE PHYSICAL GAME

Svoboda is skinny as a rail. He is not going to go out of his way to make a big hit, is not that strong along the boards or in front of the net. But he rides an opponent out of the play well.

Svoboda is not going to sacrifice his body consistently. He will hit, but will not devote a great deal of his ice time to throwing his body in front of shots or other opponents; he has too many other responsibilities.

Svoboda is not without a mean streak, however. He has a full vocabulary of stick fouls in his repertoire, is as likely to high stick you as he is to trip you, And there are times when fury gets the better of him.

THE INTANGIBLES

It is expected Svoboda will crank up his level of play this year. As was the case in Montreal, he will be asked to lead the offense from the blue line; but in Buffalo, there is a great deal more experience on the defense. He won't have to be the elder statesman, at age 26. So his production should increase significantly with greater freedom on a more offensively volatile team.

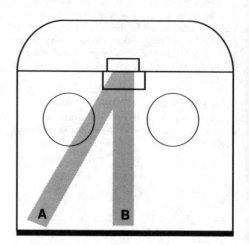

TONY TANTI

Yrs. of NHL service: 10
Born: Toronto, Ont.; Sept. 7, 1963
Position: Right wing
Height: 5-9
Weight: 190
Uniform no.: 19
Shoots: Left

Career statistics:

GP	G	A	TP	PIM
697	287	273	560	661

1991-92 statistics:

GP	G	A	TP	+/-	PIM	PP	SH	GW	GT	S	PCT
70	15	16	31	−4	100	6	1	0	1	133	11.3

LAST SEASON
Goal total increased eight.

THE FINESSE GAME
Tanti's offense has slid backward; he has lost some quickness and his shot isn't as lethal as it once was. But he has used his energy to raise the level of his defensive skills and make himself a better all-around player.

With his forechecking and his tenaciousness, Tanti has made himself a threat to come up with a play off the transition, has made himself a more consistently dependable contributor with a higher-level work ethic.

Because he has lost some confidence in his touch around the net, Tanti scores now on tip-ins, rebounds and broken plays rather than goal-scorers' goals. Rarely now will he skate the puck, make a quick move, go in and fire top shelf.

There still are flashes of first-rate hand skills; he will flip a nice little backhand pass to a teammate that lands, fat as a saucer, and skips right onto the stick tape. The trouble is, he doesn't always make it to the proper guy, and sometimes Tanti will force a pass instead of taking the puck to the net.

THE PHYSICAL GAME
Tanti basically gets abused by the larger players — which is just about everybody. But he throws his body around a lot, too. At the end of the night, at least some of Tanti's bruises are self-inflicted, and that is something of a change from prior years, when he didn't seem to get involved as much. Now, he dives for pucks, makes extra-effort plays and is much more involved in the game.

THE INTANGIBLES
Tanti doesn't want to be a player who is traded all the time. He wants to win, wants to play on a winner. He played hard enough every night to convince his teammates he wants to contribute. He makes errors of commission now, instead of omission, and has made himself a relevant third-line player.

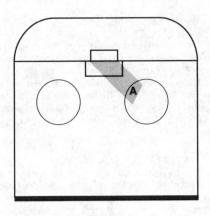

RANDY WOOD

Yrs. of NHL service: 5
Born: Princeton, N.J.; Oct. 12, 1963
Position: Left wing
Height: 6-0
Weight: 195
Uniform no.: 11
Shoots: Left

Career statistics:

GP	G	A	TP	PIM
336	108	89	197	298

1991-92 statistics:

GP	G	A	TP	+/-	PIM	PP	SH	GW	GT	S	PCT
78	22	18	40	−12	86	7	1	3	0	215	10.2

LAST SEASON

Obtained from New York Islanders, Oct. 25, 1991, with Pat LaFontaine and Randy Hillier for Uwe Krupp, Pierre Turgeon, Dave McLlwain and Benoit Hogue. Third straight year of at least 20 goals, 40 points and 74 games.

THE FINESSE GAME

Wood is a very direct player, without a hint of subtlety to his game. He is going to the net with the puck, and that, basically, is that. Nothing fancy, nothing achieved through a quick move.

A powerful straight-ahead skater, Wood can beat a defenseman with outside speed and strength. He gets to the openings and creates openings with his speed. He creates breakaways with his speed and sometimes even scores on them. He makes things happen. He does not allow a moment of comfort to any opponent who has the puck,

Wood is a good penalty killer, he will not hesitate to block a point shot with his shin guards and always is a threat to start a shorthanded break off the play. He is more than up to duty on the power play as he is more than willing to pay the price in front of the net.

His goals are going to be deflections and knock-you-over strength plays. He has a very hard shot but very little touch. He is not going to deke and score. Wood should go to a museum and study Dave Andreychuk's hands.

THE PHYSICAL GAME

Wood's physical grit is not to be underestimated. He is strong and solid and makes the most of his size. He plays a 'big' game, does not hesitate to throw a shoulder into your chest, will drive defensemen straight into their own goalies, and will always be the guy scrumming for the puck along the boards.

THE INTANGIBLES

Wood is a very annoying opponent. His work ethic, persistence and tenaciousness up and down the wing make you think of the Capitals' Kelly Miller, his ability to aggravate makes you think of the Devils' Claude Lemieux.

His consistency of effort and durability are unmistakable. What you get in Wood is lean, strong hockey that makes the team better.

If Wood would accept himself as a 20-goal scorer, he'd probably relax and get 30 or 35; yet he is convinced he's a scorer, which he is not. He is a player who checks, and who scores once in a while but who more often will fake a goalie into mezzanine and fail to finish the play.

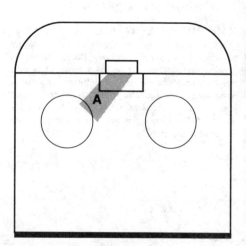

CALGARY FLAMES

CRAIG BERUBE

Yrs. of NHL service: 4
Born: Calahoo, Alta.; Dec. 17, 1965
Position: Left wing
Height: 6-1
Weight: 205
Uniform no.: 16
Shoots: Left

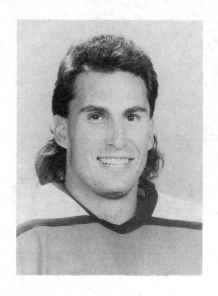

Career statistics:

GP	G	A	TP	PIM
311	22	37	59	1,112

1991-92 statistics:

GP	G	A	TP	+/-	PIM	PP	SH	GW	GT	S	PCT
76	6	11	17	−5	264	1	0	1	0	69	8.7

LAST SEASON

Obtained from Toronto, Jan. 2, 1992, with Alexander Godynyuk, Gary Leeman, Michel Petit and Jeff Reese for Doug Gilmour, Kent Manderville, Jamie Macoun, Ric Nattress and Rick Wamsley.

THE FINESSE GAME

Berube is getting there, skating-wise, but he's still on the slow side. He goes to the front of the net, but doesn't have a lot of hand quickness for finesse plays; he's going to score off scrambles and strength.

He is not much for carrying the puck, not much for beating a defender one-on-one. But Berube has improved now to the point where he will make a bit of a rush, drive a defenseman back, then hook a backpass between his skates.

Without the puck, will not be stopped if an opponent is in his way. He has some agility. He will go one direction, then another, trying to get around someone screening him off the play as the puck enters the attacking zone; then Berube simply will push the guy out of the way and go finish his check.

THE PHYSICAL GAME

Berube is as tough as they come. He can, and will, fight any heavyweight; and he will win, not just hold his own. He has a chance to win every time he drops his gloves.

For someone of limited skills, Berube gets a lot of room. He is unpredictable. You never know when he's going to 'lose it,' and players respect that for their own safety.

THE INTANGIBLES

Berube is very improved player, a good competitor who wants to contribute more from an offensive standpoint. He played for four teams in less than a year more because the acquiring teams wanted him than because the former teams wanted to get rid of him.

His curve remains upward; if Berube remains physical but cuts down on needless penalties, something between 10 and 15 goals should be attainable.

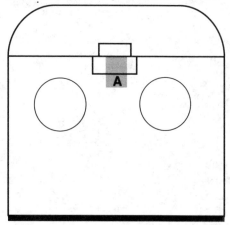

THEOREN FLEURY

Yrs. of NHL service: 3
Born: Oxbow, Sask.; June 29, 1968
Position: Center
Height: 5-6
Weight: 160
Uniform no.: 14
Shoots: Right

Career statistics:

GP	G	A	TP	PIM
275	129	148	277	605

1991-92 statistics:

GP	G	A	TP	+/-	PIM	PP	SH	GW	GT	S	PCT
80	33	40	73	0	133	11	1	6	0	225	14.7

LAST SEASON

Plus-minus plummeted 48 goals. Goal production dropped 18, point production dropped 31. Scored at least 30 goals, 30 assists and 60 points for third consective season. Goal total was second on team. Six game-winning goals led team.

THE FINESSE GAME

Whatever the cause last season, Fleury seemed to lose some fire and some confidence. He stopped blasting shots at every opportunity and started looking to pass. Coming off a 51-goal year, Fleury probably figured teams would key on him and his wings would be open, but it did not quite work that way. He had lots of scoring chances but did not finish them as well last season as the year before.

Fleury still has a change of gears. He can go from fast to laser in a second, which has allowed him to survive at his size. Fleury does a good job of getting the puck, moving it and getting it back. When you deny him the return pass, though, you force his wings into plays they can't or don't want to make.

One thing teams have tried against Fleury is to use defensemen or checkers who can use their reach on him — thereby forcing him to shoot earlier or to change his shooting angle. Of course, Fleury can use his outside speed on most of the larger, clumsier defensemen.

THE PHYSICAL GAME

Opponents started to take advantage of his size, play more physical against him. Teams now don't give him an inch to use his greatest asset, his speed. Teams let him shoot, but limit his playmaking. That leaves the puck handling to other players who might not be as good at it.

THE INTANGIBLES

His 51-goal season two years ago should not have been a fluke. What enabled him to reach the all-star level was the heart he showed; he played a big man's game like a big man and the spark he added meant so much. If Fleury decides not to put those attributes forward constantly, his fall from grace could come that much quicker than a larger player.

When he doesn't have extra desire, that extra zip, especially away from the puck, Fleury becomes ordinary. He scored 33 goals, including six winners, and did not get one voting point in all-star balloting in league-wide voting.

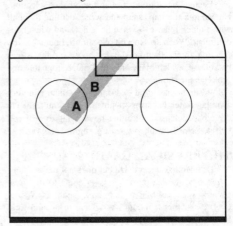

GARY LEEMAN

Yrs. of NHL service: 9
Born: Toronto, Ont.; Feb. 19, 1964
Position: Right wing
Height: 5-11
Weight: 175
Uniform no.: 11
Shoots: Right

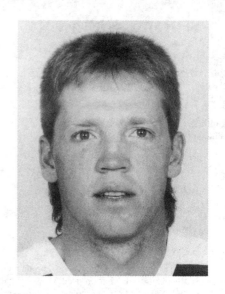

Career statistics:

GP	G	A	TP	PIM
574	178	237	415	500

1991-92 statistics:

GP	G	A	TP	+/-	PIM	PP	SH	GW	GT	S	PCT
63	9	19	28	−12	81	4	0	0	0	141	6.4

LAST SEASON

Obtained from Toronto, Jan. 2, 1992, with Craig Berube, Alexander Godynyuk, Michel Petit and Jeff Reese for Doug Gilmour, Kent Manderville, Jamie Macoun, Ric Nattress and Rick Wamsley. Missed eight games due to sprained right ankle, two due to charley horse, four due to suspension. Plus-minus improved by 13.

THE FINESSE GAME

Although he has good stickhandling abilities and a very good view of the ice, Leeman is at his best as a finisher more than as a playmaker. Rather than be the forward who beats the first three opponents and makes a saucer pass for someone else to put away, Leeman is better as the player who gets open, accepts that pass and makes the last move to beat the last defender.

Leeman has a great shot and good shot selection. He can mix the slap, snap and wrist, drilling them all with a quick release — when he is hot, and when he is confident. When he's in a bit of a slump, Leeman starts thinking about when he should shoot, and that slows his release, which makes his shot more stoppable and prolongs the slump.

While he has good endurance, Leeman is a very average skater in terms of power. He is not able to drive past defensemen; either he is going to beat you by finesse or he probably isn't going to beat you.

THE PHYSICAL GAME

Leeman has decent size but does not make extensive use of it. The puck seems to come to the great players such as Mario Lemieux, such as Wayne Gretzky; at times, though, you have to go and fight for it and Leeman isn't often seen in those battles.

THE INTANGIBLES

There is tremendous controversy about Leeman's competitiveness.

One perception of him is that he's a player who wants to win, who isn't loud on the bench or in the dressing room but who will stand up for himself or his team when push comes to shove. Another perception of Leeman is that if those things are true, he has a hard time making people believe it — that his heart, determination and willingness to pay the price for success are in profoundly short supply.

The consensus is, Leeman is not getting the most out of his abilities, for whatever reason.

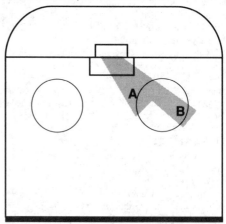

AL MacINNIS

Yrs. of NHL service: 8
Born: Inverness, N.S.; July 11, 1963
Position: Right defense
Height: 6-2
Weight: 195
Uniform no.: 2
Shoots: Right

Career statistics:

GP	G	A	TP	PIM
678	174	512	686	794

1991-92 statistics:

GP	G	A	TP	+/-	PIM	PP	SH	GW	GT	S	PCT
72	20	57	77	13	83	11	0	0	1	304	6.6

LAST SEASON

Plus-minus dropped by 29 goals. Goal production dropped by eight overall and seven power play despite virtually the same number of shots. Missed eight games due to separated left shoulder. Led Flames defensemen in scoring and tied for fourth among NHL defensemen. Led team in assists. Reached 20-goal plateau third consecutive season, fifth time in six. Reach 70-point plateau sixth consecutive season.

THE FINESSE GAME

MacInnis is not hugely mobile, but uses his stick extremely well defending against the rush to compensate for any lack of range. He is fairly agile, capable of a sharp stop-and-start sequence, but is not facile when he has to turn and stride to chase a puck. He does spring instantly and effortlessly into the rush, but has some outside speed and will use it.

He gambles at times on the transition, and as a consequence doesn't always make the sensible decisions in his defensive zone. But MacInnis is an exceptional offensive asset — smart when he jumps into the rush, because he sees the ice very well and spots the holes. If somebody gets him the puck, a legitimate scoring opportunity will unfold.

MacInnis' shot alone makes him a weapon and forces the other team to defend differently. He takes a huge backswing, but a quick downstroke still qualifies it as a quick release.

His point shot is so hard, glass-breaking hard, bone-breaking hard, that he is a threat to score simply when driving the puck into the attacking zone from center ice. Goalies have to defend against the threat of a shot before they can cheat behind the net. But even when MacInnis merely drills the puck around the boards, it moves with such zip, they have to be quick to reach it and strong to stop it.

THE PHYSICAL GAME

MacInnis has good size but is not especially physical. He plays aggressively on defense and handles himself adequately in front of the defensive net but is not a punishing hitter.

THE INTANGIBLES

If he had Brian Leetch's skating ability, MacInnis would be unstoppable; of course, if Leetch had MacInnis' shot, Leetch would be unstoppable. Different people do different things well and overall, MacInnis does two things best: shoot and compete. He gets frustrated at times, tries to force things and ends up making a bad pass or taking a bad penalty; but is committed to the game and to getting better.

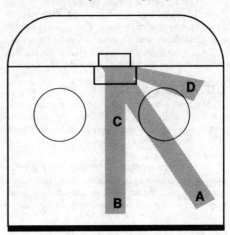

SERGEI MAKAROV

Yrs. of NHL service: 3
Born: Chelyabinsk, Russia; June 19, 1958
Position: Right wing
Height: 5-8
Weight: 175
Uniform no.: 42
Shoots: Left

Career statistics:

GP	G	A	TP	PIM
226	76	159	235	159

1991-92 statistics:

GP	G	A	TP	+/-	PIM	PP	SH	GW	GT	S	PCT
68	22	48	70	14	60	6	0	2	0	83	26.5

LAST SEASON

Goal production dropped eight. Scored at least 20 goals, 40 assists and 70 points third consecutive season.

THE FINESSE GAME

Makarov has super-elite finesse abilities in every aspect. Tremendous hand skills and view of the ice enable Makarov to see a player driving to the net and put a pass through three pairs of legs, straight to his teammate's stick tape for a tap-in. Makarov can make a play like that while in motion, while standing still, while standing on his head.

His skating isn't what it used to be, but Makarov has exceptional balance and strength on the puck. You simply cannot knock it away from him. A lot of defensemen can't compete with him. He'll beat one checker, a second, then try to beat a third; except everyone else on the team is waiting for the puck.

Makarov has a great deal of elusiveness, which you can't teach, and is unbelievably creative. If some players' thoughts are two moves ahead of the play, his are in the next time zone ahead. Except when he tries to be creative, he doesn't shoot; 83 shots on net in a season is WAY too low — even if you're playing with such finishers as Joe Nieuwendyk and Gary Roberts.

THE PHYSICAL GAME

Makarov is not shy. He is strong enough physically to dominate entire shifts because he protects the puck with his body so well. Teams tried to be aggressive on him, run him out of town, but it didn't stop Makarov.

The boards and corners are the weakest part of his game. If he has the puck along the wall, he'll take a hit to make play, but he won't go and outwork somebody to get it. He gets hooked and held but is too proud to dive.

THE INTANGIBLES

The North American game is starting to rise to Makarov's skills at a time when his speed is carrying him back to the level of most of the players he competes with and against. A reduction of the hooking and holding that has sabotaged him would treat NHL audiences to Makarov's artistry.

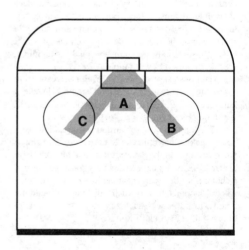

FRANK MUSIL

Yrs. of NHL service: 6
Born: Vysoke Myto, Czechoslovakia; Dec. 17, 1964
Position: Left defense
Height: 6-3
Weight: 215
Uniform no.: 3
Shoots: Left

Career statistics:

GP	G	A	TP	PIM
416	25	68	93	810

1991-92 statistics:

GP	G	A	TP	+/-	PIM	PP	SH	GW	GT	S	PCT
78	4	8	12	12	103	1	1	0	0	71	5.6

LAST SEASON

Games played increased 11 from prior season and penalty minutes dropped 57. Point total dropped nine, plus-minus remained constant.

THE FINESSE GAME

Musil is a confident skater—not quick, but strong — who plays a scrappy game. He is an especially effective penalty killer because he is alert away from the puck and steps way up to challenge.

Musil stops and starts quickly. He keeps his legs moving and gets the puck out of the defending zone with second- or third-effort. Nice lateral movement helps him cut off a right wing's lane, and Musil always tries to finish the play, Ulf Samuelsson-style, with a subtle elbow or a jab at the ankle.

On the attack, Musil is not fast and does not try to be. He uses his head, stays within the limits of his speed. He is more deliberate, calm and composed. He tends to turn to his forehand, protecting the puck, but has the balance and wrist strength to make a turn with the puck on his backhand.

Overall, he makes a good first pass and rarely seems flustered under pressure. While not overly creative offensively, Musil is able to make the simple, direct play. The same goes for the defensive one-on-one play.

THE PHYSICAL GAME

Musil generally makes sure his man is at least inconvenienced, if not run completely out of the play. He initiates. He steps up. He punishes in front of his net. He is big man and uses the size to the utmost. His upper body is so strong that when he bear-hugs you, you can't move.

THE INTANGIBLES

Musil is a stabilizing force on the defense. He works, plays well off his partner, keeps the front of the net clear, gets the job done.

He is probably a No. 5 defenseman, but Musil outworked people to gain the fourth spot.

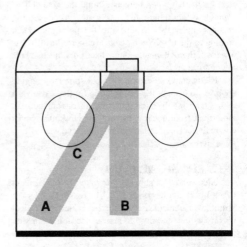

43

JOE NIEUWENDYK

Yrs. of NHL service: 5
Born: Oshawa, Ont.; Sept. 10, 1966
Position: Center
Height: 6-1
Weight: 195
Uniform no.: 25
Shoots: Left

Career statistics:

GP	G	A	TP	PIM
388	219	197	416	180

1991-92 statistics:

GP	G	A	TP	+/-	PIM	PP	SH	GW	GT	S	PCT
69	22	34	56	−1	55	7	0	2	1	137	16.1

LAST SEASON

Goal production dropped 23, plus-minus dropped 20 goals, shots dropped 85. Missed season's first 11 games due to cartilage surgery on right knee. Goal total tied for fourth on team. Marked fifth consecutive season with at least 20 goals.

THE FINESSE GAME

Nieuwendyk's knee seems to limit him. When you lose speed, you lose that ability to get into the fray to make plays. He gets there later now, but he still has tremendous instincts with the puck and is tremendously creative.

Nieuwendyk has the magic hands. He's in the top five in the league for hands, up there with Mario Lemieux and Wayne Gretzky. Playmaking probably is his strong suit, but when he gets around the goal, Nieuwendyk is not going to miss many initial scoring chances; he's quick reacting to the puck and quick coming to the net. When pucks are there, he still gets to a lot of them, using the quick hands that he also puts to good use on face-offs.

Nieuwendyk became a 50-goal scorer by paying the price in front of the net, fighting for that extra yard of ice and using the hand skills he gained from lacrosse more than from hockey. He was able to knock pucks down, deflect them, react to rebounds, and was willing to be in that area in the first place.

THE PHYSICAL GAME

Nieuwendyk, a game player, takes the punishment to get his goals; he used to play lacrosse, so he's not afraid of a confrontation. But he is not a physical player; he gets the urge to scrap once in a while and acts on it, but is not chippy by any means.

THE INTANGIBLES

Nieuwendyk struggled somewhat last season with the burdens of leadership; he had a lot on his mind. The team had a bad year, he was captain and player rep, he had the knee, and he didn't put up the numbers people have come to expect of him. The people asked to lead aren't always natural at it; Nieuwendyk will succeed if he becomes mentally stronger, stays within himself and comes to understand the responsibility that comes with his status.

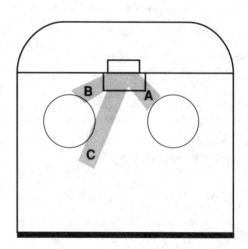

JOEL OTTO

Yrs. of NHL service: 7
Born: St. Cloud, Minn.; Oct. 29, 1961
Position: Center
Height: 6-4
Weight: 220
Uniform no.: 29
Shoots: Right

Career statistics:

GP	G	A	TP	PIM
527	129	203	332	1,274

1991-92 statistics:

GP	G	A	TP	+/-	PIM	PP	SH	GW	GT	S	PCT
78	13	21	34	−10	163	5	1	3	0	105	12.4

LAST SEASON

Missed two games due to sprained right ankle.

THE FINESSE GAME

Otto is the prototype defensive power center. He has great size and just the right element of unpredictability to make a few opponents nervous.

Despite his predominantly defensive role as a checker, a nullifier, it frustrates Otto that he is not more productive offensively. He has good hockey sense on the defensive side of the puck, he understands the game defensively, and he's willing to pay the price defensively. But his lack of confidence offensively almost ties him in knots.

Otto has played a fair amount on the power-play — the Tim Kerr role in front of the net — but hasn't had the point production to warrant it. Still, he is such a dominant physical presence in front, you figure a puck is going to bounce in off him eventually.

His skating isn't great. Otto never will be a speed burner, a breakaway guy, but he does have quickness for his size. His hands are adequate, but more suited to face-offs than finesse goal scoring.

THE PHYSICAL GAME

Otto is raw-boned and strong as an ox; the ultimate face-off man. He'll take the first face-off of just about every penalty-killing situation and, late in the game, will take just about every face-off everywhere.

Most of his goals are just from overpowering people down low. The prototypical Otto goal: he drives through the defensemen, stations himself in front, and gets goals off his knees, his pants, his body. He's always in action, always involved.

THE INTANGIBLES

More of a leader than people tend to recognize, he has a great work ethic. You can't have a complete team of guys like Joel Otto, but you need two or three — especially in the playoffs.

He is a gritty, dogged competitior. He's got the tough miles on him. He also is a coach's dream. He does what coaches ask him to do, and gets a lot of responsible roles because of that.

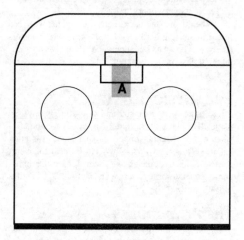

MICHEL PETIT

Yrs. of NHL service: 9
Born: St. Malo, Que.; Feb. 12, 1964
Position: Right defense
Height: 6-1
Weight: 205
Uniform no.: 7
Shoots: Right

Career statistics:

GP	G	A	TP	PIM
565	70	179	249	1,308

1991-92 statistics:

GP	G	A	TP	+/-	PIM	PP	SH	GW	GT	S	PCT
70	4	23	27	−15	164	4	0	1	0	129	3.1

LAST SEASON

Obtained from Toronto, Jan. 2, 1992, with Craig Berube, Alexander Godynyuk, Gary Leeman and Jeff Reese for Doug Gilmour, Kent Manderville, Jamie Macoun, Ric Nattress and Rick Wamsley. Plus-minus improved by 19 goals. Missed four Flames games due to back spasms, one due to concussion.

THE FINESSE GAME

Petit is a tremendously skilled player—and a right shot, to boot.

A strong skater who more than holds his own in speed matchups against fast forwards, Petit has splendid lateral mobility and range that allow him to cheat over to the left side for a challenge. He has the balance to succeed with poke checks or sweep checks, and uses his reach at every opportunity.

When he has the puck, Petit uses the net well as a shield in starting his breakout plays, and he controls nicely—even when being pursued. He makes an accurate first pass on the breakout and has a very hard point shot.

THE PHYSICAL GAME

Petit has very good size and is a willingly physical player. He plays an extremely aggressive game, finishes every checking opportunity and uses his stick extensively against opponents. He is mean in front; tries to punish people, make them think twice about coming back for more. And when he fights, he handles himself well.

THE INTANGIBLES

Petit gets into trouble because his concentration level varies. He will be focused when defending a rush or carrying the puck, but his thoughts seem to wander when he doesn't have it or when a quick decision is needed. He'll come to the bench for a change and create a two-on-one against his partner; he'll drift out of position every so often—usually at the worst possible time.

He has a hard time recognizing which player he should defend against, and he doesn't put himself in position to use his skills.

And it is that one missing ingredient, focus, which has kept him an average/slightly-above-average player who can be replied upon only in the middle 15 minutes of a period.

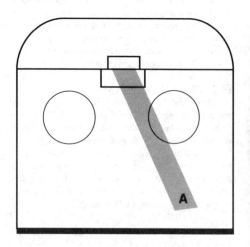

PAUL RANHEIM

Yrs. of NHL service: 3
Born: St. Louis, Mo.; Jan. 25, 1966
Position: Left wing
Height: 6-0
Weight: 195
Uniform no.: 28
Shoots: Right

Career statistics:

GP	G	A	TP	PIM
204	63	64	127	59

1991-92 statistics:

GP	G	A	TP	+/-	PIM	PP	SH	GW	GT	S	PCT
80	23	20	43	16	32	1	3	3	0	159	14.5

LAST SEASON

Games played increased by 41, goal output increased by nine, point total by 13. Led team in short-handed goals.

THE FINESSE GAME

There are not many better pure skaters in the league than Ranheim, who has the sheer power and leg strength to blow past opponents and who puts that asset to exceptional use while killing penalties.

Ranheim has a great release and a rocket for a wrist shot, which he uses far more than the slap shot. His ability to shoot in stride catches a lot of goalies by surprise, as does his ability to shoot as he cuts to the middle. Ranheim barely got any power-play time; most of his goals were earned during full-strength situations.

He is not especially creative, but his top-rank skating and shoooting skills would make you think he'd be a bigger asset from a scoring standpoint. He would be if he were more committed to blowing past guys and paying a price—one he easily could afford, given his size and strength—for in-tight chances. Ranheim does it sporadically instead of consistently.

THE PHYSICAL GAME

Ranheim plays big. He isn't vicious or sneaky-dirty. He could use a bit of Dale Hunter's venom. Ranheim is not quite as willing to initiate physically as he is willing to accept contact.

THE INTANGIBLES

Ranheim was an enigma last year, as were the Flames. For a guy with all the characteristics of greatness, he just didn't put up the numbers he should have.

He has speed galore, good size, good strength. He simply has a hard time finishing what he starts. He's got the whole package to be a power forward in the league, a 40-goal scorer, a right-handed Kevin Stevens; but there's something missing around the net. You don't know whether he'll get one goal in the first 19 games, as he did last season, or 22 over the final 60—as he also did last season.

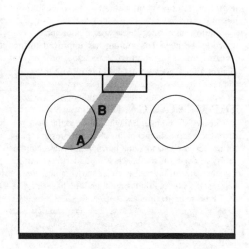

JEFF REESE

Yrs. of NHL service: 2
Born: Brantford, Ont.; Mar. 24, 1966
Position: Goaltender
Height: 5-9
Weight: 170
Uniform no.: 35
Catches: Left

Career statistics:

GP	MINS	GA	SO	GAA	A	PIM
86	4,266	287	2	4.04	3	22

1991-92 statistics:

GP	MINS	GAA	W	L	T	SO	GA	S	SAPCT	PIM
20	1,000	3.42	4	7	3	1	57	500	.898	12

LAST SEASON

Obtained from Toronto, Jan. 2, 1992, with Alexander Godynyuk, Gary Leeman, Michel Petit and Craig Berube for Doug Gilmour, Kent Manderville, Jamie Macoun, Ric Nattress and Rick Wamsley.

THE PHYSICAL GAME

Technically, Resse is sound — similar to Mike Vernon, although less spectacular and less capable athletically. Reese stands up, challenges the shooters well, makes himself big as possible in the net and covers the upper corners nicely.

He has worked to improve his game, although work remains to be done on his consistency. However, he plays a more active role in the game now, coming out to meet the play, ranging from the net to move the puck, using his stick to deflect any pass he can reach. Reese also has refined his rebound control: he is directing the puck more often, and letting the puck hit him less often.

Agile and mobile, Reese does a good job of recognizing the play. His skating has improved to the point where he is not fused to one goal post or the other if a puck goes up for grabs and Reese thinks he can reach it.

THE MENTAL GAME

Reese is a competitor with better skills than his record suggests. Some of his more impressive performances last season came in the relief role, and the ability to come off the bench is an underrated trait in a goaltender. Strangely, when he starts games, Reese has coaches holding their breath until he has survived the first five or 10 minutes.

THE INTANGIBLES

Reese keeps his head in the game. He is a good citizen, a responsible player who knows his role and knows he belongs there. Reese is a solid, reliable backup goaltender who really has not had a chance to ply his trade on a good team.

ROBERT REICHEL

Yrs. of NHL service: 2
Born: Most, Czechoslovakia; June 25, 1971
Position: Center
Height: 5-10
Weight: 170
Uniform no.: 26
Shoots: Left

Career statistics:

GP	G	A	TP	PIM
143	39	56	95	56

1991-92 statistics:

GP	G	A	TP	+/-	PIM	PP	SH	GW	GT	S	PCT
77	20	34	54	1	34	8	0	3	0	181	11.0

LAST SEASON

Goal total tied for fourth on team. Point total was fifth best among Flames forwards.

THE FINESSE GAME

Reichel's best asset is his shot. You don't think a player that small would be able to gun it past a goaltender, but he does. He has a quick release and good velocity. Plus, his shot gets there; the big thing is getting shots through to the net, and he does that. He needs one shot to score, while other guys need three.

He complements his shot with the ability to stickhandle in extremely confined quarters, but hands aren't his only resources. His puck savvy and hockey sense make him useful on the power play; he is very good at creating scoring opportunities for other players.

Reichel is a natural scorer because of his shot and because of his timing. But he needs to increase the pace of his play and significantly improve his conditioning, stamina and leg power. Imagine what he could do if he could keep up with the play.

THE PHYSICAL GAME

Reichel is not physical at all. He plays a soft game, plays smaller than his size, which IS small. If the puck is in open ice, he'll win the race because he knows he won't get hit. Along the wall, he has less eagerness to win those races for loose pucks.

THE INTANGIBLES

Reichel has more than his share of major-league skills, but doesn't compete enough nights. But that will come. He is only about eight months older than Petr Nedved, yet his production has been substantially higher than Nedved's.

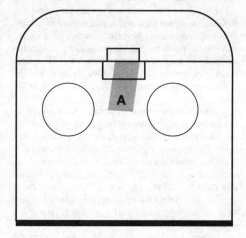

GARY ROBERTS

Yrs. of NHL service: 5
Born: North York, Ont.; May 23, 1966
Position: Left wing
Height: 6-1
Weight: 190
Uniform no.: 10
Shoots: Left

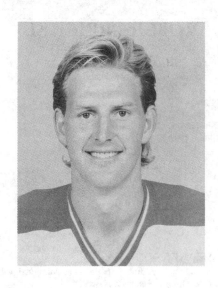

Career statistics:

GP	G	A	TP	PIM
411	154	142	296	1,310

1991-92 statistics:

GP	G	A	TP	+/-	PIM	PP	SH	GW	GT	S	PCT
76	53	37	90	32	219	15	0	2	3	196	27.0

LAST SEASON

Goal total surpassed career high by 14 and marked second time in three seasons he has scored at least 39. Assist and point totals also were career high. Goal total was third-best in NHL, point total was 17th. Shooting percentage led NHL. Set club records for goals and points by a left wing. Became first NHL player to record 50 goals and 200 penalty minutes in season. Led team in power-play goals. Missed three games due to whiplash injury.

THE FINESSE GAME

For someone who entered the league as a scrapper, Roberts has surprisingly soft hands in front of the net. When the opportunity is there to score, he does not miss often. When he gets the puck, Roberts does not make the mistake of holding on too long. He wastes no time in front of the net or along the boards; if he doesn't have an immediate play, he throws it to the net.

The big improvement in Roberts has come in his one-on-one skills. In his earlier years, he used to try to beat a defender one-on-one but his feet would not carry him through the critical moment. Now, he at least has reason for confidence in his straight-ahead skating speed, has the puckhandling skills to succeed and gains a respectful amount of space from many defensemen. He even tries an occasional inside move now, although he hasn't perfected that play and just ends up in bad ice.

Roberts is not an overly agile skater. He has the strength and balance to drive to the net, although occasionally, he loses his balance and needs to use the goaltender to cushion his fall. That keeps the netminders alert and sometimes keeps them very distracted.

THE PHYSICAL GAME

Roberts will pay the price in all situations to get to the net. He has tremendous determination to capitalize on second-effort opportunities. He creates a lot of space with his physical nature. Roberts is strong on his feet, so he doesn't get knocked down often in the slot. He also uses tremendous strength along the boards.

THE INTANGIBLES

Roberts is a heart-and-soul player who is tremendous leader on and off the ice. He is respected not only by teammates but by opponents. He comes to play every night and is somebody every team would want. He has done a fine job in controlling his temper, and would be even more valuable to his team if he continued to improve in that area.

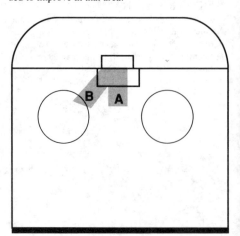

RONNIE STERN

Yrs. of NHL service: 3
Born: Ste Agathe, Que.; Jan. 11, 1967
Position: Right wing
Height: 6-0
Weight: 195
Uniform no.: 22
Shoots: Right

Career statistics:

GP	G	A	TP	PIM
182	19	18	37	887

1991-92 statistics:

GP	G	A	TP	+/-	PIM	PP	SH	GW	GT	S	PCT
72	13	9	22	0	338	0	1	1	0	96	13.5

LAST SEASON

Totals for goals, assists, points and penalty minutes all were career highs.

THE FINESSE GAME

Stern is not a great, powerful skater. He has trouble with quick turns at high speed, but he's able to kill penalties because he has enough straight-ahead speed to pressure the puck, enough agility to react, and he does a pretty good job with his stops and starts in the corners. He also has decent acceleration to the puck and a decent first step.

Though he is a nothing-fancy player who plays primarily in a checking role, Stern has good instincts in the attacking zone. He doesn't just go to one place and stop if he doesn't have the puck; he'll use anticipation and go to where the puck might go.

Stern hardly is a deft stickhandler — hands, for now, are a problem — but he will help himself by getting the puck and moving it, rather than holding on or trying to carry it. Most of his goals are going to come from mucking and grinding and deflections off him in front, but he has shown ability to score the occasional pretty goal.

THE PHYSICAL GAME

Stern is extremely tough, a physical forechecker and a willing fighter. He will battle for the puck and win more than his share of those battles. He will create space for his linemates, which makes him appropriate on a line with a finisher.

Stern wants to compete physically, wants to go to the net. He has Gary Roberts' attitude, but he doesn't have Roberts' touch around the net.

THE INTANGIBLES

Stern shows up every night, plays his heart out and is respected by his teammates. An aggressive player with a good work ethic and impressive pride, He is showing signs of becoming a leader. He is a solid, character player, a Phil Bourque without the finishing skills.

Stern is developing confidence in himself and could end up scoring in the 20-25-goal range if he starts converting the turnovers he forces through forechecking.

But he needs to cut down on his foolish penalties. At this stage of his development, he needs to prove how tough he is by skating away from confrontations, rather than by accepting every challenge.

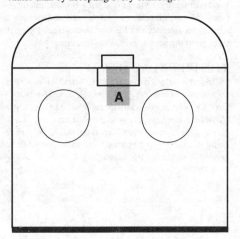

GARY SUTER

Yrs. of NHL service: 7
Born: Madison, Wis.; June 24, 1964
Position: Left defense
Height: 6-0
Weight: 190
Uniform no.: 20
Shoots: Left

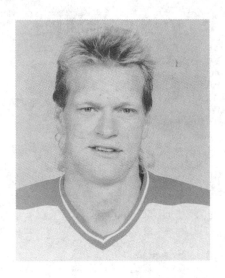

Career statistics:

GP	G	A	TP	PIM
511	101	370	471	738

1991-92 statistics:

GP	G	A	TP	+/-	PIM	PP	SH	GW	GT	S	PCT
70	12	43	55	1	126	4	0	0	0	189	6.3

LAST SEASON

Assist total was third-best on team, point total ranked second among Flames defensemen. Marked fifth consecutive season of at least 40 assists. Missed 10 games due to bruised right knee.

THE FINESSE GAME

The more defined responsibility Suter is given, the better. He wants to be told what to do and wants to play within those confines as opposed to reading the play and reacting to it.

Suter is a powerful, natural skater. He defends well against the rush, and you can count on him to skate the puck out of the defensive zone. And he moves the puck well, although sometimes he does not recognize the proper passing outlet as quickly as he should. Sometimes he makes a pass where he thinks a player should be, without seeing there's no way the player can reach that destination.

Things improve during the power play. Suter is a good partner to Al MacInnis during manpower advantages, because he realizes who the gun is. Suter has a strong, accurate shot of his own and can get the puck through to the net, or he can make a smart pass.

THE PHYSICAL GAME

Suter is a solid bodychecker who defends very tenaciously below the goal line. He cranked Wayne Gretzky, you may recall, in the Canada Cup. Suter plays best when he plays like he's ticked off. He'll give you the stick and earn his turf out there, and you're going to have to earn yours if you want space, but he doesn't always play that way.

THE INTANGIBLES

Suter is an elite athlete when it comes to conditioning and strength. He has explosive skills, but needs to give himself a better chance to use them. He has to become better at reading and reacting, has to take charge of games, has to bring a hard edge to the rink a little more consistently.

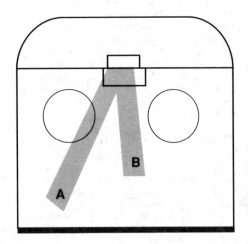

MIKE VERNON

Yrs. of NHL service: 7
Born: Calgary, Alta.; Feb. 24, 1963
Position: Goaltender
Height: 5-9
Weight: 170
Uniform no.: 30
Catches: Left

Career statistics:

GP	MINS	GA	SO	GAA	A	PIM
355	20,048	1,120	4	3.35	28	120

1991-92 statistics:

GP	MINS	GAA	W	L	T	SO	GA	S	SAPCT	PIM
63	3,640	3.58	24	30	9	0	217	1,853	.883	8

LAST SEASON

Games played ranked sixth in NHL, minutes played tied for sixth. Played in at least 40 games for sixth consecutive season, at least 50 games for fifth time in six seasons. Minutes played and loss totals were career highs.

THE PHYSICAL GAME

Vernon plays a stand-up style and makes himself as big in the net as he can. He makes excellent use of his glove and tries to catch everything — a trait he learned in his youth because he did not have quality protective gear.

Technically, Vernon is sharp. While he is very quick, and does a good job of recovering position for a second shot, reflexes remain his key asset. He has used his reactions to advantage for years.

He has the skating skills to reach the puck behind the net, but does not have the stick skills to make any appreciable plays. His forehand clears aren't always strong enough to get out of the zone, and his backhand clears are even weaker.

Vernon is much better with the stick as a defensive implement. He is very alert and aggressive when the puck is in the corners, and uses the big, Billy Smith sweepcheck when a forward is trying to set up an office behind the net.

THE MENTAL GAME

Vernon is a hard-nosed, competitive goaltender who comes out and challenges, plays by the seat of his pants but plays hard and battles. He is always talking and chirping, and it is difficult to get him off his game.

THE INTANGIBLES

Vernon performed quite a bit better than the team did in the first 50 games and often was the sole reason the team was able to get a point or two. He struggles mainly with allowing weak goals at bad times; it wasn't so much that his performance was poor in many games, but some of the crushing goals came at awful times.

There were major distractions: His contract status was up-for-grabs, the fans were on him. Still, it appears time for a change. Even if not many GMs seem to consider him a top goaltender, Vernon is one of the very few current netminders with a Stanley Cup ring.

CAREY WILSON

Yrs. of NHL service: 8
Born: Winnipeg, Man.; May 19, 1962
Position: Center
Height: 6-2
Weight: 205
Uniform no.: 33
Shoots: Right

Career statistics:

GP	G	A	TP	PIM
530	165	251	416	575

1991-92 statistics:

GP	G	A	TP	+/-	PIM	PP	SH	GW	GT	S	PCT
42	11	12	23	−6	37	4	2	2	0	74	14.9

LAST SEASON

Missed 31 games due to rib cage surgery, one due to hip pointer.

THE FINESSE GAME

Wilson is a player who has a much better time of things in special-teams situations, because there is more open ice. He is good on the power play; he is more confident with the puck because he is not going to be punished physically. The extra space gives him time to make plays, to use his hockey sense and stick-handling skills.

Meanwhile, he kills penalties well because he can be strong on face-offs — he crouches way down for good leverage and strength — and knows what to do to slice time off the clock.

Wilson is reasonably strong on the puck and protects it well with his body; there aren't many opponents who can take the puck away from him. He runs into problems when he overhandles the puck, because he boxes himself in and takes away chances to get people scoring opportunities.

This is especially true at the blue line; Wilson creates a lot of offsides because players break wide when they think he's going to carry across, only to have Wilson hold that extra instant after they've committed. Other times, he will make a low-percentage pass in traffic and a turnover will result.

THE PHYSICAL GAME

A good, but not great skater, Wilson at times will give up the puck rather than accept a hit. At other times, when an opponent is vulnerable and just begging to be body-slammed, Wilson will turn away, rather than finish — which suggests he absolutely is not a physical player. Often he will leave a drop pass instead of taking the puck to the net; also, instead of going one-on-one with a defenseman, Wilson will pull up short and pass, or simply bury the puck behind the net.

There are times, however, when Wilson gets clobbered because he wouldn't give up the puck to save his body. Sometimes he keeps working along the boards, keeps his legs driving and keeps the puck in play. He hits at times. So he is a somewhat physical player, but one who absorbs more than he initiates. He is capable of playing physical hockey, but tends not to.

For a player with his size, Wilson gets knocked around too easily. He is more effective against less physical players, less effective against very physical players. The perimeter is where he can use his skills best.

THE INTANGIBLES

Wilson is versatile. He can play as a No. 2, 3 or 4 center and can play wing too. He plays the game in the manner that's best-suited to the way he wants to play, which is not to take too much punishment. It's just too bad he doesn't have more drive and determination to use his size.

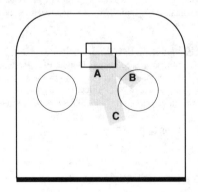

TRENT YAWNEY

Yrs. of NHL service: 4
Born: Hudson Bay, Sask.; Sept. 29, 1965
Position: Left defense
Height: 6-3
Weight: 192
Uniform no.: 18
Shoots: Left

Career statistics:

GP	G	A	TP	PIM
262	19	64	83	335

1991-92 statistics:

GP	G	A	TP	+/-	PIM	PP	SH	GW	GT	S	PCT
47	4	9	13	−5	45	1	0	0	0	33	12.1

LAST SEASON

Obtained from Chicago, Dec. 16, 1991, for Stephane Matteau.

THE FINESSE GAME

Yawney has skating ability for a big man. When he has time, he moves the puck creatively; when he is challenged, though, he often throws it away without finding his outlets.

Yawney sees the ice well and reads defensive situations well, but his lack of aggressiveness impedes his overall play. He tries to play it safe, is always back, but gets beat, anyway, at times.

He simply doesn't do anything to bowl you over. Yawney shows up, does his job and gets off. Some people could do the same thing and be termed 'quietly efficient.' Yawney, instead, is conservative to a fault.

If he reverts to prior form, though, Yawney will be a fifth defenseman. Some people would like to think he's better, but he doesn't have enough zip to his game.

THE PHYSICAL GAME

Yawney is a very soft player. Guys just run roughshod over him when they realize he isn't going to do anything to deter this behavior. He is more of a pusher than a hitter. He will not commit himself to physically confronting a player and separating him from the puck, so he has a difficult time in front of net containing his man or establishing his position.

THE INTANGIBLES

He could have an interesting year playing for Dave King, as Yawney had his best sccess with King on the Canadian National Team and Canadian Olympic Team. He also is far more comfortable on the acres of ice at the Saddledome than on the backyard pond in Chicago; he can go behind the net for the puck knowing he isn't going to get plowed.

CHICAGO
BLACKHAWKS

ED BELFOUR

Yrs. of NHL service: 2
Born: Carman, Man.; Apr. 21, 1965
Position: Goaltender
Height: 5-11
Weight: 182
Uniform no.: 30
Catches: Left

Career statistics:

GP	MINS	GA	SO	GAA	A	PIM
149	8,206	376	9	2.74	3	80

1991-92 statistics:

GP	MINS	GAA	W	L	T	SO	GA	S	SAPCT	PIM
52	2,928	2.70	21	18	10	5	132	1,241	.894	40

LAST SEASON

Five shutouts were career high. Recorded consecutive shutouts Mar. 10-14. Started 25 consecutive games from Nov. 7-Jan. 2. PIM total set club record for goaltenders.

THE PHYSICAL GAME

It is fascinating to watch Belfour perform. Some goaltenders are cartoon characters, but Belfour unmistakably is impressionist art with that deep crouch, the feet wide apart in his stance, the butt way back, the stick planted in the five hole, the catching hand held so high, the eagles atop his helmet standing vigil. There is no stance like it; you can stare at that stance for hours, like a painting in a museum, and wonder how he can move at all with his feet so wide apart and so much weight planted on his inside edges.

Belfour is on his knees a lot, but rarely on his side. He covers a huge amount of net, but doesn't skate that much; as the puck moves and the angle changes, he pivots and flows to the new location.

Belfour anticipates. Belfour challenges. Belfour defies. He rarely does what you expect him to do, except if you expect him to stop the puck.

He is unorthodox on stuff attempts. When a player walks out from the corner or behind the net, the normal approach for a goaltender is to step out on the curl of the crease and move with the shooter. Belfour, however, drops to one knee, plants the length of his stick along the ice to take away the low shots, and lunges out at the puck — forcing the attacker to rush. If the shooter buries a high shot to the vacant upper half of the net, congratulations; the percentages still go with Belfour's tactic.

He is a very good skater, actually; but he is on his knees so much, you forget. At the same time, when he goes down, he recovers well for the second shot — if there is one, because he surrounds the shots very well with his equipment and generally controls the caroms very well.

Belfour also loves to handle the puck, and does it well; he is strong enough to wrist the disc off the glass and out of the zone. He has the nerve and the confidence to go to the corner with two men for the puck.

THE MENTAL GAME

Belfour seems to stop all the rockets, only to be confused every so often by the change-ups. Still, he plays an active, involved game that keeps him sharp. He's up, he's down, he's out, he's in. He's smothering the puck, blocking passes with his stick. But he's in control; he concentrates very nicely.

THE INTANGIBLES

Belfour was brilliant in the first three rounds of the playoffs, then seemed to be eaten alive by first-time jitters in the finals. He'll be a better goalie for having gone through it, and Belfour will be better still with goalie coach Vladislav Tretiak around more this season. Tretiak was a master at keeping the game simple; Belfour at times is a master at making the position complicated. Often that hurts him more than it helps.

KEITH BROWN

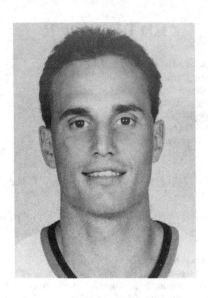

Yrs. of NHL service: 13
Born: Cornerbrook, Nfld.; May 6, 1960
Position: Right defense
Height: 6-1
Weight: 192
Uniform no.: 4
Shoots: Right

Career statistics:

GP	G	A	TP	PIM
779	62	260	322	815

1990-91 statistics:

GP	G	A	TP	+/-	PIM	PP	SH	GW	GT	S	PCT
57	6	10	16	7	69	2	1	1	0	105	5.7

LAST SEASON

Games played improved by 12 from prior season, but marked third straight campaign in which he missed at least 13 contests. Goal total was six-season high, but went without a road goal for at least second consecutive season. Shot total increased by 34.

THE FINESSE GAME

Brown is an agile, quick skater who turns smoothly in either direction and covers lots of ice with his first step toward the puck.

On defense, he reads the play well and uses his range to cut off an attacker's options, then seals off his check on the boards. On offense, the telling strength of Brown's skating is his ability to race behind the net for the puck, collect it at full speed or close to it, and not have to stop before coming out (on his forehand or his backhand) to start a rush up ice. That kind of play requires a unity of foot, hand and head, and Brown combines those components with apparent ease — even when being pursued, even when the pursuer is hacking his arms and stick.

Thus Brown also is suited perfectly to starting the power-play rush from behind his net. He uses the cage nicely as a shield, takes a quick look, and runs the charge.

From the point, Brown moves the puck intelligently. He will fake the big slap, a threat in its own right, and will slide a sharp pass down low to a teammate at the side of the net.

THE PHYSICAL GAME

Brown is a steady all-around player, but he is much more a finesse defenseman than a physical one. He gets the physical job done when there are confrontations, but does it cleanly and quietly. He controls his temper but doesn't let people take advantage of his good nature.

THE INTANGIBLES

Brown has had lots of shoulder troubles the past few seasons, and his absence badly hurt the Blackhawks' defensive depth in the Stanley Cup Finals. He is a devoted athlete, one of the club's strongest players, but his skills — plus a huge dose of dedication in the weight room — have helped him survive.

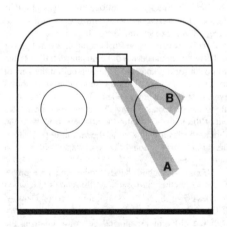

ROB BROWN

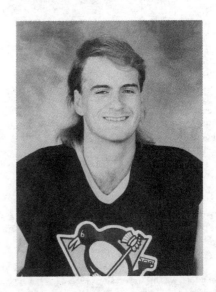

Yrs. of NHL service: 5
Born: Kingston, Ont.; April 10, 1968
Position: Right wing
Height: 5-11
Weight: 185
Uniform no.: 22
Shoots: Left

Career statistics:

GP	G	A	TP	PIM
335	151	193	344	479

1990-91 statistics:

GP	G	A	TP	+/-	PIM	PP	SH	GW	GT	S	PCT
67	21	26	47	−15	71	16	0	3	2	106	19.8

LAST SEASON

Acquired from Hartford, Jan. 24, 1992, for Steve Konroyd. Blackhawks became his third team in 14 months. Goal total was career low, point total was lowest in five years, but so was PIM.

THE FINESSE GAME

Brown has lovely hands for passing, for scoring and even for taking the occasional face-off. He knows what to do with the puck, and while he is not keen at all on contact if it can be avoided, he is not averse to luring a bunch of defenders his way, then sending the puck to the player they should have been checking.

Brown is better known for his ability to put the puck away. He scores from close range more often because he is an opportunist. He will not turn up his nose at nudging a loose puck six inches into an empty net; a goal is a goal.

Part of his scoring ability is touch. Part of it is an accurate shot that he can place just about anywhere. Part of it is that his skating skills aren't overly conducive to leading a rush and driving a big bomb past the goaltender from the wing. He isn't fast. Often he gets to the plays just as stuff is beginning to happen; somebody else starts the scrambles, Brown arrives to finish them — as the trailer who buries a drop pass with a one-timer, as the guy who uses his strength and balance to plow into traffic for a loose puck at the goalmouth.

You'll notice his puck skills have been prominently mentioned; that is because his game is more flawed away from the puck. He does, however, know how to get open. He'll be the guy 20 miles from everybody else, hiding at the side of the goalie, waving his stick in the air, wordlessly proclaiming, "I'm open! I'm open!" and hoping a teammate with the puck sees the signal.

THE PHYSICAL GAME

Brown bumps behind the net or in the corners and occasionally — for instance, if the score is close — will accept a crosscheck in front while looking for a deflection or rebound. But Brown is not going to knock a guy off the puck in the corner, carry him to the net on his back and muscle in a shot.

It is rather strange that he has such a big mouth for a player who isn't at all likely to back up tough talk. It is even stranger opponents allow them to infuriate them as much as Brown does.

THE INTANGIBLES

A hefty dose of discipline may have been just what the doctor ordered for this talented youngster, who has spent too much of his career tripping over a bad work ethic. You know the guy can score, that his versatility makes him an asset. What you don't know is whether attitude problems will continue to make him a liability and a disappointment. The belief here is that Rob Brown has seen the light and will give the Blackhawks the scoring they need desperately.

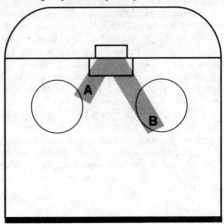

CHRIS CHELIOS

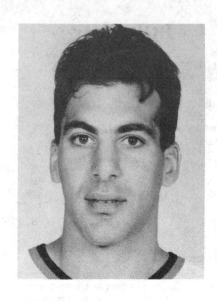

Yrs. of NHL service: 8
Born: Chicago, Ill.; Jan. 25, 1962
Position: Right defense
Height: 6-1
Weight: 186
Uniform no.: 7
Shoots: Right

Career statistics:

GP	G	A	TP	PIM
559	93	336	429	1,220

1990-91 statistics:

GP	G	A	TP	+/-	PIM	PP	SH	GW	GT	S	PCT
80	9	47	56	24	245	2	2	2	1	239	3.8

LAST SEASON

Goal total matched five-season low. Full-season point total was his lowest since 1986-87, when he had 11-33-44 in 71 games.

THE FINESSE GAME

One of the top two-way defensemen in the league, Chelios adheres to the philosophy that his fundamental responsiblity is to get the puck as far from his net as possible. And he does whatever needs to be done to achieve that end. Chelios will skate the puck out ably, pass it out, chip it off the glass; the method doesn't matter as much as the result.

And he couldn't care less how it looks. Though a fine puck-handler of eminent skill, Chelios clearly doesn't feel he has to make the big play or the big rush every time he has possession. He favors a forehand pass up the right-wing boards from behind the net, but will use any short passing option. If no passing lane opens, Chelios will carry the puck to the red line and do something with it; at worst, he will bury it behind the opposition's net. At best, he will score from inside range or outside with a sizzling slap shot that he gets off quickly by using a small windup.

Without the puck, Chelios uses his special mobility and speed to cut off the ice. He is especially smooth on turns to his right, and covers a tremendous amount of ground laterally. He does not give up on a play and hardly is intimidated by a two-on-him break. He will not concede the blue line and often causes the other team to be offside by forcing puck carriers to make decisions before they want to.

Chelios fills out his game with very solid special-teams work. While killing penalties, he is exremely aggressive and uses his skating skills to advantage, challenging all the way to the side boards. On the power play, he quarterbacks well, using the slap shot or working to the open man. And he keeps the puck in at the point extremely well.

THE PHYSICAL GAME

Chelios is a chippy, brash, yappy player who wants the last word and often gets it. His self-confidence on the ice borders on arrogance, yet it seems a critical component to his game; Chelios projects a feeling that he's unbeatable, better than his opponent and dares his opponents to do something about that. He will bump and bang, will stand right in there with the Proberts and Clarks. If you want to play dirty, he can roll in the swill with anybody in the league.

While he is mellow off the ice, Chelios is a hothead on it, vulnerable to penalties that come either in the wrong situation or for the wrong reason. It wouldn't kill him to control himself a bit.

THE INTANGIBLES

Chelios can handle all the ice time in the world. He virtually never will get beaten because he made a lazy play. Every time you look up, he is doing something. We wondered last year why he needed 187 shots to score 12 goals; this year, we wonder why he needed 239 shots for his nine goals.

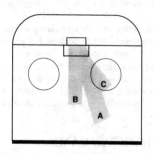

GREG GILBERT

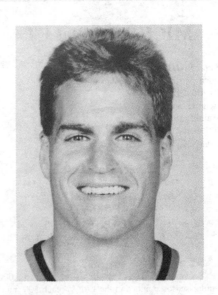

Yrs. of NHL service: 10
Born: Missisauga, Ont.; Jan. 22, 1962
Position: Left wing
Height: 6-1
Weight: 190
Uniform no.: 14
Shoots: Left

Career statistics:

GP	G	A	TP	PIM
621	122	183	305	471

1990-91 statistics:

GP	G	A	TP	+/-	PIM	PP	SH	GW	GT	S	PCT
50	7	5	12	+4	35	0	0	1	0	45	15.6

LAST SEASON

Missed games due to broken ankle. Totals for goals, assists and points all were three-season lows, plus-minus plunged by 10 goals, shot total dropped 53.

THE FINESSE GAME

While Gilbert's goal total for last season is very nearly the perfect summation of his finesse skills, it is hopelessly inadequate in describing his value. Most of the time, he doesn't carry the puck any longer than it takes a teammate to get open. Most of the time, when he doesn't have the puck, he is working to get it so he can move it again.

So he sprints to the corners, in order to be the first man to the puck the defenseman has drilled there. He gets there more with strength and balance than with speed, takes the hit, and then does something with the puck.

Gilbert has enough hands and enough speed to pick up the puck deep in the defensive zone, beat the first forechecker, then get it to the red line and dump it. Then, he either will resume the chase or, exhausted, will head for the bench.

If he scores, it is from close range. Most of the time, he is the checking wing on the line; if he has the puck, he is looking to get it deep more than he is looking to score.

THE PHYSICAL GAME

Gilbert forces turnovers with his forechecking. He works along the boards and keeps the puck alive until a teammate comes along to take possession or until he simply wears out the opposing player.

Gilbert lives in the corners and finishes a high percentage of checks. He takes a hit to make a play. He cycles, carries defenders to the front of the net and takes personal pride in beating his check back into the play after contact.

THE INTANGIBLES

Gilbert is a determined, dedicated hockey player. He battled back from a knee injury that could have ended his career. He does not take 'no' for an answer very often. His work ethic is worthy of respect.

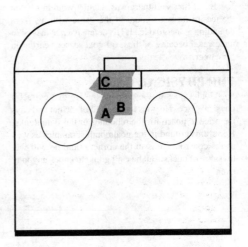

MICHEL GOULET

Yrs. of NHL service: 13
Born: Peribonka, Que.; April 21, 1960
Position: Left wing
Height: 6-1
Weight: 195
Uniform no.: 16
Shoots: Left

Career statistics:

GP	G	A	TP	PIM
970	509	569	1078	756

1990-91 statistics:

GP	G	A	TP	+/-	PIM	PP	SH	GW	GT	S	PCT
75	22	41	63	+20	69	9	0	4	0	176	12.5

LAST SEASON

Became 30th player in NHL history to reach 1,000 regular-season points and the 17th to reach 500 regular-season goals. Scored 20 goals or more in his 13th consective season. Goal production dropped by five, plus-minus by seven.

THE FINESSE GAME

Goulet may have lost some speed, but he still has the hands, still has the touch, still puts pucks away. He will score occasionally with a boomer from the flank, but prospers more by following his instincts to the net for his own rebounds, or those nice passes from Jeremy Roenick.

An up-and-down wing who can work the power play or help kill penalties, Goulet remains a decent bet for 20-25 goals and 60-70 points. He is a thoughtful playmaker who passes the puck well to the front of the net or the point.

But if that's all there was, Goulet wouldn't be on the ice in the last minute of the game with his team defending a one-goal lead. His defensive play has been underrated because of those 50-goal seasons earlier in his career.

THE PHYSICAL GAME

Goulet goes to the parts of the ice that extract a physical price. He goes to the front of the net and pays the price to poach for the rebounds or the slam dunks. He scrums around in the goalmouth scrambles as well as the confrontations in the corners, and he will win his share of pucks. But he isn't going to knock anybody over.

THE INTANGIBLES

Goulet still keeps up, he's useful on the power play and he just got to play in the Stanley Cup final. Desire for another kick at that can should serve as a powerful motivator this season; he doesn't have many chances left.

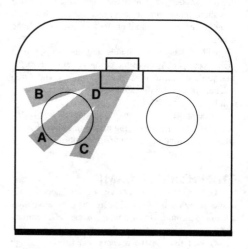

DIRK GRAHAM

Yrs. of NHL service: 8
Born: Regina, Sask.; July 29, 1959
Position: Right wing
Height: 5-11
Weight: 198
Uniform no.: 33
Shoots: Right

Career statistics:

GP	G	A	TP	PIM
581	180	225	405	686

1990-91 statistics:

GP	G	A	TP	+/-	PIM	PP	SH	GW	GT	S	PCT
80	17	30	47	−5	89	6	1	1	0	222	7.7

LAST SEASON

Goal output dropped by seven to his lowest since 1984-85. Plus-minus dropped by 17 goals after he won Frank Selke Award as top defensive forward. Played all 80 games for third time in four seasons and played 70 or more for seventh consecutive campaign.

THE FINESSE GAME

Graham is a plowhorse, persistent and insistent. He keeps driving. He shifts his weight well on his skates, leans in on a defenseman and drives deep into enemy territory. And he pursues the puck extremely well. He will jab at three different puck carriers before he finally nudges the puck free, grabs the turnover and bursts the other way.

He is a heady player, as well. Unlike a player who will force a turnover, then have no idea what he wants to do, Graham is a step ahead mentally; the plan is in place instantly, and regularly, the plan calls for Graham to take the puck to the net.

Toward that end, Graham has good speed and skating strength along with very good balance, all of which also are especially useful on the shorthanded breakaways his penalty killing creates.

As a result, he is a coach's dream: a defensive player who converts a fair share of the offensive chances his defense creates.

THE PHYSICAL GAME

Graham pays the price to make a play. He goes to the net for deflections and screens. He is unstoppable in the corners, continually driving his legs through the checks of defensemen attempting to pin him along the wall. One effort is not enough for him; Graham still has plenty of second-effort determination to spare.

THE INTANGIBLES

It is an emblem of the respect Graham merits that he is captain of a team that has so many worthy leaders. He earns that respect every night, and never was that truer than before the last game of last season's Stanley Cup Final, when he promised his teammates he would play the game of his life — only to back it up with a first-period hat trick that wiped out three Pittsburgh leads.

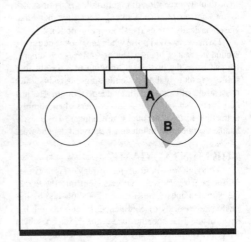

DOMINIK HASEK

Yrs. of NHL service: 2
Born: Pardubice, Czech.; Jan. 29, 1965
Position: Goaltender
Height: 5-11
Weight: 165
Uniform no.: 31
Catches: Left

Career statistics:

GP	MINS	GA	SO	GAA	A	PIM
25	1,209	52	1	2.58	0	8

1991-92 statistics:

GP	MINS	GAA	W	L	T	SO	GA	S	SAPCT	PIM
20	1,014	2.60	10	4	1	1	44	413	.893	8

LAST SEASON

Also played 20 games for Indianapolis of IHL.

THE PHYSICAL GAME

Hasek is a very impressive goaltender on a number of levels, but the thing that strikes you over and over again is the strength of his fundamentals.

He keeps his stick squarely between his pads as he moves laterally. A lot of goaltenders 'fly open' as they go side-to-side, leaving an inviting, easy-to-hit space between the legs. Hasek doesn't make that mistake, and he doesn't leave any five hole as he drops to his knees; he squeezes the knees together on the way down, rather as Ed Belfour does.

Hasek always lets the shooter make the first move on a breakaway. He is so confident in his lateral ability, so absolutely exceptional in getting his pads or skates to low shots and has such an excellent glove hand that Hasek basically leaves the shooters no options.

He has very good poise when the puck is bouncing around in front of the net, and his reflexes are superb. He can be in the process of moving to his right, but still can react to a shot that ends up going to his left.

Hasek still plays a little deep, though. He just dares you to shoot for those low corners, then, nimbly, butterflies to take the pucks on his pads. He doesn't handle the puck much, but he's better at it than he was.

THE MENTAL GAME

Although he would prefer to play, Hasek comes off the bench very well and gets right into the game. He is tremendously confident in his skills and he has many skills worthy of confidence; he can make a big save on the first shot he faces, and if he does it in Chicago, Hasek can really get the fans frothing.

THE INTANGIBLES

Hasek has 'Trade Bait' written all over him. He seems capable of playing way more than 20 games in a season, and probably could — for any number of other teams. Watching Ed Belfour play is educational, but frustrating; at 27, Hasek is approaching prime goaltending years and may be worth more now than after another season of part-time employment.

MIKE HUDSON

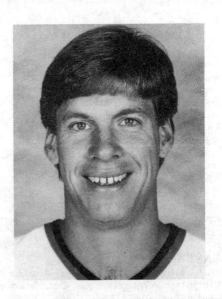

Yrs. of NHL service: 4
Born: Guelph, Ont.; Feb. 6, 1967
Position: Center/left wing
Height: 6-1
Weight: 201
Uniform no.: 20
Shoots: Left

Career statistics:

GP	G	A	TP	PIM
220	37	52	89	232

1990-91 statistics:

GP	G	A	TP	+/-	PIM	PP	SH	GW	GT	S	PCT
76	14	15	29	−11	92	2	1	2	0	97	14.4

LAST SEASON

Totals for games played, goals and points were career highs, while assist total was three-season high and one short of career best. Road goal production jumped by six, to seven.

THE FINESSE GAME

Hudson's game is speed, and properly so, as he is one of the better pure skaters in the league. He can accelerate extremely well, to a speed he can maintain from one end of the rink to the other. Speed also helps on the defensive end of the puck, as few people in the league are going to skate away from him.

But the hands have to get softer. He'll get hit on the tape with a pass and not be able to control the puck. As a result, he is not a great scorer. Because he's so fast, he can really cause a defenseman problems and can get open; a lack of finishing touch cuts into the impact of that skill, however.

THE PHYSICAL GAME

Hudson is not shy; he finishes checks, throws the shoulder. And he's strong; he stays with his man very well after face-offs.

THE INTANGIBLES

Hudson is a good third center; not more, not less.

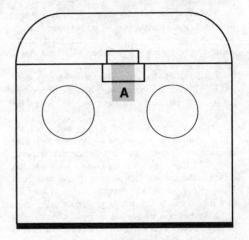

IGOR KRAVCHUK

Yrs. of NHL service: 1
Born: Ufa, Russia; Sept. 13, 1966
Position: Right defense
Height: 6-1
Weight: 200
Uniform no.: 3
Shoots: Left

Career statistics:

GP	G	A	TP	PIM
18	1	8	9	4

1991-92 statistics:

GP	G	A	TP	+/-	PIM	PP	SH	GW	GT	S	PCT
18	1	8	9	−3	4	0	0	1	0	40	2.5

LAST SEASON

Joined Blackhawks after winning gold medal with Unified Team at Winter Olympics. Captained Soviet squad at Canada Cup.

THE FINESSE GAME

Kravchuk arrived with most parts of the finesse package nicely in place.

He has exceptional mobility and turns with an ease that should make him the envy of at least three quarters of the defensemen in the NHL. He has no difficulty whatever performing a 360-degree whirl and makes his pivots without losing much speed.

On the attack, Kravchuk joins the rush very well, and he will do it at the right time because he sees the ice so well. He keeps the puck moving, keeps the tempo high.

Inside the zone, Kravchuk is shifty and smart. He will wind up for a shot, which will tease an opposing defenseman to drop. Then the defenseman is trapped, though, as Kravchuk slides a pass to a wing who has darted to the spot the defenseman should have been filling. Kravchuk also is more than able to hold his own if he is one-on-one with a goaltender.

Kravchuk will not hesitate to fire an accurate pass into the middle of the ice; Russian defensemen exploit that often-available space far more often than most North Americans. But he will dump the puck into the attack zone if he has no better play; he is not stubborn about tactics and does not try to turn the North American game into something it isn't.

THE PHYSICAL GAME

Kravchuk absorbs all the bumps, but also gets a piece of more than a few trespassers in this goalmouth and will throw a nice hip check in open ice. He will clutch and grab, seal his check along the boards, as though he has spent most of his life in the Norris Division. Kravchuk also sets a moving screen on a forechecker, to buy some time so his partner or goalie can move the puck.

Strong enough that he can use his stick effectively to slow down opponents, he uses that tactic to extra effect in combination with his mobility. Kravchuk leaves skaters no place to go, then directs them to where HE wants them to end up.

THE INTANGIBLES

Kravchuk made the NHL adjustment with relative ease, and, immediately upon arriving in Chicago, insisted people start calling him "Gary." From the appearance of his debut season, they will call him anything he asks for a number of years to come.

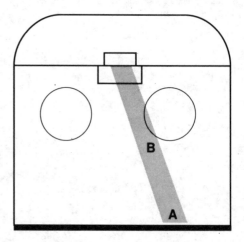

FRANTISEK KUCERA

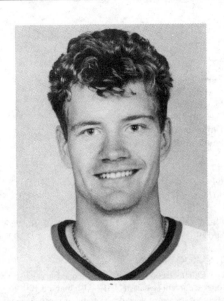

Yrs. of NHL service: 2
Born: Prague, Czech.; Feb. 3, 1968
Position: Left defense
Height: 6-2
Weight: 205
Uniform no.: 6
Shoots: Left

Career statistics:

GP	G	A	TP	PIM
101	5	22	27	68

1990-91 statistics:

GP	G	A	TP	+/-	PIM	PP	SH	GW	GT	S	PCT
61	3	10	13	3	36	1	0	1	0	82	3.7

LAST SEASON

Games played and goal totals were career highs. Played seven games in minors.

THE FINESSE GAME

Kucera is a gifted, fluid skater with some very nice hockey sense. His puck-handling skills are good, not great. He is not an end-to-end skater.

In the attacking zone, however, he pinches up the boards, knowing he has more than enough range to regain position if the puck turns over.

In the defensive zone, he makes a nice first pass on the breakout. He is just steady enough to get the job done, doesn't make glaring errors and is a pretty good defender against one-on-one rushes.

THE PHYSICAL GAME

Physical strength was a problem for Kucera last season. He was weak grinding out the one-on-one battles in front of the net, away from the puck. He is a pretty good open-ice hitter and accepts being hit. He does not back down in muscle matchups, and that is a positive; but Kucera needs to bulk up.

THE INTANGIBLES

Kucera needs to establish himself in front of the net, needs to compete harder physically. But that could come with increased experience and ice time.

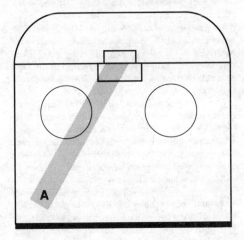

STEVE LARMER

Yrs. of NHL service: 10
Born: Peterborough, Ont.; June 16, 1961
Position: Right wing
Height: 5-11
Weight: 189
Uniform no.: 28
Shoots: Left

Career statistics:

GP	G	A	TP	PIM
807	371	482	583	427

1990-91 statistics:

GP	G	A	TP	+/-	PIM	PP	SH	GW	GT	S	PCT
80	29	45	74	+10	65	11	2	3	0	292	9.9

LAST SEASON

Extended consecutive games-played streak to 800, longest current streak in NHL. Also marked 10th consecutive season of scoring 20 goals or more. Production dropped 27 points from career-high campaign in prior season. Road goal production dropped by 20, from 27 to seven.

THE FINESSE GAME

A very good skater with jolting first-step acceleration and fine balance, Larmer turns some speed into more speed by also accelerating on the glide and skating out of his turns. He takes advantage of his speed by driving toward the blue line, forcing the defensemen to retreat, then pulling up at the top of the face-off circle — freezing the defensemen while he checks the options.

Larmer needs time to get off the big slap shot on occasion, and while that gives goalies a chance to set for the drive, it still arrives with accuracy and power. His snap shot is wickedly hard, a bolt of lightning, and Larmer makes the shot more effective by disguising extremely well where he intends to put the shot; he will look low and fire high, so goalies can't cheat.

Exceptional hand-eye coordination makes Larmer an accurate passer, helps him bat pucks out of the air, and makes him one of the better players in the league at deflecting point shots. Combined with his skating, the hand-eye skill enables Larmer to succeed at an extremely challenging position: being a left shot on right wing.

Larmer is intelligent away from the puck, which makes him an asset as a penalty killer. He reads, anticipates, uses smart positioning of body and stick to close the passing lane, then steals the pass and slices seconds off the clock.

THE PHYSICAL GAME

Larmer thrives in the corners and eagerly ties up a man so a teammate can get the puck. He dishes out solid, powerful hits and does a good job of making contact in the neutral zone. He is, simply, all-business; in the business of hockey, the business is contact and Larmer ably handles his share.

He also gets crunched a fair amount of the time because you can't always see who's coming when you're playing the off-wing. Larmer takes it in stride.

THE INTANGIBLES

Larmer perseveres, gets the most out of himself. If he is stopped by six good saves on six good scoring chances, he will turn that seventh shot into a critical goal instead of saying, 'It's not my night' and going home early. He shows up for work, he competes efficiently and productively, and he expects to win.

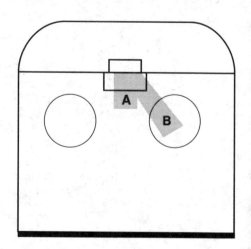

JOCELYN LEMIEUX

Yrs. of NHL service: 5
Born: Mont-Laurier, Que.; Nov. 18, 1967
Position: Right wing
Height: 5-10
Weight: 200
Uniform no.: 26
Shoots: Left

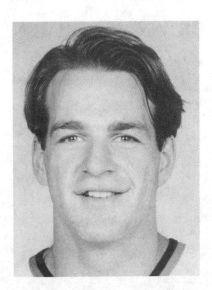

Career statistics:

GP	G	A	TP	PIM
295	37	39	76	443

1990-91 statistics:

GP	G	A	TP	+/-	PIM	PP	SH	GW	GT	S	PCT
78	6	10	16	−2	80	0	0	1	0	103	5.8

LAST SEASON

Games played marked career high. Goal total matched second best of career. Plus-minus improved by five from prior season, while penalty minutes dropped by 39 and shot total improved by 14.

THE FINESSE GAME

For all the physical chaos he creates, Lemieux actually has some nice finesse ability. He has enough hand skills to be trusted with an occasional face-off. He has a good touch with the puck and a good view of the ice; he sees the passing option, and moves it before the window of opportunity closes. Lemieux also is able to feather an accurate pass to a teammate at the last second — just before getting flattened by some defenseman, who may have been waiting weeks for one good crack at him.

Otherwise, he is mostly a power forward, thanks to a bullish skating style that has its genesis in good balance. He puts his head down and reaches top speed in a relatively short span of time. Lemiex keeps his legs churning with short little steps and keeps possession of the puck with his hand quickness. It takes a heckuva shot, even from behind, to knock him off his skates.

Lemieux is not big on dekes; this is pretty much a straight-ahead player who uses a strong wrist shot or a ripping slap shot that keeps goalies honest.

THE PHYSICAL GAME

Lemieux crashes the corners, throws his weight around, hits and gets hit with equal eagerness. He is a daredevil, a demon, a demolition derby reject who eagerly dives for pucks and outworks people to create scoring chances. He wants to be first to the puck, wants to force turnovers. He likes to squirrel around behind the net, draw people to him, then flip little grenade passes in front—hoping they'll explode in the goalie's face.

Lemieux is as much fun as a faceful of ice cubes. He could not care less about his physical well-being, could not care less about who he antagonizes, and seems to get special pleasure out of launching himself at Bob Probert.

THE INTANGIBLES

Can you imagine what it was like in the Lemieux home when Jocelyn and his brother, Claude, were kids? The two of them are off the gauge. Although Claude is the more talented, and the more annoying, Jocelyn more than earns his ice time—and opponents' respect.

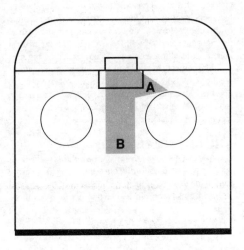

BRYAN MARCHMENT

Yrs. of NHL service: 2
Born: Toronto, Ont.; May 1, 1969
Position: Left defense
Height: 6-1
Weight: 200
Uniform no.: 2
Shoots: Left

Career statistics:

GP	G	A	TP	PIM
95	7	14	21	289

1990-91 statistics:

GP	G	A	TP	+/-	PIM	PP	SH	GW	GT	S	PCT
58	5	10	15	−4	168	2	0	0	0	55	9.1

LAST SEASON

Totals for games, goals, assists, points and PIM all were career highs.

THE FINESSE GAME

Marchment's game right now is an assortment of parts that need some nuts and bolts to connect the pieces into one functioning mechanism. He is dangerous and unpredictable, but there are times when that danger threatens Marchment's team as much as the opposition.

His passing, for instance, can have tremendous shock value. Sometimes he bricks passes that even the softest hands could not control. Sometimes the tape he hits is wrapped on the stick of an opponent. Sometimes you want him fined for handling the puck at all. But he tries, at least, as though he knows you learn better from mistakes than from never trying anything.

Marchment isn't much of a skater. He has no noticeable speed and often ends up on the ice after contact, whether he has initiated it or not. He doesn't have much agility and tends to struggle with a change of direction. He will, however, chug into the rush at the right time and he will step WAY up in the neutral zone to at least threaten a puck carrier with a big hit.

Marchment has decent defensive anticipation, positions himself properly and picks off a pass. He dives to block shots, even with a big lead. He uses the snap shot for quick-release situations and can one-time a point shot off an alley-oop pass.

THE PHYSICAL GAME

Marchment loves to throw the solid hip check in open ice, loves to go for the big bang along the boards, eagerly challenges in the physical areas of the ice, and he will fight. He is big and strong and he uses those tools.

THE INTANGIBLES

Marchment is tough and willing. He is a collection of rough edges that will be smoothed only by playing time, experience and patient guidance. Until then, he will make mistakes and his team will have to live with them, because they come from effort. His heart is in the right place, for sure; simply, there are times when it doesn't seem connected to his head or his hands.

STEPHANE MATTEAU

Yrs. of NHL service: 2
Born: Rouyn-Noranda, Que.; Sept. 2, 1969
Position: Left wing
Height: 6-4
Weight: 210
Uniform no.: 32
Shoots: Left

Career statistics:

GP	G	A	TP	PIM
102	21	27	48	157

1990-91 statistics:

GP	G	A	TP	+/-	PIM	PP	SH	GW	GT	S	PCT
24	6	8	14	5	64	1	0	0	0	38	15.8

LAST SEASON

Obtained from Calgary, for defenseman Trent Yawney, Dec. 16, 1991. Missed majority of season due to calcium growth in left thigh.

THE FINESSE GAME

Matteau's skating is a tough read because it seems to change from game to game. One night, he is moving very well and giving the appearance of speed. Another night, he seems to be loping — arriving eventually where he wants to be. He is an upright skater, who doesn't have much knee bend or ankle flex in his push-off; he doesn't seem to have much of a first step some nights, does not appear to have much quickness on other nights.

Yet, despite a seeming shortage of power, he usually covers ground. He gets to the front of the net for rebounds, although when he gets there, again he seems too upright; that cuts into his balance, because his weight is not distributed well, and it cuts into his reach.

Although seemingly limited, Matteau is used on right wing at times. He is a pretty good passer, although not a very creative one. Occasionally, it seems you can hear him thinking when he's carrying the puck. His hands are not as good as his instincts.

THE PHYSICAL GAME

Generally, Matteau is assigned physical, checking roles and generally he uses a hard edge in carrying out the assignment—especially along the boards. He gets a high percentage of his goals from in front; someone will send a puck across the goalmouth and Matteau will slam it in nicely. He also is placed in front of the net on certain power plays.

There are times, though, when he wastes his size: When he turns away instead of following through on a check and when he gets outmuscled along the boards. That should not happen.

THE INTANGIBLES

Unmistakably, Matteau is most effective when he's involved. An outward lack of intensity should not be misinterpreted. He wants to win and wants to do well.

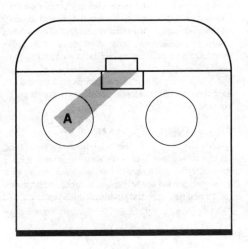

BRIAN NOONAN

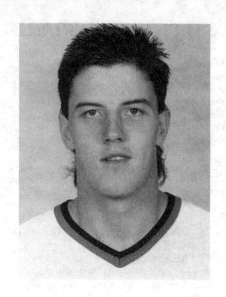

Yrs. of NHL service: 3
Born: Boston, Mass.; May 29, 1965
Position: Center/right wing
Height: 6-1
Weight: 192
Uniform no.: 10
Shoots: Right

Career statistics:

GP	G	A	TP	PIM
202	33	50	83	161

1990-91 statistics:

GP	G	A	TP	+/-	PIM	PP	SH	GW	GT	S	PCT
65	19	12	31	9	81	4	0	0	2	154	12.3

LAST SEASON

More than doubled his prior career-high goal total. Set team record by scoring all seven Blackhawk goals over two-game span, Dec. 27-29. Goal and point totals were career highs.

THE FINESSE GAME

Finesse is the name of Noonan's game. He has superb stickhandling skill and is capable of beating any defenseman in the league one-on-one—not with speed but with his finesse moves and shiftiness. A defenseman has to play the body to have a prayer against Noonan.

If he were more confident in his shot more often, Noonan would have more streaks like that two-game stretch in December, when he scored all seven of the Blackhawks' goals. Noonan has a real nose for the net, but ends up converting less than half his chances, however, because he squeezes the stick too tight or hits his shots high, wide or into the goalie. His release on the slap shot isn't too quick, so it's easier to time; Noonan gets the snap and the wrist away more quickly.

He also could use a little better vision of the ice. He'll have a guy open for a headman pass and fail to move the puck.

A versatile player, Noonan can play all three forward positions, plus defense. He can run a power play from the point, if needed.

THE PHYSICAL GAME

Noonan is game. He competes. He isn't the world's strongest player, isn't going to initiate a hit, but will try to win a race to the puck in a corner. He is sluggish coming out of combat, though, and at times gets beaten back into the play from the boards.

THE INTANGIBLES

An excellent youngster who works hard on his game, Noonan can't play a 200-foot game with 190 feet worth of self-esteem. He has the skill but still needs the will.

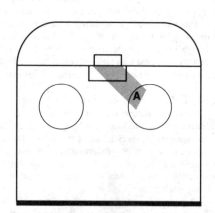

JEREMY ROENICK

Yrs. of NHL service: 4
Born: Boston, Mass.; Jan. 17, 1970
Position: Center
Height: 6-0
Weight: 200
Uniform no.: 27
Shoots: Right

Career statistics:

GP	G	A	TP	PIM
257	129	152	281	236

1990-91 statistics:

GP	G	A	TP	+/-	PIM	PP	SH	GW	GT	S	PCT
80	53	50	103	+23	98	22	3	13	0	234	22.6

LAST SEASON

Goal total was career high and club single-season record for centers. Point total was a career high. Winning-goal total was a club record. Power-play goal total matched club record.

THE FINESSE GAME

Absolutely all the tools, in what seems to be an unbreakable tool box.

Roenick is so strong. He can rifle a heavy wrist shot under the crossbar from 30 feet; yet his touch is so sweet, he can roof a backhand in tight. He keeps the puck way out to the side so nobody can touch it. His hand speed is right there with his foot speed.

Roenick is so fast. He shifts from defense to offense in an instant because of exceptional acceleration to the puck and just-as-good acceleration with it. He has reason to start the transition frequently, because he usually caused the turnover and collected it. And his skating skill is not limited, by any means, merely to speed or acceleration. He can make a 360-degree spin in a phone booth, and he changes direction beautifully.

Roenick is so smart. He knows when to hold the puck, when to move it and where. He does a splendid job of identifying the passing target and getting him the puck. He has such a great sense of where the late man is and when he is arriving, it seems at times as though Roenick has eyes in the back of his head. He is always in the right place because he sees the entire ice, always uses the right shot to keep goalies guessing. If he slapped the first two shots of the game, he'll mix in a wrist shot to keep options open.

THE PHYSICAL GAME

Roenick lives in the corners and commutes to the end boards by way of the front of the net. Night in and night out, he is one of the most physical players in the NHL. And if he isn't a demon, a raw nerve, on a given evening, you know something is gravely wrong.

The way Roenick throws his body around, you would think he is testing the strength limits of bone and tissue.

Your first effort might match his, your second effort might match his, but your third effort won't come close to his. It isn't just that he plays bigger than his own size; he plays bigger than just about everyone else's size. He plays positively every foot of every rink, takes all the punishment you can hand out and keeps coming.

THE INTANGIBLES

Don't imagine, from all these nice words, that Roenick is a one-man team or believes himself to be. While one of the top 10 players in the league, easily, Roenick is ultra-team. Which brings up a question:

Roenick is hardly the guy to make an issue of it, and it hardly affects his play, but where is this guy's letter? Of course the Blackhawks are well-stocked with leadership and role models, but it is difficult to think of any NHL player more deserving of a captain's 'C' or, at least, an alternate's 'A.'

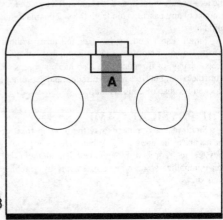

STEVE SMITH

Yrs. of NHL service: 7
Born: Glasgow, Scotland; Apr. 30, 1963
Position: Left defense
Height: 6-4
Weight: 215
Uniform no.: 5
Shoots: Left

Career statistics:

GP	G	A	TP	PIM
461	55	193	248	1,384

1990-91 statistics:

GP	G	A	TP	+/-	PIM	PP	SH	GW	GT	S	PCT
76	9	21	30	23	304	3	0	1	0	153	5.9

LAST SEASON

Obtained from Edmonton, for defenseman Dave Manson and a third-round choice in 1993, on Oct. 2, 1991. Goal total dropped by four but still was third-best in his career. Assist total dropped 20, to three-year low. Plus-minus improved by nine. Point total was a career low for a full season. Penalty minutes jumped 111 and were a career high.

THE FINESSE GAME

A giant man with a huge, powerful skating stride, Smith became confident-enough in his puck-handling skills last season that it was no surprise to see him trying one-on-one moves off a rush. At times, he even tried to split the opposing defense. Not that long ago, Smith would have gotten to the moment of truth, then would have backed off or looked for a pass; in Chicago, he became willing to 'go for it.'

He remained a conscientious defender, of course — one who makes subtle use of his size as often as he makes obvious use of it. When he steps up to challenge a point shot, the shooter attempting to get the puck past Smith has virtually no chance of hitting the net with his drive; to get the puck past so big an obstacle, the puck is almost certain to go wide.

Also, superior balance allows him to drop to one knee, drag his back skate and place his stick flat along the ice — while in motion. That shuts off a tremendous amount of any passing lane from the sideboards to the middle.

Smith skates well for his size and turns without effort. He has a shiftiness and a good, but not quite great, change of direction. He also has a strong shot from the point, but fires wide with some and gets others blocked because of a big windup.

THE PHYSICAL GAME

Smith makes opponents pay the price in front of the net and at the side boards. When he leans on people, they feel the scoreboard may have fallen on them. He can immobilize some opponents merely by grabbing their sticks.

Because he is so tall, it is natural for Smith to hit most players high — around the shoulders. Smith would be utterly devastating if he hit lower, so players are mushed along the boards, unable to get their hands free, unable to build a bridge over the puck with their bodies and wriggle away.

THE INTANGIBLES

Last season Smith took a big step toward the consistent excellence that has been predicted for him. He got a ton of ice time, worked all kinds of special teams and critical situations. He became more of a leader than a follower.

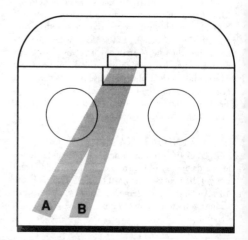

BRENT SUTTER

Yrs. of NHL service: 11
Born: Viking, Alta.; June 10, 1962
Position: Center
Height: 5-11
Weight: 180
Uniform no.: 12
Shoots: Left

Career statistics:

GP	G	A	TP	PIM
755	305	355	660	791

1990-91 statistics:

GP	G	A	TP	+/-	PIM	PP	SH	GW	GT	S	PCT
69	22	38	60	-10	36	8	1	3	1	206	10.7

LAST SEASON

Acquired with Brad Lauer from Islanders for Steve Thomas and Adam Creighton, October 25, 1991. Scored 20 or more goals for 11th consecutive season.

THE FINESSE GAME

Strength and desire are the major components of his competitive display. Finesse skills, such as an accurate wrist shot served up with a quick release, more or less just come along for the ride. He is more of a tractor on skates than a sports car.

While most other players are delighted with the freedom open ice affords, Sutter seems to prefer profoundly confined space, where it's him against you, his strength against yours, his desire against yours. He will use upper-body strength to pin you against the boards, balance plus lower-body strength to try to kick the puck free. He will hold off a man with one hand, move the puck with the other, drive to the net to make something happen.

Sutter will bury a rebound, will convert a two-on-one pass from 15 feet or closer, will tip in a point shot while he's being tackled by a defenseman.

THE PHYSICAL GAME

When the situation calls for hockey bravery, Sutter always is somewhere in the first wave of soldiers. He always can be counted on, especially in the series-long wars during the playoffs, when he takes so many face-offs against the opposition's top face-off man or second-line center. Sutter gets hurt, plays hurt, strives every shift. He doesn't hit as much as he bumps or gets a piece of a guy, but nobody ever has an easy night against him.

THE INTANGIBLES

Brent Sutter never feels he has finished his dues. He worked with his hands on his parents' farm and he works with his hands now as a laborer for his brother Darryl. He does honest work for honest pay, never leaves until he has given everything to help win.

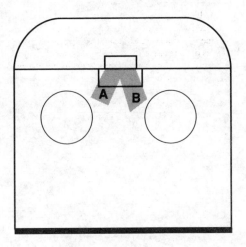

DETROIT RED WINGS

SHAWN BURR

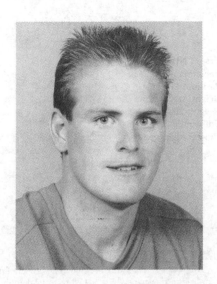

Yrs. of NHL service: 7
Born: Sarnia, Ont., July 1, 1966
Position: Left wing
Height: 6-1
Weight: 180
Uniform no.: 11
Shoots: Left

Career statistics:

GP	G	A	TP	PIM
486	122	169	291	600

1991-92 statistics:

GP	G	A	TP	+/-	PIM	PP	SH	GW	GT	S	PCT
79	19	32	51	26	118	2	0	3	1	140	13.6

LAST SEASON

Goals three-season low. Points two-season high. Missed one game with flu.

THE FINESSE GAME

Burr was a big scorer in junior hockey, but with all of the talented scorers on the Red Wings, he has carved out a niche for himself as a checker. He doesn't have the skating ability to have the same kind of scoring success in the NHL. He is choppy and his mobility and lateral movement are average to fair.

Burr is very smart and plucky, and his never-say-die attitude makes him an excellent forechecker despite his skating style. He has lost some of his time on the penalty-killing unit to Sergei Fedorov, who is much more of a shorthanded scoring threat than Burr.

Not especially creative offensively, he will still get his 15-20 goals by digging for loose pucks around the net. He is a converted center who can take defensive zone draws.

THE PHYSICAL GAME

Despite not having a great body, Burr hits hard and stands up players in open ice. He bangs in the corners and is pugnacious and chippy. He really aggravates his opponents: sometimes he aggravates his own team.

Burr tends to get worn down over the course of a season because his physical style takes its toll on him. He has never been one to keep himself in great condition, which doesn't help.

THE INTANGIBLES

Burr is a mystery to his coaches who can't decide if he is underachieving or if he has just established himself as a hard-knocking two-way center. Appar-ently there are other teams who would be happy to ponder the question because he is much sought after in trade talks.

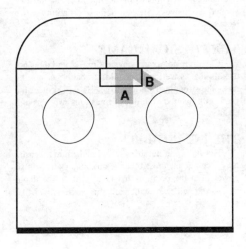

JIMMY CARSON

Yrs. of NHL service: 6
Born: Southfield, Mich.; July 20, 1968
Position: Center
Height: 6-1
Weight: 200
Uniform no.: 12
Shoots: Right

Career statistics:

GP	G	A	TP	PIM
432	217	223	440	169

1991-92 statistics:

GP	G	A	TP	+/-	PIM	PP	SH	GW	GT	S	PCT
80	34	35	69	17	30	11	0	3	0	150	22.7

LAST SEASON

All scoring totals three-season highs. Tied for team lead in power-play goals. Led team in shooting percentage. One of four Red Wings to play in all 80 games. Played all 80 for fourth time in career.

THE FINESSE GAME

Carson can score in a number of ways, and much of his attack comes from his good skating. He will fake a shot high between the circles, move on his forehand to the right and try a snap shot. He will curl out from behind the net left to right, and send a pass back against the grain to his left.

Carson has speed, but is not a well-balanced skater. He is too straight-legged and needs to bend his knees more.

A good puckhandler, especially in open ice, he overhandles occasionally at the blue line, and must be spotted defensively. He is a defensive liability down low.

THE PHYSICAL GAME

Carson is not a very physical player and does not use his size as well as he should, probably because he lacks the strength from leg drive. He will protect the puck with his body but doesn't push his way through checks.

THE INTANGIBLES

His skills and numbers would make him at least a No. 2 center on most other teams, but Detroit is so powerful at the position that he's third on the depth chart (and will be challenged this season by Mike Sillinger). Expect Carson to be dealt during the season as the Red Wings pursue a big defenseman.

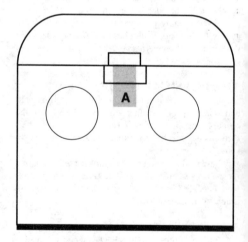

TIM CHEVELDAE

Yrs. of NHL service: 3
Born: Melville, Sask.; Feb. 15, 1968
Position: Goaltender
Height: 5-11
Weight: 180
Uniform no.: 32
Catches: Left

Career statistics:

GP	MINS	GA	SO	GAA	A	PIM
167	9573	550	4	3.48	10	10

1991-92 statistics:

GP	MINS	GAA	W	L	T	SO	GA	S	SAPCT	PIM
72	4236	3.20	38	23	9	2	226	1978	.886	6

LAST SEASON

Tied for NHL lead in goalie wins. Led NHL goalies in games and minutes played. Games played, minutes played, wins career highs. GAA career best.

THE PHYSICAL GAME

Cheveldae, the workhorse, is a good stand-up goalie with above average skills in almost all areas. He covers his angles well and has a great glove hand. He may be one of the best catchers in the league.

His puckhandling is the weakest part of his game, being merely adequate. With a lot more work on this area, Cheveldae would move into the ranks of the NHL's top goalies. He is a very strong skater, so he gets to the puck fine, but doesn't do a good job of moving it.

Cheveldae has a good stance. He is over his edges perfectly and plays a very controlled game physically and doesn't sprawl. He has good concentration and command of his body.

Cheveldae moves well laterally, and uses his stick to keep his five hole covered as he takes a big step to one side. He reacts quickly to a deflection or a redirection. He recovers well for a second shot.

THE MENTAL GAME

A very mature player with great composure, he is very cool under fire and obviously can handle the stress of a heavy workload, at least mentally. Cheveldae can have a tough night but the next morning arrives at practice like it never happened. He never loses confidence or gets uptight.

He doesn't get overly excited by a bad goal or a big save and always stays ready for the next shot. Cheveldae has been a winner at every level he has played.

THE INTANGIBLES

Cheveldae allowed some very soft goals during the playoffs. The Red Wings had every intention of giving him less work last season (they acquired Vincent Riendeau in October but he was promptly injured in his first game for Detroit). While it's entertaining to watch Cheveldae during the season as he plays night after night, he is no marathon man and needs his playing time cut back to be a better goalie in the post-season.

STEVE CHIASSON

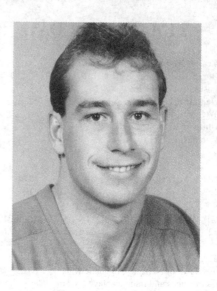

Yrs. of NHL service: 6
Born: Barrie, Ont.; Apr. 14, 1967
Position: Left defense
Height: 6-0
Weight: 205
Uniform no.: 3
Shoots: Left

Career statistics:

GP	G	A	TP	PIM
310	42	117	159	609

1991-92 statistics:

GP	G	A	TP	+/-	PIM	PP	SH	GW	GT	S	PCT
62	10	24	34	22	136	5	0	2	1	143	7.0

LAST SEASON

Second in scoring among team defensemen. Goals and points two-season highs. Missed four games from suspension from 1991 playoffs. Missed 14 games with ankle injury.

THE FINESSE GAME

Chiasson has a great shot, as hard as almost anyone's, and he can score from the top of the circle. His drives would be much more deadly if his lateral mobility improved, because then he could glide across to the middle a la Brian Leetch and become a tremendous scoring threat. Since he gets considerable time on the power play, that manoeuvre would help him open things up.

Not a great skater, he gets there, but it doesn't look pretty. To become a really good defenseman, he has to get better in his skating. That is about all that's missing in his game.

He sees the ice and moves the puck quickly out of the zone or joins the rush.

THE PHYSICAL GAME

Chiasson has got a mean streak. He is not a real fighter, but is mean and competitive. He is strong in the corners and in front of his net and likes being physical.

THE INTANGIBLES

Chiasson is close to being the best defenseman on the Red Wings, but without better skating he will never progress to the next level as an NHL defenseman.

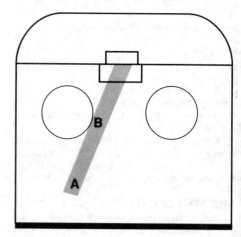

DINO CICCARELLI

Yrs. of NHL service: 12
Born: Sarnia, Ont.; Feb. 8, 1960
Position: Right wing
Height: 5-10
Weight: 175
Uniform no.: 22
Shoots: Right

Career statistics:

GP	G	A	TP	PIM
825	444	416	860	920

1991-92 statistics:

GP	G	A	TP	+/-	PIM	PP	SH	GW	GT	S	PCT
78	38	38	76	−10	78	13	0	7	0	279	13.6

LAST SEASON

Acquired for Washington for Kevin Miller, June 20, 1992. Led Capitals in goals. Third on Caps in scoring. Tied for Caps lead in game-winning goals. Tied for second on Caps in power-play goals. Games played and all scoring totals two-season highs.

THE FINESSE GAME

Ciccarelli is an extremely annoying player to face. A persistent forechecker, he will pressure the defense, chasing the puck. If he doesn't get it or the man, he will chase back up ice and badger the heels of whoever gets it. He will whack, hook, slash and yap.

Ciccarelli finishes a lot of checks in the attacking corners, often with authority. He always seems to be in front of the net, playing the price. He also takes a big slapper coming in off the wing.

More of a finisher than a starter, he doesn't make great passes. His goal scoring is not as consistent as it was.

Ciccarelli is a very mobile skater with instant speed. He can shake defenders because he is more agile than most of them, using a change of direction that catches them leaning the wrong way.

THE PHYSICAL GAME

Ciccarelli never coasts, and always works hard. He does most of his goal scoring from around the net, where the camping fee is the attention he gets from his checkers. He is one of the game's top divers, and while the referees ignore most of his belly-flops, he'll draw one every other game or so to give his team a power play — which he will happily stay out on the ice for.

THE INTANGIBLES

Ciccarelli gives the Red Wings a tremendous finisher and experience on the right side. He has slowed down a little, but had a big rebound year last season and is still a goal-scorer and can still be a game-breaker. He strengthens what is already an awesomely talented crew in Detroit.

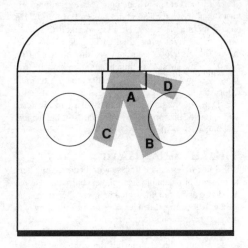

SERGEI FEDOROV

Yrs. of NHL service: 2
Born: Pskov, C.I.S.; Dec. 13, 1969
Position: Center
Height: 6-1
Weight: 191
Uniform no.: 91
Shoots: Left

Career statistics:

GP	G	A	TP	PIM
157	63	102	165	138

1991-92 statistics:

GP	G	A	TP	+/-	PIM	PP	SH	GW	GT	S	PCT
80	32	54	86	26	72	7	2	5	0	249	12.9

LAST SEASON

All scoring totals career bests in second NHL season. Second on team in assists, points, game-winning goals and shots. Finalist for 1992 Selke Trophy.

THE FINESSE GAME

Call him Ultra Man. Fedorov is ultra agile, ultra accurate and ultra fast. His finesse skills are impeccable. He can handle the puck at great speed and uses dekes even coming out of the defensive zone. He makes a tight turn with the puck on his backhand, which requires great wrist strength and exceptional balance.

Fedorov avoids traffic. He passes out of it to open ice with marvelous vision, and sees everything. He just floats above the ice, gliding like a hovercraft. His lateral mobility is scary. He likes to take the defense wide on the right wing, then curl inside with a forehand. He gets a low, accurate wrist shot off in a hurry.

Fedorov attracts so much attention that he frequently draws two or more defenders to him, opening up ice for his linemates.

Defensively, he has eyes in the back of his head, and is one of the top two-way forwards in the league. His defensive reads are near-perfect.

THE PHYSICAL GAME

Since we associate finesse with Fedorov, it's hard to think of him as a physical player, but he is. He has good size and strength, which he uses when he has to, although he prefers open ice play and intimidating with his speed and reputation.

Fedorov is improving on draws, although he has to do a better job of tying up the opposing face-off man.

THE INTANGIBLES

Did anyone say sophomore slump? Fedorov was even better in his second year than in his impressive freshman season, and he's only getting better. There is no limit to what he will be able to accomplish in the NHL.

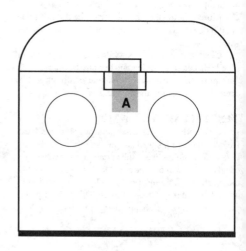

BRENT FEDYK

Yrs. of NHL service: 3
Born: Yorkton, Sask.; Mar. 8, 1967
Position: Right wing
Height: 6-0
Weight: 195
Uniform no.: 14
Shoots: Right

Career statistics:

GP	G	A	TP	PIM
162	24	32	56	88

1991-92 statistics:

GP	G	A	TP	+/-	PIM	PP	SH	GW	GT	S	PCT
61	5	8	13	−5	42	0	0	1	0	60	8.3

LAST SEASON

Goals, assists and points half (or fewer) of career bests in 1990-91. Missed four games with shoulder separation. Missed three games with strained back.

THE FINESSE GAME

On a team of scoring stars, Fedyk can get overlooked, but he plays a valuable role as a third line checking winger. He has limited skills, but has improved with experience.

Very strong defensively, he never causes uneven situations in the neutral zone, and he reads plays very well.

Fedyk was a good scorer in junior and in the minors, and seems to have the capability to be a 20-goal man. He has a good release on his shot, which he likes to use from the right circle in, but he doesn't finish well on his scoring chances. Despite lots of opportunities, most nights he can't buy a goal.

THE PHYSICAL GAME

Fedyk isn't a punishing hitter. He checks but doesn't crunch, and isn't as aggressive or chippy as some of his coaches would like. It's not that he is shy of the physical game, he just doesn't have an agitator's personality.

THE INTANGIBLES

Fedyk needs to show more consistency and intensity, and has to start producing more offense—which he can do without sacrificing his excellent defensive work.

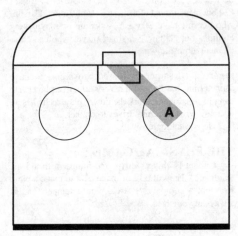

GERARD GALLANT

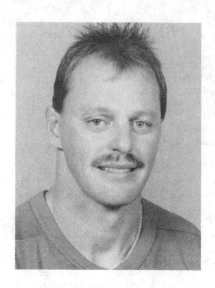

Yrs. of NHL service: 8
Born: Summerside, P.E.I.; Sept. 2, 1963
Position: Left wing
Height: 5-10
Weight: 185
Uniform no.: 17
Shoots: Left

Career statistics:

GP	G	A	TP	PIM
496	197	240	437	1412

1991-92 statistics:

GP	G	A	TP	+/-	PIM	PP	SH	GW	GT	S	PCT
69	14	22	36	16	187	4	0	1	1	116	12.1

LAST SEASON

Games played and all scoring totals two-season highs. Second on team in PIM. Missed six games with hand injury. Served one game automatic suspension for second stick major of season. Missed six games with strained back.

THE FINESSE GAME

Gallant is an up-and-down grinder with great hockey sense, but his scoring touch has tailed off and he lost his spot on the left side of Steve Yzerman. Gallant played most of the season with Jimmy Carson, who doesn't have Stevie Y's skating or playmaking abilities, but Gallant is a smart player who can complement almost anyone.

He is not a great skater, and a serious back injury that required surgery a season ago seems to have sapped him, but he is still a very effective player. He can kill penalties or work the power play, as he has an accurate wrist shot and drives to the net.

He is weak defensively.

THE PHYSICAL GAME

Gallant is chippy, dirty, and jumps in to aid his teammates. He will take or make a hit to make a play. He's got a competitive streak and a temper, and is always in your face.

THE INTANGIBLES

Gallant is a leader by example, and while his physical skills have deteriorated somewhat, he is a valuable player to have in the lineup. He is a team man.

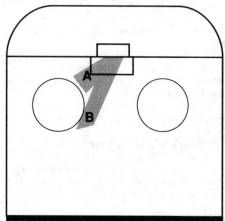

MARK HOWE

Yrs. of NHL service: 13
Born: Detroit, Mich.; May 28, 1955
Position: Left defense
Height: 5-11
Weight: 185
Uniform no.: 2
Shoots: Left

Career statistics:

GP	G	A	TP	PIM
807	215	314	529	216

1991-92 statistics:

GP	G	A	TP	+/-	PIM	PP	SH	GW	GT	S	PCT
42	7	18	25	18	18	6	0	0	0	63	11.1

LAST SEASON

Games-played was three-season high, but fourth straight year he played 52 games or fewer. Missed 24 games due to broken thumb, missed six due to lower-back troubles. Led team in plus-minus.

THE FINESSE GAME

Howe still does all the hockey things as well as he was doing them years ago. He just does them a touch slower now.

His mind unmistakably is the key instrument in his finesse game. He reads the play so well, and virtually always makes the proper choice. He moves the puck so well. He's so smart; Howe always knows when to jump into the rush, when to cheat down low on the power play. And when he is healthy, Howe remains one of the fleeter defensemen on his team.

Here is Howe, defending against a rush: he catches a guy, gives him no place to go, reaches in, takes the puck and says goodbye. So smooth, so elegant. He makes it look so easy, cuts off the ice so successfully, and yet if it were as easy as Howe makes it look, there would be trucks full of great defensemen in the NHL.

Howe calms everything down or picks everything up. He is in control virtually at all times. He is an exceptional leader with exceptional enthusiasm for the game, even for practices. He sets the focus.

THE PHYSICAL GAME

Howe accepts all the banging with a shrug, as though he can't imagine what guys think they've achieved if they knock him down. He is a gentleman, a stylist, has been one his entire career—a Lady Byng should-have-been. Howe doesn't need to blast a guy to get the puck. He uses something else: skill.

THE INTANGIBLES

Howe is 37, but there is no question he can play well a few more years. One way of looking at it is, his body is falling apart. Another way of looking at it is, he is well-enough rested, after all these partial seasons, to continue contributing—at least on a part-time basis—until he is almost as old as his famous father was when he retired. The Flyers will miss him.

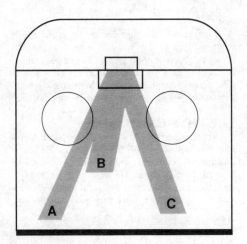

VLADIMIR KONSTANTINOV

Yrs. of NHL service: 1
Born: Murmansk, C.I.S.; Mar. 19, 1967
Position: Right defense
Height: 5-11
Weight: 176
Uniform no.: 16
Shoots: Right

Career statistics:

GP	G	A	TP	PIM
79	8	25	33	172

1991-92 statistics:

GP	G	A	TP	+/-	PIM	PP	SH	GW	GT	S	PCT
79	8	25	33	25	172	1	0	2	0	102	7.4

LAST SEASON

First NHL season. Second among NHL rookies in plus-minus. Missed one game with back injury.

THE FINESSE GAME

Konstantinov is an exceptional skater with speed, agility, lateral mobility and balance. It didn't take long for Konstantinov to become one of the best defensemen on the Red Wings, and he was used in all clutch situations. By the end of the season, he was No. 1 on Detroit's defense depth chart by many scouts' estimations.

Not an offensive defenseman, he can move the puck. He is very creative and can lead or jump into a rush, but he won't be found too deep near his own net. He has a good shot from the point, but prefers to work the puck in down low with a pass rather than take the shot.

Konstantinov has great hockey sense and is just about unflappable. He is used on the first penalty-killing unit because of his great skills and positioning. He doesn't get caught running around. Detroit's decision to pair him with steady Brad Marsh (now gone to Toronto) helped Konstantinov break into the NHL.

THE PHYSICAL GAME

Konstantinov showed a liking for the North American style of play from his first few games. He can be abrasive and obnoxious, and just wait until he learns to speak English better. He lacks size and strength along the boards, but he is a competitor and will throw his body around. He's also a very good shot blocker.

THE INTANGIBLES

Konstantinov was captain of the Red Army team before coming to the NHL and his leadership showed on the ice. Despite all the attention focused on Nicklas Lidstrom, it was this Russian rookie who was probably the Red Wings' best defenseman overall last season. Expect him to play even more of a dominating role with Detroit this season.

NICKLAS LIDSTROM

Yrs. of NHL service: 1
Born: Vasteras, Sweden; Apr. 28, 1970
Position: Left Defense
Height: 6-1
Weight: 176
Uniform no.: 5
Shoots: Left

Career statistcs:

GP	G	A	TP	PIM
80	11	49	60	22

1991-92 statistics:

GP	G	A	TP	+/-	PIM	PP	SH	GW	GT	S	PCT
80	11	49	60	36	22	5	0	1	1	168	6.5

LAST SEASON

First NHL season. Third in NHL in plus-minus. Led NHL rookies in assists and plus-minus. Tied for third in NHL rookie scoring. Led team defensemen in scoring. Second on team in assists. One of four Red Wings to appear in all 80 games. Finalist for 1992 Calder Trophy.

THE FINESSE GAME

Outstanding speed, an excellent point shot and heady play made Lidstrom one of the standouts of a strong rookie crop last season.

He helped turn the Detroit defense into a much better breakout unit. He will look up the middle for outlet passes, and the Red Wings have so many gifted skaters up front that they may be the best counterattacking team in the league.

That the Detroit power play wasn't more effective with Lidstrom working the point is something of a puzzle, unless there is a problem with too many quarterbacks (Lidstrom, Steve Yzerman and Sergei Fedorov) all being on the ice at the same time. He has a good, hard, accurate shot from the point. He doesn't cheat in much beyond the tops of the circles.

Lidstrom's work in his own end needs some improvement. The physical part of his play isn't quite up to NHL All-Star calibre yet, but there are so many strong components to his game that he is certainly future Norris Trophy material.

THE PHYSICAL GAME

Lidstrom has quiet toughness, as he showed when he went into smaller buildings like Chicago Stadium and was not intimidated. He isn't a physical player, and will try to slide away to avoid hits, but he won't do it at the expense of losing the puck. It's just a smarter way for him to play, since he is usually able to maintain control of the puck or body position on the puck carrier. He is strong on his skates, with excellent balance, and is a solid hitter.

THE INTANGIBLES

"St. Nick" had a slow second half, which probably cost him the Calder Trophy, but a slugish finish is not unusual for European players in their first season of NHL competition. He broke in at a tough position, and for much of the year was the Red Wings' best defenseman.

BRAD McCRIMMON

Yrs. of NHL service: 13
Born: Dodsland, Sask.; Mar. 29, 1959
Position: Right defense
Height: 5-11
Weight: 197
Uniform no.: 2
Shoots: Left

Career statistics:

GP	G	A	TP	PIM
969	75	291	366	1151

1991-92 statistics:

GP	G	A	TP	+/-	PIM	PP	SH	GW	GT	S	PCT
79	7	22	29	39	118	2	1	1	0	94	7.4

LAST SEASON

Second in NHL and on team in plus-minus. All scoring totals four-season highs. PIM second-highest of career.

THE FINESSE GAME

A player doesn't need a "C" or an "A" stitched to his sweater to be a leader, as McCrimmon has proven night after night throughout his career. He is a stay-at-home defenseman who knows the game inside out.

An excellent support defenseman, McCrimmon has good skills but is not an offensive player. He makes the safe play, making his first pass simple, direct and accurate.

McCrimmon is a leader in the room and is a well-conditioned athlete who works hard all year to maintain his edge. And he still approaches the game like a rookie. He wants the coaches to stay on him, to let him know what he's doing wrong.

A good penalty killer, he has slowed down but reads plays and uses his experience.

THE PHYSICAL GAME

McCrimmon exacts a toll when anyone comes into his zone. He makes people pay a price to beat him or get body position on him, and he is mean when he grinds in the corners and in front of his net. Age has become an issue, since he will yield the blue line and give attackers just a little bit more room than he used to.

THE INTANGIBLES

Could there be a more underrated defenseman than McCrimmon? He has played alongside such top-notch defensemen as Mark Howe, Al MacInnis and, now, Nicklas Lidstrom, without a lick of credit. That's how the low-key McCrimmon likes it, but we'll give him his due. Maybe those fellas wouldn't have been as great without him.

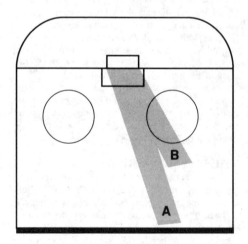

KEITH PRIMEAU

Yrs. of NHL service: 2
Born: Toronto, Ont.; Nov. 24, 1971
Position: Left wing/center
Height: 6-4
Weight: 220
Uniform no.: 55
Shoots: Left

Career statistics:

GP	G	A	TP	PIM
93	9	22	31	189

1991-92 statistics:

GP	G	A	TP	+/-	PIM	PP	SH	GW	GT	S	PCT
35	6	10	16	9	83	0	0	0	0	27	22.2

LAST SEASON

Goals and points two-season highs despite playing less than half a season in second NHL year.

THE FINESSE GAME

Yet another a center that the Red Wings have converted to a winger, Primeau came up through junior as a skilled passer but has adjusted eagerly to his role as a grinder.

Primeau needs to add more quickness. He is a good skater once he gets going, but he has to improve his first few strides. Lower body workouts might help.

As he continues to get more ice time, he will gain more confidence in his skills, which are considerable. He drives well to the net but has to release his shot quicker. Primeau scored 57 goals (and had 70 assists) in his last season of junior with Niagara Falls, so he obviously has nice scoring instincts.

He can take face-offs and will tie up his man on the draw. He hasn't seen much penalty-killing duty, but he could do the job and will sacrifice his body to block shots.

THE PHYSICAL GAME

Primeau loves to hit. He's a big kid and uses his size well. He still has trouble winning some one-on-one battles because he needs better balance, but he is very powerful. With better leg drive, he'll be almost unstoppable in front of the net. He is very intelligent and mature, and his reflexes are still playing catch-up to his body.

THE INTANGIBLES

Primeau will be a 30-goal scorer and a gifted power forward. The question is whether it will happen this season or next. He's already a frightening size,

and we're not sure he's stopped growing. Some scouts predicted he would be the best of the crop of 1990 (a draft year that included Jaromir Jagr, Derian Hatcher, Petr Nedved, Owen Nolan and Mike Ricci).

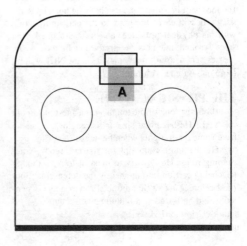

BOB PROBERT

Yrs. of NHL service: 6
Born: Windsor, Ont.; June 5, 1965
Position: Left wing
Height: 6-3
Weight: 215
Uniform no.: 24
Shoots: Left

Career statistics:

GP	G	A	TP	PIM
328	93	106	199	1523

1991-92 statistics:

GP	G	A	TP	+/-	PIM	PP	SH	GW	GT	S	PCT
63	20	24	44	16	276	8	0	1	0	96	20.8

LAST SEASON

Games played and all scoring totals four-season highs. Probert is prohibited by U.S. Immigration from playing any of the team's games in Canada. Led team in PIM.

THE FINESSE GAME

We're starting to sound like a broken record, because we say it year after year, but Probert has exceptional finesse skills for a thug. He piles up points and penalty minutes with equal elan.

His hands are quicker for punching than shooting. Even his wrist shot takes a while to release, but he gets extra room because most defensemen are leery of him, and he makes the most of the time people give him. He is a good stickhandler who can make a tight turn and keep the puck on his backhand.

Probert is a very good skater, strong and balanced. He goes well in traffic, and can kick the puck up to his stick. He will carry the puck to the net, intimidating with his physical presence, and he has a quick first step. Around the net, he pretty much does as he pleases. There aren't many players in the NHL willing to go one-on-one with him.

THE PHYSICAL GAME

Probert is one of the toughest, meanest players in the NHL. He has great size and strength, but he can have some quiet nights when he doesn't get riled up.

He has utter contempt for the enforced goalie-running rules. He will try to make it look as though he's being carried into the net by the defenseman, but most referees aren't that dumb. Probert gets his penalties, but he'll trade it to thump a netminder.

THE INTANGIBLES

A power forward with the skills to score 30 goals — and would if he did miss playing all those games in Canada — his well-publicized off-ice problems will continue to dog him. If Probert stays clean, his on-ice reputation will overshadow the other.

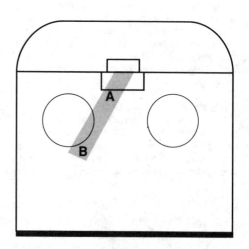

YVES RACINE

Yrs. of NHL service: 3
Born: Matane, Que.; Feb. 7, 1969
Position: Left defense
Height: 6-0
Weight: 185
Uniform no.: 33
Shoots: Left

Career statistics:

GP	G	A	TP	PIM
151	13	71	84	150

1991-92 statistics:

GP	G	A	TP	+/-	PIM	PP	SH	GW	GT	S	PCT
61	2	22	24	−6	94	1	0	0	0	103	1.9

LAST SEASON

Goals career low. Assists and points two-season lows. PIM career high.

THE FINESSE GAME

Racine has some very good finesse skills. He can carry the puck with nice speed, take the puck off the boards and make a turn on the backhand. He will control the puck and hold off the forechecker.

He is a rangy, agile skater. He has a very long reach and likes to poke check the puck away from the attacker, while maintaining a good position with his body. He doesn't always react well under pressure, sometimes overhandling or giving up the puck. More experience should solve that problem.

Racine has improved his speed but he needs more strength to take the body.

He has a good shot from the point.

THE PHYSICAL GAME

Racine needs to play stronger, and be able to work the boards one-on-one. He knows how to hit the body and will hit, but not hard enough. He does not have true NHL strength for the kind of defensive style he will have to play.

THE INTANGIBLES

Racine is steadily improving but still needs to improve his strength. As we noted in HSR last season, defensemen need at least five years to develop and Racine is only in his third. He could be worth the wait.

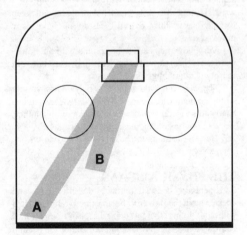

91

RAY SHEPPARD

Yrs. of NHL service: 5
Born: Pembroke, Ont.; May 27, 1966
Position: Right wing
Height: 6-1
Weight: 182
Uniform no.: 26
Shoots: Right

Career statistics:

GP	G	A	TP	PIM
292	124	99	223	77

1991-92 statistics:

GP	G	A	TP	+/-	PIM	PP	SH	GW	GT	S	PCT
74	36	26	62	7	27	11	1	4	1	178	20.2

LAST SEASON

Signed as a free agent, Aug. 5, 1991. All scoring totals best since rookie season (1987-88). Tied for team lead in power-play goals. Second on team in goals.

THE FINESSE GAME

Sheppard played most of the season with Steve Yzerman, and made a good complement because he is a finisher. Sheppard is very sharp around the net with a quick shot, either a snap (with little backswing) or a wrist. He doesn't have great balance but will keep forging forward through traffic. He doesn't have many moves.

Very slow, he needs to be spotted with quick forwards. He has slow, heavy feet, and does not turn sharply. Chug, chug, chug.

Sheppard can make some nice plays. His arms are strong enough that he can hold off a defender with one hand and shovel the puck to a teammate with another. He has good vision and has a good short game.

He is weak along the boards and poor one-on-one defensively.

THE PHYSICAL GAME

Sheppard doesn't initiate, doesn't fight and doesn't have the power to be an effective hitter. He's willing to go into the corners, but doesn't win a lot of battles. He is better off hanging in front of the net and letting his linemates feed him.

THE INTANGIBLES

Sheppard has to play with the right people to be effective, and the Red Wings found that combination last season. He isn't a very dynamic player, but he was a pretty exciting free agent signing for Detroit, which signed him away from the Rangers without compensation.

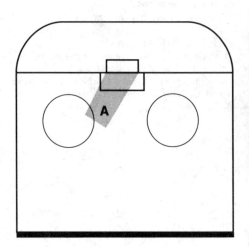

PAUL YSEBAERT

Yrs. of NHL service: 2
Born: Sarnia, Ont.; May 15, 1966
Position: Left wing/center
Height: 6-1
Weight: 190
Uniform no.: 21
Shoots: Left

Career statistics:

GP	G	A	TP	PIM
151	55	67	122	77

1991-92 statistics:

GP	G	A	TP	+/-	PIM	PP	SH	GW	GT	S	PCT
79	35	40	75	44	55	3	4	3	1	211	16.6

LAST SEASON

Led NHL in plus-minus. Third on team in scoring. Games played and all scoring totals career highs in second full NHL season.

THE FINESSE GAME

Ysebaert has good offensive sense—always did, and he made his reputation as a scorer in college and the minors (he led the AHL in scoring in 1989-90). It was his defensive game that needed work, and he has improved dramatically there. Of course, not all of the credit for his Plus-Minus Award is Ysebaert's and he is quick to point out his linemates—Sergei Fedorov and Shawn Burr—are excellent defensive forwards. Ysebaert is still weak one-on-one defensive, so don't start readying the Selke Trophy, but he is more responsible.

And he has proven he can score at the NHL level. He is a finisher and will grind around the net for his chances. He goes to the net and works hard. He has a scorer's shot, hard and accurate with a quick release.

Ysebaert is a deceptive skater who gets his jump with his first three or four steps. He will drive wide with the puck, then come to the net when the ice opens up as defenders are mesmerized by Fedorov through the middle. He doesn't carry the puck well, but knows what to do with it when he gets it in tight.

THE PHYSICAL GAME

Ysebaert is still a little soft physically, although he has worked to improve his upper-body strength. He doesn't win many one-on-one battles along the boards.

THE INTANGIBLES

Now that Ysebaert has made it as an NHLer, let's all learn to give him the respect he deserves and pronounce his name correctly (EYES-a-bart). You'll be hearing it often enough from p.a. announcers around the league.

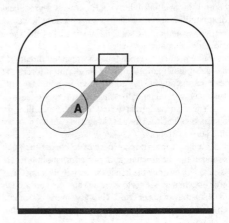

STEVE YZERMAN

Yrs. of NHL service: 9
Born: Cranbrook, B.C.; May 9, 1965
Position: Center
Height: 5-11
Weight: 183
Uniform no.: 19
Shoots: Right

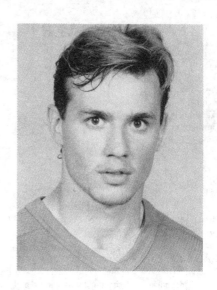

Career statistics:

GP	G	A	TP	PIM
673	387	516	903	432

1991-92 statistics:

GP	G	A	TP	+/-	PIM	PP	SH	GW	GT	S	PCT
79	45	58	103	26	64	9	8	9	0	295	15.3

LAST SEASON

Eighth in NHL in scoring. Sixth in league in goals. Topped 100-point mark for fifth consecutive season. Led NHL in shorthanded goals. Tied for second in NHL in game-winning goals. Led team in goals, assists, points, game-winning goals, shorthanded goals and shots.

THE FINESSE GAME

Yzerman uses all of the ice. For a center, he doesn't spend much time in the middle. He is such a strong, beautiful skater that he likes to weave around from wing to wing. Yzerman is very light on his skates and has very deep edges for gravity-defying balance. He can stop on a dime and give a nickel change, and control the puck all the time. He creates a great deal of scrambling in the defensive zone because he has so many high-tempo moves, and never makes the same move twice in a row.

Yzerman is a tremendous shorthanded threat. He has great anticipation, and his acceleration forces the team on the power play to be more cautious. He kills penalties with the equally dangerous Sergei Fedorov.

Yzerman has great wrist strength, and likes to operate from behind the net, where he can make a play or a stuff attempt.

He has a few flaws. He loves to handle the puck so much that he is often guilty of overhandling it. He is not a persistent backchecker, and will sometimes give up when he seems to have a skater covered, much to the dismay of his defense. He's also merely adequate on face-offs. Despite that, he is among the NHL's elite centers.

THE PHYSICAL GAME

Yzerman is a very solid player who uses his body well. He's not a punishing hitter, but then who wants to see him risk injury? He goes into traffic and, with his hand and foot skills, wins most of the one-on-one battles for the puck.

THE INTANGIBLES

Is this town big enough for Yzerman and Sergei Fedorov? Yzerman was troubled by trade rumors before last season (one of the reasons he got off to a slow start, which only made matters worse), and he is likely to hear them again this season. He adjusted to his reduced ice time, however. Trading him would be a mistake. Yzerman and Fedorov can co-exist, and Yzerman is too much the heart of this team, one that is very close to being a Cup contender.

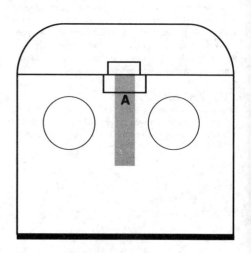

EDMONTON OILERS

KELLY BUCHBERGER

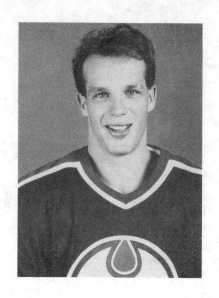

Yrs. of NHL service: 4
Born: Langenburg, Sask.; Dec. 2, 1966
Position: Left wing
Height: 6-2
Weight: 210
Uniform no.: 16
Shoots: Right

Career statistics:

GP	G	A	TP	PIM
283	31	40	71	800

1991-92 statistics:

GP	G	A	TP	+/-	PIM	PP	SH	GW	GT	S	PCT
79	20	24	44	9	157	0	4	3	1	90	7.3

LAST SEASON

Production increased by 17 goals, 23 assists, 36 shots. Shorthanded goal total led team and tied for fourth in NHL. PIM declined fourth consecutive season. Plus-minus improved 15 goals.

THE FINESSE GAME

Buchberger has a huge stride and moves very well, which plays nicely into the hell-bent style he elects to play. He makes himself an effective forechecker as well as a very useful penalty killer by combining reach and range with his size and willingness to hit.

Buchberger has the confidence to try finesse moves now. He tried splitting defenses last year, tried dekes to the backhand. And and while his puckhandling skills weren't up to that challenge last season, that doesn't mean they won't be this season. He was more than capable of controlling the puck one-handed, while off-balance, and using the other hand to fend off a defender while driving to the net. He has more than enough ability to play the off-side well.

Clearly, shots went in last season that hadn't gone in the year before — probably because he put more of them on net and sent fewer of them off the glass. Coming off a three-goal season, Buchberger got four goals while killing penalties; he established two-way credentials, earned respect as something more than a hitter.

THE PHYSICAL GAME

A defenseman may think Buchberger has been finished on a play, but is stunned and saddened to learn that is not the case. Buchberger remains an effort player with more rough edges than ever will be polished, but who compensates in hustle for the lack of greater hockey gifts. He makes plays from his knees, from his belly. He doesn't stop until he's on the bench.

THE INTANGIBLES

A solid breakthrough season such as last year's should make Buchberger hungrier to show he can do even better in 1992-93. He has the heart, he has shown the determination and almost unquestionably was the most improved player in the league. Now he must show his skills have not yet reached their limits.

Could there be a letter waiting for his sweater? It's up to him. He is an excellent team player — one who will do anything to win and one who must command respect in the room for the improvements to his game. When you talk about leadership by example, Buchberger's name must be among the first mentioned.

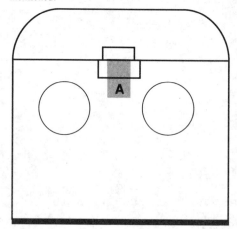

VINCENT DAMPHOUSSE

Yrs. of NHL service: 6
Born: Montreal, Que.; Dec. 17, 1967
Position: Left wing
Height: 6-1
Weight: 185
Uniform no.: 21
Shoots: Left

Career statistics:

GP	G	A	TP	PIM
474	156	262	418	315

1991-92 statistics:

GP	G	A	TP	+/-	PIM	PP	SH	GW	GT	S	PCT
80	38	51	89	10	53	12	1	8	1	247	15.4

LAST SEASON

Production improved by 12 goals (on same total shots as prior season), four assists and 16 points to career-high levels. Plus-minus zoomed 41 goals. Game-winning goal total led team and tied for third in NHL. Led team in goals, assists, points and shots.

THE FINESSE GAME

Damphousse has superb balance and fine agility with the puck; he's like a slalom skier. A very strong first step to the puck makes him a worthy penalty killer, while his skating, puckhandling and scoring skills make him a fixture on the power play.

He has an intimidating, explosive burst of speed — plus other skating assets and hand skills that make it even more of a weapon, because he can make moves while going what looks like 90 miles per hour. On the very same rush, Damphousse will shield the puck with his body, use a wonderfully deceptive weight-shift fake to the inside and lure the defenseman into attempting a poke check. That accomplished, he will then go back outside, tuck the puck inside the defenseman's feet and say bye-bye. The goalie, of course, is toasted by a backhand under the crossbar.

Damphousse is capable of accelerating on the crossover, a skill basically reserved for the elite skaters; most of the time, crossovers seem to slow a person down. And he has fairly exceptional stamina; he can keep driving for the net after long, exhausting shifts have worn out everybody else on the ice.

THE PHYSICAL GAME

At the end boards, Damphousse will accept a hit, kick the puck to a teammate, then beat the defenseman back into the play. He will score second-effort goals with the same willingness he has to make the dazzling finesse moves pay giant rewards. He is not a great defensive player and will not grind much.

THE INTANGIBLES

Last year's HSR said, "If all the pieces fit right, Damphousse could produce his first 100-point season this year." We missed by 11 points. This year, there should be no way he misses the century mark.

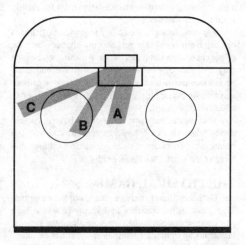

MARTIN GELINAS

Yrs. of NHL service: 3
Born: Shawinigan, Que.; June 5, 1970
Position: Left wing
Height: 5-11
Weight: 195
Uniform no.: 20
Shoots: Left

Career statistics:

GP	G	A	TP	PIM
193	49	48	97	126

1991-92 statistics:

GP	G	A	TP	+/-	PIM	PP	SH	GW	GT	S	PCT
68	11	18	29	14	62	1	0	0	0	94	11.7

LAST SEASON

Goal production dropped nine, point production dropped 11, but plus-minus improved 21 goals. Shot total decreased by 30 in just five fewer games than 1990-91.

THE FINESSE GAME

Gelinas came to the NHL as a scorer, which only made sense, given his acceleration, puck-handling skills, quick release and hard shot. His talents are suited ideally to the give-and-go, as Gelinas makes an authoritative first pass and then powers for the holes — creating openings, even if none originally exists.

Gelinas seems dedicated, however, to mastering the checking and defensive aspects that were not required of him in the Quebec League. He seems intent on adding balance to his game and turning himself into a player whose offensive chances stem most frequently from a defensive base.

For now, though, the ability to grind outstrips his offensive attributes. He gets scoring chances because of his speed, but struggles on the finishing end of the play. So, although he will chip in with the odd goal, he is more useful as a checker who works hard both ways while putting his strength and skating power to all-around use.

Then again, the same thing could have been said about Adam Graves before last season, and his goal output went from seven to 26. Sometimes things that were going wrong start going right.

THE PHYSICAL GAME

Gelinas willingly plays a clean, but very competitive game in the trenches and seems to win a high percentage of pucks in the corner or along the boards. He stands up in tough situations and will not be intimidated. He is energetic, determined and solidly built

THE INTANGIBLES

Gelinas still has things to learn, but he wants to learn and will apply himself — as is indicated best by the substantial improvement in his plus-minus rating.

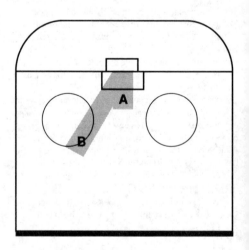

BRIAN GLYNN

Yrs. of NHL service: 3
Born: Iserlohn, West Germany; Nov. 23, 1967
Position: Right defense
Height: 6-4
Weight: 215
Uniform no.: 6
Shoots: Left

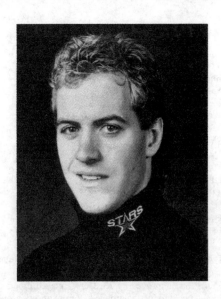

Career statistics:

GP	G	A	TP	PIM
205	17	44	61	219

1991-92 statistics:

GP	G	A	TP	+/-	PIM	PP	SH	GW	GT	S	PCT
62	4	18	22	−5	30	0	1	0	1	82	4.9

LAST SEASON

Obtained from Minnesota, Jan. 21, 1992, for David Shaw. Point total was a career high.

THE FINESSE GAME

Glynn has more offensive instincts than offensive skills. He is a big boy with rather sluggish feet, thus is more likely to join a rush than lead one. He has a good shot from the point on the power play, but doesn't use it much.

Often, that is because there isn't much time to get it off. Glynn is trusted with bringing the puck up ice on the power play, but often is on the second unit — which means well under a minute remains in the advantage. So by the time he gets the puck into the zone there is even less time. And by the time someone feeds him for a shot, there is even less time before the power play ends. Glynn thus ends up being the transition guy, playing the last part of the power play and the critical first seconds at even strength after it.

Glynn struggles with lateral movement, but compensates by making good use of his reach. It is all-important that he keeps his skates churning, however; if he commits to a poke check at the blue line and doesn't get the puck on someone's outside move, he doesn't have the explosive recovery that enables him to catch up.

THE PHYSICAL GAME

Glynn does not use his size to advantage often enough. He uses his strength to control opponents, but shows little taste for a rougher, tougher game that would make him more of a force.

THE INTANGIBLES

Consistency and intensity are issues for Glynn, who already has done a fair amount of bouncing around in just a few NHL seasons. Sometimes it takes big players longer to get the hang of the game; sometimes it takes big defensemen even longer. Suffice it to say, though, this is an important year for Glynn to show signs of progress.

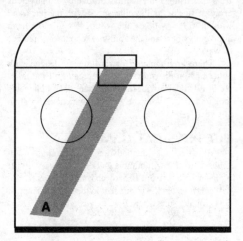

PETR KLIMA

Yrs. of NHL service: 7
Born: Choamutov, Czechoslavakia; Dec. 23, 1964
Position: Left wing
Height: 6-0
Weight: 190
Uniform no.: 85
Shoots: Right

Career statistics:

GP	G	A	TP	PIM
481	215	162	377	385

1991-92 statistics:

GP	G	A	TP	+/-	PIM	PP	SH	GW	GT	S	PCT
57	21	13	34	−18	52	5	0	0	0	107	19.6

LAST SEASON

Plus-minus plummeted 42 goals, just one season after it had improved by 33. Games played dropped 13 and goal production dropped 19 from prior season. Shot total declined 97.

THE FINESSE GAME

Klima was the best player in the press box a lot of nights last season. Hands that should have been spraying shots to all four corners of the net were put to use ushering popcorn, hot dogs and soda to his mouth — which should serve as a warning to anybody thinking about picking him in a pool this year.

When he feels like playing, and when the coach feels like using him, Klima can deploy a marvelous array of finesse skills: elite speed with the puck and without it, flashy fakes, the willingness to shoot from almost anywhere and the ability to score in any number of ways.

There aren't many forwards in the league with better one-on-one moves. Klima creates all the time. He is a daredevil with the puck, can make opponents look foolish . . . when he wants to, which wasn't often last year.

THE PHYSICAL GAME

Klima can take the body and show strength when he wants to. He will bump a guy off the puck, will lift a player's stick from behind and strip the puck. He will control a puck with his feet in the corner. You just never can be sure when these events will occur.

THE INTANGIBLES

Only Klima knows the real reason his stunning hockey skills are being wasted. There are grunts out there who would do anything for half his ability; Klima does almost nothing with all of his. Here's hoping he finds a place he wants to play, a coach for whom he wants to play, a manager who can afford to pay him and a complete change of attitude.

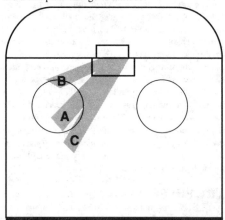

KEVIN LOWE

Yrs. of NHL service: 13
Born: Lachute, Que.; Apr. 15, 1959
Position: Left defense
Height: 6-2
Weight: 195
Uniform no.: 4
Shoots: Left

Career statistics:

GP	G	A	TP	PIM
965	73	295	368	1,164

1991-92 statistics:

GP	G	A	TP	+/-	PIM	PP	SH	GW	GT	S	PCT
55	2	7	9	−4	107	0	0	0	0	33	6.1

LAST SEASON

Goal total was six-season low. Assist and point totals were career lows.

THE FINESSE GAME

The question no longer is what Kevin Lowe wants to do; it is whether his body will allow him to do it. The spirit and enthusiasm remain in his approach, but the physical limitations increase; he used to give 150 percent out of choice, now he gives it out of necessity.

Lowe never ran up big point totals; he always has been the one who stayed back—the defense half of an offense-defense pair. He was the one who blocked the shots, killed the penalties, won the corners, got the puck out of danger with a crafty pass. In some ways, that role contributed to the punishment his body endured; in other ways, it may have enabled him to play longer.

He endures now on wit and savvy, a little more clutch-and-grab because he has slowed considerably. Lowe knows what it takes, does what it takes. He never forces the long pass when a short one will do; never tries to beat a man with the puck when he can chip it out off the boards or the glass. Positionally, he is unmatched.

THE PHYSICAL GAME

You are talking here about an intelligent man, and an intelligent player. Lowe does not need to show how tough he is, and nobody will show their toughness by running Lowe. He finishes, hits and accepts being hit, but he has much better things to do with his time than to fight.

THE INTANGIBLES

Lowe always has been an injury waiting to happen; but while in past years he was able to play with some broken appendage or torn tissue, last season literally was more painful than any of its predecessors. There is not a single sacrifice Lowe has refused to make for his team; he is the symbol of grace and dignity, the epitome of Oiler class and success. The hope is that he can get through this year by spending more time on the ice than in the trainer's room.

101

NORM MACIVER

Yrs. of NHL service: 3
Born: Thunder Bay, Ont.; Sept. 1, 1964
Position: Right defense
Height: 5-10
Weight: 180
Uniform no.: 36
Shoots: Left

Career statistics:

GP	G	A	TP	PIM
182	18	87	105	104

1991-92 statistics:

GP	G	A	TP	+/-	PIM	PP	SH	GW	GT	S	PCT
57	6	34	40	20	38	2	0	3	0	69	8.7

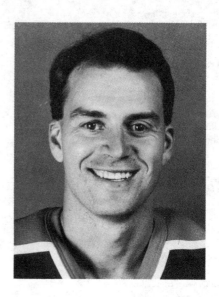

LAST SEASON

Figures for games, goals, assists, points and PIM were NHL career highs.

THE FINESSE GAME

While he has played only 182 NHL games, Maciver has been with NHL organizations for six seasons, playing a fill-in role capably because of the finesse skills that are more difficult to find than you may think. He doesn't play a lot of games, because of his size and the general absence of a physical aspect. Maciver does not always play a lot in the games for which he dresses, because his role is specialized mostly to the open-ice situations: power play, penalty killing and four-on-four.

With the exception of Paul Coffey, the Oilers for years have used a smallish, quick-ish player to bring the puck up ice on the power play. Remember Risto Siltanen? Reijo Ruotsalainen? Now Maciver receives the bulk of his ice time in that role. He has good hand skills: he can carry the puck up from behind the net, get to the center line and set the half-court game in motion. He has a good view of the ice and decent control of matters from the point.

Maciver doesn't have a bomb from the blue line, but when you play with finishers and can get your shots through to the net, the assists will come. There is nothing spectacular about his play, but that plus-20 is an attention-getter. If your main asset is special teams and your club still scores 20 more even-strength or shorthanded goals than it gives up when you're out there, you're doing something right.

THE PHYSICAL GAME

Maciver thunderbombed Chris Chelios with a high stick at the side boards in the playoff series against Chicago, but that was much more the exception than the rule. People had to be saying, "Did Normie just do what I think he did?" He is, granted, more of a stick-checker than a bodyslammer, but Maciver generally keeps his stick at legal height and shoulders people gently out of the play. He shoves, pushes, but generally is no threat to anyone's well-being.

THE INTANGIBLES

Maciver had his most productive NHL season after being named the AHL's top defenseman for 1990-91. At 28, some of his best years may lie ahead.

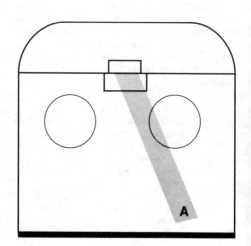

102

CRAIG MacTAVISH

Yrs. of NHL service: 11
Born: London, Ont.; Aug. 15, 1958
Position: Center
Height: 6-1
Weight: 195
Uniform no.: 14
Shoots: Left

Career statistics:

GP	G	A	TP	PIM
770	173	212	385	564

1991-92 statistics:

GP	G	A	TP	+/-	PIM	PP	SH	GW	GT	S	PCT
80	12	18	30	−1	98	0	2	1	0	86	14.0

LAST SEASON

Played all 80 games for fifth consecutive season. Scored 10 or more goals and 30 or more points in ninth consecutive season.

THE FINESSE GAME

MacTavish is a dedicated defensive player with enough of a scoring touch to convert some of the opportunities created through persistent checking by his line. He is a splendid checking-line center, is good on face-offs and is very good/excellent away from the puck. MacTavish knows who to cover, when to take a chance, when to hang back; he is an aristocrat of anticipation.

He can rag the puck nicely to chop time off the clock in penalty-killing situations. At even strength, he will get the puck and move it promptly; he is well aware the puck moves more quickly than he does, thus MacTavish becomes quicker by moving the puck quicker.

That does not mean he is slow; despite his tenure, he is quite agile, flexible and fit. More, it means MacTavish is not especially a natural in any of these endeavors. His only innate gifts are his work ethic and hockey sense; the rest is the result of practice, application and effort.

THE PHYSICAL GAME

You always find MacTavish where the turnovers are. You always find him diving in front of a shot while killing penalties. You always find him carrying an opponent or two on his back. He won't stop, won't be stopped.

THE INTANGIBLES

MacTavish is so strong positionally, so smart, so mentally tough, so important when his team is defending a lead. He was a team captain during Kevin Lowe's absence last season, an entirely appropriate call. After all these seasons, he remains a competitor, remains a source of key plays—even big goals—when they are needed most.

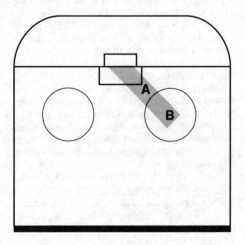

DAVE MALEY

Yrs. of NHL service: 6
Born: Beaver Dam, Wis.; Apr. 24, 1963
Position: Center/left wing
Height: 6-2
Weight: 205
Uniform no.: 12
Shoots: Left

Career statistics:

GP	G	A	TP	PIM
354	41	68	109	784

1991-92 statistics:

GP	G	A	TP	+/-	PIM	PP	SH	GW	GT	S	PCT
60	10	17	27	8	104	1	0	1	0	73	13.7

LAST SEASON

Obtained from New Jersey, Jan. 12, 1992, for Troy Mallette. Set career-highs in goals, assists and points.

THE FINESSE GAME

Maley isn't very fast, which keeps him at least one line lower than he could play. He has some smarts, some hand skills, some scoring skills, but the slow-motion aspect limits him to checking-line duty.

Away from the puck, Maley needs to depend on anticipation a lot, because he needs something of a head start to end up in the right place at the right time. He is very strong on his skates, very responsibile defensively and capable of making his opponent pay on the scoreboard for a turnover.

His goals come off muscle stuff in front of the net. He will bury a rebound off a scramble, tip in a point shot, pot a wrist shot from the slot.

THE PHYSICAL GAME

Maley will take the hit if he can get there in time. He will work the corners for all he's worth, whether he's the first man on the wall or the second. Maley has something of a short fuse when push comes to punch, because he steps onto the ice with that slightly ticked off attitude that too few players remember to bring from the dressing room.

THE INTANGIBLES

Watch Maley before he leans in for a face-off: he ALWAYS looks back at his goalie to make sure the he's ready. Whether it's in the offensive zone or the defensive zone, Maley doesn't want any surprises; if the goalie isn't watching, Maley waits. It is just a little thing, but it tells you how much he cares. Most of the other centers, if not all of them, just wait until the linesman is ready; there's a big difference.

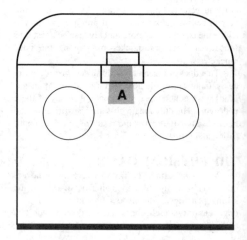

DAVE MANSON

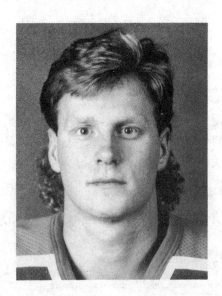

Yrs. of NHL service: 6
Born: Prince Albert, Sask.; Jan. 27, 1967
Position: Left defense
Height: 6-2
Weight: 202
Uniform no.: 24
Shoots: Left

Career statistics:

GP	G	A	TP	PIM
409	54	120	174	1,397

1991-92 statistics:

GP	G	A	TP	+/-	PIM	PP	SH	GW	GT	S	PCT
79	15	32	47	9	220	7	0	2	0	206	7.3

LAST SEASON

Production jumped 18 points, although plus-minus dropped 11 goals. Shot total increased 52 and was second-most on team. Penalty minutes went up by 29 and led team.

THE FINESSE GAME

His shot is a remarkable weapon. Like Al MacInnis, Manson is a legitimate scoring threat from anywhere past the center line and is an imposing force for a power play. He does not seem to favor carrying the puck; when he sets up the power-play breakout from behind his net, Manson prefers to make a short pass up the middle than to gain the red line and dump the puck. At even strength, he still prefers to get the puck and move it.

Manson is light on his feet; but his ability to make a 360-degree spin in a very small space while carrying the puck also testifies to good agility for a big player, plus fine balance, plus commendable wrist strength. He also will use decent speed to charge into an offensive rush every so often, although he isn't much for dekes and fancy shots.

Manson is a good enough skater to step up while defending a play in the neutral zone. He tends to gamble and does not always make that move at the proper time; but there also are instances when he seems to scare a guy off the puck merely by faking as though he was preparing to deliver The Big Hit.

THE PHYSICAL GAME

Manson is doing an increasingly good job of controlling his strength and using it cleanly. He remains an intimidating, menacing storm center in front of his net; players do not want him finishing checks on them.

THE INTANGIBLES

Speculation was that while GM Glen Sather matched the offer sheet Manson had signed, there was no way Manson still would be in Edmonton once Sather actually had to start autographing paychecks in October. Manson is a very valuable commodity — a young-but-experienced, physical, top-level two-way defenseman who has just enough danger in his game to keep both teams alert.

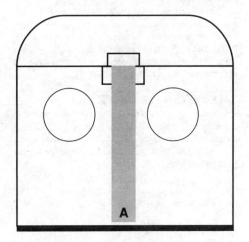

SCOTT MELLANBY

Yrs. of NHL service: 6
Born: Montreal, Que.; June 11, 1966
Position: Right wing
Height: 6-1
Weight: 205
Uniform no.: 27
Shoots: Right

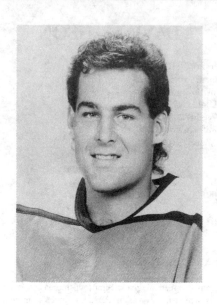

Career statistics:

GP	G	A	TP	PIM
435	106	141	247	891

1991-92 statistics:

GP	G	A	TP	+/-	PIM	PP	SH	GW	GT	S	PCT
80	23	27	50	5	197	7	0	5	0	159	14.5

LAST SEASON

Point total was fourth on team. Goal total was four-season high. PIM total was career high.

THE FINESSE GAME

Mellanby is not the world's smoothest skater; he is not the most fluid on turns. But he has a decent burst of speed straight-ahead, which helps him drive into the attacking zone in a dump-and-chase game.

Mellanby has a finesse move or two, plus a decent scoring touch. He will move to the right across the slot, then shoot back, against the grain, to his left. He has 11 game-winning goals in two seasons, and while that statistic might not mean much, 11 winners matches Tony Granato's total for the same span and is just one behind Vincent Damphousse, a much more accomplished scorer.

He is alert and responsible away from the puck, more from the defensive sense than the offensive sense. He would have more goals if he spotted the holes and jumped to them in the attacking zone, but tends more to look for an opponent to be near just in case the puck turns over.

THE PHYSICAL GAME

Mellanby hits eagerly. He is especially active in the attacking zone, of course, forechecking aggressively. He is better, though, in confined areas where it is just Mellanby, a defenseman and a tango for the puck in a corner.

THE INTANGIBLES

He is not going to make it on his hockey gifts alone; Mellanby needs to flesh out the bones of his game with hard work. He knows that, accepts it, and plays as though honored by the privilege of wearing an NHL sweater. Desire is the turbodrive of his game.

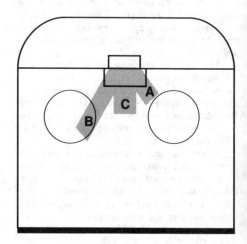

CRAIG MUNI

Yrs. of NHL service: 6
Born: Toronto, Ont.; July 19, 1962
Position: Right defense
Height: 6-3
Weight: 200
Uniform no.: 28
Shoots: Left

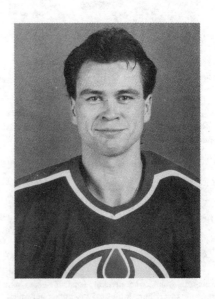

Career statistics:

GP	G	A	TP	PIM
440	24	78	102	431

1991-92 statistics:

GP	G	A	TP	+/-	PIM	PP	SH	GW	GT	S	PCT
54	2	5	7	11	34	0	0	0	0	38	5.3

LAST SEASON

Missed late-season action due to March knee surgery. Games played was six-season low.

THE FINESSE GAME

Muni is a defensive defenseman because there is no offense to his game. He doesn't have the skating range for it, doesn't have the hand skills for it, and he doesn't have the personal taste for it, either.

There is nothing wrong with that. A specialist is a specialist, and Muni's specialty is getting his team out of trouble. He can handle a night against the opposition's top offensive line or the opposition's toughest line. Muni is capable in any situation, but is an outstanding penalty killer (he blocks shots so well), and is extremely capable in one-on-one confrontations.

Muni has an extremely long reach, which he uses to compensate for a fairly significant lack of range. He does not skate poorly, but he is not fast or hugely mobile. The reach helps him defend against rushes to the outside.

THE PHYSICAL GAME

Muni is big and strong and tough—both mentally and physically. He has hurt enough people with checks that there must have been a fair amount of cheering around the league when a New Jersey player returned the favor and put Muni on the operating table. But you don't play defense to make friends . . . at least, Muni doesn't.

THE INTANGIBLES

Muni doesn't raise a lot of waves. He comes to work with a shovel and a lunch pail (dinner bucket?) most game nights, and has given a full, honest effort when all is said and done.

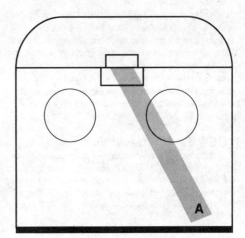

JOE MURPHY

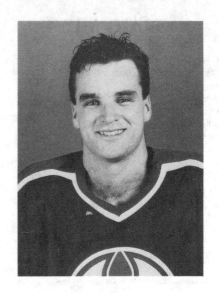

Yrs. of NHL service: 5
Born: London, Ont.; Oct. 16, 1967
Position: Right wing
Height: 6-1
Weight: 190
Uniform no.: 8
Shoots: Left

Career statistics:

GP	G	A	TP	PIM
312	83	82	165	214

1991-92 statistics:

GP	G	A	TP	+/-	PIM	PP	SH	GW	GT	S	PCT
80	35	47	82	17	52	10	2	2	2	193	18.1

LAST SEASON

Production improved by eight goals, 12 assists. Point total was second on team. Totals for goals, assists and points were career highs. Plus-minus improved 15 goals and led team forwards. Shot total jumped 52.

THE FINESSE GAME

Murphy has tremendous speed and the confidence to make something happen with it—the spirit to try to beat you with it.

Without the puck, he forechecks aggressively. With the puck, he will try to split the defense on a rush, rather than make a safer play that leads to smaller rewards. He scores with an effective wrist shot or a slap shot that doesn't lose its zip over longer distances; Murphy can bury pucks from the circles.

He also handles the puck well. He will make a smart pass to open ice, but also sees the late man charging into a play and will get the puck to that player. Murphy also can be trusted with the first face-off of a penalty kill.

THE PHYSICAL GAME

Murphy will throw the big hit in open ice or confined space. He will win a puck in a corner. He will use his size and strength camping in front of the net for screens and deflections. If it is needed, Murphy has a healthy mean streak on standby.

THE INTANGIBLES

Murphy is becoming mentally tougher, is turning into a big-game player. He is showing leadership and character. He wants to succeed, wants to reach a higher level. Last season, his breakthrough season, followed a year of improvement. This season, the challenge will be to continue the climb.

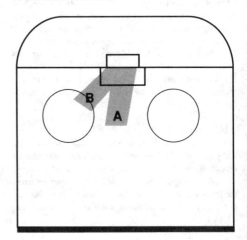

BERNIE NICHOLLS

Yrs. of NHL service: 11
Born: Haliburton, Ont.; June 24, 1961
Position: Center
Height: 6-0
Weight: 185
Uniform no.: 9
Shoots: Right

Career statistics:

GP	G	A	TP	PIM
755	384	533	917	921

1991-92 statistics:

GP	G	A	TP	+/-	PIM	PP	SH	GW	GT	S	PCT
50	20	29	49	4	40	7	0	2	0	117	17.1

LAST SEASON

Obtained from New York Rangers, Oct. 4, 1991, with Louie DeBrusk and Steven Rice for Mark Messier. Was fourth among team scorers. Games played was 10-season low. Production dropped five goals, 19 assists.

THE FINESSE GAME

Nicholls is an equal opportunity center; the right wing is going to get as many passes as the left wing. There are centers in the league who look more for the 'natural' pass, to the linemate on their forehand; in Nicholls' case, that would be the left wing. When he has time and space, though, he positions his body in such a way that the forehand pass to the right side is not a problem. And when he doesn't have time and space, he can brick the hard forehand pass to the left wing or still flip a fat, soft saucer pass on the backhand to his right wing.

He can bat pucks out of the air easily, which always makes him a threat to deflect shots. Rather than plant himself in front of a goaltender, Nicholls will feed the point for a shot, wait until the defenseman is committed in the windup, then drive to the net so he can arrive the same time the puck does — improving his chances of a tip or a rebound.

He wouldn't qualify as a fast skater, necessarily, but he is strong on his feet. Nicholls can absorb a big hit in the corner and not go down. He also is fairly shifty.

Nicholls handles the detail work with ease, if not consistency. He finds the proper passing option, makes a sharp first pass out of the zone. He covers the point when one of his defensemen rushes deep into the attacking zone. He pays attention to his point man while killing penalties. He locks off his opposing center after winning a face-off.

THE PHYSICAL GAME

Nicholls will pay some attention on defense and tends to stay on the plus side of the ledger. Generally, he will tie up an opponent's stick or simply stand in front of him — winning through positioning — more than taking the player out with a shoulder hit.

He has a nasty side. He isn't much of a battler, although he spends a fair amount of time in the corners and wins some pucks. He checks more with the stick than with the body, but he will shove a guy — or shove back.

THE INTANGIBLES

Nicholls is so creative, has such good hockey sense. He just KNOWS things some people never seem to learn.

Whether he knows as much as he thinks he knows is another question, but Nicholls certainly knows how to get goals, how to set up goals, how to see the big picture and focus it. Most of the time, you can tell he's thinking; some of the time, you wonder if he was thinking at all. Bernie's Bernie.

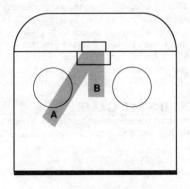

BILL RANFORD

Yrs. of NHL service: 6
Born: Brandon, Man.; Dec. 14, 1966
Position: Goaltender
Height: 5-10
Weight: 170
Uniform no.: 30
Catches: Left

Career statistics:

GP	MINS	GA	SO	GAA	A	PIM
263	14,652	813	6	3.33	12	38

1991-92 statistics:

GP	MINS	GAA	W	L	T	SO	GA	S	SAPCT	PIM
67	3,822	3.58	27	26	10	1	228	1,971	.884	4

LAST SEASON

For third consecutive season recorded career highs in games played and minutes played. Matched career high for victories. Games played total was tied for second in NHL.

THE PHYSICAL GAME

It would be difficult to name a more patient goaltender than Bill Ranford, who simply refuses to buy the first fake thrown at him. He is so programmed to ignore the first fake on a breakaway, in fact, that you'd probably score by just shooting without any fakes at all.

Confidence in his lateral movement has a lot to do with Ranford's patience. He moves with the shooter extremely well, does a nice job of keeping the five hole closed, and simply forces you to make a near-perfect shot to beat him.

He is agile, quick and alert. When he drops to his knees, Ranford is right back up quickly for a second shot. He makes compact motions and always seems prepared to move in any direction for any shot. Ranford makes very few desperation sprawls. He stops the puck and controls the carom.

And Ranford is extremely active with the stick. He always is ready for passes from the corners or behind the net and gets a lot of them with his stick. On the offensive side, he handles the puck extremely well — he gets to the pucks drilled hard around the boards and zings them up to teammates when possible.

But he isn't perfect. Ranford gets into stretches when he keeps his hands extremely low, and he also gets into stretches when he plays a touch deep in the net.

THE MENTAL GAME

Ranford is tremendously confident, as he should be. He has won a Stanley Cup, he has won a Conn Smythe and he has been a Canada Cup MVP. He has accomplished a great deal, but always works to improve — to keep his skills sharp and make them better.

THE INTANGIBLES

Ranford hardly has struggled to maintain Grant Fuhr's goaltending legacy of excellence. He is calm, but hardly is a show-off. When it enters a game in front of a goaltender such as Ranford, any team would have to feel its chances of winning are very good indeed.

LUKE RICHARDSON

Yrs. of NHL service: 5
Born: Ottawa, Ont.; Mar. 26, 1969
Position: Right defense
Height: 6-3
Weight: 215
Uniform no.: 22
Shoots: Left

Career statistics:

GP	G	A	TP	PIM
353	13	55	68	674

1991-92 statistics:

GP	G	A	TP	+/-	PIM	PP	SH	GW	GT	S	PCT
75	2	19	21	−9	118	0	0	0	0	85	2.4

LAST SEASON

Plus-minus improved 19 goals. PIM total dropped by 120.

THE FINESSE GAME

Richardson is not much for the offensive aspect of defense. He will carry the puck a few strides, then either dump it into the attacking zone or make a pass with it. He is not a natural puck carrier; Richardson does not see the ice especially well, which cuts into his options. He has a good shot from the point, which he keeps low and on-target, but does not use extensively.

Richardson prefers to have the game come to him. He skates well, moves backward nicely and with good balance. He has above-average lateral mobility, but seems still to need experience and confidence in facing the rush.

In the defensive zone, Richardson is still getting a handle on when to stay in front and when to challenge the corners. He needs more patience, needs to improve his reads.

THE PHYSICAL GAME

Hitting, especially in open ice, is high on Richardson's list of fun activities. Fighting is not. He starts confrontations and finishes them when he has to, but prefers clean, bone-rattling, get-the-smelling-salts hits.

THE INTANGIBLES

Richardson, obtained from Toronto in the Grant Fuhr trade, is another example of Oiler GM Glen Sather's fascinating trademark, which we call "drafting in reverse." Time and again, Sather trades older players for guys who were top-dozen draft picks those years when Edmonton wasn't drafting until much later. By the time Sather obtains these players, they at least have played in the minors; he has a much better idea whether they can compete—a luxury not enjoyed by the teams which originally drafted these kids.

Sather did the same thing in the trades of Mark Messier, Paul Coffey, Wayne Gretzky and Steve Smith, to name four.

Richardson was the seventh pick overall in 1987, a year Edmonton did not pick until 21st overall (Peter Soberlak). By the time Sather obtained him, Richardson had played 278 NHL games with Toronto. Now, while there still is work to be done on his game, Richardson is closer to a finished product; yet he also is still young enough and valuable enough to bring something in a trade if things don't work out in Edmonton.

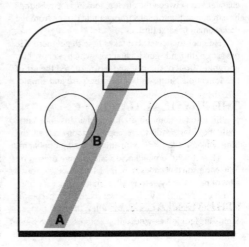

CRAIG SIMPSON

Yrs. of NHL service: 7
Born: London, Ont.; Feb. 15, 1967
Position: Left wing
Height: 6-2
Weight: 195
Uniform no.: 18
Shoots: Right

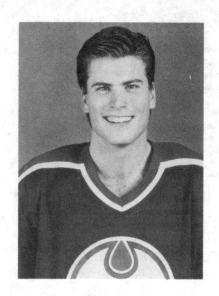

Career statistics:

GP	G	A	TP	PIM
528	211	213	424	589

1991-92 statistics:

GP	G	A	TP	+/-	PIM	PP	SH	GW	GT	S	PCT
79	24	37	61	8	80	6	0	2	0	128	18.8

LAST SEASON

Plus-minus improved 16 goals. Power-play production dropped nine goals and overall goal total dropped six to six-season low. Was third on team in goals, assists and points.

THE FINESSE GAME

Being a right-hand shot on the left wing can be difficult, but Simpson does a nice job overcoming the hardships and taking advantage of off-wing benefits.

Simpson has nice, soft hands that allow him to accept a hard pass on his backhand without disrupting his stride as he crosses the blue line. He can return the favor, because his backhand passes are strong and accurate, and he can flip them over defenders' sticks.

No speedster, he is not a player who drives down the wing with the puck, beats a defenseman with outside speed, then overwhelms the goalie from the face-off circle. Simpson stands out more in the scoring-chance area between the circles, looking for rebounds he can convert before absorbing a pile driver from the defenseman nearest him.

He goes to the net, but takes time to get there. He has strength and good balance, which keeps him upright in front of the net, and has mastered the art of the deflection. Simpson is a finisher, pure and simple.

THE PHYSICAL GAME

Simpson is annoying enough that his nickname could be 'Bart,' for the creepy cartoon kid on the Simpsons TV show. He is an antangonizing opponent.

Thus it is little wonder so many people unload on him. Simpson does not scrap much—in fact, he draws a lot of penalties by getting killed at least once a game. Those are penalties willingly served by the perpetrators, who seem to feel better after they've popped Simpson, feel it was worth it.

THE INTANGIBLES

His goal production last season was low — for him. The only other NHL players to score 24 goals last season were Peter Stastny and Glenn Anderson, both of whom are way on the downside of their careers.

It should be noted, however, that Simpson hoisted himself into plus territory. While his lack of speed leaves him behind the play a lot, he worked last season to catch up as best he could. He appeared to give up some offense for the sake of defense, which is something a team guy does.

It should be noted, as well, that those 24 goals came on 128 shots and his prior season's 'batting average' was 30 for 143 (21.0%), for a two-season aggregate of 54 for 271 (19.9%). Nothing wrong with that.

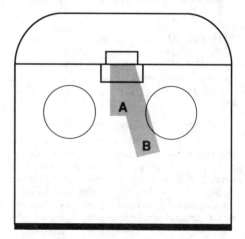

GEOFF SMITH

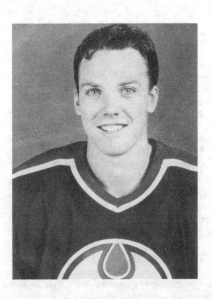

Yrs. of NHL service: 3
Born: Edmonton, Alta.; Mar. 7, 1969
Position: Left defense
Height: 6-3
Weight: 200
Uniform no.: 25
Shoots: Left

Career statistics:

GP	G	A	TP	PIM
207	7	39	46	150

1991-92 statistics:

GP	G	A	TP	+/-	PIM	PP	SH	GW	GT	S	PCT
74	2	16	18	-5	43	0	0	0	0	61	3.3

LAST SEASON

Plus-minus declined 18 goals. Assist total was career high.

THE FINESSE GAME

Smith is a very talented skater, very light on his feet. He has good lateral movement and nice range, but tends to employ those assets in a stay-at-home game rather than use the fancy feet on offense. His fundamental body position is right out of the textbook; he "sits in the chair" while skating backward, his chest up, which helps him turn to either side with equal ease.

Smith is patient with the puck in the corner. He will hold it and make a decent play with it even if he is about to get hit. On offense, Smith makes intelligent passes to the right spot on the ice; he's got an IQ. He doesn't just make the same pass every time. He will move to his right to open some ice, then pass back to his left. Other times, he will drill one up the middle.

Smith also does a very underrated, taken-for-granted thing: he doesn't shoot much (in fact, he doesn't shoot nearly enough), and he doesn't have a challenging shot at all, but he does an excellent job of getting the puck to the net. He doesn't shoot it off the glass, doesn't bonk it off shinguards; he gets the shot to the goalie, so it's a potential goal every time.

Away from the puck, Smith is alert. He looks around for signs of potential trouble rather than getting hypnotized by the play. He switches well with his partner, if the situation requires it, and can handle himself on the right side. In other words, Smith uses his head — which is why he is used in all situations, against all the opposition's lines.

THE PHYSICAL GAME

Smith always puts his stick on his man. He isn't a hatchet man, by any means; if anything, he is too much of a model citizen in front. But he puts his stick on his man the way players "hand check" in basketball — just to let you know he's there, to keep you just off-balance enough, to make you think twice about trying anything foolish.

He uses the stick more than the body, but he bumps in the corners and finishes checks. He's more of a pusher than a banger, but he beats his man back into the play a major portion of the time. Smith also uses the stick well to pick off passes.

THE INTANGIBLES

The last minute of a period tells you a lot about what a coach thinks of his players, and Smith is out there a lot in the closing minute, when you don't want to give up a goal and go into the dressing room ticked off. A coach can be confident in using him. Nothing fancy is going to happen, but nothing bad is going to happen, either. This is a trustworthy defensive defenseman with underrated offensive ability.

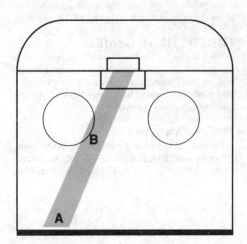

ESA TIKKANEN

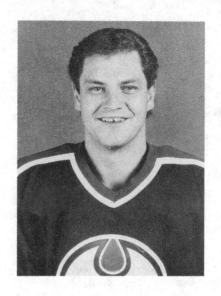

Yrs. of NHL service: 7
Born: Helsinki, Finland; Jan. 25, 1965
Position: Left wing
Height: 6-1
Weight: 200
Uniform no.: 10
Shoots: Left

Career statistics:

GP	G	A	TP	PIM
456	164	239	403	683

1991-92 statistics:

GP	G	A	TP	+/-	PIM	PP	SH	GW	GT	S	PCT
40	12	16	28	−8	44	6	2	1	0	117	10.3

LAST SEASON

Severe shoulder separation caused Tikkanen to play fewer than 67 games for first time in six seasons. Plus-minus declined by 30 goals.

THE FINESSE GAME

Since he is an excellent skater, has fine poise while handling the puck and solid passing skills, you'd figure Tikkanen for a top scorer. He has good moves in-close and a strong shot that he releases quickly and accurately.

Tikkanen is so versatile and skilled, it would not be surprising to see him play a game on defense if there was some kind of emergency and no repacement was available. As it is, he can perform capably at any of the forward positions. He can win face-offs. He can bring the puck up ice on the power play or run the show from the right point. He can kill a penalty, block a shot, tie up a man away from the puck. He can check/shadow the other team's top offensive threat, can produce the key goal off a turnover or the pretty goal off a one-on-one play.

Yet, he really doesn't pile up the points. If there is any problem, it is concentration; small wonder, with all the activities in which Tikkanen involves himself.

THE PHYSICAL GAME

If you play for the other team, Tikkanen wants to ruin your night, wants to get under your skin and right into your gall bladder. He considers the evening at least partially wasted if he has not annoyed you into some out-of-character behavior.

THE INTANGIBLES

For all his antics on the ice, on the bench, in the dressing room, Tikkanen is a serious athlete and conscientious teammate. He is a dependable, important, character player; his full recovery from last season's disastrous shoulder injury is vitally important to his team's chances of success.

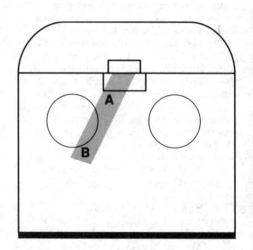

RON TUGNUTT

Yrs. of NHL service: 4
Born: Scarborough, Ont.; Oct. 22, 1967
Position: Goaltender
Height: 5-11
Weight: 150
Uniform no.: 32
Catches: Left

Career statistics:

GP	MINS	GA	SO	GAA	A	PIM
156	8,481	578	1	4.09	4	6

1991-92 statistics:

GP	MINS	GAA	W	L	T	SO	GA	S	SAPCT	PIM
33	1,707	4.08	7	18	3	1	116	855	.881	2

LAST SEASON

Obtained from Quebec, March 10, 1992, with Brad Zavisha, for Martin Rucinsky.

THE PHYSICAL GAME

Tugnutt does well when he stands up, comes out of his net to challenge the shooters and lets the puck hit him. His assets include a good glove hand, quick feet and pretty good concentration.

Things get a little ragged, though, when Tugnutt gets into a reflex mode and loses control of his game. Sometimes, for no good reason, he will drop to his knees before a shot is released, then get beaten by a shot that would have hit him in the chest if he had stood up. Other times, he will get into five hole trouble as he moves across the crease to stay with a shooter.

The biggest challenge, though, is for Tugnutt to improve his puck-handling. It is a necessity in today's game, and defensemen appreciate the help.

THE MENTAL GAME

Tugnutt must still be pinching himself. He can start thinking about being a first-shot goalie now, whereas in Quebec, he had to be a first-, second- and third-shot goalie. That makes a big difference in your mindset.

THE INTANGIBLES

Tugnutt still is improving and could develop into a good goaltender. Backing up Bill Ranford, he has a chance to grow into the NHL without facing the pressure he faced in Quebec.

HARTFORD WHALERS

MIKAEL ANDERSSON

Yrs. of NHL service: 6
Born: Malmo, Sweden; May 10, 1966
Position: Center/left wing
Height: 5-11
Weight: 185
Uniform no.: 34
Shoots: Left

Career statistics:

GP	G	A	TP	PIM
264	39	50	111	46

1991-92 statistics:

GP	G	A	TP	+/-	PIM	PP	SH	GW	GT	S	PCT
74	18	29	47	18	14	1	3	1	0	149	12.1

LAST SEASON

Games played and all point totals career highs. Led team in plus-minus.

THE FINESSE GAME

What a difference a termination contract makes. In last year's HSR, we told you that Andersson was a speedy, skilled player who talents went to waste because of his play on the perimeter and lack of involvement.

Last season, Andersson was game in and game out the most consistent performer on the Whalers, surpassing anything we (or anyone else) had seen in past.

Andersson is a small and quick skater with good puck control skills. He is absolutely deadly on a breakaway, just about unstoppable. He uses a move like Pat LaFontaine, pulling the puck to his backhand for the shot, and he does it at such a pace that the goalie cannot get across quickly enough to stop it.

Andersson does not shoot enough and sometimes overhandles the puck. He gained confidence with his increased ice time, but he does need a coach to stay on him.

THE PHYSICAL GAME

Where Andersson once avoided crowds like a hermit, last season he was more mature, more committed and showed more willingess to play in traffic. He was part of Hartford's most effective line over the course of season with Sanderson and Holik, anchoring the line, and it showed in plus/minus. He is responsible defensively and killed penalties, and he played hurt.

THE INTANGIBLES

Andersson became a free agent after the 1991-92 season. The Whalers would be wise to hang on to him, since they have so few skaters with any kind of offensive flair. On any other team, Andersson might be just an average forward, but he is more valuable to the Whalers. His reputation has certainly improved after last season, but will he play as well this year without the pressure of playing for a contract?

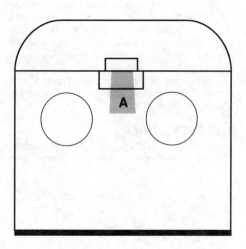

ADAM BURT

Yrs. of NHL service: 3
Born: Detroit, Mich.; Jan. 15, 1969
Position: Left defense
Height: 6-0
Weight: 195
Uniform no.: 6
Shoots: Left

Career statistics:

GP	G	A	TP	PIM
176	15	30	45	267

1991-92 statistics:

GP	G	A	TP	+/-	PIM	PP	SH	GW	GT	S	PCT
66	9	15	24	−16	93	4	0	1	0	89	10.1

LAST SEASON

Games played and all point totals career highs.

THE FINESSE GAME

Burt saw some time on the point on the power play, but that was probably more by default than design. He has limited hand skills and his decision-making process is slow. Burt is uncertain about when to pinch and often gets caught in no man's land.

Burt has some offensive ability, but the biggest hangup is his confidence, or lack thereof. It keeps him from realizing his potential, which is more than he has shown so far in the NHL.

Burt has a powerful shot. He handles the puck okay, but could improve there. If he established a more physical presence, it would give him more time and room to work offensively.

He is an excellent skater with terrific mobility.

THE PHYSICAL GAME

Burt will play aggressive defensively, but he does not use his body as well as he should. He plays a containment defense, forcing the attacker to the outside well, but he needs to clear his crease better when the play is in tight. He plays very straight up and is knocked off balance much too easily

Burt is a willing but not very good fighter. He has a touch of meanness in him and will use his stick. He is more reactive than initiating.

THE INTANGIBLES

Burt came back last season following serious knee surgery, and there is little doubt that injuries have slowed his development. If he can stay healthy, Burt may overcome some of the inconsistencies in his play to develop into a solid everyday defenseman.

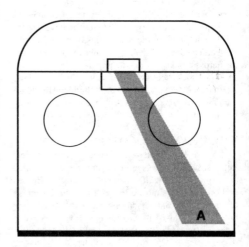

ANDREW CASSELS

Yrs. of NHL service: 2
Born: Bramalea, Ont.; July 23, 1969
Position: Center
Height: 6-0
Weight: 192
Uniform no.: 21
Shoots: Left

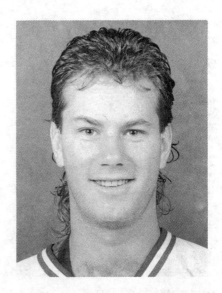

Career statistics:

GP	G	A	TP	PIM
127	19	49	68	40

1991-92 statistics:

GP	G	A	TP	+/-	PIM	PP	SH	GW	GT	S	PCT
67	11	30	41	3	18	2	2	3	0	99	11.1

LAST SEASON

Acquired from Montreal for 1992 second-round draft pick, Sept. 17, 1991. Games played and all point totals career highs.

THE FINESSE GAME

It takes some time for Cassels to get up to speed. His acceleration is labored, but once he gets going he has a pretty long stride and fair speed.

Cassels can't move too quickly because his hand skills won't keep pace. He is very good with the puck but has a tough time doing things at high tempo. Cassels has good hockey sense, but there's a softness to him and he has to become mentally tougher and be more of a committed player.

He has a strong wrist shot that he releases quickly and accurately. His balance and soft hands would make him a natural in traffic, but he doesn't work as consistently there as he should.

THE PHYSICAL GAME

Cassels uses his body more willingly in the attacking zone than back on defense. He crashes to the front of the net well, and is pretty good along the boards when there is a chance he will get the puck. Overall, Cassels lacks the speed and strength to be very effective physically. He has to decide that that's what he wants and put forth the effort.

THE INTANGIBLES

Cassels is a good team person who is at this stage an average NHL player. He is an untapped resource who could be a very good player with the right spark. Cassels improved over the second half of the season, due in part to the leadership of Murray Craven. Cassels is easy-going by nature, not a self-starter, but if someone pushes the right buttons he could be a real surprise this season.

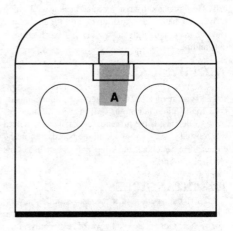

YVON CORRIVEAU

Yrs. of NHL service: 5
Born: Welland, Ont.; Feb. 8, 1967
Position: Left wing
Height: 6-1
Weight: 202
Uniform no.: 20
Shoots: Left

Career statistics:

GP	G	A	TP	PIM
220	40	28	68	296

1991-92 statistics:

GP	G	A	TP	+/-	PIM	PP	SH	GW	GT	S	PCT
38	12	8	20	5	36	3	0	0	0	69	17.4

LAST SEASON
Goals and points totals career highs.

THE FINESSE GAME
Sometime in the past year, someone went up to this policeman and took away his handcuffs. Unfettered, Corriveau started to develop into a solid NHL player.

Corriveau has good size and strength with nice skills. Inconsistent in the past, he dedicated himself more to learning the game, and utilized the best aspects of his talent. He is not a good skater laterally, but has good straight-ahead quickness that only surfaced this season. Corriveau made it his business to drill his way to the net.

Confidence added a big edge to his game, and he was one of the Whalers' best performers in the playoffs. He has a good wrist shot and uses it well going forward so that he is in position to fight for a rebound. He is hardly a natural talent, but his work ethic is outstanding.

time power forward, but he is a team guy and is improving to become a regular contributor. He has the potential to play some dominant games, as he did in the playoffs.

THE PHYSICAL GAME
Corriveau loves to hit and will earn room for himself and his linemates. The Whalers used him alongside little John Cullen late in the season; it was a nice fit, since Cullen needs the protection. Corriveau is a hard worker and is very strong along the boards and in the corners. He can check and kill penalties because of his physical presence.

THE INTANGIBLES
Corriveau spent part of the season in the minors, but after joining the Whalers late in the season became one of their most effective forwards, especially in the playoffs. That might not say much for the rest of the Hartford forwards, but it speaks volumes for Corriveau's desire. He lacks all the necessities to be a big

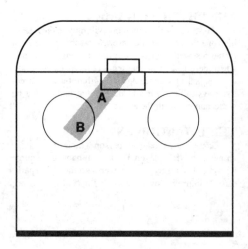

MURRAY CRAVEN

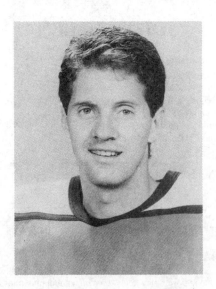

Yrs. of NHL service: 10
Born: Medicine Hat, Alta.; July 20, 1964
Position: Left wing
Height: 6-2
Weight: 185
Uniform no.: 12
Shoots: Left

Career statistics:

GP	G	A	TP	PIM
630	180	313	493	365

1991-92 statistics:

GP	G	A	TP	+/-	PIM	PP	SH	GW	GT	S	PCT
73	27	33	60	−2	46	9	4	1	1	152	17.8

LAST SEASON

Acquired from Philadelphia with a second-round draft pick for Kevin Dineen. Led team in goals and shorthanded goals. Second on team in points. Goals four-season high.

THE FINESSE GAME

Craven is not an instinctive scorer because of limited hockey sense, but he works hard to keep himself in the right position. He uses his good size and speed to go to the net. An excellent passer in tight quarters, he passes well off his backhand as well as his forehand.

Craven has a great wrist shot and most of his goals come off his close range shots. He also has a very good slapshot.

Craven has very good speed but it goes unrecognized because he doesn't use it as well as he could. That speed, combined with his size, would make Craven an even more dangerous player.

Craven can play all three forward positions. Although he is used mainly on the wing, he is Hartford's best faceoff man and usually steps in to take draws. He also works the point well on the power play, although the Whalers did not use him there as much as the Flyers did.

Craven has a long reach and is a good stickhandler. He can beat a defensemen one-on-one because of his speed and reach.

THE PHYSICAL GAME

Craven can be a very good defensive forward because he is willing to backcheck and use his body. He is a very heads up player and will bang, but is not a devastating checker.

THE INTANGIBLES

Craven is a complete hockey player, perhaps the only one on the Whalers. If he continues to get a lot of ice time alongside Cullen, Craven will cash in his share of scoring chances. He surfaced as team leader in Hartford, on a team that really needed one.

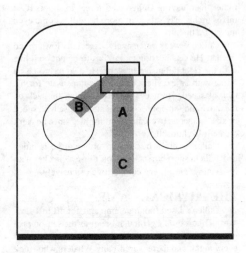

JOHN CULLEN

Yrs. of NHL service: 4
Born: Puslinch, Ont.; Aug. 2, 1964
Position: Center
Height: 5-10
Weight: 185
Uniform no.: 11
Shoots: Right

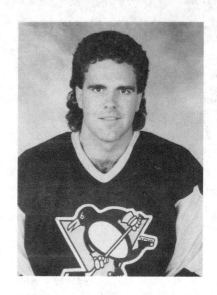

Career statistics:

GP	G	A	TP	PIM
306	109	219	328	501

1991-92 statistics:

GP	G	A	TP	+/-	PIM	PP	SH	GW	GT	S	PCT
77	26	51	77	−28	141	10	0	4	0	172	15.1

LAST SEASON

Led team in assists and scoring. Tied for first on team in power play goals. Last on team in plus-minus. All point totals three-year lows following career best in 1990-91. PIM total career high.

THE FINESSE GAME

Cullen is one of the game's top playmakers, a creative passer with exquisite timing and touch. Cullen uses a munchkin-sized stick, in order to keep the puck under control and close in to his body and feet. It is very difficult for opponents to knock the puck away from him. They have to go through Cullen in order to get the puck. He is willing to take a hit to make the play, holding on to the puck until a teammate is open. His peripheral vision is among the best of the league's top centers.

Like most playmakers, Cullen doesn't shoot enough. That allows defenders to anticipate a pass rather than playing Cullen as a threat to shoot. If he mixes up his play selection more he will become even more of a threat.

Cullen is weak defensively, especially low around the net. He gets his points, but has to be put on a line with the right defensive players. He also has to be on a line with an excellent skater to compensate for his lack of speed. He needs someone to get the puck on the move and someone to intimidate defense with speed or size, someone to create room for him since he can't create it for himself.

Cullen is not a fast skater, although he is quick and agile in short bursts. He won't lose a checker with his skating. He is very competitive offensively.

THE PHYSICAL GAME

Cullen missed training camp and got off to a slow start. Things didn't get much better as the season progressed. Cullen was a marked man and was battered every night, and there weren't any Whalers who stood up while their top player was getting bashed all over the ice. The hard-working Cullen never quits, but there is only so much abuse a body can take. Physically, he has to come into camp at his peak and maintain it through the season, because he needs every step he can get.

THE INTANGIBLES

Cullen learned what it was like to be a No. 1 center with a weak supporting cast. Opponents focused on shutting down Cullen, and he lacked the size and strength to win that kind of battle. The Whalers have to get more help for Cullen (they're looking at the big rookie Patrick Poulin as a linemate) or it will mean another frustrating season for him.

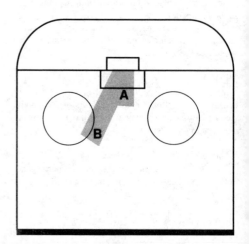

RANDY CUNNEYWORTH

Yrs. of NHL service: 8
Born: Etobicoke, Ont., Canada; May 10, 1961
Position: Left wing
Height: 6-0
Weight: 190
Uniform no.: 7
Shoots: left

Career statistics:

GP	G	A	TP	PIM
458	133	149	282	757

1991-92 statistics:

GP	G	A	TP	+/-	PIM	PP	SH	GW	GT	S	PCT
39	7	10	17	−5	71	0	0	1	0	63	11.1

LAST SEASON

Missed 41 games with a broken left fibula.

THE FINESSE GAME

Cunneyworth has good straight-ahead speed with a good shot. He has above average hand skills and scores most of his goals from in tight around the net. He is a good passer and likes to work a give-and-go in deep.

Cunneyworth has good balance, but his speed seems to have been sapped by his injury and the lack of muscle condition that went along with his layoff. He will have to apply himself conscientiously during the off-season, because much of his game relies on his skating ability.

Since he came back to see a regular role with the Whalers during the playoffs, there will be a spot for him on their roster. He is a reliable checking forward and his experience should not be undervalued.

THE PHYSICAL GAME

Cunneyworth will hit and be an agitator, and his effectiveness is dependent on his ability to play the body. He runs into trouble when he chases the puck. Cunneyworth is not a big player but he has good size and will make hits in any zone of the ice.

THE INTANGIBLES

Injuries and age have taken their toll. Although Cunneyworth still has some value as a role player and third line checker, his skills are on the decline and he will have to fight for a job this season — even on the lowly Whalers. He is a terrific team player, which may help keep him in the league where another player of his ability would be on his way out.

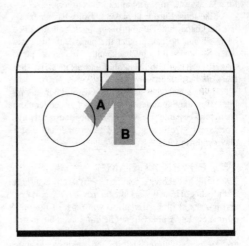

BOBBY HOLIK

Yrs. of NHL service: 2
Born: Jihavla, Czechoslovakia; Jan. 1, 1971
Position: Left wing/center
Height: 6-3
Weight: 210
Uniform no.: 24
Shoots: Right

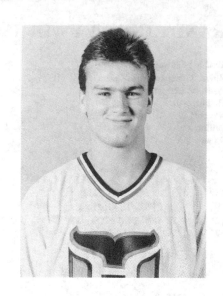

Career statistics:

GP	G	A	TP	PIM
154	42	46	88	157

1990-91 statistics:

GP	G	A	TP	+/-	PIM	PP	SH	GW	GT	S	PCT
76	21	24	45	4	44	1	0	2	1	207	10.1

LAST SEASON

Matched rookie goal total in second NHL season. PIM less than half of rookie year.

THE FINESSE GAME

The curse of expectation overshadowed what was a solid season for Holik in his sophomore year. From the blue line in, Holik is one of the strongest forwards in the NHL, and he was one of the best forwards on the Whalers, although many people were disappointed by his production.

Holik is on his way to being a very good power forward. He has good size amd when he shows a willingess, is great in traffic and in the corners.

Like most European players, Holik has an excellent backhand shot. He controls the puck well and since he is so big, he can protect the puck with his body when he carries it on his backhand. An average playmaker, he has a good slap shot and a fair wrist shot that could use improvement.

He is a lackadaisical checker who either has no interest in playing defense or does not yet understand the defensive game. He works hard, but doesn't always work smart. Holik was drafted as a center but won't play center in NHL.

THE PHYSICAL GAME

Holik has shown a real taste for the physical part of the game. He will work the boards and the corners, and has the skating strength to win most of the one-on-one battles. Holik will not be inimidated but is still learning how his size and speed could intimidate others. He plays with enthusiasm and needs to generate force.

THE INTANGIBLES

One of the major disappointments for the Whalers last season, Holik doesn't appear to want to pay the price to be a good player in the NHL. A bizarre hypothesis offered for his laissez faire attitude last season was the Holik was in love. Maybe new head coach Paul Holmgren will be able to light a fire under Holik and give Cupid a hotfoot. He has room for improvement.

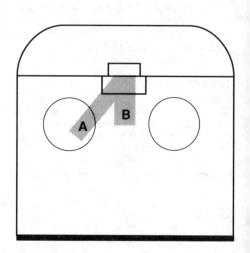

STEVE KONROYD

Yrs. of NHL service: 11
Born: Scarborough, Ont.; Feb. 10, 1961
Position: Left defense
Height: 6-1
Weight: 195
Uniform no.: 5
Shoots: Left

Career statistics:

GP	G	A	TP	PIM
802	38	181	219	784

1991-92 statistics:

GP	G	A	TP	+/-	PIM	PP	SH	GW	GT	S	PCT
82	4	24	28	−1	97	1	0	0	0	126	3.2

LAST SEASON

Acquired from Chicago for Rob Brown on Jan. 24, 1992. Played complete regular season schedule for first time in career (extra games due to trade). Missed four games with the flu. No goals in 1990-91. Points six-season high. PIM four-season high.

THE FINESSE GAME

Konroyd is a stay-at-home defenseman who relies on his smart positional play. He partners almost any defensemen well, since he sticks to a very basic game.

He moves the puck very well and could do more offensively. However, Konroyd seems to have set some boundaries for himself and he seldom dares himself to push the envelope. He is a consistent player and night in and night out will deliver the same steady performance.

Konroyd is used to kill penalties and also works on the second unit on the power play. He has a presence on a team because of his experience, and adds a degree of quiet leadership.

Konroyd is an intelligent defenseman who reads plays well and will get involved in a rush in a limited way.

THE PHYSICAL GAME

Konroyd has some physical ability but does not play to size. He blocks shots well, and will hit when he has to, but it is far from being his favorite part of the game. He plays well below his size.

THE INTANGIBLES

Although he has played on four different teams in his NHL career, Konroyd has never missed the play-offs. There may or may not be a coincidence there.

Konroyd is a versatile player to have in a lineup. While not a star, he is capable of contributing more than the average NHL defenseman.

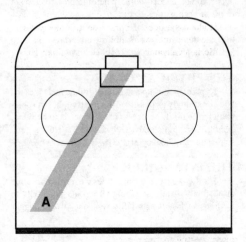

NICK KYPREOS

Yrs. of NHL service: 3
Born: Toronto, Ont.; June 4, 1966
Position: Left wing
Height: 6-0
Weight: 195
Uniform no.: 9
Shoots: Left

Career statistics:

GP	G	A	TP	PIM
175	18	19	37	484

1991-92 statistics:

GP	G	A	TP	+/-	PIM	PP	SH	GW	GT	S	PCT
65	4	6	10	−3	206	0	0	0	0	28	14.3

LAST SEASON

Penalty total was career high. Goal total dropped five, assists total dropped three.

THE FINESSE GAME

If Kypreos is going to score at all, he has to get very close to the net. Kypreos plays an in-tight game, paying all the prices and taking all the hits, so scoring from there should not be difficult. He makes it seem extremely difficult despite an accurate, heavy shot that should be a scorer's dream.

Coming down the wing and breaking to the net, Kypreos will put a tremendous amount of pressure on a defenseman. His agility and mobility aren't too bad and his ability to turn is about average. But skating out of the turns is something he doesn't do well, and that puts Kypreos a step behind when the play moves out of the attacking zone.

Without the puck, Kypreos doesn't always identify his defensive responsibility and rarely is used against the opposition's potent offensive line.

THE PHYSICAL GAME

Kypreos skates up and down his lane and takes the body as strongly as possible. It's a dirty job, but somebody has to do it; he does whatever needs to be done, even giving up his body to make a play. He's a good soldier for any hockey army.

THE INTANGIBLES

Hard as we try, there are times we make inaccurate projections. And ascribing 15-goal potential to Kypreos in last year's HSR was one of our bigger blunders. As long as we're in the business of ripping players, we have to rip ourselves for that blotch on our vision. Let's see him reach 20 goals for his career before we come close to predicting he could get almost that many in a season.

Still, ability to score is not the reason he is on the team. Kypreos is intense, full of energy, good in the dressing room and great to have on the team. He knows his role, plays it to his utmost.

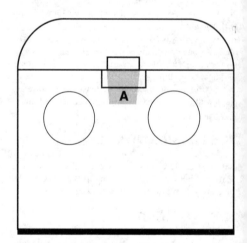

RANDY LADOUCEUR

Yrs. of NHL service: 10
Born: Brockville, Ont.; June 30, 1960
Position: Left defense
Height: 6-2
Weight: 220
Uniform no.: 29
Shoots: Left

Career statistics:

GP	G	A	TP	PIM
680	24	106	130	1056

1991-92 statistics:

GP	G	A	TP	+/-	PIM	PP	SH	GW	GT	S	PCT
74	1	9	10	−1	127	0	0	0	0	59	1.7

LAST SEASON

Games played three-season high. PIM total six-year high.

THE FINESSE GAME

Ladouceur is a stay-at-home defenseman who could do a little travelling, but is loath to do so. Ladouceur is very reluctant to venture offensively out of his own end. He plays the percentages so much, never taking risks, and is very much afraid to deviate from his ultra-basic play.

Ladouceur could help out more because he does log so much ice time. He has shown an average point shot, and doesn't like to carry the puck or try to make a fancy play. He is strictly dump and hope.

His skating is average, but he plays such a strong positional style that he is seldom caught out of position or chasing the puck carrier. He will go down to block shots, often too quickly.

THE PHYSICAL GAME

Ladouceur has limited physical skills but will always give a coach what he has. He takes the body and works very hard. He is willing to carry out whatever plan the coaching staff maps out for him.

THE INTANGIBLES

Ladouceur is a quiet team leader, well respected by his teammates and very coachable. The things that keep him in the league are his upbeat attitude and his desire to remain an NHL player.

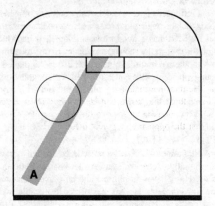

FRANK PIETRANGELO

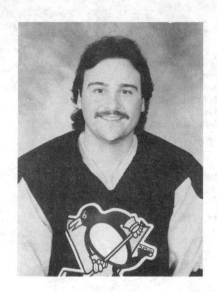

Yrs. of NHL service: 5
Born: Niagara Falls, Ont.; Dec. 17, 1964
Position: Goaltender
Height: 5-10
Weight: 185
Uniform no.: 40
Catches: Left

Career statistics:

GP	MINS	GA	SO	GAA	A	PIM
92	4784	320	1	4.01	1	28

1991-92 statistics:

GP	MINS	GAA	W	L	T	SO	GA	S	SAPCT	PIM
10	531	3.62	5	2	1	0	32	286	.888	0

LAST SEASON

Acquired from Pittsburgh for future considerations on March 10, 1992. Games played, minutes played and wins career lows. GAA career best.

THE PHYSICAL GAME

Pietrangelo showed so many good qualities in his brief stint with Hartford at the end of last season that he could be a true No. 1 goalie, but first he has to prove himself over the long haul. We just don't know yet if it was a flash in the pan or not.

Pietrangelo is very quick with good reactions. He reads the play well and moves with the puck across the net well. He has a good glove and quick feet. While with Pittsburgh, he showed a tendency to flop too much and to leave rebounds, but with Hartford he played a sound, stand-up style and controlled his rebounds well.

He does not handle the puck well, but with more playing time and more confidence may show better ability in that area.

THE MENTAL GAME

Pietrangelo is a very poised, controlled person emotionally. He doesn't have roller coaster highs and lows. He believes in himself and he played that way for the Whalers. He has performed especially well under playoff pressure, as he did in 1991 during the Penguins ride to the Stanley Cup and in a thrilling seven-game series against Montreal with the Whalers (see stats below).

THE INTANGIBLES

Be careful what you wish for, you might get it. Pietrangelo was trapped in Pittsburgh behind solid No. 1 goalie Tom Barrasso for two seasons, and was unhappy in the backup role. Traded to the Whalers, he instantly became their top man (over Peter Sidorkiewicz and Kay Whitmore). He had a strong playoffs (2.68 GAA, .922 save percentage over seven games) and will be asked to shoulder the burden this year. He has to prove himself behind a weak team. He is a very strong team man, which isn't always the case with goalies.

128

PATRICK POULIN

Yrs. of NHL service: 0
Born: Vanier, Que.; Apr. 23, 1973
Position: Left wing
Height: 6-1
Weight: 208
Uniform no.: 37
Shoots: Left

Career statistics:

GP	G	A	TP	PIM
1	0	0	0	2

1991-92 statistics:

GP	G	A	TP	+/-	PIM	PP	SH	GW	GT	S	PCT
1	0	0	0	-1	2	0	0	0	0	0	.0

LAST SEASON
Has yet to play full season in NHL.

THE FINESSE GAME
Poulin, the Whaler's first-round draft pick in 1991, joined the team late in the season and in the playoffs took a spot on the first line with John Cullen and Pat Verbeek. The speed of NHL play took some adjusting to, especially playoff speed, but Poulin did not look out of place. He can be expected to stick this season with a team desperate for a scoring hero.

Poulin is a very good skater with quickness and balance. He gets good drive from his legs and can shift speeds and lose a defender. Poulin has the hand skills to go with his speed. He has a strong wrist shot and slap shot, and was a mainstay on the power play for his junior team, St-Hyacinthe of the QMJHL. His junior coach has compared him to Joe Nieuwendyk, but some scouts compared him to Vincent Damphousse — meaning, on nights when Poulin shows up, he can be a devastating offensive force. But on those nights when he doesn't, he's a disaster.

Poulin has sharp hockey instincts and very good hands. He sees the ice very well and is an intelligent player, poised beyond his age. Poulin was not in awe of where he was or who he was playing with. Poulin is very strong on his skates. During the playoffs, he went head to head with Mike McPhee and sent McPhee flying.

THE PHYSICAL GAME
Poulin is a good size and uses his body well along the boards and in the corners. He forechecks aggressively, and generally minds his checking assignment. Like most players fresh out of junior (especially the Quebec league), Poulin's defensive game needs fine-tuning, but he is way above average already. He appears to have the ability and the instincts to learn new disciplines. The knock on Poulin has been his lack of intensity and consistency.

THE INTANGIBLES
Given the bleak atmosphere in Hartford—GM Ed Johnston was fired after the Whalers took Montreal to seven games in the first round of the playoffs, the team is in financial trouble, and their home playoff games failed to sell out — Poulin will have to concentrate solely on his on-ice development and ignore the off-ice distractions. Although happy to be drafted by an American team instead of playing in his native Quebec, he will face another kind of pressure as a blue chip prospect for a red ink team. He seems to have the leadership characteristics to push through that. If it sounds like we're excited about his prospects, we are.

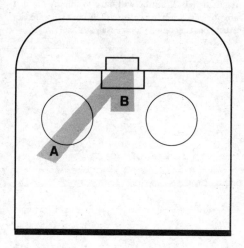

TODD RICHARDS

Yrs. of NHL service: 0
Born: Robbinsdale, Minn.; Oct. 20, 1966
Position: Defense
Height: 6-0
Weight: 190
Uniform no.: 46
Shoots: Right

Career statistics:

GP	G	A	TP	PIM
8	0	4	4	4

1991-92 statistics:

GP	G	A	TP	+/-	PIM	PP	SH	GW	GT	S	PCT
6	0	0	0	-2	2	0	0	0	0	3	.0

LAST SEASON

Has yet to play full NHL season.

THE FINESSE GAME

Richards will make it to the NHL on the strength of his skills, but in order to stay there he will have to improve in other areas.

Richards is an intelligent player who sees the ice very well. He saw some time on the point on the power play, where he put his offensive instincts to work. He has a good shot from the point and is a very poised player. Richards does not like to carry the puck, preferring to dish off as soon as possible.

Size is a problem for him, and he needs to improve on his strength and endurance.

THE PHYSICAL GAME

Richards hasn't yet learned to use his size to his best advantage and often loses his man in front of the net. He came out of college hockey (University of Minnesota) where aggressive body work was not a required course, but he will have to improve in that area to win a job, since his offensive skills are not exceptional enough to compensate.

THE INTANGIBLES

Richards saw some playing time in the playoffs and may move up to be the fifth or sixth defenseman on Hartford's depth chart.

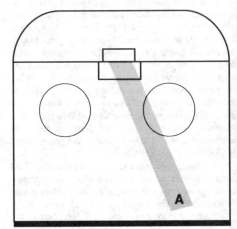

GEOFF SANDERSON

Yrs. of NHL service: 1
Born: Hay River, Northwest Territories; Feb. 1, 1972
Position: Center
Height: 6-0
Weight: 185
Uniform no.: 8
Shoots: Left

Career statistics:

GP	G	A	TP	PIM
66	14	18	32	18

1991-92 statistics:

GP	G	A	TP	+/-	PIM	PP	SH	GW	GT	S	PCT
64	13	18	31	5	18	2	0	1	0	98	13.3

LAST SEASON

First year in NHL.

THE FINESSE GAME

The Whalers are taking some of the green out of their uniforms. Now they have to take it out of Sanderson.

Here is some very raw material, which, with maturity, could grow into an impressive NHL talent. An exceptional playmaker, Sanderson sees his options well and has amazing instincts in tight and in traffic. He has deceptive speed and good balance, which helps him in those situations.

Sanderson doesn't shoot enough when he is in close, looking instead for the clever play. His preferred shot is coming in on the defense and trying to blow it by the goalie. He usually blows it by the net as well. Sanderson would be better served getting in a few strides tighter, since he has a good slapshot that he gets away quickly.

THE PHYSICAL GAME

Sanderson needs to improve on his upper body strength. He can be outmuscled by opposing centers on draws, and will lose some one-on-one battles in front of the net, but he is in no way intimidated and will continue to scrap for the puck. He is competitive on every shift.

THE INTANGIBLES

Sanderson ranks as one of the game's sleepers. He is an underrated, two-way forward who is capable of becoming a great player. Sanderson was involved in an auto accident where he was slightly injured, and he may have to improve his off-ice habits.

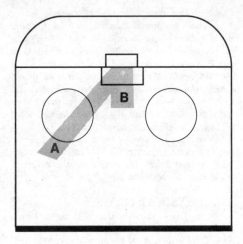

PAT VERBEEK

Yrs. of NHL service: 9
Born: Sarnia, Ont.; May 24, 1964
Position: Right wing
Height: 5-9
Weight: 195
Uniform no.: 16
Shoots: Right

Career statistics:

GP	G	A	TP	PIM
699	279	270	549	1660

1991-92 statistics:

GP	G	A	TP	+/-	PIM	PP	SH	GW	GT	S	PCT
76	22	35	57	−16	243	10	0	3	0	163	13.5

LAST SEASON

Tied for team lead in power-play goals. Led team in PIM. Third on team in goals and assists, tied for third in points. Goals total lowest since 1984-85. Points total three-season low.

THE FINESSE GAME

Verbeek was embarrassed by his production last year. He should be.

A pure shooter and consistent goal scorer, Verbeek's contribution sagged with his lack of commitment. When he is involved, the gritty forward will barge through the NHL's biggest defensemen to get to the net to score. Verbeek was a center in junior and is a capable playmaker, but he lives by his shot.

Verbeek is a powerful skater with a square build. His low center of gravity makes it impossible for bigger players to knock him off-balance. Verbeek is an excellent man to have on the power play because of his fearlessness in front of the net. He will tip and screen and whack and chop for a loose puck, and drive a goalie to distraction. Verbeek has very strong arms and wrists, and can flick in a shot one-handed while holding off a defender with his other hand.

With the right people, he can be effective; he needs people to get him the puck. Most effective coming in late and drilling the shot, Verbeek is not much of a grinder or cornerman himself.

THE PHYSICAL GAME

Verbeek is small but solid, and has a nasty temperament. Not all of his usually high penalty minutes come from toughness, however. Verbeek takes sublimely stupid penalties, and at the most crucial times. He cost the Whalers some games this year with the bad penalties he took (and since he's not on the referees' Christmas card list, he seldom gets the benefit of the doubt on a call). He spends far too much time in the penalty box for a scorer of his calibre.

THE INTANGIBLES

Verbeek took the Whalers to salary arbitration, a long, drawn-out process that resulted in his winning an $825,000 annual salary (more than three times his old salary). The distraction of the money war wore on Verbeek; his outspoken comments during the season wore on management. He might have bought some time with the departure of Ed Johnston. The new regime (headed by Brian Burke) is likely to give him a clean slate, and the feeling here is that Verbeek will rebound with a strong season.

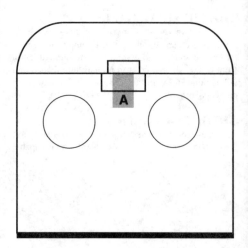

ZARLEY ZALAPSKI

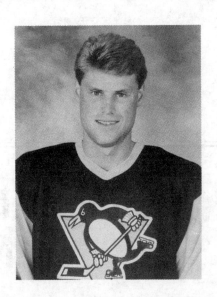

Yrs. of NHL service: 4
Born: Edmonton, Alta.; Apr. 22, 1968
Position: Defenseman
Height: 6-1
Weight: 210
Uniform no.: 3
Shoots: Left

Career statistics:

GP	G	A	TP	PIM
280	56	142	198	282

1991-92 statistics:

GP	G	A	TP	+/-	PIM	PP	SH	GW	GT	S	PCT
79	20	37	57	−7	116	4	0	3	1	230	8.7

LAST SEASON

Led team defensemen in scoring. Tied for third on team in points. Led team in shots. Career high in goals, points and PIM.

THE FINESSE GAME

Zalapski is a terrific skater with speed and agility — going forward. He lacks agility backward, which is a dreadful flaw for a defenseman and which is why he is a much better offensively than back in his own zone.

Zalapski's forward acceleration and anticipation allow him to go wide and get involved in attacking rushes. He has good hand skills and can either carry the puck or make a play with a pass. Zalapski is a good point man on the power play. He one-times the puck well but he is less effective when he is put on the left point, where he tried to overshoot. He could take a little off his shots to allow his forwards a better chance at redirecting the shot. Zalapski is not an intelligent shooter and tends to just blast away.

Zalapski is inconsistent mentally. He doesn't concentrate and gets a little spacy, sometimes in the middle of a rush coming at him. He needs to mature and may improve in that area. Zalapski has to decide whether he wants to do what his abilities will allow him to do, if he is willing to play that price.

THE PHYSICAL GAME

Zalapski does not use his body well. He has a very solid build and has tremendous power, but he allows himself to be outmuscled by players he should be taking the measure of. He keeps himself in fairly good condition, but endurance is a bit of a problem.

He prefers to play the stick rather than the man, and while he can pick off a few passes that way and start a counterattack, he more often gets beaten.

THE INTANGIBLES

Zalapski must get mentally tougher if he is to take the next step from being an average defenseman to a being good one.

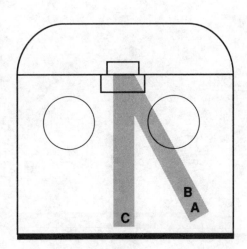

LOS ANGELES KINGS

PETER AHOLA

Yrs. of NHL service: 1
Born: Espoo, Finland; May 14, 1968
Position: Left defense
Height: 6-3
Weight: 205
Uniform no.: 26
Shoots: Left

Career statistics:

GP	G	A	TP	PIM
71	7	12	19	101

1991-92 statistics:

GP	G	A	TP	+/-	PIM	PP	SH	GW	GT	S	PCT
71	7	12	19	12	101	0	0	0	1	74	9.5

LAST SEASON

First NHL season. Led team in plus-minus.

THE FINESSE GAME

Much of Ahola's ability was hidden under a bushel basket last season. He has offensive skills the Kings haven't tapped into fully. He can carry the puck or jump into the play, but wasn't encouraged to do so. Ahola has an average shot but above average hands to go along with very good skating ability. With defensemen like Rob Blake and (late in the season) Paul Coffey in the Kings' lineup, Ahola may continue to be urged to remain a stay-at-home defenseman.

In that department, Ahola gets high marks as well. He reads plays very well. His skating is above average, and gives him the mobility and the agility to competently play against just about any forward or attack that might come at him.

His shot is average at best but he does get it through. Ahola will often make a clever play, not just a play. He sees openings and jumps into the play, or he can carry the puck and start a rush. Ahola appears to have the instincts to do even more.

THE PHYSICAL GAME

Ahola has good size but has yet to establish a physical presence on the ice. The question is how down and dirty does he want to get? Is he willing to bloody his nose? He has to be willing to block shots and maintain his peak game through all kinds of resistance.

THE INTANGIBLES

Ahola has the potential to become one of the Kings' top four defensemen, a real steal as a free agent signing. He established himself as a capable defenseman in his first season, but has the potential to develop into a much better player. The skills and sense are there, but his willingness to pay the price will determine whether or not he reaches the next NHL level.

ROB BLAKE

Yrs. of NHL service: 2
Born: Simcoe, Ont.; Dec. 10, 1969
Position: Right defense
Height: 6-3
Weight: 215
Uniform no.: 4
Shoots: Right

Career statistics:

GP	G	A	TP	PIM
136	19	47	66	231

1991-92 statistics:

GP	G	A	TP	+/-	PIM	PP	SH	GW	GT	S	PCT
57	7	13	20	−5	102	5	0	0	0	131	5.3

LAST SEASON

Games played and all scoring totals career lows in second full NHL season. Missed 15 games with shoulder sprains. Missed six games with sprained knee ligaments. Missed two games with flu.

THE FINESSE GAME

Blake has been touted as an offensive defenseman, but for all of his natural talent, don't expect to find him among the league's top-scoring blueliners. Blake does have a huge slap shot, but that leads to troubles in other departments. He does not one-time a shot well — a valuable skill for a defenseman trailing into the attack. He does not rush well, and will never control the ice from one end to the other.

Offensively, he doesn't see the ice nearly as well as he does defensively, and he lacks the creativity to be much of a quarterback. His big shot is effective only when it gets through, but he frequently takes so long to wind up that it is easily blocked. When he is in a groove, Blake will fake the big slapper, fake the checker, and seek other options, but he doesn't always make those decisions quickly enough.

Blake is a powerful skater, quick and agile, and with good balance. He is a very efficient player, with little wasted motion, and generally opts for the smart, safe play defensively (this stands out on a squad of risk-takers).

After the Kings' late-season acquisition of Paul Coffey, the two were paired on the point on the power play, and that combo should be very productive, especially if the Kings get a power forward to tip and screen in front.

THE PHYSICAL GAME

Blake is one of the hardest hitters in the King's lineup. He has very good size and is willing to use it. He was not known for this in his rookie season, so either the coaching staff has been working on that phase of his game or Blake was smart enough to know that on a team of finesse players somebody has to pay a price physically.

When he is healthy, Blake is a prominent and valuable member of the Kings, and is capable of logging up to 24-28 minutes of ice time. Kings coaches consider him to be a quality person and quality player, and he is probably future captain material.

THE INTANGIBLES

When the Kings traded Steve Duchesne to Philadelphia last season, the message was clear: Blake is ready to carry the offensive load. Blake wasn't. He is not a big-time rushing defenseman and too much was expected too soon of the sophomore blueliner, especially with the expectations coming off his All-Rookie Team season. Injuries only added to Blake's confidence problems. The Kings may have pegged Blake as a Ray Bourque type, but he should develop into a more physical, less offensively involved player like Scott Stevens. It's not a bad substitute, as long as Blake is willing to grow into that role.

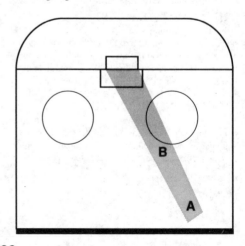

PAUL COFFEY

Yrs. of NHL service: 12
Born: Weston, Ont.; Jun. 1, 1961
Position: Left defense
Height: 6-0
Weight: 200
Uniform no.: 77
Shoots: Left

Career statistics:

GP	G	A	TP	PIM
873	318	796	1114	1291

1991-92 statistics:

GP	G	A	TP	+/-	PIM	PP	SH	GW	GT	S	PCT
64	11	58	69	1	87	5	0	1	0	232	4.7

LAST SEASON

Acquired from Pittsburgh for Brian Benning, Jeff Chychrun and 1992 first-round draft pick. Led Kings defensemen in scoring. Third on team in assists and points. Goals lowest since rookie season (1980-81). Games played, assists and points four-season lows. Missed five games with fractured right wrist. Missed six games with sore back. Missed three games with pulled hip muscle. Surpassed Denis Potvin to become the NHL's career leader in goals, assists and points by a defenseman.

THE FINESSE GAME

The best offensive defenseman of all time? The numbers say so, and Coffey has proven it time and again through the seasons. Coffey is easily the greatest skating defenseman of all time, and possible one of the best skaters to ever glide across the frozen ponds of North America. He can accelerate in a heartbeat, pivot in a phone booth, or leave only his passing breeze as evidence to a faked-out checker.

As good a skater as Coffey is, his hand skills are perhaps even better. Coffey can score from all over the ice. From the point, he works with a low, accurate shot, or by feathering a pass down low to a forward. He will eagerly cheat in deep and utilize a short-range wrist shot. Coffey is smart, poised and has great hockey sense.

In his prime, Coffey was one of the rare NHL players who could change the entire complexion of a game with one play. He still possesses that talent, but at age 30, his impact will not be the same as it was in his prime.

Coffey's greatest contribution remains his work on the power play.

THE PHYSICAL GAME

Coffey's weakness has long been his defensive play, and on the Kings that flaw becomes even more glaring. He does not use his body well, and because injuries have dogged him late in his career, will become even less anxious to get or take a hit. Defensively, Coffey relies on his keen anticipation to deflect shots or pick off passes.

Will Coffey body check? Sure, when it counts. The same hit he passes up in December will be one he makes in April. Nobody earns four Stanley Cup rings by being a coward.

THE INTANGIBLES

Despite all the championships he has already won and his place in the NHL record book — or perhaps because of those facts — Coffey was genuinely upset with the performance of the Kings in the playoffs, where they were eliminated in the first round without putting up much of a fight. Coffey was probably one of the top three Kings in the playoffs. He is grateful to L.A. owner Bruce McNall for reuniting him with Wayne Gretzky and Jari Kurri, and unlike some veterans who land in a cushy spot late in their careers, Coffey will not coast on the West Coast.

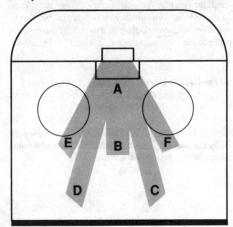

MIKE DONNELLY

Yrs. of NHL service: 5
Born: Detroit, Mich.; Oct. 10, 1963
Position: Left wing
Height: 5-11
Weight: 185
Uniform no.: 11
Shoots: Left

Career statistics:

GP	G	A	TP	PIM
229	50	40	90	131

1991-92 statistics:

GP	G	A	TP	+/-	PIM	PP	SH	GW	GT	S	PCT
80	29	16	45	5	20	0	1	4	0	197	14.7

LAST SEASON

Games played and all scoring totals career highs. Goal total surpassed previous four seasons combined (21). One of four Kings to appear in all 80 games.

THE FINESSE GAME

Donnelly earned a regular shift for the first time in his career, and deserved it. He is a hard-working forward, a type the Kings could use a few more of, and nearly achieved a 30-goal season wholly at even strength.

Donnelly is most effective from short range, from the tops of the circles in. One of his best weapons is his speed. He can toast a defenseman to the outside, and many of his scoring chances come from a 2-on-1 play that develops quickly and inside the blue line. He could develop a better change of pace to dupe a defender, rather than simply try to challenge him.

He can't overpower a goalie, but he can fool him. One of the knocks on Donnelly is that he doesn't shoot enough, but instead looks to make the play first — and he is a better shooter than passer. He is capable of scoring from the wing.

He has good anticipation and acceleration, and jumps into the holes quickly. Donnelly is a smart player defensively as well, and was a regular on the Kings' penalty-killing unit. Donnelly was an offensive star in college, but has made the adjustment to being a two-way player.

THE PHYSICAL GAME

Donnelly will always be limited by his size, which is small by today's NHL standards. Getting as much ice time as he did hurt Donnelly in a way because he wore down late in the season and had a poor playoff. He has proven he can play through most of the tough going, but it takes its toll.

THE INTANGIBLES

Donnelly is a solid player who is now a legitimate full-time NHLer. He will face pressure this season to show that last year's production was no fluke. Donnelly was very frustrated by his finish and his post-season performance, and a good start to the new season will be important to him.

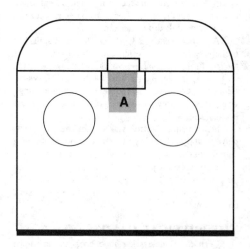

TONY GRANATO

Yrs. of NHL service: 4
Born: Downers Grove, Ill.; July 25, 1964
Position: Left wing
Height: 5-10
Weight: 185
Uniform no.: 21
Shoots: Right

Career statistics:

GP	G	A	TP	PIM
282	117	114	231	603

1991-92 statistics:

GP	G	A	TP	+/-	PIM	PP	SH	GW	GT	S	PCT
80	39	29	68	4	187	7	2	8	1	223	17.5

LAST SEASON
Tied for fourth in NHL in game-winning goals. Games played, goals, points and PIM career highs. Second in team in goals. Led team in game-winning goals. One of four Kings to appear in all 80 games.

THE FINESSE GAME
A coach's dream, Granato will do whatever is asked. He will play left wing, center or right wing, and never pouts that the constant shifting is affecting his game. He didn't see nearly enough power play time last season due to the embarrassment of riches in scoring stars on the Kings, but never complained about that either. Granato could easily have been a 45-goal scorer, perhaps even hit the magic 50 mark, if he had been given the ice time he deserved with the extra attacker.

Granato fits with anyone he plays because he makes himself fit. He adapts his own game to the benefit of his linemates. Granato's work ethic is unquestioned. He is a complementary player who is a key to that elusive quality, team chemistry.

Granato is a fast, quick skater who likes to operate down low. Most of his goals will come from within 10 feet of the net. He doesn't blast anything past a goalie, but will find the opening and, with his accurate wrist shot, will usually hit the mark. Since he is too small to operate as a power forward, he can't plant himself in front of the net. He will stay on the move, darting in and out and confounding the defensemen who try to keep track of him.

He has very strong wrists and will use his stick defensively as well, knocking down passes or sneaking up from behind to lift a puck carrier's stick and steal the puck.

THE PHYSICAL GAME
Granato is a gritty player, probably too gritty for his own good, given his size. He is tough as nails but wears down to a thumbtack by the end of a physical game or a season because he tries to play to the size of his heart instead of his body, and will lose his effectiveness.

Granato is a tenacious checker. He does not read plays well defensively, but because he will outwork the majority of his opponents, he is a solid defensive player even though he does not always make the right reads.

THE INTANGIBLES
Granato is the heart of the Kings, and was voted Most Inspirational Player by his teammates. As long as his body holds out (and he didn't miss a game last year), he will also be one of their most valuable. The Kings could use a few more like him.

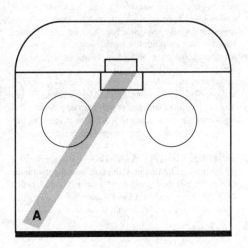

WAYNE GRETZKY

Yrs. of NHL service: 13
Born: Brantford, Ont.; Jan. 26, 1961
Position: Center
Height: 6-0
Weight: 170
Uniform no.: 99
Shoots: Left

Career statistics:

GP	G	A	TP	PIM
999	749	1514	2263	441

1991-92 statistics:

GP	G	A	TP	+/-	PIM	PP	SH	GW	GT	S	PCT
74	31	90	121	−12	34	12	2	2	1	215	14.4

LAST SEASON

Led NHL in assists for 13th consecutive year. Third in league in scoring. Led team in scoring. Goals and points career lows. Reached 100-point mark for 13th consecutive year. Missed five games due to personal reasons. Missed one game with knee strain.

THE FINESSE GAME

When Gretzky goes to the office, don't think high-rise corporate tower. Think low. Think behind the net. And if you're an opposing defenseman, start thinking about how to avoid getting another minus.

Gretzky's quiet elegance is terrifying to his defenders. It is likely that no one in the history of the game has ever seen the ice as well as Gretzky, has sought and rejected passing and shooting options, and has made the split-second pass or shot that resulted in a score.

He has such great puck control that he can dangle the puck like a minnow before a hungry fish, then when the defender makes his move, Gretzky will slither past like an eel. He is one of the few non-European players who has made a virtual living off his backhand, which allows him to protect the puck with his body.

Gretzky is the ultimate two-on-one player, because he can hold the puck, delay, and give his teammates the time and room to move up and get involved in the play.

One of the underrated aspects of Gretzky's game, and one which is developing later in his career, is his defensive ability. Gretzky could become a Selke Trophy winner and play until he's 40, if he wanted to, but that's not what people pay to see Gretzky do.

THE PHYSICAL GAME

Stanley Cup finals, Canada Cups and the long Edmonton and L.A. road trips (coupled with his fear of flying) have drained Gretzky over the seasons, and the wear and tear is beginning to show.

He has become nervous and somewhat leery about getting hurt, especially after Gary Suter's questionable check in the 1991 Canada Cup. The physical demands on him have begun to sour Gretzky on the game.

THE INTANGIBLES

Is he serious about retirement? He may well be, despite finishing third in scoring last season. Third isn't good enough for someone like Gretzky, and he will not be a player who will hang on to an NHL career even though he could be an exceptional player in a reduced role, much as the formerly high-scoring Bryan Trottier was for the past two seasons with the Stanley Cup champion Pittsburgh Penguins.

Gretzky can be expected to slip even lower in the scoring in 1992-93, and if he does not help bring a Cup to L.A. this season, we may be very close to enjoying his final season. His pride will force his departure from hockey before he has to change his game or be considered some kind of relic.

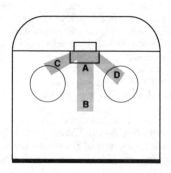

KELLY HRUDEY

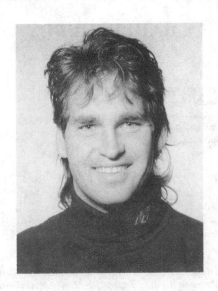

Yrs. of NHL service: 9
Born: Edmonton, Alta.; Jan. 13, 1961
Position: Goaltender
Height: 5-10
Weight: 180
Uniform no.: 32
Catches: Left

Career statistics:

GP	MINS	GA	SO	GAA	A	PIM
416	23691	1357	13	3.44	11	151

1991-92 statistics:

GP	MINS	GAA	W	L	T	SO	GA	S	SAPCT	PIM
60	3509	3.37	26	17	13	1	197	1916	.897	12

LAST SEASON

Games played three-season high. Wins matched career high. Led NHL goalies with 13 ties.

THE PHYSICAL GAME

Hrudey is a reflex goalie rather than one who relies on technique, and a goalie who lives by his reactions walks a rather fine line. Hrudey has recognized his weaknesses and in the past season worked to make his game more fundamentally sound, but in the heat of battle Hrudey abandons substance for his personal style.

Hrudey plays more like a soccer goalie, trying to use his hands to trap and control the puck instead of his feet or stick. He can be very good down low because of this quirk, but more often starts flopping around and is caught on his belly or side. He maintains his concentration well through a crowd of skaters in front.

Hrudey is a good skater and comes out of his net to help his defense. He can handle the puck very well.

Hrudey is vulnerable high, especially on the glove side, and will sometimes abandon his post and be susceptible to wraparounds.

Hrudey had his best seasons when he was paired with Bill Smith with the Islanders, and even a season ago when he and Daniel Berthiaume shared the rotation. Hrudey will be most effective when he is limited to 40-45 starts a season.

THE MENTAL GAME

Hrudey exists on emotion. He has turned in the occasional brilliant performance — his 73-save, four-overtime win over Washington in Game 7 of the 1987 playoffs was one of the greatest shows in Stanley Cup history — but he flares and then dies out, rather than putting consistent games together in any sort of streak.

THE INTANGIBLES

Hrudey's poor playoff performance was a legitimate concern to L.A. management, and the Kings will likely be shopping for either another No. 1 goalie to succeed him or a solid goalie who can share the load.

CHARLIE HUDDY

Yrs. of NHL service: 12
Born: Oshawa, Ont.; June 2, 1959
Position: Right defense
Height: 6-0
Weight: 210
Uniform no.: 22
Shoots: Left

Career statistics:

GP	G	A	TP	PIM
750	85	306	391	543

1991-92 statistics:

GP	G	A	TP	+/-	PIM	PP	SH	GW	GT	S	PCT
56	4	19	23	−10	43	2	1	0	0	109	3.7

LAST SEASON

Claimed from Edmonton by Minnesota in 1991 Expansion Draft. Acquired by Los Angeles with Randy Gilhen, Jim Thomson, and a 1991 fourth-round draft pick for Todd Elik on June 22, 1991. Missed six games with shoulder injuries. Missed 12 games with groin injury. Missed seven games with chest contusion.

THE FINESSE GAME

Huddy is a smart player and as his finesse skills have eroded over time, his head has become the most important part of his game. Huddy picks his spots offensively and does not get involved as much as he did in the past, but can still move up and join the rush.

He is confident in his decisions about when to pinch and when to back off, and makes the right choice most of the time with little of the hesitation that plagues less veteran defensemen.

Huddy's passing and stickhandling are above average. He doesn't scare anybody with his point shot, but he keeps it low and on net, making it easy for the forwards to deflect.

Huddy is an okay skater, nothing special, but he is bright enough to have himself in the right spot so that his skating deficiencies are often minimized.

THE PHYSICAL GAME

Huddy has never been a physical player, relying more on his positioning and timing to force attackers to the perimeter or to pick off a pass. As his reflexes have slowed, Huddy has become more and more vulnerable to speed coming at him, and he is more easily beaten inside or out. He must be paired with a physical partner to be effective.

THE INTANGIBLES

Huddy is no longer one of the top defensemen as he was with the Oilers, but he can add experience to the Kings as a fifth or sixth defenseman.

BOB KUDELSKI

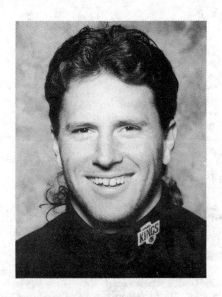

Yrs. of NHL service: 5
Born: Springfield, Mass.; Mar. 3, 1964
Position: Right wing/Center
Height: 6-1
Weight: 200
Uniform no.: 37
Shoots: Right

Career statistics:

GP	G	A	TP	PIM
254	69	51	120	162

1991-92 statistics:

GP	G	A	TP	+/-	PIM	PP	SH	GW	GT	S	PCT
80	22	21	43	−15	42	2	1	2	0	155	14.2

LAST SEASON

Games played, assists and points career highs. One of four Kings to appear in all 80 games.

THE FINESSE GAME

Kudelski will win no awards for style. He is not a pretty player, but is a tough skater who just gets to where he wants to go on desire.

Kudelski is a very intelligent player. He thinks quickly and reacts well, especially with his passing skills, which are above average. He shoots very well off the pass and can beat goalies from 25-30 feet.

Although Kudelski saw little time on the power play, he would probably be a very good asset because of his brains. He works hard to get open for a shot.

Kudelski worked hard to improve his work on face-offs, and by the end of the season became the Kings' No. 2 center (after John McIntyre) on draws, winning more than 60 percent. He kills penalties effectively.

Because Kudelski isn't a very dynamic player, he seemed to be an easier player to bounce around from position to position and role to role, and the changes did not help his game.

THE PHYSICAL GAME

Kudelski does not show an inclination for the more physical part of the game, but he is willing to hit in the offensive zone to make a play. Defensively, he covers up well for some of his more offensively involved linemates.

THE INTANGIBLES

Kudelski was a victim of L.A. management's indecision. He was projected to be the team's second-line center, but ended up spending most of his time on the wing, and his confidence suffered along with the changes. Last season was considered a disappointment. He is a solid player, and 20-25 goals a season will probably be his norm. Basically, Kudelski is a two-way center with limited skills.

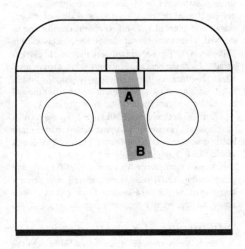

JARI KURRI

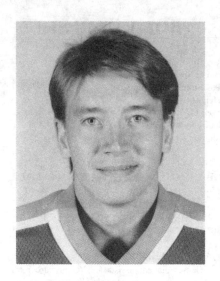

Yrs. of NHL service: 11
Born: Helsinki, Finland; May 18, 1960
Position: Right wing
Height: 6-1
Weight: 195
Uniform no.: 17
Shoots: Right

Career statistics:

GP	G	A	TP	PIM
827	497	606	1103	372

1991-92 statistics:

GP	G	A	TP	+/-	PIM	PP	SH	GW	GT	S	PCT
73	23	37	60	−24	24	10	1	3	0	167	13.8

LAST SEASON

Returned to NHL after playing 1990-91 season in Italy. Goals and points career lows. Worst plus-minus on team. Missed two games with flu. Missed two games with hip flexor. Missed three games with sprained shoulder.

THE FINESSE GAME

Kurri's favorite shot, the one that helped him score a career high of 71 goals some seasons back, was totally absent from his repertoire last season. It is the one-timer, the drive off the pass with absolutely no hesitation. Kurri misfired too many times on those opportunities in his return to the NHL. The problems really showed on the power play. Kurri was on the first unit of a power play that ranked a disappointing 10th last season.

In his prime, Kurri possessed every skill that is usually associated with European players, and he played at a world class level. His skating is exceptional, and coupled with his vision made him one of the NHL's best players in all zones. Despite his terrible plus-minus, he is a sound two-way player. He can kill penalties with the best and is always a threat to counter-attack shorthanded. Kurri's defensive game is under-rated, and last season he worked better from the red line back than from the red line in on the attack.

Kurri's shots are most effective from the tops of the circles in. He used to go to the net more in the past but last season was a perimeter player. The Kings would like to see more of his old fire return.

An excellent passer who has very soft hands and great timing, Kurri uses open ice well, but doesn't create as much of it as he used to. Once a terrific, fluid skater, he appears to have lost a step.

THE PHYSICAL GAME

Kurri is very strong and used to use his body along the wall to fight for the puck. He seems to have lost some of the physical strength that was so much a part of his game and is not as effective grinding. He can be intimidated now, which never used to be the case.

Because Kurri is such an intense, proud individual, he never let the coaching staff inside his head to know what was wrong, if anything. He had a few minor injuries during the season, but nothing major. His decline remains a puzzle.

THE INTANGIBLES

Last season was a period of readjustment for Kurri, who was expected to return to his 50-goal form and work his old magic with ex-Oiler teammate Wayne Gretzky. Those hopes never materialized, but Kurri remains a world-class player. It would not be a shock for Kurri to score 35 goals, but the days of 60 and 70 are over.

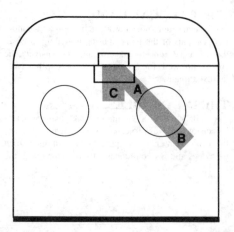

JOHN McINTYRE

Yrs. of NHL service: 3
Born: Ravenswood, Ont.; Apr. 29, 1969
Position: Center
Height: 6-1
Weight: 180
Uniform no.: 44
Shoots: Left

Career statistics:

GP	G	A	TP	PIM
201	18	39	57	357

1991-92 statistics:

GP	G	A	TP	+/-	PIM	PP	SH	GW	GT	S	PCT
73	5	19	24	0	100	0	0	1	0	40	12.5

LAST SEASON

Games played career high. Assists career high. Goals matched career low. PIM career low. Missed five games with broken nose. Missed two games with sprained thumb.

THE FINESSE GAME

McIntyre is a good defensive forward who is getting better all the time. Easily the best defensive player up front for the Kings, McIntyre is the team's top man on draws. If he fails to win a face-off cleanly, he will use his body to continue to scrap for the puck and tie up the opposing center.

McIntyre isn't merely a plodder. He is a deceptively good skater with a piston-like stride, and he has good balance which he uses in traffic to maintain position in front of the net or body an opponent in the defensive zone.

McIntyre scored only five goals last season, but that paltry total is deceptive since McIntyre showed average offensive awareness and could have had 10 or more goals. His luck with goalposts was abysmal.

THE PHYSICAL GAME

McIntyre is a baby bull with a lot of youthful courage and enthusiasm. He gives an honest effort every night. Only an average-sized player, he is extremely strong and hard-working. His reads on defensive plays improved steadily through the season.

THE INTANGIBLES

On a team that is noted for its high-flying, high-scoring stars, McIntyre gets little notice. He could well develop into a Selke Trophy contender, a Guy

Carbonneau-type who has the potential to produce around 20 goals a season. He should be playing this game with effectiveness for a very long time.

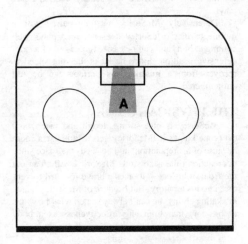

MARTY McSORLEY

Yrs. of NHL service: 9
Born: Hamilton, Ont.; May 18, 1963
Position: Right defense
Height: 6-1
Weight: 235
Uniform no.: 33
Shoots: Right

Career statistics:

GP	G	A	TP	PIM
520	63	132	195	2047

1991-92 statistics:

GP	G	A	TP	+/-	PIM	PP	SH	GW	GT	S	PCT
71	7	22	29	-13	268	2	1	0	0	119	5.9

LAST SEASON

Surpassed 2,000 PIM for career. Assists two-season low. Points three-season low. Led team in PIM. Missed three games with sprained shoulder. Missed six games with throat virus.

THE FINESSE GAME

McSorley's skills are minimal. He is a slow skater, with little speed or agility, and his hand skills are about the same.

The highlight of McSorley's offensive game is his shot. He has a strong shot from the point, and can also snap a pass in low for a teammate. McSorley does not carry the puck well, nor is he a pinpoint passer in a high tempo situation. McSorley has fair hockey sense in the offensive zone and will usually make the safe play.

Defensively, McSorley must be paired with a mobile partner. McSorley does not read plays well coming at him, and can be easily fooled out of a safe, defensive position. Since he lacks the foot speed to recover from a mistake, his partner can be left outnumbered.

THE PHYSICAL GAME

McSorley is big, strong, tough and mean, and everyone knows it. McSorley gets a little extra room because of his reputation, and he needs the space since his reaction time is so slow. McSorley will clean out the front of his net — it takes a brave forward to venture into his territory. But because of McSorley's lack of skating ability, he can't always catch what he wants to hit, and that limits his effectiveness as a body checker.

THE INTANGIBLES

McSorley is a character player who competes every night and functions in whatever role he's asked to play, whether it's as Wayne Gretzky's bodyguard up front or someone who tries to pick up his team with a fight. The problems with being asked to change roles (defense to forward and back again) is that McSorley is not very adaptable. He accepted the juggling without a gripe, but McSorley will be more effective when he can concentrate on one job because his skills are only adequate. He has to work long and hard to do a solid job at one position.

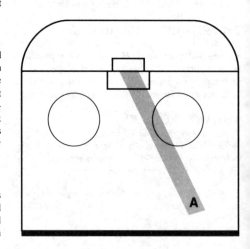

COREY MILLEN

Yrs. of NHL service: 1
Born: Cloquet, Minn.; Apr. 29, 1964
Position: Center
Height: 5-7
Weight: 168
Uniform no.: 23
Shoots: Right

Career statistics:

GP	G	A	TP	PIM
65	24	26	50	68

1991-92 statistics:

GP	G	A	TP	+/-	PIM	PP	SH	GW	GT	S	PCT
57	21	25	46	2	66	8	1	3	0	109	19.3

LAST SEASON

Acquired from New York Rangers for Randy Gilhen on Dec. 23, 1991. First NHL season. Led team in shooting percentage. Missed one game with shoulder contusion.

THE FINESSE GAME

With all of the big names in Kings jerseys last season, it was little Corey Millen who became the lifeblood of the anemic power play. Millen likes to carry the puck in and get things set up in the zone. He is a speedy center, a lightning-quick skater who can pull away from longer-legged pursuers because of his acceleration.

Millen has a hiccup style, jumping in and out of the holes in front of the net to avoid getting pasted. He is very effective at this, since through most of his playing days he has been one of the smallest players on the ice, at whatever level he has played.

Despite his lack of NHL experience, Millen is not exactly a youngster. He has a veteran's savvy and smarts, and good hockey sense. He was a solid player at the University of Minnesota and has played on two U.S. Olympic teams—which, despite their failures at the Games, have been fertile breeding grounds for NHL talents.

THE PHYSICAL GAME

Millen is smart enough to try to keep himself out of situations where he will be easily outmuscled, but the fact remains that his small stature will always limit his NHL abilities. The Kings might be wise to keep him out of the lineup on those road trips to Boston Garden, Buffalo's Aud, Chicago Stadium and the Cow Palace, where the small ice surfaces make Millen easy to find and smack around. The problem is that Millen is making himself too valuable to the Kings to be out of the lineup for long.

THE INTANGIBLES

Millen needs bigger players around him to maximize his talent. If the Kings don't get him more physical support up front, Millen will be too exhausted and banged up to be of much use, and that would be a waste. Think of how well Theo Fleury played two seasons ago when he was surrounded by the redwoods who were disguised as Calgary Flames, and you'll get an idea of what Millen may be capable of.

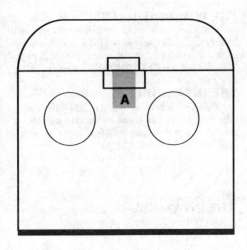

147

JAY MILLER

Yrs. of NHL service: 7
Born: Wellesley, Mass.; July 16, 1960
Position: Left wing
Height: 6-2
Weight: 210
Uniform no.: 29
Shoots: Left

Career statistics:

GP	G	A	TP	PIM
446	40	44	84	1711

1991-92 statistics:

GP	G	A	TP	+/-	PIM	PP	SH	GW	GT	S	PCT
67	4	7	11	−8	237	0	0	0	0	32	12.5

LAST SEASON

Second on team in PIM. Goals and points five-season low. Missed one game with ankle injury. Missed three games with flu.

THE FINESSE GAME

Miller's point production has never been part of his existence in the NHL. When he does contribute offensively, his goals will come from in tight. He is very strong and balanced on his skates — his fighting effectiveness stems from this as well — and can't be intimidated from the high-traffic areas.

Miller can't do a whole lot with the puck on those rare chances he gets to touch it. He is best at banging away for a loose rebound. Hard shots that deflect in off him will do so by accident, since he lacks the hand-eye coordination to redirect shots.

He has a very hard shot, but won't try to deke out a goalie with it. He simply fires away.

THE PHYSICAL GAME

Miller is intelligent enough to know his sole role is as a tough player, and he is willing to fight to keep his job. With his kind of player on the verge of being legislated out of the NHL, Miller is a dinosaur.

THE INTANGIBLES

Miller is on his way out. The game has gotten faster and Miller has gotten slower. He will have a difficult time seeing much ice this season. He was left unprotected and went unclaimed in the 1992 Expansion Draft. Only if the Kings are desperate for toughness will he get much playing time.

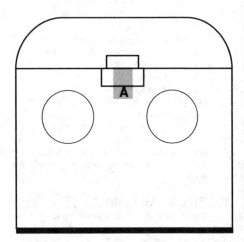

LUC ROBITAILLE

Yrs. of NHL service: 6
Born: Montreal, Que.; Feb. 17, 1966
Position: Left wing
Height: 6-1
Weight: 190
Uniform no.: 20
Shoots: Left

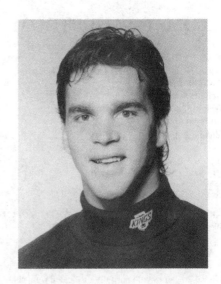

Career statistics:

GP	G	A	TP	PIM
473	285	307	592	376

1991-92 statistics:

GP	G	A	TP	+/-	PIM	PP	SH	GW	GT	S	PCT
80	44	63	107	−4	95	26	0	6	1	240	18.3

LAST SEASON

Second in NHL in power-play goals. Tied for fifth in NHL in points. Tied for seventh in NHL in goals. Reached 100-point mark for third season. Led team in goals and power play goals. Second on team in points and assists. One of four Kings to appear in all 80 games. Assists career high. Points four shy of career high (111, 1987-88). Has scored 40 or more goals in all six NHL seasons.

THE FINESSE GAME

Until Pittsburgh's Kevin Stevens enjoyed his career year last season, Robitaille reigned as the NHL's premier left wing for four seasons. Robitaille has tremendous alertness around the net. He is a natural scorer, and a puck magnet. The pass always seems to get through to him, a rebound always seems to land within stick's reach. Those events are not serendipitous. They happen because Robitaille's hockey sense puts him in the most advantageous position.

Robitaille has fabulous hands, and can score anywhere from the blue line in to the slot. He can score off the slap shot or the snap, or use his wrist shot at close range. He keeps goalies guessing because there is nothing predictable about what shot he will take. Robitaille can look high and shoot low, and he is usually among the Kings' leaders in shooting accuracy. His hand-eye coordination is excellent, and he can redirect bullet point shots.

Robitaille is an ugly skater, but that doesn't matter much. He is smart, and his anticipation often gives him the step or two to beat a defender.

THE PHYSICAL GAME

Robitaille loves scoring goals so much that he will run the gauntlet, taking hit after hit, to score. It's when he is away from the puck, especially at the other end of the ice, that Robitaille gets gun-shy. He isn't tough in the fighting sense, but he won't be intimidated and will retaliate when he is pushed too far. He does not take many bad penalties, however, since he knows he is far more valuable to the Kings on the ice.

THE INTANGIBLES

As good as Robitaille is, and has been through much of his NHL career, coaches always think there is more to his ability than he's shown. That might be due in part to the label that always seems to stick to French-Canadian players—that they never seem to be working as hard as other people think they should. But if there is a vein of gold inside his silver-trimmed jersey, no coach has been able to mine it yet.

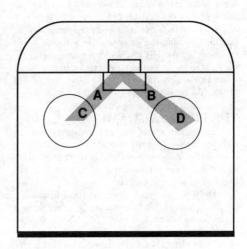

TOMAS SANDSTROM

Yrs. of NHL service: 8
Born: Jakobstad, Sweden; Sept. 4, 1964
Position: Right wing
Height: 6-2
Weight: 200
Uniform no.: 7
Shoots: Left

Career statistics:

GP	G	A	TP	PIM
552	248	293	541	767

1991-92 statistics:

GP	G	A	TP	+/-	PIM	PP	SH	GW	GT	S	PCT
49	17	22	39	−2	70	5	0	4	0	147	11.6

LAST SEASON

Games played, goals and points career lows. Missed 26 games with partially dislocated right shoulder. Served five-game suspension in stick incident.

THE FINESSE GAME

Sandstrom is an impressive blend of speed, strength and skill. When a player of his size skates with the agility and quickness of a smaller player, it adds up to an inimidating presence. Throw in a frighteningly powerful shot, and you have a nearly flawless scoring machine. Sandstrom has never produced the kind of 100-point season that might be expected from his qualities, however, and that may be tied into his emotions more than his abilities.

Sandstrom doesn't respond well to being moved in and out of the lineup, or having to change partners every few games. But because of the injuries he suffered last season, Sandstrom never firmly established his position in the Kings' pecking order. With Jari Kurri added to the lineup, Sandstrom's time on the power play all but vanished.

Sandstrom is a creative shooter and passer, and he can do everything at high speed. He will drill a shot or feather a pass. His touch with a pass is light, but his wrist and snap shots are powerful and true. Sandstrom shoots especially well on the move, and he will drive to the net for a scoring chance.

THE PHYSICAL GAME

Sandstrom is one of the more irritating players to do battle against. Chivalry is dead as far as Sandstrom is concerned. Sandstrom's creed is to do unto others whatever you can get away with, then skate like mad to desert the scene of the crime.

But he is no coward. Sandstrom will fight along the boards, using his feet, his stick or any other weapon at hand to free the puck. He will battle his way through checks and will take or mete out his share of punishment to get what he wants. He has been known to carry his stick above shoulder height. Often more like nose height.

THE INTANGIBLES

Sandstrom has to feel that he is a valued member of the team, and with all of the line shuffling the Kings put him through and with the injuries he had to cope with, Sandstrom did not feel important. If he stays healthy, Sandstrom can re-establish himself as one of the top power forwards in the NHL this season. He is still young enough and strong enough, but his performance will depend greatly on the circumstances in L.A.

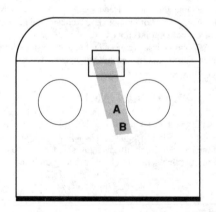

DAVE TAYLOR

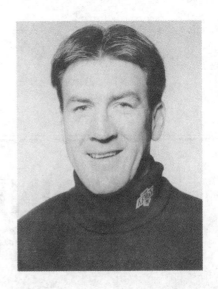

Yrs. of NHL service: 15
Born: Levack, Ont.; Dec. 4, 1955
Position: Right wing
Height: 6-0
Weight: 190
Uniform no.: 18
Shoots: Right

Career statistics:

GP	G	A	TP	PIM
1030	421	626	1047	1512

1991-92 statistics:

GP	G	A	TP	+/-	PIM	PP	SH	GW	GT	S	PCT
77	10	19	29	10	63	0	0	2	0	81	12.3

LAST SEASON

Played in 1,000th career game. All scoring totals career lows. Second on team in plus-minus.

THE FINESSE GAME

E for effort. Every night, every shift. Taylor's consistency and intensity were unmatched by almost any Kings' forward last season. He is very defensively aware and led the team's forwards in plus/minus last season.

Taylor's skills have eroded through the years, but his intelligence has minimized their deterioration. Never a great skater, and even slower now, he is careful not to get caught out of position deep in the attacking zone. He will venture down low when the opportunity is ripe, and scores most of his goals from a very close range.

Given the Kings' lack of size up front, Taylor could be better utilized as a forward who goes to the net on the power play, something that was lacking from their scheme last season.

THE PHYSICAL GAME

Taylor is an athlete who takes great pride in his physical fitness, which is one of the reasons his career has lasted as long as it has. He was the Kings' most physically present forward in most of their games last season. He is a very quiet leader who is well respected by his teammates.

THE INTANGIBLES

Taylor remains an honest competitor who has lost some physical skills but is still an effective checker who can score a key goal now and then. He will be a role player who can contribute on special teams.

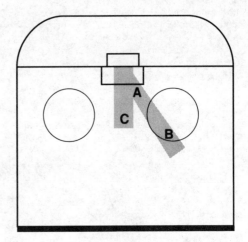

MINNESOTA NORTH STARS

BRIAN BELLOWS

Yrs. of NHL service: 10
Born: St. Catherines, Ont.; Sept. 1, 1964
Position: Left wing
Height: 5-11
Weight: 195
Uniform no.: 23
Shoots: Left

Career statistics:

GP	G	A	TP	PIM
753	342	380	722	537

1991-92 statistics:

GP	G	A	TP	+/-	PIM	PP	SH	GW	GT	S	PCT
80	30	45	75	-20	41	12	1	4	0	255	11.8

LAST SEASON

Led team in assists, which were six-season high. Second on team in scoring, third in power-play goals. Played all 80 games for third consecutive season. Points matched last season's output.

THE FINESSE GAME

Bellows is an outstanding skater, textbook perfect in terms of balance and lower body strength. He powers his way through checks around the net, which is where he does his best work offensively. Not very fast in open ice, once he establishes himself down low there are few better. He is not very tall, but he is sturdy and is a top-notch power forward.

Bellows has quick, strong hands, and will carry the puck to the net through a crowd. He is a finisher, not a playmaker. His assists will come from rebounds that his teammates pick up from following up his shots (if he doesn't beat them to the puck).

He can shoot a puck in tight or rifle a one-timer off the wing. He does not shoot well carrying the puck in at high speed, preferring to carry the puck to the net.

A sound player defensively, he occasionally loses a step and takes a bad hooking or holding penalty, but for the most part he maintains his positioning well. He is not a good man-to-man player, but needs support and will support his teammates.

THE PHYSICAL GAME

Bellows plays bigger than his size, especially on offense. A strong skater, he is a powerful force along the boards. He crashes the net, taking the body and bumping and hitting. He is a clean player whose power and intensity make his finesse skills all the more valuable. He will initiate a lot of hitting.

THE INTANGIBLES

Due to his power-play skills, he was one of the most sought-after forwards in trade talks last season. The North Stars might move the veteran to acquire one or two younger forwards to help restock their aging, creaky forwards. Bellows still has very good trade value.

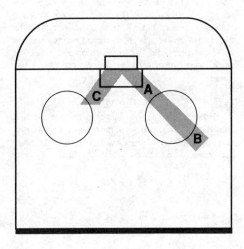

153

NEAL BROTEN

Yrs. of NHL service: 11
Born: Roseau, Minn.; Nov. 29, 1959
Position: Center
Height: 5-9
Weight: 170
Uniform no.: 7
Shoots: Left

Career statistics:

GP	G	A	TP	PIM
848	237	526	763	435

1991-92 statistics:

GP	G	A	TP	+/-	PIM	PP	SH	GW	GT	S	PCT
76	8	26	34	-15	16	4	1	1	0	119	6.7

LAST SEASON

All scoring totals career low.

THE FINESSE GAME

Broten's entire career was built on his skating, and that part of his game deserted him last season — leaving little else for him to build on except his experience. His excellent finesse skills and scoring instincts seemed to have deserted him entirely. Few players have gone from peacock to feather duster as quickly as Broten did in the past two seasons without some serious injury.

His production was the worst of his career. He didn't get himself anywhere near the number of shots or scoring chances he is expected to generate. What's gone wrong? No one seems to know the answer, since he was by all accounts healthy most of the season.

Age is obviously a factor. Broten will be 33 two months into this season. He can no longer be relied upon as a regular, but will have to be spotted in the role of an offensive specialist. He can still quarterback the power play, and has great vision and a passing knack, which resurfaced briefly near the end of last season.

THE PHYSICAL GAME

Broten is an open-ice player with little strength along the boards or in front of the net. He plays a smart game for a player of his (small) size, and the Stars don't expect him to throw his body around.

THE INTANGIBLES

Broten went to Germany at the start of the 1991-92 season, but the North Stars lured him back, and might now be sorry they did (although he showed signs of life in the playoffs). Can Minnesota be satisfied with a one-way defensive forward who is costing them $850,000 a year?

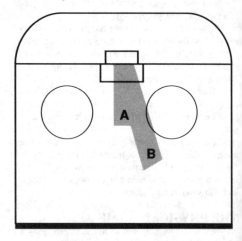

JON CASEY

Yrs. of NHL service: 5
Born: Grand Rapids, Minn.; Mar. 29, 1962
Position: Goaltender
Height: 5-10
Weight: 155
Uniform no.: 30
Catches: Left

Career statistics:

GP	MINS	GA	SO	GAA	A	PIM
265	14613	795	9	3.26	8	84

1991-92 statistics:

GP	MINS	GAA	W	L	T	SO	GA	S	SAPCT	PIM
52	2911	3.40	19	23	5	2	165	1401	.882	26

LAST SEASON

Games played, minutes played and victories three-season low. Most losses in one season. GAA three-season high.

THE PHYSICAL GAME

His style is a hybrid of reflexes and stand-up technique. A goalie who lives by his reactions dies by them when things go wrong, and Casey struggled last season. When he is on his game, he is on his feet, cutting down his angles and challenging shooters. He has a very quick glove hand, reads and anticipates plays well, and doesn't overcommit.

Casey is, to put it bluntly, a brutal stickhandler. He is indecisive and frequently gets caught 15 feet out of his net with the puck, trying to decide what to do. Opposing forwards know this, and are on him quickly. He then shoots it right into the attacker.

He isn't a great skater either, although he has improved his lateral movement.

THE MENTAL GAME

Casey made a brief trip to the minors after the mid-point of the season to regain some of his confidence after losing starts to unheralded Darcy Wakaluk. He gave up more soft goals last season and seemed affected by them. His mental toughness became a question mark instead of a certainty. Because of his unusual playing style, it's harder for Casey to regain his playing groove, but he had a respectable playoff, which could buoy him into this season.

THE INTANGIBLES

Casey took a lot of the heat after Minnesota, a surprise Stanley Cup finalist in 1991, struggled last season. He also signed a lucrative new contract (about $900,000 per annum) in November, and there were questions how it affected his desire.

SHANE CHURLA

Yrs. of NHL service: 4
Born: Fernie, B.C.; June 24, 1965
Position: Right wing
Height: 6-1
Weight: 200
Uniform no.: 27
Shoots: Right

Career statistics:

GP	G	A	TP	PIM
219	10	12	22	1157

1991-92 statistics:

GP	G	A	TP	+/-	PIM	PP	SH	GW	GT	S	PCT
57	4	1	5	-12	278	0	0	0	0	42	9.5

LAST SEASON

Games played and goals career high. Led team in PIM for second straight year. Missed one game with bruised foot. Missed six games with back spasms. Missed seven games with separated shoulder.

THE FINESSE GAME

Churla's finesse skills are negligible. He will get his goals from banging in loose pucks around the net, and is strong and brave enough to fight in the trenches in front of the crease.

His limited use results in limited ice time. He gets no ice time on special teams play, and can't be utilized in late stages of a close game. He is a slow skater and has slow reaction time.

His hands aren't tragically bad and he is able to scoop some loose pucks into the net, although the goalie usually has to be distracted elsewhere. Churla does try.

THE PHYSICAL GAME

Tough and aggressive, he plays a more disciplined style than he did a few seasons back, which makes him a more effective enforcer. He is a willing and eager fighter, but is also anxious to become more than a one-dimensional player. He doesn't have the skills to be a Bob Probert type, but can be a useful sort up front and gets his linemates a lot of room.

THE INTANGIBLES

Injuries have slowed his development over the past two seasons. With all of the finesse players the Stars are trying to break in this season, they'll need a healthy Churla around for insurance.

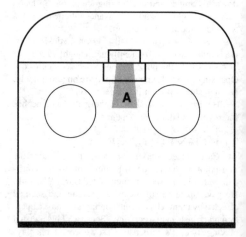

MIKE CRAIG

Yrs. of NHL service: 2
Born: London, Ont.; June 6, 1971
Position: Right wing
Height: 6-0
Weight: 180
Uniform no.: 20
Shoots: Right

Career statistics:

GP	G	A	TP	PIM
106	23	20	43	187

1991-92 statistics:

GP	G	A	TP	+/-	PIM	PP	SH	GW	GT	S	PCT
67	15	16	31	-12	155	4	0	4	0	136	11.0

LAST SEASON

Games played and all scoring totals career highs in second NHL season. Tied for third on team in game-winning goals.

THE FINESSE GAME

Craig has good vision of the ice and sees the open man. He is a creative playmaker and unselfish. He plays a smart game around his own net and can play a short game in traffic.

He has a wrist shot that he gets away quickly and has good scoring instincts (he was a linemate of Eric Lindros in the 1991 World Junior Championships). Craig needs to play with a grinding linemate to help get him the puck, since he doesn't win many corner battles.

He is an excellent skater with good speed, acceleration and balance.

THE PHYSICAL GAME

Craig does not shy away from physical play, but needs to become stronger. He is very competitive and forechecks aggressively. His defensive reads need work, but he is willing and has a sound work ethic.

THE INTANGIBLES

Craig still has had trouble getting into the Stars lineup because of his inconsistent play, but he has improved with experience and is on the verge of becoming a dependable two-way forward.

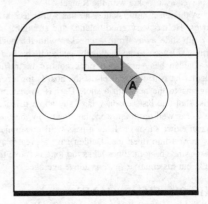

ULF DAHLEN

Yrs. of NHL service: 5
Born: Ostersund, Sweden; Jan. 12, 1967
Position: Right wing
Height: 6-2
Weight: 195
Uniform no.: 22
Shoots: Left

Career statistics:

GP	G	A	TP	PIM
347	130	112	242	122

1991-92 statistics:

GP	G	A	TP	+/-	PIM	PP	SH	GW	GT	S	PCT
79	36	30	66	−5	10	16	1	5	0	216	16.7

LAST SEASON

Led team in goals and shooting percentage. Second on team in power-play goals, fourth in scoring. Games played and all scoring totals career highs.

THE FINESSE GAME

Dahlen built on his status as an outstanding cornerman. Always strong along the boards, last season he went to the net with the same energy. He can finish around the net, and regained the finishing touch he had displayed as a rookie with the Rangers.

Although a slow skater, he has some deceptive moves. He has very good balance and strength, and can slip-slide away from a checker with the puck, turning sideways as he shields the puck with his body.

Dahlen has very good puck control in traffic, whether he is trying to peel off the boards for a pass or going to the net with a shot. He has an accurate wrist shot and last season wasn't shy about using it. He works well on the power play down low, because he can either shoot or delay a pass until a teammate has moved into open ice. Dahlen isn't a great playmaker since he sometimes takes too long to move the puck, but his creative sense is above average.

THE PHYSICAL GAME

Dahlen doesn't always play to his size. He protects the puck well on the boards, but is poor man-to-man defensively. He is not very aggressive except in the pursuit of the puck. There is a feeling that he is holding something back, because he has the skill and strength to bump his game up another notch. As good as he is, he could become even better with more physical play.

THE INTANGIBLES

Dahlen has excellent character and is well respected by his coaches and teammates. The only thing holding him back from being a better player is his skating, but the Stars seems willing to overlook that for the other things he can bring to their team.

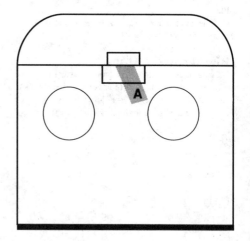

CHRIS DAHLQUIST

Yrs. of NHL service: 6
Born: Fridley, Minn.; Dec. 14, 1962
Position: Defense
Height: 6-1
Weight: 196
Uniform no.: 4
Shoots: Left

Career statistics:

GP	G	A	TP	PIM
311	13	45	58	320

1991-92 statistics:

GP	G	A	TP	+/-	PIM	PP	SH	GW	GT	S	PCT
74	1	13	14	-10	68	0	0	0	0	63	1.6

LAST SEASON

Assists career high. Points matched career high. Goals matches career low for more than 40-game season.

THE FINESSE GAME

Dahlquist is a stay-at-home defenseman with limited skills. He is a defensive defenseman with enough skills to move the puck well, but he doesn't always move it fast enough, and his team ends up trapped after he has an apparently easy chance to clear the puck.

He won't get involved in the attack; he doesn't carry the puck orgamble in deep over the blue line. Dahlquist is strong on his skates and concentrates on his defensive duties. He won't leave anybody in his wake, but he has fairly good speed and mobility up and down the ice. He is very smart positionally.

THE PHYSICAL GAME

A solid hitter, his man stays out of the play once he's been targeted. Dahlquist sometimes has trouble in open ice, but he's very solid along the boards, in the corners and in front of his net. He plays tough and smart, keeping himself out of the penalty box, although he'll get mean every now and then and throw an elbow just to keep the opposition worried.

THE INTANGIBLES

Dahlquist is an underrated, unsung player who lends nice support to a team's defense corps. As the Stars develop defensemen with a better offensive flair, this veteran will work as an effective partner for them.

GAETAN DUCHESNE

Yrs. of NHL service: 11
Born: Les Saulles, Que.; July 11, 1962
Position: Left wing
Height: 5-11
Weight: 200
Uniform no.: 10
Shoots: Left

Career statistics:

GP	G	A	TP	PIM
816	148	214	362	536

1991-92 statistics:

GP	G	A	TP	+/-	PIM	PP	SH	GW	GT	S	PCT
73	8	15	23	6	102	0	2	1	0	106	7.5

LAST SEASON

Led team forwards in plus-minus. Goals matched career low. PIM career high. Games played four-season high.

THE FINESSE GAME

Duchesne has keen defensive instincts. He knows where he should go and the quickest way to get there, and always works hard. He is one of Minnesota's top penalty killers, a special favorite of coach Bob Gainey, who made his own mark as a defensive forward with Montreal.

His numbers have steadily declined but he is more important for preventing goals. He'll still score the odd one now and again, although it's unlikely he'll ever hit double figures again.

Duchesne is a good skater with tremendous defensive hockey sense and anticipation. His conditioning is excellent and he can skate a full shift full-out. Most of his scoring chances are generated by his forechecking. He will either separate the puck carrier from the puck with a bump, or he will intercept passes. He does not have good hand skills, so his plays are limited once he has the puck. He scores from close range.

THE PHYSICAL GAME

Not an overly physical player, he is still smart and solid and knows when to pick his spots for hits. He won't skate all over the ice, willy-nilly, but will find the most efficient way to slow up the opposition's attack. When the time is right, he will sacrifice his body for the play.

THE INTANGIBLES

Duchesne is limited to the role of a checking forward, and he is able to fill that role admirably. Even as the Stars break in younger forwards, he will remain valuable for another season or so because of his experience.

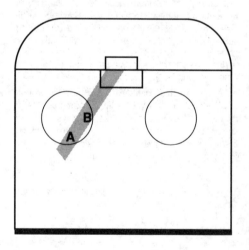

TODD ELIK

Yrs. of NHL service: 3
Born: Brampton, Ont.; Apr. 15, 1966
Position: Center
Height: 6-2
Weight: 190
Uniform no.: 14
Shoots: Left

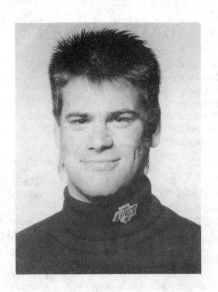

Career statistics:

GP	G	A	TP	PIM
184	46	91	137	187

1991-92 statistics:

GP	G	A	TP	+/-	PIM	PP	SH	GW	GT	S	PCT
62	15	31	46	0	125	4	3	1	0	118	12.7

LAST SEASON

Led team in shorthanded goals. All scoring totals two-season lows. PIM career high.

THE FINESSE GAME

Elik has great quickness but doesn't use it to intimidate the defense as he should. Sometimes he looks off-balance when he starts a rush, as though his hands can't keep up with his feet when he is carrying the puck.

Not a natural goal-scorer, he has a good wrist shot—or he can carry the puck to the net—but his release is slow. He doesn't use his wingers as well as he should, either, which reduces his value as a playmaker.

Elik lacks mental toughness, especially when things aren't going his way scoring-wise. Since most of his value is on offense, he is almost useless to a team when he's in a slump, and his attitude makes matters worse. When things are going well, he is almost another player entirely, cocky and confident, and willing to try more in the offensive zone.

Although he has made great strides in his own end, he still needs work defensively. He was used to kill penalties, mostly because he is aggressive and thinks offense, and because of his speed.

THE PHYSICAL GAME

Elik will use his body in the attacking zone, if not defensively. He has good size, and combined with his skating ability, can be a solid forechecker. He will go in traffic for the puck, but isn't strong enough to win the one-on-one battles. He is average on draws.

THE INTANGIBLES

Last season was a disappointment for Elik, but the Stars have faith that he can become a solid two-way forward who can score 20-25 goals a season.

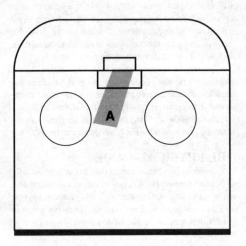

DAVE GAGNER

Yrs. of NHL service: 6
Born: Chatham, Ont.; Dec. 11, 1964
Position: Center
Height: 5-10
Weight: 180
Uniform no.: 15
Shoots: Left

Career statistics:

GP	G	A	TP	PIM
436	165	190	355	481

1991-92 statistics:

GP	G	A	TP	+/-	PIM	PP	SH	GW	GT	S	PCT
78	31	40	71	−4	107	17	0	3	0	229	13.5

LAST SEASON

Led team in power-play goals. Third on team in assists and points. Goals and points four-season lows. Missed two games with knee injuries.

THE FINESSE GAME

Few players may be prouder of being called a garbage man that Gagner. His goals come from his inner fire and determination. None of his skills are overpowering or awe-inspiring on their own, but combined with his gritty play down low, he has become a reliable scorer in the 30-40 goal range.

Knee problems over the past two season have affected his skating, which was never a strong suit to begin with, as far as speed goes. Gagner has good quickness and pressures the defense on the rush. He likes to carry to the net with a forehand-backhand-forehand move, exhibiting good puck control.

Gagner is more of a one-on-one center than a playmaker. He has good hockey sense as a shooter and uses his shot selection intelligently. He won't overpower many goalies, but he will fool them.

Although it is not the best part of his game, he has improved defensively. He is adequate on draws.

THE PHYSICAL GAME

Gagner plays much bigger than his size, especially in front of the net. He will power his way to the crease, using his strong skating stance. He is scrappy, aggressive and has good hockey courage. He doesn't wait to get hit, but tries to get the first lick in.

THE INTANGIBLES

Gagner missed only two games with knee surgery to remove cartilage, but was evidently affected by the ailment for at least half the season. He is an inspirational player who leads by example on the ice and takes few nights off.

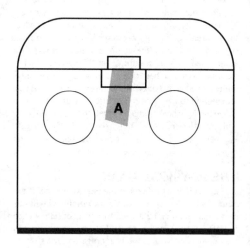

DERIAN HATCHER

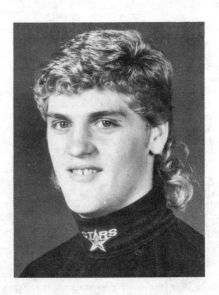

Yrs. of NHL service: 1
Born: Sterling Heights, Mich.; June 4, 1972
Position: Left defense
Height: 6-5
Weight: 205
Uniform no.: 28
Shoots: Left

Career statistics:

GP	G	A	TP	PIM
43	7	5	12	88

1991-92 statistics:

GP	G	A	TP	+/-	PIM	PP	SH	GW	GT	S	PCT
43	7	5	12	7	88	0	0	2	0	51	13.7

LAST SEASON

First NHL season. Missed 25 games with broken ankle (sustained in non-hockey accident).

THE FINESSE GAME

Hatcher has a lot of raw talent and is just learning to put all the facets together and add some polish. In the short time he was with the Stars, he moved quickly up the depth chart and ended the season as the No. 2 defenseman (after Mark Tinordi).

Coach Bob Gainey compared the young defenseman to former Montreal blueliner Serge Savard because of Hatcher's physical play and his poise and cool with the puck in his own zone.

He has good offensive instincts. His puckhandling and shooting skills are good and getting better. He has very good hands for a big man and likes to get involved in the attack. Hatcher doesn't have the speed to launch end-to-end rushes, but he will follow up the play and has the confidence to attack at the blue line. He will also sally in deep and use a wrist shot at close range and also has an effective one-timer.

Hatcher has some lack of coordination in his skating, where it looks like he's still getting adjusted as he grows.

THE PHYSICAL GAME

Ouch. This is a monster in training. Hatcher has a mean streak. He received a three-game suspension in the playoffs for hitting Detroit's Kevin Miller in the face with his stick, breaking Miller's upper jaw and cracking several teeth. He is a powerful hitter, and if his skating improves, he will be an even more dangerous hitter because skaters won't be able to avoid him. Hatcher is very strong along the boards.

THE INTANGIBLES

After he was cut from the U.S. Olympic team, America's loss became Minnesota's gain. His skills are catching up to his still-growing body. It's unfair to compare young players to others, especially to an older, established sibling, but Derian shows every sign of being as good as big brother Kevin (who plays for Washington). Hatcher can be a dominating, two-way defenseman: he's young, he will make mistakes and NHL defensemen need a few years to develop, but he's taken a big first step.

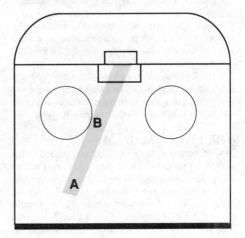

JIM JOHNSON

Yrs. of NHL service: 7
Born: New Hope, Minn.; Aug. 9, 1962
Position: Right defense
Height: 6-1
Weight: 190
Uniform no.: 6
Shoots: Left

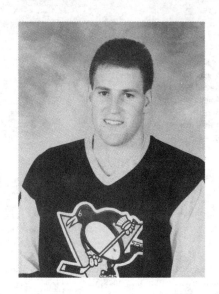

Career statistics:

GP	G	A	TP	PIM
505	19	114	133	860

1991-92 statistics:

GP	G	A	TP	+/-	PIM	PP	SH	GW	GT	S	PCT
71	4	10	14	11	102	0	0	1	0	86	4.7

LAST SEASON

Led team defensemen in plus-minus. Goals five-season high. Missed five games with knee injury. Missed two games with hamstring strain. Missed two games with separated shoulder.

THE FINESSE GAME

Johnson is a good stay-at-home defenseman who will pick his offensive spots wisely. An intelligent player all around, he is confident enough in his skating and his positioning to step up and challenge skaters at the blue line. He likes to force the play rather than wait for the attackers to come at him with speed, and his aggressive style allows his teammates to get back into the play defensively as Johnson slows down the attack.

Usually a safety valve for a more offensive defenseman, he is not allergic to the attacking zone. If you see him venturing down between the hash marks, you'll know it's a high percentage scoring play. Johnson won't take a wild shot, but will use an accurate, low wrist shot that won't be blocked.

He moves the puck well out of his own end with a crisp pass. He doesn't like to lug it, and since he's usually teamed with a finesse partner, that works out well. He is poised and doesn't rush his passes.

THE PHYSICAL GAME

His skating — he has good quickness and lateral mobility — makes him a hard checker. Johnson doesn't go running all over the ice looking to crunch people, but he never wastes an opportunity to make a hard hit, either. He is steady in front of his own net, keeping things clear for his goalie to get a good look at the shooter. He is a hard worker and an intense competitor.

THE INTANGIBLES

Johnson is a solid defensive defenseman, one who doesn't get a lot of attention because he doesn't have any flashy numbers. His plus-minus on a struggling Stars team last season is an indication of one flashy number to take note of. He is a valuable member of an improving defense corps. Johnson will help some of the younger, more inexperienced players get better.

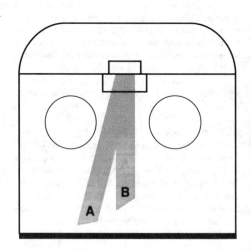

CRAIG LUDWIG

Yrs. of NHL service: 10
Born: Rhinelander, Wisc.; Mar. 15, 1961
Position: Left defense
Height: 6-3
Weight: 215
Uniform no.: 3
Shoots: Left

Career statistics:

GP	G	A	TP	PIM
745	29	128	157	750

1991-92 statistics:

GP	G	A	TP	+/-	PIM	PP	SH	GW	GT	S	PCT
73	2	9	11	0	54	0	0	0	0	51	3.9

LAST SEASON

All scoring totals two-season highs. PIM eight-season low. Missed six games with fractured foot. Missed one game with flu.

THE FINESSE GAME

Offensive skills were never part of Ludwig's game even in his prime, and it's useless to discuss them now because he's not going to change. You're not going to get big numbers from him. He doesn't lead or get involved in a rush, although he can start a breakout with a clean pass. Ludwig will stick to the blue line and take his shots from there, but there isn't much mustard on his slapper and he will more often just take the safe dump in to keep the puck deep.

You will get a big effort on defense, Ludwig is a classic stay-at-home defenseman who has long recognized his limitations and always played well within them. His skating is below average. He has big strides but not much mobility. He is intelligent enough to play a smart, conservative game. Ludwig reads the defense very well.

THE PHYSICAL GAME

The biggest pads ever seen on a non-goalie are his shot-blocking weapon. Ludwig has gotten a little slower, and shooters will try to make him commit early to going down, then step around him. Although strong, he is not much of a hitter. He prefers to tie up his man. Ludwig has a long reach and can neutralize a puck carrier while reaching in to knock the disk loose. He has a little nasty in him and will carry his stick high.

THE INTANGIBLES

Ludwig will be on the bubble this season as the North Stars have several good young defensive prospects eager to break into the NHL (among them, Tommy Sjodin and Richard Matvichuk). Even though his good buddy Bob Gainey is coach and GM, you have to wonder how much ice time Ludwig will get this season.

MIKE MODANO

Yrs. of NHL service: 3
Born: Livonia, Mich.; June 7, 1970
Position: Center
Height: 6-3
Weight: 190
Uniform no.: 9
Shoots: Left

Career statistics:

GP	G	A	TP	PIM
235	90	126	216	174

1991-92 statistics:

GP	G	A	TP	+/-	PIM	PP	SH	GW	GT	S	PCT
76	33	44	77	−9	46	5	0	8	2	256	12.9

LAST SEASON

Led team in points, shots and game-winning goals. Goals and points career highs in third NHL season. Missed three games with hip injuries.

THE FINESSE GAME

Modano has excellent offensive skills and instincts, and is a dynamic player with the potential to be a game-breaker. He excels in open ice and has every skill necessary to be a top flight forward, starting with his skating. Modano has speed, accleration, agility and balance. He can stop and start quickly.

He has the up-tempo hand skills to match his speed. He can control the puck in traffic, stickhandle through players, or blaze in with the speed and force the defense back on its heels, opening up the ice for his linemates. Modano can pass equally well on his forehand or backhand. The Stars played him on right wing but he will use all of the ice and not just skate up and down his wing. He has to play with creative thinkers who will drive to open ice, where Modano will get them the puck. He is a natural to quarterback the power play.

He also has several tremendous shots. He releases a wrist shot quickly from close range, one-times from the circles and can work the point on the power play.

Modano still plays soft but is improving. Since he is big enough to play with more power, he has to add a grinding element to his game. He needs to improve his man-to-man defense, but does have a wonderful knack for picking off passes in the neutral zone.

THE PHYSICAL GAME

Modano has been noted more for his creative side than his willingness to stand up for his teammates (and even himself), but he showed some signs last season that he can be more of a factor physically. If he does that on a more consistent basis this year, his game will take a huge stride forward, since he will earn himself room. If he plays to his size more often, he will be a powerful force.

THE INTANGIBLES

Modano is still a cut below the league's elite. He has shifts, but not a complete game, where he will dominate the action. He needs to do that on a more consistent level. Modano is developing into a top forward but needs to play with more confidence and not be so erratic.

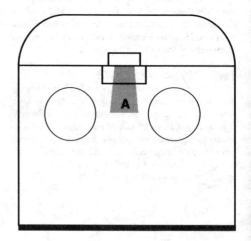

DAVID SHAW

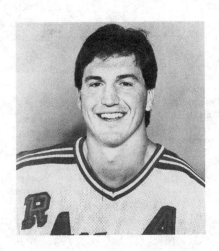

Yrs. of NHL service: 8
Born: St. Thomas, Ont.; May 25, 1964
Position: Right defense
Height: 6-2
Weight: 204
Uniform no.: 26
Shoots: Right

Career statistics:

GP	G	A	TP	PIM
456	25	103	128	529

1991-92 statistics:

GP	G	A	TP	+/-	PIM	PP	SH	GW	GT	S	PCT
59	1	9	10	−12	72	0	0	0	0	70	1.4

LAST SEASON

Acquired from Edmonton for Brian Glynn, Jan. 21. Started season with New York Rangers before trade to Oilers. All scoring totals five-season lows. Missed three games with broken ankle.

THE FINESSE GAME

Shaw has some good offensive finesse skills which he puts to good use, but he needs a little room (like on the power play). He has a nice, low bullet of a shot from the right point that he steps into with some confidence. His shots are often blocked, however, because he doesn't always look up when he's shooting. He just puts his head down and blasts away.

Injuries have robbed Shaw of some of his speed and agility. He reads defensive plays well and used to meet the challenge more aggressively at the blue line. Too often, he is now content to sit back and wait for the play to develop deeper.

Shaw has good hand skills once he gets control of the puck. He seldom rushes it, but will make cool, flat passes out of the zone.

THE PHYSICAL GAME

The physical part of Shaw's game has plummeted. He has never been the same player since he took a 12-game suspension for high-sticking Mario Lemieux. That was way back in the 1988-89 season, but it has taken its toll. He was a much more physical player before the incident. He's been plagued by injuries since then, too.

THE INTANGIBLES

Shaw is very much on the bubble in Minnesota. After being moved three times last season, it might be difficult to find a comfortable home anywhere now.

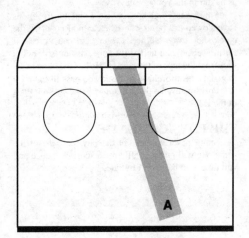

BOBBY SMITH

Yrs. of NHL service: 15
Born: North Sydney, N.S.; Feb. 12, 1958
Position: Center
Height: 6-4
Weight: 210
Uniform no.: 18
Shoots: Left

Career statistics:

GP	G	A	TP	PIM
1032	352	672	1024	909

1991-92 statistics:

GP	G	A	TP	+/-	PIM	PP	SH	GW	GT	S	PCT
68	9	37	46	−24	111	3	0	1	0	129	7.0

LAST SEASON

Surpassed 1,000 games played and 1,000 points for career. Goals career low. Assists three-season high. Points matched previous season's production. Worst plus-minus on team. Missed two games with flu.

THE FINESSE GAME

Smith has slowed a step, but he still remains a graceful skater with wiry strength. He can plant himself in front of the net and use his long reach to get his arms and stick free of the defender to take a shot. He no longer has the speed to beat defenders one-on-one as he did in his younger days.

Smith has good hockey sense but his reactions have slowed to a point where he can no longer get the quick shot away. He needs room, but can't create it for himself. When he has the time, he can still nail a shot from the tops of the circles. He has the hand skills to make a neat forehand or backhand pass in tight.

Positionally, he plays a smart game in both ends of the ice.

THE PHYSICAL GAME

Smith never excelled at the physical part of the game. He will go nto traffic for a scoring chance and will take a hit but won't initiate.

THE INTANGIBLES

At best, Smith might have one season left. His gas tank is just about empty. He can come up with a big effort in a big game — like the playoffs — but no longer has the stamina for a full season.

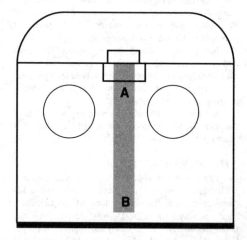

MARK TINORDI

Yrs. of NHL service: 4
Born: Deer River, Alta.; May 9, 1966
Position: Defense
Height: 6-4
Weight: 205
Uniform no.: 24
Shoots: Left

Career statistics:

GP	G	A	TP	PIM
269	15	63	78	765

1991-92 statistics:

GP	G	A	TP	+/-	PIM	PP	SH	GW	GT	S	PCT
63	4	24	28	-13	177	4	0	0	0	93	4.3

LAST SEASON

Led team defensemen in assists and points. Missed 17 games with foot palsy (from blocking Al MacInnis shot). Games played three-season low. Finalist for 1992 Masterton Trophy.

THE FINESSE GAME

Tinordi is one of the top all-around defensemen in the league. Other players have gaudier point totals, but few are following the Ray Bourque blueprint of offense, defense and leadership as well as this reformed goon.

His offensive instincts will never match Bourque's. Tinordi doesn't have the finesse skills, and doesn't try to do a whole lot more than he is capable of doing. He will pinch in aggressively at the blue line, and will crash the net, especially on the power play. He won't beat anybody one-on-one with his stickhandling, but he can overpower defensemen and goalies as he drive to the net.

Tinordi's skating is above average. He isn't quick off the mark, nor fast from end to end, but he has a long stride with good balance and lateral mobility. He can use his long reach to get around people offensively, or to reach in and knock the puck away defensively. He can move the puck once he gets it.

THE PHYSICAL GAME

Tinordi is aggressive and smart. He will goad other players into taking bad retaliatory penalties, while wasting little time in the penalty box himself. He will fight when challenged, but only to prove a point. He doesn't go looking for trouble because he knows he is one of the top players in the lineup and the Stars can't afford to lose him.

Playing with confidence and authority, he dominates his end of the ice and dares the opposition to challenge him. He can take care of himself and his teammates, and is strong along the boards and in front of his net.

THE INTANGIBLES

We predicted big things for Tinordi in last year's HSR, and they might have happened if it hadn't been for his freak injury. He came back just as strong from the career-threatening injury and, demontrating his courage, kept throwing himself in front of shots. He is now the Stars' captain and official team leader, just as he was their heart two years ago in the drive to the final. Tinordi remains the most valuable player on the team.

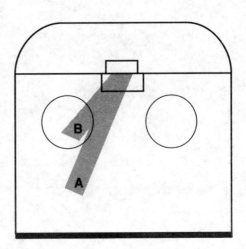

169

MONTREAL
CANADIENS

GUY CARBONNEAU

Yrs. of NHL service: 10
Born: Sept-Iles, Que.; Mar. 18, 1960
Position: Center
Height: 5-11
Weight: 180
Uniform no.: 21
Shoots: Right

Career statistics:

GP	G	A	TP	PIM
772	203	289	492	555

1991-92 statistics:

GP	G	A	TP	+/-	PIM	PP	SH	GW	GT	S	PCT
72	18	11	39	2	39	1	1	4	0	120	15.0

LAST SEASON

Won 1992 Selke Trophy. Missed eight games with injuries. Goals two-season low. Assists career low. Points four-season low.

THE FINESSE GAME

Carbonneau has a great knowledge of the game. His anticipation, poise and defensive reads have enabled him to win the Selke Trophy as the NHL's best defensive forward in three of the last five seasons.

He has slowed down some, but is still a top-notch skater with all of the best traits: quickness, agility and balance. He has lost the most in his straightaway speed, but that was never the biggest part of Carbonneau's game anyway.

A two-way checking center, Carbonneau is solid positionally. One of the bonuses used to be his regular contribution of 20 or more goals while detracting nothing from his defensive game. He can still contribute the odd goal, although his production will continue to drop. It's unlikely he'll ever score 26 again, but will instead be in the 15-18 goal range. Carbonneau has an excellent wrist shot, and likes to use it through a crowd to gain the screen. He is also a very good passer, especially in tight. Carbonneau doesn't go for many home runs, but he's a consistent singles hitter, to borrow a baseball description.

There are few better men to have on the dot for a crucial face-off than Carbonneau. His hand-eye coordination is exceptional.

THE PHYSICAL GAME

Carbonneau has a small but wiry frame and is deceptively strong. His skating balance gives him a power base and he is able to neutralize bigger forwards because of it. He is tireless and doesn't quit in his pursuit of a bouncing puck in front of the net or in pursuit of a puck carrier.

He uses his body in another way, too: Carbonneau is one of the league's best shot-blocking forwards. His timing and his willingness to sacrifice his body to deny a scoring chance made him one of the best defensive forwards over the past few seasons.

THE INTANGIBLES

Carbonneau's skills have dropped off some, and he won the Selke last year largely on reputation. There are better defensive forwards around now, although Carbonneau is still one of the very good ones. He had knee surgery during the off-season, which may affect his mobility.

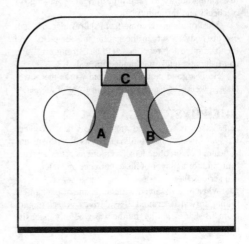

171

SHAYNE CORSON

Yrs. of NHL service: 6
Born: Barrie, Ont.; Aug. 13, 1966
Position: Center
Height: 6-0
Weight: 175
Uniform no.: 27
Shoots: Left

Career statistics:

GP	G	A	TP	PIM
420	121	166	287	891

1991-92 statistics:

GP	G	A	TP	+/-	PIM	PP	SH	GW	GT	S	PCT
64	17	36	53	15	118	3	0	2	0	165	10.3

LAST SEASON

Missed 14 games with suspensions. Goals four-season low. Assists and points two-season highs. Third on team in assists, fourth in points.

THE FINESSE GAME

Corson is an above average skater with good power and balance, but not much agility. He seems to have all the qualities of a good power forward, yet Corson hasn't always put that kind of game together. There are too many nights when he seems happy being a perimeter player, and his finesse skills are not good enough to let him succeed without playing a physical game.

Corson has good skills, though, and good hockey sense. He reads plays well in both zones. A basic player when it comes to playmaking, Corson prefers to work a short passing game with none of the fancy trimmings. As a scorer, he will drive to the net, using his skating ability to keep him upright, bouncing off of checks and through traffic.

Most of his goals come from short range. He will use his body to screen the goalie and set picks, and then scramble for rebounds. He has strong arms and can fish out a puck one-handed for a shot.

He is a good penalty killer and works the power play as well because of his work in front of the net.

THE PHYSICAL GAME

Corson is tough and aggressive when involved. He's not always smart-tough either, as his suspensions indicate. Corson often lets his emotions get away from him, and for a player of his experience and talent, that is a serious flaw.

When he's involved, Corson is one of the hardest hitting forwards around. He derives great strength from his skating ability, but he was woefully inconsistent in this category last season.

THE INTANGIBLES

It was surprising that Corson was not dealt after the 1991 playoffs, since his trade value is never likely to be as high. He is as erratic in his play as he is in his off-ice behaviour. Corson does not come to play every game and as a result, his effort falls far short of his abilities. He has about worn out his welcome in Montreal, even with a coaching change.

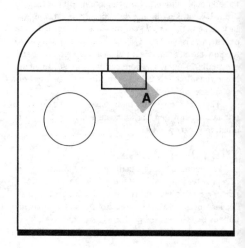

RUSS COURTNALL

Yrs. of NHL service: 8
Born: Duncan, B.C.; June 2, 1965
Position: Right wing
Height: 5-11
Weight: 180
Uniform no.: 6
Shoots: Right

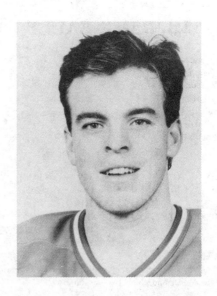

Career statistics:

GP	G	A	TP	PIM
559	172	241	423	320

1991-92 statistics:

GP	G	A	TP	+/-	PIM	PP	SH	GW	GT	S	PCT
27	7	14	21	6	6	0	1	1	1	63	11.1

LAST SEASON

Missed 53 games with shoulder injuries. Goals and points career lows for full season.

THE FINESSE GAME

Courtnall has great speed and quickness. He likes to try to burn a defender to the outside and he is often successful, although he could utliize his teammates better rather than always challenging one-on-one. His hand skills are up to tempo and he can get off a good scoring chance with speed.

Courtnall is not an instinctive scorer but he can get 30 goals a year (when healthy) because of the edge he gets by intimidating with his speed. He has an excellent wrist shot. Defensemen have to play off him because of his skating ability, and that gives Courtnall a lot of room to manuever. If he would try to create plays more, he would be even more dangerous. Usually, the opposition anticipates him taking the shot.

Courtnall works hard defensively. He can be used to kill penalties (his breakaway speed gives him short-handed potential) and he also works the power play. He won't crash the net (his size indicates that is a wise decision). Courtnall came back from his shoulder injury with most of his speed and touch intact.

THE PHYSICAL GAME

Pound for pound, Courtnall is a pretty tough player. There just aren't enough pounds to go around. Wisely, then, Courtnall avoids scrums in the corners and along the boards, and darts in and out of the openings in front of the net. He is a willing hitter in open ice, where his skating gives him a little edge. He is strong for his size.

THE INTANGIBLES

Courtnall started the off-season by marrying an actress in Los Angeles and announcing to the hockey world that he wanted a trade to the Kings, and only the Kings—as if Bruce McNall were in the market for another overpaid forward.

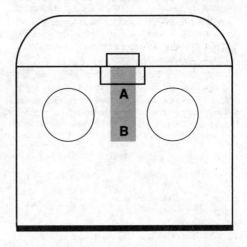

J.J. DAIGNEAULT

Yrs. of NHL service: 7
Born: Montreal, Que.; Oct. 12, 1965
Position: Left defense
Height: 5-11
Weight: 185
Uniform no.: 48
Shoots: Left

Career statistics:

GP	G	A	TP	PIM
402	26	104	130	263

1991-92 statistics:

GP	G	A	TP	+/-	PIM	PP	SH	GW	GT	S	PCT
79	4	14	18	16	36	2	0	0	1	108	3.7

LAST SEASON

Games played career high. Goals four-season high. Assists and points two-season lows.

THE FINESSE GAME

Daigneault's game is based on his offensive skills and instincts. He is an excellent skater, with speed, and that speed allows him to recover from some of his defensive mistakes.

He moves or carries the puck well at high tempo and knows when to get involved with an up-ice rush. Daigneault concentrated more on his defensive chores last season, but was effective from the point. He likes to use a long wrist shot when he gets power play time. He has very strong arms and can get an accurate, low shot through to the goalie for a rebound or a tip by his forwards. Daigneault also has a good slap shot.

His positional play has also improved.

THE PHYSICAL GAME

Daigneault lacks the size and strength to be an effective checker. He is weak along the boards, and does not clear out the front of his net. Daigneault is limited by his size, but with his skating ability seems to have the potential to be a more effective hitter. Daigneault likes to use a quick-flick poke check.

THE INTANGIBLES

Daigneault is an average player, a serviceable fifth or sixth defenseman who has improved defensively but will be on the bench in crunch time.

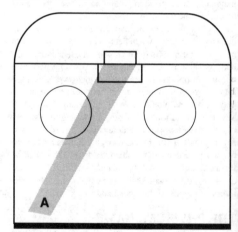

ERIC DESJARDINS

Yrs. of NHL service: 4
Born: Rouyn, Que.; June 14, 1969
Position: Right defense
Height: 6-1
Weight: 200
Uniform no.: 28
Shoots: Right

Career statistics:

GP	G	A	TP	PIM
230	18	76	94	154

1991-92 statistics:

GP	G	A	TP	+/-	PIM	PP	SH	GW	GT	S	PCT
77	6	32	38	17	50	4	0	2	0	141	4.3

LAST SEASON

Led team defensemen in scoring with career highs in assists and points. Led team defensemen in plus-minus. Missed two games due to injury.

THE FINESSE GAME

Desjardins took great strides offensively last season, gaining confidence in his abilities after a disapponting sophomore season in 1990-91. He has very good offensive instincts and likes to get involved in the attack.

Desjardins is a very good skater, with speed and balance, and surprisingly agile although he has pretty good size. He skates well backwards and can pivot quickly. Desjardins seldom gets caught running around. He is a good positional defenseman who spots his offensive chances; he doesn't gamble unless it looks like a sure bet.

Desjardins works the point on the power play and has an excellent one-timer, his favorite shot. He will skate into the middle and occasionally venture in front of the net, but his chief responsibility is defense. He is a very good passer.

THE PHYSICAL GAME

Desjardins has worked at his physical conditioning, adding muscle to a solid frame, and it has paid off. He is all business—a clean, solid, tough defenseman who will clear out the front of his net, work the wall and make his take-outs count. When he gains control of the puck, he will quickly outlet a pass or carry the puck to get his team going. He is very poised under pressure.

THE INTANGIBLES

Desjardins is not outstanding in any one area, but is good in all aspects of the game. He is a solid, all-around defenseman and should take another step forward in his development this season. Desjardins is becoming a team leader.

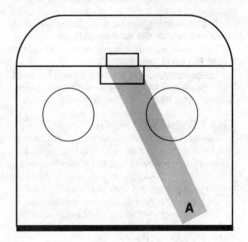

GILBERT DIONNE

Yrs. of NHL service: 1
Born: Drummondville, Que.; Sept. 19, 1970
Position: Left wing
Height: 6-0
Weight: 194
Uniform no.: 45
Shoots: Left

Career statistics:

GP	G	A	TP	PIM
41	21	13	34	10

1991-92 statistics:

GP	G	A	TP	+/-	PIM	PP	SH	GW	GT	S	PCT
39	21	13	34	7	10	7	0	2	0	90	23.3

LAST SEASON

First NHL season. Tied for second among NHL rookies in power-play goals. Led NHL rookies in shooting percentage.

THE FINESSE GAME

Dionne has great scoring instincts, which, genetically speaking, one might expect from the younger brother of Hall of Famer Marcel Dionne. He is always around the net. Don't look for a pass from Dionne, because he loves to shoot and always takes a shot rather than looking to make a play. For someone who is as accurate as he is, this is not a flaw. He does have good passing skills when he opts to make a play. Dionne will lead the man well and make an accurate and fast pass.

Dionne lacks breakaway speed, but he is a strong skater with balance and quickness. He is excellent in traffic, which is where Dionne spends most of his time. He has very good hand skills.

Dionne works hard defensively and has good hockey sense in all zones. His anticipation is excellent. Dionne is very mature for a young player.

THE PHYSICAL GAME

Dionne has size and strength, and uses both to fight his way through checks. Dionne can get his helmet knocked flying but he will maintain control of the puck and will be looking for his scoring chance. He likes to go in corners and work, and is always battling for the puck. Dionne won't be intimidated, and as aggressive as he plays, does not take bad penalties.

THE INTANGIBLES

An unsung, overage draft pick despite his family ties, the late-blooming Dionne will have to show he can sustain his half-season of rookie stardom over an entire 84-game schedule. He has the attitude, the work ethic and the skills, and should be a mainstay for a Canadiens team that is desperately seeking offense.

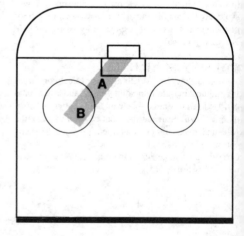

BRENT GILCHRIST

Yrs. of NHL service: 4
Born: Moose Jaw, Sask.; Apr. 3, 1967
Position: Center
Height: 6-1
Weight: 190
Uniform no.: 41
Shoots: Left

Career statistics:

GP	G	A	TP	PIM
236	46	67	113	111

1991-92 statistics:

GP	G	A	TP	+/-	PIM	PP	SH	GW	GT	S	PCT
79	23	27	50	29	57	2	0	3	2	146	15.8

LAST SEASON

Led team in plus-minus. Games played and all scoring totals career highs.

THE FINESSE GAME

Gilchrist enjoyed a career year when the defensive-minded center suddenly developed a nice scoring touch. Although he was a scorer at the junior and minor league levels, the Canadiens have a habit of shoehorning players into defensive roles, and Gilchrist willingly did it. Now that this offensive facet of his game has re-emerged, it might to difficult to hold him back.

Gilchrist is very quick, but the key to his success is his work. He is always in motion, always driving to the net, and he draws his share of penalties because he doesn't quit. Gilchrist is versatile enough to play all three forward positions.

His offensive instincts are not outstanding. He likes to buzz around the net, and that is where a majority of his scoring chances come from. Gilchrist has great balance around the net and is aggressive, but he does not abandon his defense. He is a determined forechecker and is very good on draws.

THE PHYSICAL GAME

Gilchrist has above-average strength and adequate size, although he doesn't leave an impression as a very physical player. He will take the body and generates much of his hitting from his good skating. Gilchrist is scrappy and won't back down from a challenge. He is a good team player.

THE INTANGIBLES

Gilchrist is turning into a good all-around player, a valuable member of the Canadiens because of his hard work. He is self-motivated and has worked hard to improve himself. Gilchrist now has to maintain the level he exhibited last season.

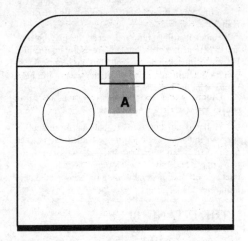

KEVIN HALLER

Yrs. of NHL service: 1
Born: Trocho, Alta.; Dec. 5, 1970
Position: Left defense
Height: 6-3
Weight: 182
Uniform no.: 14
Shoots: Left

Career statistics:

GP	G	A	TP	PIM
89	9	25	34	112

1991-92 statistics:

GP	G	A	TP	+/-	PIM	PP	SH	GW	GT	S	PCT
66	8	17	25	−9	92	3	0	1	0	85	9.4

LAST SEASON
Acquired from Buffalo for Petr Svoboda, March 10, 1992. First full NHL season.

THE FINESSE GAME
Haller is an excellent skater with a long, easy stride. He has very good lateral movement and skates well backwards.

Haller is a good scoring defenseman with a low, accurate shot and quick release (his shooting percentage in his eight games with Montreal after the trade was 22.2). He is a good passer and can make a soft pass or a hard one as the situation dictates. Haller can move the puck through traffic and can find the open man.

Haller is still green, and needs the playing time and experience to grow into a more useful competitor. He makes mistakes defensively, but the Montreal system should help him develop: Haller was +4 in his 8 games with the Canadiens.

THE PHYSICAL GAME
Haller is tall but needs to bulk up more and get stronger to handle the one-on-one battles. He is weak on the boards and in the corners, and needs to develop more upper and lower body strength. Attention to an intensive off-season conditioning program would help him tremendously.

THE INTANGIBLES
Haller has the potential to become the Canadiens' best offensive defenseman. As he gains experience, he will get more and more power play time. He has a good shot and reads his options well, and it would be no surprise to see him get around 15 goals and 50 points this season. If the Canadiens were more of an offensive-minded team, those numbers could go even higher.

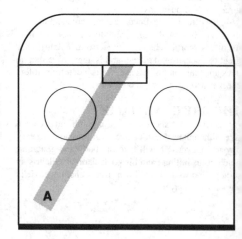

178

MIKE KEANE

Yrs. of NHL service: 4
Born: Winnipeg, Man.; May 28, 1967
Position: Right wing
Height: 5-11
Weight: 175
Uniform no.: 12
Shoots: right

Career statistics:

GP	G	A	TP	PIM
283	49	87	136	261

1991-92 statistics:

GP	G	A	TP	+/-	PIM	PP	SH	GW	GT	S	PCT
67	11	30	41	16	64	2	0	2	1	116	9.5

LAST SEASON

Missed 11 games with injuries. Career highs in assists and points.

THE FINESSE GAME

Keane is a heady, competitive player who has developed into a two-way up and down winger. There is nothing spectacular about him, but Keane is very steady defensively and will contribute a goal here and there.

Keane, who can play either wing but is better on the right side, is a very effective checker. He has the speed to forecheck and take the body and is a good penalty killer.

Keane's offensive skills are okay. He has good hand skills and can take or receive a pass with a nice, soft touch, but most of his scoring chances are generated from hard work down low.

THE PHYSICAL GAME

Keane plays bigger than he is. He is fearless and is always in somebody's face. Although he is not a fighter, Keane is always ready to come to a teammate's aid in a fracas. He will hit in all three zones, generating what power he can from his good skating ability.

THE INTANGIBLES

Keane is a dependable, hard-working forward whose game will always be limited by his lack of size, which does not suit the style he has to play in order to be effective. Keane might sneak up into the 20-goal range: if he does, the Canadiens will consider it a bonus.

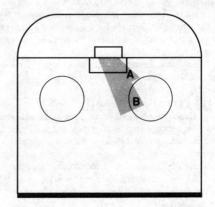

STEPHAN LEBEAU

Yrs. of NHL service: 3
Born: St.-Jerome, Que.; Feb. 28, 1968
Position: Center
Height: 5-10
Weight: 180
Uniform no.: 47
Shoots: Right

Career statistics:

GP	G	A	TP	PIM
208	64	83	147	51

1991-92 statistics:

GP	G	A	TP	+/-	PIM	PP	SH	GW	GT	S	PCT
77	27	31	58	18	14	13	0	5	0	178	15.2

LAST SEASON

Tied for team lead in game-winning goals. Third on team in scoring. Second in power-play goals. Career highs in goals and points.

THE FINESSE GAME

Lebeau has every offensive tool to be a sniper in the NHL, except for size.

Lebeau has great hockey sense. He can score with a quick-release wrist shot, or make a pretty pass. Since he is far too small to fight his own battles, Lebeau needs to work with players who will get him the puck.

Lebeau is a nifty, shifty skater. He has some straightaway speed but won't take off on many breakaways. He will key some odd-man rushes as he outfoxes a checker in open ice. He likes to come in late as the trailer. He does not have a shot that will overpower goalies, but he is a clever shooter and picks his openings.

Lebeau has defensive awareness, but still has trouble handling bigger forwards.

THE PHYSICAL GAME

Lebeau will play a physical game in the attacking zone. He will go to the front of the night and fight his way through a forest of sticks to the best of his ability, because he loves to score. You won't see the same dedication in the corners. Lebeau can disappear on some of the smaller ice surfaces, a problem in the Adams Division, which has two such buildings in Boston and Buffalo.

THE INTANGIBLES

Lebeau was a great scorer at the minor league level (70 goals, 134 points with Sherbrooke in 1988-89). The Canadiens thought he had 40-goal potential at the NHL level, but Lebeau hasn't indicated that will be the case. Size is always going to be a question mark, but if Montreal could land a beefy forward for Lebeau to team with, he could take off. For the time being, he is a solid second-line center.

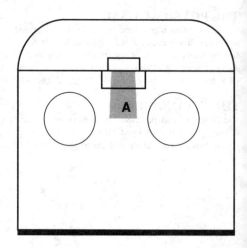

JOHN LeCLAIR

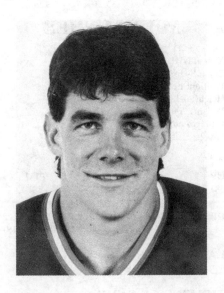

Yrs. of NHL service: 1
Born: St. Albans, Vt.; July 5, 1969
Position: Left wing
Height: 6-2
Weight: 215
Uniform no.: 17
Shoots: Left

Career statistics:

GP	G	A	TP	PIM
69	10	16	26	16

1991-92 statistics:

GP	G	A	TP	+/-	PIM	PP	SH	GW	GT	S	PCT
59	8	11	19	5	14	3	0	0	0	73	11.0

LAST SEASON

First NHL season. Missed 9 games with injuries.

THE FINESSE GAME

LeClair is a physical winger who makes good use of his size and strong skating. One of LeClair's favorite plays is to come down his off-wing, intimidating the defense with his head of steam, then faking a slap and sliding a pass across the middle.

LeClair shows creativity in the offensive zone. He passes and leads well to both sides (he can also play center), and he is a good stickhandler. LeClair has an excellent scoring touch; with a little confidence he will become more willing to shoot. He knows how to set up a play and uses his body favorably, especially in protecting the puck.

LeClair accelerates well and skates with balance and a long stride. He has good defensive awareness for a rookie.

THE PHYSICAL GAME

LeClair is a product of the University of Vermont and came to the Canadiens as a finesse player who could be tough and aggressive. The more physical part of his game is just starting to blossom. He is willing to take the body, and his skating acceleration and size make him a powerful hitter.

THE INTANGIBLES

LeClair showed steady progress through the season and has the makings of a becoming a power forward.

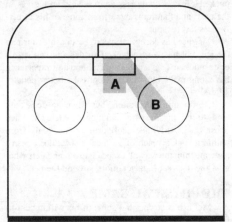

MIKE McPHEE

Yrs. of NHL service: 9
Born: Sydney, N.S.; July 14, 1960
Position: Left wing
Height: 6-1
Weight: 200
Uniform no.: 35
Shoots: Left

Career statistics:

GP	G	A	TP	PIM
581	162	162	324	581

1991-92 statistics:

GP	G	A	TP	+/-	PIM	PP	SH	GW	GT	S	PCT
78	16	15	31	6	63	0	0	1	0	146	11.0

LAST SEASON

Goals, assists and points career lows.

THE FINESSE GAME

McPhee is a two-way role player who gives his all on every shift; the problem is that those shifts are becoming more and more rare.

McPhee is very strong, with a long reach that he uses to tie opponents up or lean around them to get the puck. He has become less aggressive than he was in the past, and that took away from some of his effectiveness last season.

McPhee has deceptive speed. He doesn't churn up the ice, but has very powerful strides and can accelerate quickly. That and his anticipation and experience have long made him one of Montreal's better penalty killers.

He doesn't score often, but when he does they tend to be in pressure situations, where McPhee doesn't wilt. McPhee scores all of his goals from within a stick's reach of the goalie. McPhee doesn't have much in the way of a scoring touch and gets what goals he does score in scrambles around the net.

THE PHYSICAL GAME

McPhee is strong, but some of his willingness to fight along the boards (long one of his hallmarks) has ebbed. His balance gives him a big edge in corner wars, since checkers will bounce off him.

THE INTANGIBLES

Despite starting to slow down, McPhee is valued for his character and quiet leadership, and probably has a season or two left to contribute. He has always been an honest hockey player, one of the first to arrive for practice and the last to leave, and his dedication to the game has never been questioned.

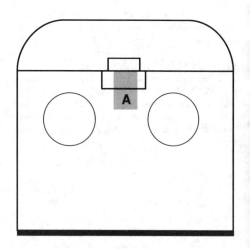

KIRK MULLER

Yrs. of NHL service: 8
Born: Kingston, Ont.; Feb. 8, 1966
Position: Left wing/center
Height: 6-0
Weight: 200
Uniform no.: 11
Shoots: Left

Career statistics:

GP	G	A	TP	PIM
634	221	376	597	658

1991-92 statistics:

GP	G	A	TP	+/-	PIM	PP	SH	GW	GT	S	PCT
78	36	41	77	15	86	15	1	7	1	191	18.8

LAST SEASON

Acquired from New Jersey with Roland Melanson for Stephane Richer and Tom Chorske, Sept. 20, 1991. Led team in goals, power-play goals and points. Second-best goals and points totals of career. Led team in game-winning goals. Best shooting percentage among team players who played more than 40 games.

THE FINESSE GAME

Muller was far and away the best forward for the Canadiens, who thought they knew what they were getting in the ex-Devils captain. They got much, much more.

A very determined player, Muller has limited skills but makes up for it with hard work. He plays his very best in close quarters. Although he is not a great open ice skater (he has some speed but no moves), his balance and strength in traffic, along with his hand skills and poise, make him one of the top players to have on the ice in a last-second scramble for a tying or winning goal.

Muller is strong on his feet and with his feet. If his stick is tied up, he will still attempt to create something by kicking the puck to a teammate. Muller is not a fancy playmaker, but a wise linemate will known enough to play off of Muller, because he will find some way to help the puck squirt loose. Most of Muller's goals come from close range. He has a good slap off the wing but seldom uses the shot.

Muller has good hand-eye coordination, and while his NHL future is as a winger, he will be used to take key draws. He is a good power-play man because of his work in front of the net and his ability to tip in shots and dig for loose pucks.

THE PHYSICAL GAME

The durable Muller has missed only 6 games out of 640 in his NHL career, despite playing at full-tilt every night. He was very mature at 18 when he broke into the NHL, and he remains a player to whom "leadership" is not just a word. He will stand up for his teammates, although he seldom gets involved in some

of the fights he did as a younger player, when he looked like the Tasmanian Devil flurrying punches.

THE INTANGIBLES

Muller was the second player chosen overall, after Mario Lemieux, in the 1984 draft, and there were some scouts who thought at the time that Muller would develop into a better player than Lemieux. Eight years and two Lemieux-led Pittsburgh Stanley Cups later, we can safely say those scouts were dead wrong. But Muller should be judged on his own merits: he is a very good all-around player who is capable of producing 80-85 points per year.

He did not have the reputation of being a good playoff performer with the Devils, but may have changed that perception with his showing with the Canadiens last season.

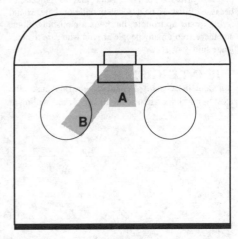

LYLE ODELEIN

Yrs. of NHL service: 2
Born: Quill Lake, Sask.; July 21, 1968
Position: Right defense
Height: 5-10
Weight: 205
Uniform no.: 24
Shoots: Left

Career statistics:

GP	G	A	TP	PIM
131	1	11	12	504

1991-92 statistics:

GP	G	A	TP	+/-	PIM	PP	SH	GW	GT	S	PCT
71	1	7	8	15	212	0	0	0	0	43	2.3

LAST SEASON

All scoring totals career highs. Second on team in PIM.

THE FINESSE GAME

Odelein has a penalty minutes per point ratio of 42:1, and that about sums up his style. He brings nothing to the table offensively, but he is some huge piece of furniture himself.

Fairly mobile for a player of his size, Odelein still needs to improve his skating and it appears as though he has worked very hard at doing so, since it did getter better last year.

Odelein's finesse skills are average on a good night, but he knows his limitations. He will not jump into a rush offensively. He will never venture in the attacking zone. Odelein will make safe passes and take the occasional shot from the point, but otherwise plays it safe, and for him, that's smart.

THE PHYSICAL GAME

Odelein is a legitimate heavyweight, although fighting does not come naturally to him. He likes to play an aggressive, physical game, and if a fight comes because of that, so be it. Odelein will not skate around trying to stir up trouble, but he is a punishing hitter, and there aren't many people around who care to challenge him.

THE INTANGIBLES

Odelein has great physical presence and makes the most of his skills. He is a good team player, willing to accept his role, and is working to improve some of the weaker parts of his game. On a team revered for its defense, Odelein is an underrated player.

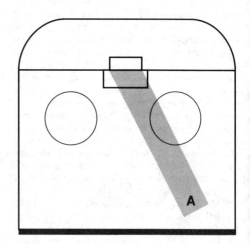

PATRICK ROY

Yrs. of NHL service: 7
Born: Quebec City, Que.; Oct. 5, 1965
Position: Goaltender
Height: 6-0
Weight: 175
Uniform no.: 33
Catches: Left

Career statistics:

GP	MINS	GA	SO	GAA	A	PIM
356	20630	934	18	2.72	24	38

1991-92 statistics:

GP	MINS	GAA	W	L	T	SO	GA	S	SAPCT	PIM
67	3935	2.36	36	22	8	5	155	1806	.914	4

LAST SEASON

Won 1992 Vezina Trophy and Jennings Trophy. Led NHL in GAA with career-low. Third in NHL in wins with career high. Tied for most shutouts in NHL with career high. Led NHL in save percentage. Tied for second in NHL in games played.

THE PHYSICAL GAME

Roy is a butterfly-style goalie who isn't as sound technically as one might think for a player of his stature and success. Roy plays somewhat of a standup style, but goes down much more quickly than students of the game like to see. When a goalie has been as successful as Roy has been for so many years, however, nobody messes with technique.

Roy is especially tough low, taking away a lot of the net with his long legs even when he flops down too quickly. He is a strong skater and jumps back to his skates right away to be poised for the next shot. A lot of shooters think the best way to beat Roy is high, but he has a pretty good glove hand. His weakness is the five hole.

Roy does not come out of his net to handle the puck and is not a very good stickhandler. His five assists last season came from quick counterattacks off his saves, not by Roy's headman passing. He leaves a lot of rebounds, but the Montreal defense is geared to play off his style.

Roy does not play his angles well, and is most effective close in, where his keen reflexes take command. He backed further and further into the net as the season wore on and he tired.

THE MENTAL GAME

Because the Canadiens score so few goals (they averaged 3.3 per game last season), Roy goes into every game knowing he has no margin for error. Many nights he was able to do that, holding opponents to 2 or fewer goals in 39 of his 66 starts. Other goalies could shake off a bad goal here or there, but not Roy, since it would often mean the difference between winning and losing. That is tremendous pressure for a goalie to face year-round. If Roy is still talking to his goal posts, they've probably started talking back.

THE INTANGIBLES

Roy is one of the top three goalies in the NHL, but it's arguable whether he is the best anymore. He let in some very soft goals in the Adams Division Final against Boston, that after a slumping second half (slumping by Roy standards). He would benefit from a solid backup goalie who could make 25-30 starts a season — and from another scorer up front. Good as he is, Roy looks like a candidate for burnout.

185

DENIS SAVARD

Yrs. of NHL service: 12
Born: Pointe Gatineau, Que.; Feb. 4, 1961
Position: Center
Height: 5-10
Weight: 175
Uniform no.: 18
Shoots: Right

Career statistics:

GP	G	A	TP	PIM
883	407	735	1142	953

1991-92 statistics:

GP	G	A	TP	+/-	PIM	PP	SH	GW	GT	S	PCT
77	28	42	70	12	73	12	1	5	0	174	16.1

LAST SEASON

Second on team in goals and points. Matched previous season's goals. Assists and points two-season highs. Tied for second on team in game-winning goals. Third on team in power play goals.

THE FINESSE GAME

The rabbit has a few grey hairs, but Savard can still produce one out of his helmet and bring back a little of the old magic now and then.

Surprisingly, Savard had a stronger second half than a first half (11-17 — 28 over the first half, 17-25 — 42 over the second). The only reason we could deduce was Savard regaining confidence in his old moves. Early in the season, he would carry the puck to the blue line and turn, not challenging the defense. Later in the year, he kept going forward and found he still had some of that zip. Savard had to create his own open ice to do his stuff.

Savard is a great two-on-one player because of his speed and skills. He is a threat to pass or shoot. He is a liability on defense, especially low in defensive zone. Savard won't be on the ice to protect a lead.

A better playmaker than scorer, Savard can overpower goalies with his strong wrist shot. He will shoot from just about anywhere from the circles in. Savard has great hockey sense and soft, soft hands for giving and receiving passes.

Savard has tremendous agility: he can stop, start, go left, pivot, turn right, pivot again — all while handling the puck and always with speed.

THE PHYSICAL GAME

Savard has always kept himself out of the corners and avoided situations where he can be outmuscled. Savard's strength is his speed and quickness. He jumps in and out of openings and uses open ice as well as just about any player in the game.

THE INTANGIBLES

The seasons of 80 and 90 points are over for Savard. He might not even match 70 again. But veteran players whose games are based on their skating (Mike Gartner, Peter Stastny), always seem to hang in the game longer than others. Savard can pace himself, pick his spots and still be a human highlight film. Spinaramas forever.

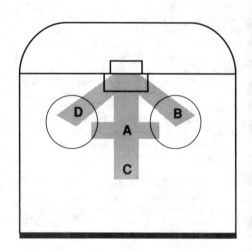

MATT SCHNEIDER

Yrs. of NHL service: 3
Born: New York, N.Y.; June 12, 1969
Position: Left defense
Height: 5-11
Weight: 180
Uniform no.: 18
Shoots: Left

Career statistics:

GP	G	A	TP	PIM
195	25	58	83	162

1991-92 statistics:

GP	G	A	TP	+/-	PIM	PP	SH	GW	GT	S	PCT
78	8	24	32	10	72	2	0	1	0	194	4.1

LAST SEASON

Led team defensemen in scoring. Career high in points.

THE FINESSE GAME

Schneider has pretty good offensive instincts and plays an overall intelligent game. He has good hockey sense and good vision of the ice. While not a great point man on the power play (the Canadiens don't really have one; Schneider is about their best), he has a good slap from the point. Schneider will also decoy the slap and work the puck in low. He will seldom skate in any deeper than the top of the circle.

Schneider moves the puck well but doesn't lead rushes, nor is he overly anxious about jumping up into the fray. Schneider's first duty in the Montreal system is to play defense, and he is conscientious about it. If he gets turned loose under a new coach, Schneider's skills might be put to better use.

A mobile skater with a good, long stride, Schneider has balance and is a change-of-pace skater who can accelerate smoothly and quickly, but lacks breakaway speed.

THE PHYSICAL GAME

Schneider is mentally tough and plays with determination, but he lacks the strength to go one-on-one with bigger forwards. He loses board battles and tries to compensate by playing a very sound positional game. Schneider will play aggressively, but he does not have good enough skills to be a purely offensive forward and isn't big enough to be physical, so he is caught between two styles and limited by his physique.

THE INTANGIBLES

We told you last year that Schneider had the potential to replace Chris Chelios and possibly develop into a defenseman worthy of Norris Trophy consideration. We would rather tear out that page (203). At the

moment, there are three defensemen on the Canadiens with more potential than Schneider (Eric Desjardins, Kevin Haller and Patrice Brisebois). It's unfair to blame Schneider for the expectations he didn't ask for.

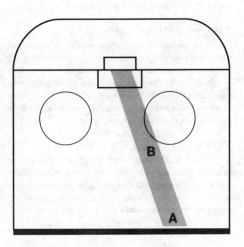

BRIAN SKRUDLAND

Yrs. of NHL service: 7
Born: Peace River, Alta.; July 31, 1963
Position: Center
Height: 6-0
Weight: 185
Uniform no.: 39
Shoots: Left

Career statistics:

GP	G	A	TP	PIM
452	73	136	209	537

1991-92 statistics:

GP	G	A	TP	+/-	PIM	PP	SH	GW	GT	S	PCT
42	3	3	6	−4	36	0	0	1	0	51	5.9

LAST SEASON

Missed 38 games with injuries. Career lows in games played and all scoring categories.

THE FINESSE GAME

Skrudland is a tenacious player who, with limited skills, has been a very effective checker. He is quick and strong, and sticks to his mark even though he is not a very agile skater. What Skrudland loses in agility, he more than makes up for with hard work and experience.

He anticipates plays well and is a tremendous forechecker because of that, forcing turnovers in the offensive zone as he badgers the puck carrier. When he gains control of the puck, Skrudland will look to make a play. He has a good short game and passes well in traffic. He is not a natural goal scorer (he's only scored more than 30 goals once in his hockey career, and that was as a junior).

Skrudland's greatest asset is his character. He is a good third or fourth line role player.

THE PHYSICAL GAME

Skrudland has a very broad skating stance, which gives him tremendous balance and a power base for checking. He seldom passes up a chance to get a piece of somebody, and he can be an irritating fellow to play against. Skrudland's stance helps him in his battles for loose pucks in front of the crease, which is where he generates most of his scoring chances.

THE INTANGIBLES

Skrudland is a great team leader who came close to being voted team captain over Guy Carbonneau in a player ballot several seasons ago. His health is a concern, since he has failed to play 60 or more games in each of the last three seasons, but when he is healthy he is a reliable and consistent defensive forward.

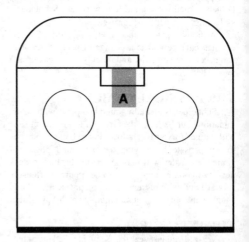

NEW JERSEY
DEVILS

CRAIG BILLINGTON

Yrs. of NHL service: 3
Born: London, Ont.; Sept. 11, 1966
Position: Goalie
Height: 5-10
Weight: 170
Uniform no.: 1
Catches: Left

Career statistics:

GP	MINS	GA	SO	GAA	A	PIM
69	3518	246	2	4.20	2	4

1991-92 statistics:

GP	MINS	GAA	W	L	T	SO	GA	S	SAPCT	PIM
26	1363	3.04	13	7	1	2	69	637	.892	2

LAST SEASON

Games played and wins career high. GAA career best. Missed two games with hamstring pull. Missed nine games with knee injury.

THE PHYSICAL GAME

A funny thing happened between 1986-87 — Billington's last sustained stint in the NHL — and last season. He became NHL goaltending material. Thrown into the fray at 19, when he was too immature physically and mentally to handle playing behind a bad Devils team, Billington appeared ruined for life.

Instead, he spent three seasons in the minors and another with the Canadian national team before getting the surprise backup role to Chris Terreri after the Devils failed to sign Sean Burke. Billington improved his angle-playing and his balance, and is thus able to cover more of the net — essential for such a small-framed goalie. He is good down low, quick with his feet, and recovers well for a second shot. Billington moves post to post quickly. Playing for a year in the Canadian Olympic program, and getting a lot of experience on larger ice surfaces, has helped Billington with his lateral movement.

Billington's major flaw remains his stickhandling, which is not NHL caliber. He used to have to switch his hands to shoot and has cured himself of that time-consuming habit, but he is still poor at stopping hard-arounds and cannot help out his defense with clearing passes, as Terreri does. He is frequently hesitant about whether to try to move the puck or leave it for his defense, and the indecision leads to scrambles around his net.

THE MENTAL GAME

Billington's greatest advancement came in this area. He was able to accept the role of part-time goalie. Billington had only one start through the first 20 games of the season, yet was able to step in and win or at least keep the Devils in the game when he did get playing time. When he wasn't playing, Billington concentrated on being a good team man — contrary to the reputation others had (rightly or wrongly) perceived about him early in his career.

When Terreri went through a slump in the middle of the season, Billington stepped in to win five straight games, then relinquished the starting role without an outward grumble. He shook off poor games and showed a tougher mental edge.

THE INTANGIBLES

Billington's season ended with arthroscopic surgery on his right knee after a teammate dumped Oilers forward Anatoli Semenov (190 pounds) on it. Billington's recovery from the surgery will be key to his continued development as an NHL goaltender. He may never be a No. 1 (although he believes he can be — an important confidence edge). He seems to be willing to accept the backup role to Terreri and always works hard to be ready for his playing opportunity.

TOM CHORSKE

Yrs. of NHL service: 3
Born: Minneapolis, Minn.; Sept. 18, 1966
Position: Right wing/left wing
Height: 6-1
Weight: 204
Uniform no.: 9
Shoots: Right

Career statistics:

GP	G	A	TP	PIM
147	31	29	60	66

1991-92 statistics:

GP	G	A	TP	+/-	PIM	PP	SH	GW	GT	S	PCT
76	19	17	36	8	32	0	3	2	0	143	13.3

LAST SEASON

Acquired from Montreal with Stephane Richer for Kirk Muller and Roland Melanson, Sept. 20, 1991. Led team in shorthanded goals. Games played and all point totals career highs.

THE FINESSE GAME

Chorske's game is determined by his breakout speed. He has real quickness that intimidates opposing defensemen and is a powerful, balanced skater. His skating ability is showcased in open ice, but his leg drive also helps him in corner and board battles.

Now the bad news. Chorske's hands haven't caught up to his feet. He can carry the puck at top speed, but when it comes to play selection — pass or shoot? — his thought-making process sometimes seems interminable. He did have a career-high 19 goals last season, but with the opportunities Chorske is able to create with his bursts of speed, he should be in the ranks of the 30-goal scorers.

Chorske has shown a nice touch with the puck, whether passing or shooting. Now with a full year's service under his suspenders, the confidence may carry through to his scoring and bump Chorske up to the next level. Chorske has not yet shown much offensive instinct, however. He is an excellent defensive forward and will become the Devils' key man on penalty-killing units.

THE PHYSICAL GAME

Chorske was on the bubble at one point in mid-season, and when it seemed his season would come down to a one- or two-game test, Chorkse responded with several huge efforts. When he is involved, Chorske becomes a solid hitter in all three zones. He is not a mean or punishing checker, but he's smart and will keep his man out of the play. He seldom misses a checking assignment. Chorkse has to use his body more consistently.

THE INTANGIBLES

One of the Devils' most solid performers during the playoffs, Chorske came to play every night and the results showed on the ice. Considered a throw-in in the Stephane Richer-Kirk Muller trade, the unknown Chorske turned out to be an unexpected bonus. He was overlooked in the Montreal system but now shows every sign of blossoming into a respected two-way player who can produce 20 goals a season.

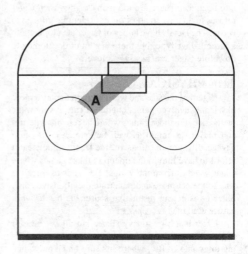

ZDENO CIGER

Yrs. of NHL service: 2
Born: Martin, Czechoslovakia; Oct. 19, 1969
Position: Left wing
Height: 6-1
Weight: 190
Uniform no.: 33
Shoots: Left

Career statistics:

GP	G	A	TP	PIM
65	14	22	36	18

1991-92 statistics:

GP	G	A	TP	+/-	PIM	PP	SH	GW	GT	S	PCT
20	6	5	11	-2	10	1	0	0	0	0	18.2

LAST SEASON
Missed 59 games with wrist surgery.

THE FINESSE GAME
Ciger came back from his wrist surgery with little of his exquisite hand skills impaired. He has good wrist, snap or slap shots, but still has the European habit of looking to fake a pass before taking a rather obvious shooting chance. His shots, when he takes them, are accurate, and he hardly ever sprays his shots wildly.

Defensively, Ciger remains a liability because of his habit of jerking his stick while he skates. He will lose or overskate the puck even when he is not being checked because of this flaw. He has to become a better one-on-one battler. He is a very quick skater and is strong on his feet.

Ciger has yet to develop the on-ice presence or reputation that forces the opposition to play off him, so he must make high-tempo plays and bull his way into open ice. There are too many nights when Ciger refuses to do this, so all of his considerable gifts go to waste. The Devils have hopes of Ciger developing into a Jaromir Jagr-type, but there is a lot of developing to do before Ciger reaches Jagr's level.

THE PHYSICAL GAME
Ciger has the size and wiry strength to play a more physically involved game, but doesn't always show the inclination. On those games where he remains a perimeter player, he might as well be scratched. Because Ciger's gifts are all offensive, the Devils simply can't afford to have him in the lineup in those games where Ciger watches from the wings. He needs to force his way to the net more and penetrate the offensive zone. Since he is not an instinctive scorer, he has to work harder at it.

Ciger is a big, sinewy skater but allows himself to get pushed off the puck too easily. He is often unwilling to go into traffic, where his sure touch and quick release would be of the utmost benefit. Ciger's wrist shot could be a potent scoring weapon.

THE INTANGIBLES
Ciger's wrist injury, which kept him sidelined until Feb. 24, postponed the judgment we pronounced last year, which was that 1991-92 would be the major test for Ciger to prove himself as NHL material. We'll just change the deadline on that to 1992-93, and repeat that time is running out for Ciger to mark his mark. Working against him might be the departure of fellow Czechoslovak Peter Stastny, who acted as Ciger's big brother on and off the ice. It might not be a bad idea for Ciger to finally stand on his own two skates.

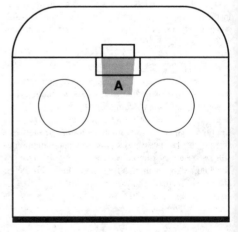

192

KEN DANEYKO

Yrs. of NHL service: 8
Born: Windsor, Ont.; Apr. 17, 1964
Position: Right defense
Height: 6-0
Weight: 210
Uniform no.: 3
Shoots: Left

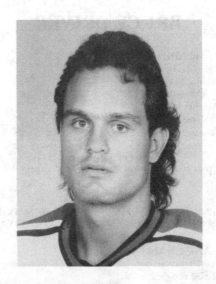

Career statistics:

GP	G	A	TP	PIM
529	24	76	100	1467

1991-92 statistics:

GP	G	A	TP	+/-	PIM	PP	SH	GW	GT	S	PCT
80	1	7	8	7	170	0	0	0	0	57	1.8

LAST SEASON

One of only three Devils to appear in all 80 games. Goals, assists, points and PIM totals career lows. Second on team in PIM.

THE FINESSE GAME

As he has matured, Daneyko has concentrated more and more on being the steady, stay-at-home defenseman. His offensive skills have always been minimal. He has an on-target slapshot with little on it, and he does not get his shot away quickly. He is not used on the power play unit.

Daneyko is a fair skater for his size, but you won't ever see him making an end-to-end dazzler like Brian Leetch. Nor does Daneyko join the rush late. He is seldom found gambling in deep around the opponent's net. Daneyko's offensive involvement is limited to a breakout pass.

Daneyko has become a smarter defenseman, but he's still no Einstein, and he doesn't have good hockey sense. He sometimes needs a beat to read a play, and occasionally that beat is enough for a fleet forward to get past him. Daneyko usually compensates for that indecision by playing back off the attacker instead of stepping up to challenge. One area where Daneyko does excel is shot-blocking and he is a mainstay on the penalty-killing unit because of that skill.

THE PHYSICAL GAME

The arrival of tough Randy McKay and Scott Stevens took some of the heat off Daneyko to be the sole protector on the ice (the trend the Devils were taking with the continued importation of European and Russian talent). Daneyko will still mix it up and take care of his teammates, and can handle himself well in a scrape. He has established enough of a reputation that he gets few challengers.

Daneyko's wild-eyed desire to hit still gets the better of him and he is wont to take ill-timed penalties (although last year's PIM total was a career low). He always will be a player who is guided by his emotions, but has to rein them in a little more effectively to avoid hurting his team (especially since he is one of the Devils' better penalty-killers).

THE INTANGIBLES

Daneyko's toughness and courage is undisputed. He was the team's Rock of Gibraltar with a fine playoff effort against the New York Rangers, despite playing most of the seven-game series with a broken bone in his hand. Daneyko wants to be thought of as a team leader and spokesman, and that desire to keep improving is evident in Daneyko's lack of complacency with his game. Unfortunately, Daneyko's poor off-ice habits frequently affect his play on ice, and coaches are dismayed by his lack of discipline.

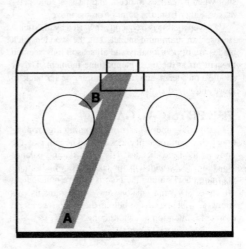

BRUCE DRIVER

Yrs. of NHL service: 8
Born: Toronto, Ont.; Apr. 29, 1962
Position: Left defense
Height: 6-0
Weight: 185
Uniform no.: 23
Shoots: left

Career statistics:

GP	G	A	TP	PIM
512	57	240	297	387

1991-92 statistics:

GP	G	A	TP	+/-	PIM	PP	SH	GW	GT	S	PCT
78	7	35	42	5	66	3	1	1	0	205	3.4

LAST SEASON

Second among team defensemen in scoring. Missed two games with flu.

THE FINESSE GAME

Driver is a fluid, almost elegant skater with deceptive speed. Nothing about Driver's style screams out, but he does everything with efficiency and little wasted movement. He can accelerate quickly, especially with the puck, and has good lateral movement and backward speed. His balance is very solid, and despite his small size (by today's behemoth NHL defenseman standards), Driver can hold his own physically with bigger opponents.

He is smart, smart, smart. Smart at reading plays, smart in his decisions to pinch or fall back, smart about whether to carry the puck or make an outlet pass. He is alert to all play options and works on both speciality teams.

Driver has a very good if not awesome arsenal of shots. His point shot is low and accurate and he gets it away quickly. Driver can also release a nice wrist shot when he carries in deep, and he is a good playmaker, either from the point or on the move.

Driver's game is frequently thwarted by his sticks. He uses an aluminum model, but the wooden stick blades are of poor quality and all season long seemed to snap off at the most inopportune moment. Driver should consider a new manufacturer, or go back to those antiquated all-wood sticks.

THE PHYSICAL GAME

Driver's game is based more on intelligent positional play than forceful checking, but he will play the body as the need dictates. His good skating balance gives him the foundation for take-outs, which aren't booming checks along the boards but are nonetheless effective. Driver's major drawback remains his strength, which seems to ebb as the season wears on despite his attention to conditioning.

THE INTANGIBLES

A captain should be a team's big-play man, but Driver last season often came up empty when the team needed him most. He was particularly disappointing on the power play, where he plays the point on the first unit. Driver seemed headed for the next level of improvement, but last season was a step backward.

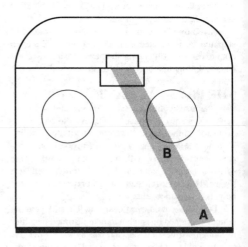

VIACHESLAV FETISOV

Yrs. of NHL service: 3
Born: Moscow, CIS; May 20, 1958
Position: Left defense
Height: 6-1
Weight: 205
Uniform no.: 2
Shoots: Left

Career statistics:

GP	G	A	TP	PIM
209	14	73	84	222

1991-92 statistics:

GP	G	A	TP	+/-	PIM	PP	SH	GW	GT	S	PCT
70	3	23	23	11	108	0	0	1	0	70	4.3

LAST SEASON

PIM career high. Assists and point totals career highs. Missed five games with suspension due to stick infraction. Missed two games with foot injury.

THE FINESSE GAME

Now a 34-year-old with countless Olympic, World Championship and NHL mileage clicked off on his hockey odometer, Fetisov remains an elegant skater and passer. Every so often Fetisov's reflexes betray him, which must be a tremendously frustrating experience for an athlete who was once judged to be the best in the world at his position.

Fetisov is an intelligent player at both ends of the ice. Defensively, he will block shots and cut down passing lanes, and with his longtime Soviet defense partner Alexei Kasatonov, formed a formidable backline duo on penalty-killing units. Offensively, he knows when to join a rush (he no longer has the speed to lead one) and when he does, he has the hand skills and the creative playmaking instincts of a forward.

Experience helps an older player compensate for lacking young legs. Fetisov positions himself very well, and he no longer makes the grandstand plays that he tried in his first year in the league (and which were often disastrous on smaller ice surfaces). He will still make the dangerous pass in front of his own goaltender, which works when he is paired with Kasatonov but sometimes backfires when he is out with another defense partner.

THE PHYSICAL GAME

See Slava hit! Fetisov showed an unexpected, remarkable taste for the physical when he crashed and clashed with some of the Rangers' bigger skaters (Jeff Beukeboom, Adam Graves, Mark Messier) in the 1992 playoffs. There was even a hidden mean streak showing — not a bad thing for one of the Russian pioneers who took such a pounding when he was introduced to North American hockey three seasons ago.

Fetisov did wear down physically late in the season, but after the 10-day layoff due to the NHL strike, was a new player in the playoffs. The grind of that caught up to him after several games, however, and the lesson seems to be to use Fetisov sparingly.

THE INTANGIBLES

Fetisov's best hockey is behind him, but while he is no longer a world class defenseman, he re-established himself as a quality NHL player last season. Fetisov was a free agent at the end of 1991-92, but indicated he would like to play another season in New Jersey. If the Devils don't overplay him, they could get another very useful season out of this seasoned competitor.

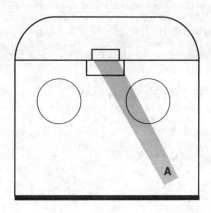

195

ALEXEI KASATONOV

Yrs. of NHL service: 3
Born: Leningrad, CIS; Oct. 14, 1959
Position: Right defense
Height: 6-1
Weight: 210
Uniform no.: 7
Shoots: Left

Career statistics:

GP	G	A	TP	PIM
193	28	74	102	162

1991-92 statistics:

GP	G	A	TP	+/-	PIM	PP	SH	GW	GT	S	PCT
76	12	28	40	14	70	3	2	1	0	107	11.2

LAST SEASON
Goals career high. Missed three games with hemorrhoid surgery.

THE FINESSE GAME
Ask most scouts who is the most underrated defenseman on the Devils and they will answer Kasatonov. Opposing scouts love his poise, work ethic and powerful skating ability. Because he doesn't possess great breakaway speed, Kasatonov has never garnered as much notice as some of the other players to come from Russia, but he has all the tools and a toolbox to put them in.

Kasatonov was more involved offensively last season and until he went inexplicably cold around January was an important factor on the power play. Kasatonov doesn't shoot bullets from the blue line (his slap shot is one of the weaker parts of his game), but he sees the ice well and works his passes. He also likes to sneak into the right circle and use his accurate wrist shot. Kasatonov will not lead a rush, preferring to start a breakout with a pass.

One of the league's better penalty-killing defensemen, an underrated Kasatonov skill is lifting the puck from deep in his defensive zone to center ice on his backhand. Few players can do it as quickly and effectively (although it is apparent he has taught some of his Devils teammates the trick). He uses this clearing technique during penalty kills and it is extremely frustrating to opponents.

THE PHYSICAL GAME
It didn't take long for Kasatonov to adapt to the more physical style of North American play. He won't be intimidated and will frequently initiate some belligerant contact. Kasatonov is not a crushing checker and the Devils would like him to get a little meaner since he has the lower body strength and agility to become a punishing hitter. Maybe playing with Scott Stevens another season will have an effect on him.

THE INTANGIBLES
Kasatonov stepped up his development last season to become the team's second-best all-around defenseman (after Stevens). The only thing lacking now is consistency. Kasatonov wore down after the mid-point of the season and didn't come on again until after the strike layoff. One big plus is that despite his offensive drought, Kasatonov never hurt the team defensively.

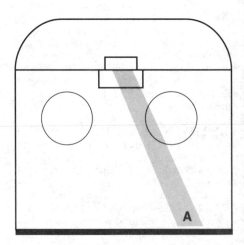

196

CLAUDE LEMIEUX

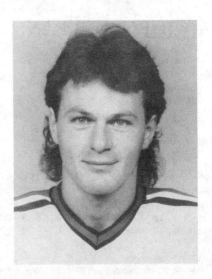

Yrs. of NHL service: 6
Born: Buckingham, Que.; July 16, 1965
Position: Right wing
Height: 6-1
Weight: 215
Uniform no.: 22
Shoots: Right

Career statistics:

GP	G	A	TP	PIM
435	168	136	304	790

1991-92 statistics:

GP	G	A	TP	+/-	PIM	PP	SH	GW	GT	S	PCT
74	41	27	68	9	109	13	1	8	3	296	13.9

LAST SEASON

Led team in goals, points, power-play goals, game-winning goals and shots. Goals and points totals career highs. Missed four games with back injury. Missed two games with ankle injury.

THE FINESSE GAME

Speed and power form the basis of Lemieux's game. He is a player who always wants the puck—so badly that he had on-ice squabbles with linemate Peter Stastny when he felt he should have received a pass and didn't. Lemieux has a wicked slapshot and shoots especially well off the fly, when he can put all of his leg drive into the shot.

Lemieux is a finisher, not a playmaker. He does not carry the puck well and those assists he does accumulate usually come from a teammate scoring off one of his rebounds. He is selfish, but then 41-goal scorers are supposed to be. Lemieux is a key Devils player on power plays, since he positions himself well for high percentage scoring attempts and is willing to battle to traffic for the puck.

Defensively, Lemieux has matured into a better player. He is sometimes guilty of leaving the zone without the puck, since he is so eager to get up ice for a scoring chance, and he sometimes leaves his mates outnumbered in the defensive zone. Lemieux saw some time killing penalties last season, and his break-away speed makes him a shorthanded scoring threat.

Fiery and ultra-competitive, Lemieux seldom takes a night off. His constant yapping may be irritating to opponents, but it is music to the Devils' ears, especially when he backs it up with the kind of numbers he posted last season. Lemieux works hard and is such an intense player that he is able to compensate for his only average hockey sense.

THE PHYSICAL GAME

Whatever it takes to win a game—gloves in the face, chops in the ribs, a hook around the wrist—Lemieux will dish it out. And take it. The problem with being on the receiving end of the rough stuff is that referees have wearied of Lemieux's over-reacting so that the boy who cried wolf doesn't draw too many penalties. No matter, Lemieux just picks himself off the ice and gains his own form of retribution, whether with a goal or physical payback.

THE INTANGIBLES

Nasty as he wants to be, Lemieux remains one of the NHL's more annoying guys. He willingly accepted the role of Mark Messier's shadow during the playoffs and was one of the reasons why Messier had such a terrible series against the Devils. Lemieux, on the other hand, had four goals. Lemieux plays at only one intensity level—high—and continued playing late in the season on a badly injured ankle because the team needed him. He will bleed for you, and score for you, and you can't ask for much more than that from an athlete. Now the pressure is on him to repeat his excellent production of last year.

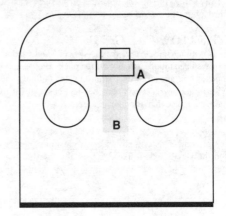

JOHN MacLEAN

Yrs. of NHL service: 8
Born: Oshawa, Ont.; Nov. 20, 1964
Position: Right wing
Height: 6-0
Weight: 200
Uniform no.: 15
Shoots: Right

Career statistics:

GP	G	A	TP	PIM
546	217	224	441	785

1991-92 statistics:

GP	G	A	TP	+/-	PIM	PP	SH	GW	GT	S	PCT
0	0	0	0	0	0	0	0	0	0	0	0

LAST SEASON

Missed entire season with reconstructive knee surgery.

THE FINESSE GAME

MacLean was injured during a 1991 exhibition game in one of those ridiculous scrums, when Islanders forward Brad Dalgarno fell on top of him in a pile-up. The injury cost the Devils the use of their potential 50-goal scorer and primary "go-to" guy. No one in the team's history has scored more clutch goals than MacLean.

Since we didn't get to see him in action last season, we'll hark back to two seasons ago and hope this is what you can see should MacLean return healthy:

Never blessed with outstanding speed, MacLean is a powerful skater who just barely seems to get where he has to be. His release on his repertoire of shots — a slap shot, a one-timer (from a standing position or in full flight), a wrist and a snap — is so incredibly quick that it enables him to get a shot away before a defender can take another stride toward him.

MacLean gets most of his goals through hard work, and is a special terror on the power play because of his ability to get into open ice or pursue the puck through traffic — and because of his desire.

THE PHYSICAL GAME

With his wide-based skating stance, MacLean has always been tough to knock off the puck. He has good hockey courage and won't be intimidated (although he will frequently take bad penalties and has to learn to take the abuse that good goal-scorers attract).

THE INTANGIBLES

More than his scoring, the Devils missed MacLean's presence in the dressing room, where a team unity was lacking. His personality and, of course, his production are needed on a team that just might be on the verge of breaking into the NHL's elite. It all rests on MacLean's ability to come back from surgery.

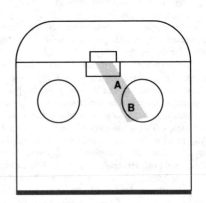

RANDY McKAY

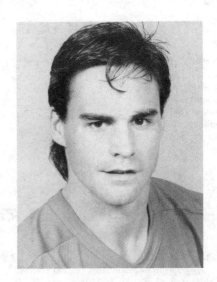

Yrs. of NHL service: 3
Born: Montreal, Que.; Jan. 25, 1967
Position: Right wing
Height: 6-1
Weight: 185
Uniform no.: 21
Shoots: Right

Career statistics:

GP	G	A	TP	PIM
163	21	29	50	480

1991-92 statistics:

GP	G	A	TP	+/-	PIM	PP	SH	GW	GT	S	PCT
80	17	16	33	6	246	2	0	1	0	111	15.3

LAST SEASON

Awarded to the Devils with Dave Barr as compensation for Detroit signing free agent Troy Crowder Sept. 9, 1991. Led team in PIM. One of only three Devils to appear in all 80 games.

THE FINESSE GAME

The combative McKay showed surprising development in his offensive skills when given more ice time by the Devils. His reactions are not lightning quick, but he has a deceptive shot that most goalies don't expect from a player of his reputation.

The only thing holding McKay back from becoming a better player is his lack of skating ability. He has a long stride, but is a bit clumsy and lacks quickness. He can hold his own in tight quarters because his balance is fair enough and his reach and strength overcome his lack of agility, but in open ice many pursuers have no trouble catching up to him, especially when he is carrying the puck.

THE PHYSICAL GAME

McKay is a legitimate heavyweight, a clean player and solid puncher that most other fighters prefer not to tangle with. McKay sticks up for his teammates. He is durable and strong with a powerful upper body.

THE INTANGIBLES

It's ironic that in trying to acquire a younger Bob Probert type—Troy Crowder—the Red Wings ended up losing just that sort of player. McKay may never be the fearsome puncher that Probert is, but he combines clutch scoring with real toughness (not just goonery), and was one of the major surprises on the Devils last season.

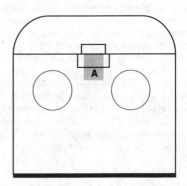

STEPHANE RICHER

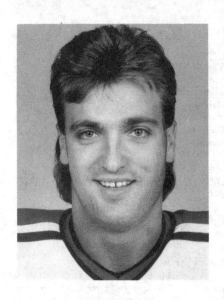

Yrs. of NHL service: 7
Born: Ripon, Que.; June 7, 1966
Position: Right wing
Height: 6-2
Weight: 200
Uniform no.: 44
Shoots: Right

Career statistics:

GP	G	A	TP	PIM
487	227	203	430	387

1991-92 statistics:

GP	G	A	TP	+/-	PIM	PP	SH	GW	GT	S	PCT
74	29	35	64	−1	25	5	1	6	1	240	12.1

LAST SEASON

Acquired from Montreal with Tom Chorske for Kirk Muller and Roland Melanson, Sept. 20, 1991. Second on team in points and goals. Goals three-season low. Missed three games with knee injury. Missed three games with groin injury.

THE FINESSE GAME

Most of Richer's game is powered by his skating, and since he was hampered most of the season by a variety of lower-body injuries (including a groin injury at the start of the season and a knee injury later in the year), the rest of his game never caught up. That Richer was able to score 29 goals at half-speed is a tribute to his scoring instincts, but still a disappointment for the two-time 50-goal scorer.

Richer has a powerful slap shot but doesn't mix it up often enough with other shots to make it even more effective. Even the best fastball pitcher needs an effective change-up. He does not work well in traffic, but does a good job of sliding around into open ice to receive a pass. Richer has an excellent one-timer when he doesn't worry about taking a big wind-up.

Richer is also a slick passer. He sees the ice and his options well, but sometimes tried too hard to force a play when he should be taking the shot himself. He has excellent hockey sense and has played center in the past. Confidence is a big factor—when Richer is in his goal scorer's groove, he wants the shot.

THE PHYSICAL GAME

Richer doesn't consistently play to his size. He has the build to be more effective as a power forward, but not the inclination. Physical problems may have played a factor in that last season. If Richer stays healthy, he should be more of an impact player for the Devils.

THE INTANGIBLES

From season to season, even game to game, one isn't sure what to expect from Richer. He can be explosive, or give you nothing. He has set a recent pattern of good season (50 goals in 1987-88), bad season (25 goals the next), good season (51 in 1989-90), bad season (31, after which he was traded). But last season broke the mold. That would mean either Richer is overdue, or he is no longer among the NHL's elite goal-scorers.

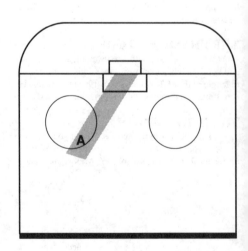

PETER STASTNY

Yrs. of NHL service: 12
Born: Bratislava, Czechoslovakia; Sept. 18, 1956
Position: Center
Height: 6-1
Weight: 200
Uniform no.: 26
Shoots: left

Career statistics:

GP	G	A	TP	PIM
892	424	754	1178	798

1991-92 statistics:

GP	G	A	TP	+/-	PIM	PP	SH	GW	GT	S	PCT
66	24	38	62	6	42	10	1	3	0	142	16.9

LAST SEASON

Second on team in assists and power-play goals, fourth in scoring. Missed nine games with virus. Missed five games with knee injury. Goals and point totals two-year highs.

THE FINESSE GAME

All of the skills that made Stastny one of the best scorers of the 80s (second only to Wayne Gretzky) are still intact. Players whose games are based on their skating quickness seem to last longest in the NHL; last season, at 35, Stastny was still showing the young'uns how it's done. Stastny had 21 goals by the middle of the season, but because he was relied upon as a No. 1 center, wore down drastically in the second half and produced only three more goals.

When Stastny is fresh, as he was at the start of the season and at the start of the playoffs after the players' strike, he ran the Devils' power play with efficiency and guile. Stastny is excellent at working the puck down low. Stastny has great vision and timing, so that he can put a puck to where a teammate will be going, and the puck is flat and soft for a quick shot. Few players can match his hand-eye coordination.

Stastny has lost some breakaway speed, but anticipates well and still possesses excellent balance, with deep edges, and lateral quickness. He is tough to knock off the puck and he can do-si-do around open-ice checks. Stastny is more of a playmaker than a shooter, although his backhand and wrist shots remain dangerous. What Stastny needs is the endurance to keep moving and skating. When he tires and is standing still, he starts to look, well, old.

THE PHYSICAL GAME

Stastny will go after the puck in traffic but prefers to leave the dirty work along the boards and corners to bigger, younger linemates — not necessarily a flaw for a playmaker as valuable as Stastny. He remains an excellent man on the draws — again, when he is rested — and he ate up Rangers forwards during the first round of the playoffs. He was the Devils' top face-off man last season.

THE INTANGIBLES

Stastny was a free agent after 1991-92, and made no secret that he would like to return with his family to Quebec. The Nordiques supposedly have a front-office job waiting for him, but after his resurgence last season, Stastny wants to play another year. The Nordiques don't have any room at center for him, but the Devils do, and if used sparingly and wisely, Stastny could contribute another valuable season.

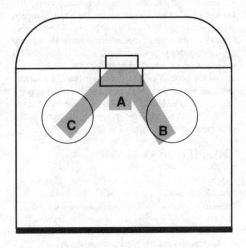

SCOTT STEVENS

Yrs. of NHL service: 10
Born: Kitchener, Ont.; Apr. 1, 1964
Position: Left defense
Height: 6-2
Weight: 215
Uniform no.: 4
Shoots: Left

Career statistics:

GP	G	A	TP	PIM
747	120	417	537	1902

1991-92 statistics:

GP	G	A	TP	+/-	PIM	PP	SH	GW	GT	S	PCT
68	17	42	59	24	124	7	1	2	0	156	10.9

LAST SEASON

Awarded to Devils as compensation for St. Louis signing free agent Brendan Shanahan. Led team defensemen in scoring. Missed 12 games with knee injury. Goals total second highest of career.

THE FINESSE GAME

Stevens had five seasons with 50 or more points while with the Capitals, but in his one season with St. Louis (1990-91) had concentrated more on his defensive role. With the Devils, whose defensemen are expected to be more involved offensively, the other facet of Stevens' game has resurfaced.

Stevens was used up front by the Devils on the power play, using his bulk to screen the goalie and distract the defensemen. He has good hands and is more effective up front than on the point. He has a hard shot but is frequently off-target.

At even strength, Stevens will sometimes make bad decisions about pinching in, leaving his partner vulnerable to an odd-man rush. Stevens sometimes has too much faith in his own stickhandling abilities, which are adequate, and he will get into trouble when he tries to carry the puck out of the defensive zone. He is better off making the safe outlet pass. Pairing him with a more mobile, puckhandling partner (the Devils plan to use rookie Scott Niedermayer, their No. 1 pick from 1991, alongside Stevens) would be a wise strategy.

Stevens was one of the most valuable members of the Devils last season. While he was sidelined with a knee injury, the team went 2-8-2.

THE PHYSICAL GAME

Stevens' physical presence is his No. 1 trait. Defensively, Stevens clears out the front of his net like a bulldozer. Because he is such a good skater, with tremendous lower body strength and agility, he is a frightening open-ice checker. The art of the submarine check has been so forgotten that Stevens sometimes draws penalties for his legal but lethal hits.

Stevens is a good fighter and will stand up for his teammates. His temper will sometimes get the better of him, allowing other team's lesser player to goad him into a scrap. He is a fierce competitor.

THE INTANGIBLES

When voting for a team MVP award was conducted last season, the joke was that the honor should go to Judge Houston, the arbitrator who awarded Stevens to the Devils. The Blues aren't laughing. Without Stevens, their team's defense was ravaged. With Stevens, the Devils' defense was immediately assessed as one of the best in the league. Stevens doesn't wear the "C", but shortly after coming to the Devils became their captain in deed if not in name. He is a respected leader who on some nights looked to be the only player out there trying. Stevens leads by example and could be the bedrock for a legitimate Cup challenge this season. His size, strength, skills and toughness make him one of the best defensemen in the game.

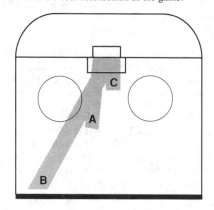

CHRIS TERRERI

Yrs. of NHL service: 5
Born: Providence, R.I.; Nov. 15, 1964
Position: Goaltender
Height: 5-9
Weight: 160
Uniform no.: 31
Catches: Left

Career statistics:

GP	MINS	GA	SO	GAA	A	PIM
157	8760	462	2	3.16	4	15

1991-92 statistics:

GP	MINS	GAA	W	L	T	SO	GA	S	SAPCT	PIM
54	3169	3.20	24	22	10	1	169	1511	.888	13

LAST SEASON

Matched career high in victories. Missed five games with back injury.

THE FINESSE GAME

Terreri is an excellent stickhandler. Sometimes he gets a little too cocky with his ability and makes a dangerous clearing attempt up the middle that gets picked off, but more frequently his stick work gives his team a huge edge. He is as much a part of the penalty-killing unit as the defensemen. Don't be surprised if Terreri becomes the next NHL goalie to score a goal.

Reflexes are the key to Terreri's game. He is not a very big goalie and has to challenge aggressively to take away some of the net. He likes to leave a tantalizing bit for the shooter on the glove side, because he is very quick with his glove hand. Terreri is also sharp down low, with quick feet. He controls his rebounds well and if he does have to go down to make a save, he pops up very quickly for the second effort.

Terreri is a good skater and roams willingly (even eagerly) out of his net to play hard-arounds and help out his defensemen. He communicates very well with his teammates so there are few miscues when handling the puck.

Terreri sometimes comes off the post to his right on plays developing from behind the goal line and leaves some stick side room. He also has some trouble with high shots.

THE MENTAL GAME

Terreri just gets tougher and tougher. He has terrific concentration through screens and scrambles. He will sometimes get beaten on a long shot or the odd scoring attempt from a face-off, but in heavy traffic and under pressure he continues to bear down. The more shots he faces, the sharper Terreri stays.

He is unaffected by bad nights. Terreri struggled through a seven-game winless streak in Nov. and Dec., but never lost his composure and regained his No. 1 status in the second half of the second. If anything, his teammates might have relied too much on Terreri, who is more than capable of winning games by himself.

THE INTANGIBLES

Frequently overlooked when top goalies are discussed, Terreri deserves more respect. He outplayed not one but two Rangers goalies during the 1992 playoffs (he had only one poor outing). Terreri is a bona fide No. 1 goalie who has proven he can be counted on in the long haul. He has a winning attitude.

KEVIN TODD

Yrs. of NHL service: 1
Born: Winnipeg, Man.; May 4, 1968
Position: Center
Height: 5-10
Weight: 175
Uniform no.: 14
Shoots: Left

Career statistics:

GP	G	A	TP	PIM
82	21	42	63	69

1991-92 statistics:

GP	G	A	TP	+/-	PIM	PP	SH	GW	GT	S	PCT
80	21	42	63	8	69	2	0	2	1	131	16.0

LAST SEASON

First full NHL season. Second among NHL rookies in scoring and assists. Tied for team lead in assists, third in scoring. One of only three Devils to appear in all 80 games. Named to NHL All-Rookie Team.

THE FINESSE GAME

Todd was one of the most unheralded players in a strong rookie crop of 1991-92, but he deserves more attention. A slow developing center (he was drafted in 1986), Todd led the AHL in assists and points in 1990-91 and he was able to carry those skills to the NHL level last season.

Not a great skater, Todd does possess a low center of gravity, using a wide-legged stance, and he gets the maximum drive from his lower body which helps him with his board and corner work. He is very wiry with deceptive strength, and he is a hungry player from the goal line to the corners.

Todd has nice hand skills, a good passing touch and an accurate wrist shot. He is a good playmaker who also likes to shoot — a nice combination since it keeps the opponent guessing.

Todd is fair on face-offs. The Devils preferred to use a veteran center on key draws last year. This is one area where experience will help Todd improve. Another area that needs some work is his defensive awareness.

THE PHYSICAL GAME

Todd was nicknamed "the Rat" for his penchant for scurrying in corners and somehow coming out with the puck. He is a tough player who won't initiate much contact (wise, given his size), but he is not easily fazed by rough stuff.

Because he is limited by his physical build, there are always some parts of the game that will elude Todd. He is willing to go in front of the net and muck, but can be easily handled by some bigger defensemen. To Todd's credit, he never quits battling for position.

THE INTANGIBLES

Todd was among the most consistent of the Devils' forwards last season. Building off a strong rookie season is difficult, but Todd didn't ease into the lineup last season, he shouldered the burden of being a No. 2 center.

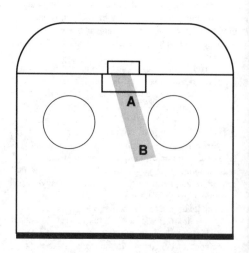

CLAUDE VILGRAIN

Yrs. of NHL service: 3
Born: Port-au-Prince, Haiti; Mar. 1, 1963
Position: Left wing/center
Height: 6-1
Weight: 205
Uniform no.: 19
Shoots: Right

Career statistics:

GP	G	A	TP	PIM
83	21	30	51	78

1991-92 statistics:

GP	G	A	TP	+/-	PIM	PP	SH	GW	GT	S	PCT
71	19	27	46	27	74	1	1	1	1	88	21.6

LAST SEASON

Led team in plus-minus and shooting percentage. Games played and all point totals career highs. Missed four games with groin injury. Missed one game with concussion.

THE FINESSE GAME

Vilgrain is a frustratingly slow mover, but his deliberate style sometimes catches opponents off-guard. The Devils sometimes used Vilgrain on the power play, where he looked woefully out of place because of the quick reactions and hockey vision needed to counter aggressive penalty killing.

Vilgrain scores most of his goals from close quarters, using a wrist shot that is strong and accurate, and he will go to the net. He is strong on his skates and scraps along the boards and in the corners for the puck. He does not shoot well driving in off the wing.

Vilgrain is surprisingly good on draws (he played a lot of center in junior and in his minor league career). If he does not win the face-off cleanly, he always does a good job of tying up the opposing center.

THE PHYSICAL GAME

One of the few blacks and the only Haitian ever to play in the NHL, you can bet Vilgrain has his own special brand of toughness. He has had to endure racial taunts through every level of junior, international, minor pro and NHL play, and has always stood up for himself without flying off the handle (with one exception — an incident this year with Quebec's Mats Sundin).

Even when he is not scoring, Vilgrain does such a good job defensively that he does not hurt his team. He is very alert and responsible.

THE INTANGIBLES

Vilgrain will always have to battle for an NHL job because his skills are marginal for an NHL player. His intensity helped Vilgrain get to the NHL and only that continued work ethic will keep him there.

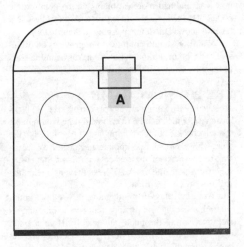

ERIC WEINRICH

Yrs. of NHL service: 3
Born: Roanoke, Va.; Dec. 19, 1966
Position: Right defense
Height: 6-1
Weight: 210
Uniform no.: 5
Shoots: Left

Career statistics:

GP	G	A	TP	PIM
173	13	66	79	114

1991-92 statistics:

GP	G	A	TP	+/-	PIM	PP	SH	GW	GT	S	PCT
76	7	25	32	10	55	5	0	0	0	97	7.2

LAST SEASON
Goal total career high.

THE FINESSE GAME
Weinrich's skating improved slightly last year, but not to the point where he could be counted on as a puck-carrying threat. Weinrich has a nice stride and can accelerate quickly, but is not a well-balanced skater and needs to work on more lower-body conditioning. He does not get good power from his legs and needs that strength to help move men out of the slot area.

Weinrich's finesse skills are very good, close to excellent. He is a solid passer and also has a good point shot. Weinrich knows when to rifle a shot and when to take a little edge off so that his shot can be tipped in. He has a tendency to get flustered under pressure, however, and had more problems on the point on the power play than you would expect a player of his talent level to show. His defensive play is inconsistent.

Weinrich should continue to improve as on offensive contributor, although he will never be in the class of the elite scoring defensemen.

THE PHYSICAL GAME
Weinrich does not always play to his size. He lacks meanness, which can be overlooked if he would make takeout checks, but his skating hasn't developed to the point where his checks eliminate an attacker. Weinrich was paired most of the season with Scott Stevens, a superb checker, and maybe some of Stevens' technique will rub off on Weinrich.

Weinrich plays a good game in his own zone, where his skating and passing skills come into play to facilitate getting the puck out quickly. He has some trouble reading plays coming at him fast, although he has improved in their area, especially at breaking up two-on-ones.

THE INTANGIBLES
Confidence still plays a major role in Weinrich's game. He needs reassurance from his coaches. A sophomore season is often a telling one for a player who had a good rookie campaign, as Weinrich did. Although probably the Devils' best defenseman during the third quarter of the season, he did not distinguish himself in the playoffs and has to play better consistently to be counted into the future plans of a team that has a good crop of offensive defensemen developing.

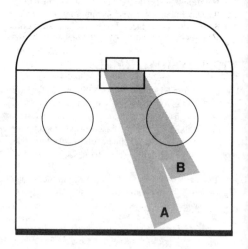

VALERI ZELEPUKIN

Yrs. of NHL service: 1
Born: Voskresensk, Russia; Sept. 17, 1968
Position: Left wing
Height: 5-11
Weight: 180
Uniform no.: 25
Shoots: Left

Career statistics:

GP	G	A	TP	PIM
44	13	18	31	28

1991-92 statistics:

GP	G	A	TP	+/-	PIM	PP	SH	GW	GT	S	PCT
44	13	18	31	11	28	3	0	3	0	94	13.8

LAST SEASON
First season in NHL.

THE FINESSE GAME
Zelepukin loves to shoot — a rarity among many Soviet-trained skaters who are taught to look to make the perfect play. Zelepukin doesn't take low percentage shots, either. He uses his excellent skating skills to always stay in motion and dart into opening around the net. He has very strong wrists, and his wrist and snap shots are very accurate. Zelepukin wastes few scoring chances. He will not shot wildly from the point. If the good quality shot is not there, Zelepukin will not take it.

He is a swift skater who thrives on a high-tempo game. Zelepukin does not skate up and down his wing, but likes to use as much of the ice as possible and works best when teamed with linemates who think creatively (he had his best games alongside Peter Stastny). Zelepukin works well down low on power plays.

Zelepukin is not much of a playmaker, although he will look to make the pass when he is out of shooting options. He has uncanny anticipation, especially in the neutral zone. He will pick off passes and quickly put his team on the attack with a rush. He is an excellent stickhandler.

THE PHYSICAL GAME
Zelepukin has shown little taste for physical play, and will have to learn to check effectively to stick in the NHL. He is not a big man, but his skating ability and balance give him an edge that many bigger players lack. He goes into traffic only with the puck.

THE INTANGIBLES
The Devils gave Zelepukin time to adjust to North American play in the minors, and the plan worked as the Russian winger stepped up to the Devils at mid-season and made an immediate impact. The impact faded, as it frequently does with European players in their first season. Zelepukin has to show he can consistently compete at the NHL level. He is well-liked by his teammates despite his problems with English. They would just like him to show more desire.

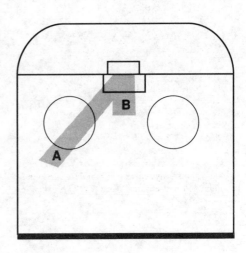

NEW YORK
ISLANDERS

ADAM CREIGHTON

Yrs. of NHL service: 9
Born: Burlington, Ont.; June 2, 1965
Position: Center
Height: 6-5
Weight: 210
Uniform no.: 11
Shoots: Left

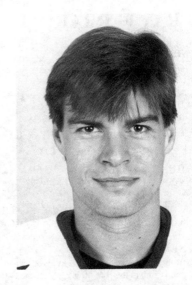

Career statistics:

GP	G	A	TP	PIM
444	132	154	286	765

1991-92 statistics:

GP	G	A	TP	+/-	PIM	PP	SH	GW	GT	S	PCT
77	21	15	36	−5	118	4	0	2	1	140	15.0

LAST SEASON

Acquired from Chicago with Steve Thomas for Brent Sutter and Brad Lauer, Oct. 25, 1991. Goal total four-season low. Missed one game with automatic suspension after incurring second stick major of season.

THE FINESSE GAME

Creighton's octopus reach helps him where his skating skills do not. His reach is so long that he can stand behind the net, reach around, and set up a play in front without ever moving his feet from the midpoint of the goal cage. When he is in front of the net, he has a nice touch with a shot. His slap shot from longer range is less of a weapon.

A painfully slow skater and not well-balanced, once he gets in gear, he has a long stride that covers a lot of ice. But by then he has given everyone else a significant head start.

He is more effective in the offensive zone than back on defense. Frankly, you don't see him back on defense much. He is so slow that if he is working in deep in the attacking zone, he is usually trapped.

THE PHYSICAL GAME

Creighton's physique begs a more forceful, commanding presence, but he doesn't use his body well enough or aggressively enough to maximize his size. On nights when he is motivated, Creighton is strong enough to drag defenders around with him or hang out in front of the net and frustrate his checkers. Those night just don't happen often enough.

THE INTANGIBLES

Creighton got off to a strong start after the trade to the Islanders, but by the end of the season was fighting for ice time on a fourth line. Unless he plays more consistently, and with more intensity, he will be in and out of the lineup as he was near the end of last season.

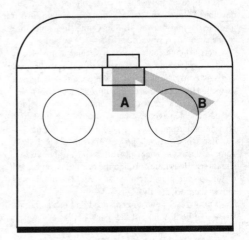

RAY FERRARO

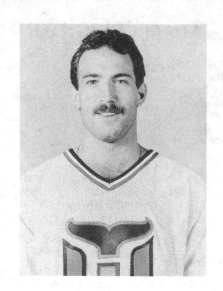

Yrs. of NHL service: 8
Born: Trail, B.C.; Aug. 23, 1964
Position: Center
Height: 5-10
Weight: 185
Uniform no.: 33
Shoots: Left

Career statistics:

GP	G	A	TP	PIM
583	216	250	466	577

1991-92 statistics:

GP	G	A	TP	+/-	PIM	PP	SH	GW	GT	S	PCT
80	40	40	80	25	92	7	0	4	2	154	26.0

LAST SEASON

One of three Islanders to appear in all 80 games. One of three Islanders to score 40 goals. Reached 40-goal mark for second time in career. Led team in shooting percentage. Tied for team lead in goals, second in points and plus-minus. Points career high.

THE FINESSE GAME

Ferraro is very quick and has good offensive moves, particularly around the net. He is a gutsy competitor who knew that in order to stay in coach Al Arbour's lineup, he had to play better defensively. He worked hard at the weaker parts of his game, and developed into a solid two-way performer who earned a trip to the mid-season All-Star Game. It's a pleasure to see such effort rewarded.

Ferraro contributes to both special teams. He is good at working the puck down low on the power play, and saw considerable time on the penalty-killing unit as well. His greatest area of improvement was in his defensive work down low, and he proved that increased defensive awareness often leads to better scoring opportunities.

Ferraro is a heads-up passer with a good short game deep in the zone, in traffic and in give-and-go situations. He is quick around the net and is very good on the power play because he sees his options and moves the puck alertly.

Ferraro lacks end-to-end speed and has a choppy stride, but he is quick off the mark and is very agile.

THE PHYSICAL GAME

Able to play wiry-tough, he is willing to stand in front of the net and take his whacks. He had a memorable game against the Rangers when John Vanbiesbrouck cracked him half a dozen times across the ankles; Ferraro screamed at the referee but never budged. He is very gritty and protects the puck well.

THE INTANGIBLES

Ferraro graduated willingly into the role of team spokesman as most of the veteran Islanders were traded or were sidelined by injuries. The responsibility suited him on and off the ice, and he was one of the Islanders' mosts consistent forwards. Another 35-40 goal season (we predicted a mere 30 in last year's HSR) should be in the offing.

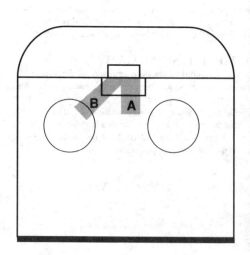

MARK FITZPATRICK

Yrs. of NHL service: 4
Born: Toronto, Ont.; Nov. 13, 1968
Position: Goaltender
Height: 6-1
Weight: 190
Uniform no.: 29
Catches: Left

Career statistics:

GP	MINS	GA	SO	GAA	A	PIM
107	6100	354	3	3.48	6	30

1991-92 statistics:

GP	MINS	GAA	W	L	T	SO	GA	S	SAPCT	PIM
30	1743	3.20	11	13	5	0	93	949	.902	8

LAST SEASON
Won 1992 Masterton Trophy. Missed 10 games with symptoms of eosinophilia myalgia syndrome. Missed two games with bruised back. GAA career best for full season.

THE PHYSICAL GAME
Fitzpatrick is a butterfly-style goalie with exceptional quickness for a player of his size. Big goalies are usually vulnerable low and with pucks in their skates, but Fitzpatrick is faster with his feet than most tall netminders. He does have some trouble with his lateral movement and gets beaten on quick plays cutting across in front of him.

He does not handle the puck well. This may be part of the Islanders' system, since their defense improved greatly last season, but it appears to be more of an adjustment on the team's part to Fitzpatrick's flaw. He does not stop pucks well behind the net (although he has gotten better), nor does he move the puck quickly to his teammates, and this is the area where he needs the most improvement.

Fitzpatrick is at his best when he stays on his feet and challenges the shooters with his big frame taking away much of the net. He does not recover well for a second shot if he has to scramble. He has a good glove hand.

THE MENTAL GAME
Fitzpatrick has a tendency to lose his focus once in a while, and those lapses usually cost him. When a goalie as big as Fitzpatrick lets in a long, soft one, he can look very bad, but he will not let a bad goal affect him for long. He has worked closely with Islanders' goalie coach Bill Smith, one of the best all-time money goalies, and some of his development can be credited to Smith. Fitzpatrick has big-save capacity.

THE INTANGIBLES
Fitzpatrick is battling EMS, a potentially fatal disease. It can flare up at any time, as it did just prior to training camp last season, and he must carefully regulate his medication and training regimen. He has the mental edge and skills to become a No. 1 goalie. His future is limited solely by his medical condition.

211

PATRICK FLATLEY

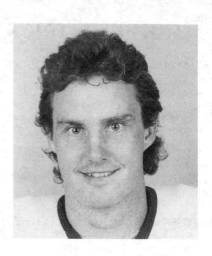

Yrs. of NHL service: 9
Born: Toronto, Ont.; Oct. 3, 1963
Position: Right wing
Height: 6-2
Weight: 195
Uniform no: 26
Shoots: Right

Career statistics:

GP	G	A	TP	PIM
467	120	222	342	524

1991-92 statistics:

GP	G	A	TP	+/-	PIM	PP	SH	GW	GT	S	PCT
38	8	28	36	14	31	4	1	0	0	76	10.5

LAST SEASON

Missed 42 games with surgery on broken thumb. Games played and goals total lowest since 1983-84. Third season playing 41 or fewer games.

THE FINESSE GAME

Flatley is a solid two-way forward with a tremendous work ethic. He is very effective along the boards and in tight quarters.

Taken piece by piece, there is little impressive about Flatley's game. He is a slow skater and his hand skills are only adequate. It is his relentless play that separates him from being an average player; he is a good grinder at both ends of the ice.

Flatley flounders in open ice because of his choppy stride, but he works well in traffic and in the corners because he is very strong on his skates and on his stick. He has good balance and is tough to knock off his feet.

In front of his own net, he fights for loose puck and has a good scoring touch, especially with a wrist shot. An intelligent veteran player, he doesn't panic under pressure and usually gets a good scoring chance even when the heat is on.

THE PHYSICAL GAME

Flatley will make hits or take late hits to make a play, which is one of the reasons he bought a time share in the trainer's room. He will sacrifice his body along the wall to wait until the last possible moment to make a play, and in doing so, leaves himself vulnerable to a hit.

When healthy, he remains the team's top corner and boards man. But health has become a serious matter for Flatley, who has played 41 or fewer games three times in the past five seasons.

THE INTANGIBLES

Named captain after the Brent Sutter trade. Heart and soul, Flatley has driven other players around him to work harder. But injuries have taken such a toll on him that his inspirational leadership is often sidelined. He can't help it: it's the only way he knows how to play.

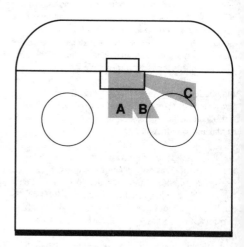

GLENN HEALY

Yrs. of NHL service: 5
Born: Pickering, Ont.; Aug. 23, 1962
Position: Goaltender
Height: 5-10
Weight: 175
Uniform no.: 35
Catches: Left

Career statistics:

GP	MINS	GA	SO	GAA	A	PIM
212	11775	751	4	3.82	7	73

1991-92 statistics:

GP	MINS	GAA	W	L	T	SO	GA	S	SAPCT	PIM
37	1960	3.80	14	16	4	1	124	1045	.881	18

LAST SEASON

Missed 10 games with fractured right thumb. Missed 13 games with surgery to repair severed right index finger. Minutes played four-season low.

THE PHYSICAL GAME

Healy is a scrambler, small and quick, and he relies on his reflexes rather than technique. Scouts see a lot of flaws in his game but grudgingly admit that whatever he's doing works for him, since he was very effective last season.

He does not play his angles well, and usually leaves a good rebound for the opposition because he doesn't do a very good job on the first save. Fortunately, his recovery time is quick and he regains his feet fast. Healy seldom gets beaten cleanly; the goal will come on a third or fourth effort with Healy down and out.

Because he is a small goalie, he can be easily screened, but he has good concentration and picks the puck up in a crowd well.

Not a very good puckhandler, he does not stop hard-arounds well and hardly moves the puck at all.

THE MENTAL GAME

Healy is mentally tough, and can shake off bad games and some strange injuries. He returns sharply from being sidelined (whether by coach's decision or injury), because he will work efficiently in practice (not necessarily long and hard, though — games take a lot out of him because of his style of play).

THE INTANGIBLES

Healy was asked to be a No. 1 goalie and thought of himself as such, but if he can adjust to being a No. 2 goalie behind a healthy Mark Fitzpatrick, the Islanders will have a very solid duo in net. Depending on Fitzpatrick's recuperation, Healy may only see 25 starts this season.

BENOIT HOGUE

Yrs. of NHL service: 4
Born: Repetigny, Que.; Oct. 28, 1966
Position: Center/right wing
Height: 5-10
Weight: 190
Uniform no.: 33
Shoots: Left

Career statistics:

GP	G	A	TP	PIM
268	75	112	187	342

1991-92 statistics:

GP	G	A	TP	+/-	PIM	PP	SH	GW	GT	S	PCT
75	30	46	76	30	67	8	0	5	0	149	20.1

LAST SEASON

Acquired from Buffalo with Pierre Turgeon, Uwe Krupp and Dave McLlwain for Pat LaFontaine, Randy Wood, Randy Hillier and future considerations Oct. 25, 1991. Led team in plus-minus. Best production of career.

THE FINESSE GAME

There is a lot of pizzazz in Hogue's game when he is in the mood, and the early-season trade that sent him to the Islanders clearly improved his frame of mind. Given ice time on both specialty teams (he had never played the power play with the Sabres), he added jump to both.

Hogue played wing primarily, but was used to take key defensive-zone draws. He was one of the Islanders' best face-off men, with good anticipation and hand quickness.

Hogue has become a solid two-way player, with an offensive flair. He has good speed, and the vision to jump into openings. He has good hand skills and can handle the puck at a high tempo.

He has a very hard wrist and snap shots. He is also an excellent passer, which made him a dangerous man on the power play because opponents couldn't key off either tendency. A good finisher in tight, he can also blast a strong shot from the top of the circle.

THE PHYSICAL GAME

Hogue is not a big checker but he is a strong man-to-man player who will lean on an opponent and keep him from getting in the play. He always seems to position himself well so that he can get involved quickly in a counterattack, and showed very good instincts in all zones. A very hard worker and a crunch-time player, Hogue is tough to play against.

THE INTANGIBLES

A noted malcontent in Buffalo, where he complained about the treatment of French-Canadian athletes, Hogue underwent a personality transplant in the move to Long Island. He never even complained about the traffic. A happy Hogue was a successful Hogue, and he finally showed the consistency he had lacked with the Sabres.

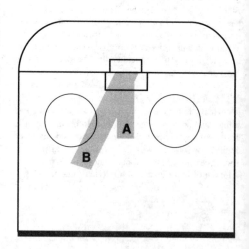

DARIUS KASPARAITIS

Yrs. of NHL service: 0
Born: Elektrenai, Lithuania; Oct. 16, 1972
Position: Left defense
Height: 5-11
Weight: 187
Uniform no:
Shoots: Left

Career statistics:

GP	G	A	TP	PIM
0	0	0	0	0

1991-92 statistics:

GP	G	A	TP	+/-	PIM	PP	SH	GW	GT	S	PCT
0	0	0	0	0	0	0	0	0	0	0	0

LAST SEASON

Played for Moscow Dynamo. Drafted in the first round, fifth overall, in 1992.

THE FINESSE GAME

Kasparaitis is a good skater with balance and speed. A member of the gold medal-winning C.I.S. team at the 1992 Albertville Olympics, Kasparaitis was one of the less flashy members of the squad as he concentrated on his defensive responsibilities. Still, he was one of the most impressive players for the champions.

One of the things scouts like most about Kasparaitis is that he has met every challenge as the quality of his competition improved. He is an excellent passer, moving the puck quickly and accurately, even when pressured. Kasparaitis does not get flustered when he is being pressed. He will be a crunch-time player, since he wants to be on the ice in key situations and wants the puck.

He plays a very sound positional game, which will need to adapt to the smaller NHL ice surfaces. He has indicated he can handle the faster pace of the game.

Kasparaitis was drafted as much for his personality as his skills. The dour Soviet coaches must have been scratching their heads over this breezy, confident Lithuanian. Kasparaitis has very good desire and attitude, but the Islanders may want to keep an eye on his off-ice activities.

THE PHYSICAL GAME

The major question mark is his size, but he is built along the same lines as Pat Stapleton, the former Blackhawk who had a long and solid NHL career. Kasparaitis uses his blocky build effectively, especially since he is such a good skater. He plays well in the corners, and does try to move out skaters from in front of the net. He will find that more difficult in the NHL than it was in Europe.

THE INTANGIBLES

Islanders general manager Bill Torrey thought enough of Kasparaitis to trade a second-round draft pick to Toronto in order to move up three positions in the first round to nab him. Torrey believes that the stocky defenseman was the one player in this year's draft capable of stepping into the NHL right away. Kasparaitis will be in an Islanders uniform this season if Torrey can come to terms with Dynamo, with whom he has a year left on his contract. Plans are to pair him with another Russian the Islanders hope to sign, Vladimir Malakhov. By the way, Kasparaitis was available at age 18 in the 1991 draft, but there were no takers.

DEREK KING

Yrs. of NHL service: 5
Born: Hamilton, Ont.; Feb. 11, 1967
Position: Left wing
Height: 6-1
Weight: 200
Uniform no.: 27
Shoots: Left

Career statistics:

GP	G	A	TP	PIM
309	98	144	242	154

1991-92 statistics:

GP	G	A	TP	+/-	PIM	PP	SH	GW	GT	S	PCT
80	40	38	78	-10	46	21	0	6	2	189	21.2

LAST SEASON

One of three Islanders to score 40 goals. One of three Islanders to appear in all 80 games. Tied for team lead in goals. First on team, fifth in NHL in power-play goals. Tied for team lead in game-winning goals. Third on team in scoring. Goals more than double any previous season's best.

THE FINESSE GAME

King must have been one of those kids who could study for an exam with the television blaring and a road crew blasting away with dynamite outside his open window. His concentration around the net is unwavering.

He has remarkable hand skills. We said in last season's edition that King was capable of scoring 40 goals, and he made us look smart. Of course, the coaches felt that way all along, and it was just a matter of finally wringing out that potential. An increased dedication to his off-ice conditioning was a factor, since he reported to camp in what might have been the best shape of his career. His improved stamina allowed him to take longer shifts without chugging off in search of oxygen.

A finisher, he needs to play with someone who gets him the puck. The Islanders had been without a playmaking center since Bryan Trottier's departure, but Pierre Turgeon proved to be the perfect complement for King. One of the game's best young centers, Turgeon allows King to head for the net confident that the puck will get through to him. And King knows just what to do with it.

Defensively, his game still needs work. He is not a great skater, and when he is caught out of position, he can't hustle back to cover up for his mistake.

THE PHYSICAL GAME

King is solid and bears up well under the increased attention he's been receiving in front of the net. He does a fair job of avoiding bad retaliatory penalties. Now that he has seen his reward of 40 goals, King is willing to pay the price.

THE INTANGIBLES

The departure of Brent Sutter and Pat LaFontaine put more responsibility on King as a team leader. Quiet off the ice, he shouted with his scoring on the ice. Maybe the burden was just what King needed to mature. Now the pressure is on him to maintain his off-ice conditioning and hard work, and repeat his 40-goal effort. Consistency is the one aspect of his game that has hurt him in the past.

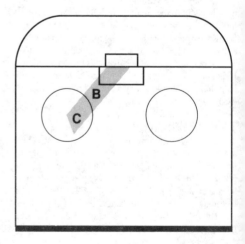

216

UWE KRUPP

Yrs. of NHL service: 6
Born: Cologne, West Germany; June 24, 1965
Position: Right defense
Height: 6-6
Weight: 235
Uniform no.: 4
Shoots: Right

Career statistics:

GP	G	A	TP	PIM
386	31	107	138	429

1991-92 statistics:

GP	G	A	TP	+/-	PIM	PP	SH	GW	GT	S	PCT
67	8	29	37	13	49	2	0	0	0	128	6.3

LAST SEASON

Acquired from Buffalo with Pierre Turgeon, Benoit Hogue and Dave McLlwain for Pat LaFontaine, Randy Wood, Randy Hillier and future considerations, Oct. 25, 1991. Missed eight games with left knee injury. Games played and all offensive totals two-season lows.

THE FINESSE GAME

Krupp is a solid two-way defenseman, a steady and consistent performer who can help out in any area of the ice and in any game situations. He moves the puck very well and has some offensive ability.

You would figure Krupp for a bullet point shot, and Krupp does have one. The problem is that it takes him so long to tee up that the shot is easily blocked or he misfires. Unable to one-time the puck, he has to stop the pass before getting a shot away. He has a strong, low wrist shot that he should use more often. When he works the point on the power play, he gets more time to shoot than at even strength. He is also more effective when he one-times his shot.

Krupp sees his outlet passes well and sends in a lot of his forwards on odd-man rushes. He does not always see the play as well in the offensive zone, and will often look to shoot first rather than make a pass.

He reads the rush well coming at him. If an opponent gets a step, it's not always enough because Krupp's reach compensates. He is a very good penalty killer.

THE PHYSICAL GAME

Krupp is one of the biggest players in the NHL. He doesn't hit hard because he doesn't have to; he needs only to take a stride to cover his half of the ice, and he effectively wraps up an opponent. He is a solid penalty killer, and since he covers so much ice, is good at blocking shots.

Despite his gentle nature, he beat Brendan Shanahan in a fight early in the season. He then helped Shanahan up and inquired if he were hurt. Only Shanahan's pride was bruised.

THE INTANGIBLES

Krupp is one of the less heralded NHL defensemen (mostly because his point totals aren't exciting), but he is one of the better blueliners around, and seldom has a bad night.

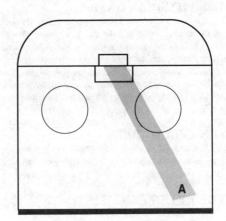

TOM KURVERS

Yrs. of NHL service: 8
Born: Minneapolis, Minn.; Sept. 14, 1962
Position: Right defense
Height: 6-2
Weight: 195
Uniform no.: 28
Shoots: Left

Career statistics:

GP	G	A	TP	PIM
519	72	264	336	259

1991-92 statistics:

GP	G	A	TP	+/-	PIM	PP	SH	GW	GT	S	PCT
74	9	47	56	-18	30	6	0	1	0	132	6.8

LAST SEASON

Led team defensemen in scoring. Points three-season high.

THE FINESSE GAME

One of the game's premier power-play specialists, Kurvers is a quarterback with good vision and passing skills. His passing from the left point is one of the reasons why left wing Derek King was able to connect for 21 power play goals.

He controls the puck at the point, using a good low slap shot. He has good lateral movement, gliding along the blue line, and he has a real knack for keeping the puck in after the penalty killers try to knock it out.

Kurvers is a fluid skater who moves well when carrying the puck. He is very intelligent when rushing, and seems to do everything almost effortlessly.

He does not gamble in deep as often as he used to, perhaps mindful of the criticism of his defensive play.

THE PHYSICAL GAME

Kurvers doesn't use his size well and usually opts for the finesse move (a poke check or sweep check) rather than bodying an attacker. He has to be paired with a hitting, stay-at-home partner to be effective. A minus-26 at mid-season, after injuries forced him into more even-strength situations, he played with more intensity and had a stronger second half, even killing penalties.

THE INTANGIBLES

Kurvers is a cerebral player who will brood over a bad game. Increased ice time has helped confidence, but he must be spotted defensively. He is most effective in purely offensive situations. Left unprotected in the 1992 Expansion Draft—and with Scott Lachance, Jeff Norton and possibly two Soviet defensemen coming into the lineup this season—he will be struggling for ice time.

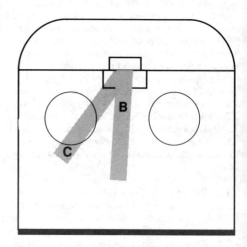

SCOTT LACHANCE

Yrs. of NHL service: 0
Born: Charlottesville, Va.; Oct. 22, 1972
Position: Left defense
Height: 6-1
Weight: 197
Uniform no.: 7
Shoots: Left

Career statistics:

GP	G	A	TP	PIM
17	1	4	5	9

1991-92 statistics:

GP	G	A	TP	+/-	PIM	PP	SH	GW	GT	S	PCT
17	1	4	5	13	9	0	0	0	1	20	5.0

LAST SEASON

Made NHL debut after Olympics; will be entering first full NHL season.

THE FINESSE GAME

As Lachance progressed from high school to college to international play to the NHL, his game rose to each level. He is an extremely capable offensive player, not flashy like Brian Leetch, but with great instincts and the skating and hand skills to complement his smarts. He handles the puck well whether carrying or passing.

Lachance is a strong skater with a good stride and can accelerate quickly. He skates well laterally and backwards, and turns quickly.

Lachance plays the point well with a good, low slap. He is poised under pressure, whether on the point on the power play or under siege in his own zone. He sees the ice very well and has good anticipation.

Defensively, his game is very advanced for a young player. He is sound positionally and is willing to sacrifice his body either to make a check or block a shot. Lachance wants to mold his game after Ray Bourque. He couldn't pick a better role model.

THE PHYSICAL GAME

Lachance is still growing, and while he will never be a devastating checker he is solidly built and getting stronger. He is an aggressive player in all zones, and reads plays well coming at him. He has to improve his work in the corners, but has the attitude that indicates he will work to shore up his few flaws. He is a tough competitor.

THE INTANGIBLES

After underwent arthroscopic knee surgery in October during Team USA's pre-Olympic tour, his return was uninspiring, but he played in the World Junior tournament, then showed gradual improvement during the Olympics. He began hitting his stride as he made his NHL debut with the Islanders late in the season, and shows every sign of being the offensive defenseman the team has sorely missed ever since Denis Potvin's retirement. If this weren't the Year of Eric Lindros, Lachance would be a top Calder Trophy candidate. He is capable of becoming an outstanding NHL defenseman.

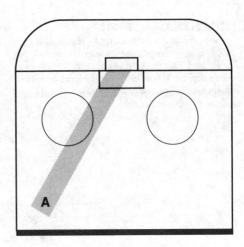

CLAUDE LOISELLE

Yrs. of NHL service: 10
Born: Ottawa, Ont.; May 29, 1963
Position: Center
Height: 5-11
Weight: 195
Uniform no.: 10
Shoots: Left

Career statistics:

GP	G	A	TP	PIM
558	86	113	199	1010

1991-92 statistics:

GP	G	A	TP	+/-	PIM	PP	SH	GW	GT	S	PCT
75	7	10	17	-24	115	1	0	1	0	101	6.9

LAST SEASON

Acquired from Toronto with Daniel Marois for Ken Baumgartner and Dave McLlwain, March 10, 1992. Points matched last year's career low for full season.

THE FINESSE GAME

Loiselle isn't blessed with much finesse skill. He is a good skater, wide-based with a solid stance, and gets much of his strength from his powerful lower body. He is not very big, but has always played bigger because his skating technique is so sound. Most of his scoring chances come from around the net. He is not easy to budge, and will scrap for the puck in traffic with adequate hand skills.

Loiselle shines when penalty killing. He is a smart, tenacious forechecker.

He has been in and out during the past few seasons. If he can ever get his game back together on a consistent basis, he can be a sound defensive forward.

THE PHYSICAL GAME

Loiselle can be aggravating to play against. He will bump with his body and whack with his stick. He can hit hard, but needs to improve his conditioning and his desire. Both of those commodities have been in short supply over the past few seasons.

THE INTANGIBLES

Loiselle is a role player, a hard worker who has made the most of his limited skills throughout his career. He is on the bubble now.

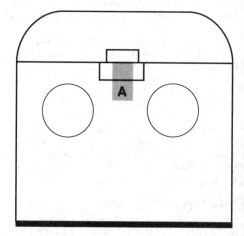

220

DANIEL MAROIS

Yrs. of NHL service: 4
Born: Montreal, Que. Oct. 3, 1968
Position: Right wing
Height: 6-0
Weight: 190
Uniform no.: 24
Shoots: Right

Career statistics:

GP	G	A	TP	PIM
297	108	85	193	364

1991-92 statistics:

GP	G	A	TP	+/-	PIM	PP	SH	GW	GT	S	PCT
75	17	16	33	−34	94	4	0	0	0	159	10.7

LAST SEASON

Acquired from Toronto with Claude Loiselle for Ken Baumgartner and Dave McLlwain, March 10, 1992. Plus-minus worst on team (he carried over a minus-36 from Toronto). Goal total career low.

THE FINESSE GAME

Marois has the skills to be a top NHL finisher. A very good skater, he cuts to the net with quick acceleration. He is a clever player who uses a wide selection of shots. Marois can rifle a shot off the wing, or in close will use a hard, accurate wrist shot. He releases all of his shots quickly.

He is a good passer and will take a check to make a play. Good with the puck in his skates, he is able to kick an errant pass to up his stick and barely break stride. Marois should see considerable power-play time.

He worked defensively with New York but needs more defensive intensity.

THE PHYSICAL GAME

Marois will get in front of the net and create chaos, but last season did not use his body as effectively as he should. In the past, he has used his body well and showed he would not be intimidated. Once he regains that desire, the rest of his game will take off.

THE INTANGIBLES

The Islanders succeeded with two major reclamation projects in Pierre Turgeon and Benoit Hogue last season. This year, they'll take on a third in this former 39-goal scorer. Marois was hurt by the departure of Vincent Damphousse from the Leafs last season and didn't get another chance to play with a solid center. The Islanders are deep at that position, and Marois should get ample chance to prove himself with his new team.

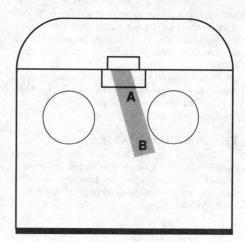

RICH PILON

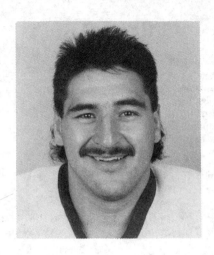

Yrs. of NHL service: 4
Born: Saskatoon, Sask.; April 30, 1968
Position: Left defense
Height: 6-0
Weight: 200
Uniform no.: 47
Shoots: left

Career statistics:

GP	G	A	TP	PIM
201	2	26	32	582

1991-92 statistics:

GP	G	A	TP	+/-	PIM	PP	SH	GW	GT	S	PCT
65	1	6	7	−1	183	0	0	0	0	27	3.7

LAST SEASON

Second on team in PIM. Missed four games with lacerated tip of right index finger. Missed three games with personal leave.

THE FINESSE GAME

Pilon is a stay-at-home defenseman with little ability to contribute offensively. His stickhandling is average, and he never ventures in deep in the offensive zone. Since he will not make plays from the blue line, his only option is to fire a shot, and it's not much of a slapper. He does not join the rush, but he will carry the puck to get out of trouble in the defensive zone.

An above-average skater, he is very strong on his feet. His lateral movement needs improvement, but his agility is not awful. Pilon's skating speed allows to be a powerful checker. He must improve his reads and needs to work better positionally. He is a good shot-blocker.

Pilon has slightly damaged vision in one eye, and must wear a face shield. Both affect his ability to see plays develop, and he will make passes in his own zone into dangerous areas.

THE PHYSICAL GAME

Strong and tough, he is a mean, punishing hitter. He will stand up for his teammates, and he will initiate, although that means taking bad penalties, which he does too often. Pilon has tremendous physical presence and he probably scares more than a few opponents.

THE INTANGIBLES

Pilon took a step backwards last season. His development was undoubtedly impeded by the career-threatening eye injury that he suffered in 1989. He is only an average NHL defenseman now, but he once had the potential for more.

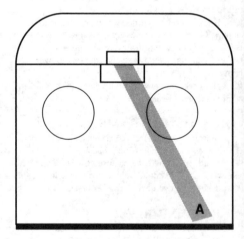

STEVE THOMAS

Yrs. of NHL service: 8
Born: Stockport, England; July 15, 1963
Position: Left wing
Height: 5-11
Weight: 185
Uniform no.: 32
Shoots: Left

Career statistics:

GP	G	A	TP	PIM
463	179	210	389	578

1991-92 statistics:

GP	G	A	TP	+/-	PIM	PP	SH	GW	GT	S	PCT
82	30	48	78	8	97	3	0	3	1	245	12.2

LAST SEASON

Acquired from Chicago with Adam Creighton for Brent Sutter and Brad Lauer on Oct. 25, 1991. Reached the 30-goal mark for third time in career. First on team in shots, second in assists, fourth in scoring. All scoring totals two-season high after career lows in 1990-91.

THE FINESSE GAME

Intensity has always been what drives Thomas. If there is such a thing as too much intensity, then he's got it. He has great speed, but doesn't always think to use it wisely, and is sometimes too far ahead of the play to do his teammates any good. He will blast away at shots when a more subtle move would do, but there isn't much subtle about him.

Thomas can intimidate with his speed, but since he doesn't have many fancy moves, his best hope is for the defenseman to back off and give him room for a slap or snap shot coming off the wing. He is not much of a playmaker. Once a linemate gives Thomas a pass, he doesn't expect to get it back.

Although he is still so overanxious to go on the attack that he will leave the zone early, he has improved defensively. He is a streaky, emotional player.

THE PHYSICAL GAME

Thomas is a good forechecker whose speed adds a lot of power to his hits. Small but powerfully built, he is not intimidated and will use his body along the boards and in the corners. He has quick feet and good balance, and will win some battles by kicking at a loose puck. Feisty, he hates to lose a game or a one-on-one contest.

THE INTANGIBLES

Thomas has shown flashes of brilliance, but on a consistent basis, he seems to be lacking that little something that would lift him above average. There are many nights when Thomas is "on," however, and on those nights he is a tremendous force.

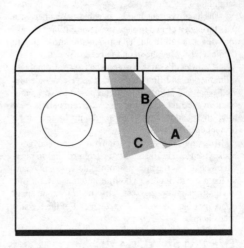

PIERRE TURGEON

Yrs. of NHL service: 5
Born: Rouyn, Que.; Aug. 29, 1969
Position: Center
Height: 6-1
Weight: 203
Uniform no.: 77
Shoots: Left

Career statistics:

GP	G	A	TP	PIM
391	160	250	410	135

1991-92 statistics:

GP	G	A	TP	+/-	PIM	PP	SH	GW	GT	S	PCT
77	40	55	95	7	20	13	0	6	0	207	19.3

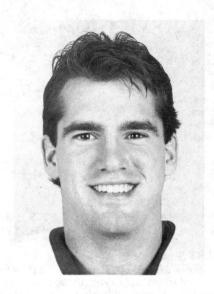

LAST SEASON

Acquired from Buffalo with Benoit Hogue and Uwe Krupp for Pat LaFontaine, Randy Wood, Randy Hillier and future considerations, Oct. 25, 1991. Led team in assists and points. One of three 40-goal scorers on team. Best numbers since posting career highs in 1989-90. Second 40-goal season of career.

THE FINESSE GAME

Turgeon has great offensive skills and the right package to go with them. He has size and strength, along with speed and quickness, and can pass or shoot with equal ability. Wingers have to be alert because his pass can get through a tangle of legs and stick to find their tape, or his shot will set up a rebound scramble.

He has excellent hands, capable of feathering a pass through a crowd to a teammate or hitting a streaking winger in full flight. That touch also allows him to cradle a pass when he is on the receiving end.

A powerful skater, Turgeon has very strong legs, a fluid stride and first-step quickness. He is agile and well-balanced. He needs to put his power to work more often in the high-traffic areas, where his skills give him a tremendous edge over the competition, but he prefers open-ice play.

Turgeon has superb peripheral vision and good hockey sense. He likes to work from behind the net, where he draws the attention of the defense and opens up ice for his wingers, who trail into the play for one of his radar-like passes. His neutral zone play improved, but his work in his own end of the ice still needs help.

THE PHYSICAL GAME

Turgeon has never shown much mental toughness. While he has the skills to move into the NHL's elite centermen, he won't do so without earning more respect with his work ethic and desire. He does not relish physical play and can be taken out of a game by a team that does a good job of harassing him that way.

THE INTANGIBLES

Turgeon took a step back in Buffalo after the acquisition of Dale Hawerchuk. The trade to the Islanders made Turgeon a No. 1 center again, and the role was just what he wanted. He is coming into his own and could stamp himself this season as one of the game's stars. Much of that will be shown as the improving Islanders battle for a playoff position in a very tough division.

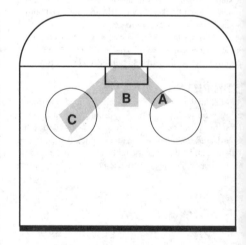

DAVID VOLEK

Yrs. of NHL service: 4
Born: Prague, Czechoslovakia; June 18, 1966
Position: Left wing
Height: 6-0
Weight: 185
Uniform no.: 25
Shoots: left

Career statistics:

GP	G	A	TP	PIM
308	82	132	214	157

1991-92 statistics:

GP	G	A	TP	+/-	PIM	PP	SH	GW	GT	S	PCT
74	18	42	60	0	35	4	1	2	0	167	10.8

LAST SEASON

Point total career high. Missed two games with pulled rib cage muscle.

THE FINESSE GAME

Volek has good offensive skills and instincts, and seems to always be around the net and in the slot in good scoring position. However, he missed a lot of goals this season which means he may not be as good a finisher as a player of his calibre should be. Either that, or his intensity level has gone way, way down.

A strong skater with good balance, he isn't easy to knock off his feet. He can get around a defenseman with a good deke, and handles the puck well while moving so he is in good position for a shot. He has a backhand shot which he doesn't use enough.

Volek is intelligent enough to be an effective player on both the power play and penalty killing. Although he can be a soft player defensively five-on-five, he seems to apply himself better when his team is working shorthanded.

THE PHYSICAL GAME

Volek has a wiry strength and is a very good skater, yet loses a lot of man-to-man battles. Since he seems to have the capability to be more involved, it would behoove him to regain the scrappy form he showed a season ago. He can be mentally and physically tough.

THE INTANGIBLES

Bothered in the first half of the season by the departure of Pat LaFontaine — his best friend on the team — and by a contract dispute, he settled down and finished the season well once the latter was settled. The Islanders projected him as a 30-goal scorer, but it appears that he won't be living up to those expectations.

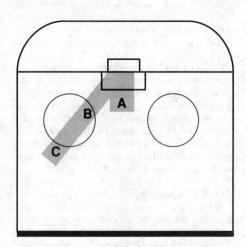

MICK VUKOTA

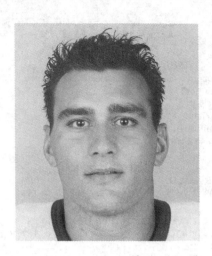

Yrs. of NHL service: 5
Born: Saskatoon, Sask.; Sept. 14, 1966
Position: Right wing
Height: 6-2
Weight: 195
Uniform no.: 12
Shoots: Right

Career statistics:

GP	G	A	TP	PIM
275	9	20	29	1086

1991-92 statistics:

GP	G	A	TP	+/-	PIM	PP	SH	GW	GT	S	PCT
74	0	6	6	−6	293	0	0	0	0	34	0.0

LAST SEASON

Led team in PIM. Only NHL player, other than goaltenders, with 70 or more appearances to fail to score a goal.

THE FINESSE GAME

Even a tough guy should be able to score the odd goal now and then, but Vukota has very limited offensive ability. It's hard to believe, but he once actually scored a hat trick in an NHL game. Now it would seem a miracle if he got three in a season.

The game has become faster, and Vukota has not been able to keep pace. His skating is slow, his shot release is slow and his thinking process is slow. He has some straight-ahead speed, but little quickness or mobility, so he is easily out-manoeuvred. He will fight along the boards for the puck, but his hand skills are below average, so he can't do much with it once he gets it.

THE PHYSICAL GAME

Vukota is a tough role player who will hit and take the body. He is a good fighter who will stand up for his teammates, but saw so few shifts that he tried to make an impact every time he did get on the ice, and usually ended up taking bad penalties. Although he understands his role as an enforcer, he just has to get smarter at it. He's one of the few tough guys the Islanders have, and they may need him.

THE INTANGIBLES

Vukota had limited ice time last season, and should any rule changes be enacted by the NHL to legislate fighting out of the game, he will have an even tougher time getting off the bench (or even into uniform). Like many of the league's policemen, he is a good team man who always sticks up for his teammates.

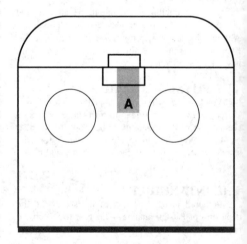

226

NEW YORK
RANGERS

TONY AMONTE

Yrs. of NHL service: 1
Born: Hingham, Mass.; August 2, 1970
Position: Right wing
Height: 6-0
Weight: 185
Uniform no.: 33
Shoots: Left

Career statistics:

GP	G	A	TP	PIM
79	35	34	69	55

1991-92 statistics:

GP	G	A	TP	+/-	PIM	PP	SH	GW	GT	S	PCT
79	35	34	69	12	55	9	0	4	0	234	15.0

LAST SEASON

Was a finalist in voting for Calder Trophy as NHL rookie of the year. Goal total was one short of matching club record for rookies. Led NHL rookies in goals and points. Shot total was second, assist total was fourth among league freshmen. Missed one game due to concussion.

THE FINESSE GAME

Amonte has fine acceleration, foot speed and skating strength, and makes ample use of those tools to turn himself into a threat. He never stops moving, but controls his speed with great maturity; though he plays a speed game, he waits at the blue line until the puck crosses and causes very few offsides.

Though troubled by giveaways early in the season, Amonte grew more careful with the puck as time passed and also worked on his defense. His heart is in the right place—he looks for his linemates all the time — and his passing is quite good for a left shot who plays the right side.

Amonte is blessed with a quick release, plus hand-eye coordination that makes his one-timers a devastating weapon. He gets extra style points for regularly hitting the goalie's water bottle with his rockets under the crossbar. Amonte also makes frequent use of the wrist shot, off his back foot, with his weight going away from the net. He will use the backhand and snap shot to good effect as well.

THE PHYSICAL GAME

There isn't an awful lot of physical strength to his game, but Amonte makes as much use as possible of what he has. He keeps the legs driving despite various hits and slashes. He goes to the front of the net to bury rebounds and he wades eagerly into the traffic to try for deflections. He also gets involved at the side boards and uses his feet nicely to control the puck. And he often tries to lift a defender's stick with his own to steal the puck.

Amonte had a target on his back for a lot of the season. A hot-shot rookie who scores a lot is going to get his share of abuse and Amonte took it all. He kept coming back when often there were nights someone with less mental toughness would have disappeared or gotten into a fight or taken a dumb penalty.

He showed tremendous discipline and mental toughness, absorbed the punishment and kept coming; if he hadn't, he'd never have been heard from again. Though he passed the physical test, he will be challenged again this season.

THE INTANGIBLES

Amonte benefited tremendously from playing on Mark Messier's line in his rookie season, but it would be unfair to lay all the credit at Messier's feet. Amonte was the guy who put the pucks away, the guy who brought hunger and enthusiasm to the rink. The guy who played with youthful eagerness and something approaching a veteran's polish.

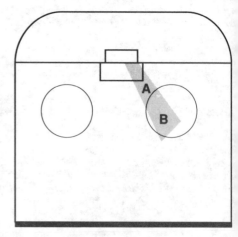

JEFF BEUKEBOOM

Yrs. of NHL service: 6
Born: Ajax, Ont.; Mar. 28, 1965
Position: Right defense
Height: 6-4
Weight: 215
Uniform no.: 23
Shoots: Right

Career statistics:

GP	G	A	TP	PIM
340	13	67	80	855

1991-92 statistics:

GP	G	A	TP	+/-	PIM	PP	SH	GW	GT	S	PCT
74	1	15	16	23	200	0	0	0	0	48	2.1

LAST SEASON

Obtained from Edmonton, Nov. 12, 1991, for David Shaw. Plus-minus improved by 17. Missed four games due to suspension, one due to back spasms. PIM total was third-most on team.

THE FINESSE GAME

Beukeboom is a tractor-trailer on skates, slow-moving but powerful. He is not agile. He does not change directions well, though he seems more fluid on the pivot to the left than to the right. He has a huge first step to the puck, but that just about does it for his acceleration.

Still, this player is aware of his limitations. Beukeboom uses his reach to angle players toward the corner and make up for the shortcomings in mobility. He has more than enough balance to try a poke check or sweep check at the defending blue line, and enough mobility to recover quickly if the poke attempt does not succeed.

And he is smart. If he has time, Beukeboom makes smart turns to open ice as he goes back to chase a puck, which gives him a chance to grab a look over his shoulder to see if an opponent is bearing down on him. Thus he knows in advance what he wants to do with the puck instead of having to size up his options while being checked.

Beukeboom also makes nice reads away from the puck. With it, though, he keeps things simple: a couple of strides, a strong first pass and back into the woodwork. He gets it and moves it.

THE PHYSICAL GAME

Beukeboom loves to hit, loves to use his size. He's just a brute. In open ice or along the boards, he'll smear you. If he gets one good lick in, he immediately wants to get another. He'll hit you because you just hit one of his teammates. He'll hit you because he feels like it. And he'll really hit on the road. His attitude makes him a player opponents worry about from a physical standpoint — with good cause.

Beukeboom blocks shots fearlessly and often ends up playing in pain as a consequence. A player of fierce strength, he will place one opponent under each arm in the corner, then kick the puck free.

THE INTANGIBLES

Beukeboom will never be accused of using style to hide his substance. He is strictly a defensive defenseman, which is what he needs to be as Brian Leetch's partner. In that regard, he is the perfect complement and is more than happy to let Leetch be the stylist and the gunner. It is not the easiest role to play (everybody has an ego) but Beukeboom is perfect at it.

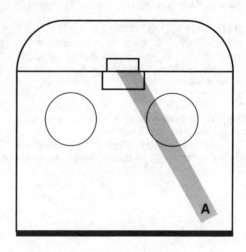

PAUL BROTEN

Yrs. of NHL service: 2
Born: Roseau, Minn.; Oct. 27, 1965
Position: Right wing
Height: 5-11
Weight: 190
Uniform no.: 37
Shoots: Right

Career statistics:

GP	G	A	TP	PIM
134	22	24	46	146

1991-92 statistics:

GP	G	A	TP	+/-	PIM	PP	SH	GW	GT	S	PCT
74	13	15	28	14	102	0	3	1	0	96	13.5

LAST SEASON

Established career highs in games played, goals, assists and points. Penalty minutes increased by 84.

THE FINESSE GAME

Broten has better puck skills than you might expect of a checker. He's got some very good hockey smarts and some very good pond-hockey moves, doubtless developed by playing against two stronger older brothers.

This player simply loves the race for the puck. It captures the whole spirit of his game — chasing, harrying, pestering you into a fury. Broten has decent speed and is able to change directions very well on the glide. In the neutral zone, especially in penalty-killing situations, Broten almost crouches — getting the length of his stick on the ice to close off passing lanes. But he is not agile or shifty. He is very solid on his skates, and can continue moving after getting bombed with a check.

The bottom line is, he gets the puck deep or he gets it to the net. When he shoots, there is mustard on the puck; he isn't running any benefits for goalies.

THE PHYSICAL GAME

If he happens to skate through the crease or happens to run into somebody who doesn't have the puck, that's their problem. Broten plays very much the kind of game that asks, ''What are you going to do about it?''

Broten works hard along the wall. He cycles. He keeps the legs going as long as possible, he'll carry a player along with him if he can.

And his promixity to Kris King has helped Broten master certain diving techniques that get laughs, but draw occasional penalties, from the referees. Broten will make sure that when he falls to the ice behind the play, he slaps the ice hard with his stick so the referee will look back, see Broten down, and call a hooking penalty on the guy next to him.

THE INTANGIBLES

Ranger management long felt it was impossible for Broten to play his hell-bent, spitfire kind of game on a consistent basis, but Broten earned his spot in the lineup every night. He made it impossible for the Rangers to bench him for long. He works, he scraps, he yaps, gives you all he can give and all the other team can stand. A real in-your-face attitude that ticks off the opposition's top stars or lowliest grunts.

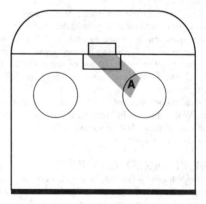

JOE CIRELLA

Yrs. of NHL service: 9
Born: Hamilton, Ont.; May 9, 1963
Position: Right defense
Height: 6-3
Weight: 210
Uniform no.: 6
Shoots: Right

Career statistics:

GP	G	A	TP	PIM
684	60	198	258	1,237

1991-92 statistics:

GP	G	A	TP	+/-	PIM	PP	SH	GW	GT	S	PCT
67	3	12	15	11	121	1	0	0	0	58	5.2

LAST SEASON

Missed 10 games due to strained back. Goal total was three-season high and second highest of past five seasons.

THE FINESSE GAME

When they ran into injury and depth problems last season, the Rangers had enough confidence in Cirella's ability to station him on the left side, and Cirella did the best he could to meet the challenge. He got in trouble against players with outside speed, because he is not quick of foot and had to make a decision—skate with the guy and angle him or try to play the body. Sometimes, the decision plus the direction change cost him a half-second and the guy got position anyway, which forced Cirella to hook or hold.

Cirella also saw some time on the power play, because the right point is a place where Roger Neilson tends to experiment somewhat. Sometimes he'll put a forward there, sometimes he'll put a defenseman there who is good, simply, at throwing the puck to the net to make something happen. Cirella can do that.

He has a decent touch with the puck (some stunning giveaways notwithstanding). He makes a decent first pass. He has a decent release on his slap shot from the point, and the shot has some heat on it.

THE PHYSICAL GAME

Cirella is becoming scrappier now, late in his career, than he was. He played nastier last season, probably because the option probably was play nastier or not play at all. And he scraps in a team way; last season, he even stood up for Tie Domi once, which is something you notice.

THE INTANGIBLES

This is an experienced player who has been a survivor and who will continue to be. He gets beat, but not from lack of effort. Cirella makes himself more valuable than his skills. He'll go over to the left side; he'll make something happen on the power play—or try. And that's what gets him ice time over a No. 5 or a No. 6 who can't do those things.

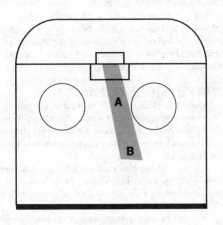

TIE DOMI

Yrs. of NHL service: 2
Born: Windsor, Ont.; Nov. 1, 1969
Position: Right wing
Height: 5-10
Weight: 195
Uniform no.: 28
Shoots: Right

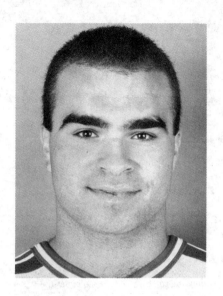

Career statistics:

GP	G	A	TP	PIM
72	3	4	7	473

1991-92 statistics:

GP	G	A	TP	+/-	PIM	PP	SH	GW	GT	S	PCT
42	2	4	6	−4	246	0	0	1	0	20	10.0

LAST SEASON

Missed eight games with sprained knee.

THE FINESSE GAME

Domi's skating ability helps him be an effort player. He is first to a lot of pucks and he is eminently capable of doing something with the disc once possession is gained.

He will lead a occasional rush, hook a drop pass to a teammate, then go to net for a rebound. He will power behind the net, get someone to chase him, then will throw the puck in front or, occasionally, use his strong wrist shot to get the puck on net.

Domi has the courage to try things, even if they don't work. He will make a backhand pass. He'll try a one-timer, even if he falls on his head.

His passing generally is underrated, but some subtleties remain that he still needs to grasp. There are times on a two-on-one when a flip pass is needed, to get over a defenseman's stick; but he'll throw it flat and get it picked off. There are similar occasions when he'll forego a shot to force a pass to a more talented teammate who has a lesser angle.

THE PHYSICAL GAME

Domi hits clean, but hits as hard as he can. He makes every defenseman pay a price. He will fight any and all heavyweights. And he is starting to get good at drawing penalties from frustrated opponents who don't like getting hit.

It doesn't matter how hard you hit if you can't get there while the target is available; Domi gets there, with power and balance. A low center of gravity makes him extremely strong on his skates.

You might expect Domi to get thrown around because of his size, and that happens sometimes when he's fighting someone with a much longer reach. But generally, when he hits, he keeps his balance; and when he gets hit, he usually doesn't go down — although the guy who hit him might.

THE INTANGIBLES

Domi doesn't get to play much, so when he's out there, you know he's going to make something happen. He's going to get noticed, whether it is by an opponent or by a referee. He keeps trying and doesn't stop working; even on his belly, he'll try to clear a puck out of danger.

There was a season-long battle to control Domi's emotions. He is a fiery fellow. But it seemed toward the end, that the battle was being won. He is likely to play more this year; he needs ice time.

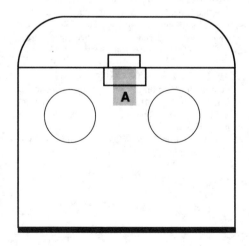

JAN ERIXON

Yrs. of NHL service: 9
Born: Skelleftea, Sweden; July 8, 1962
Position: Left wing
Height: 6-0
Weight: 195
Uniform no.: 20
Shoots: Left

Career statistics:

GP	G	A	TP	PIM
511	52	156	208	157

1991-92 statistics:

GP	G	A	TP	+/-	PIM	PP	SH	GW	GT	S	PCT
46	8	9	17	13	4	0	1	0	0	51	15.7

LAST SEASON

Missed 33 games because of various injuries, including 16 due to back troubles, nine due to neck troubles and six due to rib injury. Has not played more than 58 games in any of past four seasons, has played as many as 70 only once in past eight, but has not missed a playoff game since 1985-86.

THE FINESSE GAME

Effort, hustle, positioning, tenaciousness and hockey sense make all the difference in Erixon's game. Positioning, especially, is a key to the way he makes his living. He makes a player with the puck go around him, or through him, which is not easy, because Erixon is very smart and does a good job covering ground.

Erixon skates very well; generally, if he leaves his feet, it is by choice, because he is very difficult to knock down. He does a very good job of pursuing the puck. While killing penalties, he gouges giant chunks of time off the clock by playing keepaway with the puck; he'll accept three or four hits, move the puck a few feet, pin it against the boards, take a few more whacks and hacks, then kick the puck to his stick and clear it to a teammate.

Offensively, though, he is a bust. He shows you flashes, scores a couple of goals with moves you knew he was capable of making, and then his hands go back in storage.

THE PHYSICAL GAME

Erixon has tremendous wrist strength to control the puck with one hand. He has the leg strength for drive that keeps the puck alive along the boards and in the corners. And has the mental strength to accept the punishment he always seems to absorb.

He is a splendid forechecker who complements skating skills with hockey sense that helps him cut off the rink on a player with the puck. Erixon does not hit so much as he finishes, eliminates, rubs out. But he also pressures the puck carrier into turnovers, and his success is unquestioned as a shadow of the other team's top offensive threat.

THE INTANGIBLES

As valuable a contributor as Erixon is, health has been a problem almost from the start of his career. And while he is so exceptionally dependable in the games he plays, he is rehabilitating a work-related injury almost constantly. How much more punishment he can take is a legitimate question.

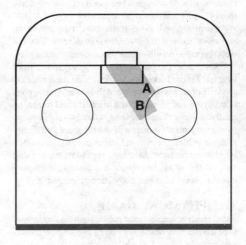

MIKE GARTNER

Yrs. of NHL service: 13
Born: Ottawa, Ont.; Oct. 29, 1959
Position: Right wing
Height: 6-0
Weight: 190
Uniform no.: 22
Shoots: Right

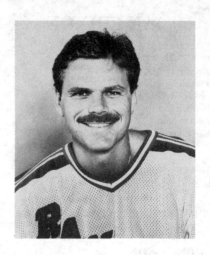

Career statistics:

GP	G	A	TP	PIM
1,005	538	501	1,039	918

1991-92 statistics:

GP	G	A	TP	+/-	PIM	PP	SH	GW	GT	S	PCT
76	40	41	81	11	55	15	0	6	0	286	14.0

LAST SEASON

Became first player in NHL history to reach milestones of 500 regular-season goals, 500 assists, 1,000 points and 1,000 games all in same season. Missed three games due to suspension. Reached 40-goal plateau a third consecutive season and became third player in league history to score 30 or more 13 consecutive seasons.

THE FINESSE GAME

Much of Gartner's game stems from his speed, and his eagerness to use it. In fact, his speed, power and remarkable acceleration sometimes hurt as much as they help: Gartner constantly is on the hunt for a timing/breakaway pass at the attacking blue line, and always makes sure his skates are onside as he accepts the puck. He then covers about 10 feet with the next sizzling stride, but linesmen constantly call him, or the pass, offside — even when taped replays regularly show Gartner's skates were legal.

Gartner could avoid those calls if he stayed an extra foot on the neutral-zone side of the blue line, but feels that tactic would negate the advantage of the play.

Sometimes the play works, however, and Gartner long has favored top corner, glove side on his breakaways. For all his outside speed, however, Gartner has virtually no inside move; and after all these years, he hardly is likely to develop one.

Other times, Gartner will use his speed and agility to drive behind the net and come out from the other side for a wraparound attempt. He favors the big slap shot off the wing, but mixes in a cunning wrist shot that has plenty of upper-body strength behind it.

THE PHYSICAL GAME

Gartner's penalty total may be misleadingly low, as he plays a very physical game and gets a tremendous amount of ice time. And while he certainly is an outside shooting threat, Gartner is by no means a perimeter player.

When the puck is at the point, he'll always post-up in front of the net, looking either to draw the attention of a defenseman, to screen the goalie or to attempt a deflection. Gartner eagerly cycles in the corners. He drives to the net and makes maximum use of his size, speed and strength.

And he does virtually all of it within the rules, though he regularly is crosschecked, hacked and tripped as opponents try to slow or stop him.

THE INTANGIBLES

Despite his achievement and tenure, Gartner earns the respect of his peers every night with a work ethic that most rookies would do well to emulate. There is a desperation to his game as the Stanley Cup continues to elude him; though he is in remarkable shape for one so travelled, he is not getting any younger. He does not have many chances left.

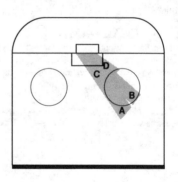

RANDY GILHEN

Yrs. of NHL service: 4
Born: Zweibrucken, West Germany; June 13, 1963
Position: Center
Height: 6-0
Weight: 190
Uniform no.: 16
Shoots: Left

Career statistics:

GP	G	A	TP	PIM
287	38	40	78	186

1991-92 statistics:

GP	G	A	TP	+/-	PIM	PP	SH	GW	GT	S	PCT
73	10	13	23	2	28	0	1	0	0	99	10.1

LAST SEASON

Obtained Dec. 23, 1991, from Los Angeles for Corey Millen. Goal total was second best of his career.

THE FINESSE GAME

Gilhen is not a gifted skater in the least. His stride lacks power, it takes him a while to get going, and isn't very fast, really, once he reaches top speed.

But he can play center and left wing, versatility which gets him in the lineup more often and on the ice more often than if he played only one position. He does a responsible job defensively as the 'third man high' in the attacking zone, and swoops to an uncovered area of the ice if a teammate has gambled on offense.

Gilhen doesn't get many shots because he doesn't have the puck much. Offense is not his role, so 10 goals actually is a fairly creditable output.

THE PHYSICAL GAME

Gilhen gets the dirty-work jobs, like winning the first face-off of a penalty kill in the defensive zone. He gets to scrum in the sludge along the boards. He does it, does it well, because it keeps him in the league.

THE INTANGIBLES

Gilhen is a good guy for a dressing room, a respectable elder who seems an attentive listener as well as a good speaker, a fellow who is important to the team's chemistry. He just knows how to fit in, how to make himself valuable.

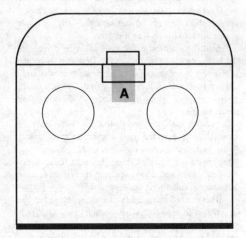

ADAM GRAVES

Yrs. of NHL service: 4
Born: Toronto, Ont.; April 12, 1968
Position: Left wing
Height: 6-0
Weight: 185
Uniform no.: 9
Shoots: Left

Career statistics:

GP	G	A	TP	PIM
297	49	70	119	801

1991-92 statistics:

GP	G	A	TP	+/-	PIM	PP	SH	GW	GT	S	PCT
80	26	33	59	19	139	4	4	4	0	228	11.4

LAST SEASON

More than doubled his career total in goals. Marked career highs in goals, assists and points.

THE FINESSE GAME

Graves is a prototype left wing, because in the NHL these days, that position goes to the plowhorse for the playmaking center and the scoring right wing. The left wing initiates a play, then passes to the scorers on his line, and Graves does those things extremely well. As a bonus, Graves put away lots of the chances his forechecking created last season — suggesting he is coming into his own as a scorer.

Still, it is almost a surprise when he drives into the left-wing circle and takes the first shot of a rush. It is a very good shot — low, hard and heavy — and it creates rebounds. But he isn't a first-shot scorer; his goals come off going to the net and shooting from closer range.

Skating isn't his greatest asset, but Graves is smooth on his feet and agile enough to react quickly to the surprise arrival of a puck. His balance and strength cannot be questioned, because he is always banging bodies and always scrumming in the war zones but never seems to get knocked down.

This overall strength, combined with the fact that he has played center, enables a coach to use Graves be used on face-offs. He can even be trusted to win draws in the defensive zone. And he is an effective penalty killer who always makes sure to finish the check on his point man, driving him, at least temporarily, off the blue line.

THE PHYSICAL GAME

A solid grinder with skill, Graves is much more likely to win a one-on-one battle of strength than a one-on-one finesse battle with a goalie. His nightly duty is to neutralize A) the other team's better offensive defenseman or B), the other team's biggest defenseman. Graves checks Paul Coffey, Kevin Hatcher or Sylvain Cote and Petr Svoboda, Al MacInnis, Uwe Krupp or Kjell Samuelsson. He bangs them hard, fronts them up ice effectively and keeps them from joining the play. His physical presence often forces them to rush plays, or to make plays they don't want to make.

Graves will hit anybody, anywhere, anytime. He'll hit a defenseman to free the puck. He'll hit in the corners. He'll fight if you messed with his teammates. He wakes up the crowd, wakes up his bench and keeps the intensity high.

THE INTANGIBLES

Graves is a first-, second- and third-effort player wrongly branded for his slash of Mario Lemieux last spring. He doesn't play that way, he doesn't need to play that way. He plays hard and tough and he's a nightmare to play against, but he is no cheapshot.

The question, though, is whether Graves was in any way scarred by the outcry for his head. Suspensions have a more profound effect on most players than you might think.

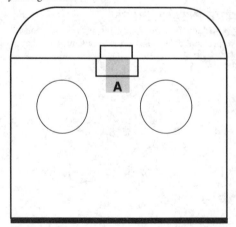

MARK HARDY

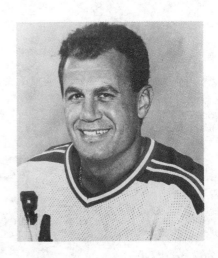

Yrs. of NHL service: 13
Born: Semaden, Sweden; Feb. 1, 1959
Position: Left defense
Height: 5-11
Weight: 195
Uniform no.: 14
Shoots: Left

Career statistics:

GP	G	A	TP	PIM
844	65	290	355	1,177

1991-92 statistics:

GP	G	A	TP	+/-	PIM	PP	SH	GW	GT	S	PCT
52	1	8	9	33	65	0	0	1	0	42	2.4

LAST SEASON

Missed 24 games due to separated right shoulder, five due to sprained back. Plus-minus was second best on team.

THE FINESSE GAME

Hardy has the wheels to get to the loose pucks. He has the confidence in his ability to skate the puck out of the defensive zone and make something happen on the other side of the red line. He has good range, good mobility, the hands to start a quick transition game and a good sense of when to jump into the rush.

And he has the smarts. Hardy will get wrapped up in offense occasionally, but he sees the ice pretty well and uses a healthy helping of hockey sense to decide when to go deep and when to play cautiously. When he loses the puck, he works hard to get it back.

Since he has two goals over three seasons, you know Hardy generally does not shoot to score. He shoots to get the puck to the net so somebody else can score. He shoots to cause a rebound, to set up a deflection. The odd time, he will fake a shot, get an opponent to drop in front, then skate around the guy and try to make a play. Twice last season, he and partner James Patrick led two-on-one rushes.

THE PHYSICAL GAME

A steady defenseman who plays within himself, Hardy always tries to get a piece of his man. If he can't shoulder his check, he will at least put the stick on him and make some presence felt. He is a trusted penalty killer who will throw himself in front of point shots. He shows up for the wars in front of the net, but is not big enough or strong enough to just man-handle people; Hardy is more likely to nullify the player's stick and use his smarts to gain advantage.

THE INTANGIBLES

Hardy receives respect because he has respect for the game and for his job. That respect translates into dependability on the ice in virtually any situation, including four-on-four, and consistent workmanship.

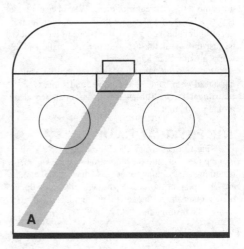

KRIS KING

Yrs. of NHL service: 4
Born: Bracebridge, Ont.; Feb. 18, 1966
Position: Left wing
Height: 5-11
Weight: 210
Uniform no.: 19
Shoots: Left

Career statistics:

GP	G	A	TP	PIM
277	30	33	63	836

1991-92 statistics:

GP	G	A	TP	+/-	PIM	PP	SH	GW	GT	S	PCT
79	10	9	19	13	224	0	0	2	0	97	10.3

LAST SEASON

Plus-minus improved by 14 goals, although goals, assists and points total dropped while PIM increased by 48 over prior season. Collected first two game-winning goals of his career.

THE FINESSE GAME

There is something to be said for momentum, and King probably is the one to say it. He isn't the world's greatest stickhandler, and he knows it; but he makes the effort, getting up a big head of steam as he drives up the left side. And while he may lose the puck once or twice in the process, momentum often carries him directly to the place the puck bounces to; King reclaims it as though that is the way he planned it all along — not so much a rush but two or three passes to himself.

He is a muscle guy first, a checker, a preventer of goals more than a creator of them. When he scores, it is with a bomb of a slap shot that carries every ounce of strength in his being . . . or it is one of those pucks he just throws at the net — better the goalie should worry about it than King should.

But King does skate well in a straight line, churning ahead with balance and power and some type of centrifugal force. Turns give him a small world of problems, though.

THE PHYSICAL GAME

King finishes every check possible. He's always looking for a hit, and the bigger, the better. And there is nothing 21st Century about his game; if you and he are scrapping at the boards, he will give your upper body a giant shove, move you off the puck, and snap it toward a teammate.

THE INTANGIBLES

King is much more head and heart than hands and feet. He gives you positively every molecule of himself; he doesn't save a thing for tomorrow night's game, which is why he plays in tomorrow night's game.

And he loves to agitate opponents, which make him an effective checking-line player and the perfect foil for right wings like Claude Lemieux.

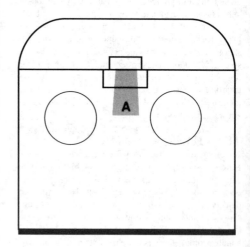

JOEY KOCUR

Yrs. of NHL service: 7
Born: Calgary, Alta.; Dec. 21, 1964
Position: Left wing
Height: 6-0
Weight: 210
Uniform no.: 26
Shoots: Right

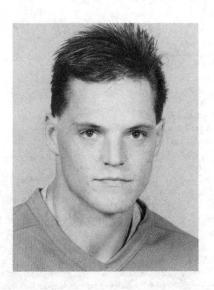

Career statistics:

GP	G	A	TP	PIM
455	63	59	122	1,871

1991-92 statistics:

GP	G	A	TP	+/-	PIM	PP	SH	GW	GT	S	PCT
51	7	4	11	-4	121	0	0	2	0	72	9.7

LAST SEASON

Missed one game due to suspension, 22 due to various injuries. Two winning goals improved his career total to 11.

THE FINESSE GAME

Kocur plays an intimidating game, but his finesse skills have nothing to do with the intimidation. His skating is okay, straight ahead, but direction changes are troublesome. He has a hard enough shot, but will do most of his scoring from scrambles, deflections and rebounds.

Kocur will go to the boards and tie up a wing or defenseman, which leaves the puck free for a teammate. He'll get the puck deep, then go to work to get it back. He'll go to the front of the net and force a defenseman to grab him.

But his main role is that of The Great Equalizer. You put out your tough guy, I'm going to put out Mr. One Punch Knockout. You run my goalie, Joey K. will be paying your goalie a visit.

THE PHYSICAL GAME

While there is no mistaking that his right hand is his meal ticket, the fact remains this player can, at times, be found on the ice in the last minute of a game with the Rangers protecting a one-goal lead. The fact is, along with his punching strength, Kocur is physically strong enough to skate through the interference after a defensive-zone draw and get out to try to block or hurry the shooter at the point. Sometimes it works, sometimes it doesn't.

Strength also allows Kocur to camp in front of the net and plant his stick on the ice, providing a nice big target for his point men. He's gotten more than a few deflection goals that way. How strong is he? In a game against Pittsburgh last season, Kocur shot a puck THROUGH the net.

THE INTANGIBLES

A team benefits from his contribution in the dressing room, needs his toughness. Kocur is a persistent, give-you-everything type of player. But he has been giving everything for a long time; his body is battered from the sacrifice.

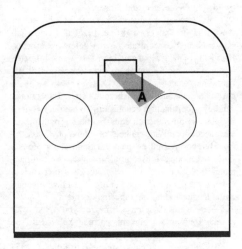

BRIAN LEETCH

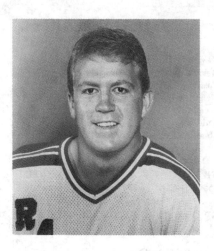

Yrs. of NHL service: 5
Born: Corpus Christi, Tex.; March 3, 1968
Position: Left defense
Height: 5-11
Weight: 192
Uniform no.: 2
Shoots: Left

Career statistics:

GP	G	A	TP	PIM
317	74	257	331	44

1991-92 statistics:

GP	G	A	TP	+/-	PIM	PP	SH	GW	GT	S	PCT
80	22	80	102	25	26	10	1	3	1	245	9.0

LAST SEASON

Won Norris Trophy as NHL's top defenseman after becoming fifth defenseman in league history to reach 100 points. Led NHL defensemen in scoring.

THE FINESSE GAME

Leetch still has trouble finishing some of the brilliant rushes he makes into the attacking zone, but he's getting better at it. A deep pushoff puts the power in his skating stride while his hands, eyes and head all work in perfect unison to choreograph his dashes up ice: he sees the holes, jumps into them with speed and agility, and stickhandles around virtually every obstacle in his path.

If he wants to buy time until a teammate gets open, Leetch will stickhandle laterally in the neutral zone, draw a checker or two, then feather a perfect pass. If he wants to take the puck to the net, Leetch now has the confidence — and the command of his skills — to try to split the defense and score.

His offense is always dictated by the score, though. If the Rangers don't need a goal, Leetch will stay back and concentrate on the defensive aspects. His vision of the ice and anticipation is so good, Leetch always seems to know where the puck is going. His lateral movement is so good, Leetch always seems to cut off the ice and get to the puck first. Exceptional hand-eye coordination enables him to bat pucks out of the air — a plus at both ends — and strength on his stick accounts for any number of intercepted passes.

His scoring figures speak for themselves. He is a fairly exceptional passer in all manners; he can one-touch it, pass on the forehand or hook a drop pass. He governs the point on the power play as well as anybody in the league and his shot is a major threat.

If he were all offense, though, you'd see a lot more two-on-ones against his partner. You hardly see any. When Leetch is caught deep in the attacking zone, he makes sure to get back, and he more than has the skating speed to do so.

THE PHYSICAL GAME

He does not play a vigorous physical game, but the Rangers probably wouldn't want him to, anyway. Leetch will play your stick, he'll stick his butt in your way, but that is the most you can expect of him most nights. He isn't going to grind. He'll go in the corners and work for the puck, but when he hits, he hits high, which makes it easier for opponents to wriggle away in the corners.

THE INTANGIBLES

Brian Leetch still wants to get better, wants to be known for consistent excellence, and over the course of time, he will achieve that aim. Mark Messier taught him some lessons about winning and wanting more every day. Leetch took the advice and turned himself into a Norris winner. Now comes the next step up: to repeat after signing a big-money contract.

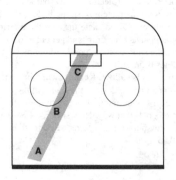

MARK MESSIER

Yrs. of NHL service: 13
Born: Edmonton, Alta.; Jan. 18, 1961
Position: Center
Height: 6-1
Weight: 210
Uniform no.: 11
Shoots: Left

Career statistics:

GP	G	A	TP	PIM
930	427	714	1,141	1,198

1991-92 statistics:

GP	G	A	TP	+/-	PIM	PP	SH	GW	GT	S	PCT
79	35	72	107	31	76	12	4	6	0	212	16.5

LAST SEASON

Obtained from Edmonton, Oct. 5, 1991, for Bernie Nicholls, Louie DeBrusk and Steven Rice. Became only fourth 100-point scorer in Rangers history.

THE FINESSE GAME

One of the remarkable skaters in the game, Messier makes acceleration, speed, agility, balance, strength and stamina all work to his benefit. He controls the pace of the rush and the game.

Defensemen know he's going to be faster going forward than they are going backward, so they have to concede territory and Messier makes use of that time and space. He'll stop short with the puck, let everyone else react, then check his options and find the proper target with a precise pass.

He's got nice hands, a nice passing touch and nice smarts. He'll carry behind the net from the goalie's left, then throw the puck back in front against the grain —a goalie's nightmare. He will go to the net and one-touch an alley-oop pass from a teammate. He will muscle a bullet over the goalie's glove hand.

Messier isn't much for one-on-one moves. He is more of a power guy when he gets near the net, and there are limits to his puck movement. Sometimes, as he runs the power play from the side boards, Messier tries to force passes through people. Other times, decisions have to be made long before he seems to make them; too many seconds click off the clock.

But when his team needs a goal to get on the scoreboard first, to take the lead, to pull even, to grab a game that is sitting on the table, Messier scores it or sets it up. He always finds a new way to beat you, which is what makes him a premier player.

THE PHYSICAL GAME

A specimen of stunning physical strength, Messier only steamrolled a couple of players last season. He bumped people, but New Yorkers spent lots of time wondering when his vaunted physical presence would show itself more regularly.

The fear factor of playing against him doesn't seem to be there as much as it used to be. Defensemen still worry about his speed, but he didn't give them much reason last season to worry that he'd knock their teeth out. On the other hand, a lot of that could be the tremendous respect Messier commands on the ice and the amount of room defenders give him.

THE INTANGIBLES

Messier was everything to his team last season because he set higher and higher expectations for himself, for the Rangers, even for the coaching staff. The team got some ambition, at long last. It got a taste of what is required for success. Messier wants to win, and you better want to win, too.

Now, nearing 31, with a lot of hockey behind him, Messier must do it all, and more, over again — a far greater challenge than doing it the first time. Do not mistake the challenge placed in front of him and the responsibility heaped on his shoulders: to make Stanley Cup champions of the Rangers. Nothing less.

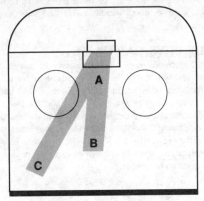

SERGEI NEMCHINOV

Yrs. of NHL service: 1
Born: Moscow, Russia; Jan. 14, 1964
Position: Center
Height: 6-0
Weight: 205
Uniform no.: 13
Shoots: Left

Career statistics:

GP	G	A	TP	PIM
73	30	28	58	15

1991-92 statistics:

GP	G	A	TP	+/-	PIM	PP	SH	GW	GT	S	PCT
73	30	28	58	19	15	2	0	5	0	124	24.2

LAST SEASON

Game-winning goal total was third on team. Shooting percentage ranked fourth in league. Scored all but nine of his points at even strength. Had more points on road (33) than at home (25). Missed seven games due to sprained knee.

THE FINESSE GAME

Nemchinov is a solid two-way player of good skills—a smooth, strong skater who plays at a steady, controlled speed whether he has the puck or is working to get it. He has a long stride, very good balance and very good hand-eye coordination; even if a pass is coming in his skates, Nemchinov is able to keep focused on the net, bend deeply to accept the off-target pass, and still aim an accurate shot on net.

Nemchinov changes directions easily on the glide but struggles somewhat with quick starts and stops. He isn't a dancer on skates, isn't very agile or shifty, but he is an effective playmaker in the attacking zone and a dedicated backchecker on defense.

Though his goal production was quite high last season and his shooting percentage was excellent, that statistic is a tad misleading. His release on the snap shot can be a trifle slow. And because he always seems to want the perfect shot, he often sends three or four shots wide for every one he makes the goalie worry about.

THE PHYSICAL GAME

Nemchinov uses his body nicely to protect the puck and will throw his back or his shoulder into a defenseman while retaining possession. But he has to play with linemates who are alert without the puck; he will create open ice for them by drawing the attention of defensemen, but they have to be alert enough to read the play and react. Generally, he gets a pass to the place they should be, but sometimes the puck simply goes up for grabs.

Nemchinov willingly blocks point shots while killing penalties, and he is not without sly tricks. He'll wedge himself into the corner with a player and hold the opponent's stick so a teammate can come and get the puck.

THE INTANGIBLES

If there is a trademark to Nemchinov's game, it is his steadiness. A veteran of high-level competition, Nemchinov never tries to do more than he is capable of doing. By staying within his strengths, by exploiting his two-way skills, he can be an extremely solid third-line center.

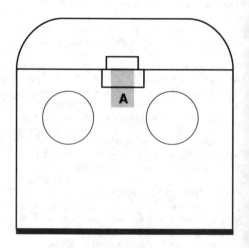

JOHN OGRODNICK

Yrs. of NHL service: 13
Born: Ottawa, Ont.; June 20, 1959
Position: Left wing
Height: 6-0
Weight: 205
Uniform no.: 25
Shoots: Left

Career statistics:

GP	G	A	TP	PIM
909	396	419	815	258

1991-92 statistics:

GP	G	A	TP	+/-	PIM	PP	SH	GW	GT	S	PCT
55	17	13	30	6	22	3	0	4	0	110	15.5

LAST SEASON

Rangers were 34-18-2 with him in lineup. Missed four games due to back spasms, one due to wrist injury.

THE FINESSE GAME

Ogrodnick no longer is much of a threat to score with a bomb from the wing. He just doesn't get the puck much in that area of the ice any more, and certainly is not used in a role where he is depended on for offense.

In fact, last season, he wasn't depended on for much of anything. Though an effective short-game player who can score trash goals off scrambles or deflections, Ogrodnick needed to score consistently to stay in the lineup; he saw less and less action after scoring 10 goals in the first 20 games.

Ogrodnick is a good skater. He is quick for his size, gets his feet wide apart for extensive strength. He has a powerful shot, and gets it off rather quickly. He makes a decent pass, although it's a marvel Ogrodnick propels the puck at all, given the mutilated stick blade he favors.

THE PHYSICAL GAME

Although he will throw an occasional check, Ogrodnick doesn't initiate much physically. He isn't a player for a dump-and-chase game, because he isn't likely to smear a defenseman and dish the puck.

Ogrodnick still can be considered a physical player, however, because he goes to physical areas of the ice. In his quest for rebounds or deflections, he absorbs the punishment in front of the net. He darts into the scrambles to poach for loose pucks. He goes into the corners and can be an effective cycler. He has very good balance and is very hard to knock down.

THE INTANGIBLES

Something about his play has thrown off Ranger coaches since Michel Bergeron was coach, but those rare times he gets out of the doghouse, Ogrodnick still produces very decent numbers. For the amount he played last year, and given that he lost both linemates in the expansion process, 17 goals is exceptional output and convincing evidence of his ability to set hassles aside when game time comes.

It says here he still has something to offer an NHL team. The fact is, he still has something to offer a Rangers team that is hardly overstocked on the left side, but it's past time for a new address — for his sake.

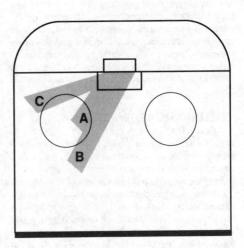

JAMES PATRICK

Yrs. of NHL service: 8
Born: Winnipeg, Man.; June 14, 1963
Position: Right defense
Height: 6-2
Weight: 205
Uniform no.: 3
Shoots: Right

Career statistics:

GP	G	A	TP	PIM
605	99	339	438	478

1991-92 statistics:

GP	G	A	TP	+/-	PIM	PP	SH	GW	GT	S	PCT
80	14	57	71	34	54	6	0	1	0	148	9.5

LAST SEASON

Plus-minus improved by 39 goals, point total increased by 12. Assists total was career high, scoring total was sixth among all NHL defensemen.

THE FINESSE GAME

James Patrick skates faster laterally than some players can skate forward. He skates backward faster than most players can skate forward. He is nimble, agile, able to stop on a dime and start on a penny. So he has no trouble reaching the puck, and he has the hands and the vision of the ice to do something with it once possession is gained.

Patrick prefers to pass more than to shoot, prefers the safe play to the risky one. He's a guy who can go behind his net on a power play, beat a forechecker, skate the puck to the red line and dump it in the zone to start the half-court game. If that's so easy to do, how come half the league always seems to be looking for someone who can do it?

Patrick jumps into the play nicely — sometimes for gap control, sometimes for support, sometimes for offense—and uses a quick release. His shot is accurate enough to weave through traffic and probably is an underrated aspect of his game; he started making things happen with it in the second half last season, once he had recovered strength after a wrist injury had hindered him.

THE PHYSICAL GAME

Patrick is a finesse player in a physically demanding position. He gets involved. He bumps. He shoulders people. He stands up at the blue line. But he isn't much for the one-on-one battles in the corners or in front of the net; the stick is his primary checking tool.

Sometimes his reluctance about physical play cuts into his skating asset. Though he is agile and has no trouble turning, and uses those tools in angling forwards toward the corners, Patrick sometimes has trouble with moves to his outside. Sometimes he has to put a hook on a guy and hold on for the ride.

In penalty-killing situations, Patrick's greatest asset is exceptional range, discipline and hockey sense. He easily can go to the corners to harry the puck-carrier into making a decision, then can get back in time to regain position and try to block a shot if the puck gets to the point. He does a good job of getting the puck clear of the zone during shortages.

Patrick also is strong on his stick and on the puck. He occasionally drives to the net with the puck, occasionally skates through checks, but he leaves you wanting more.

THE INTANGIBLES

James Patrick makes you wonder, "Is that all there is?" With his size, with his skating skill, with his touch, you speculate what kind of player Patrick would be if he added an element of risk, of danger — if he had some riverboat gambler in him, if he just shed the shackles of caution every once in a while and said, "I'm GOING for it."

But then it always comes back to the fact that this, by choice, is a spectacularly unspectacular player. And if you trade him, you always run the risk of not appreciating what he brings to the game until you don't have those qualities on your team any more.

MIKE RICHTER

Yrs. of NHL service: 3
Born: Abington, Pa.; Sept. 22, 1966
Position: Goaltender
Height: 5-10
Weight: 185
Uniform no.: 35
Catches: Left

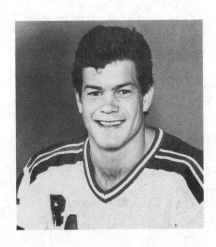

Career statistics:

GP	MINS	GA	SO	GAA	A	PIM
109	6,215	320	3	3.09	4	10

1991-92 statistics:

GP	MINS	GAA	W	L	T	SO	GA	S	SAPCT	PIM
41	2,298	3.11	23	12	2	3	119	1,205	.901	6

LAST SEASON

Save percentage tied for fifth in NHL. Shutouts were his first in NHL. Won 20 or more games for second consecutive season. Won skills competition at all-star game in hometown Philadelphia. Missed 12 games due to torn groin muscle.

THE PHYSICAL GAME

Richter is capable of winning games by himself. The higher the shot total, the greater the Rangers' chance of winning some nights. He seems to thrive on the work, although he creates some of it by failing to control rebounds as well as he will in time.

The rebounds are the result of Richter being more a shot blocker than a shot absorber. He uses his pads a lot, uses his body a lot, but doesn't use his gloves that much, so the puck tends to fly free.

Exceptionally athletic, extremely strong in the legs and trunk, especially explosive to his left, Richter may have the best lateral movement of any goalie in the NHL. He really drives into the puck on passes across the goalmouth and can take your breath away by stealing sure goals.

But he makes the game harder on himself than it should be because of his reluctance to use his stick in defensive situations. He doesn't get passes out of the corners or passes from behind the net, so he ends up facing point-blank shots. He'll use an occasional poke check if a guy is cutting in, but that remains more the exception than the rule.

Still, his stance is excellent, he is able to move in any direction. He recovers well for second shots. Teams tend to test him low stick and high glove, but Richter will face a hail of long shots this season after a Ron Francis drive beat him from outside the blue line in Pittsburgh and turned around Game 4 of the Patrick Division Final.

THE MENTAL GAME

It is difficult to say how much fun Richter had last season. There were times when it seemed he was working, not enjoying, and enjoyment appears a key element of his performance. His statistics improved in a lot of areas, though, the team was successful, and Richter played a big role in that success.

THE INTANGIBLES

Richter is solid positionally, splendid laterally and strong reflexively. He makes you hurry your plays, forces you to make a very good shot to beat him most of the time. He was an All-Star on merit last midseason.

Shortcomings in stick skills keep him from being the complete package, though, and he knows it. Still, there is plenty of time for him to add them to his substantial repertoire.

DARREN TURCOTTE

Yrs. of NHL service: 3
Born: Boston, Mass.; March 2, 1968
Position: Center
Height: 6-0
Weight: 180
Uniform no.: 8
Shoots: Right

Career statistics:

GP	G	A	TP	PIM
241	95	101	196	130

1991-92 statistics:

GP	G	A	TP	+/-	PIM	PP	SH	GW	GT	S	PCT
71	30	23	53	11	57	13	1	4	1	216	13.9

LAST SEASON

Scored 25 goals or more for third consecutive season. Notched at least one hat trick for fourth consecutive year. Missed four games due to sore ribs, five due to foot troubles.

THE FINESSE GAME

You could call him "Air Turcotte" for his skating ability. He seems to glide above the ice and cover a tremendous amount of ground with each stride. This is a player who makes things happen, who drives defenses back with his speed and puck control.

Speed helps Turcotte in two other areas. He is an effective penalty killer because he can challenge the points and is always a threat for the odd shorthanded goal. He also reaches top speed very quickly, which makes him a top-level breakaway threat and more than keeps opposing defensemen honest. And on the other side of the puck, Turcotte uses his speed to hurry the puck carrier on the forecheck.

Turcotte is a close-range scorer who favors a quick-release one-timer, snap shot or wrist shot over the big slap. He can finesse the puck into the net or muscle it with equal ease. The method doesn't matter; Turcotte makes sure on his chances, and he seems to score when it matters, when the pressure's on.

A good dose of hockey sense makes Turcotte a trustworthy player in key situations. He handles a tremendous amount of defensive assignments against the better centers in the league, but also gets time at the right point on the power play because of his offensive skills.

THE PHYSICAL GAME

Turcotte cannot be termed a physical player; he accepts being hit more than he initiates. But he willingly does what he can to gets his nose dirty. He takes the puck to the net on offense. He challenges the point man while killing penalties, and always is getting his feet in front of point shots.

THE INTANGIBLES

Darren Turcotte centered a checking line last season, played with linemates of underwhelming offensive skills, and still scored 16 even-strength goals — a jump of seven from the prior season. That's a coach's dream. He is a sparkplug. You'd have to figure he'd be centering the second scoring line on any other team.

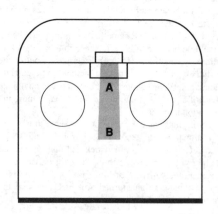

JOHN VANBIESBROUCK

Yrs. of NHL service: 8
Born: Detroit, Mich.; Sept. 4, 1963
Position: Goaltender
Height: 5-9
Weight: 175
Uniform no.: 34
Catches: Left

Career statistics:

GP	MINS	GA	SO	GAA	A	PIM
401	22,623	1,306	12	3.46	24	194

1991-92 statistics:

GP	MINS	GAA	W	L	T	SO	GA	S	SAPCT	PIM
45	2,526	2.85	27	13	3	2	120	1,331	.910	23

LAST SEASON

Went 12-0-3 his final 15 games at home and finished with 8-0-1 overall streak, during which he permitted just 11 goals. Save percentage tied for second in NHL. GAA was fourth in league. Reached double figures in victories at home and on road for first time since 1987-88. Missed five games due to back spasms.

THE PHYSICAL GAME

Vanbiesbrouck does a very nice job of staying square with the puck and always knows where the net is. He is extremely aggressive, and virtually never gives up a goal because he is doing too little; he goes down swinging. He stands up well, virtually never goes down early, and can react to deflections.

Vanbiesbrouck has tremendous confidence in his ability to use his stick. And while that shows most often in the offensive aspects, when he wings the puck off the boards or straight down the middle of the ice, it is his use of the stick as a defensive weapon that earns him more points. He has great trust in the poke check and uses it very effectively on breakaways and cut-ins. And he uses the stick to block any pass he can reach from the corners, end boards or side boards.

He is a fundamentally strong goaltender who always challenges the shooters. He plays out of the inverted-V, crouched, seemingly planted on his inside edges, but is able to explode to any direction. He is quick on low shots and has a good-to-excellent glove.

Vanbiesbrouck is extremely patient and confident in one-on-one conflict, even against the slithery types like Mario Lemieux or Pavel Bure. He bites less now on the first move. It is as though he makes the shooter worry about him, when usually it is the goalie who is supposed to worry about the shooter.

THE MENTAL GAME

This goalie can play, and excel, in big games. He has a very good handle on the situation and can make the home crowd loud with a big save and a dramatic smother on the rebound. He has a good grasp of when his team needs a face-off and when to keep the puck in play.

Vanbiesbrouck gets in a little trouble when he gets frustrated. He will let up occasionally if the score is lopsided, but he tightens the screws if the game gets close.

THE INTANGIBLES

Vanbiesbrouck really has grown up, has matured, has come to grips with the realities of goaltending for a living — which mean don't get too high or too low — and now is one of the mentally tough competitors in the league. He stole points last season the way he did in 1986, regularly carried the team, even though he had to sing for his supper every night.

DOUG WEIGHT

Yrs. of NHL service: 1
Born: Mt. Clemens, Mich.; Jan. 21, 1971
Position: Center
Height: 5-11
Weight: 195
Uniform no.: 39
Shoots: Left

Career statistics:

GP	G	A	TP	PIM
53	8	22	30	23

1991-92 statistics:

GP	G	A	TP	+/-	PIM	PP	SH	GW	GT	S	PCT
53	8	22	30	-3	23	0	0	2	0	72	11.1

LAST SEASON

Missed 14 games due to injury, including nine because of chip fracture in wrist.

THE FINESSE GAME

Weight is stocky, thick and as enthusiastic as a puppy with a slipper. He's no speedster, but he has good balance, decent quickness, a good first step and an acceptable change of direction that enables him to get open for a return pass.

His hands are pretty good. Weight makes use of the wrist shot and the snap shot and passes equally well to both sides. Because he sees the ice well and anticipates well, he can spot a breaking teammate and throw a pass to an open space so the wing can skate into it with speed.

Weight has no problem with close quarters. He almost seems to like it or feel more comfortable in a one-on-one corner battle, as he likes to use his feet on the puck.

THE PHYSICAL GAME

Weight is strong on his skates and strong on his stick, which makes him respectable on face-offs. He hits hard, hits solid and hits as often as possible; he never met a check he didn't want to finish.

Mixed in is a healthy amount of spirit. He is an energetic forechecker and backchecker, a bull-terrier kind of player who always seems to be nipping.

Weight is on the yappy side and he is not sheepish about expressing himself. The fact is, when he controls that emotionalism and makes it work for him, Weight adds an attractive dimension to his game. He needs to

play that way to do well; he just can't go overboard with it. But on those sleepy February nights against Hartford, Weight can provide a nice little wake-up call if he wants to.

THE INTANGIBLES

Weight is a player to watch for the future. He is eager, wants to improve and is brutally honest with himself every night about whether he did all he could. Off last season, he has more the look of a solid checking-line center than a scorer, although 15 or 20 goals shouldn't be too much to ask.

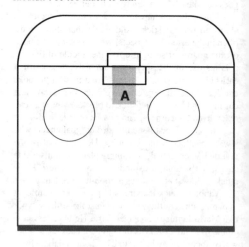

OTTAWA SENATORS

LAURIE BOSCHMAN

Yrs. of NHL service: 13
Born: Major, Sask.; June 4, 1960
Position: Center
Height: 6-0
Weight: 185
Uniform no.: 16
Shoots: Left

Career statistics:

GP	G	A	TP	PIM
939	220	341	561	2164

1991-92 statistics:

GP	G	A	TP	+/-	PIM	PP	SH	GW	GT	S	PCT
75	8	20	28	9	121	0	0	2	0	89	9.0

LAST SEASON

Claimed from New Jersey in 1992 Expansion Draft. Goals career low.

THE FINESSE GAME

Once a good defensive forward with a good scoring touch (he had four seasons with 25 or more goals), Boschman provides hardly any offense anymore. He still is a hard worker and most of his goals will come from his grinding around the net. Boschman is also smart enough to be a shorthanded threat. He lacks breakaway speed, but is a deceptive skater and will occasionally surprise the defense.

Boschman's role as a checker is diminishing, however, since he lacks the speed and the strength to keep up with the league's top centers. The Devils even stopped using Boschman in that role in the second half of last season, utilizing their better-skating centers instead, even though they lacked Boschman's defensive knowledge.

THE PHYSICAL GAME

Boschman's skills are on the decline, but he can still be a very pesky, in-your-face checker. He is very good at getting away with holding penalties, making it look as if he were the injured party instead of the guilty one. He is not a quitter and is very tenacious, using his wiry strength in battles along the boards.

THE INTANGIBLES

Boschman is strictly a defensive forward who is on his way out. The Devils didn't use him against other team's top lines as they once did, nor did Boschman take many key face-offs. To his credit, Boschman remains a hard worker and an honest player who will give you what he's got, but most nights that isn't enough.

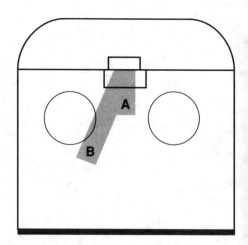

250

MARK FREER

Yrs. of NHL service: 1
Born: Peterborough, Ont.; July 14, 1968
Position: Center
Height: 5-10
Weight: 185
Uniform no.: 37
Shoots: Left

Career statistics:

GP	G	A	TP	PIM
59	6	9	15	18

1991-92 statistics:

GP	G	A	TP	+/-	PIM	PP	SH	GW	GT	S	PCT
50	6	7	13	−1	18	0	0	2	0	41	14.6

LAST SEASON

Claimed from Philadelphia in 1992 Expansion Draft. First NHL season.

THE FINESSE GAME

Freer had good numbers as a junior with Peterborough and in the Flyers system with Hersey, but has not been able to play the game on a consistent, quality basis in the NHL.

Freer has good hockey sense. Since he is a small player, he likes to glide around until the defense forgets about him, then slide in the back door. He doesn't have much on his shot and scores most of his goals from sneaking in to the side of the net.

A fair skater with average mobility, he can be used to kill penalties because he has good anticipation.

THE PHYSICAL GAME

Freer lacks size and strength; while he was been put into a checking role with the Flyers, he may lack the frame to match up well against opposing forwards. Players are getting bigger and more mobile, and Freer doesn't have the skating speed to overcome his other weaknesses.

THE INTANGIBLES

Freer saw limited ice time with the Flyers, but will be given more responsibilities with the expansion Senators. He could become a solid NHL citizen, but that will depend on how he's used and how his scoring develops. Right now, Freer appears to lack the skills to be much of a scorer and is too small to be an effective checker . . . none of which bodes well for a successful career.

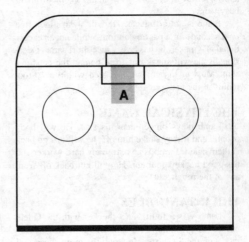

MARK LAMB

Yrs. of NHL service: 5
Born: Ponteix, Sask.; Aug. 3, 1964
Position: Center
Height: 5-9
Weight: 180
Uniform no.: 7
Shoots: Left

Career statistics:

GP	G	A	TP	PIM
199	26	55	81	135

1991-92 statistics:

GP	G	A	TP	+/-	PIM	PP	SH	GW	GT	S	PCT
59	6	22	28	4	46	2	0	1	0	61	9.8

LAST SEASON

Claimed from Edmonton in 1992 Expansion Draft. Games played and assists career highs. Points matched career high.

THE FINESSE GAME

Lamb has good speed and quickness but does not have enough offensive ability to overcome his lack of size. His agility and hand skills make him a very persistent forechecker. Lamb doesn't play the body, but he will use his stick to harass the puck carrier and force a turnover. Most of his scoring chances come from his busy work.

Lamb is not a finisher. He will always look first (and second) for a passing option. While not an exceptional playmaker, he has a very nice short game. Occasionally he will sneak out from behind the net for a shot. Most of his goals are scored within a 10-foot radius of the net.

THE PHYSICAL GAME

Lamb plays bigger than his size. He will body people, and if they shake him off, he will just go back at them again. Lamb is an extremely hard worker and has good hockey courage. He will not back off from any of the rough stuff.

THE INTANGIBLES

Lamb was a fourth-line checker with the Oilers but will be given more ice time and more responsibilities with the Senators. He would be more successful playing with bigger linemates (especially one with a finishing touch), but the expansion team doesn't seem to have many of those on their roster.

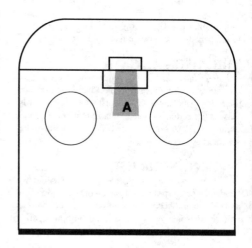

JEFF LAZARO

Yrs. of NHL service: 2
Born: Waltham, Mass.; Mar. 21, 1968
Position: Left wing
Height: 5-10
Weight: 180
Uniform no.: 14
Shoots: Left

Career statistics:

GP	G	A	TP	PIM
76	8	19	27	98

1991-92 statistics:

GP	G	A	TP	+/-	PIM	PP	SH	GW	GT	S	PCT
27	3	6	9	4	31	0	0	0	0	46	6.5

LAST SEASON

Claimed from Boston in 1992 Expansion Draft. Missed 26 games with knee injuries.

THE FINESSE GAME

Lazaro, a find out of a free-agent tryout camp two seasons ago, has tremendous speed. He has very limited finesse skills, but can handle both special teams because of his skating.

Always driving for the net, he has great balance that makes him tough to take down. He draws a lot of penalties because he always keeps his legs moving forward. Lazaro does not have a powerful shot, but he can use a good wrist shot in full stride. He can beat a defenseman wide with his speed.

Lazaro's forte is as a defensive forward. He is very smart and works hard every shift.

THE PHYSICAL GAME

Lazaro played defense at the University of New Hampshire, so he knows how to get the job done back in his own zone. He has a great deal of jump, which he uses to compensate for his lack of strength. Lazaro can pick a team up with an aggressive shift where he will go out and try to make things happen.

THE INTANGIBLES

If there is such a thing as a dynamic defensive forward, Lazaro is it. He missed more than a quarter of the season with knee injuries last year. If those injuries affect his speed, he will have lost his most valuable NHL skill.

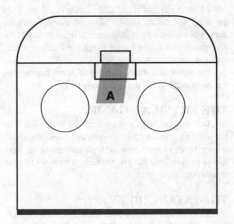

ANDREW McBAIN

Yrs. of NHL service: 9
Born: Scarborough, Ont.; Jan. 18, 1965
Position: Right wing
Height: 6-1
Weight: 205
Uniform no.: 20
Shoots: Right

Career statistics:

GP	G	A	TP	PIM
494	111	148	259	526

1991-92 statistics:

GP	G	A	TP	+/-	PIM	PP	SH	GW	GT	S	PCT
6	1	0	1	-1	0	0	0	0	0	11	9.1

LAST SEASON

Signed as free agent. Games played career low.

THE FINESSE GAME

McBain will get a lot of ice time with the Senators and will probably be on their first power play unit because of his tremendous shot — which is about the only part of his game that is NHL calibre. McBain is strong and will take root in the slot until someone works the puck to him. He has a very quick, accurate release. Most of his points will come with the man advantage.

McBain has fair speed and can carry the puck up the wing with an occasional burst of speed. When he does, you can look for him to shoot. He is not a creative playmaker and doesn't read plays well either offensively or defensively.

McBain is a liability at even strength because he has no interest in his defensive coverage.

THE PHYSICAL GAME

Despite good size and balance, he is unwilling to hit or be hit and thus has no physical presence whatsoever. Once in a while he will go into traffic to fight for the puck around the net, but only if there's a chance of scoring.

THE INTANGIBLES

McBain was a first-round draft pick (eighth overall) in 1983, but after two good seasons with Winnipeg in which he scored 32 and 37 goals, has never been

near the same kind of productive player. A streaky player, his work ethic has been been a question mark throughout his career. The Senators are his fourth NHL team, and without expansion, McBain would be spending another year in Milwaukee (where he scored 24-54-78 in 65 games last season).

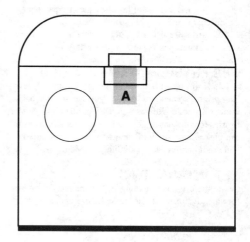

MIKE PELUSO

Yrs. of NHL service: 2
Born: Pengilly, Minn.; Nov. 8, 1965
Position: Left wing/defense
Height: 6-4
Weight: 200
Uniform no.: 44
Shoots: Left

Career statistics:

GP	G	A	TP	PIM
118	12	4	16	728

1991-92 statistics:

GP	G	A	TP	+/-	PIM	PP	SH	GW	GT	S	PCT
63	6	3	9	1	408	2	0	0	0	32	18.8

LAST SEASON

Claimed from Chicago in 1992 Expansion Draft. Led Blackhawks in PIM. Games played career high.

THE FINESSE GAME

For a player who makes his reputation with his fists, Peluso is in the NHL because of his feet. He has skating speed good enough to get in on a defenseman and intimidate that way (instead of the old-fashioned method). Peluso needs to work on his balance, though. He can be tipped over rather easily when he is going straight ahead. He skates very well backwards.

Peluso's versatility is also a plus; he can swing from back to up front and back again without becoming mentally unglued. He will get his goals from driving to the front of the net. His point shot is only average. Peluso's effectiveness on the power play will come from being used as a power forward. He doesn't have the finesse touch of the NHL's better power forwards, however.

Peluso reads plays well coming at him but does not see much offensively. As a left wing, he plays dump and chase.

THE PHYSICAL GAME

Peluso likes his policeman role too much. He often runs around looking for a fight rather than concentrating on being a hockey player. He is capable of fighting all the tough guys, but he picks his spots. Peluso is a hard, nasty body checker.

THE INTANGIBLES

So much for the new NHL teams being concerned about the rumored crackdown on fighting. Peluso was the NHL's penalty minutes champ last season. He can be expected to carry on his carnage in Ottawa.

Peluso is more than one-dimensional, however, and if he learns to curb his wilder tendencies just a tad — without losing his aggressiveness — he could turn out to be a surprisingly successful role player.

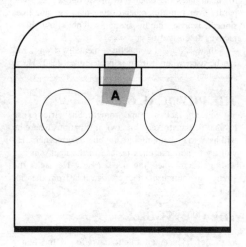

BRAD SHAW

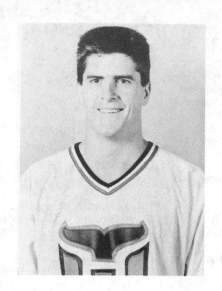

Yrs. of NHL service: 4
Born: Cambridge, Ont.; Apr. 28, 1964
Position: Right defense
Height: 6-0
Weight: 190
Uniform no.: 32
Shoots: Right

Career statistics:

GP	G	A	TP	PIM
212	11	84	95	107

1991-92 statistics:

GP	G	A	TP	+/-	PIM	PP	SH	GW	GT	S	PCT
62	3	22	25	1	44	0	0	0	0	101	3.0

LAST SEASON

Acquired by New Jersey from Hartford for future considerations. Claimed from New Jersey in 1992 Expansion Draft.

THE FINESSE GAME

Shaw is a very smart, poised player, who knows his limitations and has built up a solid style despite them. A good skater, although not overly fast, he has a fluid stride and decent acceleration. He won't rush the puck end to end, but he will start the play out of his own zone and lead a man with one of his smooth passes.

Shaw does not generate much offense, but is fair on the power play since he has good vision and reads plays well. He won't overpower anyone with his slap shot from the point, but he will keep it low and give his teammates the chance to tip or deflect it. Shaw hardly ever ventures much deeper than the blue line, since he worries that his skating will not allow him to recover defensively.

Shaw is a good competitor, mentally strong, and can be used when a team is protecting a lead. He is consistent.

THE PHYSICAL GAME

Since he lacks size and strength, Shaw tries to use his intelligence to keep him out of situations where he will have to go banging into the boards or corners. He will try to play the puck instead of the man, but is a willing hitter when the need arises. He lacks the strength to outmuscle bigger forwards from the slot area.

THE INTANGIBLES

Named to the All-Rookie Team just two seasons ago, the defenceman might have found the honor placed too much expectation on him. He is not flashy, but he is a steady, serviceable defenseman who won't do anything to hurt his team. Shaw might not win you a game, but he won't lose one for you, either.

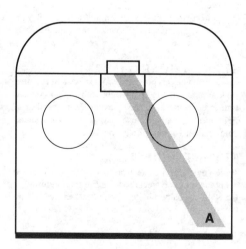

PETER SIDORKIEWICZ

Yrs. of NHL service: 4
Born: Dabrowa Bialostocka, Poland; June 29, 1963
Position: Goaltender
Height: 5-9
Weight: 180
Uniform no.: 30
Catches: Left

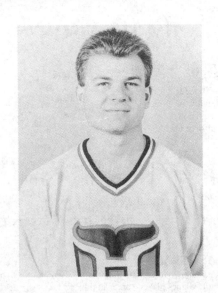

Career statistics:

GP	MINS	GA	SO	GAA	A	PIM
178	10346	575	8	3.33	9	12

1991-92 statistics:

GP	MINS	GAA	W	L	T	SO	GA	S	SAPCT	PIM
35	1995	3.34	9	19	6	2	111	940	.882	2

LAST SEASON

Claimed from Hartford in 1992 Expansion Draft.

THE PHYSICAL GAME

Sidorkiewicz has good quickness, which, added to his basically sound, stand-up game, makes him an adequate NHL goalie. Since he does not live and die by his reflexes, he is very careful to position himself well for the shot.

Sidorkiewicz is a good skater and fair handling the puck. He prefers to leave it for his defensemen to handle but he can bank the puck out of trouble if he has to. He is conservative and does not go for a home run, breaking passes up the middle to his forwards.

Since he does not recover well from a first shot if he has to go down, he has his most trouble with bang-bang plays in front. He also seems to have trouble with criss-cross plays since he does not move well laterally.

Sidorkiewicz works hard at his game on off-days.

THE MENTAL GAME

Sidorkiewicz was a No. 1 goalie in Hartford almost by default (he lost that position as soon as the Whalers acquired Frank Pietrangelo). He lacks mental toughness and is not a true No. 1 goalie, although he will inherit that role again by default in Ottawa. Bad games bother him, as does a bad goal during the course of a game. Overall, Sidorkiewicz lacks consistency.

THE INTANGIBLES

Sidorkiewicz is his own worst enemy. Confidence has been his major bugaboo and he will be in for some busy nights as the No. 1 goalie for an expansion team. It is going to be a long, tough season for him, and he might not have the personality to overcome it.

JIM THOMSON

Yrs. of NHL service: 4
Born: Edmonton, Alta.; Dec. 30, 1965
Position: Right wing
Height: 6-1
Weight: 205
Uniform no.: 25
Shoots: Right

Career statistics:

GP	G	A	TP	PIM
85	4	2	6	314

1991-92 statistics:

GP	G	A	TP	+/-	PIM	PP	SH	GW	GT	S	PCT
45	1	2	3	-1	162	0	0	0	0	24	4.2

LAST SEASON

Claimed from Los Angeles in 1992 Expansion Draft. Games played career high.

THE FINESSE GAME

Thomson is a straight line player. He has some speed, but very little agility. He does have good balance, which helps him in one-on-one battles, but he needs to work more on strength and conditioning to have a more physical presence.

He is very limited offensively, and knows it. He does not try to do anything fancy with the puck other than grind. His few points will be generated from his work in front of the net. Thomson has more skills than hockey sense at this point. If he plays with more skilled teammates, he can open up some ice for them once he establishes a more physical game.

THE PHYSICAL GAME

Thomson's role is as a tough guy, an enforcer. He could be more than a one-dimensional player, but he needs the ice time to work on the other points of his game to make himself into a hockey player and gain confidence. He didn't get the chance with L.A., but he will with the Senators.

THE INTANGIBLES

Thomson has been inconsistent his whole career and does not have much hockey sense. He will never be more than a fair NHL player. Without expansion, he probably wouldn't have an NHL job. If he develops at all, he could be a John Tonelli-type winger.

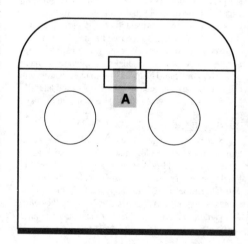

SYLVAIN TURGEON

Yrs. of NHL service: 9
Born: Noranda, Que.; Jan. 17, 1965
Position: Left wing
Height: 6-0
Weight: 200
Uniform no.: 20
Shoots: Left

Career statistics:

GP	G	A	TP	PIM
517	222	185	407	506

1991-92 statistics:

GP	G	A	TP	+/-	PIM	PP	SH	GW	GT	S	PCT
56	9	11	20	-4	39	6	0	1	0	99	9.1

LAST SEASON

Claimed from Montreal in 1992 Expansion Draft.

THE FINESSE GAME

Turgeon has marvelous hands and wonderful scoring instincts. He has scored 40 or more goals twice in his career, and loves to shoot. When he is in a confident groove, he not only gets away a first shot, quick and accurate, but follows it to the net in case of rebounds.

Injuries have changed all that. Turgeon's skating has faltered, and he is much more timid about his ability to score. Unless his confidence is restored, Turgeon will be out of the league in no time, because goals are all he has going for him. He had trouble getting playing time for Montreal — a team that was crying for goals.

Limited as a playmaker, he is not a very smart player, nor is he creative. This was a minor flaw when he was popping in goals. Now it is glaring.

Turgeon has lost his first-step quickness. He is a basic disaster on defense, absolutely clueless about where to position himself and unwilling to pay the physical price.

THE PHYSICAL GAME

Never a physical player to begin with, injuries have made Turgeon appear even more afraid of getting involved with any hitting. He carries his stick high to ward off contact. The boards and corners are uncharted waters as far as Turgeon is concerned.

THE INTANGIBLES

Few players have fallen as fast and as hard as Turgeon, who seemed on the verge of stardom after several big seasons with the Hartford Whalers, who

made him the second player taken overall in 1983. Turgeon was traded to the New Jersey Devils in 1989, and in his second season there suffered a severe abdominal pull/hernia that required surgery. He has never been the same player since.

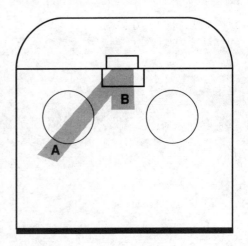

PHILADELPHIA FLYERS

KEITH ACTON

Yrs. of NHL service: 12
Born: Stouffville, Ont.; Apr. 15, 1958
Position: Center
Height: 5-8
Weight: 170
Uniform no.: 25
Shoots: Left

Career statistics:

GP	G	A	TP	PIM
863	216	335	551	1,070

1991-92 statistics:

GP	G	A	TP	+/-	PIM	PP	SH	GW	GT	S	PCT
50	7	9	16	-4	98	0	0	3	0	79	8.9

LAST SEASON

Games played was a 12-season low, as were figures for goals, assists and points. Missed 26 games due to fractured wrist sustained Nov. 27.

THE FINESSE GAME

Virtually all Acton's energies are devoted to checking now, as the only goals he is going to score are going to come off forechecking opportunities, turnovers or scrappy plays in front. Acton has quickness that gets him to the holes, and still has some speed, which enables him to pursue the puck carrier.

Acton would not have been in the league all these years without having learned from his experience. He augments splendid hockey sense with a coach's dispassionate insight. Acton knows where to go, who to cover, what to do.

Having made a study and virtually a science of face-offs, Acton also is useful for those defensive-zone draws that must be won. Acton believes he will win the draw, sees himself winning the draw, before the puck is dropped. He views face-offs as a challenge to be enjoyed, rather than an adventure in life-threatening terror, and never fails to prevent his opponent from getting to the net or the point.

THE PHYSICAL GAME

Acton does what he can in a defensive role. What he lacks in speed, which has eroded over the years, he makes up for in tenaciousness as a checker.

He will throw his body around, will go for the big hit if he can. But mainly he will try to agitate his opponent by paying him close attention, by whacking his stick and by becoming a total distraction, if possible. If he can draw a penalty from his opponent, get him off the ice at the same time or at least be a distraction, Acton has done his job.

THE INTANGIBLES

Aside from his skills as a checker, Acton still brings a hunger and competitive fire to game night. This emotion, whether real or synthetic, helps keep the bench alive and alert. It keeps the lifeblood pumping in the dressing room and it provides a better chance of winning. That, combined with his dedication to the sport and to conditioning, is how Acton stays around at such an advanced age. He has the makings of a very good coach.

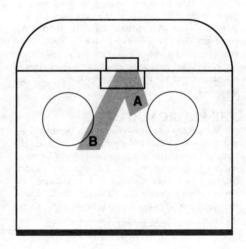

BRIAN BENNING

Yrs. of NHL service: 6
Born: Edmonton, Alta.; June 10, 1966
Position: Right defense
Height: 6-1
Weight: 195
Uniform no.: 19
Shoots: Left

Career statistics:

GP	G	A	TP	PIM
416	46	178	224	682

1991-92 statistics:

GP	G	A	TP	+/-	PIM	PP	SH	GW	GT	S	PCT
75	4	42	46	-5	134	2	0	0	0	152	2.6

LAST SEASON

Obtained from Pittsburgh (via Los Angeles), Feb. 19, 1992, with Mark Recchi and Los Angeles' first-round choice in 1992 entry draft, for Rick Tocchet, Kjell Samuelsson, Ken Wregget and a conditional pick. Led team defensemen in assists.

THE FINESSE GAME

A left shot on the right side, Benning is smooth in his turns, covers lots of ground laterally, and is heady with the puck. He knows what he wants to do before he gets it, and generally accomplishes his objective if he has a good patch of open ice in front of him.

If the space starts to get confined, Benning is an accurate passer who doesn't over-carry. He gets the puck and moves it or jumps into the rush if the opportunity avails. And he is a confident operator at the left point on the power play.

More than anything, Benning simply knows the position. He understands defense and knows where to be on the ice, with or without the puck. He may not win every loose puck or every battle in front, but he is a thinker who makes maximum use of his hockey sense. He talks; you can hear him communicating with his partner and his teammates, not leaving them on their own.

THE PHYSICAL GAME

His penalty total notwithstanding, Benning is not a very physical player and does not play very big. His size and strength limit his defensive play in the muscle match-ups along the boards, but he's very good at grabbing an opponent's stick and neutralizing. He doesn't play tough, but there is a mean streak in him; Benning doesn't always use his stick merely to propel the puck.

THE INTANGIBLES

Benning doesn't do a lot of things to draw attention to himself, but if you watch him a few games, you end up liking what you see. That doesn't make him elite, but it puts him in the top four on a lot of teams.

Ironically, his play with Los Angeles was one reason the Kings felt able to trade Steve Duchesne to Philadelphia. And his play with the Flyers may have made them feel they could trade Duchesne to Quebec.

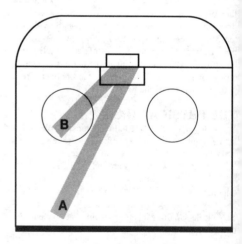

CLAUDE BOIVIN

Yrs. of NHL service: 1
Born: Quebec City, Que.; Mar. 1, 1970
Position: Left wing
Height: 6-2
Weight: 210
Uniform no.: 40
Shoots: Left

Career statistics:

GP	G	A	TP	PIM
58	5	8	13	187

1991-92 statistics:

GP	G	A	TP	+/-	PIM	PP	SH	GW	GT	S	PCT
58	5	8	13	−2	187	0	0	0	0	46	10.9

LAST SEASON

First in NHL.

THE FINESSE GAME

Everything about this hulking brute says "I am huge," but if that's all he was, Boivin would be used only in fight situations. Rather, Boivin often finds himself in a defensive matchup against one of the opposition's better wings; he is just as likely to take a penalty for holding or interference as he is for roughing or elbowing. The guy can be trusted with far more than just slugging, and he's still learning the NHL game.

For someone who is building-sized, Boivin skates well. His big, strong stride and straight-ahead speed are perfect for a dump-and-chase game, but agility allows him to change direction if the puck takes a funny bounce. Once most players get that much weight going in a certain direction, that is the route they must continue; Boivin can't exactly dart, but he CAN move.

And he stays in control of his speed, which keeps him on the ice more; referees would paint a target on his back — and his coach would have to limit the risk of using him — if Boivin simply ran around killing people on the way to the penalty box.

He also has a pretty good touch with the puck, which complements a pretty good idea of what to do with it. Boivin knows he's no magician, but he can make a pass, and it doesn't take an hour for the message to get from his head to his hands. The shot he uses most is half-wrist/half-snap, about halfway up the goalpost, from the rim of the face-off circle or the hashmark. It's accurate and effective because of quick release time.

Away from the puck, Boivin identifies his check and stays with his man well.

THE PHYSICAL GAME

Boivin's physical nature is multi-faceted. He throws his weight, without hesitation, against the other team's biggest players. He also presents a formidable physical obstacle for the finesse guys who have to get around him if they want to score. Meanwhile, when scrapping for the puck, Boivin does a good job of using his body to build a bridge over the puck, shoving an opponent out of the way and using his stick or his feet to move the disc.

If you want to fight, he wants to fight, although that, frankly, is not one of his strengths. He's still learning the subtleties of fighting the NHL masters — he's vulnerable to uppercuts — but Boivin more than holds his own most of the time.

THE INTANGIBLES

Boivin is the widebody about whom coaches dream. He has a far better handle on the game than most muscle guys. He's got hand and foot skills. He's got a head for the game. He's got a giant upside that only he can mess up.

He seems coachable, eager to learn, and it says here he'll score at least 15 goals this season. Boivin will sneak up on teams that don't take him seriously. The kid's a comer.

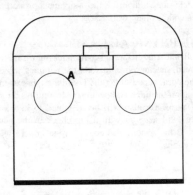

ROD BRIND'AMOUR

Yrs. of NHL service: 3
Born: Ottawa, Ont.; Aug. 9, 1970
Position: Center
Height: 6-1
Weight: 202
Uniform no.: 17
Shoots: Left

Career statistics:

GP	G	A	TP	PIM
237	76	111	187	239

1991-92 statistics:

GP	G	A	TP	+/-	PIM	PP	SH	GW	GT	S	PCT
80	33	44	77	−3	100	8	4	5	0	202	16.3

LAST SEASON

Obtained from St. Louis, Sept. 22, 1991, with Dan Quinn for Ron Sutter and Murray Baron. Totals for goals, assists, points and penalty minutes all were career high. Third consecutive season of at least 78 games. Made first All-Star Game appearance. Led team in shorthanded goals, was second on team in points, goals and assists.

THE FINESSE GAME

Brind'Amour skates with a long, powerful stride that generates good speed and acceleration. He puts his head down and burns it on the straightaways, and takes an excellent, powerful first step after stealing a puck.

He complements those assets with solid hand skills. Brind'Amour deploys a variety of shots, including a quick-release slap shot that is extremely heavy, an accurate wrist shot and a fairly powerful backhand. As long as he keeps his feet moving, Brind'Amour controls the puck well. He makes smart passes to either side and rarely makes the receiver reach too far ahead or behind. When he gets the puck and stops skating, Brind'Amour gets in trouble.

When he doesn't have the puck, Brind'Amour works hard to get it back and is a good forechecker. On defense, he identifies the assignment properly and stays with his man well.

THE PHYSICAL GAME

Brind'Amour can take the puck into traffic and succeed, he can more than get the bumping job done in the corners and along the boards. He is extremely strong on the puck and beats people with his strength and speed. He also will be delighted to knock you down, will get you with a hip check in the neutral zone. Brind'Amour also goes in front for screens and deflections.

Make no mistake: He takes no shortcuts, plays all the way to the endboards. Brind'Amour plays every foot of every rink.

THE INTANGIBLES

There would be no energy crisis if some scientist could harness this player's intensity. Brind'Amour is working hard to make that drive work in his favor, instead of to his detriment, which has been the case too often in the past. Sometimes he simply tries too hard to do too much.

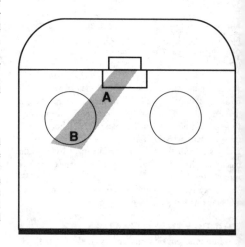

DAVE BROWN

Yrs. of NHL service: 8
Born: Saskatoon, Sask.; Oct. 12, 1962
Position: Right wing
Height: 6-5
Weight: 205
Uniform no.: 21
Shoots: Right

Career statistics:

GP	G	A	TP	PIM
523	40	43	83	1,483

1991-92 statistics:

GP	G	A	TP	+/-	PIM	PP	SH	GW	GT	S	PCT
70	4	2	6	-11	81	0	0	0	0	50	8.0

LAST SEASON

Games played was three-season high. Goal total was four-season high. Assist and PIM totals were career-low. Missed 10 games due to bruised shoulder.

THE FINESSE GAME

Brown has decent offensive instincts and continues to work on his skill level. He can make a play out of the corner after he wins the puck, can position himself in the slot for a pass, can tie somebody up in front of the net while a point shot is on the way and at times will do some good things after receiving the puck.

He is quick enough with his hands and feet to kick the puck to his skates and get off a shot in-tight. He has a rather sluggish stride, though, which often gets him to the play late and also hinders his ability to keep up if the play goes the other way. So Brown often gets caught in-between, especially in situations that require quickness or agility, and ultimately finds himself a step behind the play.

THE PHYSICAL GAME

Brown is not going to surprise anybody. Every team in the NHL knows why he is in the lineup and usually is sure to have its own heavyweight in fighting prime by the time the puck drops. Still, if Brown isn't heavyweight champ, he's darn close.

He is smarter about things now. He isn't going to shred his knuckles and splinter his fingers on a guy's helmet just for the fun of it any more. The time has to be right and the situation has to be right, so sometimes he stays on the ice and the guy who tried to bait him into a fight ends up in the penalty box.

THE INTANGIBLES

Brown still sends a message when it is needed; sometimes, it would be worth his while to send a message when it ISN'T needed. Still, it will be difficult for him to stay on the team if that is all he can provide on the ice. He is a good man for the dressing room, however, and still could be a plus if he escapes claim in the waiver draft.

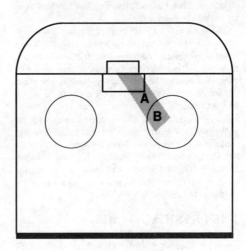

TERRY CARKNER

Yrs. of NHL service: 6
Born: Smiths Falls, Ont.; Mar. 7, 1966
Position: Left defense
Height: 6-3
Weight: 205
Uniform no.: 29
Shoots: Left

Career statistics:

GP	G	A	TP	PIM
408	31	124	155	992

1991-92 statistics:

GP	G	A	TP	+/-	PIM	PP	SH	GW	GT	S	PCT
73	4	12	16	-14	195	0	1	0	0	70	5.7

LAST SEASON

Goal total matched four-season low. Assist total was career-low. Missed four games due to suspension, three due to injury or illness.

THE FINESSE GAME

Carkner has worked on his skating virtually his entire career, and has reached a point where it seems just about as good as it's going to be. His first step to the puck seems improved. Carkner will never be fast or agile, his mobility is much more suited to cramped situations than open-ice situations and his balance is good, not great. But Carkner has some quickness and he makes use of it especially well in penalty killing situations, when he challenges the puck all the way to the corners or sideboards.

Carkner plays a confident, aggressive game. He pinches in from the point, he jumps into the play every so often to create an odd-man rush and almost always makes use of an under-rated wrist shot that sneaks up on goalies because he gets it away quickly. The other advantage to Carkner's wrist shot is it can be tipped by a teammate in front.

Sometimes he gets a little carried away with the puck, though. When he passes the puck out of the zone, Carkner does a pretty good job. But when he skates it out, Carkner occasionally beats the first man, then just misses beating the second and ends up chasing the resultant turnover. That second quick move is still a challenge to him.

THE PHYSICAL GAME

Carkner is a game, tough player who will click out every once in a while. Though he controls his temper well now, Carkner remains successfully unpredictable. You never really know if he's going to skate away or if he's going to try to pound somebody. And that's good. You want to keep opponents guessing.

THE INTANGIBLES

Whatever difficulties he has reading the rush or the defensive coverage — part of that is trusting teammates who don't always deserve the trust — Carkner makes up for in his willingness to hit, clear the front of the net and fight anyone who drops the gloves..

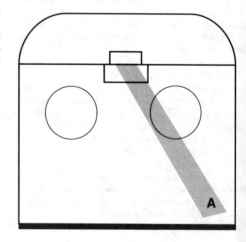

AL CONROY

Yrs. of NHL service: 1
Born: Calgary, Alta.; Jan. 17, 1966
Position: Center/right wing
Height: 5-8
Weight: 170
Uniform no.: 46
Shoots: Right

Career statistics:

GP	G	A	TP	PIM
31	2	9	11	74

1991-92 statistics:

GP	G	A	TP	+/-	PIM	PP	SH	GW	GT	S	PCT
31	2	9	11	1	74	0	0	0	0	25	8.0

LAST SEASON
First in the NHL.

THE FINESSE GAME
Conroy is an entertaining character who is always doing 90 miles-per-hour when the puck is up for grabs. He keeps those stubby legs churning and working — starting with the springy first step that cranks him up to maximum speed in just a couple of darting strides.

He breaks nicely to open ice, moves the puck with smarts and sizzle. And Conroy gets the puck to the net very quickly and accurately. He won't bring the stick all the way back for the big slap shot; he favors the snap, and is agile enough to fire it off a 360-degree pivot if the situation calls for it.

There are, of course, aspects which need improvement. Conroy can't turn right in less than an hour, and there are times when he blows reads as the play enters his defensive zone.

THE PHYSICAL GAME
You look at Conroy and go, ''Too small. The guy's gonna get killed.'' Then you watch someone try — and fail — to knock him over. When he really gets jolted, Conroy might end up taking a step backward, but that's about it; his center of gravity is so low, his balance is so good, and he gets his feet so wide apart, that it's going to take a very good check to drop him.

Despite the obvious size disadvtange, Conroy can do a decent job on face-offs. He doesn't just get involved along the boards, he works those mines to win the puck. Conroy is positively fearless. He will go to the boards with anyone and make them pay a price.

THE INTANGIBLES
If he weren't a competitor, Conroy wouldn't have made it this far. If he weren't gritty and gutty enough to put himself on the line every night, he'd be playing industrial league hockey someplace. But you get a lot more than what you see; Conroy is a spirited player who is going to outwork you because he has to simply in order to survive, in order to get another shift.

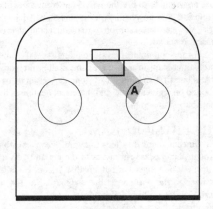

KEVIN DINEEN

Yrs. of NHL service: 8
Born: Quebec City, Que.; Oct. 28, 1963
Position: Right wing
Height: 5-11
Weight: 195
Uniform no.: 11
Shoots: Right

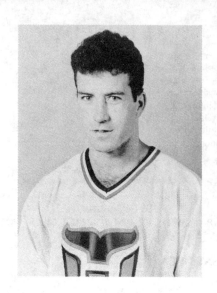

Career statistics:

GP	G	A	TP	PIM
553	240	262	502	1,151

1991-92 statistics:

GP	G	A	TP	+/-	PIM	PP	SH	GW	GT	S	PCT
80	30	32	62	-5	143	6	3	5	0	225	13.3

LAST SEASON

Obtained from Hartford, Nov. 13, 1991, for Murray Craven and Flyers' fourth-round pick in 1992. Plus-minus improved by 10. Goal, assist and point totals all increased over prior season. Games played was career high. Scored at least 30 goals for the fourth time.

THE FINESSE GAME

Strong skating ability, especially-good balance and acceleration, enable Dineen to play the hell-bent style that is his greatest attribute. He is light on his feet, and uses a spry first step to charge toward top speed — although his top speed isn't as fast as it used to be. Dineen has good straightaway speed with the puck, but sometimes gets so much momentum going, he loses control of the disc when he tries to stop short.

He is, nonetheless, a confident puck-handler who does not hesitate to use the wrist shot from the wing. While it is less powerful than his slap shot, Dineen's wrist shot can sneak up on a goaltender and at least cause a rebound.

For the amount he plays, including special teams, barely three shots in an average game really isn't many. That's one first shot off a rush, one deflection or one rebound on a given night, and that hardly captures his contribution to a game.

THE PHYSICAL GAME

Dineen keeps his legs moving, keeps skating through the checks. He drives to the net and gets all he can out of a muscular but smallish frame. He is no stranger to the corners or the endboards, and wins more than his share of loose pucks.

THE INTANGIBLES

Dineen is a hockey machine, a competitive two-way player who is a stubborn, determined opponent. He seems to supply a lot of the power, drive and leadership Rick Tocchet did, which probably is what made Tocchet tradeable. He plays like his britches are on fire and more than earns his considerable ice time; Dineen's father being the coach has nothing to do with anything.

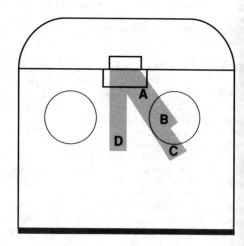

PELLE EKLUND

Yrs. of NHL service: 7
Born: Stockholm, Sweden; March 22, 1963
Position: Center
Height: 5-10
Weight: 175
Uniform no.: 9
Shoots: Left

Career statistics:

GP	G	A	TP	PIM
486	106	280	386	83

1991-92 statistics:

GP	G	A	TP	+/-	PIM	PP	SH	GW	GT	S	PCT
51	7	16	23	0	4	1	2	1	0	74	9.5

LAST SEASON

Totals for games played, goals, assists and points were career low. Shot total dropped 57 from prior season. Missed final 23 games due to cartilage damage in left knee.

THE FINESSE GAME

When he's playing well, Eklund has so much jump it looks like he's on a pogo stick. His short, little steps eat lots of ice as he accelerates quickly to top speed. Quick hands and a strong shot make Eklund a threat to score from anywhere, although last season's goal total tells you how threatening he was in 1991-92.

Smart as Eklund can be in an offensive role, he is a willing defensive player who can go against the game's premier offensive stars. The more things you can do, the more ice time you can get, the better the chance of scoring or making something happen.

Eklund has very good balance, which keeps him from wiping out even when he gets crunched along the boards.

THE PHYSICAL GAME

Eklund's lack of size limits his effectiveness down low as a center on the power play, but he gets around that by running the show from the boards side of the face-off circle. The thing is, after he has passed from there to set up a point shot, Eklund rarely goes to the net to poach for rebounds—so a strong, physical wing needs to play with him.

Still, Eklund can go into a corner with someone far larger and come away with the puck. He is a good penalty killer, because he is a threat to score a short-handed goal. And he accepts being hit; it keeps him more alert, more in the game.

THE INTANGIBLES

When he entered last season, Eklund was the Flyers' MVP and the player with the least to prove. After an awful season, in which he was the greatest disappointment on the team, Eklund arrives with the most to prove.

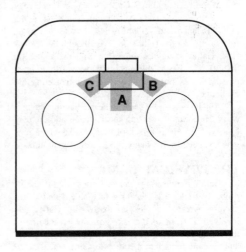

GARRY GALLEY

Yrs. of NHL service: 8
Born: Montreal, Que.; April 16, 1963
Position: Left defense
Height: 6-0
Weight: 190
Uniform no.: 3
Shoots: Left

Career statistics:

GP	G	A	TP	PIM
529	57	184	241	595

1991-92 statistics:

GP	G	A	TP	+/-	PIM	PP	SH	GW	GT	S	PCT
77	5	27	32	−2	117	3	0	1	0	125	4.0

LAST SEASON

Obtained from Boston, Jan. 2, 1992, with Wes Walz and future considerations for Gord Murphy, Brian Dobbin and a third-round choice in 1992 draft. Played at least 70 games a fourth straight season. Goal total was six-season low, penalty minutes were 33 more than prior year's career-high.

THE FINESSE GAME

Galley has decent skating speed, which helps him jump into the rush and which is a major advantage during shorthanded situations. His acceleration enables him to range all the way to the corner or sideboards to challenge for possession or at least hurry the puck carrier, yet still get back into position if the puck gets to the point.

Mobility also allows Galley to step up on a play in the neutral zone and to pinch with confidence at the point. Balance and versatility also enable him to be trustworthy on the right side, even though he is a left shot. Galley struggles somewhat with the angles on that off-side, has to shift his body awkwardly to open passing angles, but does an acceptable job meeting that challenge.

And he plays a lot because he can handle situation work. He competes on both special teams and can play four-on-four. He is a jack of many trades and a jack who has been traded many times; teams want him.

THE PHYSICAL GAME

Galley is more physical than most would credit, probably because he wears a face shield and shield players, as a rule, are less combative. But Galley gets involved in front of the net, goes into the corners, throws his body in front of shots, and makes the physical commitments that nicely complement his finesse skills to make him a balanced player.

The penalty-minute figure tells you Galley gets involved; you don't get 117 penalty minutes just by tripping people. He plays an active game, throws a big jolt every once in a while and uses his stick or his body to delay attackers trying to get to his partner.

THE INTANGIBLES

Pretty easy-going off the ice, Galley is, nonetheless, a competitor. He is a better-than-average defenseman best suited to a three-four-five role on any team. He has an excellent personality for the dressing room. He CARES.

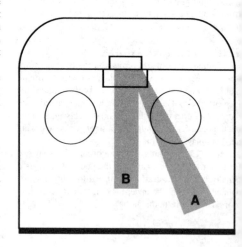

DAN KORDIC

Yrs. of NHL service: 1
Born: Edmonton, Alta.; Apr. 18, 1971
Position: Left defense
Height: 6-5
Weight: 220
Uniform no.: 6
Shoots: Left

Career statistics:

GP	G	A	TP	PIM
46	1	3	4	126

1991-92 statistics:

GP	G	A	TP	+/-	PIM	PP	SH	GW	GT	S	PCT
46	1	3	4	1	126	0	0	0	0	27	3.7

LAST SEASON
First in the NHL.

THE FINESSE GAME
Kordic plays a stay-at-home game. Part of that may be preference, part of that may be limited skating skills that would prohibit a more ambitious approach. He has a whopping stride and very nice straight-ahead ability, but has fairly heavy feet and no significant agility.

Kordic has the confidence to make an occasional rush, and will step way up for plays in the neutral zone on the defensive side of the puck.

THE PHYSICAL GAME
Do not underestimate this player's strength. Of course, he's enormous, so it would be difficult to underestimate his strength. But we're talking about his passing strength. From behind the net during one practice, this guy once hit a teammate at the blue line in the skates with a breakout pass; the pass was so hard, it knocked the teammate off his skates.

Kordic has a decent dose of discipline in his approach to the game. He knows he can fight you and will fight you, but there are lots of times when he concedes to the scoreboard or the game situation and just takes an opponent's number for later.

Nonetheless, he's huge, and he plays like it. If you want a piece of him, there is enough for everybody.

THE INTANGIBLES
Kordic comes to the rink angry and seems able to make that energy work in his favor. The Flyers broke him in slowly last season; he may be ready for more in 1992-93.

ERIC LINDROS

Yrs. of NHL service: 0
Born: London, Ont.; Feb. 28, 1973
Position: Center
Height: 6-5
Weight: 227
Uniform no.: 88
Shoots: Right

Junior Career statistics:

GP	G	A	TP	PIM
95	97	119	216	304

1991-92 statistics:

GP	G	A	TP	PIM
13	9	22	31	54

LAST SEASON

Played for Team Canada in Canada Cup, Olympics and World Junior tournaments. Also returned occasionally to Oshawa Generals while waiting to be traded by the Quebec Nordiques.

THE FINESSE GAME

The skill that has improved most is his skating. When Lindros was younger, he was just a big guy who couldn't skate very well. Now, he can hurdle a defenseman going to hip-check him, land on his feet and retrieve the puck. He doesn't get knocked down as easily, he's quicker off the mark and he protects the puck better because his balance has improved so much.

Not slick or speedy, Lindros is sneaky-fast. He worked with a personal trainer during the off-season to improve his skating technique and stride.

His entire junior career, Lindros has played against players smaller than himself, and his game has been tailored accordingly. He hasn't been the playmaker as much as he has been the finisher. Teammates give him the puck and he puts it away with a heavy, hard, accurate snap or wrist shot. But he's not a natural, gifted goal scorer, like a Mike Bossy, and he doesn't have a hair-trigger release. Lindros tries different tricks to beat a goaltender, works on a quicker release, shooting off the pass, improving his backhand. He practices shots under the crossbar and to the corners.

Lindros he can make accurate passes to either side and sees the ice well. The puck does not slow him down. His likes to beat defensemen wide, carry behind the net and feed in front.

THE PHYSICAL GAME

Lindros is supremely strong and powerful, so there aren't many defensemen who are going to move him away from the net if he decides to plant himself in front. That will be a special asset during power plays; some defensemen will give him the extra shot out of frustration and Lindros' team will get a two-man advantage.

There also are not many defensemen who are going to stand Lindros up and stop him from skating just about anyplace he wants — with or without the puck. He's able to take all kinds of punishment and not retaliate . . . until the time is right. He'll absorb a slash or a cheap shot, take your number, then try to kill you later.

THE INTANGIBLES

Lindros plays at an extremely high level for someone his age, but he is not one to be satisfied with whatever he achieves. He displays exceptional confidence for someone his age, and that should help him through what promises to be a challenging rookie season. Lots of people will be eager to take a piece out of him, which is nothing new. He won't get as much time and space in the NHL, so he might not score as much.

He has patterned himself after Mark Messier; he could do plenty worse.

ANDREI LOMAKIN

Yrs. of NHL service: 1
Born: Voskresensk, Russia; Apr. 3, 1964
Position: Left wing
Height: 5-10
Weight: 176
Uniform no.: 23
Shoots: Left

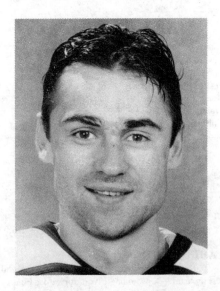

Career statistics:

GP	G	A	TP	PIM
57	14	16	30	26

1991-92 statistics:

GP	G	A	TP	+/-	PIM	PP	SH	GW	GT	S	PCT
57	14	16	30	−6	26	2	0	0	0	82	17.1

LAST SEASON

First in NHL. Was second on team in shooting percentage. Missed 16 games, through Feb. 27, due to broken thumb.

THE FINESSE GAME

Lomakin is a hockey technician who has extremely sharp open-ice, finesse moves. He likes to remain in motion at all times, so he is never caught flat-footed and is always a step closer to top speed if a burst of acceleration is necessary.

Not a sprinter, he is more sneaky-fast. He has good anticipation and a fine sense of his position. He knows how to get open for a pass, knows how to give it back during a two-on-one break, knows how to make a deft touch-pass to an open teammate. He enjoys a good pass as much as a goal, but Lomakin also shot more last season than he ever did in Russia. Twelve goals at even strength is hardly small potatoes.

If the puck turns over, Lomakin is well-schooled defensively. He always tries to make the proper play and he knows the properly play, because his thought process and hockey education is well ahead of most of his teammates. Last season, Lomakin would jump to the right hole but his teammate wouldn't get him the puck; he would make a move on a defenseman to open the proper lane, but no teammate would fill the lane.

THE PHYSICAL GAME

In the first half of the season, Lomakin would get hooked or held but would skate through the trouble without losing his footing. In the second half, while he still skated with the puck or scrapped for position in front of the net, Lomakin was something of a pushover.

While his physical conditioning was fine, Lomakin, like other players who competed in the Canada Cup, grew increasingly fatigued as the NHL season wore on. The wheels fell off his wagon, but he is a battler who will be heard from.

THE INTANGIBLES

Lomakin had a very strong start on left wing, but struggled on the right once the Flyers got into numbers troubles over there and used him on the off-side. Lomakin felt extremely comfortable with his teammates, who accepted him warmly, but did not like the way he finished the season. His personal pride was bruised and he will attempt this season to erase the bad memory.

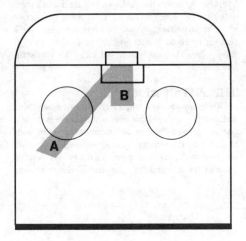

MARK PEDERSON

Yrs. of NHL service: 2
Born: Prelate, Sask.; Jan. 14, 1968
Position: Left wing
Height: 6-2
Weight: 196
Uniform no.: 14
Shoots: Left

Career statistics:

GP	G	A	TP	PIM
126	25	43	68	47

1991-92 statistics:

GP	G	A	TP	+/-	PIM	PP	SH	GW	GT	S	PCT
58	15	25	40	14	22	4	0	3	0	94	16.0

LAST SEASON

Plus-minus improved 19 goals and was second best on team — tops among Flyers forwards. Figures for goals, assists and points all were single-season personal bests.

THE FINESSE GAME

Pederson has a nice first step toward the puck and does a decent job in a straight line, although he has difficulty changing directions. He is an average or adequate skater who at times seems awkward and off-balance, doesn't seem to have much range and appears to arrive late on a lot of plays.

Pederson uses the stick to screen for his teammates, impeding a checker from reaching the puck until a fellow Flyer has moved it. Other times, possibly to compensate for a lack of speed or mobility, Pederson puts his stick in a guy's gut and hangs on for the ride.

He makes a most acceptable pass and is most effective when he moves the puck quickly. He doesn't seem much for carrying the puck. He is more productive with the wrist shot, because he has a terrific quick release; he could get 30 goals if he used it more. It takes a long time for him to get away the slap shot, however.

THE PHYSICAL GAME

Pederson seems a bit selective in using his size and strength. It seems that only when the net is in sight does his intensity and involvement in the action start to pick up. It certainly appears he could get more involved in the physical aspect of the game, in more areas of the ice, and still play the offensive role he prefers.

THE INTANGIBLES

Pederson is a tiger in the scoring-chance area, more of a lamb in most of the rest of the ice. Teams with great supporting casts can enjoy the luxury of a player whose intensity varies with the zone, but the Flyers may ask that Pederson's vigilance and willingness cover more ground. It's a 200-foot game in most rinks.

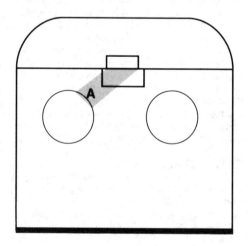

MARK RECCHI

Yrs. of NHL service: 3
Born: Kamloops, B.C.; Feb. 1, 1968
Position: Right wing
Height: 5-9
Weight: 185
Uniform no.: 8
Shoots: Left

Career statistics:

GP	G	A	TP	PIM
247	114	165	279	188

1991-92 statistics:

GP	G	A	TP	+/-	PIM	PP	SH	GW	GT	S	PCT
80	43	54	97	−21	96	20	1	5	1	210	20.5

LAST SEASON

Obtained from Pittsburgh, Feb. 19, 1992, with Brian Benning and Los Angeles Kings' first-round choice in 1992 draft for Rick Tocchet, Kjell Samuelsson, Ken Wregget and a conditional draft pick. Plus-minus declined 21 goals, point total decreased 16. Power-play goal total improved by eight, game-winning total decreased four but tied for team lead. Shots total was third on team.

THE FINESSE GAME

Recchi is a give-and-go player. He makes a sharp first pass, then jumps for the hole, ready to receive the return. Sometimes, when he gets the puck back, he'll move to his left across the high slot and catch goalies by surprise with a sharp snap shot back against the grain to his right. Other times, he'll hold the puck and look for the late man coming into the rush, which keeps the defense honest because they can't always play him to shoot.

Recchi also uses the spring in his legs to beat defensemen to the outside. It isn't great looking — Recchi has short legs and uses a short, choppy stride — but it is effective.

He is a marksman in-close, an expert finisher because he has good scoring instincts and quick hands and he pulls the trigger quickly.

THE PHYSICAL GAME

Recchi gets whacked around pretty much every night. He accepts being hit, but might get messed-with less if he plays with Eric Lindros. Stocky and solid, he doesn't get intimidated. He plays a willing game, but just can't win many muscle match-ups.

THE INTANGIBLES

The Flyers added a needed offensive dimension when they obtained Recchi from Pittsburgh, which needed the physical element it secured in Rick Tocchet. Of course, Pittsburgh reaped quicker benefits, getting Tocchet a ride in the Stanley Cup parade, but the Flyers unmistakably got long-term value in Recchi, who has added a layer of scrap to his attitude and now must add a layer of defensive attention.

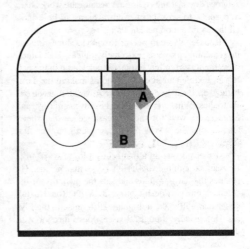

DOMINIC ROUSSEL

Yrs. of NHL service: 1
Born: Hull, Que.; Feb. 22, 1970
Position: Goaltender
Height: 6-1
Weight: 180
Uniform no.: 33
Catches: Left

Career statistics:

GP	MINS	GA	SO	GAA	A	PIM
17	922	40	1	2.60	1	2

1991-92 statistics:

GP	MINS	GAA	W	L	T	SO	GA	S	SAPCT	PIM
17	922	2.60	7	8	2	1	40	437	.908	2

LAST SEASON

First in NHL. Allowed two goals or fewer in 10 of his 14 starts.

THE PHYSICAL GAME

Roussel is very reminiscent of Patrick Roy in style and appearance, but may be more promising because he makes better use of his size and his assets. Without any particular drama, he gets to the puck. He makes extremely difficult saves look routine.

His philosophy, like Roy's, is take care of the low shots; if you're going to get beat, get beat up high by a good shot. It's all timing. If you go down early, the shooter sees everything that's available. if you go down at the right time, the shooter sees nothing. Roussel goes down at the right time because he works hard in practice to stay sharp. And this season, he'll have all the game action he can stand.

Roussel also can play a Roy-style game because his catching glove is extremely quick. His lateral movement is excellent. Roussel looks huge in the net, but is flexible and agile, capable of making the acrobatic stop on a two-on-one break without theatrical flourishes. Whatever rebounds he leaves are tiny, and he recovers well for those occasional second shots. One-on-one, he is very patient; he won't buy the first fake.

If there is one area that needs a lot of work, it is Roussel's use of the stick. He's better than he was. He reaches the hard-arounds and sets the puck up for the defense, but he doesn't move it. With Ron Hextall gone, that will make a dramatic difference in the Flyers. Defensively, though, Roussel does a nice job with the stick; he never telegraphs the poke check before he uses it.

THE MENTAL GAME

Roussel does not seem to give an inch. He's the same with a shutout going as in a blowout. He appears cool and collected, doesn't waste any motions on the ice and doesn't seem to waste a lot of time worrying. Pressure doesn't bother him; he takes the good and the bad in stride. He has good focus and good anticipation. He doesn't fall into the young goalie's trap of admiring a great save for so long that he blows an easy shot 10 seconds later.

When he struggled with cut-ins early last season, the Flyers sent him back to Hershey to work on his weaknesses and he did. When he came back, the weaknesses seemed to be gone.

THE INTANGIBLES

In his short stint last season, Roussel showed the Flyers what they had to see. He convinced them he could be trusted with the bulk of the workload if the right deal came along for Ron Hextall.

Roussel has the look of a future star. He wants to get better, and he will. The challenge for him, behind a dramatically different defense, will be to avoid being melted by the spotlight.

PITTSBURGH
PENGUINS

TOM BARRASSO

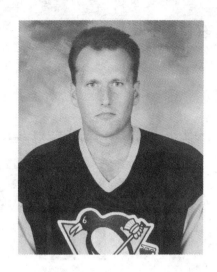

Yrs. of NHL service: 9
Born: Boston, Mass.; March 31, 1965
Position: Goaltender
Height: 6-3
Weight: 211
Uniform no.: 35
Catches: Right

Career statistics:

GP	MINS	GA	SO	GAA	A	PIM
439	25,246	1469	15	3.49	31	309

1991-92 statistics:

GP	MINS	GAA	W	L	T	SO	GA	S	SAPCT	PIM
57	3329	3.53	25	22	9	2	196	1702	.885	30

LAST SEASON

Set club record for road victories with 12. Games played was most by a Penguins goaltender since 1981-82. Missed six games due to back spasms, three due to ankle injury, two due to hand injury, one because of flu.

THE PHYSICAL GAME

Barrasso gives you the glove side, then takes it back after you've shot to what probably is his greatest strength. Barrasso is also is very good on low shots. His feet aren't lightning quick, but he gets his pads or his skates on the shots toward the corners.

He is extremely aggressive — sometimes too much so. Sometimes he over-challenges on a play and is dead meat when a forward passes behind him to a teammate rushing to the net. Barrasso is also aggressive, and effective, in the use of his stick as a defensive tool; he will use it to block any pass he can reach.

He will go all the way to the corner to control a loose puck. He is extremely eager to play the puck with his stick and is extremely confident in his puck-handling ability. He has the skating skill, the balance and the wrist strength; and — in the playoffs, at least — actually managed to direct the puck to teammates. During the regular season, he seemed to give the puck away and hurt himself as much as he helped himself.

THE MENTAL GAME

Barrasso is a player of undisputable mental toughness. He wins the big games, gets the job done, makes the key saves when the game is on the line.

And his concentration is exceptional. Especially when there is a lot of traffic in front, Barrasso seems to have a sixth sense about where the puck is coming and where he has to be as a consequence.

He also reads the play very well and has a good sense of anticipation, which enables him to get to the right place BEFORE the right time.

Barrasso also is extremely tenacious. He does not give up. If he does make the first move in a one-on-one confrontation with a shooter, he always will attempt a secondary or emergency/recovery move. And, because a lot of shooters let up once they think they've beaten him, Barrasso makes more than a few ultimate-effort stops that prevent goals.

THE INTANGIBLES

Barrasso is a winner, with the rings to prove it. He may not always look pretty, but he has heart to go with his skills. Time after time in the playoffs, when the Penguins needed him to carry them, to get them through a pressure storm on the road, Barrasso provided the key saves. He won pretty, he won ugly, but he won. And he is only now approaching his peak period.

PHIL BOURQUE

Yrs. of NHL service: 5
Born: Chelmsford, Mass.; June 8, 1962
Position: Left wing
Height: 6-1
Weight: 196
Uniform no.: 29
Shoots: Left

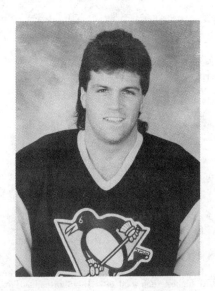

Career statistics:

GP	G	A	TP	PIM
344	75	89	164	435

1991-92 statistics:

GP	G	A	TP	+/-	PIM	PP	SH	GW	GT	S	PCT
58	10	16	26	−6	58	0	1	3	0	51	19.6

LAST SEASON

Goal and points totals were four-year lows. Missed 22 games due to injury: Foot (13), back (three), flu (three), elbow (two), concussion (one).

THE FINESSE GAME

For a player whose outstanding skill is speed, Bourque receives a tremendous amount of responsibility. He brings the puck up ice on the power play and works the left point during the advantages. He kills penalties and plays pretty much a regular shift.

There are times when uncertainty creeps into his game. Either he's going to give you speed, or he's going to give you puck movement, but he is not going to give you puck movement while at high speed. He will take a defenseman deep with his speed, but he will not always make the effort pay off, will not always make a play off the rush. Sometimes he will just run out of room.

He is very good, though, at racing behind the net and coming out from the goalie's left for a stuff shot.

THE PHYSICAL GAME

Bourque can be a very physical player. He is an effort guy who has no second thoughts about diving for a loose puck. He will take a hit to make a play, eagerly will throw one to pin a defenseman along the boards with the puck.

THE INTANGIBLES

Because he also can play defense in a pinch, Bourque's versatility complements his speed and supplements his playing time. Good left wings are not that easy to find and Bourque grades out at 'good' in most key areas.

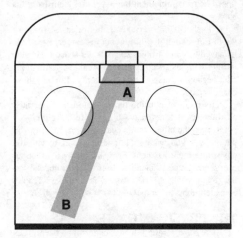

BOB ERREY

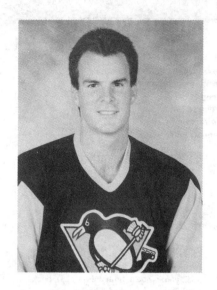

Yrs. of NHL service: 9
Born: Montreal, Que.; September 21, 1964
Position: Left wing
Height: 5-10
Weight: 183
Uniform no.: 12
Shoots: Left

Career statistics:

GP	G	A	TP	PIM
518	124	134	258	575

1991-92 statistics:

GP	G	A	TP	+/-	PIM	PP	SH	GW	GT	S	PCT
78	19	16	35	1	119	0	3	1	0	122	15.6

LAST SEASON

Nineteen goals, with none on power play, was fourth-highest such total in NHL. Shorthanded goal total was second on team. Missed one game due to foot injury, one game due to hamstring injury.

THE FINESSE GAME

Errey clearly is one of the underrated skaters in the league; he has the ability to pull away from anyone because of his explosive acceleration and speed. But that is one of the few finesse elements in his game. Speed helps complement the plays that stem from his hard work.

His shot is not very good, his release isn't very good. But seemingly, throughout his career, Errey has managed to score around 20 goals per season. He gets in tight with his speed, gets into breakaway situations a lot because of his grit as a checker, and makes those chances pay.

His main responsibility, and another underrated attribute, is as a defensive player. He's the guy you put against the other team's best forward, the guy you put out with your weakest left defenseman, to save the guy some embarrassment. Errey shuts down just about everybody he plays against, he is the best checker on his team, and he is worthy of Selke Trophy consideration.

THE PHYSICAL GAME

Errey is a scrappy, feisty, eager player who uses every ounce of his strength and still has a fairly short fuse on a fairly large mean streak. He loves to make contact — the kind of contact that gets on the highlight shows, the kind that sends guys flying. He lifts his own bench and wakes up the crowd, which is all-important when the building has gone for a nap.

For a small man, Errey is a very dangerous checker. He plays THROUGH people. He is a thick-body player who always plays through a check and never seems to bounce off one.

THE INTANGIBLES

Errey is a leader, an assistant captain and a valued team player. He doesn't take undisciplined extra penalties any more because he has matured; he's less of a hothead. He always seems to come up with a big play at a key moment. He wants the puck all the time. He wants to beat you. He wants to win.

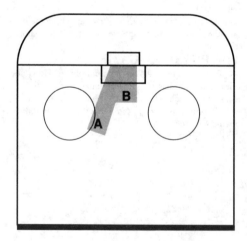

RON FRANCIS

Yrs. of NHL service: 11
Born: Sault Ste. Marie, Ont.; March 1, 1963
Position: Center
Height: 6-2
Weight: 200
Uniform no.: 10
Shoots: Left

Career statistics:

GP	G	A	TP	PIM
798	287	599	886	589

1991-92 statistics:

GP	G	A	TP	+/-	PIM	PP	SH	GW	GT	S	PCT
70	21	33	54	−7	30	5	1	2	1	121	17.4

LAST SEASON

Marked 11th consecutive season of 20 goals or more. Set up seven game-winning goals. Missed nine games due to contract dispute, one due to injured ankle.

THE FINESSE GAME

Francis is a player of fine two-way skills, which is why he always seems to be there when danger is to be created offensively or averted defensively.

He is an excellent defensive player who is depended upon to win the key defensive-zone face-offs — especially the first draw in a penalty-killing situation. Francis has a nice touch on the draws, and good hands also enable him to feather a pass to a breaking teammate. He also has a long reach, and he uses it.

Francis is strong on his feet, which helps keep his legs going in the scrums. Good balance enables him to tie up his opponent, then kick the puck to a teammate. But he is rather a gawky skater and doesn't have a lot of speed; Francis is more a player who excels at stops and starts in confined space.

He is also a responsible player who is as dilligent in front of his net as he is in the attacking zone. He has above-average drive and determination, and will not hesitate to dive toward a puck — to block a shot, to sweep the puck from the goal mouth, to chop it away from an opponent.

His offensive game is not to be overlooked, but his role behind Mario Lemieux does not call for as much scoring. He sees the ice well, distributes well and takes the hits to spring a teammate with the puck. He is, nonetheless, an unspectacular offensive player.

THE PHYSICAL GAME

Francis does not shy away from the painful places on the ice, the places where you get bruises. He goes in front of the net for deflections and rebounds, uses his strength and balance to gain position, keeps plugging away.

He does not initiate any element of threatening physical contact. He doesn't bury people. But he uses strength in the face-off battles, does his best to lock off his opposing center on offensive-zone draws, fights hard to get to his point those rare times he loses a face-off in the defensive zone.

THE INTANGIBLES

Francis inspires a sense of confidence in his teammates because he is such a dependable player. And he was an absolute tower of strengh in the playoffs last spring, stepping into the gap and playing a huge leadership role when Mario Lemieux was injured.

Francis may not seem to show much emotion on the ice, but he has tremendous desire to win and is an extremely gritty competitor. He may not be much for the spotlight, but his persistence and contribution to victory are laudatory.

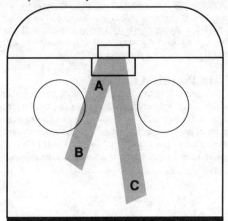

JAROMIR JAGR

Yrs. of NHL service: 2
Born: Kladno, Czechoslovakia; Feb. 15, 1972
Position: Right wing
Height: 6-2
Weight: 208
Uniform no.: 68
Shoots: Left

Career statistics:

GP	G	A	TP	PIM
150	59	67	126	76

1991-92 statistics:

GP	G	A	TP	+/-	PIM	PP	SH	GW	GT	S	PCT
70	32	37	69	12	34	4	0	4	0	194	16.5

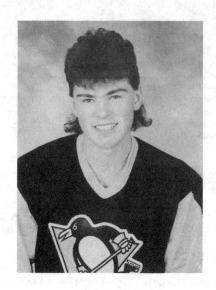

LAST SEASON

Ranked fourth on team in goals, fifth in total points. Missed 10 games due to suspension for bumping referee Ron Hoggarth at Washington, January 26. Scored 17 goals in third periods.

THE FINESSE GAME

Jagr is a multi-faceted weapon who can be a positively terrifying offensive threat. He has a nose for the net and the tools that will carry him there.

A skater of tremendous strength, power and balance, he uses his edges extremely well. He accelerates on his crossovers, is more a glider than a strider. He can lean on a defenseman, control the puck with one hand while driving to the net, and even can get off a strong one-handed shot.

Jagr loves the backhand, and knows everyone expects him to use it. So he often fakes going to the backhand, evoking the reaction he wants, then stays on the forehand and scores. He also makes extensive use of his reach and his wingspan, which often fools the goalie into aligning himself with Jagr's body rather than the puck; that opens up lots of shooting space for him to fill.

There are times when he hangs onto the puck too long, waiting for openings that never occur. But mostly, he moves it promptly and properly.

THE PHYSICAL GAME

Jagr tends to turn away from checks, rather than finish them, but there is an unmistakable physical element to his game. He seems to relish one-on-one confrontations with a defenseman or a goalie, wins many more than he loses, and couldn't care less if he has to go into the corners with two defenders converging on him.

Jagr did get quiet for a while in the Stanley Cup finals last spring when the Blackhawks used hitmen against him, which suggests intimidation attempts work occasionally. But Jagr's mental toughness is hardening and he's still growing; he's just 20 years old.

THE INTANGIBLES

Is there a player in the league who has as much fun as this guy? He loves the game, loves to play it, wants to make even better moves. And he has the benefit of not being the go-to guy, because Lemieux is there, attracting most of the checking attention and pressure. Last year, we forecast 50 goals for Jagr ''in the next season or two.'' He's on schedule.

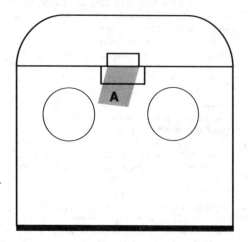

GRANT JENNINGS

Yrs. of NHL service: 4
Born: Hudson Bay, Sask.; May 5, 1965
Position: Right defense
Height: 6-3
Weight: 210
Uniform no.: 3
Shoots: Left

Career statistics:

GP	G	A	TP	PIM
229	12	28	40	542

1991-92 statistics:

GP	G	A	TP	+/-	PIM	PP	SH	GW	GT	S	PCT
53	4	5	9	−1	104	0	2	2	0	35	11.4

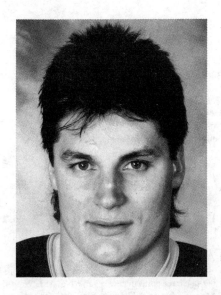

LAST SEASON

Goal total was single-season high. Tied club record for defensemen with two shorthanded goals. Games played total was career low. Missed five games due to finger injury, three due to hand injury, one due to flu.

THE FINESSE GAME

Jennings isn't much of a skater — a problem because of the position he plays and because of the physical role he must play to stay in the lineup. He can get toasted by a player with outside speed because he does not turn quickly. By the time he shifts from backward skating to forward skating, the attacker generally is past him and Jennings is forced to hold the guy or put a hook in him to prevent a scoring chance.

To his credit, though, Jennings seems aware of this limitation and had adapted his game accordingly. Jennings never tries to do too much with the puck. He doesn't throw it away too fast, but he gets the puck and moves it promptly, so he won't get into a situation where foot speed is required.

Jennings also uses his reach, which is an asset in penalty-killing situations. But lack of mobility essentially pins him to the front of the net.

THE PHYSICAL GAME

Jennings' skating also is a disadvantage in physical confrontations. When he fights, he tends to get off balance and fall down before he wants to. Along the boards, he rarely will come away with the puck because the foot quickness is not there. But he keeps the front of his net clear, punishing any opponent who comes near.

THE INTANGIBLES

Jennings is a limited player of size and strength and willingness. He keeps opposing players honest, but that isn't always enough reason for him to play every night.

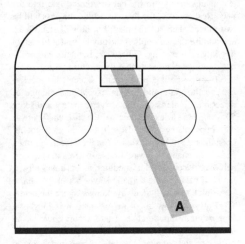

283

MARIO LEMIEUX

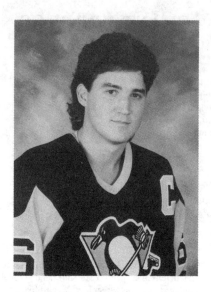

Yrs. of NHL service: 8
Born: Montreal, Que.; October 5, 1965
Position: Center
Height: 6-4
Weight: 210
Uniform no.: 66
Shoots: Right

Career statistics:

GP	G	A	TP	PIM
517	408	606	1,014	548

1991-92 statistics:

GP	G	A	TP	+/-	PIM	PP	SH	GW	GT	S	PCT
64	44	87	131	27	94	12	4	5	1	249	17.7

LAST SEASON

Won third scoring title in five seasons. Scored 1,000th career point in career game No. 513. Was on-ice for 70 of team's 72 power-play goals in games he played. Missed 13 games due to back problems, two due to shoulder injury, one because of flu.

THE FINESSE GAME

Because he is so creative, has such soft hands and is such a fine passer on the forehand and the backhand, Lemieux makes the game revolve around his whim. He can fiddle with the puck high in the zone and paralyze defenders while his wings break wide to open ice. Or he can drive the defense back with his skating power, then send a perfect pass on any number of teammates driving to the net or coming late into the play. Rest assured, the thought behind the pass will be two moves ahead of the play; but he will stand back and admire the pass only if the guy he sent it to cannot possibly miss scoring. Otherwise, Lemieux will break back into the play, available for a return pass.

Because he is a phenomenal skater who accelerates on the glide and has an exceptional change of direction, Lemieux also can drive to the net and score 50 ways. He varies the speed of the rush and controls the tempo of the game. He can bear in on a goalie, open the face of his stickblade to fake a forehand, then shoot a forehand, anyway. Lemieux loves the top corner, over the goalie's left shoulder, as a primary target, but he'll fill any hole a goalie leaves because he has a very quick release and always knows where the net is.

But you know about his offense. It is long past time to credit his defense. There are giveaways and there are takeaways, and Lemieux uses his reach and his smarts to take away the defense-to-defense pass at the point. He is as scary during the other team's power play as he is during the Penguins'.

THE PHYSICAL GAME

For all his finesse skills, Lemieux is an enormous physical presence because of his strength and his will-ingness to use his physical assets. Lemieux almost always carries the puck way out to the side, forehand or backhand, shielding it with his body and forcing a defender to reach, which guarantees the defender will be off-balance when the next move comes. Lemieux also makes a number of his best scoring plays while carrying a defender to the net, or after pulling out of the clutches of an opponent — the foremost display of his power.

THE INTANGIBLES

He is the premier player in the game, and it is about time he was recognized as such. Lemieux loses style points because people still claim he takes nights off and because he over-reacts theatrically to illegal plays against him. But there's no greater competitor when the chips are down, when the game's on the line and you need a goal or a big play. He wants to win and he wins. Any complaints about him are jealousy or sour grapes.

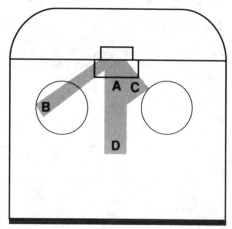

TROY LONEY

Yrs. of NHL service: 7
Born: Bow Island, Alta.; September 21, 1963
Position: Left wing
Height: 6-3
Weight: 209
Uniform no.: 24
Shoots: Left

Career statistics:

GP	G	A	TP	PIM
450	64	84	148	881

1991-92 statistics:

GP	G	A	TP	+/-	PIM	PP	SH	GW	GT	S	PCT
76	10	16	26	−5	127	0	0	1	0	94	10.6

LAST SEASON

Goal and point totals were within one of career highs. Games played total was career high.

THE FINESSE GAME

Loney used to be a slug, someone who was in the lineup only because of his willingness to mix it up. And while Loney still adds a physical element to the lineup, his more direct claim to fame now is his improved ability to read the play and act accordingly in a defensive role.

Loney can kill a penalty. He can play a responsible game in the defensive zone. He doesn't just wander around, leaving players who should be covered.

His goals are going to come from scrambles in front, from rebounds and from going to the net. He isn't going to finesse a pretty play past a goalie. His shooting range, about once a game, is 15 feet or less.

THE PHYSICAL GAME

Loney has not forgotten his roots. He is still one of the first guys over the boards if physical battles are escalating, but he is smarter now, a bit more of a diplomat than before. He is used more to restore order than to heighten turmoil. He still will fight, but it has to be for a good reason.

THE INTANGIBLES

Loney is a marginal player. He has not gotten better as much as he has gotten smarter

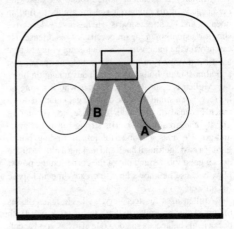

JOE MULLEN

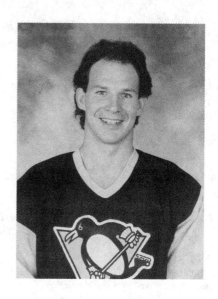

Yrs. of NHL service: 11
Born: New York City, N.Y.; February 26, 1957
Position: Right wing
Height: 5-9
Weight: 180
Uniform no.: 7
Shoots: Right

Career statistics:

GP	G	A	TP	PIM
770	400	449	849	176

1991-92 statistics:

GP	G	A	TP	+/-	PIM	PP	SH	GW	GT	S	PCT
77	42	45	87	12	30	14	0	4	1	226	18.6

LAST SEASON

Became first American-born player to record 400 goals. Goal total was third on team and tied for 11th in NHL. Marked seventh career season with 40 goals or more. Scored 80 or more points for eighth time. Missed three games due to hip/back injury.

THE FINESSE GAME

Mullen has excellent skills around the attacking net because of his quick release, his ability to find an opening and his street smarts. He has a very deceptive shot for a small man, again because of his release. He can protect the puck very well, but is not going to beat a lot of guys one-on-one because he's not super-fast and almost everybody has a reach advantage on him.

Mullen is a sneaky-quick skater who is strong on his feet. For a small man, he doesn't get knocked down much because of his wide foot base, low center of gravity and great balance. His strong suit is the give-and-go. He does a wonderful job of finding holes, giving a pass, getting it back and making a play. Mullen does a good job coming out of the corner on the power play, because he knows how to create time and space for himself.

Mullen uses his feet very well. He takes passes off his skates and nudges them to his stick in a flash because his balance is so good. He also has good acceleration, so if he steals an opponent's pass, he can break away with it. Mullen's hockey sense also makes him proficient at getting the puck out of his defensive zone; he can take an outlet pass around the boards, then beat the first forechecker and get it out.

THE PHYSICAL GAME

Mullen is not shy, but obviously size is a limitation. So he makes himself 'larger' by always keeping his stick on the ice when he forechecks. That way, he may not be a threat to crunch somebody, but he still closes down the passing lane and forces a defenseman to make a move to get past him. That tactic causes turnovers, which Mullen is more than quick enough to convert.

THE INTANGIBLES

A bona fide candidate for the Hall of Fame, simply because he made it to the NHL from the sidewalks of New York. The fact he has scored as much as he has, has played on three Stanley Cup champions, has made as much of himself as he has, tells you how much character and heart there is in this player.

When he talks in the dressing room, people tend to listen, and they should, because of Mullen's respect for the game and the sacrifices he has made to play it. This is a consummate professional who still is trying to sharpen his skills, which is why he has endured and why he still has value to a team despite his age, his size and the major knee injury that ended last season for him.

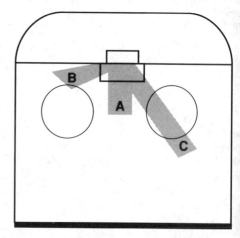

LARRY MURPHY

Yrs. of NHL service: 12
Born: Scarborough, Ont.; March 8, 1961
Position: Right defense
Height: 6-2
Weight: 210
Uniform no.: 55
Shoots: Right

Career statistics:

GP	G	A	TP	PIM
937	181	568	749	761

1991-92 statistics:

GP	G	A	TP	+/-	PIM	PP	SH	GW	GT	S	PCT
77	21	56	77	33	50	7	2	3	0	206	10.2

LAST SEASON

Finished fourth among NHL defensemen in scoring, second among defensemen in goals. Tied club record for winning goals by a defenseman. Tied club record for shorthanded goals by a defenseman.

THE FINESSE GAME

Murphy does a lot of things well, plays the game way better than he did a few years ago, because he seems to be thinking the game better than ever — seems only now to be reaching peace with the mental challenge of his position. When he broke into the league, Murphy played more like a forward who occasionally skated backward to protect his net; now, he is a much more mature player whose offense stems from a defensive base.

Most of the time now, when Murphy takes offensive risks, they are risks with a good up-side. He uses his head in deciding when to join the rush. He will cheat way into the attacking zone to steal a puck that is up for grabs; and while the opponent is guaranteed a break the other way if the puck gets past him, Murphy does a better job now of making sure he controls the disc — which leaves the other team at a disadvantage.

Murphy makes a nice first pass. He takes what's there instead of forcing something that isn't. He doesn't need to make a home run breakaway pass to the red line. He doesn't need to make a pretty play, unless it's the best option. He'll still carry end-to-end once in a while; Murphy has the skating and puck-handling skills to do it.

But the enduringly noticeable quality is his smarts. He reads the play well, positions himself well. And for a guy who handles the puck as much as he does, Murphy seems to give it up less. He also uses the right shot for the situation; rather than wind up for the big bomb, for example, he makes extensive use of the wrist shot and increases his point production as a result.

THE PHYSICAL GAME

Murphy still plays the puck more than the man, still has his share of lapses in front of his net. He absolutely is a finesse player in a physically demanding position, but he more than gets the job done.

THE INTANGIBLES

Murphy probably would get more attention if he drew more attention to himself, but he plays a game that must be described as quietly effective. In fact, he was one of the better two-way defensemen in the league last season, but Brian Leetch stole the headlines by scoring more than 100 points.

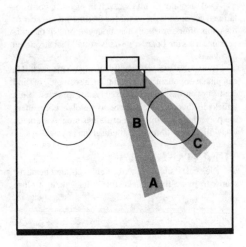

JIM PAEK

Yrs. of NHL service: 1
Born: Seoul, Korea; April 7, 1967
Position: Left defense
Height: 6-1
Weight: 195
Uniform no.: 2
Shoots: Left

Career statistics:

GP	G	A	TP	PIM
53	1	7	8	45

1991-92 statistics:

GP	G	A	TP	+/-	PIM	PP	SH	GW	GT	S	PCT
50	1	7	8	0	36	0	0	0	0	33	3.0

LAST SEASON
Missed 14 games due to surgery to repair finger tendon on left hand.

THE FINESSE GAME
Paek is a player who does a lot better in open ice than in confined space. He plays into his assets by keeping the puck in motion. He gets it and moves it. He does nothing fancy, nothing glamorous; he just chips the puck out of the zone and keeps dangerous things from occurring.

And every so often, just to keep you honest, he'll throw a sharp breakout pass straight up the middle of the ice. He uses his head out there, but he almost never draws any attention to himself.

The guy virtually never shoots. He is very strictly a stay-at-home defenseman.

THE PHYSICAL GAME
Paek may not do all that well in physical confrontations. He spends an awful lot of time on the seat of his pants after somebody has bounced him in the corners or along the boards; so he is not all that strong on his skates.

He is, however, extremely strong on his stick. He can pin an opponent's stick on the ice, can pick off and control even the hardest passes. And, in order to get knocked down, you still have to involve yourself in the play; there are many other defensemen with much less willingness to involve themselves physically.

THE INTANGIBLES
Paek carries himself extremely well, and he never seems to make the mistake that kills you in a close game. He already has stood up to many challenges under great pressure and has never failed in the face of that stress.

KJELL SAMUELSSON

Yrs. of NHL service: 6
Born: Tyngsryd, Sweden; October 18, 1958
Position: Right defenseman
Height: 6-6
Weight: 235
Uniform no.: 23
Shoots: Right

Career statistics:

GP	G	A	TP	PIM
446	31	97	128	753

1991-92 statistics:

GP	G	A	TP	+/-	PIM	PP	SH	GW	GT	S	PCT
74	5	11	16	1	110	0	0	1	0	91	5.5

LAST SEASON

Obtained from Philadelphia, along with Rick Tocchet and Ken Wregget, in three-way trade February 19, 1992. Missed one game due to shoulder injury, one due to flu.

THE FINESSE GAME

A lot of Samuelsson's game is based on his phenomenal reach and his ability to make it work so much to his advantage. With those incredibly long arms, and incredibly long stick, Samuelsson seems to take half the rink away from any forward coming down his side.

Add to that an extremely long stride, which more than enables Samuelsson to keep up with most of the forwards in the league and angle them to the bad ice. There, they have to try to pass through him or throw the puck up for grabs before he comes to smear them along the boards.

Samuelsson is one of the last players in the world to make a rush. In fact, he doesn't seem to want much to do with the puck. Once he gains possession in the defensive zone, he'll look for a breakout pass; but most of the time he is content to crank it off the boards and simply get it out of the zone. This makes him effective against a heavy forecheck, because the marauding forwards then are caught coming hard into the zone.

The rare times he gets the puck as far up ice as the neutral zone, Samuelsson always makes sure to get the puck deep in the other end, so the opposition has to skate another 150-odd feet before meeting him again.

THE PHYSICAL GAME

Samuelsson can be an extremely effective checker without throwing the big hit on a player. All he has to do is reach you and lean on you with his 230-odd pounds; you aren't going anyplace and you certainly aren't going to beat him back into the play.

There also are times when he is a very annoying opponent. He lays his stick on you, he wraps arms around you, puts his hands on you, leans his body on you, puts his glove in your face, says something rude. He's always making somebody say, 'Get the heck OFF me.'

When it comes down to paying the price instead of making someone else do it, Samuelsson is first in line. He is very effective challenging point shots and making the shooters fire wide; first they have to get the puck past him, then they have to get it past the goalie. That isn't easy. Samuelsson also will block a lot of shots and will use his reach to intercept a lot of passes.

THE INTANGIBLES

This is a player who doesn't rattle easily or often. Just about all he cares about it getting the puck out of the zone, which makes him the perfect guy for defending a lead late in the game.

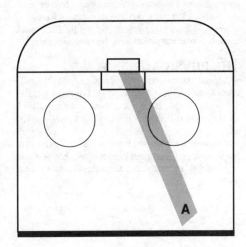

ULF SAMUELSSON

Yrs. of NHL service: 8
Born: Fagersta, Sweden; March 26, 1964
Position: Left defense
Height: 6-1
Weight: 195
Uniform no.: 5
Shoots: Left

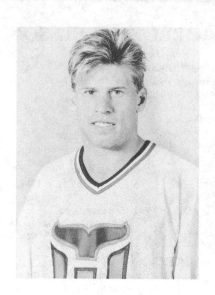

Career statistics:

GP	G	A	TP	PIM
539	33	162	195	1353

1991-92 statistics:

GP	G	A	TP	+/-	PIM	PP	SH	GW	GT	S	PCT
62	1	14	15	2	206	1	0	1	0	75	1.3

LAST SEASON

Goals scored represented a career low, games played was second lowest of his career. Lost four games because of surgery for removal of bone chips from right elbow, two because of hip injury, two because of flu, one due to hand injury.

THE FINESSE GAME

Samuelsson is a solid package, an extremely well-built athlete who virtually never takes a backward step on someone else's terms. If you're trying to get to his net, you have to go around him or through him; and neither is especially easy, as Samuelsson is a good (not great) skater who relies on his balance and strength.

Utter fearlessness makes Samuelsson an excellent defender, as great lateral mobility makes him more or less impossible to beat one-on-one. While he is a fine skater laterally, Samuelsson doesn't have much straight-line speed. While he's not a plodder, the puck slows him down.

At the same time, he is the Penguins' most effective penalty-killing defenseman because of he challenges the puck aggressively and blocks shots eagerly.

Samuelsson has a very big shot, but he isn't a big scorer and is never going to be, as he isn't quick enough in read the situation in the offensive zone.

THE PHYSICAL GAME

Samuelsson plays as though big hits are the only checks you're allowed to throw. He is extremely nasty in front of the net, and makes it clear that a crosscheck awaits any forward who wants to set up shop in the slot.

Samuelsson will use his hip or his knee to hit you. He will hit you high or submarine you, but you will be hit if he can reach you. If you get hurt, it's your problem.

At the same time, Samuelsson accepts life on the receiving end of the bruises, and not just from physical contact. He is always ready to block shots, especially if his team has two players in the penalty box, and will always try to grab a piece of any skater attempting to get past him.

THE INTANGIBLES

Samuelsson has become more disciplined, because he regularly is asked to play against the other team's better players and constantly is reminded he is of no value in the penalty box. Still, Samuelsson is an agitator, an in-your-face kind of player who always keeps putting pepper in the stew. If he gets you thinking more about killing him than about winning the game, Samuelsson has done his job perfectly.

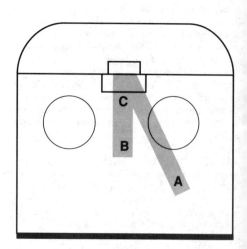

PAUL STANTON

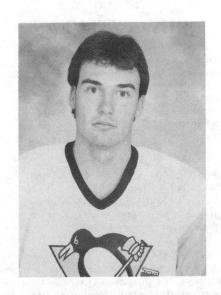

Yrs. of NHL service: 2
Born: Boston, Mass.; June 22, 1967
Position: Right defense
Height: 6-1
Weight: 200
Uniform no.: 22
Shoots: Right

Career statistics:

GP	G	A	TP	PIM
129	7	26	33	100

1991-92 statistics:

GP	G	A	TP	+/-	PIM	PP	SH	GW	GT	S	PCT
54	2	8	10	−8	62	0	0	0	0	70	2.9

LAST SEASON

Missed 16 games due to ligament damage in right knee.

THE FINESSE GAME

Stanton appears to prefer having the play come at him, rather than head toward the play.

A strong first step and good acceleration to top skating speed enables him to jump into the rush explosively, but Stanton doesn't exploit that asset much. He'd rather stay back, on call, and is more comfortable with less flamboyant responsibilities. He generally chooses to pass the puck out of the defensive zone rather than to skate with it; he advances the puck effectively, but quietly.

Foot skills also give Stanton confidence to pinch up the boards at the attacking blue line, but offensive situations in general seem to confuse him. He doesn't shoot much at all, and there are times when he'll try to make a play at the blue line instead of simply getting the puck deep.

But he is a solid defender against the rush, because he can angle players off to bad ice. Stanton has fabulous, underrated lateral movement, and balance allows him to use the poke check at the blue line.

THE PHYSICAL GAME

Stanton worked hard to improve his physical play, to become stronger along the boards and in the corners. And he will throw an occasional hip check in open ice. Still, he uses his stick to check more than his body. He sometimes is extremely careless with his clearing attempts and has been known to give up the puck under pressure.

THE INTANGIBLES

Stanton is a steady player who is improving. He won't ever be dominant, but he's very adequate and he works hard.

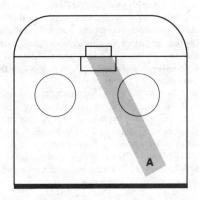

KEVIN STEVENS

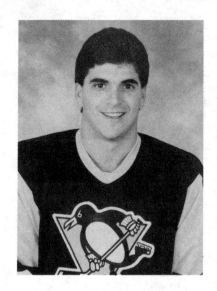

Yrs. of NHL service: 5
Born: Brockton, Mass.; April 15, 1965
Position: Left wing
Height: 6-3
Weight: 217
Uniform no.: 25
Shoots: Left

Career statistics:

GP	G	A	TP	PIM
276	140	161	301	583

1991-92 statistics:

GP	G	A	TP	+/-	PIM	PP	SH	GW	GT	S	PCT
80	54	69	123	8	252	19	0	4	0	325	16.6

LAST SEASON

Set record for points in a season by an American-born player. Was first player to record more than 100 points and 200 penalty minutes in same season. Set NHL record for points by a left wing in one season. Point total was second in NHL.

THE FINESSE GAME

Stevens' statistics in points and penalty minutes speak for themselves in describing his game. He was the NHL's definitive power forward last season.

Stevens has a good sense of when to drive to the net, go for the holes or look for the pass from behind the goal line. He gets to those holes more because of skating prowess and leg strength than because of quickness or agility. He scores from the holes because of his fast release, combined with strength, and hand-eye coordination that allows him to one-time the puck well.

Stevens doesn't necessarily need the element of surprise, because his shot is strong enough to beat most goalies. But he gives goaltenders more than they can handle. Especially on the passes from behind the net, goalies have to change their focus from behind the net to in front, they have to gauge where Stevens is — even if they've already stolen a look — and then they have to react to his strong shot.

His strength in the slot is reminiscent of Tim Kerr in his devastating prime. Mario Lemieux lays those big, fat saucer passes out between the face-off circles and Stevens snaps them in from the hashmarks. He also is expert at deflecting point shots, which makes him a varied threat. He can bury a rebound, convert a deflection, score off a rush and collect a hat trick without making the same play twice.

THE PHYSICAL GAME

For a guy his size, Stevens hits with authority but seems at times to hate being hit. He is so confident in his skating strength and balance that almost any time he ends up flat on the ice, Stevens believes a penalty should be called.

Stevens uses his size and strength to intimidating advantage; it gets him extra room. But while he finishes most checks, Stevens is not always an eager banger. He's one of the truly nice guys off the ice, and sometimes, he's too nice on it.

Still, you don't pile up 252 penalty minutes for genteel play. And only the truly exceptional can bang AND score for 80 games, plus playoffs.

THE INTANGIBLES

Stevens has worked hard to improve, to reach All-Star respectability, and has two Stanley Cup rings for his reward. It should be noted he got his nose above the line, into 'plus' status.

Plus 8 on 123 points, however, suggests a bit of work on defense remains for this player, for whom the sky seems to be the limit.

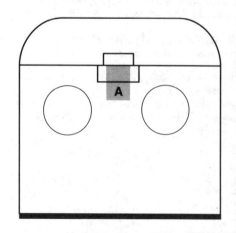

RICK TOCCHET

Yrs. of NHL service: 8
Born: Scarborough, Ont.; April 9, 1964
Position: Right wing
Height: 6-0
Weight: 205
Uniform no.: 92
Shoots: Right

Career statistics:

GP	G	A	TP	PIM
550	229	463	492	1734

1991-92 statistics:

GP	G	A	TP	+/-	PIM	PP	SH	GW	GT	S	PCT
61	27	32	59	15	151	8	1	2	1	166	16.3

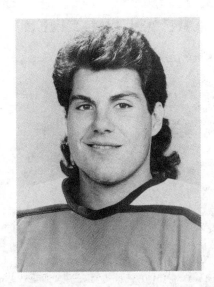

LAST SEASON

Reached 20-goal mark a sixth consecutive season. Surpassed 100 PIM an eighth straight season. Missed 19 games due to injuries: heel (10), knee (five), jaw (three), eye (one). Plus-minus improved 13 goals.

THE FINESSE GAME

Tocchet is a strong skater, in that he has good balance and some explosiveness, but he is not agile or especially quick. He has difficulty changing direction quickly and he makes an extremely wide turn, which often leaves him more behind the play than he wants to be.

But he gets to the physical, confrontation areas of the ice, where he feels most at home. He drives to the front of the net and draws a defender's attention. He powers to the side boards and into the corners and wars for the puck, but his proficiency is in winning the puck, more than doing something with it after gaining possession.

He does have finishing skills—a strong wrist shot from the slot and a powerful slap shot from the circles. He will score his goals by burying rebounds, converting deflections or finishing scrambles in front, because he is not often knocked down and always is willing to pay a price. Tocchet also is a good give-and-go player, because what speed he has is in the straightaways, and his shot off the wing is quite good.

THE PHYSICAL GAME

Tocchet has been a willing hitter throughout his career, but emotionalism still gets him in trouble during the regular season. He can have a guy lined up for a solid hit, but often feels the need to leave his feet, adding emphasis to the check; and all that tends to do is draw the attention of the referee for two needless minutes in the penalty box. In the playoffs, discipline takes over and Tocchet tends to skate away from the stupid stuff.

All the banging over the years has taken a physical toll. Tocchet too often has come back too early from an injury and then has had to spend more time rehabilitating. But he is getting smarter about that, and still does a good job of sparking his team with a big hit or a big play.

THE INTANGIBLES

Tocchet benefitted from the change in scenery, provided the hard edge the Penguins wanted and needed from the right side. He gave them a physical advantage, added to their competitive spirit with his drive and desire to win. He remains a player you want on the ice in the first and last minute of a period.

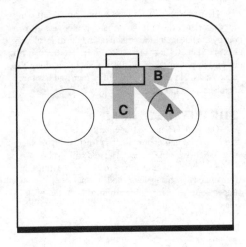

BRYAN TROTTIER

Yrs. of NHL service: 17
Born: Val Marie, Sask.; July 17, 1956
Position: Center
Height: 5-11
Weight: 195
Uniform no.: 19
Shoots: Left

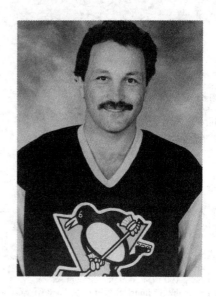

Career statistics:

GP	G	A	TP	PIM
1238	520	890	1410	876

1991-92 statistics:

GP	G	A	TP	+/-	PIM	PP	SH	GW	GT	S	PCT
63	11	18	29	-11	54	3	1	0	2	102	10.8

LAST SEASON

Is 20th on NHL all-time games-played list. Goal total is 13th in NHL history. Missed 14 games due to knee injury, two due to back injury, but still played 11 more games than prior season. Plus-minus declined 16 goals, but goal production improved by two.

THE FINESSE GAME

Trottier keeps the game simple, and remains an effective part-time player as a result. He doesn't try to overreach his capabilities, and uses supreme hockey sense to steer deliberately through the hockey waters with all those speedboats flying around.

You see the smarts in his game when a loose puck is up for grabs. Years ago, Trottier might have left his position to chase after the puck; now, he looks around first. That way, if a teammate has a better chance of reaching the puck, Trottier doesn't get in the way. And if the puck turns over, Trottier is that much closer to the person he should be checking — an extra step that matters.

He is the perfect forward to line up on left wing for important draws. If the primary center gets thrown out by the linesman, the person taking the draw merely has six Stanley Cup rings. Moreover, Trottier can fill in on the power play, or do just about anything the coach asks. He is a splendid utility man and has more than accepted that role.

THE PHYSICAL GAME

One of Trottier's trademarks always was his strength, and that endures. He is trustworthy on face-offs (defensive zone, especially) and still a solid work-horse when the puck is along the boards. Trottier has tremendously strong legs, and his balance, plus his upper-body strength, allows him to keep the puck in play.

Trottier also has not lost his penchant for hitting, an aspect powered by the drive in his legs. When he hits you, you know you've been whacked.

THE INTANGIBLES

Now that he's older, Trottier spends more and more time in the weight room, more and more time preparing himself for the next game and whatever his role in it will be. He is getting by now on his head and his smarts, more than whatever is left of his skills.

And yet, that is more than enough to keep him in an NHL lineup. The lessons he has learned, the lessons he can teach, have been invaluable. Beyond that, he still gets a giant kick out of being a hockey player.

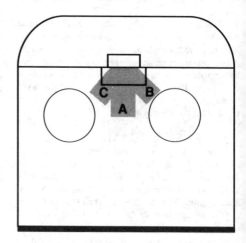

QUEBEC
NORDIQUES

JAMIE BAKER

Yrs. of NHL service: 1
Born: Ottawa, Ont.; Aug. 31, 1966
Position: Center
Height: 6-0
Weight: 190
Uniform no.: 28
Shoots: Left

Career statistics:

GP	G	A	TP	PIM
71	9	10	19	40

1991-92 statistics:

GP	G	A	TP	+/-	PIM	PP	SH	GW	GT	S	PCT
52	7	10	17	−5	32	3	0	1	0	77	9.1

LAST SEASON

First in NHL.

THE FINESSE GAME

Baker's best attribute is tremendous, explosive power in his first two steps, which gives him time to pull away from checks. His speed after that drops a bit, possibly because of a choppy stride, but still is above average.

He is a very good penalty killer. His smarts and his range make him able to check with the league's best.

Baker wins key face-offs and is not a liability in defensive zone. He will block shots and is especially good late in a game or period.

THE PHYSICAL GAME

Baker does everything at top speed, full-out. He isn't saving anything for the next shift or the next game. He is not on the ice to make friends.

THE INTANGIBLES

Baker works dilligently on off-ice conditioning and is extremely fit. He may lose ice time to more talented teammates, but he is not going to lose ice time because of being outworked.

A coach's dream, he does whatever you need him to do, and because he can come up with the big play when you need him to. He can be used, and trusted to do well, in key situations.

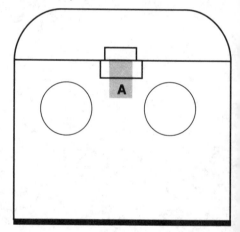

GINO CAVALLINI

Yrs. of NHL service: 8
Born: Toronto, Ont.; Nov. 24, 1962
Position: Left wing
Height: 6-1
Weight: 215
Uniform no.: 44
Shoots: Left

Career statistics:

GP	G	A	TP	PIM
526	105	144	249	473

1991-92 statistics:

GP	G	A	TP	+/-	PIM	PP	SH	GW	GT	S	PCT
66	10	14	24	−9	44	0	0	2	1	111	9.0

LAST SEASON

Games played was five-year low. Point total was a five-season low. Plus-minus declined 13 goals.

THE FINESSE GAME

Because he isn't the world's most graceful skater nor most gifted scorer, Cavallini does other things to make himself useful and productive. He draws penalties with his hustle. He succeeds because he wants the puck at least as much as his opponent, and most of the time is willing to do more to win it.

His skating skills are limited to balance and strength, especially in the straight-ahead dashes. The best of his hand skills is a sonic boom of a slap shot from the wing, although release time is a problem; he has to overpower goalies with the muscle behind the shot, because they have time to set for it.

Cavallini plays an alert, reliable game in the defensive zone. He identifies the proper check and stays with him until the danger passes.

THE PHYSICAL GAME

Cavallini will work his way down low, to the corners or behind the net, and will make a physical play on the defenseman to set up a goal. He can be valuable as a post-up guy in front on the power play. He has good size and uses it energetically.

THE INTANGIBLES

Cavallini's desire and his effort have to be contagious. You can't watch him hustle and hit and drive without wanting to do it, too. He is the perfect guy to wake up the bench, wake up the rink, to light a spark that the next line can turn into a fire.

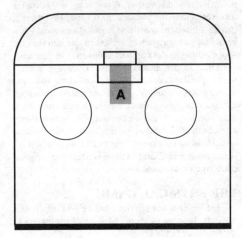

STEVE DUCHESNE

Yrs. of NHL service: 6
Born: Sept-Iles, Que.; June 30, 1965
Position: Right defense
Height: 5-11
Weight: 195
Uniform no.: ??
Shoots: Left

Career statistics:

GP	G	A	TP	PIM
460	113	235	348	483

1991-92 statistics:

GP	G	A	TP	+/-	PIM	PP	SH	GW	GT	S	PCT
78	18	38	56	−7	86	7	2	3	0	229	7.9

LAST SEASON

Goal, assist and point totals all were four-season lows. Plus-minus declined 26 goals. Shot total increased 58 and led team. Led Flyers defensemen in goals and points.

THE FINESSE GAME

Duchesne is a fast, agile skater who changes direction instantly to either side because his balance is so good. He boasts fine lateral movement and should help the Nordiques spend a great deal less time in their defensive zone this season, as one of his real strengths involves getting the puck out of trouble. He moves it quickly to start the transition game, skates it out when he has to, and always is ready to activate into the play — something he does as well as anybody in the game.

Once in the attacking zone, Duchesne doesn't waste time. He keeps the puck in well at the point and moves it quickly and is good at one-timing the puck.

Duchesne also doesn't overstay his welcome those occasions he goes deep on the attack; he gets in there, assesses the risk, and gets out if there is too much to lose. He has a very good sense of anticipation, always seems ready with Plan B if there is a turnover or some other type of emergency.

THE PHYSICAL GAME

Duchesne is not physical, but he gets in people's way, gets position on them and stops their progress to teammates or to the net.

THE INTANGIBLES

Duchesne always puts up the numbers, and can be counted on for creativity and confidence on the offensive side of the puck. He never seemed happy in Philadelphia, and may be energized by a return to his home province.

STEVEN FINN

Yrs. of NHL service: 6
Born: Laval, Que.; Aug. 20, 1966
Position: Left defense
Height: 6-0
Weight: 198
Uniform no.: 29
Shoots:

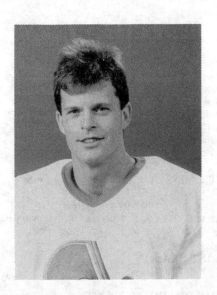

Career statistics:

GP	G	A	TP	PIM
405	20	48	68	1,129

1991-92 statistics:

GP	G	A	TP	+/-	PIM	PP	SH	GW	GT	S	PCT
65	4	7	11	−9	192	0	0	0	0	63	6.3

LAST SEASON

Plus-minus improved by 17 from prior season, PIM dropped 36, although he played six fewer games.

THE FINESSE GAME

Finn is slow, so all those games in smaller Adams Division building are a help because range is less of a requisite. But what he lack in quickness of foot, Finn tries to makes up for with quickness of thought; there is very little patience in his defensive game, and often he acts or reacts to a play before he has taken an extra moment to read it properly.

When he maintains control of his emotions, Finn does the unspectacular things that are the basis of his job and his best hope of success. He angles players to bad ice, tries to pry the puck loose, then makes sure the other guy isn't going to get it. He goes behind the net to grab the puck and make a quick breakout pass.

Finn will shoot from the point occasionally, more in hope of a deflection than in the expectation of scoring. His shot is designed as a defensive weapon; the closer the puck is to the opposing net, the farther it is from his defensive zone.

THE PHYSICAL GAME

Finn will elbow, slash, high stick or render you unconscious, if at all possible. The question used to be how he ever propelled the puck, since his stick always seemed to be probing the large intestines of anyone wearing the other uniform. There does not seem much chance he will mellow.

Finn is not much for fighting, but he does a good job as equalizer when any of his team's finesse players is being bullied. There are instances,though, when he gets into trouble with needless extra penalties at bad times.

THE INTANGIBLES

Every defense needs a mean streak, a guy who plays on the edge of sanity, and Finn is the hard-working, hard nose who handles that role well. But there is more to him than an acid stomach; along with standing up for his teammates, Finn communicates with them. You can hear him barking help and instructions on the ice, rather than leaving them on their own.

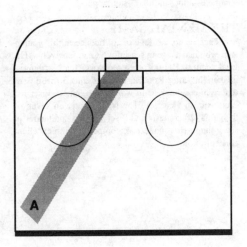

STEPHANE FISET

Yrs. of NHL service: 1
Born: Montreal, Que.; June 17, 1970
Position: Goaltender
Height: 6-0
Weight: 175
Uniform no.: 31
Catches: Left

Career statistics:

GP	MINS	GA	SO	GAA	A	PIM
32	1,661	117	1	4.27	0	8

1991-92 statistics:

GP	MINS	GAA	W	L	T	SO	GA	S	SAPCT	PIM
23	1,133	3.76	7	10	2	1	71	646	.890	8

LAST SEASON
First NHL season.

THE PHYSICAL GAME
Thanks to the exceptional quickness of his legs and his extremely sharp reflexes, Fiset prefers a butterfly style that dares shooters to aim at the upper corners. He puts a bigger worm on the hook by keeping his catching hand low, but gets away with it a lot of the time because he has fast hands.

Fiset is very good in close, where it is more difficult to get a puck over him but under the crossbar, but more of a question mark on long shots and angle shots. He leaves a lot of junk around the net, pucks up for grabs, and seems to do an awful lot of guess work.

His skills are not bad, but his technique could improve. He makes pucks hit him, and that's good; he scrambles a lot, and that's not so good.

THE MENTAL GAME
There is no shortage of confidence in this youngster, who had a strong season with a defensively AHL weak team in Halifax, then took over the Nordiques' goaltending after Ron Tugnutt was traded to Edmonton. While neither team won many games, Fiset led each team in victories. The Nordiques won seven of their final 20 contests and Fiset was the goaltender in six of them. He is an intense competitor with excellent concentration.

THE INTANGIBLES
A lot is predicted for Fiset, who needs experience and playing time to improve his reads of the play and build his professional portfolio. But the signs of a solid competitor are there; he was only three victories under .500 on a team that was 28 victories under .500.

ADAM FOOTE

Yrs. of NHL service: 1
Born: Toronto, Ont.; July 10, 1971
Position: Right defense
Height: 6-1
Weight: 180
Uniform no.: 52
Shoots: Right

Career statistics:

GP	G	A	TP	PIM
46	2	5	7	44

1991-92 statistics:

GP	G	A	TP	+/-	PIM	PP	SH	GW	GT	S	PCT
46	2	5	7	−4	44	0	0	0	1	55	3.6

LAST SEASON
First in NHL.

THE FINESSE GAME
Foote is very aptly named, because he is a skating wizard and because he plays in the Adams Division. He has a very nice first step and extremely impressive quickness. He can reach top speed from a standing start in a very short period of time and can jump into the rush very well. He has lots of range and covers acres with his mobility; Foote is very good laterally.

So he wins the races to the corners, bumps a guy and takes the puck. Foote has good balance and, as a result, a good reach.

It would be a problem, though, if he were named Adam Hands, because he isn't as gifted from that standpoint. He all but refuses to shoot, though he has an accurate slap shot. He plays the right point on the power play more because he sees the ice, because he a keen sense of where and how to move the puck; he takes a look at the target area before he makes a pass. But it is still the foot skills that make Foote a player to watch closely in the future.

THE PHYSICAL GAME
It also would be a problem if he were named Adam Strength. Foote needs to improve his grinding and play a more physical game to survive the battles in the corners or in front of his net.

THE INTANGIBLES
Foote has good anticipation. He reacts well in most situations. He is a player of promise, whose future depends on his ability to flesh out his physique and his game.

ALEXEI GUSAROV

Yrs. of NHL service: 2
Born: Leningrad, Russia; July 8, 1964
Position: Right defense
Height: 6-2
Weight: 170
Uniform no.: 5
Shoots: Left

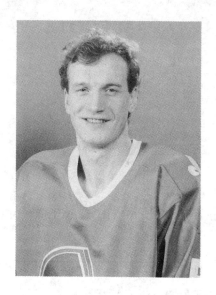

Career statistics:

GP	G	A	TP	PIM
104	8	27	35	34

1991-92 statistics:

GP	G	A	TP	+/-	PIM	PP	SH	GW	GT	S	PCT
68	5	18	23	-9	22	3	0	1	0	66	7.6

LAST SEASON

Goal, assist, point and PIM totals were career highs.

THE FINESSE GAME

Gusarov moves very well, but sometimes that asset becomes a liability. There are times when he seems to be all over the place, every place but where he should be; he will be off in a corner at a time when he should have been in front, or some such thing. When he roams, Gusarov compromises his partner. There is nothing wrong with using your range aggressively, but Gusarov doesn't yet pick all the right times to stay close to the net.

He has pretty good poise with the puck, however; Gusarov knows what he wants to do with the puck when he gets it, and will make a sharp first pass up the middle. He has a good head for the power play, a decent head for when to pinch up the boards and when to join the rush. He is confident on the backhand in open ice.

Gusarov takes a big windup on his shot from the point, which slows down the release, but still gets it off — about once a game.

THE PHYSICAL GAME

Gusarov uses his size, finishes checks, steps up to challenge the play at the blue line or in the neutral zone. He uses his reach, makes a poke check and starts a counter-attack.

THE INTANGIBLES

Gusarov is a bit of a gambler, which is not necessarily a bad thing. But he is still getting his skates wet, learning the league and the forwards and needs to get better in his one-on-one reads in the pressure zones — in the corners and the front of the net.

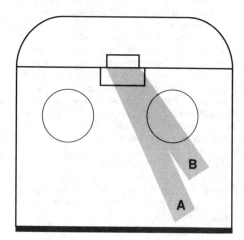

RON HEXTALL

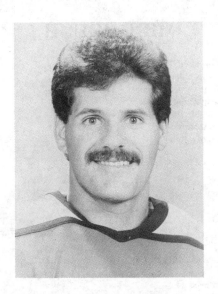

Yrs. of NHL service: 6
Born: Brandon, Man.; May 3, 1964
Position: Goaltender
Height: 6-3
Weight: 192
Uniform no.: 27
Catches: Left

Career statistics:

GP	MINS	GA	SO	GAA	A	PIM
281	16,237	886	4	3.27	15	380

1991-92 statistics:

GP	MINS	GAA	W	L	T	SO	GA	S	SAPCT	PIM
45	2,668	3.40	16	21	6	3	151	1,294	.883	35

LAST SEASON

Totals for games played, minutes and victories all increased for third consecutive season. Shutout total was career best. Missed nine games due to tendinitis in right shoulder, six games due to suspension.

THE PHYSICAL GAME

Hextall is an extremely aggressive goaltender and comes way out of the net to challenge the shooters. He never will be accused of underplaying a shot, but compared to earlier in his career, Hextall is almost chained to his net. He used to be a sucker for a first fake, but that also is less an issue now.

Hextall is very quick, flexible enough to catch and control the ankle-high shots that most other goaltenders turn into rebounds. His short game has improved because he is standing up more, striving for less extravagant movements. He is more compact in his motions, is staying with the shooter better. Hextall also is taking smaller steps to move with the play as the puck carrier slides through the low slot, thereby doing a better job of keeping his five hole closed.

His use of the stick remains a major asset. Hextall has tremendous wrist strength and skating balance, so he can rifle the puck out of trouble. He also can zip the puck up the middle to a teammate on the power play. He is more than willing to gamble, go to the corner for a loose puck, and then wing it out of danger.

THE MENTAL GAME

Hextall concentrates well. He stays with the puck through traffic and gets a piece of deflected shots. But he will allow a soft goal every now and then.

He still leads the world in complaints to referees after opposition goals, though. It is one thing to be confident enough to think you're better than every shot you face; it is a good thing to have a fiercely competitive nature. A goaltender has to accept that occasionally, somebody's shot will be better than he is, though, and Hextall seems never to have seen a goal against that wasn't the result of crease interference or a high stick.

THE INTANGIBLES

It has been a long time since Hextall has been able to get through a season, start to finish, without having to vault some type of obstacle. Suspensions have been a problem, injuries have been a problem, and now, Hextall confronts a season as a former Flyer for the first time. That will mean more adjustments, on and off the ice.

MIKE HOUGH

Yrs. of NHL service: 5
Born: Montreal, Que.; Feb. 6, 1963
Position: Right wing
Height: 6-1
Weight: 190
Uniform no.: 18
Shoots: Left

Career statistics:

GP	G	A	TP	PIM
286	60	75	135	392

1991-92 statistics:

GP	G	A	TP	+/-	PIM	PP	SH	GW	GT	S	PCT
61	16	22	38	−1	77	6	2	1	0	92	17.4

LAST SEASON

Goal, assist and point totals were career high. PIM dropped 34.

THE FINESSE GAME

Hough is a Greg Paslawski clone, but is not nearly as quick. He does all the dirty jobs — the checking role, the penalty killing, the unheralded stuff in the pits — and does them without significant contribution from his feet. He is the winger who frees the puck so the scorers on his line can bury it.

Hough is a strong skater and has far greater success when he can drive the play to a confined area, which plays into his limited assets. He scrums in the corners a lot, uses muscle to gain the puck more than quickness.

Despite limited offensive skills, Hough will go to the net for grit goals.

THE PHYSICAL GAME

Hough is rough and tough. He works well defensively and will take the body. He is a solid hitter and can punish with his body slams; he may not be quicker than many players, but an upright Hough always will be quicker than the guy he just knocked down.

Hough also uses his size in front of the goalie. He will cut through the slot just as a point shot arrives, screening the goalie or at least distracting him.

THE INTANGIBLES

You notice when Hough isn't effective, because it hurts the team. It takes a keen eye to notice he played when Hough does the job well, because he is so smooth, so efficient.

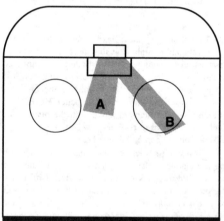

KERRY HUFFMAN

Yrs. of NHL service: 3
Born: Peterborough, Ont.; Jan. 3, 1968
Position: Left defense
Height: 6-3
Weight: 205
Uniform no.: ??
Shoots: Left

Career statistics:

GP	G	A	TP	PIM
203	22	60	82	152

1991-92 statistics:

GP	G	A	TP	+/-	PIM	PP	SH	GW	GT	S	PCT
60	14	18	32	1	41	4	0	2	0	123	11.4

LAST SEASON

Totals for games played, goals, assists, points and PIM all were career highs. Missed five games due to injury or illness.

THE FINESSE GAME

Huffman's offensive skills far outstrip his defensive abilities. He is versatile enough to be able to play on the right side. He turns very smoothly to either side. He gains the blue line with enough speed that the opposing defense has to back off out of respect for his skills. He is agile and mobile enough to get the puck out of his zone, and brings the puck up like a point guard during power plays.

He also has the smarts and the view of the ice, plus the hands, to handle an assignment on the point.

The trouble, as far as decisions are concerned, starts in the defensive end. Huffman takes some startling risks, and often has made passes directly through his own goalie's crease.

THE PHYSICAL GAME

His physical aspect is limited. He bumps and seals his checks off against the boards. Otherwise, he is not especially assertive, although he has more than enough range to reach people and finish on them.

THE INTANGIBLES

Huffman was coming on at the end of last season. He was starting to produce, the fans stopped booing and he started gaining some confidence. He was playing better in the defensive end of the ice.

Then he got traded, which seems to send him back to square one in some regards and served up another challenge to his mental toughness.

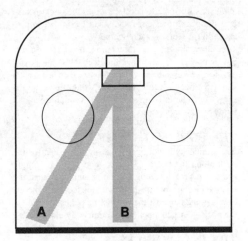

VALERI KAMENSKY

Yrs. of NHL service: 1
Born: Voskresensk, Russia; April 18, 1966
Position: Left wing
Height: 6-2
Weight: 198
Uniform no.: 17
Shoots: Right

Career statistics:

GP	G	A	TP	PIM
23	7	14	21	14

1991-92 statistics:

GP	G	A	TP	+/-	PIM	PP	SH	GW	GT	S	PCT
23	7	14	21	−1	14	2	0	1	0	42	16.7

LAST SEASON

First in NHL. Playing time was limited due to broken leg suffered in preparation for Canada Cup.

THE FINESSE GAME

Kamensky has tremendous speed and quickness, plus the one-on-one skills that could make him a 40-goal scorer. He covers lots of ground with an extremely long stride, and complements that asset by needing just a few steps to reach top speed.

Kamensky knows where to go with the puck, what to do with it. He is a very gifted passer, able to make passes that almost are reminiscent of soccer more than hockey; the pass goes into a patch of open ice, which allows his linemate to accelerate into the puck or take it at the peak of stride, rather than having to stop to accept it or, worse, reach behind.

Kamensky is a commanding presence on the power play; he would have quarterbacked the power play for the Russian team in the Canada Cup last season had it not been for the injury. He would have run the show from the left-wing sideboards, which opens all kinds of passing options.

THE PHYSICAL GAME

Kamensky is not aggressive in the scraps for the puck along the boards. He has good skating strength and a good reach, though. If he is pinned against the boards, he can work the puck with his feet. If someone else is pinned against the boards, he pokes around for the puck — or gets open while somebody else does.

THE INTANGIBLES

A broken leg suffered in the pre-season kept Kamensky out until the very late stages of the campaign and may have been one of the determining factors in costing the Nordiques a playoff spot. So the first half of this season will be pretty much a learning experience for him; but that still leaves time for his game to reach top speed in the stretch drive.

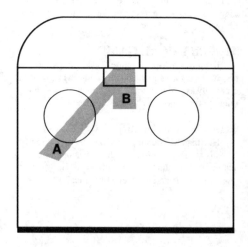

CLAUDE LAPOINTE

Yrs. of NHL service: 1
Born: Lachine, Que.; Oct. 11, 1968
Position: Center
Height: 5-9
Weight: 173
Uniform no.: 47
Shoots: Left

Career statistics:

GP	G	A	TP	PIM
91	15	22	37	90

1991-92 statistics:

GP	G	A	TP	+/-	PIM	PP	SH	GW	GT	S	PCT
78	13	20	33	−8	86	0	2	2	0	95	13.7

LAST SEASON

First full NHL season.

THE FINESSE GAME

Lapointe always drives to net with the puck, always makes things happen once he gets to the slot or the goalmouth. He does a good job on face-offs, and when he's focused on an assignment, he is a very effective role player.

Lapointe is very smart in his defensive zone. The main assets of his game are on the defensive side of the puck, but Lapointe is able to do some positive things offensively.

THE PHYSICAL GAME

A tenacious checker, Lapointe always seems to get a piece of his man, always seems to make somebody earn their territory. He is a scrappy player who loves to play along the wall, who uses effort to make up for a lack of size.

THE INTANGIBLES

This is an underrated player. Defensively speaking, given his lowly draft status, Lapointe is not that far removed from comparison to Guy Carbonneau. He is very solidly built and always seems to be reminding opponents of that fact.

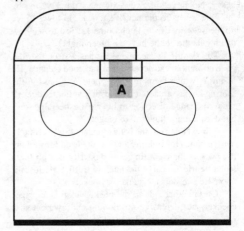

OWEN NOLAN

Yrs. of NHL service: 2
Born: Belfast, N. Ireland; Feb. 12, 1972
Position: Right wing
Height: 6-1
Weight: 195
Uniform no.: 11
Shoots: Right

Career statistics:

GP	G	A	TP	PIM
134	45	41	96	290

1991-92 statistics:

GP	G	A	TP	+/-	PIM	PP	SH	GW	GT	S	PCT
75	42	31	73	−9	181	17	0	0	1	190	22.1

LAST SEASON

Goal total jumped 39, power-play goal total increased 17. Assist output improved 21. Plus-minus improved 10. Shots increased 136.

THE FINESSE GAME

Nolan's shot qualifies as pure dynamite. It's very heavy, Nolan gets it away extremely quickly, and by the time it gets to the net, it's a pea. He loves to tee up the one-timer from the hashmarks, just to see how much guts the goalie has on a given night.

His skating is deceptive. He has a strong stride, good straight-ahead acceleration and good balance. He is quick, which helps him get open for a pass in the scoring-chance area, but is not overly agile. He doesn't seem to change direction to his right especially well, but does a more fluid job to the left.

While Nolan has the hands for shooting, definitely has the hands for fighting and has the head for moving the puck at the right time, his dexterity is a problem when he tries to carry the puck in traffic. He loses it a lot. He is a finisher, not a playmaker.

On the other side of the puck, Nolan is an eager checker, but defensive positioning and awareness is not a surpassing strength.

THE PHYSICAL GAME

Nolan is always going to the net or trying to get to the net. He will hit anyone in the league and will fight anyone in the league. He loves to initiate contact, but also will take a hit to make a play. He's as tough as nails and will fight for every inch of ice. If pushed, he very definitely pushes back.

THE INTANGIBLES

Nolan has a tremendous amount of desire, and he certainly seemed frustrated by the amount of losing he has had to endure during his time in Quebec. He slowed down a bit offensively after a positively sizzling start because of the checking attention he faced, but that opened things up for Mats Sundin.

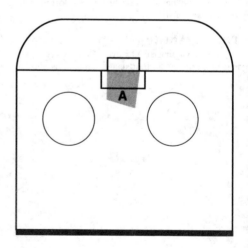

308

GREG PASLAWSKI

Yrs. of NHL service: 8
Born: Kindersley, Sask.; Aug. 25, 1961
Position: Right wing
Height: 5-11
Weight: 190
Uniform no.: 23
Shoots: Right

Career statistics:

GP	G	A	TP	PIM
562	167	161	328	155

1991-92 statistics:

GP	G	A	TP	+/-	PIM	PP	SH	GW	GT	S	PCT
80	28	17	45	−12	18	5	1	4	1	134	20.9

LAST SEASON

Goal total improved by 17, assist total by six, shot total by 59. Winning-goal total led team.

THE FINESSE GAME

Paslawski has some nice skating skills and isn't much for the heavy going, but he also is not the pure finesse player his low penalty total would suggest. He can jump to the holes, drive to the net and play a scrappy, competitive game. He can make a 360-degree pivot and wheel a backhand shot at the net from the slot. He stops sharply, gets the puck, moves it and starts the transition to offense quickly from deep in the defensive zone.

Skating skills also make Paslawski useful on special teams. While his overall package doesn't exactly merit much power-play time, Paslawski uses his skating skills to make himself viable during advantages. He has enough strength, balance and will to come out from behind the net, run the defensive gauntlet and step in front for a stuff try. Killing penalties, his skating and determination power his pursuit of the puck.

Paslawski also is a fairly effective checker, a defensive wing who will score an occasional goal.

THE PHYSICAL GAME

Paslawski, on many nights, is the hockey version of the baseball player who gets his uniform dirty. He will compete, will play tenaciously on the forecheck. He is a meat-and-potatoes kind of player who is valuable to an organization because he will do the dirty jobs.

THE INTANGIBLES

Palawski has survived in the NHL making himself a player people want on their team. He is a plugger, a character player, a worker best pegged for the third or fourth line.

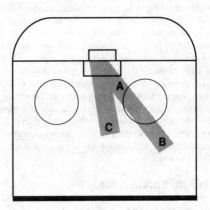

309

MIKE RICCI

Yrs. of NHL service: 2
Born: Scarborough, Ont.; Oct. 27, 1971
Position: Center
Height: 6-0
Weight: 190
Uniform no.: ??
Shoots: Left

Career statistics:

GP	G	A	TP	PIM
146	41	56	97	157

1991-92 statistics:

GP	G	A	TP	+/-	PIM	PP	SH	GW	GT	S	PCT
78	20	36	56	−10	93	11	2	0	0	149	13.4

LAST SEASON

Games played improved 10. Production improved 16 assists, although goal total dropped one from rookie output. PIM more than doubled.

THE FINESSE GAME

Ricci has good speed, but nothing that makes you go, 'Wow!' He is strong on his skates, able to turn with ease because of quality balance, but it is one aspect of his game that could use improvement.

Ricci is clever with the puck and has a good sense of when to pass, when to shoot, which makes him a viable power-play quarterback from the sideboards at the right-wing face-off circle. Along with being sure, his hands are quick; Ricci can dish the puck at the last second if he sees a checker approaching.

He can score from anywhere. Ricci can put a backhand under the crossbar from in close when most of the other forwards in the league would put it in the third row of the balcony. Superb hand-eye coordination makes him expert at deflections and batting the puck out of the air, which also helps on draws.

Moreover, he has an awareness of where to be — which is something you can expect from Peterborough graduates — and makes a good transition to defense when the puck turns over. He is extremely alert defensively and is a good penalty killer, because he always wants the puck and always works to get it when he doesn't have it.

THE PHYSICAL GAME

On face-offs, Ricci takes advantage of his strength, balance and hand speed. He also finishes a lot of checks — with authority, when possible. Ricci likes to hack the arms and ankles, just to let you know he's there, and goes to the parts of the ice where you have to pay a price.

He's good in the corners and will take on two defenders if necessary. He is strong enough to control the puck after getting crunched. He does the dirty work willingly, tries to carry the puck (and a defender) to the net from the sideboards.

THE INTANGIBLES

Ricci is an extremely intense, antagonizing, yappy competitor who still is working on his discipline. He is very scrappy, very determined, very persistent, but also very mature. He is a tremendous character player, a leader. That solid background, gained at the Dick Todd Finishing School in Peterborough, certifies him as a polished product.

Ricci had an awful 10 days last June. His father passed away after a long illness, then Ricci was part of the Eric Lindros deal. The way he responds to those adversities will give the full measure of his character.

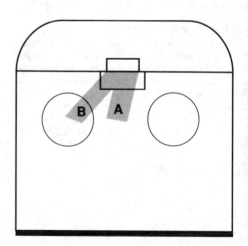

JOE SAKIC

Yrs. of NHL service: 4
Born: Burnaby, B.C.; July 7, 1969
Position: Center
Height: 5-11
Weight: 185
Uniform no.: 19
Shoots: Left

Career statistics:

GP	G	A	TP	PIM
299	139	228	367	95

1991-92 statistics:

GP	G	A	TP	+/-	PIM	PP	SH	GW	GT	S	PCT
69	29	65	94	5	20	6	3	1	1	217	13.4

LAST SEASON

Goal total dropped 19, but plus-minus improved 31 goals. Point total led team.

THE FINESSE GAME

Sakic is a phenomenal finesse player, in large part because of his stickhandling skills. He is agile, nimble, able to play in traffic and able to stickhandle in a phone booth. He is so superior with the puck on his stick, such an exceptional one-on-one player compared to 90 percent of the athletes in the league, that he's a threat to score every time he has puck.

As a result, Sakic also has the ability to make the players around him more dangerous. He can attract attention from defenders, spot open teammates and get them the puck.

Sakic is an underrated shooter — not so much because of his velocity but because of his accuracy and the quickness of his release. He can score from 20 feet or closer, but also will bury an occasional power-play shot from the right point. He can pass equally well on the forehand and backhand, and also exploits his hand quickness to win face-offs and pick off passes.

His skating is not pretty, but it's effective. If Sakic has one outstanding skating attribute, it's his ability to shift gears from an average speed, to better-than-average, very quickly. That causes problems for defensemen, because they have to turn at a time when he already has gained momentum. His balance also may be somewhat overlooked; he can absorb a pretty good jolt and remain upright.

THE PHYSICAL GAME

Sakic accepts being hit more than he will initiate contact. He will not initiate a hit unless provoked. Sakic will, however, take the puck to the net without walking on eggshells. And he will take a hit to make a play, keeps working for the puck along the boards.

THE INTANGIBLES

Sakic has had to be a leader since early in his career; he's carried the weight of the franchise since early age. He keeps the team in every game he plays. He always plays against the other team's best checker and still gets about 100 points. He has great pride in his profession, and very seldom takes a night off.

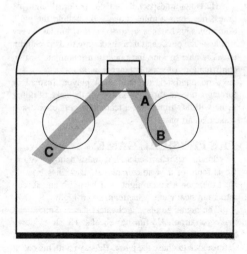

MATS SUNDIN

Yrs. of NHL service: 2
Born: Sollentuna, Sweden; Feb. 13, 1971
Position: Right wing
Height: 6-3
Weight: 185
Uniform no.: 13
Shoots: Right

Career statistics:

GP	G	A	TP	PIM
160	56	79	135	163

1991-92 statistics:

GP	G	A	TP	+/-	PIM	PP	SH	GW	GT	S	PCT
80	33	43	76	-19	105	8	2	2	1	231	14.3

LAST SEASON

Led team in shots. Goal total improved 10 from prior season, point total jumped 17.

THE FINESSE GAME

Sundin has the whole package for a prototype finesse player. He has size and strength. He has a very good shot and a very strong stick. He is a good skater in a straight line, going to the puck or with the puck. Quickness and agility help fill out the skills roster for a big player who does things many small men can't do.

Sundin has an extremely long stride, and complements that attribute with a long glide. He covers a lot of ground. That is a plus on offense, as he moves beautifully to open ice; it's also useful when he kills penalties. Sundin uses his long reach to challenge passes to the points, between the points and down the boards.

He is not an especially artistic skater, though. At times, he seems a touch slow, a bit behind the play. Sometimes his balance seems only fair; but he is very strong on the puck, and if his hands are tied up, Sundin is easily able to kick the puck to a teammate — two confirmations of good balance.

And Sundin is an intelligent player. Instead of forcing a one-on-three rush, just for the sake of doing it, he will buy time until a teammate gets open, then make a smart pass.

THE PHYSICAL GAME

Sundin has a hard edge, but doesn't show it often. He is more of a perimeter player; if a finesse game isn't there on a given night — if he is hit and forced into a physical game — he tends to struggle.

The nights he plays a physical game, Sundin can make you drool. He finishes checks. He slows down his man in the neutral zone, buying time for his defensemen to chase the puck. He stays with his check straight to the net after defensive-zone face-offs. He seals players off along the wall.

THE INTANGIBLES

Sundin is a big-ice, open-ice player trapped in a small-ice, cramped-quarters division, which is a puzzle. He has big games against teams that are less physical, has quiet nights when he gets muscled, and that is a real problem for a team that doesn't win on the road.

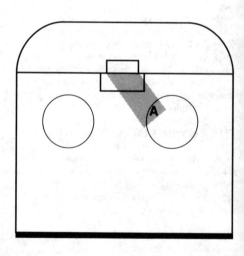

MIKHAIL TATARINOV

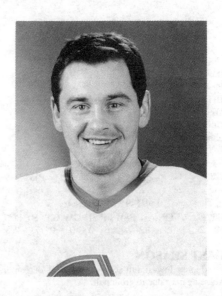

Yrs. of NHL service: 2
Born: Irkutsk, Siberia; July 16, 1966
Position: Left defense
Height: 6-1
Weight: 185
Uniform no.: 4
Shoots: Left

Career statistics:

GP	G	A	TP	PIM
131	19	42	61	154

1991-92 statistics:

GP	G	A	TP	+/-	PIM	PP	SH	GW	GT	S	PCT
66	11	27	38	8	72	5	0	1	0	191	5.8

LAST SEASON

Goal total improved by three, assist total by 12, plus-minus by 12.

THE FINESSE GAME

Tatarinov is good on his feet and has a very, very high skill level. He breaks the puck out of his defensive zone extremely well, either by rushing or passing. If you overplay him on the forecheck, he'll pass past you; if you close off the pass, he'll skate it up the ice.

He doesn't have exceptional quickness or anything resembling breakaway speed, but he is a good backward skater who has decent mobility and agility and is good laterally,

Tatarinov contributes in a number of ways in the attacking zone. He sees the open man and passes extremely well, although guilty at times of overhandling while waiting for a man to get open. His shot from the point is hard enough to break the glass behind the net.

He is, however, a liability defending against the rush. Tatarinov is not as interested in playing the defensive game at the same level as his offense. He takes chances when he shouldn't and doesn't respect other players' speed, possibly because he doesn't know the league. He courts disaster.

THE PHYSICAL GAME

Tatarinov is a finesse player who accepts there is another side to the game. He takes a hit, gives one. He will not back down from a confrontation, but he isn't likely to start one. He will not be intimidated.

THE INTANGIBLES

A player of his skill shouldn't be so inconsistent. He should be accomplishing more than he has. Tatarinov seems to take nights off. And though skaters from overseas generally have extremely high shooting percentages, his is exceptionally low.

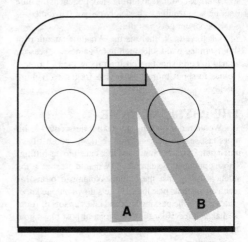

CRAIG WOLANIN

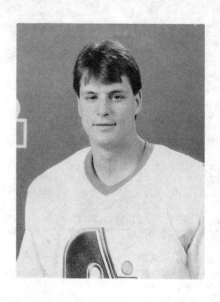

Yrs. of NHL service: 7
Born: Grosse Pointe, Mich.; July 27, 1967
Position: Right defense
Height: 6-3
Weight: 205
Uniform no.: 6
Shoots: Left

Career statistics:

GP	G	A	TP	PIM
445	23	89	112	648

1991-92 statistics:

GP	G	A	TP	+/-	PIM	PP	SH	GW	GT	S	PCT
69	2	11	13	−12	80	0	0	0	0	71	2.8

LAST SEASON
Scored lowest full-season goal total of career. Missed games due to groin pull.

THE FINESSE GAME
Wolanin's reads are improving. He knows where he should be and does what he can to get there; speed is a problem, though, and that cuts into other aspects of his play.

He concedes just a touch more blue line than he should, buying time to kick his big stride into gear against the threat of an outside speed rush. Although eager, Wolanin is neither very mobile nor overly agile; so even if he commits to hitting an opponent at the blue line, he is in trouble — basically caught flat-footed — if the opponent gets past him.

On the attack, there is the Wolanin cannon of a shot from the point, although in 69 games last season, he had to be in shooting position more than 71 times. He has to shoot more, and he has to get it off more quickly.

THE PHYSICAL GAME
Wolanin does not hit much, but he seemed to hit more last season than in prior years; he doesn't have much quickness or range, and that cuts into his hitting. Those opponents he can reach, Wolanin crushes at the sideboards; against the others, Wolanin exploits his reach as much as possible. He gets down on one knee, glides across the passing lane and takes up lots of room — makes himself larger than he is, almost plays goal against the pass.

THE INTANGIBLES
Wolanin still makes some ugly turnovers. He'll start to pass, think better of it, then try to stop himself — but too late; the puck has left his stick and gone right to a forechecker. But he is playing a smarter, more mature game and may simply be a late bloomer.

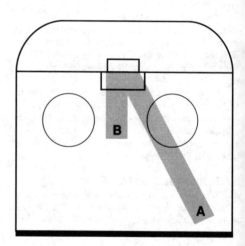

ST. LOUIS BLUES

MURRAY BARON

Yrs. of NHL service: 3
Born: Prince George, B.C., June 1, 1967
Position: Left defense
Height: 6-3
Weight: 210
Uniform no.: 6
Shoots: Left

Career statistics:

GP	G	A	TP	PIM
150	13	18	31	180

1991-92 statistics:

GP	G	A	TP	+/-	PIM	PP	SH	GW	GT	S	PCT
67	3	8	11	-3	94	0	0	0	0	55	5.5

LAST SEASON

Acquired from Philadelphia with Ron Sutter for Rod Brind'Amour and Dan Quinn on Sept. 22, 1991. Games played and assists matched career high. Missed 10 games with injuries.

THE FINESSE GAME

Baron is a good skater who moves up into the play well enough but has poor offensive sense and can't do much even though he's in the right place. He seems to have all the right skills: Baron stickhandles well and carries the puck with speed. However, everything goes awry with his shot or pass selection. Instead of hitting a headmanning forward with a hard pass, he will float a puck that is easily picked off. And when he needs to feather a pass, he fires it.

Baron doesn't have much of an assortment of shots, and is limited mostly to slaps from the left point. He seldom gambles down low, which is just as well.

For a big man, Baron has an unusually quick turn of foot. He has great straightaway speed with above-average agility.

THE PHYSICAL GAME

Baron has good size and strength but doesn't use his body well on a consistent basis. He's a little on the tame side, without real aggressiveness, and thus doesn't get the kind of respect or room a defenseman of his build is usually accorded. If Baron were more gifted offensively, this weakness could be overlooked, but Baron has to bring up the other elements of his game to be a more useful sort.

THE INTANGIBLES

Baron could be a late bloomer, especially since he possesses a skill — skating — that is hard to teach. Maybe some of the other parts of the game can be hammered home to him. If not, he will be nothing more than an average defenseman.

BOB BASSEN

Yrs. of NHL service: 7
Born: Calgary, Alta.; May 6, 1965
Position: Center/left wing
Height: 5-11
Weight: 170
Uniform no.: 28
Shoots: Left

Career statistics:

GP	G	A	TP	PIM
397	44	87	131	635

1991-92 statistics:

GP	G	A	TP	+/-	PIM	PP	SH	GW	GT	S	PCT
79	7	25	32	12	167	0	0	1	0	101	6.9

LAST SEASON

Assists career high. Goals and points two-season lows. Led Blues forwards in plus-minus.

THE FINESSE GAME

Bassen is a good checking forward who provides very little offense. His exceptional quickness and low center of gravity gives him an advantage over some bigger, lumbering skaters because Bassen can dodge this way and that, moving faster than some other players can even think.

Unfortunately, Bassen can't do a whole lot with the puck. He doesn't have great hands for passing or shooting. The Blues use him on the wing despite his size, because he is not a very good playmaker for a center. He's not much on faceoffs, and he's not much of a finisher either. His goals will come from batting in loose pucks around the net.

Bassen is a good penalty killer. He is tenacious and quick, and blocks shots like a defenseman.

THE PHYSICAL GAME

Bassen plays much bigger than his size. If you didn't see his name on the back of jersey, you would swear he was a Sutter brother. Or at least a cousin. He isn't strong enough to win many one-on-one battles, but he is scrappy and willing to go into the boards and corners, and sometimes comes away with the puck because he is so short. Bassen will sometimes squirt free, ducking underneath all the flailing elbows and high sticks.

THE INTANGIBLES

Despite his shortcomings, Bassen is a good man to have in the lineup. He is a solid team player, honest, and will accept any role uncomplainingly. He is consistent and is a defensive stalwart who can match up against many of the league's best despite spotting them six inches and 40 pounds.

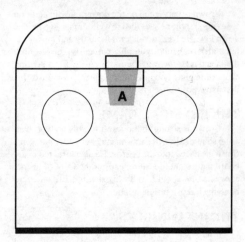

JEFF BROWN

Yrs. of NHL service: 7
Born: Ottawa, Ont.; April 30, 1966
Position: Right defense
Height: 6-1
Weight: 204
Uniform no.: 21
Shoots: Right

Career statistics:

GP	G	A	TP	PIM
432	98	230	325	280

1991-92 statistics:

GP	G	A	TP	+/-	PIM	PP	SH	GW	GT	S	PCT
80	20	38	58	8	38	10	0	2	1	214	9.3

LAST SEASON

Led Blues defensemen in scoring. Third on team in assists. One of two Blues to appear in all 80 games.

THE FINESSE GAME

Brown made his reputation as an offensive defenseman, and while he's lost none of that edge, he's also worked harder on his defense, and has turned into a good two-way blueliner.

He has a big slap shot and can let it go on the fly. He keeps it low and accurate, and creates a lot of scoring chances for the forwards who can either tip it or scramble for the rebounds.

Brown is very good on the power play. In addition to his good shot, he sees the ice well for passing options down low. He has good lateral mobility and moves the puck alertly. Brown will also cut across the ice, into the circle and down to the hash marks, for a scoring chance. He has enough skating ability to recover his defensive position.

THE PHYSICAL GAME

Brown is strong, but doesn't use his body as well as he should. He will carry an attacker wide, but won't finish the check into the boards. He also loses too many board battles and doesn't clear out the front of his net as well as he should. With his skating, Brown could be a much more efficient hitter.

THE INTANGIBLES

Improved physical play would move his rating up a notch. He appears to do everything so fluidly that it appears to be effortless, and there is always criticism that Brown isn't working hard enough. We don't think he is. Right now he is a very good defenseman, but he has the potential to be something special.

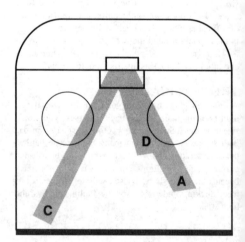

GARTH BUTCHER

Yrs. of NHL service: 8
Born: Regina, Sask.; Jan. 8, 1963
Position: Right defense
Height: 6'0"
Weight: 200
Uniform no.: 5
Shoots: Right

Career statistics:

GP	G	A	TP	PIM
691	38	126	164	1889

1991-92 statistics:

GP	G	A	TP	+/-	PIM	PP	SH	GW	GT	S	PCT
68	5	15	20	5	189	0	0	0	0	50	10.0

LAST SEASON

Missed 12 games due to foot injury. Second on team in PIM. Games played career low.

THE FINESSE GAME

There is nothing outstanding about Butcher's play, but he does a lot of small things at the NHL level. He is a stay-at-home defenseman, a solid checker and an intelligent, responsible patroller of his own blue line.

Butcher doesn't make fancy plays or get overly involved in the attack. The Blues have a very good breakout, and he will key a rush with a smart, crisp pass out of his zone and follow the play up the ice. He makes safe plays but doesn't blindly scale the puck around the boards, either.

Butcher is a average skater with average speed and below average agility, but he is experienced enough to keep himself positioned so that his defects are minimized. He is a good penalty killer because he is fearless in blocking shots.

THE PHYSICAL GAME

An agitator, he picks his spots well, trying to aggravate the right person into retaliating against him (he rarely wastes his time with less talented opponents). He is a nasty hitter and even looks mean. Butcher makes anyone think twice about going one-on-one with him in a board or corner war.

THE INTANGIBLES

The Blues made a well-criticized deal for Butcher at the end of the 1990-91 season, giving up Cliff Ronning, Geoff Courtnall, Sergio Momesso and Robert

Dirk (the Blues also obtained Dan Quinn, whom they gave up with Rod Brind'Amour in the nearly equally disastrous Ron Sutter/Murray Baron deal). The Butcher trade wouldn't look as bad if the Blues had not lost Scott Stevens in the Brendan Shanahan signing. Butcher would have added depth to the defense corps in a support role, instead of being asked to BE the defense corps.

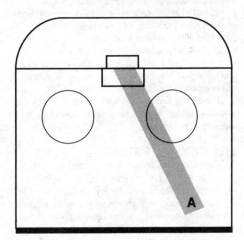

PAUL CAVALLINI

Yrs. of NHL service: 6
Born: Toronto, Ont.; Oct. 13, 1965
Position: Left defense
Height: 6-1
Weight: 210
Uniform no.: 14
Shoots: Left

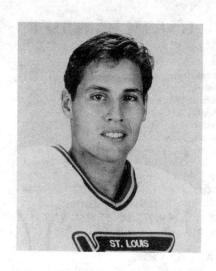

Career statistics:

GP	G	A	TP	PIM
356	28	120	159	578

1991-92 statistics:

GP	G	A	TP	+/-	PIM	PP	SH	GW	GT	S	PCT
66	10	25	35	7	95	3	1	2	1	164	6.1

LAST SEASON

Second among team defensemen in scoring. Goals, assists and points were identical to previous season's career highs. Missed 13 games with injury.

THE FINESSE GAME

Cavallini loves to get involved in the attack. A fine all-around skater, with speed, agility and balance, he is extremely confident in his skating skills and tries to force a lot of plays. He will challenge at his blue line and will pinch in and forecheck in the attacking zone.

He has improved his defensive reads and is smarter about when to pinch, rather than recklessly start pursuing the puck in the attacking zone.

Cavallini reads offensive plays very well. He has good hockey vision, and will start plays out of his own end with a strong pass, or he will carry the puck, which he can do at high tempo. Cavallini trails into the play well. His best shot is a quick slap from the point. He also has a good wrister from closer range. Neither shot will overpower a goalie.

Experience and intelligence over the past few seasons have added a great deal to his already strong portfolio of finesse skills.

THE PHYSICAL GAME

Cavallini plays an effective and efficient takeout game. He is not a big or mean hitter, although he is a willing checker. He does not clear out the front of his net well, so works best paired with a more physical defenseman who will give him some support. Preferring to play the puck instead of the man, he goes for poke checks that he can turn into a counterattack.

THE INTANGIBLES

Cavallini is a steady and unspectacular player, a solid third or fourth defenseman who gives an honest effort every night. He won't do much to surprise you, nor will he do anything to disappoint you.

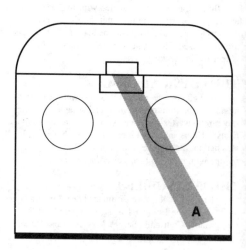

DAVE CHRISTIAN

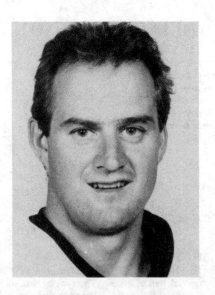

Yrs. of NHL service: 13
Born: Warroad, Minn.; May 12, 1959
Position: Right wing
Height: 5-11
Weight: 195
Uniform no.: 27
Shoots: Right

Career statistics:

GP	G	A	TP	PIM
940	336	416	752	272

1991-92 statistics:

GP	G	A	TP	+/-	PIM	PP	SH	GW	GT	S	PCT
78	20	24	44	2	41	1	3	3	0	142	14.1

LAST SEASON

Goals and points three-season lows. Assists two-season low.

THE FINESSE GAME

Christian was often the forgotten man on the Blues bench, and he can be a forgotten man once he's on the ice. He can lull a defender, and then suddenly be in striking range of the net, all alone, or trailing into the play for a quick shot. He was the Blues' Super Sub, able to fill in at all three forward positions but unable to find a comfortable niche at any one — yet he still managed to score 20 goals.

Christian has slowed down, although he tends to forget that, as many good players do. He still tries to beat defenseman wide, but he seldom gets past them and is crunched along the boards before he is able to make a play.

Much more effective in open-ice situations, where he can put his finesse skills to work, he has a good wrist shot and will still find an occasional burst of speed to jump into the holes. Christian is very patient with his shot and will wait for the goalie to commit.

THE PHYSICAL GAME

Christian has never been a strong boards or corners player and generally avoids those areas. He will battle for the puck when he is on the power play, and will work a little defensively, but he has never displayed a taste for physical play. He's not about to start at this stage of his career.

THE INTANGIBLES

A competent two-way player, he can still be useful as a third-line player and power play specialist. Christian is also the answer to a trivia question as one of the last three players from the 1980 U.S. Olympic still playing in the NHL (along with Buffalo's Mike Ramsey and Minnesota's Neal Broten).

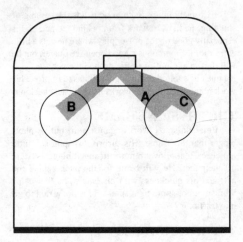

NELSON EMERSON

Yrs. of NHL service: 1
Born: Hamilton, Ont.; Aug. 17, 1967
Position: Center
Height: 5-11
Weight: 165
Uniform no.: 7
Shoots: Right

Career statistics:

GP	G	A	TP	PIM
83	23	39	62	68

1991-92 statistics:

GP	G	A	TP	+/-	PIM	PP	SH	GW	GT	S	PCT
79	23	36	59	−5	66	3	0	2	0	143	16.1

LAST SEASON

First NHL season. Fourth on Blues in points. Fifth among NHL rookies in goals. Third among NHL rookies in assists. Missed one game with suspension.

THE FINESSE GAME

Emerson probably got the least attention of the glamorous rookie crop of '92, but deserves a closer look. A good skater, with short bursts of speed, he has tremendous offensive instincts. He is a creative play-maker with a good short game down low, moving the puck crisply through weaves and finding the cutter to the net.

Extremely quick, with good hands for passing or shooting, he likes to work from behind the net, and is especially good on the power play where he gets a little extra room. Emerson is a good open-ice player, but he will dart in and out of traffic around the net.

He must be spotted defensively and has to improve his work in that area, but he works hard at backchecking.

THE PHYSICAL GAME

Emerson's size works against him, but he plays bigger than his frame. His surprise weapon is a little hip check that allows him to lift much bigger skaters off their feet. He will battle for the puck behind the net, and his quickness with his hands and feet helps him get out of some tight spots. He is not afraid to go into traffic.

THE INTANGIBLES

Emerson had an impressive rookie season (and an even better playoffs) despite not being used as well as he might have by the Blues coaches. It took Emerson a long time to get to the NHL (he was a 1985 draft pick, played four years at Bowling Green and another two in the minors), but he appears to be worth the wait.

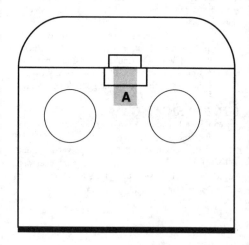

BRET HEDICAN

Yrs. of NHL service: 0
Born: St. Paul, Minn.; Aug. 10, 1970
Position: Left defense
Height: 6-2
Weight: 188
Uniform no.: 44
Shoots: Left

Career statistics:

GP	G	A	TP	PIM
4	1	0	1	0

1991-92 statistics:

GP	G	A	TP	+/-	PIM	PP	SH	GW	GT	S	PCT
4	1	0	1	1	0	0	0	0	0	1	100.0

LAST SEASON
Made NHL debut after Olympics.

THE FINESSE GAME
Hedican has explosive speed, the kind that had some scouts likening him to Paul Coffey, although he does not yet show the variety of moves that Coffey has in his repertoire. Hedican can move coast to coast in a flash.

He will carry the puck at a high tempo and can do a lot with it. He likes to rush with the puck, skating in deep and cutting across the grain from his left to his right, using the defenseman as a screen. Hedican might be too eager to look for the shot and needs to make better use of his teammates, for whom he will open up a lot of ice because of his intimidating speed.

Hedican rapidly graduated to play the point on the Blues' first power play unit. He has a strong shot from the point, with a quick release.

He gets scatter-brained defensively, to the point where he runs around and collides with his own teammates.

THE PHYSICAL GAME
Hedican is shy about getting hit, sometimes to the point where it looks as though he might be afraid of solid contact and getting hurt. The physical part of his game is not yet NHL calibre.

THE INTANGIBLES
A strong prospect, Hedican is one of the best in the Blues' system. He has shown rapid improvement late, coming out of St. Cloud State through the U.S.

Olympic team and on to the Blues, where he saw a lot of ice time in the playoffs. He needs to adjust to the physical nature of NHL play, but already is a gifted offensive defenseman.

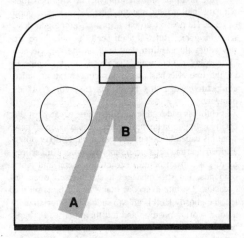

BRETT HULL

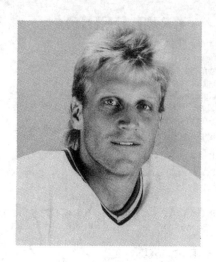

Yrs. of NHL service: 5
Born: Belleville, Ont.; Aug. 9, 1964
Position: Right wing
Height: 5-10
Weight: 201
Uniform no.: 16
Shoots: Right

Career statistics:

GP	G	A	TP	PIM
379	302	200	502	143

1991-92 statistics:

GP	G	A	TP	+/-	PIM	PP	SH	GW	GT	S	PCT
73	70	39	109	−2	48	20	5	9	1	408	17.2

LAST SEASON

Finalist for 1992 Hart Trophy. Named to First All-Star Team. Led NHL in goals and shots. Became second player in history (with Wayne Gretzky) to score 70 or more goals in three consecutive seasons.

THE FINESSE GAME

Hull is an awesome combination of foot speed, hand skills, power and intimidation — a player that comes along only once or twice in a generation. His release of a heavy, accurate shot is unbelievably quick. Unlike many players with booming shots, Hull needs no time at all to tee it up, which is just one of the reasons why he is so unstoppable.

Not an all-around great player, he kills penalties with the philosophy that the best defense is a good offense. He doesn't go out to protect a one-goal lead late in a game. But if a team needs a goal, there are few better than Hull to have out on the ice. He is a clutch player who wants the shot when the game is on the line. He has marvelous concentration and a competitive edge that belies his easy-going off-ice demeanor.

Hull has had to fine-tune his game because of the checking attention he merits. Before may people knew what his capabilities were, he was able to drive down an open lane and get a clean shot. No more. Hull scores more goals from being in front of the net and from rebounds, but still manages to get himself open on occasion. Despite everyone being aware he is on the ice, the ghostly Hull is able to suddenly materialize in a good scoring position and lull the defense. Perhaps only Mike Bossy worked that trick as neatly.

Hull loves to shoot, but isn't selfish. When the better option is a pass, he will deliver a pinpoint one. He has excellent hands and hockey sense.

Defense is a weakness, but who cares? Nobody spends their hard-earned dollars to watch Hull backcheck. He is one of the most entertaining, explosive offensive talents in the game's history.

THE PHYSICAL GAME

Hull is a power forward with consummate finesse skills. He has a burly build, is strong and balanced on his skates so he is hard to budge, and is nifty and shifty enough to win a one-on-one open ice matchup. Over, under, around and through — whatever route he has to take to the net, Hull will. He is a classy player who absorbs punishment without whining.

THE INTANGIBLES

The only question mark about Hull this season will be how he will function without his center, Adam Oates. Craig Janney moved into his spot after the trade, and the two players seemed to click well, but Janney is a smaller, less physical player than Oates, and Hull will have to make some adjustments. If the partnership is successful over the course of a long season, Hull's amazing goal total should continue to mount. If the Blues could get just one more line to click, he would get even more of a chance to shine. The glare could be blinding.

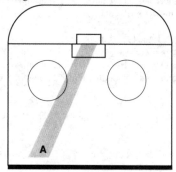

CRAIG JANNEY

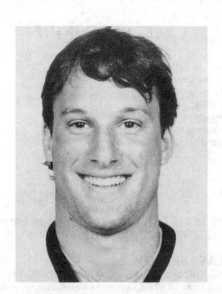

Yrs. of NHL service: 5
Born: Hartford, Conn.; Sept. 26, 1967
Position: Center
Height: 6-1
Weight: 190
Uniform no.: 15
Shoots: Left

Career statistics:

GP	G	A	TP	PIM
287	91	228	319	46

1991-92 statistics:

GP	G	A	TP	+/-	PIM	PP	SH	GW	GT	S	PCT
78	18	69	87	6	22	6	0	2	0	127	14.2

LAST SEASON

Acquired from Boston with Stephane Quintal for Adam Oates on Feb. 7, 1992. Led team in assists with career high. Second on team in points. Goals three-season low. PIM just 2 minutes less than previous four seasons combined.

THE FINESSE GAME

Janney has rightly earned the reputation as one of the best pure passers in the game. He uses a very short stick, which allows him to keep the puck in close to his feet and makes it difficult for defenders to strip him of the puck.

He sees the ice as well as any playmaker in the league. It is no accident that Cam Neely enjoyed his best season (55 goals in 1989-90) with Janney as his centerman. Since the trade to St. Louis, Janney has been teamed with another of the game's premier right wings, Brett Hull. Neely and Hull are diversely different players, but Janney's hockey sense should suit Hull just as neatly as it did Neely. He is somewhat less physical than Oates, which could be a drawback.

The major knock on Janney is that he doesn't shoot enough. Instead of looking for the scoring chance himself, he will dawdle until he spots an opening for a pass. The upside is that he is nothing short of brilliant at finding the open skater, and is willing to take a hit to make the play.

His play is weak away from the puck. He seems to have an idea of where he should be positioning himself, but the message never gets through to his legs.

THE PHYSICAL GAME

Janney enjoyed his second straight injury-free season — a positive sign, since his first two years led to some concerns about his fragility. He still does not play to his size consistently, and his play away from the puck remains a minus, although he has improved his defensive awareness. When he is hit early and often in a game, he will get headshy and coughs up the puck with no checker near him if he has to go for the puck facing the boards.

Janney uses the net exceptionally well to protect himself from attackers. He likes to set up there and is one of the NHL centers who benefited most from the rule change that added an extra foot of ice behind the net. It gives him more room to operate, and he takes advantage of it.

The increase in his penalty minutes total may be a good indication that he is getting more involved. No one wants to see him throwing punches (not with those soft hands) or wasting time in the penalty box, but no one wants a center who sleepwalks through a game, either.

THE INTANGIBLES

The question mark is how Janney will fulfill his half of the Hull and Oates team. This could be the beginning of a beautiful friendship. In the 26 games since his trade to the Blues, he assisted on 10 of Hull's 16 goals. The Blues picked up nearly five years on the deal, meaning Janney should be around a lot longer to keep feeding his sniper. But his reputation as a poor playoff performer was not changed after the Blues' first-round ouster last year.

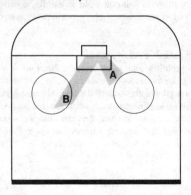

325

CURTIS JOSEPH

Yrs. of NHL service: 3
Born: Keswick, Ont.; April 29, 1967
Position: Goaltender
Height: 5-10
Weight: 182
Uniform no.: 31
Catches: Left

Career statistics:

GP	MINS	GA	SO	GAA	A	PIM
105	6056	312	2	3.09	10	12

1991-92 statistics:

GP	MINS	GAA	W	L	T	SO	GA	S	SAPCT	PIM
60	3494	3.01	27	20	10	2	175	1953	.910	12

LAST SEASON

Led NHL goalies in assists (9), the second-highest single season total in league history. Career highs in games played and wins. Career best GAA. Tied for second in NHL in save percentage.

THE PHYSICAL GAME

A fundamentally sound goalie, he helps out his team tremendously with his stickhandling ability, which is about the best in the league, despite his unorthodox style. Joseph uses a cross-handed grip on his stick and likes to whip it off the boards on his backhand. Even though he is scouted to play the puck that way, few teams have any success stopping him. He has the utmost confidence in his ability to play the puck away from the attacker.

Joseph is a strong one-on-one goalie, as he demonstrated by stopping two shooters (Minnesota's Todd Elik and Vancouver's Greg Adams) on penalty shots last season. He plays a stand-up style, challenges the shooters well and plays his angles. He has greatly improved in the area of controlling his rebounds. Where he used to use his pads to stop shots, he now guides more of them with his stick and doesn't leave them lying in dangerous areas.

He has excellent reflexes in tight and recovers quickly from a first save to be ready for a second shot. Able to move in and out of the net well, he still has some problem laterally on plays moving across in front of him.

THE MENTAL GAME

Joseph saw a lot of pucks — he faced 40 or more shots in 16 games — and was aware he was going to be in for a busy night every night. Nothing seemed to faze him. He played behind a defense that was badly stung by the loss of Scott Stevens, and won games single-handedly. Joseph earned the respect of his teammates.

His concentration is excellent. He maintains his focus during flurries and shakes off a bad goal or a bad game. He can steal games his team has no right winning.

THE INTANGIBLES

Joseph's stock rose so sharply during the season that had it been charted, the line would have been absolutely vertical. He was considered an overpaid, fragile goalie before training camp, and was offered to New Jersey as part of a compensation package for the Blues signing of Brendan Shanahan (the Devils balked and received Scott Stevens from an arbitrator's ruling). By October, Joseph had won the No. 1 job and the Blues felt confident enough to trade away Vincent Riendeau. By the end of the season, he had compiled impressive numbers despite playing behind a weak defense. If the Blues can tighten up their system under new coach Bob Plager, Joseph will no longer be one of the NHL's most underappreciated goalies.

DAVE LOWRY

Yrs. of NHL service: 7
Born: Sudbury, Ont.; Feb. 14, 1965
Position: Left wing
Height: 6-1
Weight: 195
Uniform no.: 10
Shoots: Left

Career statistics:

GP	G	A	TP	PIM
418	67	64	131	688

1991-92 statistics:

GP	G	A	TP	+/-	PIM	PP	SH	GW	GT	S	PCT
75	7	13	20	−11	77	0	0	1	0	85	8.2

LAST SEASON

Career low (for full NHL season) in goals. Two-season lows in assists and points. Missed two games with injury.

THE FINESSE GAME

Lowry has speed, and that is one quality he must learn to exploit better. He is not a very agile skater, so he won't be putting any mesmerizing dekes on a defenseman. His best hope is to bust to the outside.

Lowry does little with the puck at high tempo, however. He can shoot and likes to drive down the wing, and he will go to the net well. Lowry is a serviceable forward to use on the penalty killing unit because of his shorthanded scoring potential, but he was not used there often last season.

He does not have great hockey sense and generates little offense other than with his skating. He seems to have settled into a role as a checking forward.

THE PHYSICAL GAME

Lowry has good size and is not afraid to use it, especially when forechecking. He goes to the net very well, sometimes carrying a defender along with his speed, and he doesn't mind the traffic areas behind or in front of the net. He is not a very willing fighter.

THE INTANGIBLES

Lowry hasn't received a lot of steady ice time since his limited role as a checker put him into an overcrowded category on the Blues. He has to bring something to the table and since he does seem to have some scoring touch, maybe a coaching change will tap his talent in that area. He was left unprotected in the 1992 Expansion Draft by the Blues.

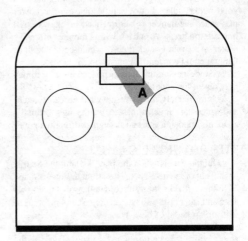

STEPHANE QUINTAL

Yrs. of NHL service: 4
Born: Boucherville, Que.; Oct. 22, 1968
Position: Right defense
Height: 6-3
Weight: 215
Uniform no.: 33
Shoots: Right

Career statistics:

GP	G	A	TP	PIM
184	8	25	33	249

1991-92 statistics:

GP	G	A	TP	+/-	PIM	PP	SH	GW	GT	S	PCT
75	4	16	20	-11	109	0	0	0	0	71	5.6

LAST SEASON

Acquired from Boston with Craig Janney for Adam Oates, Feb. 7, 1992. Career highs in games played and all scoring and PIM.

THE FINESSE GAME

Watching Quintal skate makes you want to reach for the fast forward button. Sorry, but that's as fast as he can go.

Quintal is an absolute plodder, which is a shame for him because he has some very nice finesse skills that he can't put into use because he can't get into the play. He has a very good shot from the point and is a good puckhandler, but gets little time on the power play since the danger of shorthanded breakaway past him are too great. A pairing with a mobile, offensive skater — a Brian Leetch type — would be ideal, since Quintal could concentrate on staying at home.

A nice passer, he can surprise with a headman play out of his zone.

Unfortunately, he can't hit what he can't catch, and unless an attacker has to go through Quintal's zone, his imposing size and strength do him little good.

THE PHYSICAL GAME

Quintal excels when the play is along the boards or in front of the net. There, his strength gives him the edge that he lacks in open ice. He has very good balance and can muscle all but the biggest and most insistent forwards out of his way.

A willing fighter, and a good one, he is slow to anger, which may be fortunate for many players in the Norris Division.

THE INTANGIBLES

The key word for Quintal is slow. Slow to skate, slow to think, slow to develop. He might have been more suited to the smaller ice surface in Boston, and will have to work harder now that his home rink is regulation size. His play in St. Louis last season was very inconsistent.

BRENDAN SHANAHAN

Yrs. of NHL service: 5
Born: Mimico, Ont.; Jan. 23, 1969
Position: Right wing
Height: 6-3
Weight: 210
Uniform no.: 19
Shoots: Right

Career statistics:

GP	G	A	TP	PIM
361	121	162	283	695

1991-92 statistics:

GP	G	A	TP	+/-	PIM	PP	SH	GW	GT	S	PCT
80	33	36	69	−3	171	13	0	2	2	215	15.3

LAST SEASON

Signed as free agent (Blues lost Scott Stevens to New Jersey as compensation) on July 25, 1991. One of two Blues to appear in all 80 games (he has never missed more than 15 games in any season). Second on team in goals with career high and second in power-play goals. Third on team in points. PIM total career high.

THE FINESSE GAME

Shanahan has the makings of a very good power forward, with all of the necessary skills except speed.

He has terrific hands and a quick release around the net. He'll take his punishment there, and is aggressive and confident as he battles for his scoring chances. Shanahan came up through junior as a center and will make good goalmouth passes or use a powerful wrist shot. He can one-time a shot from the circles with good velocity and accuracy.

Shanahan is strong on his skates but not fast. He lacks the first one or two steps to get an edge on a defender around the net, although once he gets going he gets up a good head of steam and can handle the puck with speed.

After coming into the league as a very young and immature 18-year-old, he's done a lot of growing up, but still sulked when he didn't get to play with Brett Hull and Adam Oates (later Craig Janney) on the Blues' top line. Nobody can blame him, but Shanahan needs to be more of a leader and less of a whiner if he wants to be the kind of player we think he truly desires to be.

THE PHYSICAL GAME

Shanahan needs a hit or two early to get going, and he will often make it himself. If he doesn't, Shanahan starts thinking too much like a finesse player, and that is when he is least effective.

A real scrapper when he came into the league, he felt he had to prove himself with his new team and was a battler again last season. He will play hurt and won't be intimidated. He's legitimately tough.

THE INTANGIBLES

We told you last year that Shanahan would be in a uniform other than the Devils' by 1991-92, and he was — at great cost to the Blues, and in a way, to Shanahan. He got off to a slow start due to the pressure involved with his signing and the Blues losing an all-star defenseman in Stevens. Once Shanahan got rolling (after all, the arbitrator's decision wasn't his fault), he was a steady contributor to the Blues and is very capable of hitting the 40-goal mark this season. Shanahan is capable of becoming an "A" player, but needs to improve his skating or that won't happen.

Speaking strictly from a media standpoint, he's a delightful interview and one of the most open, refreshing athletes around.

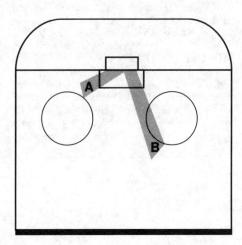

RICH SUTTER

Yrs. of NHL service: 9
Born: Viking, Alta.; Dec. 2, 1963
Position: Right wing
Height: 5-11
Weight: 188
Uniform no.: 23
Shoots: Right

Career statistics:

GP	G	A	TP	PIM
670	124	135	259	1165

1991-92 statistics:

GP	G	A	TP	+/-	PIM	PP	SH	GW	GT	S	PCT
77	9	16	25	7	107	0	1	3	0	113	8.0

LAST SEASON

Goals career low for full NHL season. Assists five-season high. Points two-season low. Missed three games with injury.

THE FINESSE GAME

Sutter, the younger and less talented of the Blues brothers' twins, is an up-and-down winger whose primary contribution is as a checker. He generates little offense, because his finesse skills are average at best.

Not a good skater, he has some power and straight-ahead speed, but his balance is average at best and he lacks agility. Sutter doesn't handle the puck well on the move. Nor does he have much of a shot. All of his goals come from hard work around the net, battling for loose pucks and tip-ins.

Sutter shines defensively, because he reads plays well and is a relentless forechecker who will hound a puck carrier to distraction.

THE PHYSICAL GAME

Like most of the Sutters (if not all), Rich plays bigger than his size. He is annoying, pesky and always in your face. He takes the body on every shift, but despite all his hitting, is an ineffective player since he can't do anything with the puck once he wins it.

THE INTANGIBLES

Putting both the twins on one team, as the Blues did last season when they acquired Ron from Philadelphia in a trade, might not be the best of ideas. This Sutter might be the least offensively gifted of the six brothers who made it to the NHL, and that is made more glaring when he plays on the same team with one

who is more talented. Despite his lack of touch, he will provide anything else his team needs in the way of effort in whatever department his talent allows him to contribute. But with the departure of his brother the coach, Sutter — who was left unprotected in the Expansion Draft — might be smart not to sign a long-term lease.

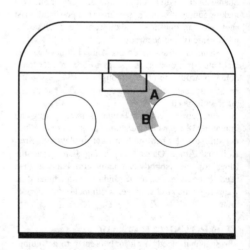

RON SUTTER

Yrs. of NHL service: 10
Born: Viking, Alta.; Dec. 2, 1963
Position: Center
Height: 6-0
Weight: 180
Uniform no.: 22
Shoots: Right

Career statistics:

GP	G	A	TP	PIM
623	156	249	405	945

1991-92 statistics:

GP	G	A	TP	+/-	PIM	PP	SH	GW	GT	S	PCT
68	19	27	46	9	91	5	4	1	1	106	17.9

LAST SEASON

Acquired with Murray Baron from Philadelphia for Rod Brind'Amour and Dan Quinn on Sept. 22, 1991. Missed 12 games with injury. Led Blues in shooting percentage. Goals and points two-season highs.

THE FINESSE GAME

The Blues expected too much of Sutter in his role as the team's No. 2 center. He is more suited to centering a checking line, where he can provide more offense than the average defensive forward while giving up nothing in his checking role.

An honest, hard-working forward, Sutter is highly competitive. He is the Blues' best face-off man, and maybe one of the tops in the league, with quick hand speed and anticipation. If he doesn't win the draw cleanly, he will tie up the opposing center and work with his feet to kick the puck to a teammate.

All of his finesse skills are enhanced by his remarkable work ethic. Sutter doesn't have a great skating style—he has a rather graceless, choppy stride —but is quick enough to jump into holes. His pursuit of the puck is keyed by desire. An aggressive forechecker, he scores most of his goals through opportunistic work around the net.

Defensively, Sutter reads plays well and anticipates, which compensates for his lack of skating speed.

THE PHYSICAL GAME

Opponents know when they have been in a game against a Sutter. He plays the body very well, even though he is usually smaller than the player he's battling with. Excellent lower body strength gives him a great foundation for battling in the corners, even though his balance in open ice is not as good. He bounces off of most checks and stays upright. Sutter will not be intimidated.

THE INTANGIBLES

In the tradition of his older brothers, Ron has developed into more of a defensive center — despite the efforts of Brian, the Blues' ex-coach, to use him as a No. 2 center. Sutter will not score many more than 20 goals in a season, but he will consistently provide the work ethic and on-ice leadership that the family is rightly famous for.

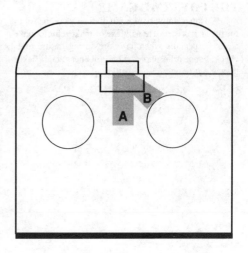

RON WILSON

Yrs. of NHL service: 12
Born: Toronto, Ont.; May 13, 1956
Position: Center
Height: 5-9
Weight: 180
Uniform no.: 18
Shoots: Left

Career statistics:

GP	G	A	TP	PIM
706	100	195	295	359

1991-92 statistics:

GP	G	A	TP	+/-	PIM	PP	SH	GW	GT	S	PCT
64	12	17	29	10	46	5	2	2	0	100	12.0

LAST SEASON

Missed one game with injury. Goals 10-season high. Assists and points two-season low. Second among team forwards in plus-minus.

THE FINESSE GAME

A veteran checker with speed and quickness, Wilson can provide a little offense. He is a very smart player, a strong forechecker who can do something with the puck once he wins a boards or corner battle. Wilson has good offensive moves. A shifty skater, he will decoy a checker with a slow start, then dart to the outside before cutting to the net. More of his scoring chances are generated off forced turnovers than rushes into the zone.

Wilson doesn't always see the ice and his scoring chances well. He has become a fourth-line forward with limited ice time.

THE PHYSICAL GAME

Wilson is not very big, but his savvy compensates for his lack of size. He will take or make a hit to make a play, especially when he is pressuring on the forecheck, but he relies more on his quickness and reflexes to stay out of one-on-one battles.

THE INTANGIBLES

Wilson was scratched 15 games due to coach's decision, and as a checker has a hard time getting into a lineup that is seeking more offense to bolster Brett Hull.

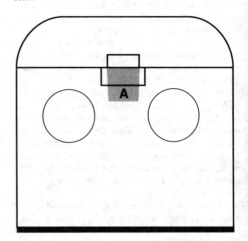

RICK ZOMBO

Yrs. of NHL service: 7
Born: Des Plaines, Ill.; May 8, 1963
Position: Right defense
Height: 6-1
Weight: 195
Uniform no.: 4
Shoots: Right

Career statistics:

GP	G	A	TP	PIM
417	17	93	110	488

1991-92 statistics:

GP	G	A	TP	+/-	PIM	PP	SH	GW	GT	S	PCT
67	3	15	18	1	61	0	0	0	0	48	6.3

LAST SEASON

Acquired from Detroit for Vincent Riendeau, Oct. 18, 1991. Missed nine games with injury. Games played, assists and points four-season lows. Goals three-season low.

THE FINESSE GAME

Zombo is a steady, stay-at-home type who won't provide many surprises on any given night. On any given night, he might not even get noticed. His style is so low key that, much like a referee on good night, he is so efficient that nothing stands out—yet the work gets quietly done.

With his adequate skills, he will move up into the play to help the offense on occasion, but he won't be leading any rushes. But he has a very nice passing touch, and can feather or fire a pass. He does not have much of a scoring touch, however.

Zombo reads plays very well and plays well positionally. He will get involved in the attack, trailing in low as the late man. He doesn't have a great skating style, but he has a good stride with very good balance. His skating gives him great range when he is killing penalties, and he reads plays well defensively and seldom gets caught out of position.

THE PHYSICAL GAME

Zombo will give every effort to win one-on-one battles in front of his net and along the boards. He's not the biggest, meanest hitter around, but his takeouts will be sound. He could use more strength.

THE INTANGIBLES

Zombo was a very calming influence among a blueline corps that lacked leadership last season. He is an honest, hard-working defenseman who hardly ever gives less than his best.

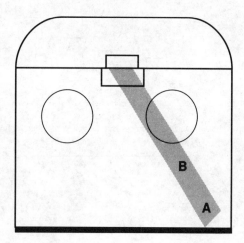

SAN JOSE SHARKS

PERRY BEREZAN

Yrs. of NHL service: 9
Born: Edmonton, Alta.; Dec. 5, 1964
Position: Right wing/center
Height: 6-2
Weight: 190
Uniform no.: 16
Shoots: Right

Career statistics:

GP	G	A	TP	PIM
350	58	71	129	251

1991-92 statistics:

GP	G	A	TP	+/-	PIM	PP	SH	GW	GT	S	PCT
66	12	7	19	-26	30	4	1	2	0	112	10.7

LAST SEASON

Signed as free agent Oct. 10, 1991. Goal total matched career high. Tied for team lead in shorthanded goals. Missed five games with knee injury. Missed one game with concussion.

THE FINESSE GAME

Most of Berezan's attention in recent seasons has been to function as a defensive forward. He has good speed that allows him to forecheck well, but he plays softer than most defensive forwards, so he fails to excel in this area. Berezan is basically a checker who can score the odd goal.

Berezan does not have much of a scoring touch and scores most of his goals from in front and in the low slot. He is not a gifted playmaker. Berezan plays a smart game away from the puck and keeps himself in the game mentally by his positional play. He will take his lumps in front of the net, but rather than use his body he will tug at the defenseman's skates with his stick and try to keep him off-balance.

He saw some time on the power play, more by default than design.

THE PHYSICAL GAME

Berezan does the minimal amount of physical work required to get the job done. He will establish good position along the boards and get in people's way, but he's not that hard to take off the puck and he won't win many one-on-one battles either. Berezan has good balance and will go into traffic areas.

THE INTANGIBLES

Expansion prolonged Berezan's NHL career. He has had trouble with injuries and is only a third or fourth line player on an expansion team where his contributions are limited.

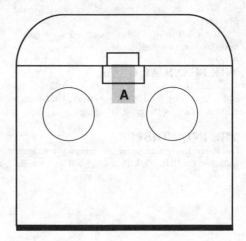

DAVID BRUCE

Yrs. of NHL service: 4
Born: Thunder Bay, Ont.; Oct. 7, 1964
Position: Right wing
Height: 5-11
Weight: 185
Uniform no.: 15
Shoots: Right

Career statistics:

GP	G	A	TP	PIM
215	46	36	82	305

1991-92 statistics:

GP	G	A	TP	+/-	PIM	PP	SH	GW	GT	S	PCT
60	22	16	38	-20	46	10	1	1	0	137	16.1

LAST SEASON

Led team in power-play goals. Second on team in goals, third in scoring. Games played and all scoring totals career highs. Missed last eight games of season with a hernia.

THE FINESSE GAME

Bruce has a good shot but does not release it quickly. He needs time to get his shot away, but he does not create ice for himself with his speed or his physical play and his supporting cast hasn't improved enough to give him that kind of help yet. Almost half of his goals came on the power play, when the extra attacker did give him that extra half-step or half-second to execute.

Bruce has straight ahead speed and some quickness, but is not very agile.

THE PHYSICAL GAME

Bruce is not a very big player but is willing to hit and accepts being hit. He will get involved but doesn't relish this facet of the game.

THE INTANGIBLES

Bruce has yet to prove he can play consistent hockey at the NHL level. He was a good scorer at the minor league level (leading the IHL with 64 goals for Peoria in 1990-91) and is getting the ice time to prove himself with the Sharks.

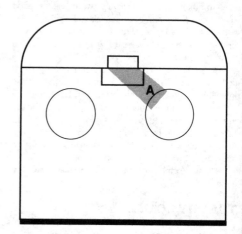

DEAN EVASON

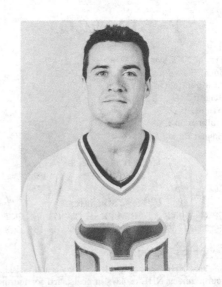

Yrs. of NHL service: 8
Born: Flin Flon, Man.; Aug. 22, 1964
Position: Center
Height: 5-10
Weight: 180
Uniform no.: 8
Shoots: Right

Career statistics:

GP	G	A	TP	PIM
525	101	167	268	713

1991-92 statistics:

GP	G	A	TP	+/-	PIM	PP	SH	GW	GT	S	PCT
74	11	15	26	-22	94	1	0	1	0	88	12.5

LAST SEASON

Points career low. Goals two-season high. Acquired from Hartford for Dan Keczmer, Oct. 2, 1991. Missed one game with flu. Missed two games with stomach injury.

THE FINESSE GAME

Evason is a gritty, feisty, competitive forward whose desire outpaces his skills. He is an average skater who has lost some quickness over the past season or two, but he compensates by working harder.

Evason doesn't generate much offense with his shot or his playmaking. Most of his goals will come from digging for loose pucks in front of the net. He is adept at getting away a quick, strong wrist shot from close range. He can work the power play because of the extra open ice.

Although lacking great hockey sense, Evason makes a good penalty killer because he won't quit skating or badgering a puck carrier. He will force turnovers with his tenacity.

He wins his share of face-offs.

THE PHYSICAL GAME

Evason plays much bigger than his size. He won't be intimidated, but as much as he would like, he simply can't win the one-on-one battles because he gets outmuscled.

THE INTANGIBLES

Evason is a solid defensive forward and a hard worker. He is a good team man who leads by example. On a team with numerous forwards at about the same talent level, Evason sticks out because of his effort.

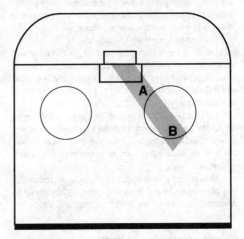

PAT FALLOON

Yrs. of NHL service: 1
Born: Foxwarren, Man.; Sept. 22, 1972
Position: Center/right wing
Height: 5-11
Weight: 192
Uniform no.: ??
Shoots: Right

Career statistics:

GP	G	A	TP	PIM
79	25	34	59	16

1991-92 statistics:

GP	G	A	TP	+/-	PIM	PP	SH	GW	GT	S	PCT
79	25	34	59	−32	16	5	0	1	2	181	13.8

LAST SEASON

First NHL season. Led team in goals and assists. Fourth among NHL rookies in goals, tied for fourth in assists. Missed one game with bruised thigh.

THE FINESSE GAME

Scouts call Falloon a natural, because everything seems to come so easily to him and it looks like he has a good time playing hockey. But Falloon works hard for his scoring opportunities. He has good offensive skills but has to work hard, and does, through his skating. He has good quickness and acceleration and jumps into holes for his scoring chances.

Falloon has very soft hands and is an excellent stickhandler. He will make a pass on his forehand and backhand, and his shot selection is varied. He can score on a blast from the point, or work the puck low and utilize his strong wrist shot. He sees the ice very well offensively.

Falloon is a superb two-on-one player. He comes across the blue line with speed and forces the defenseman to stand up to brace for the slap shot. Then he can cut wide or slide a pass across to the player breaking with him.

However, Falloon doesn't have a clue defensively. His plus-minus is not at all deceptive and he needs to drastically improve his backchecking and defensive awareness.

THE PHYSICAL GAME

The stocky Falloon is not physically imposing, but he uses his size and balance to the best of his advantage. He is unafraid to go into the corners or in traffic, where he works as well as he does when he's in open ice. Because he is one of the few highly skilled players on the Sharks, Falloon draws the lion's share of attention from the opposition's best checking lines. He has to learn to keep fighting his way through those checks until the Sharks come up with better support in the form of bigger wingers.

THE INTANGIBLES

After a slow start, Falloon improved during the season to demonstrate the traits that made him the second pick overall (after Eric Lindros) in 1991. Veteran Doug Wilson was named the Sharks' first captain, but Falloon should be the next. He will become the expansion team's leader, a leader by example and hard work. However, there is a question if he will ever develop into a complete player.

The Sharks have to worry about hurting Falloon mentally or physically. Too many seasons in a negative environment could be detrimental.

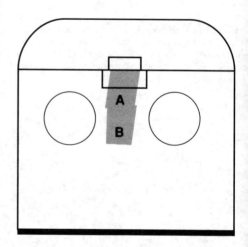

PAUL FENTON

Yrs. of NHL service: 7
Born: Springfield, Mass.; Dec. 22, 1959
Position: Left wing
Height: 5-11
Weight: 180
Uniform no.: 22
Shoots: Left

Career statistics:

GP	G	A	TP	PIM
411	100	83	183	198

1991-92 statistics:

GP	G	A	TP	+/-	PIM	PP	SH	GW	GT	S	PCT
60	11	4	15	-39	33	3	2	1	0	96	11.5

LAST SEASON

Acquired from Hartford for Mike McHugh on Oct. 18, 1991. Worst plus-minus on team. Goals four-season low. Assists career low for full season. Missed four games with head injury.

THE FINESSE GAME

Fenton's skating and hand skills are average, but he has carved out an NHL niche based on his head and hard work. He has great anticipation and some quickness, making him a very strong forechecker. He will pop in the occasional goal by forcing a turnover and whacking away at loose pucks.

Fenton can get a quick shot away from close range, and that's about it. He has no shot otherwise, nor does he have any breakaway speed to beat anybody one-one-one. His contributions will stem from his work as a checker.

THE PHYSICAL GAME

Fenton lacks size and strength but plays as much of a hitting game as those limitations will allow him. He will wade into the action in the front of the net even though he can be easily dislodged by bigger defensemen. Defensively, Fenton loses most of his board and corner battles, although he gives it his best shot.

THE INTANGIBLES

Fenton is a character player who has never made himself invaluable to any one team (the Sharks are his seventh NHL club). His job in San Jose is hardly safe, either, since Fenton's skills are average or worse.

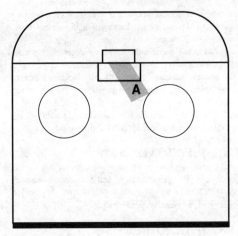

339

LINK GAETZ

Yrs. of NHL service: 1
Born: Vancouver, B.C.; Oct. 2, 1968
Position: Left defense
Height: 6-2
Weight: 210
Uniform no.: 23
Shoots: Left

Career statistics:

GP	G	A	TP	PIM
65	6	8	14	410

1991-92 statistics:

GP	G	A	TP	+/-	PIM	PP	SH	GW	GT	S	PCT
48	6	6	12	-27	324	3	0	0	0	73	8.2

LAST SEASON

Games played and all scoring totals career highs. Led team in PIM. Despite missing almost half the season, fourth in NHL in PIM. Missed four games with hand injury. Missed three game with knee injury. Missed four games with shoulder injury. Missed 12 game with suspensions. Missed last three games of season with injuries suffered in auto accident.

THE FINESSE GAME

"Missing Link" is an inconsistent mess. When his life is straight, Gaetz is a devastating blend of size and skill. An excellent skater for a big man,, he is strong on his skates, and balanced.

Gaetz has some nice offensive instincts. He handles the puck well and can rush with it or make hard, flat passes, leading his target well. He has a strong shot from the point and saw some time on the power play.

The downside is that he has considerable off-ice problems which affect his availability and his play.

THE PHYSICAL GAME

Gaetz is quite a package — size, strength and meanness. He will instigate, and few people want to go with him because he is a legitimate tough guy. He takes bad, aggressive penalties.

THE INTANGIBLES

The Sharks are fervently hoping that Gaetz will be slowed down by the auto accident (which resulted in his being comatose for several days). A recovering alcoholic, Gaetz has been given the benefit of the doubt by some very sympathetic men in the San Jose system who value his talent and don't want to give up on a young man. But to us, Gaetz is more trouble than he's worth.

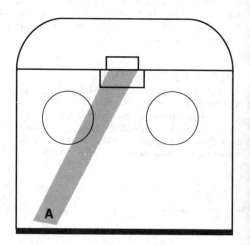

JOHAN GARPENLOV

Yrs. of NHL service: 2
Born: Stockholm, Sweden; Mar. 21, 1968
Position: Left wing
Height: 5-11
Weight: 183
Uniform no.: 10
Shoots: Left

Career statistics:

GP	G	A	TP	PIM
99	24	29	53	26

1991-92 statistics:

GP	G	A	TP	+/-	PIM	PP	SH	GW	GT	S	PCT
28	6	7	13	13	8	1	0	1	0	34	17.6

LAST SEASON

Acquired from Detroit for Bob McGill and an eighth round draft pick, Mar. 10, 1992. All totals below 1990-91 rookie season.

THE FINESSE GAME

Garpenlov is a strong skater with good balance. On those nights when he is involved, he will carry puck through checks. Garpenlov has some very nice offensive skills and when he has some room will be a creative playmaker. He doesn't shoot nearly enough, since his speed gets him into good scoring areas. He will be alone in front of the net and will overhandle the puck rather than take a shot.

Because he gets the extra room he needs to generate offense, Garpenlov works very well on the power play. He likes to work down low, catching the skater coming in late with a feed. His own shots come from low on the left side. He can one-time a shot nicely with accuracy.

THE PHYSICAL GAME

Garpenlov is not a physical player, and needs open ice to be effective. He will go into traffic with the puck, but doesn't continue to drive to the net and gets rid of the puck, not always making a smart play with it. North American-style hockey is not his forte.

THE INTANGIBLES

Garpenlov started his career as a center and despite his defensive softness, he might be better off if the Sharks gave him a try there, since he can't or won't pay the physical price necessary to succeed as a winger in the NHL. Garpenlov couldn't crack the Red Wings' lineup at the start of last season, and was in the minors before the Sharks dealt for him. He will be an offensive force for San Jose.

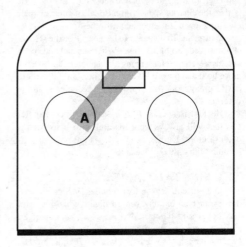

JEFF HACKETT

Yrs. of NHL service: 2
Born: London, Ont.; June 1, 1968
Position: Goaltender
Height: 6-1
Weight: 175
Uniform no.: 30
Catches: Left

Career statistics:

GP	MINS	GA	SO	GAA	A	PIM
85	4484	278	0	3.72	2	12

1991-92 statistics:

GP	MINS	GAA	W	L	T	SO	GA	S	SAPCT	PIM
42	2314	3.84	11	27	1	0	148	1366	.892	8

LAST SEASON

All totals and GAA career highs. Missed seven games with groin/hamstring injury. Missed two games with sinus infection. Missed four game with knee injury. Missed last two games of season with mono.

THE PHYSICAL GAME

Hackett might have had the busiest glove in the NHL last season. It wasn't necessarily catching pucks. It was whomping down on any loose bit of rubber within his range. Playing behind a very inexperienced defense, Hackett took few chances. San Jose's centers were pretty good on draws, making his conservation approach to the game fairly effective. The downside is that the Sharks spent a great deal of time in their own zone even if they did control the draw.

Getting his first chance to be a No. 1 goalie, Hackett improved part of his game. Where he had once been indecisive about challenging the shooter, he became more bold and played his angles better (although there is still great room for improvement technically in the latter area).

Hackett is not much of a skater or puckhandler and that will always limit his ability to help out his defense more. He has good reflexes but remains vulnerable high on the glove side.

THE MENTAL GAME

In a difficult season for a goalie, Hackett showed himself to be a battler even on nights when his team was hopelessly outclassed (i.e., about 76 out of 80 nights). Hackett seldom lost a game for his team, and kept them in games when they were badly outshot. His maturity will be tested again this season and, as the team improves slowly around him, so will his confidence.

THE INTANGIBLES

Always sensitive to criticism (he was upset with our assessment of him last year, despite our opinion that he would be the steal of the Expansion Draft for the Sharks), Hackett needs to become a little less paranoid and more self-confident. He wants to be a No. 1 goalie for a franchise that played five different men in goal last season. It would really help to have a veteran around to help him instead of one (i.e., Brian Hayward) who is competitive with him.

342

KELLY KISIO

Yrs. of NHL service: 10
Born: Peace River, Alta.; Sept. 18, 1959
Position: Center
Height: 5-9
Weight: 183
Uniform no.: 11
Shoots: Right

Career statistics:

GP	G	A	TP	PIM
620	189	350	539	644

1991-92 statistics:

GP	G	A	TP	+/-	PIM	PP	SH	GW	GT	S	PCT
48	11	26	37	−7	54	2	3	2	0	68	16.2

LAST SEASON

Games played and goals totals career low for full season. Tied for team lead in shorthanded goals. Missed 18 games with ankle injury. Missed two games with abdominal strain. Missed two games with knee injury. Missed last eight game of season with shoulder injury.

THE FINESSE GAME

All of Kisio's modest skills are enhanced by his determination and work ethic. Kisio is not a very good skater, and he has lost a step in the past season, but he positions himself well and works so hard that this is not as severe a flaw as it would be with some other players.

Very good in traffic, he has good hand skills and remains focused while scrapping for rebounds around the net. Kisio has very strong wrists and can backhand a shot from the slot. He is very good on faceoffs.

Kisio always gets back on defense. He is an excellent penalty killer with excellent hockey sense and tenacity. He does not have breakaway speed but is a shorthanded scoring threat because he forces turnovers. Kisio also plays well on the power play.

THE PHYSICAL GAME

Injuries have prevented Kisio from playing more than 51 games in each of the last two seasons. You have to wonder how many games he will be able to suit up for this season if the beat(ing) goes on. Kisio doesn't know how to play any other game other than one where he is involved in battling for the puck along the boards and in the corners, and that leaves him vulnerable to hits, usually by bigger players. Even when he is down on his knees, Kisio will still be involved trying to gain control of the puck.

THE INTANGIBLES

If it weren't for fax lag, Kisio would have been playing with the Chicago Blackhawks for the Stanley Cup. Just minutes after the NHL trade deadline, the 'Hawks tried to register a deal that would have brought him to Chicago Stadium. Instead, the NHL rejected the trade as moving too late, and he remained a Shark. He should sue for a playoff share. Kisio would be most effective if he could be dealt to a contending team, where he would be a valuable role player.

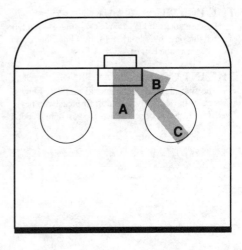

BRIAN LAWTON

Yrs. of NHL service: 8
Born: New Brunswick, N.J.; June 29, 1965
Position: Left wing/center
Height: 6-0
Weight: 190
Uniform no.: 9
Shoots: Left

Career statistics:

GP	G	A	TP	PIM
462	107	146	256	389

1991-92 statistics:

GP	G	A	TP	+/-	PIM	PP	SH	GW	GT	S	PCT
59	15	22	37	−25	42	7	0	1	0	131	11.5

LAST SEASON

Signed as free agent August 9, 1991. Did not play in NHL in 1990-91. Tied for fourth on team in scoring. Missed three games with foot injury. Missed eight games with tendonitis in his knee. Missed three games with tonsillitis.

THE FINESSE GAME

The Sharks were smart enough to use Lawton as a center — instead of a wing, where he played during his previous NHL stints. Since he is not a very good skater and is not particularly strong, keeping him out in the middle of the ice where he has room to generate more offense was the best option. Lawton is not a great playmaker, nor does he have great hands, but his skills were sufficient enough to cover up for the absence of good hockey vision. He has some moves in open ice but is wasted in close quarters, where he does not have the skating or hand quickness to function.

Lawton has good anticipation and has improved as a defensive player and checker. He will hustle back to help out defensively and was used to kill penalties.

THE PHYSICAL GAME

Lawton does not play a physical game. He is a fair size but does not play to it, and shows little interest in hockey as a contact sport.

THE INTANGIBLES

The first player drafted overall in 1983, Lawton was one of those highly touted draft picks who never lived up to expectations. He made the best of his second (last?) chance with the Sharks last season. However, Lawton was benched (when healthy) six times in the last 21 games of the season and will get less ice time as the Sharks acquire better, younger talent.

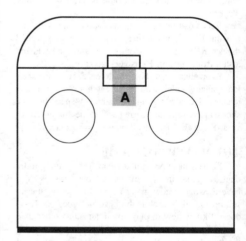

BRIAN MULLEN

Yrs. of NHL service: 10
Born: New York, N.Y.; Mar. 16, 1962
Position: Left wing
Height: 5-10
Weight: 180
Uniform no.: 19
Shoots: Left

Career statistics:

GP	G	A	TP	PIM
751	242	348	590	386

1991-92 statistics:

GP	G	A	TP	+/-	PIM	PP	SH	GW	GT	S	PCT
72	18	28	46	−14	66	5	3	1	0	168	10.7

LAST SEASON

Second on team in assists and scoring. Tied for team lead in shorthanded goals. Goals and points totals career lows. Missed six games with knee injury.

THE FINESSE GAME

Mullen's speed has always been the key to his game and even though he is losing a few m.p.h., he is still a quick and dangerous forward. He is very agile, with great balance, and has great lateral mobility. Mullen works well down low, even though he is on the small side, because he darts in and out of openings so quickly.

Sound defensively, he can quickly help his team on a counterattack rush. There are few forwards better at taking a pass off the off-wing boards in full stride. And Mullen will shoot from anywhere. The most absurd shots, from the strangest angles, seem to find the net and have some velocity on them.

Mullen can kill penalties and is always a short-handed threat. He has a weakness two-on-one in that he thinks pass first. Opponents know that, and can usually anticipate him giving up the shot to make a play.

THE PHYSICAL GAME

Mullen plays to the utmost of his physical abilities. He won't knock anybody into the seats, but he will bump and pester, and has such good hand speed that even by just distracting an opponent he can often come away with the puck. Mullen moves the puck quickly and victimizes the player who lost the disc and is usually caught flat-footed.

THE INTANGIBLES

Mullen is one of the great stories in hockey, as he and his brother Joe (of the Pittsburgh Penguins) grew up playing roller hockey in the tough Hell's Kitchen neighborhood of New York City. Their late father worked at Madison Square Garden and Brian became a stick boy for the Rangers while playing juior hockey in New York and New Jersey. You can't help but root for a player like this, and Mullen appears to have a few good seasons left in him for the Sharks.

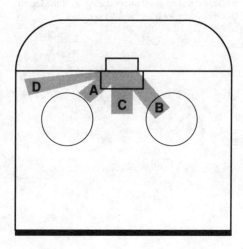

JEFF ODGERS

Yrs. of NHL service: 1
Born: Spy Hill, Sask.; May 31, 1969
Position: Left wing
Height: 6-0
Weight: 195
Uniform no.: 36
Shoots: Right

Career Statistics:

GP	G	A	TP	PIM
61	7	4	11	217

1991-92 statistics:

GP	G	A	TP	+/-	PIM	PP	SH	GW	GT	S	PCT
61	7	4	11	-21	217	0	0	0	0	64	10.9

LAST SEASON

Signed as free agent Sept. 3, 1991. First NHL season. Second on team in PIM. Missed four games with hand injury.

THE FINESSE GAME

Odgers lacks the hockey sense to be used in any situation other than even strength. He loves to forecheck, yet he can't be used to kill penalties because he gets caught in deep. Odgers lacks the hand skills and the offensive instinct to work on the power play. He does a lot of running around and gets caught out of position.

Odgers has some speed and balance, but only if he is travelling in a straight line. He has little mobility and agility. The pace of the game often seems too much for him. He is a hard worker.

THE PHYSICAL GAME

Odgers will takes the body and play tough. He loves to forecheck and will get in very quickly on a goalie, even such good puckhandlers as Ron Hextall. Odgers takes a lot of aggressive penalties.

THE INTANGIBLES

Odgers is a role player whose role is extremely limited.

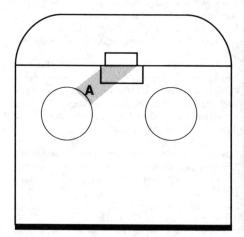

346

MIKE RATHJE

Yrs. of NHL service: 0
Born: Mannville, Alta.; May 11, 1974
Position: Defense
Height: 6-5
Weight: 203
Uniform no.:
Shoots: Left

1991-92 junior statistics:

GP	G	A	TP	PIM
67	11	23	34	109

LAST SEASON

Drafted in first round, third overall, in 1992 Entry Draft.

THE FINESSE GAME

Rathje has concentrated on playing defense, but he has very good offensive skills, especially for a player of his size.

He skates very fluidly for a big man, forwards and backwards, and is fairly agile—but it won't hurt that he'll be breaking into the NHL on a smaller ice surface (185' by 85').

A good passer, he can also lug the puck out of his zone. His playmaking decisions are getting better the more the tries to do. He has a good shot from the point.

THE PHYSICAL GAME

Rathje has excellent size and strength which he uses to advantage all over the ice. He has not always played with confidence, but when he does, he is a punishing hitter. He will clear his crease and is very strong along the boards and in the corners. He needs to be more intense on a consistent basis.

THE INTANGIBLES

What scouts like most about Rathje—aside from the obvious physical attributes—is that his improvement over the last half of last season surpassed so much of the projections. Rathje may not be ready for the NHL yet, but the Sharks might be forced to hurry him along and he could be in their lineup next season, even though he has junior eligibility left with Medicine Hat (WHL).

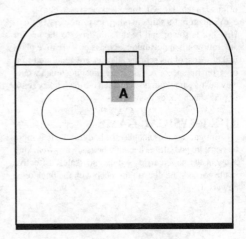

DAVE SNUGGERUD

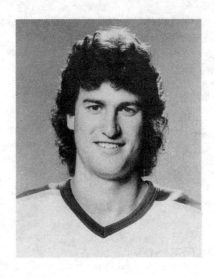

Yrs. of NHL service: 3
Born: Minnetonka, Minn.; June 20, 1966
Position: Left wing
Height: 6-0
Weight: 190
Uniform no.: 18
Shoots: Left

Career statistics:

GP	G	A	TP	PIM
226	26	47	73	118

1991-92 statistics:

GP	G	A	TP	+/-	PIM	PP	SH	GW	GT	S	PCT
66	3	16	19	-15	45	0	0	0	0	94	3.2

LAST SEASON

Acquired from Buffalo for Wayne Presley, March 9, 1992. Failed to play all 80 games for first time in NHL career. Goals and points totals career lows.

THE FINESSE GAME

Snuggerud's speed and anticipation make him one of the better penalty killers around. He is not much of a shorthanded scoring threat (although he had four a season ago in Buffalo), because he doesn't think offense much. He will forecheck aggressively.

Snuggerud's skills in other areas are very limited. His shot is so-so, and he doesn't drive to the net for any follow-up opportunities. Nor is he a creative playmaker. Most of his scoring chances are generated simply from his speed. A little more finishing touch would elevate his game, but he may not have the hockey sense to play much better than he has shown.

THE PHYSICAL GAME

Snuggerud does not play the body well. He is more terrier than pit bull, a checker who is always whacking away at the puck carrier's stick and skates. Effective in the corners, he doesn't do much with the puck once he gets it.

THE INTANGIBLES

Snuggerud is, at best, a third-line player who can contribute defensively.

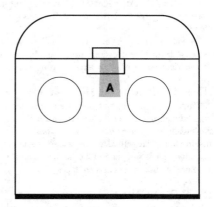

RAY WHITNEY

Yrs. of NHL service: 0
Born: Edmonton, Alta.; May 8, 1972
Position: Center
Height: 5-9
Weight: 160
Uniform no.: 43
Shoots: Right

Career statistics:

GP	G	A	TP	PIM
2	0	3	3	0

1991-92 statistics:

GP	G	A	TP	+/-	PIM	PP	SH	GW	GT	S	PCT
2	0	3	3	-1	0	0	0	0	0	4	.0

LAST SEASON

Started season with Cologne (West Germany). Played for San Diego (IHL) before joining Sharks at end of season.

THE FINESSE GAME

Whitney is a nifty skater who plays a smart, small man's game. He is at his best in open ice, where he can use his quick moves to avoid bigger, slower checkers.

Whitney has great vision and hockey sense, and nice, soft hands for shooting or passing. He doesn't have an overpowering shot, but he gets a lot on his wrist and snap shots and picks his corners.

After turning pro with the independent San Diego Gulls of the IHL last season, he scored 36-54 — 90 in 63 games. The NHL will be another big step for him.

THE PHYSICAL GAME

Whitney is not tough, like Theo Fleury, and for that reason his small stature will be a deterrent. But he does play with intensity and will go through traffic in pursuit of the puck if a scoring chance looms.

THE INTANGIBLES

Whitney was drafted in the second round in 1991 with the intention of giving him a season of seasoning (the Olympic route was planned). Instead, Whitney signed to play in West Germany but played only a few games before leaving in a contract dispute. Barred from competing in the NHL until after March 15 since he was still eligible to play junior, Whitney showed some spark in his two games in San Jose. He was Falloon's linemate in junior at Spokane, and the Sharks hope to rekindle some of that old fire. But he will always be limited by his size.

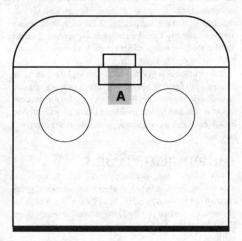

349

NEIL WILKINSON

Yrs. of NHL service: 3
Born: Selkirk, Man.; Aug. 16, 1967
Position: Left defense
Height: 6-3
Weight: 180
Uniform no.: 5
Shoots: Right

Career statistics:

GP	G	A	TP	PIM
146	6	29	35	314

1991-92 statistics:

GP	G	A	TP	+/-	PIM	PP	SH	GW	GT	S	PCT
60	4	15	19	−11	97	1	0	0	0	95	4.2

LAST SEASON

Games played and all point totals career highs. Missed four games with groin injury. Missed three games with eye injury. Missed 13 games with back spasms.

THE FINESSE GAME

Probably the best all-around defenseman on the Sharks last season, Wilkinson is equally effective in both zones without being dominant in either. Although he isn't a great rushing defenseman, when he sees an opportunity he will carry the puck. He is a right-handed shot who played the left side, but Wilkinson was deft enough to center passes off his backhand. He saw some time on the power play. He has a good, low shot and is also a good passer. He is capable of doing more offensively than he showed last season, but the Sharks obviously needed him to play a more defensive role and he emphasized that.

Wilkinson is a good skater, although he has some trouble with his foot speed when backskating and can be beaten to the outside. Most opposing forwards seem to know this and he has to learn to read plays better so he can establish an angle and force the rusher into the boards.

THE PHYSICAL GAME

Wilkinson has good size and strength, and can play tough. He needs to develop more physical presence on the ice — as yet, he hasn't earned a whole lot of respect. More upper-body conditioning might help. He will stand up for his teammates and is a pretty good battler.

THE INTANGIBLES

Wilkinson is one of the Sharks with the most potential. Nothing about his game really stands out, but he is solid in many areas.

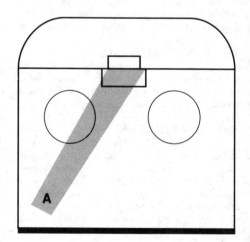

DAVID WILLIAMS

Yrs. of NHL service: 1
Born: Plainfield, N.J.; Aug. 25, 1967
Position: Right defense
Height: 6-2
Weight: 195
Uniform no.: 3
Shoots: Right

Career statistics:

GP	G	A	TP	PIM
56	3	25	28	40

1991-92 statistics:

GP	G	A	TP	+/-	PIM	PP	SH	GW	GT	S	PCT
56	3	25	28	-13	40	2	0	1	0	91	3.3

LAST SEASON
Signed as free agent August 9, 1991. First NHL season. Second among team defensemen in scoring.

THE FINESSE GAME
Williams' offensive skills are superior to his defensive skills. He has a good point shot — not a rocket, but he keeps it low and it gets through. He will also gamble deep in the zone, and likes to back door looking for a feed.

Williams is an average skater who needs to improve his positional play. He is weak defensively one-on-one and needs more experience reading the rush. He does not outlet a pass from the zone easily. He tends to freeze in some defensive situations. Williams is a good passer, and perhaps with more confidence will improve.

THE PHYSICAL GAME
Williams will play a physical game but he is out of position so often that he will start running around looking for hits. He is a big kid, and with more experience and more patience could settle down.

THE INTANGIBLES
Williams would be unlikely to have a job with any team other than an expansion team.

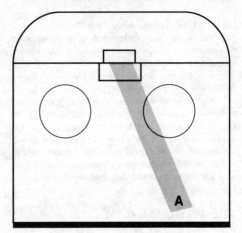

DOUG WILSON

Yrs. of NHL service: 15
Born: Ottawa, Ont.; July 5, 1957
Position: Left defense
Height: 6-1
Weight: 187
Uniform no.: 24
Shoots: Left

Career statistics:

GP	G	A	TP	PIM
982	234	573	807	790

1991-92 statistics:

GP	G	A	TP	+/-	PIM	PP	SH	GW	GT	S	PCT
44	9	19	28	-38	26	4	0	0	1	123	7.3

LAST SEASON

Acquired from Chicago for Kerry Toporowski and a second round draft choice, Sept. 6, 1991. Led team defensemen in scoring. Second-fewest games played of career. Worst plus-minus among team defensemen. Missed 10 games with thumb injury. Missed four games with ear infection. Missed three games with back injury. Missed last 19 games of season with knee injury.

THE FINESSE GAME

Wilson used to be ranked among the top offensive defensemen in the league, but those skills have dropped off sharply. His big, booming slap shot takes longer to unleash, and he doesn't always dart in for his scoring chances down low.

Wilson is valuable because of his experience and great hockey sense. He is a very good skater and an excellent stickhandler and passer. Despite playing just over half the season, he led the Sharks defensemen in scoring and ranked sixth overall on the team in scoring.

He never was that good a player defensively and with a weaker supporting cast around him now is even more ineffective.

THE PHYSICAL GAME

Wilson is a very well-conditioned athlete, but he is 35 now and age is certainly a concern, since he showed a tendency to be injury-prone over the past two seasons. He is a deceptively strong, wiry player, who doesn't bash people around but is capable of playing the body.

THE INTANGIBLES

Injuries sidelined Wilson for more than half the season and he didn't show much interest in playing when he was healthy. The Sharks need his leadership, but Wilson hasn't yet been able to provide it.

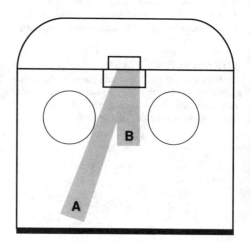

ROB ZETTLER

Yrs. of NHL service: 3
Born: Sept Iles, Que.; Mar. 8, 1968
Position: Right defense
Height: 6-3
Weight: 190
Uniform no.: 2
Shoots: Left

Career statistics:

GP	G	A	TP	PIM
154	2	20	22	257

1991-92 statistics:

GP	G	A	TP	+/-	PIM	PP	SH	GW	GT	S	PCT
74	1	8	9	-23	103	0	0	0	0	72	1.4

LAST SEASON

Games played career high. Goals and assists matched career high. Missed one game with flu.

THE FINESSE GAME

Although he was showing good signs of improvement while in the Minnesota organization, the move to San Jose last season seems to have been a setback.

Zettler does not generate much offense, but he can move the puck out of his zone by lugging it or with a pass. He is a support player, but as of yet the Sharks don't have any strong defensive players for him to complement. He's on his own and it's too much for him at this stage.

He does a lot of little things well. He is strong positionally and his skating is above average.

THE PHYSICAL GAME

Zettler has worked hard to improve his upper-body strength, but still gets knocked off the puck too easily. He will go into a boards battle with a smaller player and lose out to the munchkin. Zettler doesn't initiate enough and needs more mental toughness.

THE INTANGIBLES

Zettler hasn't given much of an indication that he wants to become a player in this league. He has some of the skills to develop into a solid, everyday player, but has to have the desire or he won't be more than an in-and-out player.

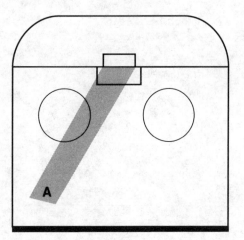

TAMPA BAY LIGHTNING

SHAWN CHAMBERS

Yrs. of NHL service: 5
Born: Royal Oaks, Mich.; Oct. 11, 1966
Position: Defense
Height: 6-2
Weight: 200
Uniform no.: 25
Shoots: Left

Career statistics:

GP	G	A	TP	PIM
200	15	47	62	208

1991-92 statistics:

GP	G	A	TP	+/-	PIM	PP	SH	GW	GT	S	PCT
2	0	0	0	-3	2	0	0	0	0	1	0.0

LAST SEASON

Claimed from Washington in 1992 Expansion Draft. Missed most of season with surgery on left knee.

THE FINESSE GAME

Chambers has adequate skills to move the puck, but he will not generate much offense. He does not join the play, and will use a so-so shot from the point that is accurate but doesn't have a lot of juice. Before his knee surgery, he did have a good degree of quickness and strength and would pinch in aggressively along the boards.

Chambers would also go to the net with the puck (we have to talk in past tense, since he appeared in only two games last season, and we don't know how he will play as he rehabs his knee).

With a good degree of hockey smarts, Chambers plays a sound positional game and was well on his well to developing into a very solid NHL defenseman before his injury.

THE PHYSICAL GAME

Chambers has good size and is a willing hitter. Again, his strength will depend on how well he comes back from his injury, since so much of his power is derived from his leg drive. He doesn't knock people into the seats, but his take-outs are effective and he keeps his man from getting back into the play.

THE INTANGIBLES

Probably the most talented defenseman available in the Expansion Draft, Chambers was still a gambler's pick. He has not indicated that he has recovered from his knee surgery and it is questionable whether he can make it back. If he does, Chambers is young enough to be a valuable contributor for many seasons.

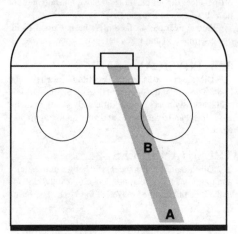

ROB DiMAIO

Yrs. of NHL service: 3
Born: Calgary, Alta.; Feb. 19, 1968
Position: Center
Height: 5-8
Weight: 175
Uniform no.: 18
Shoots: Right

Career statistics:

GP	G	A	TP	PIM
74	6	2	8	75

1991-92 statistics:

GP	G	A	TP	+/-	PIM	PP	SH	GW	GT	S	PCT
50	5	2	7	-23	43	0	2	0	0	43	11.6

LAST SEASON

Claimed from New York Islanders in 1992 Expansion Draft. Games played career high.

THE FINESSE GAME

DiMaio's finesse skills are not NHL quality. He gets most of his goals from digging around the net; he has pretty good hand skills for picking up loose pucks and getting a shot off right away. DiMaio is willing to hang out in front and try to set a screen or get a tip-in.

Stocky, with a wide skating base, he has a low center of gravity that makes it difficult to knock him off-balance. Bigger players can move DiMaio out, but he will give them a tussle first.

Above average on face-offs, he has good hand-eye coordination and takes defensive zone draws.

THE PHYSICAL GAME

DiMaio has a Mack truck attitude in a Hyundai body. The size of the opponent doesn't matter. DiMaio will fearlessly hurl his solid little body at any of them. He is feisty and aggressive, and very annoying to play against.

THE INTANGIBLES

DiMaio has been a successful scorer at the junior and minor league levels, but doesn't have the skills to make it as that kind of player in the NHL. His future is as a checker who can score the odd goal. He is a very hard worker and has good character. A good team man.

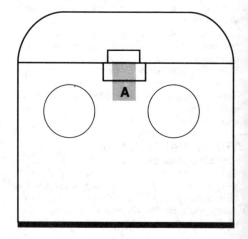

356

ROMAN HAMRLIK

Yrs. of NHL service: 0
Born: Gottwaldov, Czechoslovkia; Apr. 12, 1974
Position: Defense
Height: 6-2
Weight: 189
Uniform no.:
Shoots: Left

LAST SEASON

Drafted first overall in 1992 Entry Draft.

THE FINESSE GAME

Hamrlik is a little rough around the edges, but he has a solid foundation of skills. He is a mobile skater and can carry the puck on the rush, but is not especially offensively inclined. He has a good shot and good passing skills, but isn't creative.

Hamrlik has concentrated on his defense first. He doesn't make many mistakes and is poised under pressure. He plays well positionally and reads the play coming at him. Hamrlik is a very smart player with good instincts.

THE PHYSICAL GAME

Hamrlik always finishes his checks, and does so aggressively. He already plays a North American style of game, so shouldn't have much difficulty in making the adjustment to the NHL. How intense is he? Consider that Hamrlik nearly touched off a riot at the European Junior Tournament in Norway when he kicked the skates out from under a CIS player near the end of the game.

Hamrlik is big, powerful and aggressive.

THE INTANGIBLES

Hamrlik was the top-rated European in the 1992 draft. He has a year remaining on his contract with his hometown team of Zlin in Czechoslovkia, but the Lightning are desperate for a star and talent, and may be able to purchase his contract so he can join the NHL right away. In a draft year dominated by Europeans, Hamrlik ranked at the top of almost every scout's list.

MIKE HARTMAN

Yrs. of NHL service: 6
Born: Detroit, Mich.; Feb. 7, 1967
Position: Left wing
Height: 6-0
Weight: 190
Uniform no.: 20
Shoots: Left

Career statistics:

GP	G	A	TP	PIM
300	38	30	68	1154

1991-92 statistics:

GP	G	A	TP	+/-	PIM	PP	SH	GW	GT	S	PCT
75	4	4	8	−10	264	0	0	1	1	89	4.5

LAST SEASON

Claimed from Winnipeg in 1992 Expansion Draft.
Games played career high. Second on Jets in PIM.

THE FINESSE GAME

Although he has established his reputation as a battler, Hartman has above-average finesse skills for such a PIM monster. His problem is that he needs a great deal of time to make the pass or take the shot, and he doesn't get that time in the NHL. He has good hands and good vision, spots the open man for his passes, and could be a 20-goal scorer if he applies himself mentally.

Hartman has trouble with play back in his own zone because he gets too excited and tends to forget his own man. He has great enthusiasm that has to be curbed because he costs his team in outmanned situations.

THE PHYSICAL GAME

Hartman is a tough guy with the speed to hit and forecheck. He is an effective agitator and a tremendous competitor. Hartman starts running around too much, looking to make hits, and needs to get an emotional grip.

THE INTANGIBLES

Hartman is a good character player, very intense, and will do whatever the coaching staff asks of him.

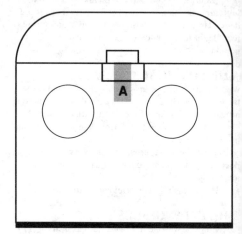

BOB McGILL

Yrs. of NHL service: 11
Born: Edmonton, Alta.; Apr. 27, 1962
Position: Right defense
Height: 6-1
Weight: 193
Uniform no.: 4
Shoots: Right

Career statistics:

GP	G	A	TP	PIM
653	16	52	68	1686

1991-92 statistics:

GP	G	A	TP	+/-	PIM	PP	SH	GW	GT	S	PCT
74	3	1	4	-37	91	0	1	1	0	62	4.8

LAST SEASON

Claimed from Detroit in 1992 Expansion Draft. Worst plus-minus on Red Wings (brought minus 34 with him in trade from San Jose).

THE FINESSE GAME

The best part of McGill's game is his competiveness. He has very limited skills, but works hard.

McGill does not get involved in the offense. He will anchor near the blue line, not gamble in deep, and does have a good, low slap shot that will get through for a tip or re-direct. McGill plays a very conservative game, since he lacks the skating ability to recover defensively.

McGill is slow, so opposing skaters can beat him wide with a good burst. McGill has improved his positional play to keep the attacker to the perimeter and not allow a break in on goal.

THE PHYSICAL GAME

McGill is an average checker who will tie up rather than take out his man. He does not skate very fast, so he doesn't generate much speed before a hit. McGill does have good balance and strength for one-on-one battles. He will block shots.

THE INTANGIBLES

McGill is an excellent fifth or sixth defenseman, but he moves up on the Lightning's depth chart to three, or maybe two, and that could be a problem.

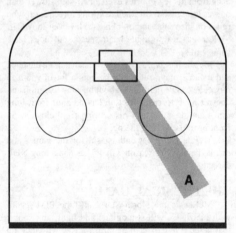

BASIL McRAE

Yrs. of NHL service: 8
Born: Beaverton, Ont.; Jan. 5, 1961
Position: Left wing
Height: 6-2
Weight: 205
Uniform no.: 17
Shoots: Left

Career statistics:

GP	G	A	TP	PIM
442	48	69	117	2061

1991-92 statistics:

GP	G	A	TP	+/-	PIM	PP	SH	GW	GT	S	PCT
59	5	8	13	−14	245	0	0	0	0	64	7.8

LAST SEASON

Claimed from Minnesota in 1992 Expansion Draft. Second on North Stars in PIM. Underwent surgery to repair severed tendon in left foot. Broke left leg.

THE FINESSE GAME

McRae has very limited finesse skills, and they will probably be undermined even more if he comes back from his leg injuries even a half-step slower than he was last season. McRae is a strong forechecker who relies on his range and quickness. Never an Indy Car, McRae has no straight-ahead speed, but does have some agility.

McRae has average hands. He can handle the puck and make a play, and since he gets a lot of room to move, he can be deliberate about his play selection and doesn't have to rush. McRae has no shot from long range and does most of his scoring from close in, in front or to the side of the net.

McRae has great enthusiasm for the game, and that is the primary reason why he has had a long NHL career.

THE PHYSICAL GAME

McRae is the North Stars' all-time PIM leader with 1,567. He will still agitate and fight, and knows that is the role expected of him. McRae will stick up for his teammates and has a huge heart. He will earn room for anyone that skates with him, because he is a feared competitor and opponents give him a wide berth.

THE INTANGIBLES

Tampa Bay GM Phil Esposito seems to have set great stock in drafting character players, and this is one of them. One of the most respected players in the

Minnesota dressing room, McRae is a role player who should be a good influence on the struggling expansion team. He is a competitor who empties his tank every night.

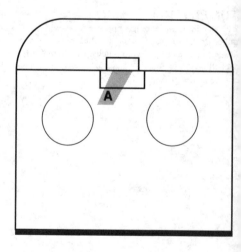

360

MICHEL MONGEAU

Yrs. of NHL service: 3
Born: Nun's Island, Que.; Feb. 9, 1965
Position: Center
Height: 5-9
Weight: 190
Uniform no.: 41
Shoots: Left

Career statistics:

GP	G	A	TP	PIM
50	5	18	23	8

1991-92 statistics:

GP	G	A	TP	+/-	PIM	PP	SH	GW	GT	S	PCT
36	3	12	15	−2	6	2	0	0	0	23	13.0

LAST SEASON
First NHL season.

THE FINESSE GAME
Mongeau is primarily a playmaker, a creative center and good passer who sees the ice well. For that reason, he is a very good power play specialist. Mongeau uses the open ice well and will work most efficiently with a finishing winger.

Mongeau is also an above-average shooter, with good accuracy. He does not drive to the net or follow up his shots.

Mongeau is not a strong player defensively and had trouble getting ice time under former St. Louis coach Brian Sutter. When the game is wide and free-wheeling, Mongeau will excel.

THE PHYSICAL GAME
Mongeau is not a very big player, or a willing hitter, and prefers to play a perimeter game.

THE INTANGIBLES
A scorer at the minor league level, Mongeau has yet to show he is able to produce the same way in the NHL. He was the first forward drafted by the Lightning, who opted for potential over proven performance.

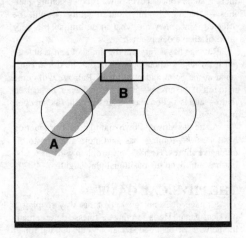

ROB RAMAGE

Yrs. of NHL service: 13
Born: Byron, Ont.; Jan. 11, 1959
Position: Right defense
Height: 6-2
Weight: 200
Uniform no.: 5
Shoots: Right

Career statistics:

GP	G	A	TP	PIM
949	134	410	544	2064

1991-92 statistics:

GP	G	A	TP	+/-	PIM	PP	SH	GW	GT	S	PCT
34	4	5	9	−4	69	2	0	0	0	63	6.3

LAST SEASON

Claimed from Minnesota in 1992 Expansion Draft. Missed 34 games with knee surgery.

THE FINESSE GAME

Ramage did not come back until very late in the season following knee surgery. Never a fast skater, there is some concern over how his other skating qualities — balance, agility and mobility — will be affected, since they are what made him such a very good offensive defenseman.

Ramage has a very good point shot and is able to get it through without being blocked; he doesn't just stand at the point and blast away. Ramage will come in to top of the circle — although no deeper, as he used to do — and is a good playmaker who will find an open man.

As he has slowed down and his point production has fallen off, Ramage has paid more attention to his defensive chores. He has some problem with his reads, but has improved his positional play slightly.

THE PHYSICAL GAME

Ramage does not go out of his way to play a physical game. He is foremost a finesse defenseman, but he will use his good size around the net and finish his checks.

THE INTANGIBLES

Ramage will add experience to the Lightning and help their power play. He has good leadership quali- ties. Should the team be able to sign Roman Hamrlik for next season, Ramage would be an ideal partner for the youngster.

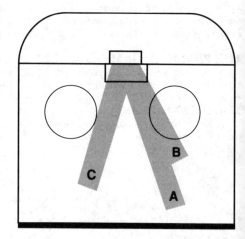

JOE REEKIE

Yrs. of NHL service: 5
Born: Petawawa, Ont.; Feb. 22, 1965
Position: Right defense
Height: 6-3
Weight: 215
Uniform no.: 29
Shoots: Left

Career statistics:

GP	G	A	TP	PIM
255	11	51	62	414

1991-92 statistics:

GP	G	A	TP	+/-	PIM	PP	SH	GW	GT	S	PCT
54	4	12	16	15	85	0	0	0	1	59	6.8

LAST SEASON

Claimed from New York Islanders in 1992 Expansion Draft. Missed 22 games with broken knuckle and surgery on left hand.

THE FINESSE GAME

Early in his career, Reekie had good enough finesse skills that he was tried out as a forward. Knee surgery put an end to that experiment, and Reekie still has limited mobility as a result of the injury. Now he generates little offense and has become a defensive defenseman.

Reekie has an unusual skating style, with a choppy stride, but he is light on his feet for a big man. Reekie has very good anticipation, which allows him to gain a step here and there. He will move the puck well out of his own end with a pass but won't carry it unless he has to.

Reekie never cheats in, sticking to the blue line. He will shoot or work a pass down low. He is not used much on the power play.

All of Reekie's skills are maximized because he is a smart player and positions himself well. He can play either right or left defense.

THE PHYSICAL GAME

Reekie has good size and strength, but his restricted range reduces his ability to be an impact hitter. He can play tough, especially in front of the net. Reekie is cool-headed and won't start running around. He keeps the front of his net clear and is strong along the boards and in the corners.

THE INTANGIBLES

The Islanders may miss Reekie more than they realize. He is an underrated, capable defenseman who made a perfect fit when rookie Scott Lachance stepped into the Islander lineup after the Olympics. Improved off-ice habits have led to similar progress on the ice. Reekie is a steady performer who has gained tremendous confidence over the past two seasons. And he is a very likeable guy.

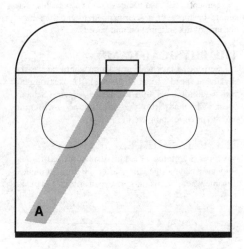

ANATOLI SEMENOV

Yrs. of NHL service: 2
Born: Moscow, CIS; Mar. 5, 1962
Position: Center/left wing
Height: 6-2
Weight: 190
Uniform no.: 19
Shoots: Left

Career statistics:

GP	G	A	TP	PIM
116	35	38	73	42

1991-92 statistics:

GP	G	A	TP	+/-	PIM	PP	SH	GW	GT	S	PCT
59	20	22	42	12	16	3	0	3	0	105	19.0

LAST SEASON

Claimed from Edmonton in 1992 Expansion Draft.

THE FINESSE GAME

Semenov has all of the finesse skills that we associate with players coming out of the Soviet system: great skating and great passing.

Semenov can also score. He likes to drive to the net and has lost any shyness about taking the shot. His shooting percentage is always high, because he will work himself (through his superior skating) into a high-percentage position before shooting. Semenov doesn't waste shots.

He is a gorgeous passer, with a cup-and-saucer pass that flips over a defender's stick and lays flat for the recipient. Semenov leads his man well and has very good hockey sense and vision.

Semenov is also defensively responsible. He should be more of a shorthanded threat than he is because of his anticipation and speed.

THE PHYSICAL GAME

Semenov plays well in traffic, where he has the slick hand speed to control the puck. He is strong but you wouldn't label him a physical player. Semenv doesn't like that part of the game but he is willing to pay the price to complete the job.

THE INTANGIBLES

Since Lightning GM Phil Esposito tried to deal Sememov back to the Oilers after the draft, it's questionable where he fits into the expansion team's plans.

But a defensive forward who can get you 20 goals should be a pretty valuable commodity, and that's just what Semenov does.

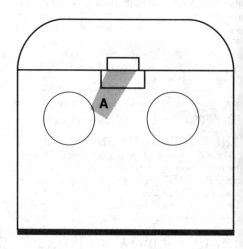

PETER TAGLIANETTI

Yrs. of NHL service: 6
Born: Framingham, Mass.; Aug. 15, 1963
Position: Left defense
Height: 6-2
Weight: 200
Uniform no.: 32
Shoots: Left

Career statistics:

GP	G	A	TP	PIM
306	14	49	63	768

1991-92 statistics:

GP	G	A	TP	+/-	PIM	PP	SH	GW	GT	S	PCT
44	1	3	4	7	57	0	0	0	0	23	4.3

LAST SEASON

Claimed from Pittsburgh in 1992 Expansion Draft.

THE FINESSE GAME

Taglianetti knows his boundaries and doesn't try to push the envelope. He is a stay-at-home defenseman who works well paired with an offensive-minded partner that likes to go wandering off all over the ice. Taglianetti will stay back and mind the store.

A limited player, he never gets involved offensively. He does not jump into the play or lead a rush. The only time Taglianetti will get anything going offensively is if the puck happens to come to him at the blue line. Even then, he won't do much more with it than fire on net; he does have a low, hard shot for the occasional point.

Taglianetti is an average skater who relies on his positional play. He does not have very good balance or agility. Despite his shortcomings, he works well on the penalty-killing unit.

THE PHYSICAL GAME

Taglianetti has good size and will hit with zest. He doesn't have as much strength as he should for someone of his build because his skating isn't that great, but he is very aggressive and uses his body to the utmost.

THE INTANGIBLES

Taglianetti can at least bring a winning attitude to the Lightning, since he played on two Stanley Cup championship teams in Pittsburgh. His work ethic and character make him a valuable player beyond his skills.

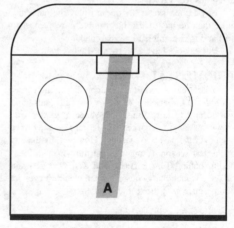

WENDELL YOUNG

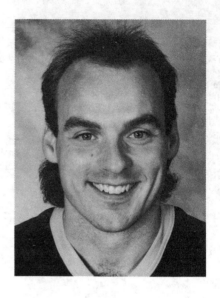

Yrs. of NHL service: 7
Born: Halifax, N.S.; Aug. 1, 1963
Position: Goaltender
Height: 5-8
Weight: 185
Uniform no.: 1
Catches: Left

Career statistics:

GP	MINS	GA	SO	GAA	A	PIM
137	6842	474	1	4.16	8	16

1991-92 statistics:

GP	MINS	GAA	W	L	T	SO	GA	S	SAPCT	PIM
18	838	3.79	7	6	0	0	53	476	.889	0

LAST SEASON
Claimed from Pittsburgh in 1992 Expansion Draft.

THE PHYSICAL GAME
Young plays a stand-up style. He concentrates on playing his angles and challenges shooters. Since he does not have quick reflexes, he runs into trouble with his rebounds and on close-in plays. Once Young goes down for a shot, he usually stays down; he doesn't regain his feet very fast.

Not a good skater, he doesn't play the puck any more than he has to. He has trouble moving post to post and is vulnerable to wraparounds.

But he does have a pretty good glove hand.

THE MENTAL GAME
Young has a good mental approach to the game. He has the experience to shake off bad goals, and works hard to keep himself in shape even when he knows his playing chances will be rare (as thay have been over the past two seasons). However, by the end of the last season Young was the third man in Pittsburgh (behind Tom Barrasso and Ken Wregget) and sulked so much that Scotty Bowman wouldn't even let him practice with the team's regulars.

THE INTANGIBLES
In six seasons with three different organizations, Young was a No. 1 goalie only once (in 1989-90, with Pittsburgh). He seemed to have no problem with his backup role, but is undoubtedly anxious to prove he can be a No. 1. Unless the Lightning find another goalie (Phil Esposito tried to pry Peter Ing away from Edmonton), he will get his shot. You can bet the Lightning will be trying to acquire another goalie right up until opening night.

TORONTO MAPLE LEAFS

GLENN ANDERSON

Yrs. of NHL service: 12
Born: Vancouver, B.C.; Oct. 2, 1960
Position: Right wing
Height: 6-1
Weight: 190
Uniform no.: 10
Shoots: Left

Career statistics:

GP	G	A	TP	PIM
900	437	516	953	871

1991-92 statistics:

GP	G	A	TP	+/-	PIM	PP	SH	GW	GT	S	PCT
72	24	33	57	-13	100	5	0	4	1	188	12.8

LAST SEASON

Finished strong, but marked third consecutive season under 30 goals. Second on team in goals. Led team forwards in shots. Missed four games due to suspension.

THE FINESSE GAME

Anderson still shows speed, but sometimes does not make as much happen with it as he used to. Some of the scoring touch appears to be gone for good.

Nonetheless, Anderson remains fast enough to beat a defenseman with speed and cut to the net. He still can come up with his share of big plays at the proper time and remains one of the modern era's better clutch players. An intelligent, creative player, Anderson knows how to get open and has the in-tight scoring touch to make a fake and roof a shot.

He always has been something of a streak player. He got just one goal in the team's first 20 games and just four in the first 42; then he started potting those passes from Doug Gilmour and the scoring flame was rekindled.

THE PHYSICAL GAME

Anderson is still just careless enough with his stick that you're never absolutely positive whether he legitimately lost his balance before bonking a guy on the head. His penalty-minute total jumped by 41.

THE INTANGIBLES

Anderson appeared utterly lost until the January trade that brought Doug Gilmour to the team and gave Anderson a center who could get him the puck. Revitalized by that development, he started playing like the scorer for whom the Leafs traded.

He ended up virtually matching his prior season's production, but those numbers are better suited to second- or third-line players. It will be interesting to see if the figure increases over a full season with Gilmour.

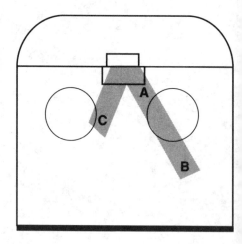

WENDEL CLARK

Yrs. of NHL service: 7
Born: Kelvington, Sask.; Oct. 25, 1966
Position: Left wing
Height: 5-11
Weight: 195
Uniform no.: 17
Shoots: Left

Career statistics:

GP	G	A	TP	PIM
333	145	94	239	1,035

1991-92 statistics:

GP	G	A	TP	+/-	PIM	PP	SH	GW	GT	S	PCT
43	19	21	40	-14	123	7	0	4	0	158	12.0

LAST SEASON

Goal, assist and point totals all improved, though his games played dropped 20 from prior season. Plus-minus worsened by nine. First season with more assists than goals. Missed 34 games due to knee injuries (two separate ligament tears) and three due to suspension.

THE FINESSE GAME

Clark's legendary spirit, toughness, heart and leadership should not blind people from the profound limitations of his all-around game. While he is a strong skater, he is neither fast nor agile nor mobile. He is a terrible playmaker. He has no identifiable passing skills. Often he is all over the ice, although he is starting to pay more attention to skating his lane. He rarely backchecks. He still takes undisciplined, too-emotional penalties.

And yet he would be a significant asset to any team deep enough to live with the 50 or 60 games a season he is healthy enough to play. Clark has a positively wicked snap shot that will go through a goalie's glove, through the net, through the boards, through the lobby and out onto Carlton Street. While he isn't going to make any plays, he will finish a load of them.

He does things well, he does things poorly. One way or the other, you notice him. One way or the other, he has an impact on the outcome.

THE PHYSICAL GAME

You to have to hold Clark to stop him, because he keeps his legs moving, keeps wriggling and struggling, keeps using his strength. He is all muscle, all mean. You want compassion, go see a clergyman; you want hard hockey, watch Wendel Clark.

THE INTANGIBLES

Clark is a bull and his body is a china shop. As each season passes, there is less cause to believe he can get through a full campaign without breaking some part of himself.

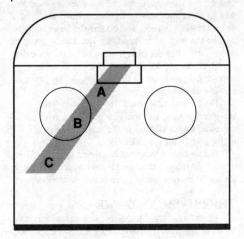

DAVE ELLETT

Yrs. of NHL service: 8
Born: Cleveland, Oh.; Mar. 30, 1964
Position: Left defense
Height: 6-1
Weight: 200
Uniform no.: 4
Shoots: Left

Career statistics:

GP	G	A	TP	PIM
614	121	267	388	668

1991-92 statistics:

GP	G	A	TP	+/-	PIM	PP	SH	GW	GT	S	PCT
79	18	33	51	−13	95	9	1	4	0	225	8.0

LAST SEASON

Led team in shots and shared team lead in game-winning goals. Second on team in assists and third on team in points. Goal total was second best of his career. Scored 10 or more goals for eighth consecutive season.

THE FINESSE GAME

Ellett is a fluid skater. He is so fluid, in fact, he at times looks like a slow-motion replay. He looks syrupy, deliberate. Ellett takes his time and tries to make sure he won't get caught if he takes the puck deep.

The skating skills are more an asset for his defense than for his offense. He has the quickness of hand and foot to make nice moves in the confined space of a defensive-zone corner, and he has the hand skills to control the puck as he heads up ice. But he tends to overhandle when decision time comes at the attacking blue line, as he doesn't have the speed to beat an opposing defenseman to the outside. So he is not an end-to-end rusher.

His passing is an asset. He has a nice touch for a sharp, crisp pass, and makes a good first pass out of the zone; he isn't afraid in the least to send a sizzler up the middle for a breakaway.

His shot from the point is a threat to score. Ellett doesn't get it away that quickly, but he gets it through the traffic to the net and keeps it low for deflections.

THE PHYSICAL GAME

Ellett looks huge. Either because of the helmet he wears or the number he wears or his on-ice manner, something about him is reminiscent of Kevin Hatcher. However, he is nowhere near the physical presence Hatcher is, and plays a rather placid game. And, of course, Ellett is left-handed.

He uses his reach, uses his size and strength. He doesn't bang, but he freezes opponents' arms with an unsubtle bear hug. He doesn't especially like to get hit, but who does?

THE INTANGIBLES

There is not an offensive defenseman in the game whose abilities are comprised of 50 percent of each category.

Brian Leetch, a 102-point scorer, still spends much more time on the defensive side of the puck than the offensive. Leetch is roughly 70 percent defense and 30 percent offense; he finished with 245 shots, 102 points and was plus 25. Phil Housley, depended on much more for offense in Winnipeg, is about 60-40 defense-to-offense; he ended up with 234 shots, 86 points and was minus 5. Ellett, is about 85-15 in defense-offense ratio (hey — it's our book, we can make up the numbers), got 225 shots, precisely half as many points as Leetch, and was minus 13.

Truly, then, Ellett is something of a defensive offenseman.

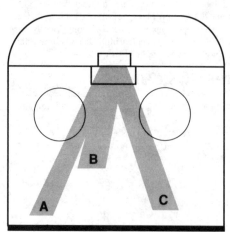

GRANT FUHR

Yrs. of NHL service: 11
Born: Spruce Grove, Alta.; Sept. 28, 1962
Position: Goaltender
Height: 5-10
Weight: 186
Uniform no.: 31
Catches: Right

Career statistics:

GP	MINS	GA	SO	GAA	A	PIM
488	27,684	1,700	11	3.68	37	58

1991-92 statistics:

GP	MINS	GAA	W	L	T	SO	GA	S	SAPCT	PIM
65	3,774	3.66	25	33	5	2	230	1,933	.881	4

LAST SEASON

Reached 20-victory milestone for eighth time in his career.

THE PHYSICAL GAME

Not enough people understand the specialness of Grant Fuhr, not enough people seem to have any interest in giving him the respect he deserves at the game's most thankless position.

Coaches watched him play 65 or 70 games with Edmonton, saw him winning Stanley Cups year in and year out, and figured their cheap-imitation goalie could do it, too. That simply is not the case. The thing that makes Fuhr so special is, he is a moose for playing time. The ideal for a No. 1 goalie in today's NHL is about 50-55 regular-season games, but coaches seem to think the top guy has to play more, not less. They're wrong.

Simply, Fuhr is the exception, not the rule. He is exceptional in his ability to handle a massive workload successfully — and with the team in front of him last year, the 55 points he got is success. His quickness remains exceptional. The speed of his feet remains unmatched. His glove is exceptional. He is a splendid skater, his puck-handling is underrated. He recovers very well for the second shots. He blows shots to the five hole at times, but makes six miracles for every one of those mistakes.

With regular seasons and playoffs and tournaments and practices and everything, Fuhr has faced about a million shots. He should be finished, washed up. But he made a weak team competitive every night and could get it into the playoffs this year.

THE MENTAL GAME

Fuhr's level of concentration is directly proportional to the score. If his team needs a big stop to keep a game close, he will provide it — and that includes the first minute of a game. If there's a breakaway right off the opening face-off, he properly can be expected to stop it. His five hole very rarely gets too big when the score is within a goal.

The other thing about Fuhr's focus is connected directly to his physical skills. Perhaps it is just a by-product of his reflexes, perhaps not; but it seems Fuhr picks up the puck off the stick five or 10 feet faster than three-quarters of the goalies in the league. While defensemen constantly are rated on their ability to "read and react," Fuhr is a master of it. He identifies the direction of the shot, and begins reacting, when most goalies would still be trying to pick up the trajectory.

THE INTANGIBLES

Fuhr had a losing record. There were times when he was booed at home. And yet he was one of the only reasons his team even challenged for a playoff spot. Sure, there were nights when he was bad, and when he is bad he is remarkably bad. And .881 isn't a Fuhr-level save percentage. But given the makeup of the team for more than half the season, it is stunning that Fuhr got points for his team in almost half his starts. Beyond that, Fuhr entered last season having played only 13 games the year before; he had some rust to scrape away.

TODD GILL

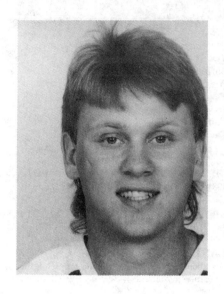

Yrs. of NHL service: 6
Born: Brockville, Ont.; Nov. 19, 1965
Position: Right defense
Height: 6-0
Weight: 180
Uniform no.: 23
Shoots: Left

Career statistics:

GP	G	A	TP	PIM
404	30	110	140	632

1991-92 statistics:

GP	G	A	TP	+/-	PIM	PP	SH	GW	GT	S	PCT
74	2	15	17	-22	91	1	0	0	0	82	2.4

LAST SEASON

Games played was a career high. Plus-minus declined 18 goals. PIM dropped 22 to three-season low.

THE FINESSE GAME

If he got two goals last season and two the year before, Gill hardly qualifies as an offensive defenseman. If he was minus-22, even though you know it wasn't ALL his fault, Gill hardly can be considered a defensive defenseman.

What he is, in fact, is a puzzle. Critics say Gill has hockey sense but simply doesn't use it all the time — doesn't think as much as he should. Other say Gill cannot think and play at the same time — that the game has to be automatic for him or he starts to struggle.

So, damned either way, Gill gets stuck between two labels. If he plays within his limitations — moves the puck quickly, makes the short pass instead of the long pass, stays out of dangerous situations, he is fine. When he tries to play outside his limitations, he is woeful; and he tries to do more than he is capable of doing when the fans at home start getting on him.

Bottom line: Gill is a sixth defenseman with average overall skills and a good enough shot to get some time on the second power play.

THE PHYSICAL GAME

Gill is a little small, but he has a lot of heart. He must play physical to be successful, or even relevant, because once he thinks he's got it made, the trouble starts.

THE INTANGIBLES

Toronto's fans may hate him, but Gill brings a lot of intangible qualities to the dressing room. He is not that big, but he sticks up for his teammates. He has lots of guts, is a good team player. How much longer he will be a good team player with Toronto is a reasonable question.

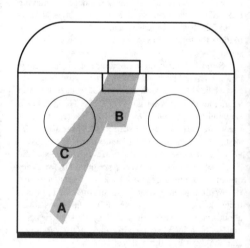

DOUG GILMOUR

Yrs. of NHL service: 8
Born: Kingston, Ont.; June 25, 1963
Position: Center
Height: 5-11
Weight: 185
Uniform no.: 93
Shoots: Left

Career statistics:

GP	G	A	TP	PIM
690	245	453	698	582

1991-92 statistics:

GP	G	A	TP	+/-	PIM	PP	SH	GW	GT	S	PCT
78	26	61	87	25	78	10	1	4	1	168	15.5

LAST SEASON

Obtained from Calgary, Jan. 2, 1992, with Jamie Macoun, Ric Nattress, Rick Wamsley and Kent Manderville, for Craig Berube, Alexander Goynyuk, Gary Leeman, Michel Petit and Jeff Reese. Power-play goal total jumped eight, PIM total dropped 64. Led team in goals, assists, points and plus-minus. Scored 85 points or more sixth consecutive season.

THE FINESSE GAME

Gilmour is not a natural skater; he is good, but not great. He is, however, extremely smooth, agile and nimble. He has enough speed to win a race to the puck, enough power to drive the defense back from the blue line before pulling up and looking for a late man entering the play as a trailer.

He will not storm across the blue line and blast a shot at the goalie, unless he thinks the goalie will leave a rebound available for a teammate. Rather, he goes to work in the scoring-chance area between the hashmarks; he has magic hands in-close, can score easily on a deke or by banging in a rebound. He also has a feather-light, computer-accurate passing touch, which is how he gets 60 assists a season, or close to it.

Gilmour is not big or hugely strong; he relies, instead, on quickness. It doesn't hurt, either, that he is among the better face-off men in the league. That asset comes in especially handy in special-team situations.

THE PHYSICAL GAME

Gilmour bumps, finishes his checks and has a feistiness that can catch fire at any time. An extremely aggressive player, he will dive in front of pucks. He also absorb whatever punishment is necessary to improve his chances — or a teammate's — of scoring.

THE INTANGIBLES

Merely by arriving last season, Gilmour revived the slumbering Glenn Anderson, helped turn him back into a productive player. Gilmour also allowed Peter Zezel to drop down to the No. 2 slot, where he is more capable and comfortable. The former Flame became invaluable, untouchable, a major component in Leafs leadership and a significant reason there is some optimism at Maple Leaf Gardens heading into this season.

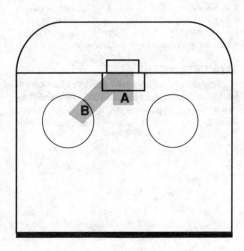

GUY LAROSE

Yrs. of NHL service: 1
Born: Hull, Que.; Aug. 31, 1967
Position: Center
Height: 5-9
Weight: 175
Uniform no.: 11
Shoots: Left

Career statistics:

GP	G	A	TP	PIM
44	9	6	15	41

1991-92 statistics:

GP	G	A	TP	+/-	PIM	PP	SH	GW	GT	S	PCT
34	9	5	14	-8	27	0	0	0	0	60	15.0

LAST SEASON

Obtained from New York Rangers, Dec. 26, 1991, for Mike Stevens.

THE FINESSE GAME

Larose is not a great skater, but he certainly gets where he wants to go, which is as near the puck as possible. He is not fast, but he has quickness and some acceleration; he can get a good head of steam going and make it turn into something.

Larose started somewhat slowly, but began getting points in bunches once he started gaining his confidence. A good work ethic complements decent all-around skills. He does things properly, but unspectacularly.

THE PHYSICAL GAME

A scrappy, feisty hustler, Larose really works to get to the puck and wants to win the battles to get it. He will punch your face if that's what is required, which keeps the fans involved and alert.

THE INTANGIBLES

Already a fan favorite around Maple Leaf Gardens for his grit and eagerness, Larose is serenaded by chants of 'Guy,' when he's on the ice. Wants to play, wants to win, wants to work. No team can have too much desire, and Larose clearly elevates Toronto's level of that ingredient. Another fine pickup, at very little cost, by Cliff Fletcher.

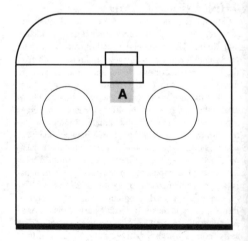

JAMIE MACOUN

Yrs. of NHL service: 9
Born: Newmarket, Ont.; Aug. 17, 1961
Position: Left defense
Height: 6-2
Weight: 197
Uniform no.: 34
Shoots: Left

Career statistics:

GP	G	A	TP	PIM
625	65	197	262	682

1991-92 statistics:

GP	G	A	TP	+/-	PIM	PP	SH	GW	GT	S	PCT
76	5	25	30	10	71	3	0	0	0	129	3.9

LAST SEASON

Obtained from Calgary, Jan. 2, 1992, with Doug Gilmour, Ric Nattress, Rick Wamsley and Kent Manderville, for Craig Berube, Michel Petit, Jeff Reese, Gary Leeman and Alexander Godynyuk. Plus-minus declined by 19 but was second best on team.

THE FINESSE GAME

Macoun is an underrated offensive player. He is agile, quick for his size and uses his skating assets in a number of ways. As he leaves the defensive zone with the puck, Macoun shields the puck well with his body and is capable of beating the first checker one-on-one with a head fake and a change of speed. If he is following the puck up ice, he has a good feel for the proper times to jump into the play.

He also uses his discipline and smarts in tight situations, such as penalty killing. He doesn't get sucked into chasing an attacker behind his net. And when the puck is in his partner's corner, Macoun is alert for back-door passes that might be coming to his side of the ice. Accordingly, he stays in position and takes care of HIS man — eliminating the passing option — rather than trying to slide over for his partner.

He has a strong shot from the point, and always will try to block point shots at the other end of the ice.

THE PHYSICAL GAME

Macoun makes sure you know he's out there and will make you pay for territory. He gets a piece of every opponent possible and will, as Pat LaFontaine knows very well, add emphasis to his strength by using his stick. Macoun's primary concern is his man; the puck will take care of itself.

THE INTANGIBLES

Macoun makes things happen. He plays an active, involved game at both ends. His addition went a long way toward stabilizing Toronto's defense, while adding a player with Stanley Cup-winning experience to the Leafs' dressing room.

KENT MANDERVILLE

Yrs. of NHL service: 1
Born: Edmonton, Alta.; April 12, 1971
Position: Left wing
Height: 6-3
Weight: 200
Uniform no.: 18
Shoots: Left

Career statistics:

GP	G	A	TP	PIM
15	0	4	4	0

1991-92 statistics:

GP	G	A	TP	+/-	PIM	PP	SH	GW	GT	S	PCT
15	0	4	4	1	0	0	0	0	0	14	0.0

LAST SEASON

Joined team after playing for Team Canada in Winter Olympics. Obtained from Calgary, Jan. 2, 1992, with Doug Gilmour, Jamie Macoun, Ric Nattress and Rick Wamsley for Craig Berube, Alexander Godynyuk, Gary Leeman, Michel Petit and Jeff Reese.

THE FINESSE GAME

Manderville is a good skater with light feet who put those abilities to work in a defensive posture during his late-season appearance. He can stop and start quickly, with good agility, while his acceleration and long stride add a nice dimension to his range — all qualities that help make him a useful penalty killer. Away from the puck in the defensive zone, Manderville delays forecheckers trying to harry his defensemen, while in the attacking zone, Manderville does a good job as the 'third man high.'

At this stage of his pro development, his skating skills may be ahead of his offensive skills. Manderville gets the puck and moves it, and does a good passing job in the attacking zone. But he hasn't shown much touch in-close; he had scoring chances he did not finish.

However, he has a quick release on the snap shot, knows how to get open, and certainly is big enough to drive to the net to create opportunities.

THE PHYSICAL GAME

Manderville's strength could improve. He rubs out opponents in the corners and along the boards, but is not yet at the stage where he demands respect or commands extra space.

THE INTANGIBLES

Manderville is an intense, determined competitor, and the suspicion is that his offensive dimension will emerge once he gets a little more comfortable with the pro game. He put up decent scoring numbers from midget to Jr. B to Cornell, and while he may still end up needing a break-in period in the AHL, the Leafs are not so deep on the left side; they may let him get some on-the-job training.

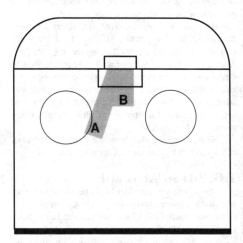

DMITRI MIRONOV

Yrs. of NHL service: 1
Born: Moscow, Russia; Dec. 25, 1965
Position: Left defense
Height: 6-2
Weight: 191
Uniform no.: 15
Shoots: Right

Career statistics:

GP	G	A	TP	PIM
7	1	0	1	0

1991-92 statistics:

GP	G	A	TP	+/-	PIM	PP	SH	GW	GT	S	PCT
7	1	0	1	-4	0	0	0	1	0	7	14.3

LAST SEASON

Joined Leafs after competing for gold-medal Unified Team at Winter Olympics.

THE FINESSE GAME

A right shot on the left side, Mironov hardly could be considered an elite skater. He has some agility and okay ability to pivot (to the inside shoulder, to the right, every time), but skates more as though wearing ankle weights. When Mironov keeps his skates moving — lumbering, but covering ground — he is far more successful than when he tries to make plays while on the glide.

While he hardly explodes to the puck, Mironov nonetheless is extremely effective in his one-on-one coverage down low — in the scoring-chance area and behind the net. He wins a high percentage of those confrontations by getting body position on his man and thus gaining advantage on the puck.

Mironov has okay hands; he will hold the puck until a checker is very near, then can move it accurately to a teammate. But he shows no signs of eagerness to involve himself in the offense. He will work the puck away from the end boards, skate with it a few strides and move it, rather than make a charge into the attacking zone.

THE PHYSICAL GAME

Mironov reminds us of Kjell Samuelsson because he is tall, uses his arms and his reach and seems simply to collapse on top of a player like a giant octopus, rendering him useless and frustrated. He isn't much of a hitter, but Mironov nullifies very well by getting a piece of his man with the stick or with a hug, or by leaning on his man.

He finishes hard on his man when he can lift the guy's stick from behind and get the player off balance as they head to the boards. But when that does not occur, Mironov ends up too upright on his skates, and lurches off balance into his hits. The guy he hit then can escape from the boards, while Mironov has to regain his balance before rejoining the play.

THE INTANGIBLES

Mironov is a major step in the right direction for a team that is very much in need of defensive overhaul. While much more effective than flashy, Mironov has an air of competence, even under pressure, and has enough variety in his game to command a lot of ice time.

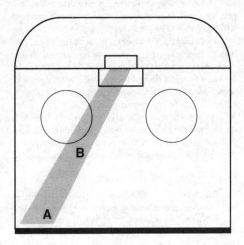

DAVE McLLWAIN

Yrs. of NHL service: 5
Born: Seaforth, Ont.; Jan. 9, 1967
Position: Center
Height: 6-0
Weight: 190
Uniform no.: 7
Shoots: Left

Career statistics:

GP	G	A	TP	PIM
303	61	65	126	186

1991-92 statistics:

GP	G	A	TP	+/-	PIM	PP	SH	GW	GT	S	PCT
73	10	18	28	−9	36	1	1	2	0	91	11.0

LAST SEASON

Obtained from Islanders by Toronto, March 10, 1992, with Ken Baumgartner for Daniel Marois and Claude Loiselle. Obtained by Islanders from Buffalo, Oct. 25, 1991, with Pierre Turgeon, Uwe Krupp and Benoit Hogue for Pat LaFontaine, Randy Hillier, Randy Wood and future considerations. Obtained by Buffalo from Winnipeg, Oct. 11, 1991, with Gord Donnelly, Winnipeg's sixth-round pick in 1992 draft, plus future considerations for Darrin Shannon, Mike Hartman and Dean Kennedy.

THE FINESSE GAME

McLlwain has good speed and quickness, decent agility, a strong first step to the puck and the lateral mobility to cut off options in the neutral zone. That is why he is used way more in penalty-killing and defensive situations than in even strength matchups.

His major asset is the ability to win face-offs, so McLlwain often is deployed for the first draw of a penalty kill. He pursues the puck extremely well and will score the occasional shorthanded goal.

McLlwain is a lot better without the puck than with it, largely because of the sense of anticipation that compensates for a significant lack of size and strength. He knows he isn't going to blast anybody off the puck, so he anticipates where a pass might go, and has occasional success being in the right place at the right time.

He will make an offensive foray every so often. And those times he actually wins a puck at the offensive endboards, he will try to come out from behind the net to attempt a stuff shot from the goalie's side.

THE PHYSICAL GAME

McLlwain does all he can to get a hook on his man. That is about the extent of his physical aspect because he does not have a great deal of strength. This becomes a major problem when he is trying to cover a man in front of the net; he simply cannot compete in strength stand-offs against most of the league's forwards.

While he tries to bump, McLlwain tends to bounce off the people he hits. He does, however, do an effective job of blocking off his opposing center after a face-off; he makes every possible effort to keep that center away from his point or his goal, depending on the zone.

THE INTANGIBLES

McLlwain never got a chance to unpack last season. He 'hit for the cycle,' getting traded three times in five months and playing in each of the NHL's four divisions, because decent utilitymen clearly are in demand. Without significantly more strength, and more bite in his game, though, the demand could ebb rapidly.

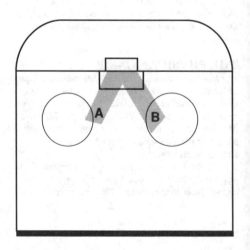

RIC NATTRESS

Yrs. of NHL service: 10
Born: Hamilton, Ont.; May 25, 1962
Position: Right defense
Height: 6-2
Weight: 210
Uniform no.: 2
Shoots: Right

Career statistics:

GP	G	A	TP	PIM
492	22	125	147	348

1991-92 statistics:

GP	G	A	TP	+/-	PIM	PP	SH	GW	GT	S	PCT
54	2	19	21	−1	63	0	0	1	0	66	3.0

LAST SEASON

Obtained from Calgary, Jan. 2, 1992, with Jamie Macoun, Rick Wamsley, Doug Gilmour and Kent Manderville, for Craig Berube, Alexander Godynyuk, Gary Leeman, Michel Petit and Jeff Reese. Missed 16 games due to knee injury, four others due to bruised foot.

THE FINESSE GAME

Nattress does everything fairly well, does nothing exceptionally well. He knows his way around the defensive zone, is a depth guy who knows how to cover for an offensive partner — and thus gets to play one pair higher than his skills would dictate.

He is versatile enough to play the left side, and he has some decent skating skills. His basic play is to keep the attacker wide and prevent the cut-in, but Nattress is smart enough and poised enough to more than hold his own against a two-on-one break. He steps up nicely in the neutral zone to cut off the ice and challenge the puck carrier, and while that doesn't make him fast or quick, it makes him competent.

Nattress is not going to score on anything other than a point shot. The few times he rushes, he seems to get caught deep in the attacking zone without getting a great deal accomplished.

THE PHYSICAL GAME

Though not a physical player, Nattress will block a shot. He is tough around the net, will punish people either with his body or his stick, but is not a force — not a source of fear.

THE INTANGIBLES

What you see is almost exactly what you're going to get. Nattress was minus-one last season, minus-one the season earlier. He had 63 penalty minutes last season, 63 penalty minutes the season before. He did, however, team with Jamie Macoun to give the Leafs some much-needed defensive depth.

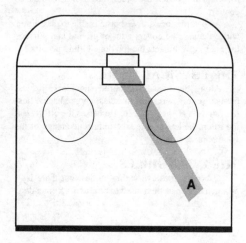

MARK OSBORNE

Yrs. of NHL service: 11
Born: Toronto, Ont.; Aug. 13, 1961
Position: Left wing
Height: 6-2
Weight: 205
Uniform no.: 21
Shoots: Left

Career statistics:

GP	G	A	TP	PIM
733	190	285	475	899

1991-92 statistics:

GP	G	A	TP	+/-	PIM	PP	SH	GW	GT	S	PCT
54	7	13	20	-10	73	0	2	0	0	66	10.6

LAST SEASON

Obtained from Winnipeg, March 10, 1992, for Lucien DeBlois.

THE FINESSE GAME

Osborne has enough size and enough jump in his stride that if he went to the left a little more, he still could score 15 or 20 goals in a season.

He is a strong player who quickly can turn a defensive situation into an offensive one. He will win a loose puck or grab an outlet pass at the side boards and will move it quickly, setting the give-and-go in motion. He will go to the net — although not as much as he used to — and will poach for a return pass or a rebound to convert.

A versatile forward, Osborne is able to play either wing. Because he covers a lot of ground and pursues the puck well, he gets the job done killing penalties.

THE PHYSICAL GAME

Along the boards, Osborne shoulders, jostles, bumps, scraps, wrestles, muscles, chops, hacks, hustles, strives. He gets a piece. He makes the effort. But too often, he lets people take unfair advantage of his good nature.

THE INTANGIBLES

Osborne gives everything he has; but there isn't as much to give as there used to be. He is a tremendous team player, useful in the dressing room, but would be more of a lineup fixture if he put some oomph back in his game.

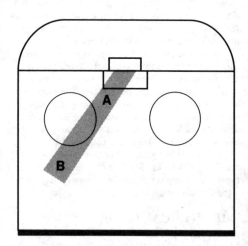

ROB PEARSON

Yrs. of NHL service: 1
Born: Oshawa, Ont.; Aug. 3, 1971
Position: Right wing
Height: 6-1
Weight: 180
Uniform no.: 12
Shoots: Right

Career statistics:

GP	G	A	TP	PIM
47	14	10	24	58

1991-92 statistics:

GP	G	A	TP	+/-	PIM	PP	SH	GW	GT	S	PCT
47	14	10	24	−16	58	6	0	0	1	79	17.7

LAST SEASON

First in NHL. Led team in shooting percentage. Fifth on team in power-play goals. Among NHL rookies, was ninth in goals, fourth in power-play goals and fourth in shooting percentage.

THE FINESSE GAME

Pearson is a good skater, not a great one. He has a good burst of speed, breaks for the openings and drives to the net, but his shot and scrappy approach are greater assets than his skating skill.

Pearson has some hockey sense, too. He knows when to shoot and when to pass, is smart around the net, sees the open man and gets him the puck.

He can get ferocious velocity on his snap and slap shots. He has scored virtually every place he has played, and shows significant signs of being a future NHL sniper as well. In midget hockey, Pearson scored 68 goals in 72 games; he added junior seasons of 48 and 63 goals, and threw in 15 tallies over 27 AHL games last season.

Since scoring skills got Pearson to the NHL, there is a natural deficiency in his defensive game at even strength. While he is working to learn that aspect, he loses ice time to checkers late in the game if his team is trying to protect a lead.

THE PHYSICAL GAME

Pearson uses his body in the corners and along the boards. He goes to the net. And he can be obnoxious. He does some showboating when he scores, which is infuriating. He yaps, tries to get people off their game. He is hard-nosed, more likely to use the stick than to fight, and is generally abrasive.

THE INTANGIBLES

Pearson's work ethic improved after his stay in the AHL, and he seems determined to reach the promise people see in him. He has desire and drive, gives an effort at home and on the road, and knows he has a lot of work to do on his game.

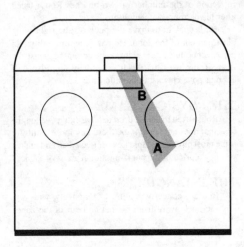

BOB ROUSE

Yrs. of NHL service: 8
Born: Surrey, B.C.; Apr. 18, 1964
Position: Right defense
Height: 6-2
Weight: 210
Uniform no.: 3
Shoots: Right

Career statistics:

GP	G	A	TP	PIM
573	23	114	137	1,066

1991-92 statistics:

GP	G	A	TP	+/-	PIM	PP	SH	GW	GT	S	PCT
79	3	19	22	−20	97	1	0	0	0	115	2.6

LAST SEASON

Tied career high in assists. Fifth on team in penalty minutes.

THE FINESSE GAME

Rouse is all right offensively, chips in occasionally with an offensive play, but unmistakably favors a defensive aspect in his game. He stays at home and leaves most of the rushing — and skating — to such as Dave Ellett.

Rouse is nowhere near as capable with the puck and knows enough to stay within his limits. Ellett, meanwhile, would not be able to rush as much if not paired with a more defense-minded partner. However, his monster-sized minus can be viewed a significant reflection of the number of two-on-ones Rouse faced after his partners got caught up ice.

He is content to drive the puck off the right-wing glass and out of the zone. He has decent mobility and pivots smoothly to his right as he retreats against the rush. Rouse uses his reach effectively and also will attempt poke checks at the blue line.

He will block shots, will grab and hold to prevent scoring chances, will send you out of the rink barely having noticed he played.

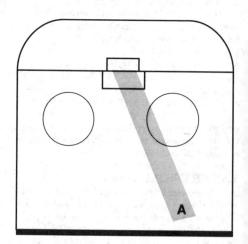

THE PHYSICAL GAME

Rouse used to scrap, used to have extensive toughness that does not seem to be there any more. Still, he is the most physical Maple Leaf defenseman and makes you pay a price in the confrontational areas of the ice.

THE INTANGIBLES

Rouse is concerned, almost exclusively, with getting the puck away from his net and out of the zone.

JOE SACCO

Yrs. of NHL service: 2
Born: Medford, Mass.; Feb. 4, 1969
Position: Left wing
Height: 6-1
Weight: 190
Uniform no.: 24
Shoots: Right

Career statistics:

GP	G	A	TP	PIM
37	7	9	16	6

1991-92 statistics:

GP	G	A	TP	+/-	PIM	PP	SH	GW	GT	S	PCT
17	7	4	11	8	4	0	0	1	0	40	17.5

LAST SEASON

Rejoined Leafs after playing for Team USA at Winter Olympics.

THE FINESSE GAME

Sacco is strong and solid on his feet, although not hugely quick or agile. He always is on his wing, so you know where he's going to be if you need an outlet for an emergency pass. He waits dependably at the top of the circle for his outlet pass and then looks up ice for further developments.

Without the puck, Sacco gravitates towards the right wing as the disc enters the zone. He accepts a pass on his backhand, accelerates to slightly above-average speed, but then seems to get slightly hand-cuffed by the weight of making offensive decisions. Sacco seems to lack either the hands or the confidence to face goalies one-on-one. It could be confidence, for he seems somewhat indecisive in the scoring-chance area, but that confidence will come with experience.

While he is waiting, if a two-on-one emerges, Sacco prefers to make a play; rather than taking the puck deep for a one-on-one move, he will aim a low shot toward the goalie's right pad — virtually guaranteeing a rebound for his fellow attacker if that other wing is driving toward the net.

Sacco will use the wrist shot from in close but will take the big slap from behind the circle on a rush up the wing. He gets the shot away pretty quickly and always keeps the puck low.

THE PHYSICAL GAME

Sacco always seems to have a strong grip on his opponent's stick away from the play. He shoulders in the neutral zone, grabs the other guy's stick until possession is determined, then goes about his business. Sacco also does a very effective job of nullifying his man away from the puck, so his defenseman will have the time and space to move it.

But he doesn't seem very strong; if he has good strength, he is inconsistent in his application of it.

THE INTANGIBLES

Seven goals in 17 games certainly suggests he is capable of scoring in the NHL, but there is proving to be done. His skills are not such that they can guarantee him a job; he has to earn one.

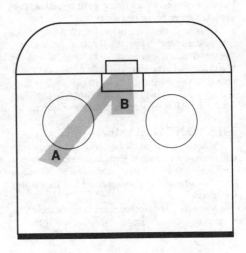

RICK WAMSLEY

Yrs. of NHL service: 11
Born: Simcoe, Ont.; May 25, 1959
Position: Goaltender
Height: 5-11
Weight: 185
Uniform no.: 30
Catches: Left

Career statistics:

GP	MINS	GA	SO	GAA	A	PIM
404	22,963	1,272	12	3.23	9	50

1991-92 statistics:

GP	MINS	GAA	W	L	T	SO	GA	S	SAPCT	PIM
17	885	4.14	7	7	0	0	61	444	.879	0

LAST SEASON

Obtained from Calgary, Jan. 2, 1992, with Doug Gilmour, Jamie Macoun, Ric Nattress and Kent Manderville, for Craig Berube, Alexander Godynyuk, Gary Leeman, Michel Petit and Jeff Reese.

THE PHYSICAL GAME

Wamsley has not lasted all these years without learning, and his experience provides valuable survival skills now. He uses smarts to compensate for dwindling skills.

Wamsley stands up well, which is a key. The bigger he makes himself, the less net shooters see, the more effective he is going to be and the less he will have to depend on quickness he does not have.

The more he stands up, the better the chance a puck will hit him—the better the chance he will force a shooter to fire wide. Wamsley isn't much to the corners; his gloves and skates are not as fast as in his earlier years. So he takes away the middle of the net and forces shooters to earn their goals by picking corners with lower-percentage shots.

Of course, there are times when Wamsley faces emergencies which favor the shooters. He does not have much lateral movement, so he struggles with the one-timers and bang-bang plays. And his recovery for second shots is suspect.

Stick-wise, he will not be confused with Ron Hextall for the ability to wing the puck out of danger.

THE MENTAL GAME

Wamsley is a good backup, because he is not consistent enough to carry a team as the top gun over a long period of time but is steady enough for fill-in duty. His attitude and disposition are fine for the secondary role.

And you can never have too many Stanley Cup rings in your dressing room. Wamsley was with Calgary's Cup-winner, that alone makes him an asset.

There aren't many teams who can put a Cup champion (Fuhr) in goal and have another on the bench.

THE INTANGIBLES

Wamsley may end up as the No. 2 man in Toronto this season, but that does not designate him as No. 2 in the organization; that role most likely will be filled by Felix Potvin, who will carry the workload for St. John's rather than play an occasional game if Fuhr needs a night off.

PETER ZEZEL

Yrs. of NHL service: 8
Born: Toronto, Ont.; Apr. 22, 1965
Position: Center
Height: 5-9
Weight: 200
Uniform no.: 25
Shoots: Left

Career statistics:

GP	G	A	TP	PIM
551	170	305	475	327

1991-92 statistics:

GP	G	A	TP	+/-	PIM	PP	SH	GW	GT	S	PCT
64	16	33	49	-22	26	4	0	1	0	125	12.8

LAST SEASON

Missed 10 games due to knee cartilage damage and five other games due to another knee injury. Second on team in assists. Fourth on team in points.

THE FINESSE GAME

Zezel profited tremendously from the addition of Doug Gilmour to the Leafs' lineup last season. Gilmour is a much better passer and touch player than Zezel is, and attempting to provide those assets was a strain for someone who is more of a No. 2 or 3 than a No. 1.

He is the key face-off guy. He is strong on his skates, without being speedy or flashy about it. He gets where he wants to go, forechecks well, pursues the puck. He has good power and balance. He drives into the draws, then drives into the center against whom he faced off.

Zezel is not a great natural scorer. He has a good snap shot, makes a good pass, but does not have a great view of the ice. He thinks about getting the puck to the net. He thinks about his defensive assignment (the minus 42 over two seasons notwithstanding), but lacks tenaciousness for one-on-one defense.

THE PHYSICAL GAME

Zezel is a solidly built player who does not get pushed around, but who also does not do a lot of his own pushing. When he gets in front of the net, defensemen find it difficult to knock him down.

THE INTANGIBLES

Intensity and focus are problems for Zezel. Inconsistency is a problem for Zezel. Hockey sense is a problem for Zezel. Effort is NOT a problem for Zezel.

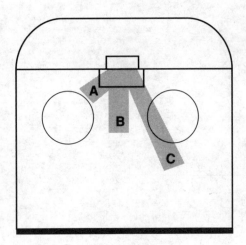

VANCOUVER CANUCKS

GREG ADAMS

Yrs. of NHL service: 8
Born: Nelson, B.C.; Aug. 1, 1963
Position: Left wing
Height: 6-3
Weight: 185
Uniform no.: 8
Shoots: Left

Career statistics:

GP	G	A	TP	PIM
523	203	203	406	171

1991-92 statistics:

GP	G	A	TP	+/-	PIM	PP	SH	GW	GT	S	PCT
76	30	27	57	8	26	13	1	5	0	184	16.3

LAST SEASON

Games played, point and PIM totals were four-season highs. Reached 30-goal milestone for second time in three seasons, third time in five seasons, fourth time in seven seasons. Fifth on team in scoring, third in goals. Power-play goal total led team. Plus-minus jumped 13 goals.

THE FINESSE GAME

Before leaving the Canucks, Igor Larionov said in his entire career, he never had played with a more unselfish linemate than Adams. There aren't many higher compliments.

Adams has great speed, a hard shot from the wing and may be the team's best player at driving to the net. He never takes the easy way, though; instead, he takes the straightest path. If there are people in the way, Adams usually takes a checker or a defenseman with him, often ends up bouncing off posts or crossbars, and usually ends up paying some kind of physical price for having attempted the scoring play.

While he often gets up a head of steam, steps into the puck and shoots from the wing, that is always a second option. Adams prefers to try to beat the defenseman one-on-one first, get closer to the net and then shoot.

Adams always was an attentive checker in the defensive zone, but his play there improved this season and he hoisted himself to the plus side.

THE PHYSICAL GAME

The way he goes to the net makes Adams anything but a perimeter player. While he is not an eager hitter, his rushes to the net qualify him as a significantly physical player.

He is not a fighter, but no opponent is going to intimidate him. He more than accepts the checking attention he receives as the top-scoring left wing on his team, but merely works harder to shed the checker rather than getting frustrated into a penalty he has no interest in taking.

THE INTANGIBLES

Adams is a quiet man, easy-going off the ice, so if you want a catch-phrase for him, it is "quietly efficient." He is an extremely underrated, extremely important scorer and an extremely important player who also is a gentleman; that makes him no less of a game player, however.

DAVE BABYCH

Yrs. of NHL service: 13
Born: Uxbridge, Ont.; May 23, 1961
Position: Left defense
Height: 6-2
Weight: 215
Uniform no.: 44
Shoots: Left

Career statistics:

GP	G	A	TP	PIM
813	122	468	590	709

1991-92 statistics:

GP	G	A	TP	+/-	PIM	PP	SH	GW	GT	S	PCT
75	5	24	29	−2	63	4	0	1	0	148	3.4

LAST SEASON

PIM total was seven-season high. Goal total was career low. Point total was third among Canucks defensemen.

THE FINESSE GAME

Babych knows the game, knows the position, understands the situations, so he keeps things simple and gets the job done.

He has almost no speed, but he has a good touch with the puck. Babych can made a sharp first pass out of the zone, and while there are certain games when he seems not to join the rush at all, there also are certain games when he jumps eagerly into the play. He won't accept a drop pass and drive to the net for a fake; more, he will shoot off the pass to create a rebound or will make a return pass.

Babych has a heavy, Denis Potvin-style wrist shot from the point. It can be tricky and can create rebounds, thereby producing a significant percentage of his assists.

THE PHYSICAL GAME

Babych hits hard — he is strong as an oak tree in front of the net — but he's not mean about it. Babych uses his strength the way Larry Robinson used his in the late stages of his career, keeping a guy pinned to the glass, preventing him from getting back into the play first, gaining body position rather than putting an opponent in the third row of seats.

THE INTANGIBLES

Babych was one of Vancouver's best defensemen in the playoffs. He enjoys the competitive challenge and met it well. He is not an 'old' 31; he has some playing time left.

PAVEL BURE

Yrs. of NHL service: 1
Born: Moscow, Russia; Mar. 31, 1971
Position: Left wing
Height: 5-11
Weight: 176
Uniform no.: 10
Shoots: Left

Career statistics:

GP	G	A	TP	PIM
65	34	26	60	30

1991-92 statistics:

GP	G	A	TP	+/-	PIM	PP	SH	GW	GT	S	PCT
65	34	26	60	0	30	7	3	6	0	268	12.7

LAST SEASON

First in the NHL. Was a finalist for Calder Trophy. Among NHL rookies, was second in goals, tied for second in power-play goals, first in shots and short-handed goals, tied for first in game-winners. Second on team in shots. Set Canucks rookie record for goals and points. Led team with 17 road goals.

THE FINESSE GAME

Bure uses the space his blistering speed creates. He drives defensemen off the blue line, then leaves a drop pass for a teammate trailing the play. There are coaches who can name you 24 places where drop passes should not be made, Pacific Coliseum in Vancouver being one of them, but Bure succeeds with the play more times than he gives the puck away.

His skating skills are such that he can stop on a dime and be off, instantly, in another direction. That stands whether he has the puck or doesn't; he seems almost as fast with the puck as without it.

Bure carries the puck way out to the side, shielding it nicely with his body. He will drill a breakaway pass up the middle and generally will move the puck intelligently. Bure also has exceptional balance; he gets hit hard but does not go down.

THE PHYSICAL GAME

Bure plays much bigger than he is — he really throws his body around — but there are limits. There are times when he will gain advantage with a move, but will not be strong enough to muscle past the defenseman to capitalize on it; as a result, the puck beats the defenseman but Bure doesn't.

THE INTANGIBLES

The first seeds of poisonous unrest among NHL governors were planted when John Ziegler awarded Bure's rights to Vancouver in an extremely controversial and unpopular ruling. Ziegler is gone now, those seeds having grown into a giant tree that fell on his presidency.

Bure, meanwhile, endures. He excites, he becomes the focal point of the game action every second he is on the ice. The buzz that goes through the crowd when he gathers the puck is reminiscent of those nights in the Montreal Forum when marvelling throngs murmured "Guy! Guy!" as Guy Lafleur began his dashes toward immortality.

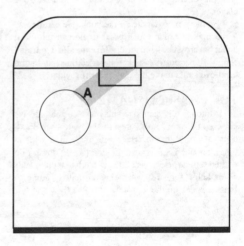

GEOFF COURTNALL

Yrs. of NHL service: 8
Born: Victoria, B.C.; Aug. 18, 1962
Position: Left wing
Height: 6-1
Weight: 190
Uniform no.: 14
Shoots: Left

Career statistics:

GP	G	A	TP	PIM
577	215	228	443	781

1991-92 statistics:

GP	G	A	TP	+/-	PIM	PP	SH	GW	GT	S	PCT
70	23	34	57	−6	118	12	0	3	0	281	8.2

LAST SEASON

Led team in shots and power-play points (27). Shot total was club record. Scored fewer than 30 goals and 60 points for first time in five seasons. PIM total was career high. Plus-minus declined 22 goals. Missed 10 games due to chronic fatigue.

THE FINESSE GAME

Despite struggling all season against the effects of chronic fatigue, Courtnall continued to be an offensive weapon with good speed and a blistering shot off the wing. He remains a prototype give-and-go player who will make a sharp first pass, burn for the hole, then blast from the face-off circle for the majority of his goals.

At the same time, Courtnall is shifty enough on occasion to beat the first man coming out of the zone. He is a good neutral-zone player, a better attacking-zone player and only a fair-to-average defensive-zone player.

He has a nice handle on the puck. He can finesse it (he makes a nice touch pass) or he can muscle it under the crossbar from the circle or the slot. Courtnall simply flicks out his stick for deflections, and solid hand-eye skills make the play pay off regularly.

THE PHYSICAL GAME

Although a decent-sized player, Courtnall always has used the stick, rather than his body, to keep opponents at arm's length. He chops away, and will, at times, shoulder a player at the boards. He doesn't do it often, but he does it just often enough that opponents never know for sure whether Courtnall is going to finish a check on them or not.

THE INTANGIBLES

Courtnall is a scorer, and 23 goals is not a scorer's year. If the Canucks had the best season in history with Courtnall barely functional, imagine what might happen if he returns to 35-goal form. It would be a small personal victory if Courtnall made it to opening night with the Canucks; he has been with a different team at the start of each of the past three seasons.

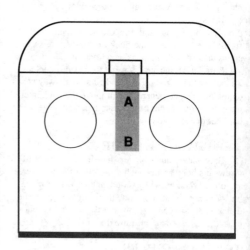

GERALD DIDUCK

Yrs. of NHL service: 7
Born: Edmonton, Alta.; Apr. 6, 1965
Position: Right defense
Height: 6-2
Weight: 207
Uniform no.: 4
Shoots: Right

Career statistics:

GP	G	A	TP	PIM
454	36	93	129	909

1991-92 statistics:

GP	G	A	TP	+/-	PIM	PP	SH	GW	GT	S	PCT
77	6	21	27	−3	224	2	0	1	0	128	4.7

LAST SEASON
Goal total was three-season high. PIM were a career high and were second most on team.

THE FINESSE GAME
Diduck has good speed. He is one of the better skating defensemen in the league. He is mobile enough to jump into the play, and likes to do it all the time, but plays more effectively when he uses a little discipline and isn't up with every rush.

Diduck has a strong shot, but isn't good enough one-on-one to step into the every play, anyway. So he concentrates now on getting the puck and making a pass to his partner or looking for a first pass out of the zone to the wing. That way, he can follow the play up ice, keeping a respectful distance and keeping his options open; if there's a turnover, Diduck is in position, and if an offensive chance opens up, he is available.

THE PHYSICAL GAME
One of Diduck's most important contributions last season was to hit hard and play tough. He went as amok as possible in front of the net, had the skating speed to get to the hit and the toughness to fight; he is a very good fighter. People did not like to play against him. The key for Diduck, from a physical standpoint, is to remain in control while playing that physical style; he gets in trouble when he starts running around and making diagonal breakout passes.

THE INTANGIBLES
Playing for Pat Quinn has been a good thing for Diduck, who needed to be focused on his responsibilities, told specific duties so he wouldn't have to figure them out for himself.

Now, he pretty much knows when to go up ice and when not to; he is in better control and is getting more out of himself. Diduck always had talent; what he needed was direction, and now he's getting it.

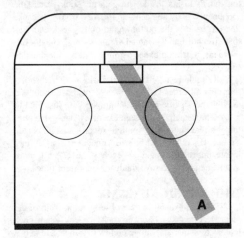

391

ROBERT DIRK

Yrs. of NHL service: 3
Born: Regina. Sask.; Aug. 20, 1966
Position: Left defense
Height: 6-4
Weight: 218
Uniform no.: 22
Shoots: Left

Career statistics:

GP	G	A	TP	PIM
177	5	13	18	401

1991-92 statistics:

GP	G	A	TP	+/-	PIM	PP	SH	GW	GT	S	PCT
72	2	7	9	6	126	0	0	0	1	44	4.5

LAST SEASON

Games played, goals, assists and points all were career highs.

THE FINESSE GAME

We are not talking here about one of the world's great skaters, nor are we talking about anything resembling an offensive threat. Dirk is a defensive defenseman, start to finish. He is the guy you pair with the offensive talent, because you know Dirk will be back to face the two-on-one after his partner was caught deep in the attacking zone when the puck turned over.

If players are going to beat him, it will be with outside speed. Dirk does a nice job pivoting to his right on moves to his inside; he gets his stick across the opponent's body and can seal the forward off, because the left hand is the bottom hand on his stick and thus the strength hand — and Dirk is strong. He doesn't have as much quickness going left on the outside moves.

It should be noted that while Dirk bothered shooting only 44 times last season, one of those shots tied a November game against Winnipeg with just 6:25 to play. The tie helped the Canucks turn a one-game winning streak into an eventual seven-game unbeaten streak. His other goal helped Vancouver start a nine-game unbeaten streak; so even if he doesn't score many, he seems to save them for important times.

THE PHYSICAL GAME

Dirk is physical in the corners and in front of the net. He often just happens to be nearby when push comes to shove and shove comes to punch. He gets a piece of any opponent he can reach. He makes an effort, dives for those pucks to which his feet will not carry him.

THE INTANGIBLES

Dirk is a depth player who has improved with experience, who stays within his limits and who has gotten better at reading the play. He will force you to beat him, more than he will beat himself.

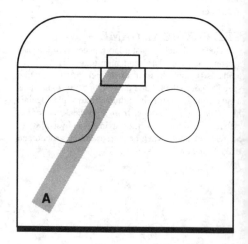

TOM FERGUS

Yrs. of NHL service: 11
Born: Chicago, Ill.; June 16, 1962
Position: Center
Height: 6-3
Weight: 210
Uniform no.: 15
Shoots: Left

Career statistics:

GP	G	A	TP	PIM
690	230	337	567	479

1991-92 statistics:

GP	G	A	TP	+/-	PIM	PP	SH	GW	GT	S	PCT
55	15	23	38	-10	21	6	0	3	0	103	14.6

LAST SEASON

Claimed on $5,000 waiver from Toronto, Dec. 18, 1991. Games played was three-season high.

THE FINESSE GAME

For $5,000, Pat Quinn got himself what probably qualifies as the NHL bargain of the year. Fergus needed a team to believe in him, Quinn made sure the Canucks were that team; in response, Fergus got them 15 goals, did some good work on the power play and won some key face-offs.

Fergus has fair-to-decent speed and fair-to-decent agility. He has very acceptable size, and while he does not make extensive use of that asset, he always seems to be there when a loose puck is up for grabs.

Fergus always has been a skilled passer, and makes effective use of his wrist shot for scoring from between the circles. He did a better job last season of getting the puck — then getting rid of it with a shot or pass, rather than holding too long, as has been his history. Fergus also was more attentive defensively; he spent lots of time against the top opposition scorers, which accounts for the healthy minus.

THE PHYSICAL GAME

When the puck is in the corners, Fergus will be there, too — waiting for some other teammate to engage an opponent in combat for the puck. Once that engagement begins, Fergus will join in to make it an odd-man battle in his team's favor. But he won't often be the first guy into the fray.

He will go to the front of the net on the power play, but will keep moving as a floating screen. He won't plant himself in front and make himself a target for a crosscheck-minded defenseman.

THE INTANGIBLES

The mathematics is very simple, very precise: Tom Fergus scores a goal every three games. He was a little under that average last season, but did an acceptable job in the No. 3 slot — especially considering what the Canucks paid to get him.

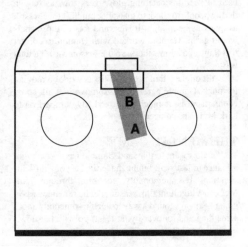

TROY GAMBLE

Yrs. of NHL service: 2
Born: New Glasgow, N.S.; Apr. 7, 1967
Position: Goaltender
Height: 5-11
Weight: 195
Uniform no.: 35
Catches: Left

Career statistics:

GP	MINS	GA	SO	GAA	A	PIM
72	3,804	229	1	3.61	1	22

1991-92 statistics:

GP	MINS	GAA	W	L	T	SO	GA	S	SAPCT	PIM
19	1,009	4.34	4	9	3	0	73	518	.859	8

LAST SEASON

Played 26 fewer games and 1,424 fewer minutes than preceding season.

THE PHYSICAL GAME

Gamble is a reaction-type goalie who needs to play a lot to stay sharp. Last season, virtually the only playing time he got was in practice.

When he is on his game, Gamble is extremely quick and his lateral movement is as fast as anyone's; he also is expert at using the poke check on breakaways and cut-ins. When he is on his game, he is spectacular and exciting; when he is watching lots of hockey, his assets corrode.

One benefit of last season was that he got loads of time to work with goalie coach Glen Hanlon. Gamble used to keep his catching glove very low, as though daring people to shoot to that side, but his glove wasn't as quick as he thought it was, and lots of those shots would go in. Gamble worked with Hanlon to correct that flaw, and a few others, so the season wasn't a total waste.

Still on the "things to do" list is work on moving the puck. Gamble barely used to move it at all, so by comparison, he is much improved. By comparison to Kirk McLean, he needs a lot of work.

THE MENTAL GAME

Goalies want to play and Gamble never really got a chance to last year, but he made the best of a difficult situation. His personality got him through Kirk McLean's highlight film season, but he remained easygoing—always found a way to needle somebody about something and (outwardly, at least) go with the flow.

THE INTANGIBLES

Did Gamble play less because he wasn't as good as the prior year? Nope. McLean got on a roll right from the start of last season, while Gamble lost 7-6 in his first start and never got anything going at all. Gamble did not win until December 12—the team's 32nd game and his fifth—and did not start consecutive games until March.

DOUG LIDSTER

Yrs. of NHL service: 8
Born: Kamloops, B.C.; Oct. 18, 1960
Position: Right defense
Height: 6-1
Weight: 200
Uniform no.: 3
Shoots: Right

Career statistics:

GP	G	A	TP	PIM
595	59	223	282	490

1991-92 statistics:

GP	G	A	TP	+/-	PIM	PP	SH	GW	GT	S	PCT
66	6	23	29	9	39	3	0	2	0	89	6.7

LAST SEASON

Missed 13 games due to separated shoulder. Games played was three-season low. Plus-minus improved 15. Shot total decreased 68. Finished second in scoring among team defensemen.

THE FINESSE GAME

Lidster is a dependable two-way player. He has the skating range to cut off the ice on almost any forward in the league and has the hands to get the puck up ice right away on the transition to offense.

While he does not rush as much as he used to, Lidster has a good amount of offensive smarts. Lidster can work the point on the power play and also knows his way around making a rush or joining one. He will hold the puck, and let the defense completely out-think itself as to what Lidster plans. The defense will anticipate and react to what they think he is going to do, then he will do nothing — until the defense has committed.

Overall, Lidster is a defenseman who can be trusted in the last minute of a period or of a game, when his team is trying to protect a narrow lead. He is not looking for points as much as he is looking to make the safe play, and virtually always gets that job done.

THE PHYSICAL GAME

Lidster finishes checks, is fairly rude in front of his net but must be considered a finesse player with physical attributes irregularly displayed. He could use more strength on the boards.

THE INTANGIBLES

Unfairly, attitude has been something of an albatross for Lidster. People expect a lot from him and question his desire when he does not reach the level of those expectations. Still, he ranks high on Vancouver's depth chart and is always in top shape.

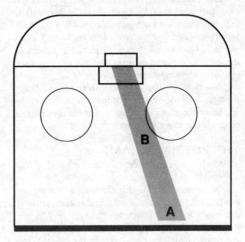

TREVOR LINDEN

Yrs. of NHL service: 4
Born: Medicine Hat, Alta.; April 11, 1970
Position: Right wing
Height: 6-4
Weight: 205
Uniform no.: 16
Shoots: Right

Career statistics:

GP	G	A	TP	PIM
313	115	139	254	274

1991-92 statistics:

GP	G	A	TP	+/-	PIM	PP	SH	GW	GT	S	PCT
80	31	44	75	3	99	6	1	6	1	201	15.4

LAST SEASON

Led team in scoring for second consecutive season. Plus-minus improved 28 goals. Totals for assists and points were career bests. Shared team lead in game-winning goals. Goal total was second on team.

THE FINESSE GAME

Linden has such a long stride and such a long reach, it looks as though his first step toward the puck covers 20 feet or more. That's helpful, as Linden remains a bit gangly as a skater and for some reason, despite his size, can be angled to the boards and stopped.

Despite those long arms, Linden seems to take too much time getting off his shots. He is quicker in starting the transition game; instead of holding the puck for an hour and coming to an eventual decision, Linden gets it and moves it with a quick pass. He distributes the puck very well; at times, he passes too much instead of shooting more.

Nonetheless, he is a fluid, smooth player who is strong enough to score from deep in the face-off circle and powerful enough to turn scrambles into muscle goals from in front of the net.

THE PHYSICAL GAME

Linden plays an important, effective physical role without the puck.

On the rush, he will drive straight to the net and will take a defenseman with him in the hope of creating open space for a teammate.

And on the power play, Linden does something else that is smart and subtle to create openings. When the puck is at the point, he sets up in front of the net and wrestles with the defense to produce traffic in front of the goalie. When the puck is at the side boards, Linden moves up higher, between the circles, opening his forehand and forcing the penalty killers to make a decision. If the defenseman on that side steps up to cover Linden, space will open behind the defenseman; if a forward collapses to cover him, a point shot will open up.

Sometimes, though, Linden moves away from the net when a shot is on the way. That helps if there is a rebound, but it hurts if there is no screen.

THE INTANGIBLES

He scores 30 goals a year, plays every game, gives everything he has, makes a whopping improvement in his defense and is a potential all-star, for sure. Yet Linden still leaves you wondering — unfairly, of course — if there's more. It seems as though he is still putting the pieces of his total game together; the next thing to be added is a mean streak and just a little more selfishness.

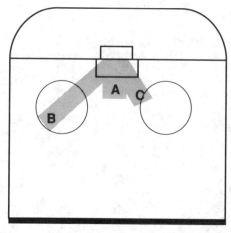

JYRKI LUMME

Yrs. of NHL service: 4
Born: Tampere, Finland; July 16, 1966
Position: Right defense
Height: 6-1
Weight: 207
Uniform no.: 21
Shoots: Left

Career statistics:

GP	G	A	TP	PIM
241	22	88	110	183

1991-92 statistics:

GP	G	A	TP	+/-	PIM	PP	SH	GW	GT	S	PCT
75	12	32	44	25	65	3	1	1	0	106	11.3

LAST SEASON

Led team defensemen in scoring. Plus-minus improved by 40 goals. Totals for goals, assists, points and PIM were career highs, although his shot total dropped 51 from prior season.

THE FINESSE GAME

A left shot who plays the right side, Lumme carries the bulk of the defense's offensive responsibility. He scored more goals last season than he had in the entirety of his career, and that contribution unmistakably played a role in the Canucks' success.

Lumme skates the puck up ice from behind the net and makes a strong first pass to set the attack in motion. He virtually always plays the puck, uses good anticipation to pick off passes, then almost instantly puts the transition game in gear with a smart outlet pass of his own.

Lumme covers a lot of ice with his stride, an attribute which comes in handy during special-team situations. He uses that mobility while killing penalties to challenge the puck from the corners to the side boards and almost always gets back to the slot in time to prepare for a shot from the point. Similarly, at even strength, he can pinch up the boards, knowing he can regain position if the puck turns over.

On the power play, Lumme keeps the puck in well at the point and uses lateral movement to slide to the center of the blue line and run the show from there.

THE PHYSICAL GAME

Lumme makes absolutely no pretense of being a physical player. He makes maximum use of his reach and mobility precisely for the purposes of avoiding physical contact, uses his stick to check way more than his body. He accepts being hit, but will not do anything much beyond occasionally pushing somebody from the other team.

THE INTANGIBLES

Lumme's improvement last season was a capsule view of the Canucks' improvement: more goals scored, more prevented, more production through focused effort and commitment, more consistency through greater confidence.

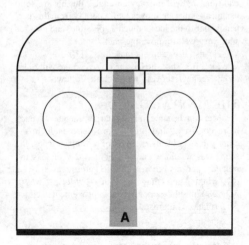

KIRK McLEAN

Yrs. of NHL service: 5
Born: Willowdale, Ont.; June 26, 1966
Position: Goaltender
Height: 6-0
Weight: 177
Uniform no.: 1
Catches: Left

Career statistics:

GP	MINS	GA	SO	GAA	A	PIM
258	14,688	818	10	3.34	10	24

1991-92 statistics:

GP	MINS	GAA	W	L	T	SO	GA	S	SAPCT	PIM
65	3,852	2.74	38	17	9	5	176	1,780	.901	0

LAST SEASON

Among NHL goalies, was third in GAA, tied for first in victories and shutouts, tied for fifth in save percentage. Established career bests in all departments. Set club record for victories.

THE PHYSICAL GAME

McLean stands up well, does a good job of remaining in position for shots and does an above-average job directing or controlling his rebounds.

He keeps his movements compact and without flourish, which makes it much easier to recover his stance. He is quick for his size and uses his reach to catch and control pucks; the Oilers seemed to be shooting high glove in the playoffs, and that proved a fatal error on their part.

McLean occasionally will play a shooter's body instead of the puck, which can make a huge difference in the amount of open net available to a shooter. The odd time, he will misplay an angle. But his are solid technical skills: he moves well laterally, remains perpendicular to the ice as much as possible, and uses his stick very well to move the puck.

He also is extremely tenacious. If he drops on his side for a first shot, he has the poise and the will to try an emergency/recovery move on the follow.

THE MENTAL GAME

McLean became much sharper mentally, much more consistent and much more dependable in the close games last season. In 17 of his appearances, the score was within a goal either way for at least 60 minutes, and his record in those games was 8-2-7, a .670 winning percentage. In 1990-91, McLean was 0-5-2, .280, in such games, so the improvement in clutch performance is unmistakable.

THE INTANGIBLES

McLean rebounded from a sub-par season in 1990-91, just as HSR predicted he would, and had the definitive breakthrough season among NHL goaltenders. McLean hiked his save percentage from .867 despite facing nearly twice as many shots as in the prior season. He doubled his career shutout total. Nine times he got only two goals of support — not two or fewer but precisely two — but posted a 4-3-2 record for 10 of the team's 96 points; in 1990-91, under the same circumstances, he was 0-5-1. The fact that two of his shutouts came by 1-0 scores also offers perspective on McLean's season.

Can he do it again? Not likely. No disrespect, but 3,852 minutes take a bite out of you, first of all. Second, when you put up numbers like that, it is difficult to repeat them. Still, he merits mention among the league's best.

SERGIO MOMESSO

Yrs. of NHL service: 8
Born: Montreal, Que.; Sept. 4, 1965
Position: Left wing
Height: 6-3
Weight: 215
Uniform no.: 27
Shoots: Left

Career statistics:

GP	G	A	TP	PIM
397	98	130	228	953

1991-92 statistics:

GP	G	A	TP	+/-	PIM	PP	SH	GW	GT	S	PCT
58	20	23	43	16	198	2	0	3	0	153	13.1

LAST SEASON

Scored 20 goals for second time in three years. Third on team in PIM.

THE FINESSE GAME

Momesso has size, strength, some straight-ahead power and some agility.

He is not a great player; he has established that over the seasons people have waited for him to put a dominant campaign together. But he can surge up the wing and take the big, heavy slap shot from the circle. He can drive to the net. He can score on a deflection or a rebound because of his strength and balance. He can work the corners and pry the puck loose from the boards.

Momesso attends to the defensive aspect as well, which is evidence of his work ethic, because he hardly could be considered fast. He does a decent job of staying with his man; when you look at replays, you don't see him at the bottom of the screen while a goal against is being scored at the top of the screen. He stays in the play responsibly.

THE PHYSICAL GAME

Momesso is big and he plays big most of the time. He is just unpredictable enough to keep people wary of when he might feel like snapping, when he might feel like playing enormous.

He is a formidable opponent when he is playing with a chip on his shoulder. He gets extra-extra room those nights, because people who generally stay away from him retreat even farther; that challenges Momesso to skate harder, so there will be no way they can stay away from him or get away from him.

THE INTANGIBLES

You could do plenty worse than have Sergio Momesso as your third left wing.

He scores and he bangs, but he is never going to put up Kevin Stevens/Gary Roberts numbers. He will get the job done at both ends of the rink and he will only hurt you if you trade him and try to replace him, because then you realize good No. 3s are very tough to find.

Momesso is a good No. 3, which means you don't have to ask your No. 2 left wing to play down one spot and you don't have to ask your No. 4 to play better than he can. That matters. You can't win without structure.

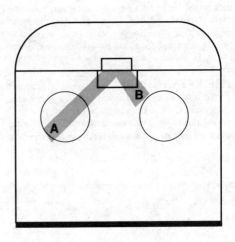

DANA MURZYN

Yrs. of NHL service: 7
Born: Regina, Sask.; Dec. 9, 1966
Position: Left defense
Height: 6-3
Weight: 205
Uniform no.: 5
Shoots: Left

Career statistics:

GP	G	A	TP	PIM
466	33	99	132	824

1991-92 statistics:

GP	G	A	TP	+/-	PIM	PP	SH	GW	GT	S	PCT
70	3	12	15	15	145	0	1	0	0	99	3.0

LAST SEASON

Plus-minus improved 22 goals and was fifth best on team. PIM increased 107.

THE FINESSE GAME

Murzyn's puck skills are pretty good. He makes a good pass. He understands the game well.

But he gets into trouble when his feet stop. Either he is too heavy or he is not strong enough to carry his playing weight, but Murzyn always has to be striding or gliding because when he gets caught flat-footed, he is a goner.

Other than that, Murzyn brings a pretty good shot to the barn, but has to be talked into using it. The shot is low and accurate, it can be tipped; but it isn't going to be much of a weapon if a goalie barely sees it only once a game.

THE PHYSICAL GAME

Big as he is, Murzyn doesn't play big. He doesn't back down, but he isn't a very good fighter. Either he doesn't have the balance or he doesn't have the upper body strength, or he simply does not have the fight in him. Murzyn will scrap, but he won't go looking for one.

THE INTANGIBLES

To stay in the league, you have to have some quality that makes you better than the guy who isn't playing that night. You look at Murzyn and wonder, sometimes, what his quality is. He doesn't use the size,

he doesn't use the shot. If it was easier to tell exactly what kind of defenseman Murzyn really is, it might be easier to tell if he's playing the role well or not.

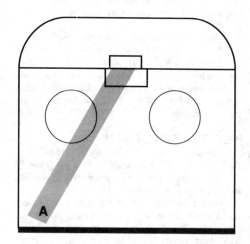

PETR NEDVED

Yrs. of NHL service: 2
Born: Liberec, Czechoslovakia; Dec. 9, 1971
Position: Center
Height: 6-3
Weight: 178
Uniform no.: 19
Shoots: Left

Career statistics:

GP	G	A	TP	PIM
138	25	28	53	56

1991-92 statistics:

GP	G	A	TP	+/-	PIM	PP	SH	GW	GT	S	PCT
77	15	22	37	−3	36	5	0	1	1	99	15.2

LAST SEASON

Plus-minus improved 18 goals. Games played, goals, assists, points and PIM all increased over rookie season.

THE FINESSE GAME

Nedved has good balance and agility, nice quickness and above-average speed. He makes the speed more of a weapon by shifting gears and keeping the opposing defensemen guessing his pace.

With his hand skills and overall skills, he should have had a lot more than the 22 assists he got last season. Nedved can feather a soft lead pass that a linemate can pick up with a good head of steam, or he can fire a brick through a tiny opening to a teammate who is open now but won't be open long. Also, because Nedved keeps his options open, he can hold the puck until a checker is in his face before dishing off accurately.

Two seasons ago, admittedly against junior competition, Nedved scored 65 goals; last season, he barely had that many shots. That won't do. He has the ability to do well on either special team, plus enough creativity and a good enough view of the ice to run the power play from the point if he is asked. Things would open up if he took the puck to the net more often.

THE PHYSICAL GAME

Nedved does well on face-offs, again because of his hand quickness. He was grittier on draws last season, getter better body position and locking off his man after the drop.

Nedved can control the puck with his skates if his hands are locked up by an opponent, but still needs to be stronger. While he does pretty well in traffic, he is not overly keen on throwing his body around and remains very much a stick checker.

He is, however, starting to play with more emotion, is starting to fight back a bit from the punishment people will hand him until he makes them stop.

THE INTANGIBLES

Nedved has gone from an explosive scorer to an offensive non-entity in a very short span of time, making him a dilemma for the people who play hockey pools; his skills make you figure he might explode at any time, but his numbers don't justify a high-round pick.

With the departure of Igor Larionov, however, Nedved may get more ice time and a giant opportunity to do bigger and better things. In preparation for that challenge, Nedved spent all summer in the weight room, adding bulk to his upper body in the hope of adding muscle to his offensive output.

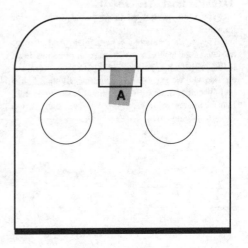

GINO ODJICK

Yrs. of NHL service: 2
Born: Maniwaki, Que.; Sept. 7, 1970
Position: Left wing
Height: 6-2
Weight: 220
Uniform no.: 29
Shoots: Left

Career statistics:

GP	G	A	TP	PIM
110	11	7	18	644

1991-92 statistics:

GP	G	A	TP	+/-	PIM	PP	SH	GW	GT	S	PCT
65	4	6	10	-1	348	0	0	0	0	68	5.9

LAST SEASON

PIM total increased 54 from prior season and set a team record. Point total also was NHL career high. Missed six games due to suspension.

THE FINESSE GAME

Odjick is not much of a skater. In fact, there are times it seems he decelerates instead of accelerates—times when he will get some momentum for the first few strides but will not be able to sustain the pace.

Still, he goes to the net, gets knocked down, gets up and chases the puck again. If a defenseman is knocking him down, maybe somebody else will have more time and space in which to make a play; Odjick will take that trade any day. Maybe, because of his effort, the defenseman will have to hold him or tackle him and take a penalty; Odjick will take that trade as well.

He gets his few goals from in front of the net. He will score off a scramble or a rebound, but will not finesse a puck past a professional goalie.

THE PHYSICAL GAME

You think he got all those penalty minutes for hooking?

This guy's a puncher, a patrolman. And whether he stays in the league many more seasons comes down to the levels he is capable of adding to his game. Players like Odjick get into the league as fighters. Then they become hitters. Third, they learn to check. Fourth, the really good ones, the players such as Bob Probert, become viable scorers.

THE INTANGIBLES

Odjick will stop at nothing in his efforts to 1) keep his job, 2) help the team win. If it takes throwing a big hit or absorbing one, starting a fight or finishing one, taking a shot or blocking one, Odjick will make the attempt.

The question is whether he can make the step up and become a presence on the ice instead of a character.

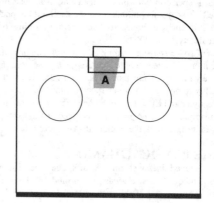

ADRIEN PLAVSIC

Yrs. of NHL service: 2
Born: Montreal, Que.; Jan. 13, 1970
Position: Right defense
Height: 6-1
Weight: 206
Uniform no.: 6
Shoots: Left

Career statistics:

GP	G	A	TP	PIM
79	6	22	28	86

1991-92 statistics:

GP	G	A	TP	+/-	PIM	PP	SH	GW	GT	S	PCT
16	1	9	10	4	14	0	0	0	1	21	4.8

LAST SEASON

Returned to Canucks Feb. 28 after playing in Winter Olympics.

THE FINESSE GAME

Plavsic is a very rangy, agile skater with good lateral ability. He doesn't just cover ground going in reverse; he actually is FAST backward. He has fine balance and flexibility, can attempt a poke check and regain position quickly if the attempt fails.

When the puck turns over in the offensive zone, Plavsic identifies his assignment well and, while not lightning quick, hustles to position to face the counterattack. In the defensive zone, he has enough confidence and skill that, under pressure in a corner, he will make a play — even if it's just a simple reverse —instead of simply hacking the puck out off the glass.

Plavsic also has the poise, plus the hands, to make a pass to a teammate at the last second before being checked. He leads the man well with a pass that has some zip on it, but isn't so hard that it bounces off the guy's stick.

THE PHYSICAL GAME

Plavsic has good size and uses it aggressively in the corners and the front of the net. He is a useful penalty killer, will block shots, and accepts a hit to make a pass. Supported by good balance, Plavsic also uses his reach well.

THE INTANGIBLES

A graduate of Dave King's National Team program, Plavsic is an extremely competent defenseman who has more offensive tools than he showed after the Olympics last season. This is a player of promise.

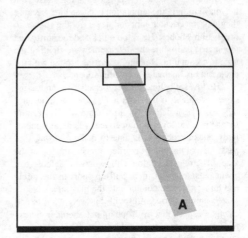

CLIFF RONNING

Yrs. of NHL service: 5
Born: Vancouver, B.C.; Oct. 1, 1965
Position: Center
Height: 5-8
Weight: 175
Uniform no.: 7
Shoots: Left

Career statistics:

GP	G	A	TP	PIM
271	84	124	208	88

1991-92 statistics:

GP	G	A	TP	+/-	PIM	PP	SH	GW	GT	S	PCT
80	24	47	71	18	42	6	0	2	1	216	11.1

LAST SEASON

Led team in assists. Assist and point totals were career high. Goal total matched career high. Shot total increased 103 from prior season. Plus-minus improved 18 goals. Finished second on team in scoring

THE FINESSE GAME

Ronning always is trying to make something happen. He speeds up the tempo of the game because he is an extremely frustrating opponent. Big defensemen just drool at the sight of a target Ronning's size, but they have to fight the temptation to chase him, because they will never catch him and never get the chance to break all his bones. He is too quick and too shifty and too smart, and while the defensemen are fighting the urge to cream him, Ronning is darting around with the puck and his linemates are getting open.

He loves it behind the net, because he can use the cage as a shield; if the defensemen are watching him, they can't be watching for a linemate who is burning for the net. He loves it in open ice, where he is tauntingly out of reach but is able to make a strong first pass. One of his other favorite haunts is the top of the face-off circle; Ronning will worry a defenseman about outside speed, then pull up short in the circle and hit a teammate coming into the play late.

Ronning is so skillful with his weight shifts and change of speed that by dropping one shoulder, he can fake an opponent into the third row. Then, with one quick stride, he drives through the opening he just created, dances to the net and finishes the play with a powerful shot. He also will fake a shot, freeze the defenseman, move to the left with the puck and shoot back toward his right. You never know what's coming with this guy, which is why he is so effective.

THE PHYSICAL GAME

Ronning knows he's going to get killed along the boards, so he lets the bigger buys do the shoving; he stays a few feet away, jabbing and probing with his stick like a long-billed bird after a worm. Other times, he'll hook a guy's arm, force him off balance, and pry the puck away that way.

He also knows he gets in trouble when defenders can use their reach on him, so he shields the puck nicely with his body. Since he is so short, his center of gravity is lower—providing nice balance and keeping him on his skates.

THE INTANGIBLES

Ronning has spent a lifetme overcoming prejudice against his size, so it should be no surprise at all that mentally, he is extremely tough. He rises to every occasion, lifts his game when it is needed, and is more dependable than many of his far larger counterparts.

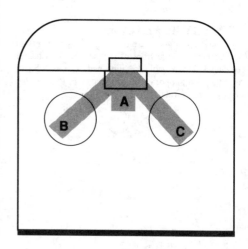

JIM SANDLAK

Yrs. of NHL service: 6
Born: Kitchener, Ont.; Dec. 12, 1966
Position: Right wing
Height: 6-4
Weight: 220
Uniform no.: 25
Shoots: Right

Career statistics:

GP	G	A	TP	PIM
417	90	97	187	661

1991-92 statistics:

GP	G	A	TP	+/-	PIM	PP	SH	GW	GT	S	PCT
66	16	24	40	22	176	3	0	2	1	122	13.1

LAST SEASON

Scored at least 15 goals for fifth time in six NHL seasons. Plus-minus improved 42 goals. Shot total increased 34. PIM increased for fourth consecutive season. Tied career high in points. Missed 14 games due to sprained wrist and sprained knee.

THE FINESSE GAME

There are times when Sandlak's hands, legs and head don't quite seem to mesh. Sometimes he will know where he wants to go and what he wants to do, but his feet won't get him there. Or he will be in the right place with the right idea, but his hands won't execute the play he needs from them. So he gets 15 goals a year instead of the 30 or more he would get if all the pieces meshed more often.

He is confident enough, willing enough to risk a low-percentage play. He will go one-on-two and try to split the defense, but he has neither the dexterity of hand nor the speed of foot to meet the challenge.

Sandlak won't beat a defenseman up the boards with the puck. He doesn't have the balance to maximize his reach. So he ends up taking what he can get, although there is no questioning his effort.

THE PHYSICAL GAME

In the absence of sure-fire finesse skills, Sandlak plays to his physical assets. He finishes checks, bangs when the big hit is there. Indeed, he has to hit to be effective. By doing so, Sandlak creates more room for his linemates, makes them bigger.

THE INTANGIBLES

Sandlak is one of many Canucks whose plus-minus rating soared last season, which shows his willingness to work on weaknesses, reflects his determination to be better and confirms the integrity of his commitment to the game.

Also, it should be pointed out that the Canucks won four games in overtime last season and Sandlak set up the winner in two of them.

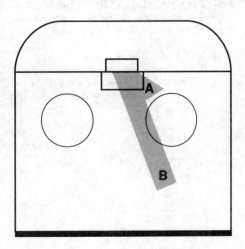

GARRY VALK

Yrs. of NHL service: 2
Born: Edmonton, Alta.; Nov. 27, 1967
Position: Right wing
Height: 6-1
Weight: 205
Uniform no.: 23
Shoots: Left

Career statistics:

GP	G	A	TP	PIM
124	18	28	46	122

1991-92 statistics:

GP	G	A	TP	+/-	PIM	PP	SH	GW	GT	S	PCT
65	8	17	25	3	56	2	1	2	0	93	8.6

LAST SEASON

Plus-minus improved 26 goals.

THE FINESSE GAME

Valk has a peculiar skating style. He's a bit knock-kneed, so he isn't pretty to watch. But he gets where he needs to go and he has some quickness.

A consistent, hard-working role player, he is a third- or fourth-line plugger who isn't going to score a lot of goals but is a game player.

Valk kills penalties well and is a good forechecker because he has good jump to the puck. He stays in tremendous shape. He does fine on a good forechecking line, but is not going to be out there when you're down two goals with 10 minutes to go.

THE PHYSICAL GAME

Valk is strong and tough, a skating pepperpot. And when the gloves come off, he's a very good fighter.

THE INTANGIBLES

Valk has a tremendous work ethic and has found a role for himself as a third-line guy who goes out and bangs and plays obnoxiously. He is not quite as ornery as Ronnie Stern, whose role he assumed after Stern was traded to Calgary.

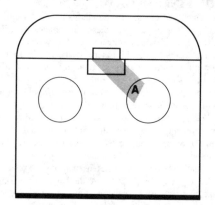

406

RYAN WALTER

Yrs. of NHL service: 14
Born: Burnaby, B.C.; April 23, 1958
Position: Center
Height: 6-0
Weight: 200
Uniform no.: 9
Shoots: Left

Career statistics:

GP	G	A	TP	PIM
978	261	382	643	936

1991-92 statistics:

GP	G	A	TP	+/-	PIM	PP	SH	GW	GT	S	PCT
67	6	11	17	6	49	1	1	0	0	73	8.2

LAST SEASON

Games played was three-season high. Was named Bud Light Man of the Year for his charity work.

THE FINESSE GAME

Walter makes his living on the defensive side of the puck. He is a checker, a defensive specialist, a penalty killer, a face-off winner.

He has enough jump in his step to be a useful player in the neutral zone. He cuts the ice off well, which disrupts the passing lanes. He finishes checks on the puck carrier if he's near enough.

While killing penalties, he reads the situation well; if a defenseman goes to the side boards to challenge the puck, Walter drops back to cover the spot the defenseman vacated.

He uses his head on offense, as well. When he doesn't have the puck, Walter works to get open and stay open for a pass. He doesn't just throw his hands up in disgust and skate away if the puck carrier has his head down and doesn't see Walter is available.

THE PHYSICAL GAME

After all these seasons, Walter remains a strong, physical player who still gets a big piece of you at every opportunity. He also dives to block shots and uses his strength in every possible way. Most notably, he is trusted with the pivotal first face-off of a penalty-killing situation.

THE INTANGIBLES

Walter has spent the bulk of his career leading the NHL in citizenship, in charity work, in elevating the image and ideals of his teammates and his sport and, basically, making his world better. His intangibles far outstrip his tangibles as an athlete at this stage; but with the 1,000-game milestone very much in sight, Walter more than deserves the chance to play at least until that threshold is crossed.

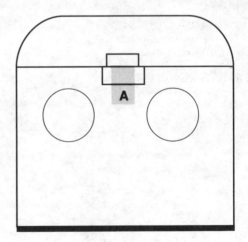

WASHINGTON
CAPITALS

DON BEAUPRE

Yrs. of NHL service: 12
Born: Kitchener, Ont.; Sept. 19, 1961
Position: Goaltender
Height: 5-9
Weight: 165
Uniform no.: 33
Catches: Left

Career statistics:

GP	MINS	GA	SO	GAA	A	PIM
474	26,884	1,568	12	3.50	4	206

1991-92 statistics:

GP	MINS	GAA	W	L	T	SO	GA	S	SAPCT	PIM
54	3,108	3.20	29	17	6	1	166	1,435	.884	30

LAST SEASON

Games, minutes played and victories were career highs. Victory total set club record. Became first Capitals goalie to win 20 or more three consecutive seasons.

THE PHYSICAL GAME

Beaupre is another goalie whose primary concern is taking away the low shots and letting the rest take care of itself. He used to be a flopper, but while he still goes down a lot and still depends on quickness, he plays more in control now. Even if there are times when he is not in good position for a second shot, he doesn't face many because he controls his rebounds well and his defenseman control the front of the net well.

He employs more of a standup style. While some other goalies' idea of following a shooter across the slot is to take two steps and fall down, Beaupre is a good skater and stays with the shooter well. He does an especially good job of moving to his right with the shooter while remaining limber and ready to kick in that direction if the shot heads toward the lower corner.

Beaupre doesn't use the stick much as an offensive tool, but will clear the puck pretty effectively when he absolutely must. More often, he tends to stop the puck behind the net and leave it for his defensemen. With as many mobile defensemen as Washington has, that seems to be the proper plan. Defensively, he will block any passes he can reach.

Otherwise, Beaupre has a good, quick glove, moves well laterally and has a good sense of anticipation that allows him to get a piece of bang-bang plays.

THE MENTAL GAME

Beaupre likes the challenge. He can come up with the big stop on a consistent basis and can be depended upon especially to keep the score close if the team gets off to a slow start.

THE INTANGIBLES

A contract squabble provided an early distraction for him last season, but Beaupre persevered and played a very significant role in his team's successful campaign. His teammates are confident with him behind them.

PETER BONDRA

Yrs. of NHL service: 2
Born: Luck, Russia; Feb. 7, 1968
Position: Right wing
Height: 5-11
Weight: 180
Uniform no.: 12
Shoots: Left

Career statistics:

GP	G	A	TP	PIM
125	40	44	84	89

1991-92 statistics:

GP	G	A	TP	+/-	PIM	PP	SH	GW	GT	S	PCT
71	28	28	56	16	42	4	0	3	0	158	17.7

LAST SEASON

Set career highs in games, goals, assists and points. Plus-minus improved 26 goals. Goal production jumped 16.

THE FINESSE GAME

Bondra has stunning speed and acceleration, which he uses to reach the puck and then to win the puck. He also uses that weapon in a defensive role, as he is more than capable of catching an opponent from behind, lifting his stick and stripping away the puck.

Bondra is extremely dangerous on the backhand, which confirms upper-body and wrist strength, complemented by excellent balance. He likes to come out from behind the net at the goalie's right and make things happen; and he has more than enough strength to retain possession while doing so.

With the puck, he is a threat to score every time on the ice; Bondra puts teams on the defensive, forces them to react either to his speed or his touch. He was much more productive offensively because he started getting more pucks on the net instead of spraying drives too high and too wide.

Away from the puck, he does a good job as the third-man-high.

THE PHYSICAL GAME

Bondra is not a physical player, but will take the puck to the net from the corner during a power play, just for the sake of causing confusion and trying to make something happen. He bumps and finishes checks. In down-low coverage, he ties up the man — and, just as important — the man's stick. Bondra is a good, persistent, man-to-man defender and he does NOT go down when he is hit.

THE INTANGIBLES

The Capitals are looking for big things from this player, who gave them a taste of exceptional play more regularly last season as he grew more familiar with the league. He became a more rounded two-way force after entering the league with something of a "who needs defense?" approach.

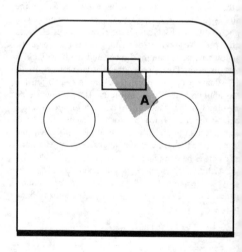

RANDY BURRIDGE

Yrs. of NHL service: 6
Born: Fort Erie, Ont.; Jan. 7, 1966
Position: Left wing
Height: 5-9
Weight: 180
Uniform no.: 12
Shoots: Left

Career statistics:

GP	G	A	TP	PIM
325	131	159	290	325

1991-92 statistics:

GP	G	A	TP	+/-	PIM	PP	SH	GW	GT	S	PCT
66	23	44	67	−4	50	9	0	3	0	131	17.6

LAST SEASON

Had career bests in assists, power-play goals and points. Appeared in first all-star game. Missed 14 games due to torn left-knee ligaments. Plus-minus was five-season low.

THE FINESSE GAME

A scoring spree in the early stages last season made Burridge much more of a two-way threat than he had been considered. His wrist shot is extremely quick and Burridge packs plenty of power behind it, which makes it a natural for creating rebounds that other teammates can put away.

By shooting more, Burridge hiked his assist total 31 from the prior season, although he played only four more games than in 1990-91. His shot also got him more time on the power play, with a personal increase of eight power-play goals the result.

Quickness makes Burridge useful in penalty-killing situations. He uses short strides and lateral quickness to win the races to the puck, and uses his wits to do something with it once he has gained possession.

THE PHYSICAL GAME

Another proud product of the Peterborough juniors, Burridge makes the most of his physical assets and tries to play a bigger man's game with his heart and strength. Rather than suffer from limited size, Burridge makes it work to his advantage; it isn't easy to knock him down because his center of gravity is low. He'll get to the boards or the corners first, absorb the initial hit, then try to use his feet to keep the puck alive or move it to a teammate.

THE INTANGIBLES

Burridge is an effort player, a spark plug who suffered a very serious knee injury but still had a career season. For a player who depends on quickness, the question is whether he can come all the way back to prior form. If he can't, though, it certainly won't be from lack of hustle.

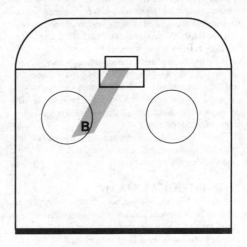

BOB CARPENTER

Yrs. of NHL service: 11
Born: Beverly, Mass.; July 13, 1963
Position: Left wing
Height: 6-0
Weight: 190
Uniform no.: 11
Shoots: Left

Career statistics:

GP	G	A	TP	PIM
757	274	320	594	698

1991-92 statistics:

GP	G	A	TP	+/-	PIM	PP	SH	GW	GT	S	PCT
60	25	23	48	−3	46	6	1	6	2	171	14.6

LAST SEASON

Signed as free agent from Boston, June 30, 1992. Tied for lead in power-play goals on Bruins. All scoring totals two-season highs following career lows in 1990-91. Missed 12 games with knee injuries. Missed eight games with calf injury.

THE FINESSE GAME

Throughout his career, the best part of Carpenter's game has been generated from his physical play, but he is no mere bump and grinder. He has very good finesse skills (project his goals over an 80-game season last year and he would have been a 30-35 goal scorer), which he uses to great advantage in traffic situations. He has to work hard for his goals. He once thought of himself of a more glamorous player (especially after scoring 50 goals in his fourth season in the league), but once he disabused himself of that notion, Carpenter actually became a better player.

He has good skating speed, although he won't get many style points from the judges. His skating has suffered from some of the leg injuries and operations he's undergone in the past year. Carpenter is still strong on his skates, although his rink-length dashes are a thing of the past.

His experience is considerable. He can play all three forward positions, and is used to kills penalties and work on the power play.

THE PHYSICAL GAME

Because of his injury, Carpenter could not play in back-to-back games. He lost muscle tone recovering from surgery, and understandably was not as strong a player as he could have been if fully healthy. His stamina was also a problem. He does not play as aggressively as he did before the injuries.

THE INTANGIBLES

That Carpenter was playing at all last season was something of a miracle, following his recovery from a shattered kneecap late in 1990-91. He can still be an effective forward and contribute around 50 points a season if the Capitals are cautious with his regimen and his playing time, and spot him wisely.

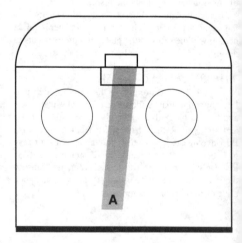

SYLVAIN COTE

Yrs. of NHL service: 7
Born: Quebec City, Que.; Jan. 19, 1966
Position: Left defense
Height: 5-11
Weight: 185
Uniform no.: 3
Shoots: Right

Career statistics:

GP	G	A	TP	PIM
460	42	90	133	178

1991-92 statistics:

GP	G	A	TP	+/-	PIM	PP	SH	GW	GT	S	PCT
78	11	29	40	7	31	6	0	2	0	151	7.3

LAST SEASON

Obtained from Hartford, Sept. 8, 1991, for Washington's second-round pick in 1992 draft. Set career highs in goals, power-play goals, assists and points. Plus-minus improved 24 goals.

THE FINESSE GAME

Cote has some very nice puck skills and a willingness to use them. He will drill a breakout pass up the middle and will make the backhand pass with confidence. He will bring the puck to the net from the left point with a strong shot, although he isn't the most accurate shooter in the world.

He is a nice combination of deft hands and light feet. Cote has a long stride, very good lateral movement and moves very well laterally across the defensive slot. He is very agile, makes exceptional stops and starts in tiny spaces and has splendid acceleration which enables him to headman the puck and distribute it nicely.

Cote can, at times, show good hockey sense — an area in which he improved last season. He seems to know when a rush is needed, when simply to gain the red line and get the puck deep. And he doesn't try to force what isn't there; if the rush is there, he makes it and if the dump-in is needed, he buries the puck in a corner.

He does a good job seeing the ice offensively, but his vision seems limited on the other side of the puck. Cote's defensive reads are improving, but there are times when his speed merely enables him to run around, out of position.

THE PHYSICAL GAME

Cote is more a finesse player than a physical player. He doesn't have size, but he has strength and quickness; he gets to the offensive player and finishes his checks, ties people up.

THE INTANGIBLES

Hockey terminology is light years behind in so many areas. Except in this book, for example, defensemen are not referred to by which side of the ice they play. And there is no accurate term for blueliners like Cote, who play offense far better than they play defense — until now, that is. The best way to refer to Cote is as "an offenseman."

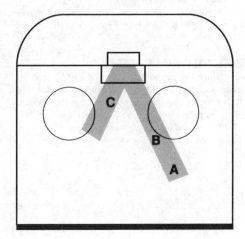

JOHN DRUCE

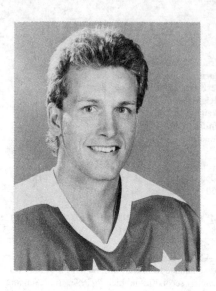

Yrs. of NHL service: 4
Born: Peterborough, Ont.; Feb. 23, 1966
Position: Left wing/right wing
Height: 6-1
Weight: 200
Uniform no.: 19
Shoots: Right

Career statistics:

GP	G	A	TP	PIM
240	57	64	121	199

1991-92 statistics:

GP	G	A	TP	+/-	PIM	PP	SH	GW	GT	S	PCT
67	19	18	37	14	39	1	0	3	0	129	14.7

LAST SEASON

Marked second consecutive season of 19 goals or more. Plus-minus improved 10 goals, though assist total dropped 18 and point total dropped 21.

THE FINESSE GAME

Having come to the NHL with defensive skills that outstripped his offense, Druce continued working last season on developing his offensive repertoire — with limited results. He has a quick snap shot from the right alley and occasionally will beat a goaltender from the circle. Generally, however, he scores from closer to the net, where he can use his strength and persistence on rebounds and loose pucks.

Druce is very comfortable with the defensive game, and can accept any checking assignment because he has good quickness and straight-ahead speed that allows him to keep up with almost any check. He accelerates well without the puck, but seems to slow down while carrying it.

Accordingly, Druce makes a pass and then drives up the wing to set up a return pass, or powers to the net.

THE PHYSICAL GAME

Druce has size and strength and a good head for penalty killing. He finishes a lot of checks, does the heavy work along the side boards and in the corners. He goes in front of the net, battles with at least one defenseman and plays a physical, but generally clean, game. He'll fight if you want.

THE INTANGIBLES

Druce is a solid two-way player with good skills. He puts up decent numbers and probably deserves more recognition than he gets, but he's most content to stay in the background and let the others have the spotlight

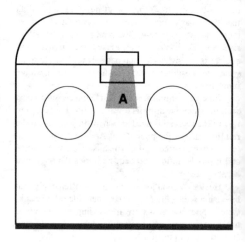

414

KEVIN HATCHER

Yrs. of NHL service: 7
Born: Detroit, Mich.; Sept. 9, 1966
Position: Right defense
Height: 6-4
Weight: 225
Uniform no.: 4
Shoots: Right

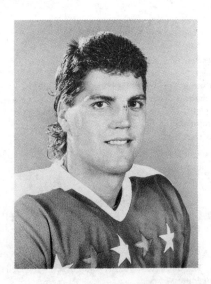

Career statistics:

GP	G	A	TP	PIM
530	99	208	307	779

1991-92 statistics:

GP	G	A	TP	+/-	PIM	PP	SH	GW	GT	S	PCT
79	17	37	54	18	105	8	1	2	1	246	6.9

LAST SEASON

Plus-minus improved 28 goals to rank third on Capitals, first among team defensemen. Production dropped seven goals, 13 assists. Penalty minutes increased 36.

THE FINESSE GAME

One appealing thing Hatcher does is use his head when he goes back for the puck. Even under pressure, he takes a look over his shoulder to see what's coming and what options are available, so that when he grabs the puck behind the net, he can make his decisions, and his moves, more quickly and appropriately. He evaluates, looks before he leaps, doesn't simply throw the puck around without a purpose.

Hatcher is very poised with the puck, skating it up the middle on the power play and starting the half-court game with a smart pass or a solid hard-around. He is more than strong enough to keep control of the puck while being hooked and hacked, is more than confident in offensive skills that make him a good rusher and a strong shooter. He can beat goalies from the blue line or in front with a powerful shot he's never reluctant to use.

Mobility, and reach, also allow Hatcher to cheat over and overload the left side against a rush, which he does often because he can still get back if the puck goes to the place he vacated. He is not perfect on his reads, and can get caught flat-footed every once in a while, but someone who plays as much as he does is going to mess up on occasion.

THE PHYSICAL GAME

Hatcher stands up at the blue line and can intimidate players off the puck. Because he has good acceleration and is a smooth skater who covers a lot of ground laterally, Hatcher can force attackers to make a move they don't like or to shoot before they want to. He is an obvious physical force who makes every opponent pay a price; when he hits, he can devastate. He doesn't fight much, because the Capitals need him on the ice.

THE INTANGIBLES

Hatcher is a player who depends on his forwards for help in standing up to the rush, but one who also gives his forwards confidence that he is there for them if they need him. A motivated, intense competitor, he gives his team a better chance of winning every night, and made himself much more valuable last season by sacrificing some of his offense to play better defense.

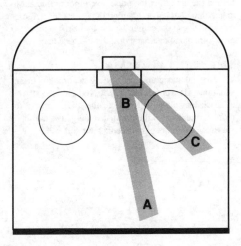

JIM HRIVNAK

Yrs. of NHL service: 1
Born: Montreal, Que.; May 28, 1968
Position: Goaltender
Height: 6-2
Weight: 185
Uniform no.: 39
Catches: Left

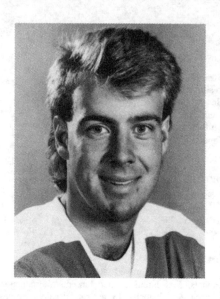

Career statistics:

GP	MINS	GA	SO	GAA	A	PIM
32	1,646	97	0	3.54	1	0

1991-92 statistics:

GP	MINS	GAA	W	L	T	SO	GA	S	SAPCT	PIM
12	605	3.47	6	3	0	0	35	274	.872	0

LAST SEASON

Games played, victory and GAA all were NHL career bests.

THE PHYSICAL GAME

Hrivnak plays a stand-up style but will go down, when the situation calls for it, in either of two ways: he will use the half-V and kick a puck to the corner, or he will lie on one side and stack the pads. The problem with that move is, when he employs it, Hrivnak is not always quick to get back on his feet; generally, he will lie on the ice in that position until the play ends.

He challenges well out of a very tight stance. There is very little space between his pads, and it takes virtually a perfect shot to beat him through the five hole. He also has a good glove and does a decent job controlling rebounds. If there is a weakness, it is to his stick side, as he doesn't always stride into pucks shot in that direction.

One real problem with Hrivnak, which seems to stem from a lack of skating skills, is an elemental unwillingness to handle the puck. He is reluctant to go behind the net to get the puck, even more reluctant to do anything but leave it behind the net for his defensemen. He does not seem to be the goalie a coach would pick for a game against a dump-and-chase team.

THE MENTAL GAME

Hrivnak has come up very big in some important situations. He wants to play in the NHL, always strived to reach that plateau. He takes the NHL game a lot more seriously than the minor-league game, but there are times when his game seems a bit soft.

THE INTANGIBLES

Hrivnak's work ethic has been questioned, and that is a tough tag to shed when you're trying to step up to the next level. Expansion year or no expansion year, points are going to be too much at a premium to be trusted to someone who doesn't work hard enough. So either Hrivnak gets a fire lit under him or he'll probably spend more time simmering, and seasoning, in Baltimore.

DALE HUNTER

Yrs. of NHL service: 12
Born: Petrolia, Ont.; July 31, 1960
Position: Center
Height: 5-10
Weight: 198
Uniform no.: 32
Shoots: Left

Career statistics:

GP	G	A	TP	PIM
918	249	511	770	2,676

1991-92 statistics:

GP	G	A	TP	+/-	PIM	PP	SH	GW	GT	S	PCT
80	28	50	78	−2	205	13	0	4	1	110	25.5

LAST SEASON

Point production jumped 12 goals, 20 assists. Plus-minus improved 20 goals. Goal total matched career high, point total was second best. Played in at least 76 games, and collected at least 200 penalty minutes, for fifth straight season with team.

THE FINESSE GAME

So much of Hunter's reputation deals with his physical game that his smarts away from the puck too often go under-recognized. Hunter knows so well that a center's job is more than winning face-offs and making passes; a center is obliged to create space for his linemates, and Hunter is among the craftiest in the league at doing so.

Hunter will make a pass at the center of the blue line and generally do either of two things: he will drive directly to the net, taking at least one defenseman with him, and mushing everything in front of the goalie and causing any of amount of distraction in front. Or he will curl to open ice, his stick on the ice and available immediately for a return pass, and find another way to set a screen on the goalie or a 'legal' pick on a defenseman.

When he has the puck, Hunter does a good job of holding it, daring the defense to come to him, while waiting for his wings to break to open ice. He also is poised and experienced enough to pull back into the neutral zone and regroup if there is no play at the attacking blue line; if he charges again and there still is no play, Hunter will get it deep and go to work on the short game.

When he doesn't have the puck, he'll always get his body in the way of an opponent, buying some time for a teammate who may have possession.

THE PHYSICAL GAME

Hunter only knows one way to play the game, which is to play to his strength. And the way to do that is to go straight ahead. He isn't much for turning or agile finesse plays. He comes straight at you, gets right in your face, gets the stick on you and cuts off your play so you can't manoeuvre him into something he can't do.

On draws, Hunter shortens way up on his stick and gets way down low, using his leg strength and back strength to win the puck. That low stance also enables him to drive his shoulder into the chest of his opposing center, locking that center off and buying time for a point shooter or a defenseman.

And make no mistake: winning means more to Hunter than following every rule. He will hit you, charge you, elbow you or fight you if it's going to help him win.

THE INTANGIBLES

You look at his size, you look at his age, you look at the miles on his tires and you wonder how he does it — how he could play so significant a scoring role while still having so much impact away from the puck. At this stage, a somewhat smaller role probably would keep him fresher; but it hardly pays to keep so valuable a player on the bench.

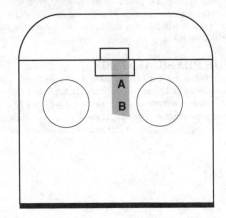

AL IAFRATE

Yrs. of NHL service: 8
Born: Dearborn, Mich.; March 21, 1966
Position: Right defense
Height: 6-3
Weight: 220
Uniform no.: 34
Shoots: Left

Career statistics:

GP	G	A	TP	PIM
580	104	211	315	850

1991-92 statistics:

GP	G	A	TP	+/-	PIM	PP	SH	GW	GT	S	PCT
78	17	34	51	1	180	6	0	1	1	151	11.3

LAST SEASON

Goal total tied for team lead among defensemen. Goal total increased by eight, assist total by 11. Was plus for only second season of his career.

THE FINESSE GAME

Iafrate is such a good skater, so light on his feet despite his size, that being a left shot on the right side hardly poses a problem. He can skate the puck out of trouble instead of just flinging the puck out off the glass. He can spin away in either direction from a forechecker or a challenger at the point, blast a shot on net and still be back in plenty of time if the shot doesn't get through or there's a quick transition play.

An agile, fluid skater for such a hulking specimen, Iafrate can go end-to-end when he's in the mood—or, at the very least, can jump easily into the play. His cannon shot stays low for deflections (if anyone has the nerve); Iafrate can shoot through a goalie as much as past a goalie.

Good lateral movement, with and without the puck, allows him to slide into the center of the blue line on the power play and set up more options. Iafrate also uses his head to advantage. Because he knows the threat posed by his slap shot, Iafrate will take the big windup to freeze the goalie and the defense, then will slide the puck down low to a forward at the side of the net. He also will fake the slap bomb and use a strong wrist shot that surprises goalies.

THE PHYSICAL GAME

Iafrate is not averse to hurting someone with a monster hit and seems to subscribe to the belief that strength is a terrible thing to waste. He will run you over, he will get in your face. He will make your night a long one, because he will compete in all areas of the ice.

THE INTANGIBLES

Iafrate is at his best when he allows his considerable skills to emerge naturally, rather than when he tries to do too much. He remains a somewhat erratic player, though still well within reach of the elite defensive echelon.

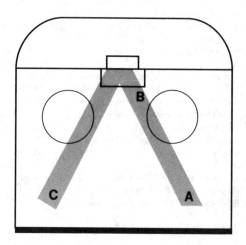

CALLE JOHANSSON

Yrs. of NHL service: 5
Born: Goteborg, Sweden; Feb. 14, 1967
Position: Left defense
Height: 5-11
Weight: 205
Uniform no.: 6
Shoots: Left

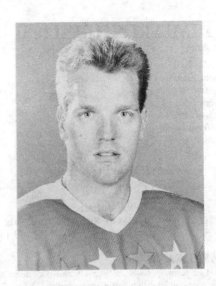

Career statistics:

GP	G	A	TP	PIM
360	40	170	210	171

1991-92 statistics:

GP	G	A	TP	+/-	PIM	PP	SH	GW	GT	S	PCT
80	14	42	56	2	49	5	2	2	0	119	11.8

LAST SEASON

Led team's defensemen in points. Set career highs in goals, assists and points for second consecutive season. Goal, power-play goal, shorthanded goal and point totals increased fourth consecutive season.

THE FINESSE GAME

It is a pleasure to watch Johansson skate. He is agile, mobile and excellent at moving up ice with the play. Speed, balance and strength allow him to race full-bore toward a puck behind the net, then pick up the disc without stopping and make an accurate pass. He is confident, even on the backhand, and likes to have the puck in the key situations.

Johansson moves the puck nicely with a good first play, then has more than enough speed and offensive instinct to jump up and be available for a return pass. He keeps the gap tight as the puck enters the attacking zone, which opens more options; he is available to the forwards if they need him for offense, and is closer to the puck if it turns over. He has a low, accurate shot that can be tipped, but unselfishness at times gets the better of Johansson, who would rather pass than score.

On defense, he reads the rush, sees the ice and reacts smartly. He also plays well off his partner; if his defense-mate wants to step up on a play, Johansson slides over to cover the vacated space. He has good anticipation and good quickness.

THE PHYSICAL GAME

Johansson absolutely gets involved in the pits and often gives up his own body to make a more effective breakout pass. He will hold and hold the puck, lure an opponent into a hitting opportunity that can't be passed up, then will crank the puck to a waiting teammate who now has a free odd-man situation to exploit up the ice.

Johansson also seals his checks off along the boards and holds his opponent's stick. He's very strong on his feet and very rarely gets beaten one-on-one.

THE INTANGIBLES

A little more confidence and assertiveness wouldn't hurt. Johansson is an underrated player because of his unselfishness and also because he underrates himself. He could believe a little more in his own talent.

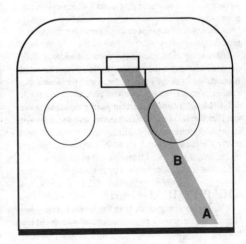

419

DIMITRI KHRISTICH

Yrs. of NHL service: 2
Born: Kiev, Russia; July 23, 1969
Position: Center/left wing
Height: 6-2
Weight: 190
Uniform no.: 8
Shoots: Right

Career statistics:

GP	G	A	TP	PIM
120	49	51	100	56

1991-92 statistics:

GP	G	A	TP	+/-	PIM	PP	SH	GW	GT	S	PCT
80	36	37	73	24	35	14	1	7	0	188	19.1

LAST SEASON

Led team in power-play goals and plus-minus. Tied for team lead in game-winning goals. Goal total jumped 23, as did assist total. Plus-minus jumped 25.

THE FINESSE GAME

Khristich is a key to the Capitals' power play. He plants himself at the post to the goaltender's right, his forehand open and available, and waits for a crossing pass from whoever is stalling for time to the goaltender's left. Every NHL team knows the play, every coach tells his team to watch for it, but Khristich still runs up his power-play goal total. The pass comes across the goalmouth, just out of the goalie's reach and Khristich slams it in.

Of course, if a defenseman goes to Khristich away from the puck, then whoever is holding it can work a two-on-one against the other defenseman. That can force a forward to cheat down low, which opens up a point shot. So Khristich, just by standing where he likes to stay on the power play, is causing all kinds of chaos.

But if he didn't have the special hand-eye coordination to convert the passes, all this would be moot. Instead, you get an idea of the multi-purpose threat Khristich poses.

Khristich is not a dazzling skater with an impressive, powerful stride. He covers ground, though, changes directions fairly quickly and moves the puck pretty well. He can make a rush in open ice, picking up steam gradually and finishing the play with a heavy wrist shot that sizzles to the upper corners.

THE PHYSICAL GAME

Khristich is responsible in the neutral zone, challenging the puck with poke checks and sweep checks, looking to create a turnover. While killing penalties, he does a good job challenging point shots — playing them goalie-style, so the point shooter has to get it past Khristich, as well as the goaltender.

He goes into the nasty areas of the ice, as well. When the puck goes to the boards, so does Khristich, who willingly uses his muscle in the traffic. If defensemen think he's going to be easy to ride off the puck, Khristich surprises them with his strength.

THE INTANGIBLES

Khristich wants to score goals, and will keep trying different methods to attain that objective. The expectation is that he will continue to improve as his NHL experience broadens and he learns more about the goaltender flaws he can exploit. Figure him for another season of 30-plus goals.

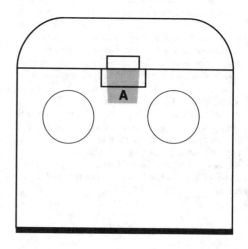

420

TODD KRYGIER

Yrs. of NHL service: 3
Born: Northville, Mich.; Oct. 12, 1965
Position: Left wing
Height: 5-11
Weight: 180
Uniform no.: 21
Shoots: Left

Career statistics:

GP	G	A	TP	PIM
197	44	46	90	254

1991-92 statistics:

GP	G	A	TP	+/-	PIM	PP	SH	GW	GT	S	PCT
67	13	17	30	−1	107	1	0	1	0	127	10.2

LAST SEASON

Had 30 points for third consecutive season. Goal and assist totals also matched prior season.

THE FINESSE GAME

Krygier's surpassing asset is his speed up the wing and his willingness to use it to his advantage. He is first to a lot of loose pucks and always is a breakaway threat because of his exceptional acceleration; he would be more of a breakaway threat, however, if he was able to make moves at top speed more consistently.

To offset this problem, Krygier sometimes uses a reverse change of speeds: he will cross the blue line at a blistering pace on a breakaway, forcing the goalie to prepare to make a decision quickly. Then he will slow down and do what he wants at a slightly slower tempo, which keeps him in control of his tools. Usually, Krygier will end up scoring on a hard wrist shot from the slot; such a shot normally would not pose a threat to a goaltender, but it sneaks through at times because the goalies are trying to guess his next move.

Krygier will use outside speed to greater advantage on his forehand side and will cap the rush with a slap shot. He doesn't have much of an inside move, however, and doesn't control the puck as well when forced to rush on the right-wing side. Though he is asked occasionally to take face-offs and will, at times, lug the puck up ice, his hands are not as quick as his feet; this player can start a transition game better than he can finish it.

THE PHYSICAL GAME

Krygier is not that strong on the puck. And while he is first to a lot of pucks, he does not do much with them once he has won the race; that would require him to 'stay in the pocket' like a quarterback and take the pounding. He prefers to nudge the puck ahead and race after it.

At the same time, Krygier also uses his speed to backcheck. He will catch players from behind and try to bump them off the puck. He's also effective in a penalty-killing role, as speed enables him to pursue the puck.

THE INTANGIBLES

Krygier has come a long way for someone who played on an outdoor rink at the University of Connecticut. He makes you forget his collegiate days at a Division II school. Clearly, he has made something of himself; just as clearly, he can do more.

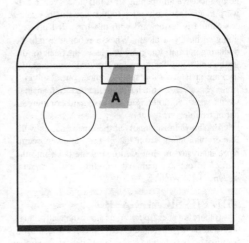

ROD LANGWAY

Yrs. of NHL service: 14
Born: Formosa; May 3, 1957
Position: Left defense
Height: 6-3
Weight: 215
Uniform no.: 5
Shoots: Left

Career statistics:

GP	G	A	TP	PIM
973	51	278	329	829

1991-92 statistics:

GP	G	A	TP	+/-	PIM	PP	SH	GW	GT	S	PCT
64	0	13	13	11	22	0	0	0	0	32	.0

LAST SEASON

Games played and assists totals were three-season highs. Was a plus for 14th consecutive season and is culumative plus-290 lifetime. Missed seven games due to broken toes, five due to groin pull, one due to concussion.

THE FINESSE GAME

Still a very smooth skater with a good, long first step toward the puck, Langway knows it's too late in his career to be challenging and off-balance at the blue line. So he concedes a little room, but buys himself an extra few feet in his retreat, and just when a forward thinks he's beaten Langway to the outside, he soon finds himself in the corner with no place to put the puck and Langway about to lean 215 pounds on him.

Discipline, and somewhat diminished range, keep Langway from challenging all the way to the corners in penalty killing situations. If he goes to the corner, he might leave an opening in front; moreover, a forward in a corner isn't going to hurt you much.

Similarly, a forward with his arms tied up isn't going to hurt you at all. When a rebound might be bouncing in front, Langway will leave the puck for the goalie and tie up the opposing forward who might be hacking at it. That's a subtle choice, but a so-very-smart one; loads of less-experienced defensemen would take a 50-50 chop at the puck and hope it gets out of trouble.

He shows those smarts at the other end, as well. Rather than shoot from the point, Langway seems more interested in simply throwing the puck into the traffic in front so a teammate can tip the disc or set a screen.

THE PHYSICAL GAME

If there's a puck up for grabs along the wall, Langway will tie up his man and leave the disc loose for a teammate. He puts his stick on you, puts his body on you, he holds your stick. He uses his reach extremely well — leans the length of his stick on the ice to block passing lanes — and always seems to know what he wants to do with the puck once he's picked it off.

Langway also uses various wiles to slice seconds off the clock during penalty-killing situations. He utterly nullifies a forward in the corner but keeps the puck in play with his feet or by jamming his stick between the forward's skates. You look up and there's 15 more seconds gone from the advantage, and the puck barely has budged. Other times, he'll establish control, take the big wind-up to clear the puck, and an opposing forward will simply peel off, conceding the play. Langway then will just stand there — tick, tick, tick — until a forward comes to challenge. Then he hacks it down ice, so instead of, say, 10 seconds, he's killed 15.

THE INTANGIBLES

Langway is one of the smartest defensemen in the league. Physically, he is battered, but the mind remains stiletto-sharp. He is putting 14 seasons of NHL education to exceptional use.

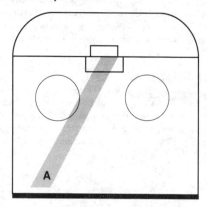

PAUL MacDERMID

Yrs. of NHL service: 8
Born: Chesley, Ont.; April 14, 1963
Position: Right wing
Height: 6-1
Weight: 205
Uniform no.: 23
Shoots: Right

Career statistics:

GP	G	A	TP	PIM
560	102	132	234	1,166

1991-92 statistics:

GP	G	A	TP	+/-	PIM	PP	SH	GW	GT	S	PCT
74	12	16	28	−6	194	2	0	2	1	92	13.0

LAST SEASON

Obtained from Winnipeg, March 2, 1992, for Mike Lalor. Penalty minutes increased 66, point total dropped eight.

THE FINESSE GAME

MacDermid is extremely strong on his skates, but doesn't have a lot of speed or drive and is not going to try to fool himself into imagining he has finesse skills. He will lug the puck a few strides, then bury it along the end board and go to work. He is a straight-ahead skater who has a hard time changing direction at top speed and really has to slow down if the puck's path changes.

Offensive skills are required occasionally, and MacDermid deploys them from strength areas. He has excellent balance, which keeps him upright when the dominoes are falling during scrambles in front. He will score second-effort goals by going to the net and will fight off the first check or two to do so.

THE PHYSICAL GAME

MacDermid is a hard player who skates up and down his wing hungry for his next hit. He is big, strong and uses the muscle to the maximum. It often takes two opponents to stop him along the boards. When he hits, you feel it. He plays a bruising style that doesn't have much use for anything else than dumping an opponent.

THE INTANGIBLES

We forecast about a dozen goals for MacDermid last year and he was right on the money. Dare we predict 20 for him this year? He's a hard-nosed player who will get the ice time, because he'll be checking the other team's hot shot.

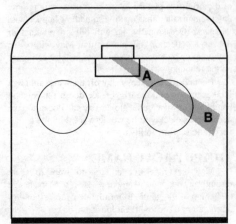

ALAN MAY

Yrs. of NHL service: 3
Born: Barrhead, Alta.; Jan. 14, 1965
Position: Left wing
Height: 6-1
Weight: 200
Uniform no.: 16
Shoots: Right

Career statistics:

GP	G	A	TP	PIM
225	18	25	43	746

1991-92 statistics:

GP	G	A	TP	+/-	PIM	PP	SH	GW	GT	S	PCT
75	6	9	15	-7	221	0	0	1	0	43	14.0

LAST SEASON

Led team in penalty minutes for third consecutive season, although total dropped (43) for second consecutive season. Production improved five points. Goal total was one short of career high.

THE FINESSE GAME

May has good quickness and decent speed but rarely uses those assets to offensive profit. Because he is much more intent on giving a good hit than on making a good scoring play, he often takes himself out of the offensive picture by picking or screening on a defenseman rather than making something happen with the puck. Occasionally, he will bury a rebound or convert a deflection, but more often, May will be the guy tying up a defenseman so someone else can score on the rebound.

He has a decent, heavy shot off the wing, although it takes time to pull the trigger. He doesn't have good hand quickness (with his gloves on) and doesn't make decisions as quickly as he would want. Simply, he has very little scoring ability.

THE PHYSICAL GAME

May is competitive enough to want to skate through any opponent at any time. He is used to change the tempo of the game, to intimidate or to respond to intimidation tactics by the opposition.

He gets used a lot in fight situations, but often last season turned those confrontations into hugging matches. He will 'turtle' at times, and while it occasionally draws the extra two minutes out of his antagonist, it does nothing for May's reputation as a tough guy. He can fight with both hands and will compete against larger opponents.

He often is the first man in on the forecheck, and is a skater of sufficient strength and balance that he can get in to the corner, give a hit on the defenseman and remain upright.

THE INTANGIBLES

May is a fourth-line guy all the way, although he can become a better player and has great desire to. He is a hard worker, very intense and strong, but there is a reason his career-high is seven goals.

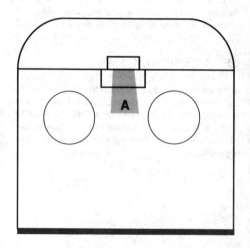

424

KELLY MILLER

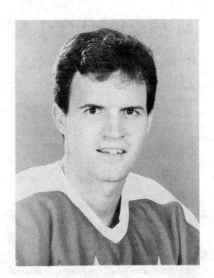

Yrs. of NHL service: 7
Born: Lansing, Mich.; Mar. 3, 1963
Position: Left wing
Height: 5-11
Weight: 196
Uniform no.: 10
Shoots: Left

Career statistics:

GP	G	A	TP	PIM
552	113	178	291	309

1991-92 statistics:

GP	G	A	TP	+/-	PIM	PP	SH	GW	GT	S	PCT
78	14	38	52	20	49	0	1	3	0	144	9.7

LAST SEASON

Set career high in assists and points, while plus-minus was second on team. Assist total increased fourth consecutive season.

THE FINESSE GAME

Miller still uses that time-worn 360-degree spin-o-rama move from the left-wing boards every so often. The right defensemen rarely fall for it, but it's still worth doing because Miller correctly wears a checker's tag and you never know when he might surprise somebody. His goals come from turnovers, from going to the net and from determination more than anything else. He just gets the puck deep, goes after it, moves it and works from there.

His stronger suit is his play away from the puck, as he unmistakably is one of the NHL's premier defensive forwards. Miller hustles, harries, ties up his man, pressures the puck and does anything he can to gain or regain possession. In the hockey wars, he is an all-important infantry leader at the front of the charge.

Miller's game is quickness and speed, using his body and going to the net. He is intelligent, reads off situations very well and is a top penalty killer. He stops and starts extremely well, like a collie herding sheep.

THE PHYSICAL GAME

Miller is always poking and probing for the puck in the corners and along the endboards. He always has his stick on you, is always in your way. He willingly takes a hit to make a play and always seems to bounce back for more.

THE INTANGIBLES

Miller remains a determined, persistent, mentally tough competitor who knows he wants to win and is willing to outwork you every shift in order to do so.

His offense is coming around a little, making him more of a two-way threat, but he seems to remain more comfortable as the leader in the pack of hounds that tries to flush the puck out for the hunters — or, in Washington's case, the Hunters.

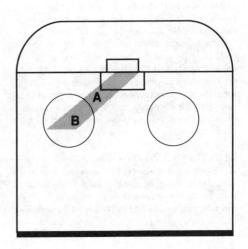

MICHAL PIVONKA

Yrs. of NHL service: 6
Born: Kladno, Czechoslovakia; Jan. 28, 1966
Position: Center/left wing
Height: 6-2
Weight: 198
Uniform no.: 20
Shoots: Left

Career statistics:

GP	G	A	TP	PIM
432	125	213	338	234

1991-92 statistics:

GP	G	A	TP	+/-	PIM	PP	SH	GW	GT	S	PCT
80	23	57	80	10	47	7	4	2	1	177	13.0

LAST SEASON

Led team in scoring. Third straight season with at least 20 goals and 60 points. Totals in points, assists, and plus-minus were career highs. Production increased on both special teams.

THE FINESSE GAME

Pivonka is extremely useful in special-teams situations, as there is more open ice when fewer players are on it. He then can make use of his size, strength and quickness more on his terms than on an opponent's.

He has all the finesse skills you could want. Pivonka skates well. He shoots well, mixing a quality wrist shot with a very good slap shot. He handles the puck well, forcing the defenseman to retreat and taking whatever areas of the ice he wants. During in-close situations, Pivonka is smart enough and quick enough to fake a shot and make a move on a goaltender, rather than simply drill the puck into the netminder's pads. He also sees the ice well.

Pivonka also shows his training and discipline away from the puck by keeping his stick on the ice. Of course, it's a small detail, but watch a game and see how many players need to use their stick for balance, the way a tightrope-walker uses a pole. Pivonka's balance is fine, and his stick being on the ice more often helps him control pucks that bounce away from other players.

THE PHYSICAL GAME

Pivonka doesn't mind hard work or a banging game. He will take and give a hit and will stay involved in the game. But he is not a physically assertive player and would rather score with a shot from the perimeter than take the puck to the net.

At the same time, he did better in one-on-one defensive confrontations this season because he became stronger on the puck.

THE INTANGIBLES

By leading the team in scoring, by mixing a degree of determination in with his skills, and making himself more of an impact player, Pivonka came closer to telling the hockey world he wanted to step up to the next level. Pivonka showed he had higher expectations of himself and raised not only his own play but his team's. There are more steps available on the ladder.

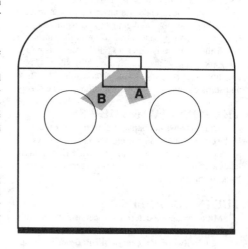

MIKE RIDLEY

Yrs. of NHL service: 7
Born: Winnipeg, Man.; July 8, 1963
Position: Center
Height: 6-1
Weight: 200
Uniform no.: 17
Shoots: Left

Career statistics:

GP	G	A	TP	PIM
541	204	292	496	271

1991-92 statistics:

GP	G	A	TP	+/-	PIM	PP	SH	GW	GT	S	PCT
80	29	40	69	3	38	5	5	3	0	123	23.6

LAST SEASON

Finished fifth in team scoring. Shorthanded goal total tied for second in league. Reached 20-goal mark for seventh straight season, but point total dropped third consecutive season and assist total was four-season low.

THE FINESSE GAME

Ridley is extremely strong on his skates and has very good balance, which makes him a one-on-one threat against most defensemen in the league. He has a healthy amount of hockey smarts and uses tremendous lower-body power for the drive that helps achieve his aims.

Hand quickness also is a Ridley weapon; he can accept a pass and surprise a goaltender with his fast release that he absolutely must use more frequently. He makes accurate passes, even on the backhand. There are times, though, when he is a bit stubborn with the puck, holding a bit too long at the attacking blue line instead of throwing it into the corner and going to work.

Ridley plays a 200-foot game and comes all the way back on defense to break up a number of plays. That helps his offense, as he regains possession of the puck; ironically, it also may take away a bit of his offense, as lots of times Ridley starts a rush from deep in his defensive end of the ice.

Still, he prevents at least as many goals as he scores and is a very solid two-way player.

THE PHYSICAL GAME

Ridley will throw the big hit and dislodge a player from the puck in any area of the ice. He also will do the subtly physical things, such as planting his trunk in an opponent's path along the boards, shielding the puck with his body and freeing at least one of his hands to control the disc. He pays the price in front of the net and in the pits and always makes the effort to beat his check back into the play after contact.

THE INTANGIBLES

Ridley spent another season drawing the top checkers, night in and night out. He continued to limit himself, however, with a disturbingly low shot total that made him easier to defend against. If the center won't shoot, all you have to do is check his wingers and be alert for a defenseman coming into the play late.

Nonetheless, he is a crucial-situations player. If you're protecting a one-goal lead in the final minute or battling a one-goal deficit, there is a good chance Ridley will get the job done for you.

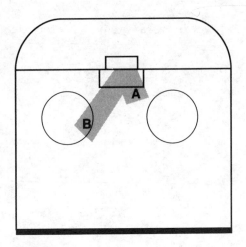

WINNIPEG JETS

STU BARNES

Yrs. of NHL service: 1
Born: Edmonton, Alta.; Dec. 25, 1970
Position: Center
Height: 5-10
Weight: 175
Uniform no.: 14
Shoots: Left

Career statistics:

GP	G	A	TP	PIM
46	8	9	17	26

1991-92 statistics:

GP	G	A	TP	+/-	PIM	PP	SH	GW	GT	S	PCT
46	8	9	17	−2	26	4	0	0	0	75	10.7

LAST SEASON

First in NHL.

THE FINESSE GAME

Barnes' speed may have been a dominant factor in junior hockey, but it isn't yet in the NHL. Nor is his quickness a source of terror to pro opponents, who simply ignore the fakes and drop Barnes on his britches.

So he barely has worked his way onto a team that specializes in finesse players. There is such a thing as working a youngster in gradually, but Barnes rarely did enough to get himself worked in more rapidly.

Barnes has a variety of finesse tools, his hands probably qualifying as the top asset. He moves the puck quickly and accurately, but also controls the puck well when necessary and will work it in traffic. He will score either with the slap shot or the wrist, mostly from around the net.

THE PHYSICAL GAME

While he plays with great determination, Barnes does not throw himself around much. He is all finesse, although he goes in the corners and shoves around in the snowpiles along the boards.

THE INTANGIBLES

The moves he used in junior don't work against defensemen who have to deal with Mario Lemieux and Steve Yzerman and Wayne Gretzky. Barnes is pretty smart, has pretty good work habits, but he's got to pick up the pace and play at a higher tempo.

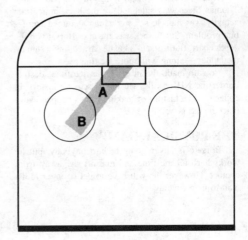

LUCIANO BORSATO

Yrs. of NHL service: 1
Born: Richmond Hill, Ont.; Jan. 7, 1966
Position: Center
Height: 5-10
Weight: 180
Uniform no.: 38
Shoots: Right

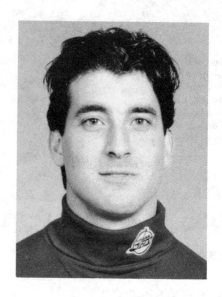

Career statistics:

GP	G	A	TP	PIM
57	15	22	37	47

1991-92 statistics:

GP	G	A	TP	+/-	PIM	PP	SH	GW	GT	S	PCT
56	15	21	36	−6	45	5	0	1	0	81	18.5

LAST SEASON
First in NHL.

THE FINESSE GAME
Borsato is a persistent player who uses a good-sized heart and a healthy helping of hockey sense to find a way to succeed. He is a below-average skater, a third-liner who plays higher because he has good offensive instincts; he knows where to go to get open, and how to make something happen.

And he works to make something happen. When Thomas Steen was sidelined by the back injury that actually was muscle spasms which stemmed from a bite problem, Stu Barnes was ahead of Borsato on the depth chart. But Borsato's hustle earned him a step up the ladder — along with more ice time.

Borsato made the most of that ice time, despite borderline NHL skills. He had a scoring history in college, has a history of making things happen every place he has gone.

THE PHYSICAL GAME
Borsato is never going to hurt anybody, but he works hard all the time and doesn't shy away from contact. However, he will have to get stronger in his man-to-man coverage.

THE INTANGIBLES
With Thomas Steen out so much last season, the Jets would have been lost without Borsato. A top-notch minor leaguer who came in and contributed, Borsato proved he could play in the NHL — and will have to do the same every day the rest of his career.

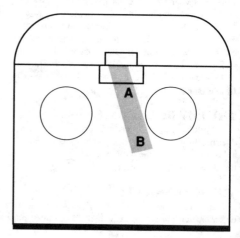

RANDY CARLYLE

Yrs. of NHL service: 16
Born: Sudbury, Ont.; April 19, 1956
Position: Left defense
Height: 5-10
Weight: 200
Uniform no.: 8
Shoots: Left

Career statistics:

GP	G	A	TP	PIM
1,033	147	498	645	1,386

1991-92 statistics:

GP	G	A	TP	+/-	PIM	PP	SH	GW	GT	S	PCT
66	1	9	10	4	54	0	0	0	0	84	1.2

LAST SEASON

Totals for goals, assists and points were career lows.

THE FINESSE GAME

While his offensive abilities used to be a major component in his game, that no longer is the case. Carlyle now survives with his hockey sense, with his knowledge of how to play the position and the game and with his ability to complement Phil Housley.

He has trouble with a high-tempo rush, at either end of the ice, which is why Housley supports Carlyle as much as Carlyle supports Housley. They can play off each other very nicely.

Carlyle still blocks shots, still gets the puck out of the defensive zone well, but most of his minutes now are going to come against the lesser offensive lights from the opposition.

THE PHYSICAL GAME

At this stage of things, Carlyle hardly has anything to prove to anyone from a physical standpoint. He gets cranky in front of the net, and hardly could be considered a polite, gracious opponent. But he sees no reason for the meaningless extra jab, extra shove.

THE INTANGIBLES

Carlyle hangs on to a job at age 36 because of his leadership. When he doesn't play, the team really misses his contribution on the bench and on the ice, so a job remains his to lose rather than his to earn. He will not play every game; there's no point to that. But he will play the important ones and still will contribute until someone better emerges.

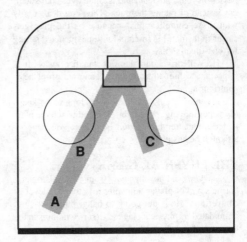

EVGENY DAVYDOV

Yrs. of NHL service: 1
Born: Chelyabinsk, Russia; May 27, 1967
Position: Left wing
Height: 6-0
Weight: 183
Uniform no.: 40
Shoots: Right

Career statistics:

GP	G	A	TP	PIM
12	4	3	7	8

1991-92 statistics:

GP	G	A	TP	+/-	PIM	PP	SH	GW	GT	S	PCT
12	4	3	7	7	8	2	0	0	0	32	12.5

LAST SEASON

Joined Jets after playing on champion Unified Team at Winter Olympics.

THE FINESSE GAME

Everything in Davydov's game stems from his exceptional skating skills. He has wonderful speed and surpassing balance, which enables him to handle the peculiarities of being a right shot on the left side. When you're playing that off-wing, you're accepting lead passes on your backhand and looking over your shoulder instead of facing the puck. Davydov deals easily with those complications, because as the play gets closer to the net, his forehand will be open and strong for one-timer shots.

He will drive into the slot and fire away. It is important to him to score; it is concrete proof he is contributing.

Davydov checks adequately, as long as he keeps his skates moving. When you stop and watch the play, it doesn't matter how much quickness you have — although he has plenty.

THE PHYSICAL GAME

Davydov did not shy away from physical contact, but he's a skill player adjusting to a tougher level of competition. He is not going to bang, but he was not intimidated by physical play his first two months in the league and did more than his share of hooking and hacking.

THE INTANGIBLES

As was the case with his countryman, Igor Ulanov, outstanding hockey abilities can be better than a passport when it comes to being accepted by your new teammates in North America. Davydov fit in very nicely.

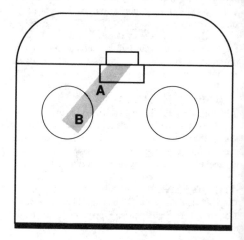

LUCIEN DeBLOIS

Yrs. of NHL service: 15
Born: Joliette, Que.; June 21, 1957
Position: Right wing
Height: 5-11
Weight: 200
Uniform no.: 23
Shoots: Right

Career statistics:

GP	G	A	TP	PIM
993	249	276	519	814

1991-92 statistics:

GP	G	A	TP	+/-	PIM	PP	SH	GW	GT	S	PCT
65	9	13	22	−2	41	0	1	2	0	90	10.0

LAST SEASON

Obtained from Toronto, March 10, 1992, for Mark Osborne.

THE FINESSE GAME

DeBlois isn't much of a skater any more; there are a lot of miles on his tires. But he plays a strong positional game and is alert away from the puck, because defense is his role now and his mind is now DeBlois' premier asset.

It plays into DeBlois' range to be the 'third man high,' in the attacking zone. He does a good job identifying his checking assignment from that spot, and also is required to cover less ground with less responsibility.

DeBlois is more than strong enough to fill in on face-offs, can even be trusted with draws in the defensive zone, and makes sure the other center never gets through him to reach the puck first after the drop.

THE PHYSICAL GAME

You can always find DeBlois plowing in the corners and along the side boards. One reason for that is a work ethic that is no less emphatic today than it was when he broke into the league. The other reason is, the longer an opponent is contained, the smaller the chance he will get to open ice and move well out of DeBlois' skating range.

DeBlois still finishes his checks, hooks and holds to keep his man from gaining speed, and does the old-style fundamental things you don't see done as much in today's game.

THE INTANGIBLES

Every day, DeBlois shows what can happen if you stay positive, keep in shape, remain dedicated to the game and earn your sweater every night. A solid example for the kids on the team.

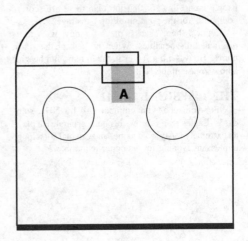

MIKE EAGLES

Yrs. of NHL service: 6
Born: Sussex, N. B.; March 7, 1963
Position: Center
Height: 5-10
Weight: 180
Uniform no.: 36
Shoots: Left

Career statistics:

GP	G	A	TP	PIM
109	7	19	26	197

1991-92 statistics:

GP	G	A	TP	+/-	PIM	PP	SH	GW	GT	S	PCT
65	7	10	17	−17	118	0	1	0	0	60	11.7

LAST SEASON

Games played increased 21, shot production increased nine, goal production jumped seven. Plus-minus declined seven.

THE FINESSE GAME

If he had any killer instinct or finishing touch, Eagles would be a lot more than a journeyman/borderline NHL player. He'd score at least three times as many goals, given the chances he creates, and would justify better than fourth-line status.

In order to get a sweater at all, Eagles has to play the checker/penalty killer role that is just as much a specialty as goal scoring. But there are a lot more people competing for that job than there are scorers competing for the position of top gunslinger.

Eagles, then, checks, plays scrappy, wins face-offs and kills penalties. When he gets goals, it's a bonus. He was a big scorer in the minors, but he's all elbow grease in the NHL.

THE PHYSICAL GAME

For someone with minimal size by NHL standards, Eagles really throws his body around. He plays an extremely feisty, acid game, and can make it a long, unpleasant evening for his opposite number.

THE INTANGIBLES

Eagles missed about six weeks last season with a broken thumb and the team just wasn't the same. He puts the pepper in the soup; the team simply seems to win when he plays and suffer when he's out.

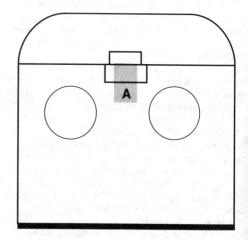

PAT ELYNUIK

Yrs. of NHL service: 3
Born: Foam Lake, Sask.; Oct. 30, 1967
Position: Right wing
Height: 6-0
Weight: 185
Uniform no.: 15
Shoots: Right

Career statistics:

GP	G	A	TP	PIM
289	115	129	244	262

1991-92 statistics:

GP	G	A	TP	+/-	PIM	PP	SH	GW	GT	S	PCT
60	25	25	50	−2	65	9	0	1	0	127	19.7

LAST SEASON

Games played dropped 20 from prior campaign, production dropped six goals, nine assists, but plus-minus improved 11 goals. Led team in shooting percentage, was fifth on team in power-play goals.

THE FINESSE GAME

Elynuik is a very good scorer who may pay a bit of a price because of his unselfishness. He doesn't simply receive the puck, put his head down and crush a shot on goal; rather, he often takes a look in front to see if someone else may have a better angle. Sometimes there is someone else available, but sometimes there isn't, and Elynuik has cost himself the better chance.

While he has very good hands, Elynuik is a sluggish skater without extensive speed. He depends more on agility and vision of the ice to spot an opening, get to it and finish the plays created for him.

Though he can make plays from the outside and score from deep in the face-off circle, Elynuik should not be considered a perimeter player. He gets involved in the scoring-chance area and clearly is successful; over the past two seasons, he has 56 goals on 277 shots, a 20.2 shooting percentage.

THE PHYSICAL GAME

Elynuik scraps for the puck, but doesn't win as many as he scraps for. He is not as strong on the puck as he'd like to be, but works in the corners and makes a nice, poised defensive play when called upon. He will backcheck on a guy, lift the player's stick and strip the puck.

THE INTANGIBLES

Elynuik is a great guy, but isn't a great leader. He knows the right things to do, but is not going to grab a teammate by the suspenders and yank him up to next level.

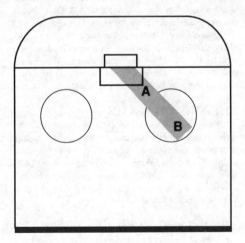

BOB ESSENSA

Yrs. of NHL service: 4
Born: Toronto, Ont.; Jan. 14, 1965
Position: Goaltender
Height: 6-0
Weight: 170
Uniform no.: 35
Catches: Left

Career statistics:

GP	MINS	GA	SO	GAA	A	PIM
158	8,680	454	11	3.14	7	10

1991-92 statistics:

GP	MINS	GAA	W	L	T	SO	GA	S	SAPCT	PIM
47	2,627	2.88	21	17	6	5	126	1,407	.910	2

LAST SEASON

Set team record for shutouts in a season. Victory total was career best.

THE PHYSICAL GAME

Essensa's main strength is, he always knows where the puck is, and is always in front of it. He is fairly compact in his motions and doesn't waste a lot of energy on theatrics. He focuses on the puck and lets it hit him.

He plays a V-style, which means he is on his knees a lot, but Essensa usually has a good sense of timing; he is established in his postion before the puck arrives, so there is less chance of getting caught 'in between' — halfway up and halfway down. He has a problem with rebounds at times, though, and doesn't always recover position perfectly for second shots.

Essensa doesn't handle the puck much or especially well. He stops the hard-arounds behind the net, and leaves them for his defensemen. Winnipeg's defense is mostly mobility and finesse, and Essensa allows them to make use of those assets.

THE MENTAL GAME

Essensa is a strong and focused competitor who stays on an even keel and avoids the high/low pitfalls younger goalies confront. Maturity tells him not every night can be great. When you face more than 1,400 shots in a season, some are going to go in; some nights, a lot are going to go in. If a stoppable shot gets past him, he does not fret about it.

THE INTANGIBLES

Essensa had a lot on his mind in the second half. As the Jets' player representative, he was a focus of attention during the strike crisis. He suffered a knee injury and missed a lot of games, then didn't get a sniff in the playoffs after producing five shutouts and a .910 save percentage during the regular season. His credentials as No. 1 target should be unassailable.

PHIL HOUSLEY

Yrs. of NHL service: 10
Born: St. Paul, Minn.; Mar. 9, 1964
Position: Right defense
Height: 5-10
Weight: 185
Uniform no.: 6
Shoots: Left

Career statistics:

GP	G	A	TP	PIM
760	224	496	720	502

1991-92 statistics:

GP	G	A	TP	+/-	PIM	PP	SH	GW	GT	S	PCT
74	23	63	86	-5	92	11	0	4	1	234	9.8

LAST SEASON

Was a finalist for Norris Trophy. Led team in assists and points. Was third on team in power-play goals, second on team in winners. Total assists and points were career highs.

THE FINESSE GAME

Because he is the whole finesse package, Housley can beat the first forechecker with his hands, a second checker with his head and a third checker with his speed. Housley is extremely fast and fluid. He has fabulous acceleration, can reach top speed within a few steps. He has a good idea of where to be on the ice and recovers quickly if he has taken an offensive chance.

When he has the puck, Housley has a feather-soft passing touch and sees the ice very well. He knows where everybody is, knows where to move it, and that becomes a major asset when the Jets are on the power play. Housley's touch is such that he can return a pass almost as quickly as it arrived to him.

Although his agility, range and use of reach would be useful in penalty killing situations, Housley is not used much under those circumstances because it burns him out. A team that has as much trouble scoring as Winnipeg needs him at full power on the power play, and Housley's low sizzlers from the point can beat a goalie or, at the least, create a rebound.

Housley plays a regular shift, which will account for at least 20 minutes per night. He also works the full two minutes of every power play, and the way things are now, teams regularly get five or more power plays a night. That's at least 10 minutes more ice time. Housley will be used to kill two-man shortages because quickness allows to him move up and challenge the points or sweep down low to protect against the pass.

Anticipation is another significant Housley asset. He has exceptional jump to loose pucks — which he then skates or passes out of the defensive zone.

THE PHYSICAL GAME

Housley gets in the way, but is not physical. It isn't his game and it would be silly for him to play it. He lacks strength in front of the net and along the boards, and plays the puck over the man virtually every time. However, he does an effective job diving to cut off passes while defending odd-man rushes.

Housley is never going to get beat to the outside. He leaves the left wing with absolutely no place to go, which forces the forward either to stop, throw the puck up for grabs, or look for the late man coming into the play. Thus Housley has changed the forward's plans, ruined his intentions; he simply used finesse force, rather than physical force, to do it.

THE INTANGIBLES

Housley has a tremendous amount of pride that might go unrecognized because of his size and his baby face. He might be perceived as a follower, but Housley does more than lead by example; he speaks up when things have to be said.

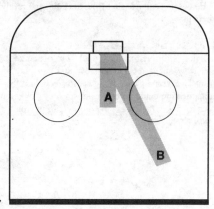

MIKE LALOR

Yrs. of NHL service: 7
Born: Buffalo, N.Y.; Mar. 8, 1963
Position: Left defense
Height: 6-0
Weight: 200
Uniform no.: 22
Shoots: Left

Career statistics:

GP	G	A	TP	PIM
458	14	74	88	505

1991-92 statistics:

GP	G	A	TP	+/-	PIM	PP	SH	GW	GT	S	PCT
79	7	10	17	25	78	0	0	1	0	74	9.5

LAST SEASON
Obtained from Washington, March 2, 1992, for Paul MacDermid. Plus-minus zoomed 48 goals. Goal production doubled career total.

THE FINESSE GAME
There is absolutely nothing fancy to Lalor's game. He is a strong defensive defenseman with some finesse skills who has his most success when he stays within his skills and gets in trouble the second he tries to go outside them.

On penalty killing, for example, Lalor steps up to challenge point shots and assumes a goaltender's stance — stickblade across the space between his skates — which is fine; the shooter has to get the puck past Lalor AND the goalie. Lalor sometimes will over-challenge a puck in the corner, though, leaving a hole in front that one of his teammates must drop down to cover.

The same is true of his puck-handling skills. Lalor moves the puck capably, and occasionally will throw a pass up the middle if the opening is there. But there also are times when he holds the puck too long and puts the puck in trouble instead of simply getting it out of the zone.

Lalor is a strong, solid skater. He has decent acceleration, acceptable range.

He has an adequate shot from the point and rarely bothers using it.

THE PHYSICAL GAME
Lalor will dive to whack pucks out of the zone. He eagerly keeps the crease clear and can play an extremely physical game. The consistency of his physical application could be better, however; Lalor often chases a puck rather than covering a man in front of his net.

THE INTANGIBLES
Lalor contributes as much intangibly as tangibly. He played on a Stanley Cup team, and that winning experience can provide a lot to a team that is short on big triumphs.

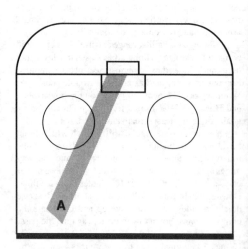

TROY MURRAY

Yrs. of NHL service: 10
Born: Calgary, Alta.; July 31, 1962
Position: Center
Height: 6-1
Weight: 195
Uniform no.: 19
Shoots: Right

Career statistics:

GP	G	A	TP	PIM
728	213	317	530	747

1991-92 statistics:

GP	G	A	TP	+/-	PIM	PP	SH	GW	GT	S	PCT
74	17	30	47	-13	69	5	2	1	1	156	10.9

LAST SEASON

Plus-minus dropped 26 goals. Production improved three goals, seven assists.

THE FINESSE GAME

Murray is a strong skater — not fast, necessarily, but extremely strong. He is a better skater than Ed Olczyk or Pat Elynuik; he gets a little more crouched for his push-off and is a little more powerful as a result. That helps him cut off the ice on the people he's checking, helps him get to the loose pucks he always is chasing.

Murray is a solid defensive player, someone you want him on the ice in the last two minutes of a close game. He takes at least half the draws you really need to win and virtually all the draws when there is a late lead to defend. Face-off skills also are a major asset in special teams situations.

Murray played every night against the best players from other team. Since he focused on checking duties rather than scoring duties, you might have expected him to be a little closer to 'even' on the plus-minus gauge. But he went through a long scoring slump, and his minus last season was worsened by the fact his team never scored many goals.

THE PHYSICAL GAME

Murray plays the man all the time, works the corners strong. He is strong on the puck all the time, and finishes every possible check.

THE INTANGIBLES

Murray is a strong, smart player and a tremendous leader. He keeps in very good shape. Murray has time left; he can play for a while yet, but his days as a scorer appear done.

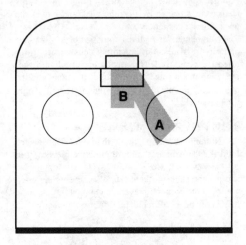

TEPPO NUMMINEN

Yrs. of NHL service: 4
Born: Tampere, Finland; July 3, 1968
Position: Right defense
Height: 6-1
Weight: 190
Uniform no.: 27
Shoots: Right

Career statistics:
GP	G	A	TP	PIM
308	25	105	130	116

1991-92 statistics:
GP	G	A	TP	+/-	PIM	PP	SH	GW	GT	S	PCT
80	5	34	39	15	32	4	0	1	0	143	3.5

LAST SEASON
Plus-minus improved 30 goals.

THE FINESSE GAME
Numminen is just a good, solid defenseman. While not particularly fast, he is fairly agile on his skates and very seldom gets beat one-on-one. He makes the right play, the easy play, that gets you out of the defensive zone.

Numminen sees the ice well and moves the puck well. He doesn't thread the needle with passes the way Phil Housley can, but he doesn't hurt his team's chances of scoring. He gets the puck and moves the puck without hesitation.

Numminen also jumps into the play when the opportunity avails. But he simply does not finish his offensive plays well. Numminen has excellent hand-eye coordination and fires a solid one-timer off the pass during the power play—which is about the only time he scores.

THE PHYSICAL GAME
Numminen bumps more than Phil Housley or Fredrik Olausson and is more effective physically to get the job done. He is able to skate with opponents and get the stick on them. He also accepts the body bombs in the corners; players load up on him because they know he won't retaliate.

THE INTANGIBLES
Numminen is a quiet, real solid person. He is never a problem in the dressing room. There is hope he might feel confident enough to show more leadership. Maybe he will.

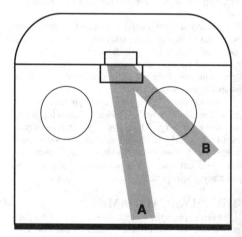

FREDRIK OLAUSSON

Yrs. of NHL service: 6
Born: Vaxsjo, Sweden; Oct. 5, 1966
Position: Right defense
Height: 6-2
Weight: 200
Uniform no.: 4
Shoots: Right

Career statistics:

GP	G	A	TP	PIM
410	68	203	271	164

1991-92 statistics:

GP	G	A	TP	+/-	PIM	PP	SH	GW	GT	S	PCT
77	20	42	62	-31	34	13	1	2	0	227	8.8

LAST SEASON

Fourth straight season with 40 or more points and 70 or more games played. Plus-minus, for second consecutive year, was worst of any regular. Led team in power-play goals.

THE FINESSE GAME

Olausson is an all-finesse player, a good/very good skater who simply does not play up to his tremendous ability. He has a powerful stride, good acceleration and at times can pull away from checkers on the strength of his step. He makes effort plays on the offensive side of the puck, leading the rush or jumping into it, but consistently is casual on the defensive side.

Olausson sees the ice extremely well; that may be his greatest attribute. He does a very good job quarterbacking from the right point, doesn't force a shot if he has a teammate open on the flank. Olausson sees the ice, sees his options. He is quick enough to change his mind and still make a good play to a secondary receiver.

If the receivers are covered, Olausson uses his strong shot from the point. He has the good sense to keep it low, so that even if the shot isn't deflected, the goalie still needs to use his pads to stop it and probably will leave a rebound bouncing in front.

THE PHYSICAL GAME

Olausson will use his stick to slow down a forechecker and buy some time for his partner, but that is about it. He is 200 pounds and won't bang. Olausson is strictly a finesse player who is going to play the puck most of the time. If he knocked a guy down, the entire organization would be hospitalized for treament of shock.

THE INTANGIBLES

How long can you go to the well with a guy who's minus 31? He is a luxury more easily afford by teams that can score enough goals to offset the ones Olausson

hands over. The Jets survive by using him more in offensive situations that focus on his strengths, and by chaining him to the bench in the last three or four minutes of the game if they're trying to protect the small lead their meager offense has provided.

Olausson could be better than he is, but doesn't seem interested in pushing himself to the top of mountain. It seems like he wants to be good, but not great — that his mail is addressed to the comfort zone.

Olausson's plus-minus (minus 53 over two seasons) speaks for itself. There is no acceptable reason for it. He should have more pride.

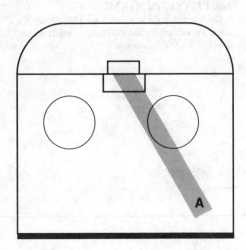

ED OLCZYK

Yrs. of NHL service: 8
Born: Chicago, Ill.; Aug. 16, 1966
Position: Center
Height: 6-1
Weight: 200
Uniform no.: 16
Shoots: Left

Career statistics:

GP	G	A	TP	PIM
600	239	330	569	590

1991-92 statistics:

GP	G	A	TP	+/-	PIM	PP	SH	GW	GT	S	PCT
64	32	33	65	11	67	12	0	7	1	245	13.1

LAST SEASON

Played 15 fewer games than previous season, but led team in goals, game-winning goals and shots on goal. Plus-minus improved 38 goals.

THE FINESSE GAME

An average skater of gradual acceleration, Olczyk makes up in smarts what he lacks in speed. He knows how to get to the holes, when to join the play late. He is someone you want to have the puck in the last 30 feet of ice.

Olczyk has a great stick and a splendid nose for the net. He knows how to score goals from close range, finds a way to do it and pays a price to do it. He also shoots well enough to beat a goaltender from 40 feet.

Olczyk does a decent job on face-offs. He uses a long stick and stands upright, as opposed to getting into a deep crouch, but is quick enough with the stick to win more than his share. That makes him useful on special teams.

THE PHYSICAL GAME

Olczyk gets in the way, but is not physical despite his size. He will use his size and strength in the corners, will get in front of the net but .

THE INTANGIBLES

Olczyk is a good team player, but is a follower rather than leader. He isn't enough of a leader to carry the full load in that category, but can do a good job in second-level leadership.

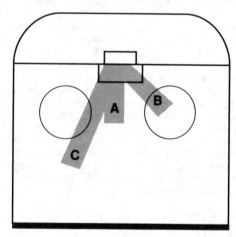

442

DARRIN SHANNON

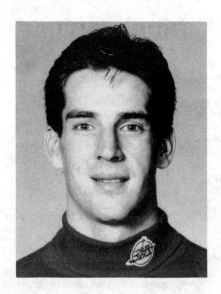

Yrs. of NHL service: 3
Born: Barrie, Ont.; Dec. 8, 1969
Position: Left wing
Height: 6-2
Weight: 200
Uniform no.: 34
Shoots: Left

Career statistics:

GP	G	A	TP	PIM
123	23	40	63	57

1991-92 statistics:

GP	G	A	TP	+/-	PIM	PP	SH	GW	GT	S	PCT
69	13	27	40	6	41	3	0	3	1	93	14.0

LAST SEASON

Obtained from Buffalo, Oct. 11, 1991, with Dean Kennedy and Mike Hartman, for Dave McLlwain, Gord Donnelly and future considerations.

THE FINESSE GAME

Shannon does not have much skating speed, quickness or range. But he has a drop of agility, a lot of balance, and even more smarts. He knows how to play the game. He knows where to be when he doesn't have the puck. He knows the puck moves faster than anyone can skate, so he keeps it moving. When he has possession and limited options, he buries the puck deep instead of getting fancy and turning it over.

On the power play, he works down low, accepts a pass from the point and wheels for a quick shot. At all times, Shannon has good poise; if he gets handcuffed by a pass that he doesn't have the range to reach, he will absorb the hit, shield the puck with his body and use his feet to control the puck.

Most of the goals he gets are coming to come from the scoring-chance area. He is a strong player who plays a strong game well and who can be counted on for solid, productive effort.

THE PHYSICAL GAME

Shannon has a physical presence without the intimidation or meanness. He is a corner man, a boards man who gets the job done effectively and cleanly but makes absolutely certain you're going to pay a price to win the puck.

THE INTANGIBLES

If he proves himself a little more, Shannon has a chance to be a leader on Winnipeg's hockey team. He may not be a big name, but teams would be wrong to overlook him. Shannon is the kind of left wing a lot of clubs would very much like to have, and he's only 22.

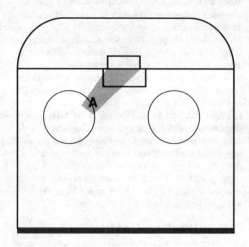

THOMAS STEEN

Yrs. of NHL service: 11
Born: Tocksmark, Sweden; June 8, 1960
Position: Center
Height: 5-10
Weight: 195
Uniform no.: 25
Shoots: Left

Career statistics:

GP	G	A	TP	PIM
763	218	461	679	632

1991-92 statistics:

GP	G	A	TP	+/-	PIM	PP	SH	GW	GT	S	PCT
38	13	25	38	5	29	10	0	0	0	75	17.3

LAST SEASON

Various injuries cost him a majority of the season, but his power-play goal total still jumped three and his plus-minus improved by eight. Fourth on team in power-play goals.

THE FINESSE GAME

Steen is a solid two-way player who comes to play every night and who always finds a way to produce a point per game. You can put any wingers at all with him and have them become productive players, because, rather than score himself, Steen is more satisfied by making a nice pass that leads to a goal. He always is getting pressure to shoot more, but he wants to make plays.

On the power play, Steen sets up office in the right-wing circle and goes to work from there—either playing catch with Phil Housley at the point or driving the puck deep for a give-and-go. Steen then will go to the net, prepared for the return pass, and is strong enough to muscle with any defender who picks him up.

Quickness of hand, foot and mind make him a tremendous offensive threat. Steen needs very little room in which to change directions; he has stopped and moved the other way with the puck before most defensemen have responded to the fact that he stopped in the first place. Tremendous stamina also allows him to make significant plays at the end of a shift, long after other players have gone to the bench.

THE PHYSICAL GAME

Steen is a physical player. He tries to take the man hard all time. He really competes. He throws the shoulder into an opponent, picks up the puck and immediately looks to make a pass. He plays off the hits extremely well, probably because he's had so much experience absorbing them over more than a decade of punishment.

THE INTANGIBLES

Last season was the third straight in which Steen played fewer than 60 games. You didn't see the real Thomas Steen. But the real Thomas Steen will be 32 years old when you see him this season.

Despite the age, Steen leads by example. He is respected tremendously for his talent and his contributions over the years.

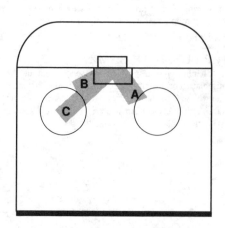

RICK TABARACCI

Yrs. of NHL service: 2
Born: Toronto, Ont.; Jan. 2, 1969
Position: Goaltender
Height: 5-10
Weight: 185
Uniform no.: 31
Catches: Right

Career statistics:

GP	MINS	GA	SO	GAA	A	PIM
43	2,092	127	1	3.64	2	12

1991-92 statistics:

GP	MINS	GAA	W	L	T	SO	GA	S	SAPCT	PIM
18	966	3.23	6	7	3	0	52	470	.889	4

LAST SEASON

Made six fewer appearances, but had just one fewer decision, than prior season.

THE PHYSICAL GAME

Tabaracci has very good athletic ability but has made himself better by changing the way he uses that attribute. He used to flop all over the place, because his athleticism enabled him to do it, but he was not as effective or as controlled a goaltender. Now, when he challenges the shooters, he relies on his angles and calls on his quickness only when it is really necessary, Tabaracci gets the job done more effectively. It is his second or third weapon now, rather than the primary one.

Now, Tabaracci stands up more and keeps the five hole closed nicely in his stance. He is out well for the first shot and does a pretty good job of controlling his rebounds and smothering them. When he doesn't, Tabaracci recovers position nicely; he is nimble enough and agile enough to kick one way on the initial shot and kick the other way on the rebound. He also has a quick catching glove.

Tabaracci has good concentration and good reflexes; he gets to the shots he sees late. He is more than mobile enough to get behind the net for pucks drilled around the boards and likes to send the puck up ice.

THE MENTAL GAME

Tabaracci has a good sense of when to smother the puck — to grab a breather for himself or rattled teammates — and when to keep it alive. He reads the tempo and the game situation well, and does what he can to turn control of those items in his team's favor.

THE INTANGIBLES

Tabaracci made good strides last season but still is learning his position and needs some patience. He wants to get to the top of his profession quickly, but in most cases, the climb is a gradual one.

445

KEITH TKACHUK

Yrs. of NHL service: 1
Born: Melrose, Mass.; Mar. 28, 1972
Position: Left wing
Height: 6-3
Weight: 218
Uniform no.: 7
Shoots: Left

Career statistics:

GP	G	A	TP	PIM
17	3	5	8	28

1991-92 statistics:

GP	G	A	TP	+/-	PIM	PP	SH	GW	GT	S	PCT
17	3	5	8	0	28	2	0	0	0	22	13.6

LAST SEASON

First in NHL. Joined Jets after playing for Team USA at Winter Olympics.

THE FINESSE GAME

This big power forward conjures comparisons to Trevor Linden, Gary Roberts and Rick Tocchet. He is a muscle forward with the skill, strength and eagerness to score gritty goals from the punishing areas of the ice. Tkachuk scores his with an excellent wrist shot that he gets off in an eyeblink.

He played in school on a line with Tony Amonte and Shawn McEachern, so there is at least some element of skating skill in his game; Tkachuk had to keep up with two of the faster skaters around.

He is a strong skater, with decent speed, but still, his foot skills could use work. While he has enough agility to change directions fairly well, he needs to add some lateral movement, some quickness. That will come, though. Tkachuk is, after all, just 20 years old; with all the banging he does, and all the times he handles the puck with his feet in the corners, you know the balance is there is abundance.

THE PHYSICAL GAME

Tkachuk is big, strong and he owns the corners. He likes physical confrontations and he has a mean streak. He isn't the greatest scorer in the game, but he makes things easier for the finishers on his line because of the space he creates for them.

When he gets the puck, he goes to the net hard or absorbs a hit to make the pass in front. He imposes his presence on defensemen, makes sure they know he's in the game and playing to win.

THE INTANGIBLES

Tkachuk is strong physically, but may be even stronger emotionally. He was Winnipeg's best forward in the Vancouver series. He handles the pressure situations extremely well. He doesn't choke. If he has to play well, he will.

Tkachuk wants to improve, and will do that, too. He has 25-30 goals in him, perhaps sooner than later, and may force his way into Calder Trophy consideration.

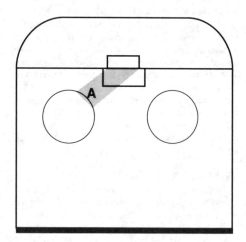

IGOR ULANOV

Yrs. of NHL service: 1
Born: Perm, Russia; Oct. 1, 1969
Position: Left defense
Height: 6-1
Weight: 198
Uniform no.: 32
Shoots: Right

Career statistics:

GP	G	A	TP	PIM
27	2	9	11	67

1991-92 statistics:

GP	G	A	TP	+/-	PIM	PP	SH	GW	GT	S	PCT
27	2	9	11	5	67	0	0	0	0	23	8.7

LAST SEASON
First in NHL.

THE FINESSE GAME
Ulanov is everything you would want in a defenseman. He is a good skater, a good puckhandler and an assertive physical factor.

He boasts impressive range because of a strong first step toward that puck. He is not fast but he covers an above-average amount of ground and fleshes out his skating asset with agility and good balance.

Ulanov has quick hands and a quick mind. He can break up a play in the neutral zone, start right into the transition game and make a strong, accurate pass to spark the offensive engine.

THE PHYSICAL GAME
Ulanov is a big boy, and he uses that size. He is physical, has a bit of a mean streak, comes to play all the time and lets you know it. Ulanov is continually whacking the hands and elbows of opposing forwards for the purpose of distraction, for the purpose of annoyance, for the purpose of establishing himself in the player's mind.

THE INTANGIBLES
Ulanov fit right in on the team because he can play. He was accepted immediately by the players, his communication skills are improving, and should, with more experience and knowledge of the league, get even better.

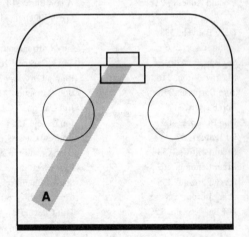

INDEX OF
PLAYERS